W9-DFV-138

Harold Pashler is Professor of Psychology
at the University of California, San Diego,
USA.

Studies in Cognition Series,
edited by Glyn Humphreys
University of Birmingham

Studies in Cognition presents authoritative
pedagogical texts for senior undergraduates
and beginning graduates, written by an
international team of leading scientists.
The books review recent developments in
a broad range of topics in cognitive science
and assume a foundational knowledge of
concepts in cognition appropriate to a
senior undergraduate level.

ATTENTION

edited by

Harold Pashler
University of California, San Diego, USA

Psychology Press
a member of the Taylor & Francis group

Psychology Press Ltd
27 Church Road
Hove
East Sussex, BN3 2FA
UK

British Library Cataloguing in Publication Data

A catalogue record for this book is available from the British Library

   ISBN 0-86377-812-7 (Hbk)
   ISBN 0-86377-813-5 (Pbk)

Cover painting *Red and Brown Formal Study* (Tempera) by Ian Hopton

Typeset by DP Photosetting, Aylesbury, Bucks.
Printed and bound in the United Kingdom by
Biddles Ltd., Guildford and King's Lynn

Contents

List of Contributors

Jon Driver, Department of Psychology, University College London, Gower Street, London WC1E 6BT, UK.

James E. Hoffman, Department of Psychology, 220 Wolf Hall, University of Delaware, Newark, DE 19716, USA.

James C. Johnston, Flight Management and Human Factors Division, Mailstop 262-4, NASA Ames Research Center, Moffett Field, CA 94035, USA.

Steven J. Luck, Department of Psychology, University of Iowa, 11 Seashore Hall E, Iowa City, IA 52242-1407, USA.

Bruce Milliken, Department of Psychology, McMaster University, Hamilton, Ontario L8S 4K1, Canada.

Michael C. Mozer, Department of Computer Science and Institute of Cognitive Science, University of Colorado, Boulder, CO 80309-0430, USA.

Harold Pashler, Department of Psychology, University of California, San Diego 9500 Gilman Drive, La Jolla, CA 92093, USA.

Bertram Scharf, CNRS Centre de Recherche en Neurosciences Cognitives, 13402 Marseille, Cedex 20, France; and Auditory Perception Laboratory, Northeastern University, Boston, MA 02115-5096, USA.

Mark Sitton, Department of Brain and Cognitive Sciences, Massachusetts Institute of Technology, Boston, MA 02139, USA.

Steven P. Tipper, Psychology Department, University of Wales, Bangor, Gwynedd, Wales LL57 2DG, UK.

Jeremy Wolfe, Center for Ophthalmic Research, Brigham and Women's Hospital & Harvard Medical School, 221 Longwood Avenue, Boston, MA 02115, USA.

Steven Yantis, Department of Psychology, Johns Hopkins University, Baltimore, MD 21218-2686, USA.

Introduction

Attention has long posed a major challenge for psychologists, whatever school of thought they may subscribe to and whatever methodologies they may employ. As with many fundamental topics in psychology, the role of attention in mental life was noticed and discussed long before psychology became an independent discipline. Augustine of Hippo (354–430) made comments on the phenomenology of attention that sound quite close to present-day intuitions about how different events in the world attract our attention (cf. Neumann, 1971). More extended descriptions of attention first appeared in writings of philosophers in the 18th century such as Christian Wolff (see Hatfield, in press, for a fascinating review of early treatments of attention).

Attention did not come to be seen as a central topic in the discipline of psychology until the 19th century, however. The major theorists of that era, including Oswald Külpe, Edward Titchener, and William James, made sustained efforts to analyze attention in some detail. These analyses started with the ordinary concept of attention, familiar to everyone, that belongs to "folk psychology"—the unsystematic but usually compelling and useful body of ideas about mental life that we use to get along in our daily lives. In folk psychology, attention appears as a sort of psychological commodity or essence that is usually, but not always, subject to voluntary control. Attention, according to folk psychology, can sometimes be devoted to sensations, resulting in an increased awareness of these sensations and better ability to remember them later. Attention can also be devoted to behaviors

1

or activities such as riding a bicycle or solving a problem. Because there is only so much attention to go around, dividing one's attention carries a cost (implicit in the demand "Can I have your full attention?"). Certain instinctive behaviors, such as breathing, and highly practiced activities, like driving, are assumed to work without attention ("automatically"). Devoting attention to these activities is believed to impair rather than enhance performance.

Writers in the late 19th and early 20th centuries generally took these everyday conceptions of attention as their starting point, and tried to systematize and extend them (Pillsbury, 1908). Some went further and attempted to reduce different aspects of attention to a single underlying essence. Mostly, these analyses were couched in phenomenological terms. For example, Titchener (1908) argued that the fundamental effect of attention is to increase "clarity". Külpe (1902), on the other hand, argued that attention enhanced the discriminability, rather than the clarity, of sensations. Others thought attention effectively increased the intensity of a stimulus, and much debate in this era focused on this particular claim. Most of the debate was based on intuitions and *a priori* considerations, but a number of interesting experiments were performed (e.g. Munsterberg, 1894; for a modern revival of this experimental tradition, see Prinzmetal, 1996).

Theoretical analysis of attention declined over the period from roughly the 1920s to the 1950s, when behaviorism dominated academic psychology (although, as Lovie, 1983, points out, attention research never became extinct as sometimes suggested). Behaviorists hoped ultimately to explain the behavior of every organism in terms of the objective history of that organism. For anyone who aspires to such a goal, attention is puzzling and downright troublesome. After all, if the consequences of presenting a stimulus depend on a person's (or perhaps an animal's) voluntary decisions about how to process this stimulus, the prospects for an all-encompassing behavioral theory seem remote.

CONTEMPORARY ATTENTION THEORY

Research on attention underwent a major revival beginning in Great Britain in the 1950s. This revival, which has continued and grown to the present day, was one of the earliest harbingers of what is sometimes called the "cognitive revolution" in psychology. A number of factors are usually cited as having sparked this revolution, including the development of digital computers and new theoretical developments in linguistics. The introduction of several obviously fruitful experimental techniques for analyzing unobservable mental processes also played an important role, however. This took place in a number of laboratories, and much of the research was motivated by practical interest in aviation and other fields where people are often subjected to sensory and cognitive overload.

One notably influential early study was carried out by Colin Cherry (1953) using the dichotic listening technique. Cherry had people listen to different messages played to the two ears through headphones (dichotic listening). When instructed to "shadow" (repeat back) either message, Cherry's subjects were able to comply. Having done so, they could describe the message they had shadowed but could report almost nothing about the unattended message. They did not even notice changes in the language in which it was spoken, nor did they notice when Cherry played a message backwards in the unattended channel. However, if the voice disappeared or there was a gross change in pitch (e.g. from a male to a female speaker), it was often noticed. Cherry concluded (1953, p.978) that "certain statistical properties [of the rejected message are] identified, but that detailed aspects, such as the language, individual words, or semantic content are unnoticed."

Cherry's interpretation alluded to a conceptual framework often called the information-processing approach to psychology. This framework invokes an idea that scarcely figured in traditional analyses of attention: that of separable mental representations or codes (Posner, 1978). While the traditional attention theorists sought to understand attention using phenomenological concepts like clarity or intensity, information-processing theorists (Cherry being an early example) assumed that the mind computes a variety of different internal descriptions or representations of even a single stimulus. This notion may have been implicit in earlier work, for example in studies of cognitive effects of brain damage (e.g. Lichtheim, 1885) and in certain learning theories (Hull, 1930), but it did not emerge prominently in psychology until the rise of cognitivism about four decades ago.

The research sparked by Cherry's observations made increasingly fruitful use of the idea of multiple codes or representations. Based on Cherry's observations of dichotic listening, and additional results of his own, Donald Broadbent formulated the first information-processing theory of attention in 1958. This theory is often referred to as the "Filter Theory" or "Early Selection Theory". According to Broadbent's theory, all messages or channels are analyzed at a "physical" (nonsemantic) level, whether or not they are attended. Physical analysis would include analyzing properties that define channels and properties of the information on these channels that do not depend on symbolic significance of language *per se* (e.g. pitch and location). Only attended messages are processed further, to the point of identification (e.g. resolving the meaning of the words). This semantic analysis, according to Broadbent, is necessarily sequential. Selection, on this scheme, occurs prior to identification (hence the term "early selection").

Not long after Broadbent formulated his theory, new experimental results began to accumulate that appeared to conflict with it, by suggesting that unattended messages must be processed more extensively than the theory would allow. Many of these studies involved auditory stimuli. Even when people try to ignore a message, psychophysiological measures sometimes demonstrate that the significance of this message has been registered by the nervous system; for example, galvanic skin conductance responses (indicating tiny emotional responses) are sometimes triggered by words previously conditioned to electric shock, even when these words are presented on an unattended channel (Corteen & Wood, 1972). Subjects shadowing a message on one channel (e.g. the left ear) will sometimes switch to shadowing the other channel when the message switches, again suggesting that the unattended material must have been analyzed semantically (Treisman, 1960). Furthermore, particularly salient stimuli such as a person's own name sometimes "grab" a listener's attention even when these stimuli are presented to an unattended channel (Moray, 1959; Wood & Cowan, 1995).

In recent decades, most attention researchers have chosen to use visual rather than auditory stimuli, partly because this allows more precise control over exactly when stimuli are processed. The findings with visual stimuli have closely paralleled those with auditory stimuli. People can, for example, select one visual object and ignore others. This is true even when the attended and unattended objects overlap spatially. As with messages played through headphones, selecting one visual object results in negligible memory for unattended objects (Rock & Guttman, 1981). As in the auditory case, however, indirect measures sometimes reveal that ignored stimuli have been processed to the point of being identified, at least on some trials. Some well known examples include the Stroop effect (in which the identity of a word slows naming of the color in which the word is printed) and so-called "flanker effects" (in which to-be-ignored stimuli can slow or speed responses to the attended stimuli that they are placed adjacent to, depending on their identity). The Moray result involving the subject's own name appears to have a visual analogue, too. Wolford and Morrison (1980) had subjects make a judgment involving two digits to the left and right of fixation; a word, sometimes their own name, was occasionally inserted briefly in the center of the visual field. Many subjects noticed and remembered their name; usually the competing task was disrupted on these trials.

To account for the evidence that unattended stimuli are semantically processed in some cases, a number of theorists proposed a radically different theory of attention, suggesting that *all* messages, attended or not, undergo semantic analysis (e.g. Duncan, 1980; Norman, 1968). This analysis was said to take place in parallel across channels and without capacity limits. This theory came to be referred to as "late selection theory", because it places attentional selection after stimulus identification in the processing stream.

The debate between early- and late-selection theory dominated research in the field of attention for several decades. While some have argued that the debate was misconceived,[1] it drew attention to a number of important and testable issues, some of which have largely been resolved. One of these is the question of how extensively unattended stimuli are processed. Results from the past 10 to 15 years now make a strong case that, contrary to late-selection theory, perceptual selectivity *is* possible, at least to some extent (see Kahneman & Treisman, 1984). When subjects are given a good opportunity to focus attention, Stroop and flanker virtually disappear (e.g. Francolini & Egeth, 1980; Yantis & Johnston, 1990). In addition, if the late-selection theory were correct, the total number of unattended stimuli should not affect the size of these indirect effects; this prediction turns out not to hold in many cases (e.g. Kahneman & Chajczyk, 1983).

The results are generally consistent with the idea that, while attentional filtering is often less than 100% successful, it nonetheless does occur, causing rejected stimuli to be analyzed less completely than attended stimuli. These results are consistent with a sort of compromise theory suggested by Treisman (1960), who proposed that filtering "attenuates" rather than completely shuts off processing of unattended stimuli. Neither early- nor late-selection accounts fit well with results of "divided attention" studies, in which people attempt to process several visual objects in parallel. On the one hand, it seems unlikely that visual object recognition is necessarily strictly sequential. For example, people seem able to identify several letters at a time (Shiffrin & Gardner, 1972). On the other hand, when demands are great enough, visual processing does seem to be subject to capacity limits (see Pashler, 1995, for a review).

Another area studied intensively during the 1950s and 1960s is the attentional limitations beyond perception, in central cognitive operations and the planning and control of action. Many studies have asked what happens when people try to perform two sensorimotor tasks concurrently. The simplest experiments of this type combined two speeded tasks such as "choice reaction time" (here, the subject responds as quickly as possible to the identity of a signal, making one of several responses depending on the identity of this signal). When two such tasks are combined, the response to the second stimulus is generally slowed, with greater slowing the closer the two stimuli are presented in time. This slowing came to be nicknamed the "psychological refractory effect". Alan Welford (1952, 1967) attributed the effect to a bottleneck in what he termed "stimulus–response translation", i.e. the mental operation of selecting which response should be made based

---

[1] In the author's view, the basic issues are not misconceived, but early- and late-selection theories both conflate several logically separable issues, including capacity limitations and the degree of attentional selectivity (Pashler & Badgio, 1985).

on the identity of the stimulus. While some reviews from this early period of dual-task research favored Welford's analysis (e.g. Smith, 1967), others were unconvinced (Kahneman, 1973).

CURRENT RESEARCH: THE SCOPE OF THIS VOLUME

The chapters in this book provide tutorials on diverse areas in contemporary attention research, where progress has been notable. The issue of early- vs late-selection theory no longer dominates attention research as it did in the past. However, that debate still provides an important context for understanding contemporary inquiry in several areas. This is especially apparent in relation to neurophysiological studies of attention, reviewed by Steven Luck in his chapter. In recent decades, researchers have begun making direct measurements of neural activity in visual areas of macaque monkeys trained to attend to certain stimuli and ignore others (Moran & Desimone, 1985). Other researchers record tiny changes in electrical potentials on the scalps of human beings, comparing neural responses to attended and unattended stimuli (so-called event related potentials or ERPs). Results from both ERPs and single-unit recordings show that the neural activity in brain areas involved in perceptual analysis is often substantially greater for attended stimuli compared to unattended stimuli. These observations suggest (although they do not quite prove) that selectivity is indeed taking place within the perceptual machinery, a conclusion that contradicts late-selection theories. Luck describes how recent results provide additional clues about the workings of attentional selection in the brain's neural machinery.

Another area where the general questions addressed by early- and late-selection theories continue to loom large is in the area of visual search (the task of attempting to find a specified target or targets in a visual display). Visual search has been a very active research topic for at least 10 years. The reasons for this are not hard to understand. First, people search the visual world all the time, and they are quite good at it; a better understanding of search seems likely to have practical value. Second, search tasks require people to process a display which may contain many objects without requiring them to remember or report anything about each of these objects. This makes the task helpful in assessing perceptual limitations apart from memory and response limitations; the two sources of limitation are otherwise liable to be confused (Duncan, 1980; Estes & Taylor, 1964). In the typical visual search task, an observer simply inspects a display to see if a target is present or not, responding "yes" or "no" (or, sometimes, saying which of several possible targets was present).

In his chapter on search, Jeremy Wolfe reviews recent research that examines how efficiently people can search for targets as a function of what sort of discrimination they must perform. A great upsurge of interest in this topic was sparked by Treisman's Feature Integration Theory (Treisman & Gelade, 1980). Feature Integration Theory was, broadly speaking, a perceptually sophisticated version of early-selection theory. The theory proposed that parallel and unselective ("preattentive") visual processing routines determine which basic features are present in the visual field, without working out which features go together with which (e.g. because they are in the same object). The original motivation for this theory was the finding that when people search for a target defined as a conjunction of features (e.g. a green T among green Os and red Ts), search seems to take place in a serial fashion (response times increase roughly linearly with number of items in the display). As Wolfe describes in his chapter, subsequent research has painted a more complex picture. Some conjunctions can be detected quite efficiently, while others, particularly those involving spatial arrangements of parts, seem very inefficient. While Feature Integration Theory contains important germs of truth, the theory nonetheless requires significant modification. Wolfe describes his own theory of search, which he calls Guided Search, which is one of the most fully developed theories in the area. The theory shares with Feature Integration some distinction between parallel feature-based processing and subsequent limited-capacity search mechanisms, but the theory substantially modifies and refines the original formulation.

Beginning at least with Helmholtz (and probably long before that), people noticed that they can attend to something that is not at the point of visual fixation. To see this for yourself, stare straight at this plus sign and, without moving your eyes, try to read off the letters immediately above or below it: +. You will probably find that you can do this without much difficulty, although you will probably also notice a strong urge to move your eyes.

This simple demonstration shows that visual attention cannot be equated with the point of fixation, and that one can shift attention in the visual field without moving the eyes. It does not follow, however, that eye movements and attention are unrelated. In his chapter, James Hoffman reviews the intriguing and controversial history of research on attention and eye movements. The findings he describes, some from his lab and some from other research centers, demonstrate that planning of eye movements entails shifting visual attention, even though the converse is not necessarily the case.

As mentioned earlier, most research on the role of attention in perception carried out in the past 15 years or so has utilized visual rather than auditory stimuli. Dichotic speech, in particular, has fallen out of favor as a stimulus material for attention research. Over this period, however, a number of very capable researchers have studied basic questions about the role of attention in hearing using relatively simple auditory events. Unfortunately, much of this research has been published in journals devoted to auditory psychophysics, and as a result it has not influenced the mainstream of attention research to the extent that it should have. The chapter by Bertram Scharf provides a thorough overview of the principal findings from this research. The literature he reviews involves psychophysical tasks such as detecting tones against a background of noise. The same issues of selectivity and attentional capacity limitations first broached by the early- and late-selection theories arise here, and the results are broadly consistent with findings of visual studies.

So far we have mostly discussed the consequences of attention (e.g. for the fate of unattended stimuli; for the efficiency with which other attended stimuli are processed). Another important set of questions concerns the determinants of attention. In the typical attention experiment, a subject is instructed to attend to stimuli on some basis chosen by the experimenter (the left ear, the letter in the middle of the screen). In ordinary life, however, the allocation of attention is not a goal in and of itself and no one tells us how to attend; rather, allocation of attention is driven by some primary goal that we have, such as reading or finding an unobstructed path on which to walk. Early attention theorists of the late 19th century were very interested in this spontaneous deployment of attention. Titchener (1908, p.194), for example, noted that attention is grabbed by novel or rare stimuli, and more recent authors such as Berlyne (1957) raised the issue as well. However, interest in the control of attention receded as the information-processing approach took hold and literatures sprang up devoted to specific tasks with specific attentional requirements. The chapter by Yantis describes one area in which information-processing research has nonetheless helped to illuminate the control of visual attention. This concerns the way in which abrupt visual onsets and, sometimes, changes of other sorts tend to "attract" attention involuntarily.

As mentioned earlier, we use the term "attention" not only to refer to limitations in perceiving multiple stimuli, but to refer to more general limitations in mental functioning—in making decisions, storing information in memory, planning actions, and so forth. The bottleneck analysis by Welford suggested that people have quite severe limitations at a post-perceptual, cognitive level, as manifested in the psychological refractory period phenomenon. The chapter by Johnston and myself reviews the literature on dual-task performance. We describe results from various labs that support Welford's early suggestion that central processing is usually and perhaps invariably sequential. Some recent results in this area suggest, however, that this sequentiality is not necessarily the result of any single brain area being responsible for particular central operations. Furthermore, the nature of these functional limits is not what one might expect from a "central processor"; for example, it seems that different stimuli can jointly help select a single response at the same time even if they cannot be used to select different responses.

Another area where there has been a marked increase in research in recent years is in the study of pathologies of attention caused by lesions of the brain. The chapter by Jon Driver focuses on the fascinating syndrome called "hemineglect". Usually caused by damage to the parietal lobes, neglect appears to reflect a selective difficulty in orienting perceptual attention to one half of space. Driver describes evidence suggesting that this pathology is attributable to a competition between lateralized brain areas that "lobby" for the allocation of attention to the opposite half of space. He also illustrates how attentional pathologies illuminate important theoretical issues relating to normal attentional function. Examples include Feature Integration Theory and the way in which attention and object segmentation are tied.

For the most part, experimental analysis of attention has been carried out with the goal of testing molar or functional hypotheses about information-processing operations, rather than underlying brain circuitry. Since the mid-1980s, however, researchers in psychology and neighboring fields such as computer science have begun attempting to model computational mechanisms of attention at a more fine-grained level. Generally, this has involved carrying out computer simulations of networks of brainlike computing elements. Mozer's chapter provides an introduction to connectionist modeling in general and current computational analyses of selective attention in particular. Without assuming any background in connectionist modeling, he takes the reader through the basic mechanics of object recognition networks and considers different ways in which attentional control might be implemented in such networks.

Harold Pashler

REFERENCES

Berlyne, D.E. (1957). Attention to change, conditioned inhibition, and stimulus satiation. *British Journal of Psychology*, *48*, 138–140.

Broadbent, D.E. (1954). The role of auditory localization in attention and memory span. *Journal of Experimental Psychology*, *47*, 191–196.

Broadbent, D.E. (1958). *Perception and communication*. London: Pergamon Press.

Cherry, E.C. (1953). Some experiments on the recognition of speech, with one and with two ears. *Journal of the Acoustical Society of America*, *25*, 975–979.

Corteen, R.S., & Wood, B. (1972). Autonomic responses to shock-associated words in an unattended channel. *Journal of Experimental Psychology*, *94*, 308–313.

Duncan, J. (1980). The locus of interference in the perception of simultaneous stimuli. *Psychological Review*, *87*, 272–300.

Estes, W.K., & Taylor, H.A. (1964). A detection method and probabilistic models for assessing information processing from brief visual displays. *Proceedings of the National Academy of Science, 52,* 446–454.

Francolini, C.M., & Egeth, H.E. (1980). On the nonautomaticity of "automatic" activation: Evidence of selective seeing. *Perception & Psychophysics, 27,* 331–342.

Hatfield, G. (in press). Attention in early scientific psychology. To appear in R.D. Wright (Ed.), *Visual attention.* New York: Oxford University Press.

Hull, C.L. (1930). Knowledge and purpose as habit mechanisms. *Psychological Review, 37,* 511–525.

James, W. (1890/1950). *The Principles of Psychology, Vol 1.* New York: Dover.

Kahneman, D. (1973). *Attention and effort.* New York: Prentice Hall.

Kahneman, D., & Chajczyk, D. (1983). Tests of the automaticity of reading: Dilution of Stroop effects by color-irrelevant stimuli. *Journal of Experimental Psychology: Human Perception and Performance, 9,* 497–509.

Kahneman, D., & Treisman, A. (1984). Changing views of attention and automaticity. In R. Parasuraman & D.R. Davies (Eds.), *Varieties of attention* (pp.29–62). New York: Academic Press.

Külpe, O. (1902). Attention. *The Monist, 13.*

Lichtheim, L. (1885). On aphasia. *Brain, 7,* 433–484.

Lovie, A.D. (1983). Attention and behaviourism. Fact and fiction *British Journal of Psychology, 74,* 301–310.

Moran, J., & Desimone, R. (1985). Selective attention gates visual processing in the extrastriate cortex. *Science, 229,* 782–784.

Moray, N. (1959). Attention in dichotic listening: Affective cues and the influence of instructions. *Quarterly Journal of Experimental Psychology, 11,* 56–60.

Munsterberg, H. (1894). The intensifying effect of attention. *Psychological Review, 1,* 39–44.

Neumann, O. (1971). Aufmerksamkeit. In J. Ritter (Ed.), (Vol 1, rev. ed., cols. 635–645) Historiches Wörterbüch der Philosophie. Damstadt: Wissenschäftliche Büchgesellschaft.

Norman, D.A. (1968). Toward a theory of memory and attention. *Psychological Review, 75,* 522–536.

Pashler, H. (1995). Attention and visual perception: Analyzing divided attention. In D.N. Osherson & S. Kosslyn (Eds.), *Visual cognition: An invitation to cognitive science* (pp.71–100). Cambridge, MA: MIT Press.

Pashler, H., & Badgio, P.C. (1985). Visual attention and stimulus identification. *Journal of Experimental Psychology: Human Perception and Performance, 11,* 105–121.

Pillsbury, W.B. (1908). *Attention.* London: S. Sonnenschein & Co. Ltd. New York: Macmillan.

Posner, M.I. (1978). *Chronometric explorations of mind.* Hillsdale, NJ: Lawrence Erlbaum Associates Inc.

Prinzmetal, W. (1996). *Phenomenology of attention.* Paper presented at the Western Attention Conference, Claremont Graduate Center, USA.

Rock, I., & Guttman, D. (1981). The effect of inattention on form perception. *Journal of Experimental Psychology: Human Perception and Performance, 7,* 275–285.

Shiffrin, R.M. & Gardner, G.T. (1972). Visual processing capacity and attentional control. *Journal of Experimental Psychology, 93,* 78–82.

Smith, M.C. (1967). Theories of the psychological refractory period. *Psychological Bulletin, 67,* 202–213.

Titchener, E.B. (1908). *Lectures on the elementary psychology of feeling and attention.* New York: Macmillan.

Treisman, A. (1960). Contextual cues in selective listening. *Quarterly Journal of Experimental Psychology, 12,* 242–248.

Treisman, A., & Gelade, G. (1980). A feature integration theory of attention. *Cognitive Psychology*, *12*, 97–136.

Welford, A.T. (1952). The "psychological refractory period" and the timing of high speed performance: A review and a theory. *British Journal of Psychology*, *43*, 2–19.

Welford, A.T. (1967). Single-channel operation in the brain. *Acta Psychologica*, *27*, 5–22.

Wolford, G., & Morrison, F. (1980). Processing of unattended visual information. *Memory and Cognition*, *8*, 521–527.

Wood, N., & Cowan, N. (1995). The cocktail party phenomenon revisited: How frequent are attention shifts to one's name in an irrelevant auditory channel? *Journal of Experimental Psychology: Learning, Memory, and Cognition*, *21*, 255–260.

Yantis, S., & Johnston, J.C. (1990). On the locus of visual selection: Evidence from focused attention tasks. *Journal of Experimental Psychology: Human Perception and Performance*, *16*, 135–149.

CHAPTER ONE

Visual Search

Jeremy M. Wolfe
Brigham and Women's Hospital & Harvard Medical School,
Boston, USA

Loosely following William James, we can assert that everyone knows that visual search tasks are because everyone does them all the time. Visual search tasks are those tasks where one looks for something. This chapter will concentrate on search tasks where the object is visible in the current field of view. Real world examples include search for tumors or other critical information in x-rays, search for the right piece of a jigsaw puzzle, or search for the correct key on the keyboard when you are still in the "hunt and peck" stage of typing. Other searches involve eye movements, a topic covered in Hoffman's chapter in this volume.

In the lab, a visual search task might look something like Fig. 1.1. If you fixate on the central asterisk in Fig. 1.1, you will probably find an "X" immediately. It seems to "pop out" of the display. However, if you are asked to find the letter "T", you may not see it until some sort of additional processing is performed. Assuming that you maintained fixation, the retinal image did not change. Your *attention* to the "T" changed your ability to identify it as a "T". Processing all items at once ("in parallel") provides enough information to allow us to differentiate an "X" from an "L". However, the need for some sort of covert deployment of attention in series from letter to letter in the search for the "T" indicates that we cannot fully process all of the visual stimuli in our field of view at one time (e.g. Tsotsos, 1990). Similar limitations appear in many places in cognitive processing.

It is important to distinguish *covert* deployment of attention from movements of the eyes. If you fixate on the asterisk in Fig. 1.2, you will find

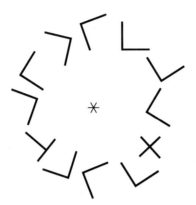

FIG. 1.1.   Fixating on the asterisk, find the X and T.

that, not only does the "T" not pop out, it cannot be identified until it is foveated. It is hidden from the viewer by the limitations of peripheral visual processing. You can identify the stimuli in Fig. 1.1 while fixating the central asterisk. This is not to say that you did not move your eyes—only that you did not need to move your eyes. For most of the experiments discussed in this chapter, eye movements were uncontrolled. While interesting, eye movements are probably not the determining factor in visual searches of the sort discussed in this review—those with relatively large items spaced fairly widely to limit peripheral crowding effects (Levi, Klein, & Aitsebaomo, 1985). For instance, when Klein & Farrell (1989) and Zelinsky (1993), using stimuli of this sort, had participants perform the search tasks with and without overt eye movements, they obtained the same pattern of reaction time (RT) data regardless of the presence or absence of eye movements. The eye movements were not random. They simply did not constrain the RTs even though eye movements and attentional deployments are intimately

FIG. 1.2.   Find the T.

related (Hoffman & Subramaniam, 1995; Khurana & Kowler, 1987; Kowler, Anderson, Dosher, & Blaser, 1995).

The basic organization of this chapter is as follows: first, some paradigmatic issues are discussed. The second section is devoted to describing the properties of preattentive processing; the processing of stimuli that occurs before attention is deployed to an item in a search task. The third section discusses the use of preattentive information by subsequent processes. A number of topics, relevant to visual search, are discussed elsewhere in this volume and not here. For example, see Luck's chapter for coverage of the electrophysiological literature.

SECTION I: THE BASIC PARADIGM

In a standard visual search, subjects look for a *target* item among some number of *distractor* items. The total number of items in the display is known as the *set size*. On some percentage of the trials, typically 50%, a target is present. On the other trials, only distractors are presented. Subjects make one response to indicate that they have found a target and another response to indicate that no target has been found. The two dependent measures that are most commonly studied are reaction time (RT) and accuracy. In studies where RT is the measure of interest, the display usually remains visible until the subject responds. RT is generally analyzed as a function of set size, producing two functions—one for target present and one for target absent trials. The slopes and the intercepts of these RT × set size functions are used to infer the mechanics of the search.

There are numerous variations on the basic search task. For instance, it can be profitable to have subjects search for any of two or more targets at once (Estes & Taylor, 1966) or to divide attention between two different search tasks. (e.g. Braun & Julesz, 1996a, 1996b; Braun & Sagi, 1990a).

Accuracy Methods

In addition to RT experiments, the second major method for studying visual search uses accuracy as the dependent measure (Bergen & Julesz, 1983; Braun & Sagi, 1990b; Eriksen & Spencer, 1969; Sagi & Julesz, 1985; Shiffrin & Gardner, 1972). In this case, the search stimulus is presented only briefly. It is followed by a mask that is presumed to terminate the search. The stimulus onset asynchrony (SOA) between the onset of the stimulus and that of the mask is varied and accuracy is plotted as a function of SOA (see Fig. 1.3). In a search where many or all items can be processed in a single step, the target can be detected even when the SOA is very short. In a search where each item must be processed in turn (e.g. Ts among Ls), the accuracy data are consistent with the view that one additional item is processed for each 40–50 msec increase in the SOA (Bergen & Julesz, 1983). That is, the

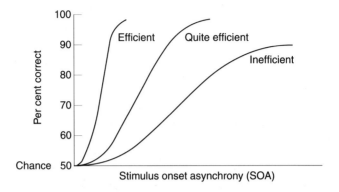

FIG. 1.3.   Easier searches can be performed with high accuracy even when a mask follows a briefly presented search stimulus with a short SOA. Harder search tasks require longer SOAs and may never reach near perfect performance.

data are consistent with a serial search.[1] Accuracy methods are of particular use if one wants to eliminate the possibility of eye movements. A stimulus can be flashed for 50 msec—too short for voluntary eye movements. Nevertheless, the internal representation of that stimulus can be searched until a mask appears several hundred msec later.

Interpreting Search Results

Returning to the RT method, it helps to begin with two extreme cases when considering the analysis of RT × size slopes. Consider a search for a red item among green distractors. As has been shown many times (e.g. Nagy & Sanchez, 1990), the number of green items makes very little difference. Either red is present or it is not. The resulting RT × set size slopes have slopes near zero msec/item. The usual inference in the visual search literature is that these results reflect an underlying *parallel search*. Apparently, all items can be processed at once to a level sufficient to distinguish targets from non-targets. The red item, if present, "pops out" and makes its presence known. In contrast, a search for a S among 2 s will produce target trial slopes of 20–30 msec/item and blank trial slopes of about 40–60 msec/item. Searches yielding this pattern of results are usually called *serial searches* because the pattern of results is consistent with a random, *serial self-terminating search* through the items at a rate of one item every 40–60 msec. The logic is as follows: On a target present trial, the target might be the first item visited by attention. It might be the last item or it might be any item in between. On average, attention will need to visit half of the items. On target

---

[1] Although a limited-capacity parallel mechanism could produce the same results; see later.)

absent (blank) trials, attention will have to visit all items in order to confirm the absence of the target. As a result, the cost of adding one additional distractor is twice as great for blank trials as for target trials and the resulting slopes of the blank trials should be twice as great (but see Horowitz & Wolfe, 1997)

The distinction between serial and parallel processes has a long history (e.g. Kinchla, 1974; Neisser, 1967; Schneider & Shiffrin, 1977; Shiffrin & Schneider, 1977; Sternberg, 1969; see Bundesen, 1996, and Kinchla, 1992, for recent reviews) The notion of a division between parallel and serial visual searches became theoretically prominent when Anne Treisman proposed her original Feature Integration Theory (FIT; Treisman & Gelade, 1980). Triesman's proposal was that many *feature searches* were parallel searches and that everything else required serial search. Feature searches are searches where the target is distinguished from distractors by a single basic feature like color, size, or motion (the list of basic features will be discussed later). "Everything else" included searches for targets defined by *conjunctions* of features. For example, in a search for a big red square among small red and big green squares, the target is defined by a conjunction of color and size. Neither the size nor the color feature alone defines the target.

Today, 15 years after the publication of the original FIT, the serial/parallel dichotomy is a useful, but potentially dangerous fiction. The strict form is no longer part of FIT (Treisman, 1993; Treisman & Sato, 1990) and it is explicitly rejected by various other models of visual search (Duncan & Humphreys, 1989; Wolfe, 1994a; Wolfe, Cave, & Franzel, 1989; Humphreys & Muller, 1993; Grossberg, Mingolla, & Ross, 1994). Nevertheless, there is a steady stream of papers that either use the dichotomy as fact or consider the strict form to be a worthy target of new research. In hope of reformulating this aspect of the debate about mechanisms of visual search, the following section presents four reasons why the serial/parallel dichotomy in visual search is deceased and ought to be allowed to rest in peace.

1. Inferring Mechanisms From Slopes is Not That Simple

For more than 20 years, Townsend and others have been warning that RT × size measures are inadequate to discriminate between underlying parallel and serial mechanisms (Atkinson, Homlgren, & Juola, 1969; Townsend, 1971, 1976, 1990). For example, parallel processing is routinely inferred from shallow target–trial slopes (e.g. 5 msec/item). However, in principle these could be the product of a serial mechanism that processes one item every 10 msec. Further, the pattern of results produced by a serial self-terminating search can also be produced by a variety of limited-capacity parallel models (e.g. Kinchla, 1974; Ratcliff, 1978; Ward & McClelland, 1989; and see Palmer & McLean, 1995, for a model employing unlimited-capacity processes). A model of this sort (loosely borrowed from Ratcliff, 1978) might look like Fig. 1.4.

The idea of a limited-capacity parallel model is that all items in the display are processed at once. Evidence accumulates at each location for the presence of a target or non-target item. Search terminates when one item crosses the "yes" threshold or when all items cross the "no" threshold. The bell curves in Fig. 1.4 are intended to show the hypothetical distribution of finishing times for target and non-target items. The rate of accumulation is dependent on the amount of the parallel *resource* that is available. Given a fixed amount of resource, an increase in set size will result in a decrease in the amount of resource per item. This will slow each item's journey to the threshold, producing an increase in RT with set size. Judicious placement of thresholds can produce the desired 2:1 slope ratios and other hallmarks of serial search. As a result, it is very difficult to distinguish between models with a serial deployment of attention and limited-capacity parallel alternatives on the basis of slope magnitudes or slope ratios alone.[2]

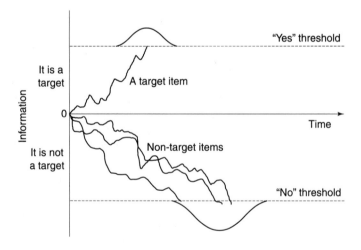

FIG. 1.4.   A limited-capacity parallel model.

---

[2] Devotees of the serial deployment of attention, including the author, think that the parallel models have to introduce "a plethora of new threshold and rate parameters" (quote from an anonymous reviewer).

2. "Strict" Serial Search Involves a Number of Unfounded Assumptions

The 2:1 slope ratio prediction relies on the assumption that target trials involve serial search through an average of half the items while blank trials involve search of all items. The blank trial assumption is undoubtedly too strong. First, it requires that search be exhaustive but that no items are ever checked twice (Horowitz & Wolfe, 1997). Second, it makes no provision for errors. Many published "serial" searches have error rates in the 5–10% range. Most of these errors are "misses", suggesting that the search ended before all items were visited. These factors complicate the 2:1 slope ratio prediction (Chun & Wolfe, 1996).

The strict model also assumes that one item is processed at a time. Several researchers propose that more than one item can be processed in a single attentional "fixation"[3] (Gilmore, 1985; Grossberg et al., 1994; Humphreys & Muller, 1993; Humphreys, Quinlan, & Riddoch, 1989; Pashler, 1987; Ross & Mingolla, 1994; Treisman, 1992). Models that propose that search proceeds from group to group (Grossberg et al., 1994) are hybrids, lying between FIT-style models and limited-capacity parallel models (see Section III).

3. The Strict Model Assumes a Fixed "Dwell Time"

Dwell time, the amount of time that attention spends at a location once it is deployed to that location, is an important parameter in attention models. Asserting that target–trial slopes of 5 msec/item reflect parallel search mechanisms assumes that such slopes could not reflect serial mechanisms operating at a rate as fast as one item every 10 msec. It assumes that the dwell time must be longer than 10 msec. Some models (e.g. Wolfe et al., 1989) explicitly assume that each item takes a fixed amount of time to process (40 msec in Wolfe et al, 1989). That cannot be strictly true. It is easy to devise stimuli that will take an appreciable amount of time to classify once attention has been deployed to their location. Conjunctions of two colors (Wolfe et al., 1990) and judgments of spatial relations (Logan, 1994) may be two examples where the dwell time at each item is significantly longer than 40–50 msec.

What if the dwell time is significantly longer than 40–50 msec/item? Assertions about long dwell times can be used to argue for parallel models of search. For example, Duncan, Ward, and Shapiro (1994) assert that the dwell time is several hundred msec long (Ward, Duncan, & Shapiro, 1996).

---

[3] An attentional fixation is theoretically analogous to an eye fixation. Attention is deployed to some location in the field for, perhaps, 50 msec. The question here is "how many items can be processed before attention is redeployed?".

If this were true, target–trial search rates of 25 or even 50 msec/item would reflect some parallel processing. This estimate of dwell time seems far too long. First, there is evidence that subjects can monitor a stream of sequentially presented items for a target letter or picture at rates exceeding eight items/sec (Chun & Potter, 1995; Lawrence, 1971; Potter, 1975, 1976). In addition, the experimental basis for the Duncan et al. claim, itself, is controversial (Moore, Egeth, Berglan, & Luck, 1996). Still, it would be an oversimplification to assume that each item in a visual search requires 50 msec to be categorized as a target or non-target.

4. Most Importantly, The Data Do Not Show a Serial/ Parallel Dichotomy

The idea that searches can be divided into two classes, serial and parallel, is an attractive notion but it is simply not supported by the data (It was better supported when Treisman first proposed it back in 1980). Results of visual search experiments run from flat to steep RT × set size functions with no evidence of a dichotomous division. The evidence shows a continuum of search results. It is important to be clear about the implications of this fact. This does not mean that distinct serial and parallel mechanisms do not exist in visual search. The Guided Search model, for example, is built around the idea that the continuum can be explained by an early parallel mechanism working in tandem with a later serial mechanism (details in Wolfe, 1994a; Wolfe et al., 1989; see also Hoffman, 1979; Kinchla, 1977). The continuum of search slopes does make it implausible to think that the search tasks, themselves, can be neatly classified as serial or parallel.

Continua of search slopes can be found in both feature and conjunction searches. In the usual version of the dichotomy between parallel and serial searches, feature searches are supposed to be parallel searches. However, if one decreases the difference between the target and the distractor attributes, feature search slopes will rise smoothly from flat "parallel" slopes to steeper "serial" slopes. Thus, a search for green among red distractors will yield slopes near zero whereas a search for green among a yellowish green will produce more classically "serial" slopes (Nagy & Sanchez, 1990). Importantly, the steep, "serial" slopes are obtained for stimuli that are still clearly discriminable—separated by much more than one "just noticeable difference" (JND—Nagy & Sanchez, 1990). Similar results can be obtained for orientation (Foster & Westland, 1996; Foster & Ward, 1991a, 1991b) and, no doubt, for any other basic feature. Feature searches can also become "serial" if the distractors are sufficiently heterogeneous. The metric of heterogenity is not trivial to describe. For example, under some circumstances a target of one color can be found efficiently among distractors of many different colors (Duncan, 1989; Smallman & Boynton, 1990; Wolfe et al., 1990), whereas, if different colors are picked, two distractor colors can yield steep search slopes for a third, target color (Bauer, Jolicoeur, & Cowan, 1996; D'Zmura, 1991). Similar effects have been observed in orientation searches with heterogeneous distractors (Alkhateeb, Morris, & Ruddock, 1990; Moraglia, 1989; Wolfe, Friedman-Hill, Stewart, & O'Connell, 1992).

In general, it is hard to argue with the Duncan and Humphreys (1989) account, which holds that search becomes harder as target–distractor similarity increases and easier as distractor–distractor similarity increases. The hard work is in the details of what "similarity" means in this context.

Turning to conjunction searches, the steep "serial" slopes of Triesman and Gelade (1980) also turn out to be at the high end of a continuum of search slopes. In the past 10 years, a range of shallower slopes has been obtained from many different types of conjunction search (Cohen, 1993; Cohen & Ivry, 1991; Dehaene, 1989; Egeth, Virzi, & Garbart, 1984; McLeod, Driver, & Crisp, 1988; McLeod, Driver, Dienes, & Crisp, 1991; Nakayama & Silverman, 1986; Sagi, 1988; Theeuwes & Kooi, 1994; Treisman & Sato, 1990; von der Heydt & Dursteler, 1993; Wolfe, 1992a; Zohary & Hochstein, 1989).

Beyond the Serial/Parallel Dichotomy: How Shall We Describe Search Performance?

If we accept that the result of RT studies of visual search do not fall into two distinct groups that can be labeled "parallel" and "serial", should we despair and declare the entire enterprise a hopeless mess? That seems too extreme. There is a clear difference between searches where the target "pops out" of the display and searches where each additional distractor makes it appreciably harder to find the target. These searches can be described as *efficient* in the former case and *inefficient* in the latter (see Fig. 1.5) Efficiency is merely a descriptive term and does not carry with it the theoretical baggage of "parallel", "serial", and so forth. Thus, search for a line of one orientation among distractors of one sufficiently different orientation is *efficient* with target–trial slopes near zero msec/item (even if the lines are defined by other little lines; Bravo & Blake, 1990). Search for a rotated "T" among rotated "L"s is *inefficient* with target–trial slopes near 20 msec/item (Egeth & Dagenbach, 1991; Kwak, Dagenbach, & Egeth, 1991). Search for some conjunctions of two features (e.g. shape and color) might be described as *quite efficient* with target–trial slopes less than 10 msec/item (e.g. Theeuwes & Kooi, 1994) but not as efficient (in this study) as conjunctions of shape and contrast polarity (slopes near zero; Theeuwes & Kooi, 1994). Finally, some searches like conjunctions of two orientations are *very inefficient* with target–trial slopes significantly greater than 25 msec/item (Bilsky & Wolfe, 1995). The use of this sort of terminology would allow the

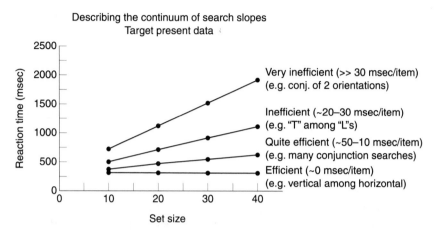

FIG. 1.5.   The continuum of search slopes can be described neutrally in terms of search "efficiency".

proponents of different models to speak about the data in a common language. It does not imply, however, an abandonment of the idea that an orderly and understandable set of underlying parallel and serial mechanisms produce the continuum of search results.

SECTION II: PREATTENTIVE PROCESSING OF VISUAL STIMULI

What Defines a Basic Feature in Visual Search?

In the heyday of the dichotomy between parallel and serial searches, a basic feature was a property that could support "parallel" visual search; that is, one that produced RT × set size slopes near zero. That definition becomes inadequate in the face of conjunction searches (Theeuwes & Kooi, 1994) or even triple conjunction searches (Wolfe et al., 1989) with near-zero slopes. One could propose that these conjunctions have featural status but this seems unparsimonious. It is one thing to propose that there are parallel processors for a set of basic features like color, orientation, size, and so forth. It is less appealing to argue for parallel representations of all the pairwise (and, perhaps, three-way) combinations of that initial list. This rapidly leads to combinatorial trouble.

Other criteria have been proposed for defining features (see Treisman's 1986 review). One of these is that basic features support preattentive texture segmentation. A region of green spots in a field of red spots will be immediately segmented from the background. Similar results would be obtained with moving spots among stationary spots, spots at one stereoscopic depth among spots at another, and so on. It has been suggested that texture segmentation, by itself, defines basic features. However, Wolfe (1992a) showed that there are cases where stimuli that produce "effortless" texture segmentation do not produce efficient search and vice versa (see also Snowden, 1996). This is illustrated in Fig. 1.6. In Fig. 1.6a, it is quite easy to find either a black vertical or a white horizontal target, but the region that is made up entirely of target items does not segregate from the background items. In Figure 1.6b, the vertical and horizontal region does segment from the oblique background. However, search for a vertical or horizontal target among oblique distractors is quite inefficient (Wolfe et al., 1992). Neither efficient search nor effortless texture segmentation is sufficient to identify a "basic feature". However, if a stimulus supports both efficient search *and* effortless segmentation, then it is probably safe to include it in the ranks of basic features. There do not seem to be any obvious exceptions to this rule.

Basic Features in Visual Search

With that preamble, this section will survey the evidence that various stimulus attributes are or are not basic features in visual search. There is reasonable consensus about a small number of basic features and more debate over several other candidates.

Color

To begin with perhaps the most straightforward case, color differences support efficient visual search and effortless texture segmentation. A long history of basic and applied research points to color as one of the best ways to make a stimulus "pop out" from its surroundings (Bundesen & Pedersen, 1983; Carter, 1982; D'Zmura, 1991; Farmer & Taylor, 1980; Green & Anderson, 1956; Moraglia, Maloney, Fekete, & Al-Basi, 1989; Smith, 1962;

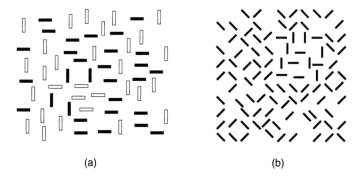

(a)   (b)

FIG. 1.6.   (a) Look for black vertical or white horizontal. (b) Look for vertical or horizontal.

Van Orden, 1993). With color, as with other basic features, we want to know what representation of the feature is used in search. Color is represented in a number of ways in the visual system. There is wavelength information at the retina. There are opponent-color representations in the relatively early stages of visual processing. At later stages of processing, there are the perceived colors of things in the world (Boynton, 1979; Lennie & D'Zmura, 1988). A few studies have looked in detail at the psychophysics of search for colored targets. Nagy and Sanchez (1990) compared JNDs for color stimuli with the color differences that would produce efficient search. The first important point to be taken from their work is that small differences between the color of targets and distractors will not support efficient search. As the difference shrinks, the slope of the RT × set size function rises. Nagy and Sanchez (1990) identified the smallest color difference that supported efficient search. This can be thought of as a *preattentive just noticeable difference* (preattentive JND). For a given target color, it is possible to create an isopter representing this preattentive JND around the target color. Nagy and Sanchez compared this isopter to the MacAdam ellipse, the isopter defined by standard JNDs for color. These two types of JNDs are quite different. The preattentive JNDs are much larger and the isopter has a different shape. This means that there are clearly discriminable pairs of colors that do not support efficient visual search. The difference in isopter shape suggests that the preattentive JNDs are created by mechanisms different than those mediating simple color discrimination. Nagy, Sanchez, and Hughes (1990) examined these effects away from the fovea with comparable results.

Jolicoeur (personal communication) notes that Nagy and Sanchez's preattentive JNDs are collected under conditions quite different from those used to determine standard JNDs. When, for example, Jolicoeur and his colleagues repeated the Nagy and Sanchez experiments with stimuli that are isoluminant with the background, they found that smaller color differences would support efficient search. It seems likely that methodological concern of this sort account for some, but not all, of the difference between preattentive and standard JNDs.

When there is more than one distractor color, efficient search is still possible but there are constraints. A number of experiments have shown efficient search for targets of unique color among at least nine distractor colors (Duncan, 1988; Smallman & Boynton, 1990 Wolfe et al., 1990). These searches with heterogeneous distractors are efficient only if the colors are widely separated in color space. When more similar colors are used, search is inefficient if the distractor colors flank the target color in color space (D'Zmura, 1991). D'Zmura has proposed that efficient search is possible whenever the target and distractor colors lie on different sides of a line drawn through color space. This is illustrated in Fig. 1.7, where Target T1 is

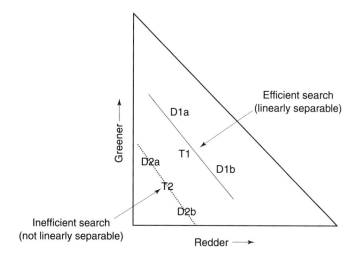

FIG. 1.7.   Linear separability in color space.

linearly separable from distractors D1a and D1b. This would correspond to something like a search for a white target among greenish (D1a) and yellowish (D1b) distractors. By contrast, T2 (bluish) would be hard to find among D2a (blue-green) and D2b (purplish) because the target is not linearly separable from the distractors. Search for T2 among D2a or D2b *alone* would be efficient. The same principle holds when more than two distractor colors are used. If the target falls inside the area of color space defined by the distractors, search is inefficient. If it falls outside, search is efficient. This linear separability account seems likely to hold only in a limited region of color space around any given target color. That is, linear separability holds if the color differences are not too large (see Bauer et al., 1996). No line in color space will explain the results of, say, Smallman and Boynton (1990) where nine different colors are used.

   In her work on color search, Treisman speaks about search for prototypical colors. She argues that it is easier to find a deviation from a prototypical color than to find the prototypical color itself. This is her account for *search asymmetries* (Treisman & Gormican, 1988). The term "search asymmetry" describes a situation where it is easier to find A among B than to find B among A. For instance, in color search it is easier to find magenta among red distractors than red among magenta. Treisman's argument is that it is easier to find the deviation from red than to find red among deviants. Another way to describe the result is to say that targets are easy to find if and only if they contain some unique basic feature information. Magenta contains "blue" and can be found by looking for blue among distractors that are not blue. Red contains red, but so does magenta. This search is less efficient because it is relatively more difficult to look for the "reddest" item or the "not blue" item. In this account, preattentive color space is divided into a few regions, a few basic colors. Indeed, many of the results with large color differences can be simulated in a model that assumes four basic colors in preattentive processing: red, yellow, green, and blue (Wolfe, 1994a). The apparently categorical description of large color differences and the linear separability account of search with smaller differences remain to be reconciled in a single description of the preattentive representation of color.

The preceding discussion of color ignores the role of black and white. Are they colors or do they represent a separate luminance feature? In some work, black and white behave like colors (Smallman & Boyntan, 1990). Bauer, Jolicoeur, and Cowan (1996) find that a middle gray is hard to find when distractors are brighter and dimmer, following the linear separability principles described earlier. However, in other work, luminance seems to act more independently. Callaghan (1984) found that brightness variation had an effect on texture segmentation tasks that were based on hue, whereas hue did not have the same impact on tasks based on brightness. Theeuwes and Kooi (1994) report that conjunctions of contrast polarity and shape are easier to find than the easiest conjunctions of color and shape. Rensink and Enns (1995), and O'Connell and Treisman (1990) also propose preattentive properties of contrast polarity that are different than the properties of color. Moreover, attention seems to affect the perception of brightness (Tsal, Shalev, Zakay, & Lubow, 1994). The topic requires more systematic research. Specifically, the systematic work on color search has been done in two dimensions of color space. It needs to be extended into the third dimension, luminance.

Orientation

Orientation is another well accepted and well studied basic feature in visual search. Some of the properties of color as a feature are seen again when we turn to orientation. Preattentive JNDs can be plotted and they are larger than traditional JNDs (Foster & Ward, 1991a). Exact values will vary with variables like line length but a reasonable rule of thumb would be that subjects can discriminate between lines that differ by 1° or 2° in orientation but require a difference of about 15° to support efficient visual search with slopes near zero msec/item. Foster and his colleagues argue that performance on simple orientation tasks can be accounted for by two broadly tuned channels, one near vertical and one near horizontal (Foster & Ward, 1991b; Foster & Westland, 1995; Westland & Foster, 1996), although they find some second-order effects that would seem to require other preattentive orientation processes (Foster & Westland, 1992, 1995). Wolfe et al. (1992)

argue for channels roughly corresponding to the categorical terms "steep", "shallow", "left", and "right" (see also Mannan, Ruddock, & Wright, 1995).

This four-channel proposal is driven by data from experiments having more than one distractor orientation. If the distractors are of heterogeneous orientations, search becomes very inefficient (Moraglia, 1989a) unless one of two conditions is met. The target can be the item having the greatest local orientation contrast with neighboring distractors as shown in Fig. 1.8a. It is immediately clear that one of the two vertical lines in Fig. 1.8a is much more salient than the other because it is more dramatically different from its neighbors. In Fig. 1.8b, the same set of lines are rearranged and the vertical targets are harder to find (Jolicoeur, 1992; Moraglia, 1989a; Nothdurft, 1991b). The same effect of local contrast is seen in color (Nothdurft, 1991a, 1993b). Doherty and Foster (1995) cast some doubt on the importance of "local" in these "local contrasts". They show little change in performance as a function of stimulus density.

The other class of efficient orientation search is search for a target that is categorically unique. Wolfe et al. (1992) find that search is quite efficient even with heterogeneous distractors, if the target is the only "steep", "shallow", "left-", or "right-tilted" item in the display. This is illustrated in Fig. 1.9 for "steep" targets.

In both panels of Fig. 1.9, the target is tilted 10° to the left of vertical and each distractor is either 40° or 60° different in orientation from the target. On the left, search is relatively efficient because the target is uniquely steep whereas on the right, search is less efficient because, while the target is the *steepest* item, it does not possess any unique categorical attribute (Wolfe et al., 1992).

The notion of four (or even of two) broadly tuned channels for the preattentive processing of orientation can go a long way toward explaining

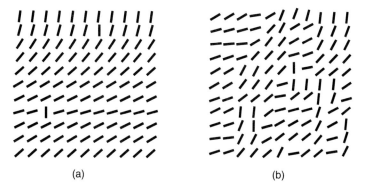

(a)   (b)

FIG. 1.8.   Find the two vertical lines in each array.

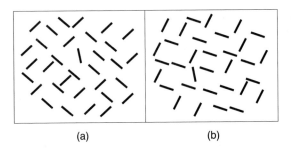

FIG. 1.9.   (a) T: –10° among D: –50° & +50°. (b) T: –10° among D: –70° & +30°.

search asymmetries in orientation search tasks. For example, it is harder to find a vertical target among distractors tilted 20° off vertical than it is to find a 20° target among vertical distractors (Treisman & Souther, 1985; Wolfe et al., 1992). In terms of four categorical orientation filters, the tilted target is easy to find because it is uniquely "tilted right" while the vertical target is merely the "steepest" item and is not categorically unique (Wolfe, 1994a). Gurnsey and Browse (1989) invoke non-linear orientation processing of a somewhat different sort to account for asymmetries in texture discrimination.

As with the luminance dimension of color, there is some question about what to do with the third dimension of orientation, slant or tilt out of the picture plane. There is good evidence for an ability to search for orientation in depth (Enns & Rensink, 1990b; Enns, 1992; Enns & Rensink, 1991; Epstein & Babler, 1990) and evidence that, like orientation in the frontal plane, some orientations in depth are easier to search for than others (Von Grünau & Dubé, 1994). He and Nakayama (1992) have provided converging evidence that visual search takes into account the slant of the perceived surface in depth (see also Aks & Enns, 1996). Orientation search is also modulated by gravitational forces (Marendaz, Stivalet, Barraclough, & Walkowiac, 1993; Stivalet, Marendaz, Barraclough, & Mourareau, 1995). One could ask if orientation in depth (slant) influences search for targets defined by orientation in the frontal plane (or vice versa). These experiments have not been done.

As might be suggested by the work on orientation in depth and by the categorical nature of preattentive orientation processing, the orientations that are processed in parallel in visual search are derived from a relatively late, abstracted representation of orientation and not from the sort of oriented luminance contrast that might drive cells in primary visual cortex. This point is underlined in experiments by Bravo and Blake (1990), Gurnsey, Humphrey, and Kapitan (1992), and Cavanagh, Arguin, and Treisman (1990). In these papers, the oriented targets in a search task are second-order stimuli—orientation based on color, texture, motion, or depth differences. It is not necessary to have an oriented edge in the luminance domain in order to have parallel processing of orientation. Illusory or subjective contours are a special case of second-order stimuli. They also appear to be available preattentively (Davis & Driver, 1994; Gurnsey et al., 1992)

In addition to the complexities of preattentive orientation processing already mentioned, one needs to consider the relationship *between* orientations. Symmetry between target and distractors makes it harder to find a 50° target among −50° distractors than to find the same target among −10° distractors, even though angular difference between target and distractors is greater in the former case than in the latter (Wolfe & Friedman-Hill, 1992a). Moreover, the angles formed by neighboring items in a display can be a clue to the presence of a target of unique orientation. That is, if there are two distractor types separated by 90° in orientation, a target of a third orientation can be found by the acute angle it will form with neighboring distractors. This works even if the orientations involved change from trial to trial (Wolfe & Friedman-Hill, 1992a). Meigen, Lagreze, and Bach (1994) report that the overall structure of the visual field modulates search performance. In their experiments, search for a tilted item was easier if the background, distractor items were colinear with each other.

The complexities of the preattentive processing of orientation are described in some detail here in part to make a larger point. It is widely held that the difficulty of a search task can be largely or even entirely explained by the similarity relationships between targets and distractors and between different types of distractors (Duncan & Humphreys, 1989). This is, no doubt, true, up to a point (Duncan & Humphreys, 1992; Treisman, 1991, 1992). However, any complete theory of visual search requires the working out of the details of preattentive similarity for each feature. They are likely to be reasonably complicated. Moreover, the rules for one feature may not generalize to another.

Curvature

Curvature is a reasonable candidate to be a basic feature. Treisman and Gormican (1988) found that curved lines could be found in parallel among straight distractors (see also Brown, Weisstein, & May, 1992; Gurnsey et al., 1992). Moreover, a search asymmetry exists. When the target is straight and the distractors are curved, search is less efficient. This suggests that curvature is a property whose presence is easier to detect than its absence. However, the alternative to curvature as a feature is that a curve might just be a point of high variation in orientation—a place where orientation is changing rapidly. Earlier assertions about the featural status of curvature (having nothing to do with visual attention) ran aground on this objection (Blakemore & Over, 1974; Riggs, 1973; Stromeyer & Riggs, 1974). Wolfe,

Yee, and Friedman-Hill (1992) tested this directly by having subjects search for curved targets among uncurved distractors that were roughly equated for local change in orientation. Efficient search for curvature remained possible (also see Cheal & Lyon, 1992; Fahle, 1991b). Only limited work has been done on the details of the preattentive processing of curvature. There is some evidence for categorical perception of curves (Foster, 1989).

Vernier Offset

Human observers are very good at detecting small departures from the colinearity of two line segments—a so-called vernier stimulus (Levi et al., 1985; Westheimer, 1979). In visual search, as shown in Fig. 1.10a, it is possible to detect the presence or absence of a vernier offset efficiently (Fahle, 1990, 1991a, 1991b; see also Steinman, 1987). Vernier offset might not be a feature in its own right. Like curvature, it could be a special case of orientation processing (Wilson, 1986). Fahle, however, has done a series of experiments that make this explanation unlikely (e.g. varying the overall orientation of the stimuli as in Fig. 1.10a). He also finds that while the presence or absence of a vernier break can be found efficiently, determining if a line is broken to the right or to the left requires attention (see Fig. 1.10b). Subjects could learn to do a left-vernier among right-vernier search, but only on the basis of an orientation cue. The ability went away when Fahle disrupted the orientation cue inherent in a stimulus composed of vernier breaks in vertical lines. As with other features, the efficiency of vernier search increases with the difference between the target and the distractors (Fahle, 1990).

Size, Spatial Frequency, and Scale

There are at least three aspects of size that need to be considered in visual search experiments. (1) A target item can have different overall dimensions than other items, e.g. search for a large item among small items.

(a)   (b)

FIG. 1.10.   It is easy to find an vernier offset even among stimuli with different orientations (a). It is much harder to find the stimulus with the vernier offset to the right among distractors with offsets to the left (b).

(2) A target item can have the same overall dimensions but can differ from other items in spatial frequency content; e.g. search for a patch of 3 cycle per degree grating among 6 cycle per degree distractors. (3) Finally, items can contain different information at different scales, e.g. Navon's stimuli in which one "global" letter was made up of a number of smaller "local" letters. Faced with an "S" made of smaller "H"s, subjects could be asked to respond at either the global or the local scale (Kinchla & Wolfe, 1979; Navon, 1977).

Beginning with size, if the size difference is sufficient, a target of one size will be found efficiently among distractors of another size (Bilsky, Wolfe, & Friedman-Hill, 1994; Duncan & Humphreys, 1992; Müller, Heller, & Ziegler, 1995; Quinlan & Humphreys, 1987; Stuart, 1993; Treisman & Gelade, 1980). In conjunction searches (see below), size behaves like a feature orthogonal to other features such as orientation and color (Dehaene, 1989; Duncan & Humphreys, 1992; Dursteler & von der Heydt, 1992). A limited amount is known about the preattentive processing of size information. In Treisman's work on search asymmetries, she found that it was harder to find small among big than big among small (Treisman & Gormican, 1988). However, given one size of distractors, it was no easier to find a bigger target than a smaller one. Interpretation of this result is complicated by the fact that all slopes were steep. Like color and orientation, it is hard to find a target that is flanked by the distractors. Looking for the medium-sized item among larger and smaller items is inefficient unless the size differences are very large (Treisman & Gelade, 1980; Wolfe & Bose, unpublished data; see also Alkhateeb et al., 1990). Like orientation, search for stimuli of different sizes can be very efficient even if the contours of the stimuli are defined by chromatic change, texture, motion, illusory contours, etc. (Cavanagh et al., 1990).

Spatial frequency and size might be the same basic feature. Spatial frequency does behave like a basic feature in simple searches and in conjunction searches (Moraglia, 1989b; Sagi, 1988, 1990) but the experiments to explore the relationship between size and spatial frequency have not been done. As in size, a medium spatial frequency target is hard to find among lower and higher frequencies (Wolfe & Bose, unpublished data).

Scale is a property of stimuli that is related to size but is probably not identical to it. Intuitively, it seems that we can examine a scene at several scales. You can search a group of people for the biggest person, or for eyeglasses, or for the presence of gold cufflinks. The visual stimulus remains the same. The scale of the search changes. Navon (1977) argued that stimuli are processed first at a coarse, global scale and somewhat later at a finer local scale. Subsequent research has made it clear that the story is not quite that simple (Kinchla & Wolfe, 1979; LaGasse, 1993; Lamb & Robertson, 1990; Lamb & Yund, 1993; Robertson, Egly, Lamb, & Kerth, 1993). For instance,

Kinchla and Wolfe (1979) showed that observers would respond more quickly to the "local" letters if the global letter was very large. The original Navon proposal may hold for unattended stimuli (Paquet, 1992). See Kimchi (1992) for a review of this literature.

Verghese and Pelli (1994) show that subjects can select a scale at which to examine a visual search display. Farell and Pelli (1993) argue that, for some tasks, it is possible to monitor two scales at the same time. Moreover, it is possible to search for an item that is defined by a conjunction of two colors if those colors are in an hierarchical relationship to one another. That is, one can search efficiently for a red whole thing with a yellow part, but not for a red and yellow thing (Wolfe & Friedman-Hill, 1992b). This works as well for searches for the objects defined by the sizes of parts and wholes (Bilsky & Wolfe, 1995), but not for orientations of parts and whole (Bilsky & Wolfe, 1995; see discussion of conjunction search in Section III).

Motion

Motion is an uncontroversial basic feature. It is intuitively clear that it will be easy to find a moving stimulus among stationary distractors (Dick, Ullman, & Sagi, 1987; McLeod et al., 1988; Nakayama & Silverman, 1986). Not surprisingly, it is much harder to find a stationary target among moving distractors (Dick, 1989). Given stimuli that are moving, it is easier to find the fast target among slow distractors than vice versa (Ivry, 1992). Short-range apparent motion stimuli support efficient search but long-range stimuli do not (Dick et al., 1987; Horowitz & Treisman, 1994; Ivry & Cohen, 1990; although there is some question as to whether this long vs short distinction is the correct one to make—Cavanagh & Mather, 1989). The apparent motion results suggest that motion differs from orientation. While a vertical stimulus will pop out amongst horizontal distractors no matter how that stimulus is made (contours derived from color, motion, luminance etc.; Cavanagh et al., 1990), only certain motion stimuli work (short-range—yes: long-range—no). This distinction is bolstered by the finding that iso-luminant motion stimuli are not available preattentively (Luschow & Nothdurft, 1993).

The broader point, worth reiterating, is that the rules for each feature need to be established for that feature and that generalization across features is risky. In the case of motion, the feature space includes axes of motion speed and direction. It is possible that these are separate features. More probably, they are aspects of a motion feature. Their interactions appear to be a bit complicated. For instance, hetereogeneity in motion direction impairs search for an item of unique speed but hetereogeneity in speed does not impair search for a unique direction (Driver, McLeod, & Dienes, 1992a). The behavior of motion stimuli in conjunction searches supports the notion that it is a basic feature (McLeod et al., 1988; Tiana, Lennie, & D'Zmura, 1989; Treisman & Sato, 1990) but a basic feature with its own, feature-specific rules (Driver, McLeod, & Dienes, 1992b; Duncan, 1995; McLeod, 1993).

Under natural conditions, retinal image motion may not reflect physical object motion. If the observer is moving (e.g. walking, driving) virtually all items in the field will move. Very little work has examined preattentive processing of the optic flow fields that result from observer motion. Braddick and Holliday (1991) found inefficient search for an expanding item among contracting items or vice versa. However, in these experiments, flow fields were local and oscillatory, not global as they would be with observer motion. Nothdurft (1993a, 1994) has done a series of experiments with gradients of motion. These are not intended to simulate observer motion but do show that the detectability of target motion depends on local distractor motion rather than on some combination of all motions present in the display. That is, a target moving upward is found efficiently if the local distractors are moving rightward even if distractors move upward in another portion of the field. In preliminary experiments with optic flow fields, observers can efficiently locate objects whose motion deviates significantly from those fields (Royden, Wolfe, Konstantinova, & Hildreth, 1996).

Shape

Probably the most problematical basic feature is shape or form. There are plenty of experiments that point toward shape features that are not reducible to orientation and curvature (e.g. Cohen & Ivry, 1991; Donderi & Zelnicker, 1969; Isenberg, Nissen, & Marchak, 1990; Quinlan & Jumphreys, 1987; Stefurak & Boynton, 1986; Theeuwes & Kooi, 1994; Tiana et al., 1989; Tsal & Lavie, 1988). However, the primitives of preattentive shape perception have been elusive. The heart of the problem is a lack of a widely agreed understanding of the layout of "shape space". Color space is a 2D plane or a 3D volume if you include luminance. One can argue about the precise axes but the general configuration is clear enough. Similarly, we know what we are talking about when we talk about orientation or size. It is much less obvious what the "axes" of shape space might be.

Several shape attributes have been suggested as candidate basic features. Perhaps the best supported is *line termination* (Julesz, 1984; Julesz & Bergen, 1983). In their paper on search asymmetries, Treisman and Gormican (1988) had subjects search for a "C" among "O"s or vice versa. Search was more efficient when the "C" was the target, suggesting that the gap or line terminators were the feature being detected. There are constraints on terminators as features. For example, whereas Julesz, using an "E" vs "S" task, had argued that a target with more terminators could be found amongst distractors with fewer terminators, Taylor and Badcock (1988) reported that inefficient, apparently serial search was required for a target with seven terminators among distractors with only two. This would be consistent with the idea that only the simple presence of terminators is detected pre-attentively. Cheal and Lyon (1992) made matters more perplexing when they got a different asymmetry. Target–trial slopes for an "S" among "E"s (two vs three terminators) were somewhat shallower than slopes for an "E" among "S"s (three vs two terminators), although neither search was par-ticularly efficient (14 msec/item for the former, 22 for the latter). Rotating the stimuli 90° to make "M"s and rotated "S"s made the searches a bit easier and maintained the asymmetry in favor of the target with fewer terminators. Enns (1986) found that the ability of terminators to support texture seg-mentation depends on the specific texture elements used. If elongated ele-ments are used the presence or absence of terminators seems ineffective.

The opposite of line termination, in some sense, is closure. There is evi-dence that something like closure is important in the preattentive processing of form. Donnelly, Humphreys, and Riddoch (1991) have a series of experiments using stimuli like those shown in Fig. 1.11. In the more efficient case there, subjects seem to be detecting deviation from a "good figure". A similar account may underlie Pomerantz and Pristach's (1989) finding that adding the same element to targets and distractors can actually improve search. Examples of their stimuli are shown in Fig. 1.12.

Elder and Zucker (1993, 1994), using somewhat similar stimuli, argue explicitly for closure as a basic feature. Their experiments do show a clear effect of closure on search. Stimuli like those of Pomerantz and Pristach (1989) support more efficient search when the figures are closed by con-necting the two lines to form a closed curve. However, Elder and Zucker's

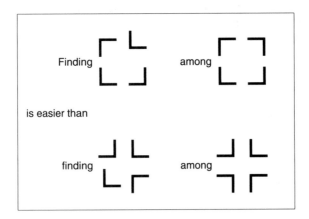

FIG. 1.11.   Stimuli redrawn from Donnelly et al. (1991).

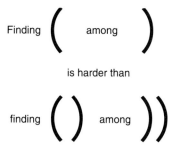

FIG. 1.12.   Stimuli redrawn from Pomerantz and Pristach (1989).

closed-curve searches are not particularly efficient, so the evidence for the featural status of closure remains somewhat ambiguous (see also Enns, 1986; Williams & Julesz, 1989).

In a more general approach to the same issue, Chen (1982) has argued for a role for topological constraints in the parallel processing of form. For instance, he would consider a "hole" to be a preattentive feature. In an illusory contour experiment, he and his colleagues report that holes could appear to migrate from one item to another even if this requires the hole to change shape (Zhou, Zhang, & Chen, 1993). It is the "holeness" that seems to be preserved. Chen's original work was criticized on methodological grounds (Rubin & Kanwisher, 1985) but subsequent work from this group tends to support a role for topology in the understanding of the preattentive analysis of form (Chen, 1990; Zhou, Chen, & Zhang, 1992).

Julesz has proposed that intersections are basic features or "textons" (Julesz, 1984, 1986; Julesz & Bergen, 1983). More recently, Bergen and Adelson have suggested that many of the demonstrations of pop-out of intersections could be explained by the operation of simple size-tuned filters with no need to invoke a mechanism sensitive to intersection (Bergen, 1991; Bergen & Adelson, 1988). Julesz and Kröse (1988) replied by filtering a texture of " + "s among "L"s to eliminate the size information. They report that texture segmentation survives this manipulation (they did not look at search tasks). However, one wonders if a simple non-linearity in early visual processing would restore the size cue to efficacy. The role of intersections as a feature in visual search tasks could benefit from further study.

Several candidate form primitives fail to support efficient visual search. "Juncture", "convergence", or "containment" (whether a dot was inside or outside a figure) were examined by Triesman and Gormican (1988). None of these produced particularly shallow RT × size functions. Biederman has proposed a set of primitives for solid shapes known as "geons" (Biederman, 1987). Although these may describe form perception for attended items, geons do not appear to be basic features (Brown et al., 1992).

Preattentive "Objects".   There is a great deal more to the perception of form than holes, intersections, terminators, and so on. This is illustrated in Fig 1.13. The same collection of local features can make a host of different objects or no object at all, if they simply gather together in one location. Is there any evidence that there is more to the preattentive processing of form than local features? Objects differ from collections of local features in at least two important ways. First, to state the obvious, they are objects. Once attention arrives, an object is not seen as collections of features. It is an object having certain featural attributes. Second, the spatial arrangement of the features is important—as for instance, in the layout of eyes, nose, and mouth in a face (Suzuki & Cavanagh, 1995).

In the original version of Feature Integration Theory, the purpose of attention was to bind features to objects (Triesman & Gelade, 1980) or, in a somewhat later formulation, to put the features in the correct "object files" (Kahneman & Treisman, 1984). More recent work shows that objects have some preattentive existence. Rensink and Enns (1995) have demonstrated that preattentive processes are sensitive to occlusion. Using stimuli like those in Fig. 1.14 in search experiments, they found that horizontal segments A and B were preattentively attributed to a single, occluded line as were C and D. Searching for "B" among A, C, & D is easy if all the segments are dissociated. B can be found because it is the longest. But if the segments are presented as shown in Fig. 1.14, "B" is hard to find because, in some sense, it does not exist.

We have conducted a series of conjunction experiments that make a similar point. In these experiments, items appear in front of and behind a lattice as schematized in Fig. 1.15. In each of the marked locations in Fig. 1.15, there are black, vertical contours. Visual search for a conjunction of color and orientation is not led astray by contours like those shown in "C"

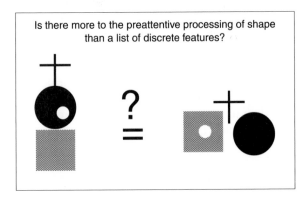

FIG. 1.13.   A problem in the preattentive analysis of form.

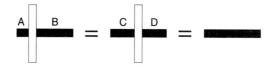

FIG. 1.14.   Preattentive processes know about occlusion.

where the relevant color is owned by the object and the relevant orientation, by the lattice (Wolfe, 1996a). Results of this sort support the idea that objects are represented preattentively.

A second line of evidence supporting the preattentive status of objects comes from experiments that compare attentional deployment to objects vs attentional deployment to spatial locations. In Duncan's (1984) experiment, the stimuli were two overlapping objects. Subjects did worse when they had to make judgments about one property of each of two objects than when they made judgments about two properties of one object (see also Baylis, 1994; Baylis & Driver, 1993, 1995a, 1995b; Gibson, 1994; Vecera & Farah, 1994). If attention is directed to objects, it seems reasonable to assume that those objects had some preattentive existence in the visual system.

Yantis and his colleagues have performed a series of experiments in which abrupt onset stimuli attract attention in visual search tasks (see Yantis's chapter in this volume, and Jonides & Yantis, 1988a; Yantis & Egeth, 1994; Yantis & Hillstrom, 1994; Yantis & Johnson, 1990; Yantis & Jones, 1991). Recently, Yantis has argued that these stimuli capture attention only if they indicate the creation of a new object—again suggesting that objects are available preattentively (Hillstrom & Yantis, 1994; Yantis, 1993; Yantis & Gibson, 1994; Yantis & Hillstrom, 1994; Yantis & Jonides, 1996).

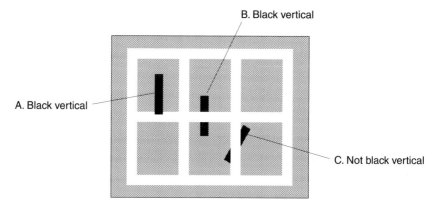

FIG. 1.15.   Preattentive processes know which objects "own" which features.

Global Shape and the Position of Local Features.   If two discriminable objects share all the same local features, it follows that the difference between them lies in the arrangement of those features. For instance, the only difference between Ƨ and S is the relative positions of the vertical lines. If the ability to process these relative positions in parallel exists, it is quite limited. Wang, Cavanagh, and Green (1994) found that subjects could search efficiently for a mirror-reversed "N" among "N"s or a mirror-reversed "Z" among "Z"s. These are searches for "novel" stimuli among well-known stimuli. The reverse searches are harder (N among mirror-N). The diagonal line in the Ns and the Zs changes orientation with mirror-reversal, providing a preattentive cue. However, the fact that this cue is only useful in the search for the mirror-reversed letters suggests some sort of sensitivity to the relationship of the diagonal lines to the vertical lines. The experiments of Heathcote and Mewhort (1993) also show that efficient search is possible on the basis of the spatial position of elements in an item. These results could reflect a preattentive sensitivity to phase information, a sensitivity that has been reported in texture segmentation experiments (Hofmann & Hallett, 1993).

Any information about spatial relationships must be fairly limited (see Tsal, Meiran, & Lamy, 1995). Searches for Ts among Ls are reliably inefficient when the Ts and Ls can be presented in several orientations (Kwak et al., 1991; Moore et al., 1996). Moreover, in a recent set of experiments, we have found no evidence for sensitivity to global shape (Wolfe & Bennett, 1996). In these experiments, subjects searched for targets among distractors that shared the same local features with the target but that differed markedly in global shape (e.g. search for a closed curve "chicken" among closed curve distractors made up of "chicken parts".) All of these searches were very inefficient (see also Biederman, Blickle, Teitelbaum, & Klatsky, 1988). The disparity between these results and results like those of Wang et al. (1994) suggest that the preattentive representation of form is still an open issue.

One final candidate for preattentive shape processing is face recognition. It seems clear that there are special-purpose mechanisms that process face information (Damasio, 1990; Farah, 1992; Kendrick & Baldwin, 1987; Purcell & Stewart, 1988; Rolls, Baylis, & Leonard, 1985; Rolls, Judge, & Sanghera, 1977; Thompson, 1980). However, visual search experiments indicate that this mechanism works on one face at a time. Searches for faces are inefficient (Kuehn, 1994; Nothdurft, 1993d; Reinitz, 1994; Suzuki & Cavanagh, 1995) although slopes are shallower than searches for non-face stimuli made of the same collection of lines and curves.

Pictorial Depth Cues

Curiously, while preattentive processing has, at best, a minimal representation of the shape of an object, there is quite good preattentive appreciation of depth cues that give 3-D structure to those objects. Enns, Rensink, and their colleagues have done a series of ingenious experiments demonstrating that efficient search is possible on the basis of 3-D appearance of stimuli. Thus, subjects can find an apparently 3-D line drawing presented among flat items composed of similar lines in similar relationships (e.g. T-junctions, Y-junctions; Enns & Rensink, 1991). They continue to do well with line drawings of targets that appear to differ only in 3-D orientation from the distractors (Enns & Rensink, 1990a, 1990b; see also Humphreys, Keulers, & Donnelly, 1994; and see Epstein & Babler, 1990; Epstein, Babler, & Bownds, 1992, for more on the preattentive processing of slant information). Sun and Perona (1996a, 1996b) have similar evidence for preattentive processing of 3-D information but argue that the cue to efficient search is a difference in the apparent reflectance of targets and distractors— a difference that is the product of the 3-D calculations.

Efficient searches can be based on shading cues to depth (Aks & Enns, 1992; Braun, 1993; Enns & Rensink, 1990a; Kleffner & Ramachandran, 1992; Ramachandran, 1988), occlusion cues (Rensink & Enns, 1995), slant from texture cues (Aks & Enns, 1993), and shadow cues (i.e. an implausible shadow pops out from among items with plausible shadows—Rensink & Cavanagh, 1993). Quite high-level cognitive factors seem to have an influence on processing of these depth cues (Brown, Enns, & Greene, 1993).

Stereoscopic Depth

Depth defined by stereoscopic cues also serves as a basic feature in visual search. Efficient search is possible when the target item lies at one depth and the distractors lie at another (Nakayama & Silverman, 1986a; see also Andersen, 1990; Andersen & Kramer, 1993). It is not necessary to have a difference in average depth between the targets and the distractors. Different directions of stereoscopic tilt will support efficient search (tilt into the page pops out from tilt out of the page—Holliday & Braddick, 1991). Further, parallel processing of stereoscopic information can influence the perceived configuration of items in search tasks (He & Nakayama, 1992). There is some limited work on searches with multiple depth planes and asymmetries in O'Toole and Walker (1993) but the preattentive representation of stereoscopic space has not been worked out.

Is There Just a Single "Depth Feature"?   It seems unlikely that there are separate parallel processes for each depth cue. More plausibly, visual search operates on a relatively "late" representation of the visual stimulus. Recall that Cavanagh et al. (1990) showed that many types of orientation stimuli would support efficient search. It didn't matter if the orientation was defined by color, texture, motion, etc. The same may hold for a feature like depth. A fair amount of depth processing occurs in parallel. Anything that makes one item appear to stand out in front of all other items ought to support efficient search. If this is true, then we can predict that different depth cues would interfere with each other if pitted against each other in search tasks. We would also predict that other depth cues, like motion parallax, should support efficient search.

If some relatively high-level depiction of depth is the basic feature for search, it would not be surprising to find that other more sensory binocular cues do not support efficient search. Eye-of-origin information is readily available in the visual system (Bishop & Pettigrew, 1986; Blake & Cormack, 1979; Hubel & Weisel, 1962). However, a target presented to the left eye among distractors presented to the right is very difficult to find. Even a perceptually salient binocular phenomenon like binocular rivalry fails to support efficient search. Binocular rivalry occurs when different, unfusable stimuli are presented at corresponding loci in each eye (Blake, 1989; Breese, 1909; Helmholtz, 1924; Levelt, 1965). It is seen as an unstable alternation between the two monocular images. It can be perceptually quite salient and is an important aspect of binocular single vision, the ability to see one world with two eyes (Wolfe, 1986). Nevertheless, efficient search does not occur for one rivalrous target in a field of fused distractors nor for a fused target among rivalrous distractors (Wolfe & Franzel, 1988; but see Koch & Braun, 1996; Kolb & Braun, 1995).

Gloss

One variant of binocular rivalry does produce efficient search. If a spot is darker than the background in the image presented to one eye and brighter in the other eye, the resulting perception is one of lustre or gloss (Bulthoff & Blake, 1989; Helmholtz, 1924; Tyler, 1983). This glossy item can be found in parallel among matte distractors and a matte target can be found amongst glossy distractors (Wolfe & Franzel, 1988). Glossy surfaces give rise to highlights. Rensink and Cavanagh (1994) show preattentive sensitivity to the location of highlights.

Some Thoughts About the Set of Basic Features in Visual Search

Learning Features?

Depending on how you count them, there appear to be about eight to ten basic features: color, orientation, motion, size, curvature, depth, vernier offset, gloss, and, perhaps, intersection and spatial position/phase. There may be a few other local shape primitives to be discovered. A dozen or so hardwired primitives does not seem unreasonable. However, there is another alternative. Perhaps we learn the primitives we need. Evidence from visual search tasks that use letters and numbers as stimuli has been used to argue for the existence of learned features (Schneider & Eberts, 1980; Schneider & Shiffrin, 1977; Shiffrin & Schneider, 1977). Much of the early work on visual search was done with alphanumeric characters (e.g. Duncan, 1980; Eriksen & Eriksen, 1974) but this, by itself, doesn't tell us anything about the featural status of the characters because the letter searches were often feature searches in alphanumeric disguise. Thus, the distinction between Xs and Os may have little to do with their status as letters and more to do with the status of "curvature", "intersection", or "terminators" as basic features. On the other hand, it has been claimed that the numeral "0" is preattentively distinguishable from a set of letters and the physically identical letter "O" is preattentively distinguishable from a set of numbers (Egeth, Jonides, & Wall, 1972; Jonides & Gleitman, 1972). This is a claim about learned categories in preattentive processing but there have been problems with replication of the result (Duncan, 1983; Krueger, 1984; Francolini & Egeth, 1979; see Kelly, Harrison, & Hodge, 1991 for related material). The finding, described earlier, that some mirror-reversed letters can be found efficiently among homogeneous arrays of non-reversed letters makes a similar claim for the learning of new features (Wang et al., 1994; see also Wang & Cavanagh, 1993). It would seem that there is some evidence supporting the position that new features can be learned or, at the very least, that subjects can learn to better utilize the signal buried in the noise of a difficult search task.

What should one make of the evidence for learned features in visual search? One might expect that a new feature that was learned in one task would be useful in another. Treisman and Vieira failed to find such transfer (Treisman, Vieira, & Hayes, 1992; Vieira & Treisman, 1988); although Wang and Cavanagh (1993) found some transfer in tasks involving the learning of Chinese characters. As noted earlier, the "O" vs "zero" effect that seemed to point to parallel processing of semantic categories has been questioned. Claims for the pop-out of novel words (Hawley, Johnston, & Farnham, 1994; Johnston, Hawley, & Farnham, 1993; see also Soraci, 1992) have recently come under methodogical attack (Christie & Klein, 1994). All of this might incline one toward skepticism about claims of learned features.

On the other hand, results like those of Wang and Cavanagh (1993; Wang et al., 1994) are very difficult to explain without invoking learning of *something*. The recent spate of papers on visual learning makes it clear that quite early stages of visual processing are subject to learning effects (e.g. Ahissar & Hochstein, 1993, 1995; Karni & Sagi, 1991, 1993; Karni et al., 1994; see Gilbert, 1994; Sagi & Tanne, 1994 for good, brief reviews). Morever, there can be no doubt that visual search performance can improve with practice (Caerwinski, Lightfoot, & Shiffrin, 1992; Lee & Fisk, 1993; Rogers, 1992; Schneider & Eberts, 1980; Sireteanu & Rettenbach, 1995). What remains in doubt is the nature of what is learned.

There is More Than One Set of Basic Features

The search for a set of visual primitives has a long history. A danger in the study of visual search is to assume that the set of primitives described for some other part of visual processing is or ought to be the set of primitives for search. Even when the same feature is found in two lists of basic features, caution should be exercised (see Shulman, 1990, for a related argument). Orientation is, perhaps, the best example because it has been so extensively studied. Cells sensitive to orientation first appear in primary visual cortex in primates. It is a convincing primitive of visual processing at that level (e.g. Hubel & Wiesel, 1974). Orientation is also a basic feature in visual search. However, the cortical orientation primitive and the preattentive orientation primitive have different properties. Preattentive processes can detect orientation differences on the order of 15° (Foster & Ward, 1991a, 1991b). Psychophysical orientation discrimination is much finer than that (Olzak & Thomas, 1986; Thomas & Gille, 1979). As noted earlier, preattentive processing of orientation appears to be categorical (Wolfe et al., 1992) and subjects can search for a uniquely oriented object defined by any number of properties; color, motion, texture (Cavanagh et al., 1990) or even other oriented elements (Bravo & Blake, 1990). All of this suggests preattentive orientation processing is several steps removed from the initial extraction of orientation information by primary visual cortex.

We don't know if the same can be said about all other features. As noted earlier, it is dangerous to assume that rules for one feature apply to another. For instance, although Nagy and Sanchez (1990) found coarse processing of color information similar to that seen by Foster and Ward (1991a) in orientation, more recent work by Bauer et al. (1995) suggests that pre-attentive color vision need not be coarse and may be well described by simple operations in a fairly low-level (non-categorical) color space. Evidence from a texture task supports the idea that color and orientation may be processed differently (Nothdurft, 1993a; Wolfe, Chun, & Friedman-Hill, 1995). See Verghese and Nakayama (1994) for different evidence that color and orientation are processed differently at a preattentive stage. For most other features, the relevant work has not been done.

The Preattentive World View

What does the preattentive world look like? We will never know directly, as it does not seem that we can inquire about our perception of a thing without attending to that thing. However, the experiments on visual search suggest that it is a world populated with objects or items that can be searched for and examined under attentional control but whose identity is not known preattentively. What is known about these objects is a listing of their surface properties. If the preattentive processing of orientation and size is any guide, the preattentive description of these surface properties is in a language similar to that used by a naive observer of an object. That is, it is big or small (not 3° of visual angle in extent). It is steeply tilted (not tilted 15° relative to vertical). Bauer et al. (1996) notwithstanding, it is probably "green" (not some wavelength or specific location in color space). (See Wolfe, 1993b, for a further discussion of this point.). To borrow terminology from Adelson and Bergen (1991), preattentive processes divide the scene into "things" and the preattentive basic features describe the "stuff" out of which perceptual "things" are made. The next section will discuss how subsequent processes use this information to find and/or identify those "things".

SECTION III. USING PREATTENTIVE INFORMATION

Preattentive information exists to be used, not as an end in itself. In the previous section, we stressed the differences between preattentive processing of various features. Whatever those differences may be, preattentive processing of any feature can be used to guide the subsequent deployment of attention. In this section, we are specifically interested in the details of how preattentive information is used in visual search tasks. Ideas about the use of preattentive information are wrapped up in more general theories of visual search. The ideas put forth here will tend to be in the context of the Guided Search model (Version 2.0—Wolfe, 1994) but an effort will be made to acknowledge places where adherents of other models might differ in the interpretation of the data.

From the vantage point of Guided Search, preattentive processes exist to direct attention to the locations of interesting objects in the visual field. There are two ways in which a preattentive process can be used to direct attention: bottom-up (stimulus-driven) and top-down (user-driven). This distinction is not new. For example, Titchener (1919), speaking very generally about attention, distinguished between "primary attention" to something that was intrinsically interesting, and secondary attention—the volitional attention to something we should attend to. In the present context, we will distinguish between top-down and bottom-up forms of pre-attentive processing.

Bottom-up Processing

If a target is sufficiently different from the distractors, efficient search is possible even if the subject does not know the target's identity in advance. Bravo and Nakayama (1992) showed this for the simple case where targets that could be red or green and distractors were whatever color targets were not. Found and Müller (1995; Müller, Heller, & Ziegler, 1995) obtained similar results with stimuli that could be distinct in color, orientation, and size (although they did find a difference between the case where targets varied within a feature vs the case were targets varied across feature types, discussed later). This summoning of attention to an unusual item is what is usually meant when the term "pop-out" is used. Bottom-up pop-out appears to be based on a local difference operator (Julesz, 1986; Nothdurft, 1991b, 1993a, 1993b). If items are grouped by feature (e.g. color), attention will be attracted to the border where the feature changes (Todd & Kramer, 1994). One consequence of this local comparator is that some features searches may actually get *easier* as set size increases. More items means greater density of items and stronger local contrasts (Bravo & Nakayama, 1992; Maljkovic, 1994). There is a continuum of pop-out. The salience of a pop-out target can be measured using standard psychophysical matching methods, matching the target salience with the salience of a luminance stimulus (Nothdurft, 1993c).

Top-down Processing

As the Titchnerian dichotomy indicates, we need preattentive processes to alert us to the presence of stimuli in the world that might be worthy of our attention. We also need to be able to use preattentive processes to deploy our attention to stimuli that we have decided are worthy of attention. That is, we need *top-down*, user-driven control of our preattentive processes. In searches for a target defined by a single feature, the clearest evidence for top-down control comes from color search tasks with very heterogeneous distractors. Even when each distractor is of a different color, it is possible to search efficiently for a target of a specified color (Duncan, 1989; Wolfe et al., 1990).

Top-down guidance of attention seems to involve a very limited "vocabulary". As discussed earlier, orientation can only be specified as "steep", "shallow", "left", "right", and "tilted" (Wolfe et al., 1992). Sizes are "big" or "small" (Wolfe & Bose, unpublished data). Vernier offset is probably "broken" or "not broken" with the direction of the break not available (Fahle, 1990). The vocabularies for most other features have not been systematically studied but there is no reason to assume that they are significantly richer. Further restrictions are imposed on these few terms. In many searches, "top-down" specifications seem to be effectively limited to one term per feature—one color, one orientation, and so on. For instance, searches for targets defined by two colors or two orientations are very inefficient (Wolfe et al., 1990). In a color × color search, the target might be red and green while the distractors are a mix of red-blue and blue-green items. These searches would be efficient if observers could use top-down processing to select the items that were *both* red *and* green. However, it appears that top-down selection of red and green selects all items that are red and all items that are green—in this case, the set of all items.

As noted in the previous discussion of size and scale, two terms per feature per search can produce efficient search when one term applies to the whole object and the other term applies to a constituent part. Thus, it is possible to search efficiently for the red thing with a green part, perhaps because it is possible to select all red whole items *and* to select all green parts and to guide attention to the intersection (rather than the union) of those two sets (Wolfe, Friedman-Hill, & Bilsky, 1994). Interestingly, this part–whole processing works for color and size but not for orientation. Searches for a vertical thing with an oblique part are as inefficient as search for a vertical and oblique thing (Bilsky et al., 1994). Beyond limited information about object structure, there is some evidence for higher-order scene properties having an influence in top-down control of search (Brown, Enns, & Greene, 1993; He & Nakayama, 1992).

In Guided Search and related models, information from top-down and bottom-up analyses of the stimulus is used to create a ranking of items in order of their attentional priority. In a visual search, attention will be directed to the item with the highest priority. If that item is rejected, attention will move to the next item and the next and so on (Wolfe, 1994). This is not the only way to understand the bottom-up, top-down distinction. For example, Braun and his colleagues have done a series of experiments where attention is tied up with a demanding task at fixation. They ask what attributes of a peripheral stimulus can still be evaluated in a brief presentation. Many of the basic features described in Section II survive this treatment (Braun, 1993, 1994; Braun & Julesz, 1996a, 1996b; Braun & Sagi, 1990a; see also Mack et al. 1992). Following William James, Braun argues that this is evidence for the concurrent activity of two types of attention—active (for the central task) and passive (for the peripheral task; Braun & Julesz, 1995). One could also argue that these results show that preattentive processing continues across the field while attention is busy elsewhere.

The division between top-down and bottom-up guidance of attention may be somewhat arbitrary. Maljkovic and Nakayama (1994, 1996) did a series of experiments in which observers had to report on the shape of a unique item in the field. For example, with color stimuli the unique item could be green among red items or red among greens. If the unique color remained constant, RTs were faster than if the color changed. This sounds like top-down, strategic control—"Select red". However, it is not under the observer's control. Predictable changes in the target color (e.g. alternating red-green-red-green over trials) produced RTs that were indistinguishable from unpredictable changes. If this is top-down control, the control comes from middle-management and not from the CEO.

Singletons, Attentional Capture, and Dimensional Weighting

The Maljkovic and Nakayama task is a variant of a singleton search. Singleton search is probably the simplest use of preattentive information in a visual search task. A single target is presented among homogeneous distractors and differs from those distractors by a single basic feature. Preattentive processing of the unique item causes attention to be deployed to that item so it is examined before any distractors are examined. As a result, RT is independent of the number of distractors presented. This account raises three questions:

1. Can irrelevant singletons attract attention?
2. Are there any irrelevant singletons that *must* attract attention?
3. If all singletons are relevant, are all singletons equivalent?

These are the topics of considerable ongoing research but, on the basis of present data, the answers appear to be: yes, no, and no. Detailed discussion of these matters (with potentially different answers) can be found in Yantis's chapter in this volume. The topic is important to an understanding of search and will be discussed briefly here. Beginning with Question 1, Yantis and his colleagues have done a series of experiments showing that the appearance of a new item can capture attention. In the basic onset paradigm, some items are created by the *onset* of stimuli while other items are created by deleting parts of existing stimuli. All else being equal, in a search through such items, attention will visit the onset stimuli first. (Jonides & Yantis, 1988b; Remington, Johnston, & Yantis, 1992; Yantis, 1993; Yantis & Johnson, 1990; Yantis & Jones, 1991). Early on, Miller (1989) raised methodological concerns about the paradigm, but these were controlled for in later experiments. Pashler (1988), using a different task, found evidence for disruption of search for a target in one featural dimension by the presence of a distractor in another. Abrupt onsets (or other indications of the creation of a new "object") seem to be the most powerful singletons. Others, like color, capture attention in some cases (e.g. Theeuwes, 1992; Todd & Kramer, 1994) but not in others (e.g. Folk & Annett, 1994).

Turning to Question 2, it seems fair to say that there are paradigms where singletons must capture attention even if the subject does not want this to occur. However, it is not the case that there exist stimuli that capture attention across all paradigms. Here we are restricting ourselves to stimuli of the sort that would be presented in a visual search experiment—for who can doubt Sully when he says "One would like to know the fortunate (or unfortunate) man who could receive a box on the ear and not attend to it?" (Sully, *The human mind*, p. 146, quoted in Ladd, 1894). Theeuwes (1991,

1992, 1993, 1994, 1995) has a series of experiments showing, in particular, the attention-grabbing abilities of color and onset stimuli (see also Remington et al. 1992). Theeuwes would like to argue against a role for top-down processing but Bacon and Egeth (1994) argue that this mandatory capture occurs only if subjects are already looking for singletons. That is, onsets do not always capture attention but, if your task requires that you look for odd events, certain irrelevant odd events (e.g. onsets) will always interfere. If your task does not involve hunting for singletons, onsets may not disturb you. For example, Wolfe (1996a) presented abrupt onset spots every 40 msec during an inefficient search for Ts among Ls and found only a small, approx. 50 msec, additive cost compared to a no-spot condition. Mandatory attentional capture by each abrupt onset would have made the search task impossible.

Turning to Question 3, if singletons capture attention when the targets are, themselves, singletons, does the nature of the singleton matter? As was noted earlier, abrupt onsets seem to capture attention more vigorously than other singletons. Beyond that, there is evidence of top-down modulation of sensitivity to singletons. Treisman (1988a) reported on experiments in which subjects searched for singletons. Different targets appeared on different trials. If all the singletons were within one featural dimension, such as orientation, RTs were shorter than if singletons were spread over several dimensions. That is, RTs were shorter for a sequence of vertical target, horizontal target, oblique target than for a sequence of red, vertical, big. Pashler (1988) also found that irrelevant singletons within a dimension caused substantial disruption. Müller et al. (1995) have done a series of experiments expanding on this finding. They replicate the basic result and argue that the cause is "dimensional weighting". Following models like Feature Integration (Treisman, 1993; Treisman & Gelade, 1980) and Guided Search (Wolfe, 1994a; Wolfe et al., 1989), they hold that there are several parallel feature processors whose output feeds a general salience map. A salience (or "activation") map is a representation of visual space in which the level of "activation" at a location reflects the likelihood that that location contains a target. This likelihood is based on preattentive, featural information. In Guided Search, attention is deployed from peak to peak in the activation map in a search for the target. Thus, search is efficient if the target generates the highest or one of the highest activation peaks, as it will in a singleton search. Müller and Found (1995) argue that the contribution of any specific feature to the salience map is controlled by a weight that can change from task to task and, indeed, from trial to trial. They find that the RT for trial "N" is contingent on the relationship between target identity on trials "N" and "N-1" (See also Maljkovic & Nakayama, 1994, discussed earlier, and Found & Muller, 1995). That is, you are faster to find a color singleton on trial N if you found a color singleton on trial N-1.

If "redness" or "greeness" is being more heavily weighted on a given trial, how is that accomplished? Is attention made to favor "red" or to favor locations (or objects) that are red? The distinction is subtle but efforts to tease these apart suggest that it is locations that are favored, not features *per se* (Cave & Pashler, 1995; Shih & Sperling, 1996).

Conjunctions

Most searches in the real world are not searches for stimuli defined by single basic features. They are searches for stimuli that are defined by conjunctions of two or more features. You don't look for "red". You look for an apple that is some conjunction of red, curved, shiny, and apple-sized. Figure 1.16 shows a standard conjunction search; in this case, for a *black vertical* line among *black* horizontal and white *vertical* lines.

Treisman and Gelade (1980), in the original Feature Integration Theory, argued that all conjunction searches were serial, self-terminating searches. Like many an attractively strong claim, this one soon came under attack. There were technical matters—Houck and Hoffman (1986) found that the McCollough effect does not require attention even though the McCollough effect is a contingent after-effect based on a conjunction of color and orientation. Pashler (1987) argued that the slope ratios of target to blank trials did not correspond to the 2:1 ratio expected for a serial self-terminating search. Ward and McClelland (1989) reported that the variance of the blank trial RTs was greater than would be predicted by a simple, serial self-terminating model of conjunction searches. However, the worst problem for the claim came from evidence that conjunction searches could be done too efficiently to be described as "serial" searches. Egeth et al. (1984) reported that subjects could restrict search to an appropriately colored subset of items (see also Friedman-Hill & Wolfe, 1995; Kaptein, Theeuwes, & Van der Heijden, 1994). Nakayama and Silverman (1986a) found efficient search for conjunctions involving stereoscopic depth. The same held true for conjunctions of various features with motion (Driver, 1992a, 1992b; Driver

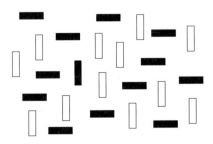

FIG. 1.16.   Conjunction search: Find the black vertical line.

et al., 1992a; McLeod et al., 1988, 1991). It seemed possible that strictly serial search was a general rule beset by a variety of exceptions, until a number of studies failed to produce serial, self-terminating results, even with the sorts of conjunction stimuli used in the original Treisman and Gelade studies. (Alkhateeb, Morland, Ruddock, & Savage, 1990; Dehaene, 1989; Moraglia, 1989b; Mordkoff, Yantis, & Egeth, 1990; Quinlan & Humphreys, 1987; Tiana et al., 1989; von der Heydt & Dursteler, 1993; Wolfe et al., 1989; Zohary & Hochstein, 1989). An important difference between the older "serial" conjunction searches and the newer, more efficient results seems to be stimulus salience. The most efficient searches occur with large differences between stimulus attributes—green vs red, vertical vs horizontal (Treisman & Sato, 1990; Wolfe et al., 1989). That said, we have been able to get very efficient results in conjunction searches with stimuli whose salience seems comparable to that reported in, for example, Treisman and Gelade (1980). We do not fully understand why conjunctions searches have become more efficient in the last 20 years.

Other Influences on Efficient Search for Conjunctions

Other constraints on the efficiency of conjunction search include stimulus density. Cohen and Ivry (1991) report that conjunction search becomes less efficient if items are packed closely together (see also Berger & McLeod, 1996). While we find that efficient search remains possible with the densities used by Cohen and Ivry (O'Neill & Wolfe, 1994; Wolfe, unpublished), it seems reasonable to assume that closer packing would, at some point, make it harder to determine which features went with which objects.

There are search asymmetries in conjunction search as there are in feature searches. However, the pattern of conjunction search asymmetries may not be obviously related to the asymmetries for the relevant features (Cohen, 1993). The topic can get quite complicated, as can be seen in an exchange of papers about asymmetrical asymmetries in motion × orientation conjunctions (Berger & McLeod, 1996; Driver, 1992b; Müller & Found, 1996; Müller & Maxwell, 1994): This may prove, perhaps, the futility of "theories of visual search that try to establish general principles that hold irrespective of the stimulus features defining the target" (Berger & McLeod, 1996, p. 114).

Conjunction search may also become somewhat less efficient with age (e.g. Zacks & Zacks, 1993; but see Plude & Doussard-Roosevelt, 1989). Given these constraints, efficient search seems possible for any pairwise combination of basic features. Triple conjunctions (e.g. search for the big, red, vertical target) tend to be *more* efficient than standard conjunctions (Dehaene, 1989; Quinlan & Humphreys, 1987; Wolfe et al., 1989). Recall also that, unlike conjunctions between two or more features, searches for conjunctions of two instances of one type of feature are generally very inefficient (Wolfe et al., 1990) unless the features are in a part–whole relationship to each other (Wolfe et al., 1994). Even then, the part–whole relationships do not lead to efficient search for orientation × orientation conjunctions (Bilsky & Wolfe, 1995).

How is Efficient Conjunction Search Possible?

If one accepts the argument that there is a limited set of relatively independent basic features, efficient conjunction search becomes a puzzle to be solved. The original argument of Feature Integration Theory was that conjunction search had to be "serial" because there was no preattentive process that could find conjunctions (Treisman & Gelade, 1980). At the heart of the Guided Search model is an argument about how attention can be *guided* to likely conjunctions by combining information from two pre-attentive processes *even* if Treisman is correct about the absence of explicit parallel conjunction processing. For example, in a search for a red vertical target, a preattentive color processor could highlight or "activate" all "red" objects and a preattentive orientation processor could highlight all "vertical (or steep)" objects (e.g. Rossi & Paradiso, 1995). If these two sources of information are combined into a salience or activation map as described earlier, objects having both red and vertical attributes will be doubly activated. If attention is directed to the locus of greatest activation, it will find red vertical items efficiently even though none of the preattentive processes involved could recognize an item as simultaneously red and vertical. (See Cave & Wolfe, 1990; Wolfe & Cave, 1989; Wolfe et al., 1989 for the original Guided Search model, and Wolfe, 1992b, 1993a; and especially 1994a for the revised Guided Search 2.0 version. See Hoffman, 1979 for an earlier model with a similar architecture. See also Swensson, 1980. See Koch & Ullman, 1985, for an earlier version of an activation or salience map.)

Revised Feature Integration Theory has a similar account for conjunction searches, although one that proposes inhibition of distractor attributes rather than activation of target attributes (Treisman, 1988b, 1993; Treisman & Sato, 1990; Treisman et al., 1992; see Friedman-Hill & Wolfe, 1992, 1995 for an argument in favor of activation rather than inhibition).

There are other accounts of these results and, more generally, of the processes of visual search. Duncan and Humphreys (1989) proposed that the feature processes were not independent of each other and that search efficiency could be understood in terms of distances in a multidimensional similarity space—distances between targets and distractors and between different types of distractors. In brief, larger differences between target and distractor tended to make search easier, while larger differences between different types of distractors tended to make search harder. Moreover, they argued for a limited-capacity parallel search mechanism, rather than the serial, item by item mechanism invoked by Treisman and by Wolfe (Duncan et al., 1994). In a subsequent exchange with Treisman, Duncan acknowledged that basic features might have a degree of independence (Duncan & Humphreys, 1992; Treisman, 1991, 1992). Part of the limited-capacity parallel argument relies on the claim that attention moves only once every few hundred msec rather than every 40 or 50 msec as required by Treisman and by Wolfe. However, as noted earlier, that estimate (from Duncan et al., 1994) seems hard to reconcile with the ability to attend to discrete events occurring much more rapidly (Chun & Potter, 1995; Lawrence, 1971; Potter, 1975, 1976). Duncan and Humphrey's stress on target–distractor and distractor–distractor similarity has been influential in interpreting experimental results and in shaping other theories of search.

Nakayama (1990) has a somewhat different account in which the demands of the task determine the scale at which items can be processed. A feature search makes minimal demands and the whole field can be processed at once. More complex searches make greater demands and cause processing to be limited to progressively smaller and smaller regions at one time. The relationship between scale and task in a model of this sort could be described in terms of the amount of information that can be processed in a single attentional fixation. Verghese and Pelli (1992) estimate this to be about 50 bits of information in one series of experiments. See Lavie and Tsal (1994) for related discussion using non-search paradigms, and see Green (1991) for an interesting analysis of model architectures of this sort.

Grouping

Several theories of search rely on grouping mechanisms to make conjunction search more efficient. Treisman (1982) has shown that conjunction search became more efficient as distractors were grouped by type. That is, in a search for red verticals, if all of the red horizontal items formed a single group, a red vertical item would pop out of that group on the basis of its orientation information alone (see Egeth et al., 1984; and see Farmer & Taylor, 1980 for similar results with feature search and also Bundesen & Pedersen, 1983). Ross and Mingolla (1994) have shown similar effects for color × color conjunctions. These grouping effects may be less marked in the elderly (Gilmore, 1985; but see Humphrey & Kramer, 1994). Most grouping accounts suggest that search can be speeded by processing and rejecting distractors in groups rather than one at a time (Grossberg et al., 1994; Humphreys, Freeman, & Muller, 1992; Humphreys & Müller, 1993; Muller, Humphreys, & Donnelly, 1994; Pashler, 1987).

Grouping effects do seem to have a role to play in search—a role that is not presently acknowledged by models like Guided Search (Duncan, 1995).

Even with small numbers of items, the sameness of two items may cause them to be treated together rather than in the strictly item by item manner of Guided Search or the original Feature Integration Theory (Baylis & Driver, 1992; Mordkoff & Yantis, 1993; Mordkoff et al., 1990). On the other hand, one burden on grouping models is to explain just how the grouping is done. For instance, Grossberg et al. (1994) make the reasonable suggestion that groups are formed by networks that group items that share a property and are not separated by other items that do not share that property (e.g. {red red} GREEN forms one red group while {red} GREEN {red} forms two red groups). However, Wolfe (1994b), using some naturalistic stimuli, showed that color × orientation searches could still be performed quite efficiently despite various colors and orientations intervening between virtually all "items" in the search. Probably a truly satisfactory model of search will need low-level grouping in addition to top-down and bottom-up selection processes.

Parallel Models

Returning to an issue raised at the start of this chapter, recall that it can be difficult to tell serial and parallel processes apart (Townsend, 1990). It makes sense, therefore, that there exist models with parallel architectures that do work similar to that done by parallel–serial architecture of Feature Integration and Guided Search. TVA (Theory of Visual Attention and FIRM (Fixed-capacity Independent Race Model) are examples of models of this kind (Bundesen, 1990, 1996; Shibuya & Bundesen, 1993; see also Logan, 1996). See Kinchla (1974) for an earlier incarnation and see also Mordkoff and Yantis (1991). In a similar spirit are models that frame the visual search problem in signal detection terms (Geisler & Chou, 1995; Palmer, 1994, 1995; Swensson & Judy, 1981) although signal detection theory is a tool that is useful across search models.

Other Issues in the Development of Attention

Eccentricity Effects

Most visual search studies ignore the effects of eccentricity. Not surprisingly, there are such effects and, not surprisingly, the main effect is that targets are located more slowly as their distance from fixation increases (Bursill, 1958; Carrasco & Chang, 1995; Carrasco, Evert, Change, & Katz, 1995; Cole & Hughes, 1984; Efron, 1990; Engel, 1971; Geisler & Chou, 1995; Lee, Jung, & Chung, 1992; Previc & Blume, 1993; Remington & Williams, 1986; Saarinen, 1993; Sanders, 1970; Sanders & Brück, 1991). In the study of attention, this effect of eccentricity is interesting to the extent that it can be seen as something more than a reflection of the general decline of acuity and sensitivity in the periphery. Evidence includes the finding that the eccentricity effect is not eliminated if the size of the peripheral targets is increased (Cole & Hughes, 1984) and the effect is dissociable from standard measures of visual fields (Ball, Owsley, & Beard, 1990). Moreover, variables like age (Ball et al., 1990; Madden, 1992; Scialfa, Kline, & Lyman, 1987), mental load (Egeth, 1977), and stress (Bursill, 1958) all have an impact on search performance that seems to be separate from their effects on measures like acuity. In one recent study, Bennett and Wolfe (1995) equated the difficulty of a visual and an auditory vigilance task and found that the visual task had an effect on eccentricity functions in a standard search paradigm whereas the auditory task did not.

Ball and her colleagues have studied an attentional visual field measure that they call "the Useful Field of View" (or "UFOV"; Sekuler & Ball, 1986). The UFOV is a measure of an attentional visual field. It is smaller in the old than in the young (Ball et al., 1988), shrinks in the presence of auditory load in older subjects (Graves et al., 1993), is not well correlated with visual fields in subjects with healthy fields (Ball, Owsley, & Beard, 1990), and correlates with automobile accidents in an elderly population (Ball et al. 1993). These UFOV studies use a task that is rather different from standard visual search tasks and it remains to be seen if these results generalize to those standard tasks.

Illusory Conjunctions

A basic tenet of Feature Integration Theory and of related models like Guided Search is that features are "bound" together by the action of attention. Even if "red" and "vertical" are at the same physical location, they are not known to be two attributes of a red vertical thing until attention arrives on the scene. It follows that errors might occur in which features are incorrectly bound together. These errors are known as "illusory conjunctions" (Treisman & Schmidt, 1982). They tend to make their appearance when stimuli are briefly presented and the visual and attentional systems are left to construct a perception of the stimuli from decaying data (although it is possible to get illusory conjunctions with continuously visible stimuli and rigorous fixation—Prinzmetal, Henderson, & Ivry, 1995). Thus, subjects may report seeing a red vertical thing in a display that contains red things and vertical things but no red vertical things. Treisman's original assertion was that preattentive features were "free-floating" and that any feature could conjoin with any other. She has subsequently declared that this free-floating terminology "got her into more trouble than anything else she ever wrote." (Treisman, personal communication). Since the original claim, there have been several papers showing varying degrees of spatial restriction on illusory conjunction formation (Cohen & Ivry, 1989; Eglin, 1987; Prinzmetal et al., 1995; Prinzmetal & Keysar, 1989; but see Tsal, Meiran, & Lavie, 1994, exp. 3). Ashby, Prinzmetal, Ivry, and Maddox (1996) present a theory of illusory conjunctions based on position uncertainty.

Part of the difficulty in interpreting the meaning of illusory conjunctions might be traced to the possibility that illusory conjunctions are not produced by a single mechanism but by two or maybe more. Specifically, there are illusory conjunctions of low-level preattentive features that may be explainable as the consequence of a loss of position information at the level of the feature integration that is important for normal conjunction searches (e.g. Cohen & Ivry, 1989). There are also illusory conjunctions that involve the meaning of stimuli, usually—but not always—words (Prinzmetal, 1991; Treisman & Souther, 1986; Virzi & Egeth, 1984). Goolkasian (1988) found illusory conjunctions in the perception of clock time. It seems entirely possible, given a degraded or decaying representation, that higher-level attributes like "meaning" might seem to migrate in the same way that preattentive features might migrate. Similar processes might be occurring at two or several levels in processing. For purposes of understanding visual search, the danger arises in assuming that there is a single mechanism of illusory conjunction and, on the basis of that assumption, being forced into risky assertions about the preattentive processing of words or other complex stimuli.

Blank Trials

One area that has received relatively little attention is the termination of visual search trials when no target is found. It is easy enough to imagine how a truly serial search is terminated. You stop searching when all items have been examined. Rules for termination of more efficient searches are less obvious. Chun and Wolfe (1996) have proposed a solution in the context of the Guided Search model. As noted earlier, Guided Search proposes that an activation map is created on the basis of preattentive processing of basic features. This map rank-orders items from the most likely to be a target to the least. Chun and Wolfe (1996) propose that search proceeds through that list until the target is found or until no items remain with activations that are above an "activation" threshold. The remaining items are deemed unlikely to be targets and are not visited by serial attention. This threshold is set adaptively. It is pressured to be more conservative in order to minimize errors and pressured to be more liberal in order to minimize RT. In addition to this threshold mechanism, Chun and Wolfe propose that some trials are terminated by guesses and that the probability of guessing increases as search time increases. This guessing mechanism could produce the few false alarms seen in the data. This model does well in accounting for the blank trial data from a range of search tasks. See Zenger and Fahle (1995) for a somewhat different account.

Inhibition of Return

The Chun and Wolfe model and, indeed, all the search models with a serial component, need to ask how attention "knows" where it has been. For instance, a serial exhaustive search on a blank trial implies that each item is examined once and only once. One could inhibit each item or location after it is visited and rejected by attention—so-called "inhibition of return" (Gibson & Egeth, 1994; Mackeben & Nakayama, 1988; Posner & Cohen, 1984; Tipper, Driver, & Weaver, 1991). Klein (1988) reported finding evidence for inhibition of return in a search paradigm. Wolfe and Pokorny (1990) failed to replicate the finding. Moreover, Pratt and Abrams (1995) cued two items and found inhibition of return only for the most recently cued one. However, if models like Guided Search have any validity, there must be some way to keep track of the loci and/or objects that have been examined and rejected in the course of a search.

CONCLUSION

PsychInfo, the online database for Psychological Abstracts, listed 761 papers when given "visual search" as a subject heading on 23 February 1996. For all that research, some very basic questions remain to be fully answered. An incomplete list might include:

1. Is there a fixed set of basic features and, if so, what is the full list? As this chapter's large section on this topic indicated, a credible list can be offered but, particularly in the area of preattentive shape/form processing, much work remains to be done.
2. What is the role of learning in preattentive processing? Specifically, when a task becomes efficient, as some tasks do with practice, is the observer building a new parallel process or isolating an attention-guiding signal from one existing preattentive process in the midst of the noise from the other processes?
3. What is an "item" in visual search? Is it an object? If so, how complete is preattentive processing of objects?
4. Whatever an item might be, is attention *always* limited to the processing of one item at a time? Alternatively, is it *ever* limited to one item at a time or are the limited-capacity parallel models a better representation of reality?
5. What happens after attention departs? If we assume that attention does *something* to the visual representation of an object, what *post-attentive* visual representation remains when attention is deployed

elsewhere? Preliminary investigation suggests that the post-attentive visual representation is the same as the preattentive representation (Wolfe, 1996b).

5. Finally, will any of the models of visual search survive the confrontation with the real world? In the real world, distractors are very heterogeneous. Stimuli exist in many size scales in a single view. Items are probably defined by conjunctions of many features. You don't get several hundred trials with the same targets and distractors. The list could go on but the point is made. A truly satisfying model of visual search will need to account for the range of data produced in the laboratory, but it will also need to account for the range of real-world visual behaviors that brought us into the laboratory in the first place.

ACKNOWLEDGEMENTS

I thank Sara Bennett, Greg Gancarz, Todd Horowitz, and Patricia O'Neill for comments on earlier drafts of this chapter. I am also grateful to Anne Treisman for various discussions and to Hal Pashler and an anonymous reviewer for excellent editorial comments. Some parts of this chapter are based heavily on my previous review of this literature in Wolfe (1994a). This work was supported by NIH-NEI grant RO1-EY05087 and by AFOSR grant F49620-93-1-0407.

REFERENCES

Adelson, E.H., & Bergen, J.R. (1991). The plenoptic function and the elements of early vision. In M. Landy & J.A. Movshon (Eds.), *Computational models of visual processing* (pp.3–20). Cambridge, MA: MIT Press.

Ahissar, M., & Hochstein, S. (1993). Attentional control of early perceptual learning. *Proceedings of the National Academy of Sciences USA, 90*, 5718-5722.

Ahissar, M., & Hochstein, S. (1995). How early is early vision? Evidence from perceptual learning. In T. Papathomas, C. Chubb, A. Gorea, & E. Kowler (Eds.), *Early vision and beyond* (pp.199–206). Cambridge, MA: MIT Press.

Aks, D.J., & Enns, J.T. (1992). Visual search for direction of shading is influenced by apparent depth. *Perception and Psychophysics, 52*(1), 63–74.

Aks, D.J., & Enns, J.T. (1993). Early vision's analysis of slant-from-texture. *Investigative Ophthalmology and Visual Science, 34*(4), 1185.

Aks, D.J., & Enns, J.T. (1996). Visual search for size is influenced by a background texture gradient. *Journal of Experimental Psychology: Human Perception and Performance, 22*(6), 1467–1481.

Alkhateeb, W.F., Morland, A.B., Ruddock, K.H., & Savage, C.J. (1990). Spatial, colour, and contrast response characteristics of mechanisms which mediate discrimination of pattern orientation and magnification. *Spatial Vision, 5*(2), 143–157.

Alkhateeb, W.F., Morris, R.J., & Ruddock, K.H. (1990). Effects of stimulus complexity on simple spatial discriminations. *Spatial Vision, 5*(2), 129–141.

Andersen, G.J. (1990). Focused attention in three-dimensional space. *Perception and Psychophysics, 47*, 112–120.

Andersen, G.J., & Kramer, A.F. (1993). Limits of focused attention in three-dimensional space. *Perception and Psychophysics, 53*(6), 658–667.

Ashby, F.G., Prinzmetal, W., Ivry, R., & Maddox, W.T. (1996). A formal theory of feature binding in object perception. *Psychological Review, 103*(1), 165–192.

Atkinson, R.C., Homlgren, J.E., & Juola, J.F. (1969). Processing time as influenced by the number of elements in a visual display. *Perception and Psychophysics, 6*(6A), 321–326.

Bacon, W.F., & Egeth, H.E. (1994). Overriding stimulus-driven attentional capture. *Perception and Psychophysics, 55*(5), 485–496.

Ball, K., Owsley, C., Sloane, M.E., Roenker, D.L., & Bruni, J.R. (1993). Visual attention problems as a predictor of vehicle crashes among older drivers. *Investigative Ophthalmology and Visual Science, 34*(11), 3110–3123.

Ball, K.K., Beard, B.L., Roenker, D.L., Miller, R.L., & Griggs, D.S. (1988). Age and visual search: Expanding the useful field of view. *Journal of the Optical Society of America A, 5*(12), 2210–2219.

Ball, K.K., Owsley, C., & Beard, B. (1990). Clinical visual field perimetry underestimates visual field problems in older adults. *Clinical Vision Science, 5*(2), 113–125.

Bauer, B., Jolicoeur, P., & Cowan, W.B. (1996). Visual search for colour targets that are or are not linearly-separable from distractors. *Vision Research, 36*(10), 1439–1466.

Baylis, G.C. (1994). Visual attention and objects: Two object cost with equal convexity. *Journal of Experimental Psychology: Human Perception and Performance, 20*(1), 208–212.

Baylis, G.C., & Driver, J. (1992). Visual parsing and response competition: The effect of grouping factors. *Perception and Psychophysics, 51(2)*, 145–162.

Baylis, G.C., & Driver, J. (1993). Visual attention and objects: Evidence for hierarchical coding of location. *Journal of Experimental Psychology: Human Perception and Performance, 19(3)*, 451–470.

Baylis, G.C., & Driver, J. (1995a). One-sided edge assignment in vision: 1. Figure–ground segmentation and attention to objects. *Current Directions in Psychological Science, 4*(5), 140–146.

Baylis, G.C., & Driver, J. (1995b). One-sided edge assignment in vision: 2. Part decomposition, shape discrimination, and attention to objects. *Current Directions in Psychological Science, 4*(6), 201–206.

Bennett, S.C., & Wolfe, J.M. (1995). Don't look, listen: When does a second task interfere with visual search? *Investigative Opthalmology and Visual Science, 36*(4), S901.

Bergen, J.R. (1991). Theories of visual texture perception. In D. Regan (Ed.), *Spatial vision,* (Vol.10, pp.114–134). Boca Raton, FL: CRC Press.

Bergen, J.R., & Adelson, E.H. (1988). Early vision and texture perception. *Nature, 333,* 363–364.

Bergen, J.R., & Julesz, B. (1983). Rapid discrimination of visual patterns. *IEEE Transactions on Systems, Man, and Cybernetics, SMC-13,* 857–863.

Berger, R.C., & McLeod, P. (1996). Display density influences visual search for conjunctions of movement and orientation. *Journal of Experimental Psychology: Human Perception and Performance, 2*(1), 114–121.

Biederman, I. (1987). Recognition-by-components: A theory of human image understanding. *Psychological Review, 94,* 115–147.

Biederman, I., Blickle, T.W., Teitelbaum, R.C., & Klatsky, G.J. (1988). Object search in nonscene displays. *Journal of Experimental Psychology: Learning, Memory, and Cognition, 14*(3), 456–467.

Bilsky, A.A., & Wolfe, J.M. (1995). Part–whole information is useful in size × size but not in orientation × orientation conjunction searches. *Perception and Psychophysics, 57*(6), 749–760.

Bilsky, A.A., Wolfe, J.M., & Friedman-Hill, S.F. (1994). Part–whole information is useful in size × size but not in orientation × orientation conjunction searches. *Investigative Opthalmology and Visual Science, 35*(4), 1622.

Bishop, P.O., & Pettigrew, J.D. (1986). Neural mechanisms of binocular vision. *Vision Research, 26,* 1587–1599.

Blake, R. (1989). A neural theory of binocular rivalry. *Psychological Review, 96,* 145–167.

Blake, R., & Cormack, R.H. (1979). On utrocular discrimination. *Perception and Psychophysics, 26,* 53–68.

Blakemore, C., & Over, R. (1974). Curvature detectors in human vision. *Perception, 3,* 3–7.

Boynton, R.M. (1979). *Human color vision.* New York: Holt Rinehart, & Winston.

Braddick, O.J., & Holliday, I.E. (1991). Serial search for targets defined by divergence or deformation of optic flow. *Perception, 20,* 345–354.

Braun, J. (1993). Shape-from-shading is independent of visual attention and may be a texton. *Spatial Vision, 7*(4), 311–322.

Braun, J. (1994). Visual search among items of different salience: Removal of visual attention mimics a lesion of extrastriate area V4. *Journal of Neuroscience, 14*(2), 554–567.

Braun, J., & Julesz, B. (1994). *Was William James right about passive, involuntary, and effortless attention?.* Paper presented at the annual meeting of the Psychonomic Society.

Braun, J., & Julesz, B. (1997). Dividing attention at little cost: detection and discrimination tasks. *Perception and Psychophysics, in press.*

Braun, J., & Sagi, D. (1990). Vision outside the focus of attention. *Perception and Psychophysics, 48*(1), 45–58.

Bravo, M., & Blake, R. (1990). Preattentive vision and perceptual groups. *Perception, 19,* 515–522.

Bravo, M., & Nakayama, K. (1992). The role of attention in different visual search tasks. *Perception and Psychophysics, 51,* 465–472.

Breese, B.B. (1909). Binocular rivalry. *Psychological Review, 16,* 410–415.

Brown, J.M., Enns, J.T., & Greene, H. (1993). Preattentive processing of line junctions can be altered by perceptual set. *Investigative Ophthalmology and Visual Science, 34*(4), 1234.

Brown, J.M., Weisstein, N., & May, J.G. (1992). Visual search for simple volumetric shapes. *Perception and Psychophysics, 51*(1), 40–48.

Bulthoff, H.H., & Blake, A. (1989). Does the seeing brain know physics? *Investigative Ophthalmology and Visual Science (Suppl.), 30*(3), 262.

Bundesen, C. (1990). A theory of visual attention. *Psychological Review, 97,* 523–547.

Bundesen, C. (1996). Formal models of visual attention: A tutorial review. In A. Kramer, G.H. Cole, & G.D. Logan (Eds.), *Converging operations in the study of visual selective attention* (pp.1–44). Washington, DC: American Psychological Association.

Bundesen, C., & Pedersen, L.F. (1983). Color segregation and visual search. *Perception and Psychophysics, 33,* 487–493.

Bursill, A.E. (1958). The restriction of peripheral vision during exposure to hot and humid conditions. *Quarterly Journal of Experimental Psychology, 10,* 113–129.

Caerwinski, M., Lightfoot, N., & Shiffrin, R. (1992). Automatization and training in visual search. *American Journal of Psychology, 105*(2), 271–315.

Callaghan, T.C. (1984). Dimensional interaction of hue and brightness in preattentive field segregation. *Perception and Psychophysics, 36,* 25–34.

Carrasco, M., & Chang, I. (1995). The interaction of objective and subjective organizations in a localization task. *Perception and Psychophysics, 57*(8), 1134–1150.

Carrasco, M., Evert, D.L., Chang, I., & Katz, S.M. (1995). The eccentricity effect: Target eccentricity affects performance on conjunction searches. *Perception and Psychophysics, 57*(8), 1241–1261.

Carter, R.C. (1982). Visual search with color. *Journal of Experimental Psychology: Human Perception and Performance, 8*, 127–136.

Cavanagh, P., Arguin, M., & Treisman, A. (1990). Effect of surface medium on visual search for orientation and size features. *Journal of Experimental Psychology: Human Perception and Performance, 16*(3), 479–492.

Cavanagh, P., & Mather, G. (1989). Motion: The long and the short of it. *Spatial Vision, 4*, 103–129.

Cave, K.R., & Pashler, H. (1995). Visual selection mediated by location: Selecting successive visual objects. *Perception and Psychophysics, 57*(4), 421–432.

Cave, K.R., & Wolfe, J.M. (1990). Modeling the role of parallel processing in visual search. *Cognitive Psychology, 22*, 225–271.

Cheal, M., & Lyon, D. (1992). Attention in visual search: Multiple search classes. *Perception and Psychophysics, 52*(2), 113–138.

Chen, L. (1982). Topological structure in visual perception. *Science, 218*, 699–700.

Chen, L. (1990). Holes and wholes: A reply to Rubin and Kanwisher. *Perception and Psychophysics, 47*, 47–53.

Christie, J., & Klein, R. (1994). *Novel popout: The true story.* Paper presented at the 35th annual meeting of the Psychonomic Society, November, 1994, St. Louis, MO.

Chun, M.M., & Potter, M.C. (1995). A two-stage model for multiple target detection in RSVP. *Journal of Experimental Psychology: Human Perception and Performance, 21*(1), 109–127.

Chun, M.M., & Wolfe, J.M. (1996). Just say no: How are visual searches terminated when there is no target present? *Cognitive Psychology, 30*, 39–78.

Cohen, A. (1993). Asymmetries in visual search for conjunctive targets. *Journal of Experimental Psychology: Human Perception and Performance, 19*(4), 775–797.

Cohen, A., & Ivry, R.B. (1989). Illusory conjunction inside and outside the focus of attention. *Journal of Experimental Psychology: Human Perception and Performance, 15*, 650–663.

Cohen, A., & Ivry, R.B. (1991). Density effects in conjunction search: Evidence for coarse location mechanism of feature integration. *Journal of Experimental Psychology: Human Perception and Performance, 17*(4), 891–901.

Cole, B.L., & Hughes, P.K. (1984). A field trial of attention and search conspicuity. *Human Factors, 26*(3), 299–313.

Damasio, A.R. (1990). Category-related recognition defects as a clue to the neural substrates of learning. *Trends in Neuroscience, 13*(3), 95–98.

Davis, G., & Driver, J. (1994). Parallel detection of Kanisza subjective figures in the human visual system. *Nature, 371*(27 Oct), 791–793.

Dehaene, S. (1989). Discriminability and dimensionality effects in visual search for featural conjunctions: A functional pop-out. *Perception and Psychophysics, 46*(1), 72–80.

Dick, M. (1989). *Parallel and serial processes in motion detection.* Unpublished PhD, Weizmann Institute, Rehovot, Israel.

Dick, M., Ullman, S., & Sagi, D. (1987). Parallel and serial processes in motion detection. *Science, 237*, 400–402.

Doherty, L.M., & Foster, D.H. (1995). *Detection of oriented line-targets in very sparse displays.* Paper presented at European Conference on Visual Perception, Tübingen, Germany.

Donderi, D.C., & Zelnicker, D. (1969). Parallel processing in visual same–different decisions. *Perception and Psychophysics, 5(4)*, 197–200.

Donnelly, N., Humphreys, G.W., & Riddoch, M.J. (1991). Parallel computation of primitive shape descriptions. *Journal of Experimental Psychology: Human Perception and Performance, 17*(2), 561–570.

Driver, J. (1992a). Motion coherence and conjunction search: Implications for guided search theory. *Perception and Psychophysics, 51*(1), 79–85.

Driver, J. (1992b). Reversing visual search asymmetries with conjunctions of movement and orientation. *Journal of Experimental Psychology: Human Perception and Performance, 18*(1), 22–33.

Driver, J., McLeod, P., & Dienes, Z. (1992a). Are direction and speed coded independently by the visual system? Evidence from visual search. *Spatial Vision, 6*(2), 133–147.

Driver, J., McLeod, P., & Dienes, Z. (1992b). Motion coherence and conjunction search: Implications for guided search theory. *Perception and Psychophysics, 51*(1), 79–85.

Duncan, J. (1980). The locus of interference in the perception of simultaneous stimuli. *Psychological Review, 87*, 272–300.

Duncan, J. (1983). Category effects in visual search: A failure to replicate the "oh-zero" phenomenon. *Perception and Psychophysics, 34*(3), 21–232.

Duncan, J. (1984). Selective attention and the organization of visual information. *Journal of Experimental Psychology: General, 113*, 501–517.

Duncan, J. (1988). Boundary conditions on parallel processing in human vision. *Perception, 17*, 358.

Duncan, J. (1989). Boundary conditions on parallel processing in human vision. *Perception, 18*, 457–469.

Duncan, J. (1995). Target and non-target grouping in visual search. *Perception and Psychophysics, 57*(1), 117–120.

Duncan, J., & Humphreys, G.W. (1989). Visual search and stimulus similarity. *Psychological Review, 96*, 433–458.

Duncan, J., & Humphreys, G.W. (1992). Beyond the search surface: Visual search and attentional engagement. *Journal of Experimental Psychology: Human Perception and Performance 18*(2), 578–588.

Duncan, J., Ward, R., & Shapiro, K. (1994). Direct measurement of attention dwell time in human vision. *Nature 369*(26 May), 313–314.

Dursteler, M.R., & von der Heydt, R. (1992). Monkey beats human in visual search. *Perception, 22* (Suppl. 2, European Conference on Visual Perception, Pisa), 12.

D'Zmura, M. (1991). Color in visual search. *Vision Research, 31*(6), 951–966.

Efron, R. (1990). Detectability as a function of target location: Effects of spatial configuration. *Brain and Cognition, 12*(1), 102–116.

Egeth, H. (1977). Attention and preattention. In G.H. Bower (Ed.), *The psychology of learning and motivation*, (Vol. 11, pp. 277–320). New York: Academic Press.

Egeth, H., & Dagenbach, D. (1991). Parallel versus serial processing in visual search: Further evidence from subadditive effects of visual quality. *Journal of Experimental Psychology: Human Perception and Performance, 17*(2), 551–560.

Egeth, H., Jonides, J., & Wall, S. (1972). Parallel processing of multielement displays. *Cognitive Psychology, 3*, 674–698.

Egeth, H.E., Virzi, R.A., & Garbart, H. (1984). Searching for conjunctively defined targets. *Journal of Experimental Psychology: Human Perception and Performance, 10*, 32–39.

Eglin, M. (1987). The effects of different attentional loads on feature integration in the cerebral hemispheres. *Perception and Psychophysics, 42*, 81–86.

Elder, J., & Zucker, S. (1993). The effect of contour closure on the rapid discrimination of two-dimensional shapes. *Vision Research, 33*(7), 981–991.

Elder, J., & Zucker, S. (1994). A measure of closure. *Vision Research, 34*(24), 3361–3369.

Engel, F.L. (1971). Visual conspicuity, directed attention, and retinal locus. *Vision Research, 11*, 563–576.

Enns, J. (1986). Seeing textons in context. *Perception and Psychophysics, 39*(2), 143–147.

Enns, J.T. (1992). Sensitivity of early human vision to 3-D orientation in line-drawings. *Canadian Journal of Psychology, 46*(2), 143–169.

Enns, J.T., & Rensink, R.A. (1990a). Scene-based properties influence visual search. *Science*, *247*, 721–723.

Enns, J.T., & Rensink, R.A. (1990b). Sensitivity to three-dimensional orientation in visual search. *Psychological Science*, *1*(5), 323–326.

Enns, J.T., & Rensink, R.A. (1991). Preattentive recovery of three-dimensional orientation from line drawings. *Psychological Review*, *98*(3), 335–351.

Epstein, W., & Babler, T. (1990). In search of depth. *Perception and Psychophysics*, *48*(1), 68–76.

Epstein, W., Babler, T., & Bownds, S. (1992). Attentional demands of processing shape in three-dimensional space: Evidence from visual search and precuing paradigms. *Journal of Experimental Psychology: Human Perception and Performance*, *18*(2), 503–511.

Eriksen, B.A., & Eriksen, C.W. (1974). Effects of noise letters upon the identification of a target letter in a nonsearch task. *Perception and Psychophysics.*, *16*, 143–149.

Eriksen, C.W., & Spencer, T. (1969). Rate of information processing in visual perception: Some results and methodological considerations. *Journal of Experimental Psychology Monograph*, *79*(2 (part 2)), 1–16.

Estes, W.K., & Taylor, H.A. (1966). Visual detection in relation to display size and redundancy of critical elements. *Perception and Psychophysics*, *1*(1), 9–16.

Fahle, M. (1990). Is vernier displacement a texton? *Investigative Ophthalmology and Visual Science, (Suppl.)*, *31(4)*, 105.

Fahle, M. (1991a). A new elementary feature of vision. *Investigative Ophthalmology and Visual Science*, *32*(7), 2151–2155.

Fahle, M. (1991b). Parallel perception of vernier offsets, curvature, and chevrons in humans. *Vision Research*, *31*(12), 2149–2184.

Fahle, M.W. (1990). *Parallel, semi-parallel, and serial processing of visual hyperacuity.* Paper presented at the SPIE: Human Vision and Electronic Imaging: Models, Methods, and Applications, Santa Clara, CA.

Farah, M. (1992). Is an object and object an object? Cognitive and Neurospsychological investigations of domain specificity in visual object recognition. *Current Directions in Psychological Science*, *1*(5), 165–169.

Farell, B., & Pelli, D.G. (1993). Can we attend to large and small at the same time? *Vision Research*, *33*(18), 2757–2772.

Farmer, E.W., & Taylor, R.M. (1980). Visual search through color displays: Effects of target-background similarity and background uniformity. *Perception and Psychophysics*, *27*, 267–272.

Folk, C.L., & Annett, S. (1994). Do locally defined feature discontinuities capture attention? *Perception and Psychophysics*, *56*(3), 277–287.

Foster, D.H., Cook, MJ. (1989). Categorical and noncategorical discrimination of curved lines depends on stimulus duration, not performance level. *Perception*, *18*(4), 519.

Foster, D.H., & Ward, P.A. (1991a). Asymmetries in oriented-line detection indicate two orthogonal filters in early vision. *Proceedings of the Royal Society (London B)*, *243*, 75–81.

Foster, D.H., & Ward, P.A. (1991b). Horizontal–vertical filters in early vision predict anomalous line-orientation frequencies. *Proceedings of the Royal Society (London B)*, *243*, 83–86.

Foster, D.H., & Westland, S. (1992). Fine structure in the orientation threshold function for preattentive line-target detection. *Perception*, *22* (Suppl. 2, European Conference on Visual Perception, Pisa), 6.

Foster, D.H., & Westland, S. (1995). Orientation contrast vs orientation in line-target detection. *Vision Research*, *35*(6), 733–738.

Foster, D.H. & Westland, S. (1996). Orientation fine-structure in line-target detection. In A. Gale, & Carr, K (Eds.), *Visual Search III*. Basingstoke, UK: Taylor & Francis.

Found, A., & Müller, H.J. (1995). Searching for unknown feature targets on more than one dimension: Further evidence for a "dimension weighting" account. *Perception and Psychophysics*, *58*(1), 88–101.

Francolini, C.M., & Egeth, H. (1979). Perceptual selectivity is task dependent: The pop-out effect poops out. *Perception and Psychophysics*, *25*(2), 99–110.

Friedman-Hill, S., & Wolfe, J. (1992). Activation vs inhibition in visual search. *Investigative Ophthalmology and Visual Science*, *33*, 1356.

Friedman-Hill, S.R., & Wolfe, J.M. (1995). Second-order parallel processing: Visual search for the odd item in a subset. *Journal of Experimental Psychology: Human Perception and Performance*, *21*(3), 531–551.

Geisler, W.S., & Chou, K.-L. (1995). Separation of low-level and high-level factors in complex tasks: Visual search. *Psychological Review*, *102*(2), 356–378.

Gibson, B.S. (1994). Visual attention and objects: One vs two or convex vs concave? *Journal of Experimental Psychology: Human Perception and Performance*, *20*(1), 203–207.

Gibson, B.S., & Egeth, H. (1994). Inhibition of return to object-based and environment-based locations. *Perception and Psychophysics*, *55*(3), 323–339.

Gilbert, C.D. (1994). Early perceptual learning. *Proceedings of the National Academy of Sciences*, *91*, 1195–1197.

Gilmore, G.C. (1985). Aging and similarity grouping in visual search. *Journal of Gerontology*, *40*(5), 586–592.

Goolkasian, P. (1988). Illusory conjunctions in the processing of clock times. *Journal of General Psychology*, *115*(4), 341–353.

Graves, M.A., Ball, K.K., Cissell, G.M., West, R.E., Whorely, K., & Edwards, J.D. (1993). Auditory distraction results in functional visual impairment for some older drivers. *Investigative Ophthalmology and Visual Science*, *34*(4), 1418.

Green, B.F., & Anderson, L.K. (1956). Color coding in a visual search task. *Journal of Experimental Psychology*, *51*, 19–24.

Green, M. (1991). Visual search, visual streams, and visual architectures. *Perception and Psychophysics*, *50*(4), 388–403.

Grossberg, S., Mingolla, E., & Ross, W.D. (1994). A neural theory of attentive visual search: Interactions of boundary, surface, spatial and object representations. *Psychological Review*, *101*(3), 470–489.

Gurnsey, R., & Browse, R.A. (1989). Asymmetries in visual texture discrimination. *Spatial Vision*, *4*(1), 31–44.

Gurnsey, R., Humphrey, G.K., & Kapitan, P. (1992). Parallel discrimination of subjective contours defined by offset gratings. *Perception and Psychophysics*, *52*(3), 263–276.

Hawley, K.J., Johnston, W.A., & Farnham, J.M. (1994). Novel popout with nonsense string: Effects of predictability of string length and spatial location. *Perception and Psychophysics*, *55*, 261–268.

He, J.J., & Nakayama, K. (1992). Surfaces vs features in visual search. *Nature*, *359*(9/17/92), 231–233.

Heathcote, A., & Mewhort, D.J.K. (1993). Representation and selection of relative position. *Journal of Experimental Psychology: Human Perception and Performance*, *19*(3), 488–516.

Helmholtz, H.v. (1924). *Treatise on physiological optics* (Southall, Trans. from 3rd German edn. of 1909). Rochester, NY: The Optical Society of America.

Hillstrom, A.P., & Yantis, S. (1994). Visual motion and attentional capture. *Perception and Psychophysics*, *55*, 399–411.

Hoffman, J.E. (1979). A two-stage model of visual search. *Perception and Psychophysics*, *25*, 319–327.

Hoffman, J.E., & Subramaniam, B. (1995). The role of visual attention in saccadic eye movements. *Perception and Psychophysics*, *57*(6), 787–795.

Hofmann, M.I., & Hallett, P.E. (1993). Texture segregation based on two-dimensional relative phase differences in composite sine-wave grating patterns. *Vision Research, 33*(2), 221–234.

Holliday, I.E., & Braddick, O.J. (1991). Pre-attentive detection of a target defined by stereoscopic slant. *Perception, 20*, 355–362.

Horowitz, T., & Treisman, A. (1994). Attention and apparent motion. *Spatial Vision, 8*(2), 193–219.

Horowitz, T.S., & Wolfe, J.M. (1997). Is visual search lost in space? *Investigative Ophthalmology and Visual Science, 38*(4), 5688.

Houck, M.R., & Hoffman, J.E. (1986). Conjunction of color and form without attention: Evidence from an orientation contingent color aftereffect. *Journal of Experimental Psychology: Human Perception and Performance, 12*, 186–199.

Hubel, D., & Weisel, T.N. (1962). Receptive fields, binocular interaction, and functional architecture in the cat's visual cortex. *Journal of Physiology (London), 160*, 106–114.

Hubel, D.H., & Wiesel, T.N. (1974). Sequence regularity and geometry of orientation columns in the monkey striate cortex. *Journal of Comparative Neurology, 158*, 267–294.

Humphrey, D.G., & Kramer, A.F. (1994). *Perceptual organization and selective attention: Age related effects.* Paper presented at the Converging Operations in the Study of Visual Selective Attention, Urbana, Illinois.

Humphreys, G.W., Freeman, G.W., & Müller, H.J. (1992). Lesioning a connectionist model of visual search: Selective effects on distractor grouping. *Canadian Journal of Psychology, 46*, 417–460.

Humphreys, G.W., Keulers, N., & Donnelly, N. (1994). Parallel visual coding in three dimensions. *Perception, 23*(4), 453–470.

Humphreys, G.W., & Müller, H.J. (1993). SEarch via Recursive Rejection (SERR): A connectionist model of visual search. *Cognitive Psychology, 25*, 43–110.

Humphreys, G.W., Quinlan, P.T., & Riddoch, M.J. (1989). Grouping processes in visual search: Effects with single and combined-feature targets. *Journal of Experimental Psychology: General, 118*(3), 258–279.

Isenberg, L., Nissen, M.J., & Marchak, L.C. (1990). Attentional processing and the independence of color and shape. *Journal of Experimental Psychology: Human Perception and Performance, 14*(4), 869–878.

Ivry, R.B. (1992). Asymmetry in visual search for targets defined by differences in movement speed. *Journal of Experimental Psychology: Human Perception and Performance, 18*(4), 1045–1057.

Ivry, R.B., & Cohen, A. (1990). Dissociation of short-and long-range apparent motion in visual search. *Journal of Experimental Psychology: Human Perception and Performance, 16*(2), 317–331.

Johnston, W.A., Hawley, K.J., & Farnham, J.M. (1993). Novel popout: Empirical boundaries and tentative theory. *Journal of Experimental Psychology: Human Perception and Performance, 19*(1), 140–153.

Jolicoeur, P. (1992). Orientation congruency effects in visual search. *Canadian Journal of Psychology, 46*(2), 280–305.

Jonides, J., & Gleitman, H. (1972). A conceptual category effect in visual search: O as letter or digit. *Perception and Psychophysics, 12*, 457–460.

Jonides, J., & Yantis, S. (1988). Uniqueness of abrupt visual onset in capturing attention. *Perception and Psychophysics, 43*(4), 346–354.

Julesz, B. (1984). A brief outline of the texton theory of human vision. *Trends in Neuroscience, 7*(Feb), 41–45.

Julesz, B. (1986). Texton gradients: The texton theory revisited. *Biological Cybernetics, 54*, 245–251.

Julesz, B., & Bergen, J.R. (1983). Textons, the fundamental elements in preattentive vision and perceptions of textures. *Bell Systems Technical Journal, 62*, 1619–1646.

Julesz, B., & Kröse, B. (1988). Features and spatial filters. *Nature, 333*, 302–303.

Kahneman, D., & Treisman, A. (1984). Changing views of attention and automaticity. In R. Parasuraman & D.R. Davies (Eds.), *Varieties of attention* (pp.29–61). New York: Academic Press.

Kaptein, N.A., Theeuwes, J., & Van der Heijden, A.H.C. (1994). Search for a conjunctively defined target can be selectively limited to a color-defined subset of elements. *Journal of Experimental Psychology: Human Perception and Performance, 21*(5), 1053–1069.

Karni, A., & Sagi, D. (1991). Where practice makes perfect in texture discrimination: Evidence for primary visual cortex plasticity. *Proceedings of the National Academy of Sciences, 88*, 4966–4970.

Karni, A., & Sagi, D. (1993). The time course of learning a visual skill. *Nature, 365*(16 Sept), 250–252.

Karni, A., Tanne, D., Rubenstein, B.S., Askenasy, J.J.M., & Sagi, D. (1994). Dependence on REM sleep of overnight improvement of a perceptual skill. *Science, 265*(29 July 1994), 679–682.

Kelly, P.L., Harrison, D.W., & Hodge, M.H. (1991). The category effect in visual selective attention. *Bulletin of the Psychonomic Society, 29*(1), 71–74.

Kendrick, K.M., & Baldwin, D.A. (1987). Cells in temporal cortex of conscious sheep can respond preferentially to the sight of faces. *Science, 236*, 448–450.

Khurana, B., & Kowler, E. (1987). Shared attentional control of smooth eye movement and perception. *Vision Research, 27*(9), 1603–1618.

Kimchi, R. (1992). Primacy of wholistic processing and global/local paradigm: A critical review. *Psychological Bulletin, 112*(1), 24–38.

Kinchla, R.A. (1974). Detecting targets in multi-element arrays: A confusability model. *Perception and Psychophysics, 15*, 149–158.

Kinchla, R.A. (1977). The role of structural redundancy in the perception of targets. *Perception and Psychophysics, 22*(1), 19–30.

Kinchla, R.A. (1992). Attention. *Annual Review of Psychology, 43*, 711–742.

Kinchla, R.A., & Wolfe, J.M. (1979). The order of visual processing: "Top-down", "bottom-up", or "middle-out". *Perception and Psychophysics, 25*, 225–231.

Kleffner, D.A., & Ramachandran, V.S. (1992). On the perception of shape from shading. *Perception and Psychophysics, 52*(1), 18–36.

Klein, R. (1988). Inhibitory tagging system facilitates visual search. *Nature, 334*, 430–431.

Klein, R., & Farrell, M. (1989). Search performance without eye movements. *Perception and Psychophysics, 46*, 476–482.

Koch, C., & Braun, J. (1996). Towards the neural correlate of visual awareness. *Current Opinion in Neurobiology, 6*, 158–164.

Koch, C., & Ullman, S. (1985). Shifts in selective visual attention: Towards the underlying neural circuitry. *Human Neurobiology, 4*, 219–227.

Kolb, F.C., & Braun, J. (1995). Blindsight in normal observers. *Nature, 377*, 366–368.

Kowler, E., Anderson, E., Dosher, B., & Blaser, E. (1995). The role of attention in the programming of saccades. *Vision Research, 35*(13), 1897–1916.

Krueger, L.E. (1984). The category effect in visual search depends on physical rather than conceptual differences. *Perception and Psychophysics, 35*(6), 558–564.

Kuehn, S.M. (1994). Impact of quality of the image, orientation, and similarity of the stimuli on visual search for faces. *Perception, 23*(1), 95–122.

Kwak, H., Dagenbach, D., & Egeth, H. (1991). Further evidence for a time-independent shift of the focus of attention. *Perception and Psychophysics, 49*(5), 473–480.

Ladd, G.T. (1894). *Psychology: Descriptive and explanatory*. New York: Scribner.

LaGasse, L.L. (1993). Effects of good form and spatial frequency on global precedence. *Perception and Psychophysics, 53*(1), 89–105.

Lamb, M.R., & Robertson, L.C. (1990). The effect of visual angle on global and local reaction times depends on the set of visual angles presented. *Perception and Psychophysics, 47*(5), 489–496.

Lamb, M.R., & Yund, E.W. (1993). The role of spatial frequency in the processing of hierarchically organized stimuli. *Perception and Psychophysics, 54*(6), 773–784.

Lavie, N., & Tsal, Y. (1994). Perceptual load as a major determinant of the locus of selection in visual attention. *Perception and Psychophysics, 56*(2), 183–197.

Lawrence, D.H. (1971). Two studies of visual search for word targets with controlled rates of presentation. *Perception and Psychophysics, 10*(2), 85–89.

Lee, D., Jung, E.S., & Chung, M.K. (1992). Isoresponse time regions for the evaluation of visual search performance in ergonomic interface models. *Ergonomics, 35*(3), 243–252.

Lee, M.D., & Fisk, A.D. (1993). Disruption and maintenance of skilled visual search as a function of degree of consistency. *Human Factors, 35*(2), 205–220.

Lennie, P., & D'Zmura, M. (1988). Mechanisms of color vision. *CRC Critical Reviews in Neurobiology, 3*(4), 333–402.

Levelt, W.J.M. (1965). *On binocular rivalry.* PhD thesis published by The Institute for Perception RVO-TNO, Soesterberg, The Netherlands.

Levi, D.M., Klein, S.A., & Aitsebaomo, A.P. (1985). Vernier acuity, crowding and cortical magnification. *Vision Research, 25*, 963–977.

Logan, G.D. (1994). Spatial attention and the apprehension of spatial relations. *Journal of Experimental Psychology: Human Perception and Performance, 20*(5), 1015–1036.

Logan, G.D. (1996). The CODE theory of visual attention: An integration of space-based and object-based attention. *Psychological Review, 103*(4), 603–649.

Luschow, A., & Nothdurft, H.C. (1993). Pop-out of orientation but not pop-out of motion at isoluminance. *Vision Research, 33*(1), 91–104.

Mack, A., Tang, B., Tuma, R., & Kahn, S. (1992). Perceptual organization and attention. *Cognitive Psychology, 24*, 475–501.

Mackeben, M., & Nakayama, K. (1988). Fixation release facilitates rapid attentional shifts. *Investigative Ophthalmology and Visual Science (Suppl.), 29*, 22.

Madden, D.J. (1992). Selective attention and visual search: Revision of an allocation model, an application to age differences. *Journal of Experimental Psychology: Human Perception and Performance, 18*(3), 821–836.

Maljkovic, V., & Nakayama, K. (1994). Priming of popout: I. Role of features. *Memory and Cognition, 22*(6), 657–672.

Maljkovic, V., & Nakayama, K. (1996). Priming of popout: II. Role of position. *Perception and Psychophysics, 58*(7), 977–991.

Mannan, S., Ruddock, K.H., & Wright, J.R. (1995). Eye movements and response times for the detection of line orientation during visual search. In J.M. Findlay, R. Walker, & Robert W. Kentridge (Eds.), *Eye movement research: Mechanisms, processes and applications. Studies in visual information processing,* (Vol. 6, pp.337–348). Amsterdam, Netherlands: Elsevier.

Marendaz, C., Stivalet, P., Barraclough, L., & Walkowiac, P. (1993). Effect of gravitoinertial cues on visual search for orientation. *Journal of Experimental Psychology: Human Perception and Peformance, 19*(6), 1266–1277.

McLeod, P. (1993). Filtering and physiology in visual search: A convergence of behavioural and neurophysiological measures. In A.D. Baddeley & L. Weiskrantz (Eds.), *Attention: Selection, awareness, and control: A tribute to Donald Broadbent* (pp.72–86). Oxford: Clarendon Press/Oxford University Press.

McLeod, P., Driver, J., & Crisp, J. (1988). Visual search for conjunctions of movement and form in parallel. *Nature, 332*, 154–155.

McLeod, P., Driver, J., Dienes, Z., & Crisp, J. (1991). Filtering by movement in visual search. *Journal of Experimental Psychology: Human Perception and Performance, 17*(1), 55–64.

Meigen, T., Lagreze, W.-D., & Bach, M. (1994). Asymmetries in preattentive line detection. *Vision Research, 34*(23), 3103–3109.

Miller, J. (1989). The control of visual attention by abrupt visual onsets and offsets. *Perception and Psychophysics, 45*, 567–571.

Moore, C.M., Egeth, H., Berglan, L.R., & Luck, S.J. (1996). Are attentional dwell times inconsistent with serial visual search? *Psychonomics Bulletin and Review, 3*(3), 360–365.

Moraglia, G. (1989a). Display organization and the detection of horizontal lines segments. *Perception and Psychophysics, 45*, 265–272.

Moraglia, G. (1989b). Visual search: Spatial frequency and orientation. *Perceptual and Motor Skills, 69*(2), 675–689.

Moraglia, G. (1989). Display organization and the detection of horizontal line segments. *Perception and Psychophysics, 45(3)*, 265–272.

Moraglia, G., Maloney, K.P., Fekete, E.M., & Al-Basi, K. (1989). Visual search along the colour dimension. *Canadian Journal of Psychology, 43(1)*, 1–12.

Mordkoff, J.T., & Yantis, S. (1991). An interactive race model of divided attention. *Journal of Experimental Psychology: Human Perception and Performance, 17*(2), 520–538.

Mordkoff, J.T., & Yantis, S. (1993). Dividing attention between color and shape: Evidence for coactivation. *Perception and Psychophysics, 53*(4), 357–366.

Mordkoff, J.T., Yantis, S., & Egeth, H.E. (1990). Detecting conjunctions of color and form in parallel. *Perception and Psychophysics, 48*(2), 157–168.

Müller, H.J., & Found, A. (1996). Visual search for conjunctions of motion and form: Display density and asymmetry reversal. *Journal of Experimental Psychology: Human Perception and Performance, 22*(1), 122–132.

Müller, H.J., & Maxwell, J. (1994). Perceptual integration of motion and form information. *Journal of Experimental Psychology: Human Perception and Performance, 20*, 397–420.

Müller, H.J., Heller, D., & Ziegler, J. (1995). Visual search for singleton feature targets within and across feature dimensions. *Perception and Psychophysics, 57*(1), 1–17.

Muller, H.M., Humphreys, G.W., & Donnelly, N. (1994). SEarch via Recursive Rejection (SERR): Visual search for single and dual form conjunction targets. *Journal of Experimental Psychology: Human Perception and Performance, 20*(2), 235–258.

Nagy, A.L., & Sanchez, R.R. (1990). Critical color differences determined with a visual search task. *Journal of the Optical Society of America A, 7*(7), 1209–1217.

Nagy, A.L., Sanchez, R.R., & Hughes, T.C. (1990). Visual search for color differences with foveal and peripheral vision. *Journal of the Optical Society of America A, 7*(10), 1995–2001.

Nakayama, K., & Silverman, G.H. (1986). Serial and parallel processing of visual feature conjunctions. *Nature, 320*, 264–265.

Nakayama, K.I. (1990). The iconic bottleneck and the tenuous link between early visual processing and perception. In C. Blakemore (Ed.), *Vision: Coding and efficiency* (pp.411–422). Cambridge: Cambridge University Press.

Navon, D. (1977). Forest before the trees: The precedence of global features in visual perception. *Cognitive Psychology, 9*, 353–383.

Neisser, U. (1967). *Cognitive psychology.* New York: Appleton, Century, Crofts.

Nothdurft, H.-C. (1991a). The role of local contrast in pop-out of orientation, motion and color. *Investigative Ophthalmology and Visual Science, 32*(4), 714.

Nothdurft, H.-C. (1993a). The role of features in preattentive vision: Comparison of orientation, motion and color cues. *Vision Research, 33*(14), 1937–1958.

Nothdurft, H.-C. (1993b). Saliency effects across dimensions in visual search. *Vision Research, 33*(5/6), 839–844.

Nothdurft, H.C. (1991b). Texture segmentation and pop-out from orientation contrast. *Vision Research, 31*(6), 1073–1078.

Nothdurft, H.C. (1993c). The conspicuousness of orientation and visual motion. *Spatial Vision, 7*(4), 341–366.

Nothdurft, H.C. (1993d). Faces and facial expression do not pop-out. *Perception, 22,* 1287–1298.

Nothdurft, H.C. (1994). Cortical properties of preattentive vision. In B. Albowitz, U. Kuhnt, R. Müzenmayer, H.C. Nothdurft & P. Wahle (Eds.), *Structural and functional organization of the neocortex,* (pp.375–384). Berlin: Springer-Verlag.

O'Connell, K.M., & Treisman, A.M. (1990). Is all orientation created equal? *Investigative Ophthalmology and Visual Science, 31*(4), 106.

Olzak, L.A., & Thomas, J.P. (1986). Seeing spatial patterns. In K.R. Boff, L. Kaufmann, & J.P. Thomas (Eds.), *Handbook of perception and human performance,* (Ch. 7). New York: Wiley.

O'Neill, P., & Wolfe, J.M. (1994). Mechanisms of visual search revealed by individual differences. *Investigative Opthalmology and Visual Science, 35*(4), 1328.

O'Toole, A.J., & Walker, C.L. (1993). Disparity as a visual primitive: The competing role of surface percepts. *Investigative Ophthalmology and Visual Science, 34*(4), 1187.

Palmer, J. (1994). Set-size effects in visual search: The effect of attention is independent of the stimulus for simple tasks. *Vision Research, 34*(13), 1703–1721.

Palmer, J. (1995). Attention in visual search: Distinguishing four causes of a set-size effect. *Current Directions in Psychological Science, 4*(4), 118–123.

Palmer, J., & McLean, J. (1995). *Imperfect, unlimited-capacity, parallel search yields large set-size effects,* Paper presented at the Society for Mathematical Psychology, Irvine, CA.

Paquet, L. (1992). Global and local processing in nonattended objects: A failure to induce local processing dominance. *Journal of Experimental Psychology: Human Perception and Performance, 18*(2), 512–529.

Pashler, H. (1987). Detecting conjunctions of color and form: Reassessing the serial search hypothesis. *Perception and Psychophysics, 41,* 191–201.

Pashler, H. (1988). Cross-dimensional interaction and texture segregation. *Perception and Psychophysics, 43,* 307–318.

Plude, D.J., & Doussard-Roosevelt, J.A. (1989). Aging, selective attention, and feature-integration. *Psychology and Aging, 4*(1), 98–105.

Pomerantz, J.R., & Pristach, E.A. (1989). Emergent features, attention, and perceptual glue in visual form perception. *Journal of Experimental Psychology: Human Perception and Performance, 15*(4), 635–649.

Posner, M.I., & Cohen, Y. (1984). Components of attention. In H. Bouma & D.G. Bouwhuis (Eds.), *Attention and performance X,* (pp.55–66). Hove, UK: Lawrence Erlbaum Associates Ltd.

Potter, M.C. (1975). Meaning in visual search. *Science, 187,* 965–966.

Potter, M.C. (1976). Short-term conceptual memory for pictures. *Journal of Experimental Psychology: Human Learning and Memory, 2*(5), 509–522.

Pratt, J., & Abrams, R.A. (1995). Inhibition of return to successively cued spatial locations. *Journal of Experimental Psychology: Human Perception and Performance, 21*(6), 1343–1353.

Previc, F.H., & Blume, J.L. (1993). Visual search asymmetries in three-dimensional space. *Vision Research, 33*(18), 2697–2704.

Prinzmetal, W. (1991). Automatic processes in word perception: An analysis from illusory conjunctions. *Journal of Experimental Psychology: Human Perception and Performance, 17*(4), 902–923.

Prinzmetal, W. (1995). Visual feature integration in a world of objects. *Current Directions in Psychological Science, 4*(2), 1–5.

Prinzmetal, W., Henderson, D., & Ivry, R. (1995). Loosening the constraints on illusory conjunctions: The role of exposure duration and attention. *Journal of Experimental Psychology: Human Perception and Performance, 21*(6), 1362–1375.

Prinzmetal, W., & Keysar, B. (1989). Functional theory of illusory conjunctions and neon colors. *Journal of Experimental Psychology: General, 118*(2), 165–190.

Purcell, D.G., & Stewart, A.L. (1988). The face-detection effect: Configuration enhances detection. *Perception and Psychophysics, 43*(4), 355–366.

Quinlan, P.T., & Humphreys, G.W. (1987). Visual search for targets defined by combinations of color, shape, and size: An examination of the task constraints on feature and conjunction searches. *Perception and Psychophysics, 41*, 455–472.

Ramachandran, V.S. (1988). Perception of shape from shading. *Nature, 331*, 163–165.

Ratcliff, R. (1978). A theory of memory retrieval. *Psychological Review, 85*(2), 59–108.

Reinitz, M.T., Morrissey, J., & Demb, J. (1994). Role of attention in face encoding. *Journal of Experimental Psychology: Learning, Memory, and Cognition, 20*(1), 161–168.

Remington, R., & Williams, D. (1986). On the selection and evaluation of visual display symbology: Factors influencing search and identification times. *Human Factors, 28*(4), 407–420.

Remington, R.W., Johnston, J.C., & Yantis, S. (1992). Involuntary attentional capture by abrupt onsets. *Perception and Psychophysics, 51*(3), 279–290.

Rensink, R., & Cavanagh, P. (1993). Processing of shadows at preattentive levels. *Investigative Ophthalmology and Visual Science, 34*(4), 1288.

Rensink, R., & Cavanagh, P. (1994). Identification of highlights in early vision. *Investigative Ophthalmology and Visual Science, 35*(4), 1623.

Rensink, R.A., & Enns, J.T. (1995). Pre-emption effects in visual search: Evidence for low-level grouping. *Psychological Review, 102*(1), 101–130.

Riggs, L.A. (1973). Curvature as a feature of pattern vision. *Science, 181*, 1070–1072.

Robertson, L.C., Egly, R., Lamb, M.R., & Kerth, L. (1993). Spatial attention and curing to global and local levels of hierarchical structure. *Journal of Experimental Psychology: Perception and Performance, 19*(3), 471–487.

Rogers, W.A. (1992). Age differences in visual search: Target and distractor learning. *Psychology and Aging, 7*(4), 526–535.

Rolls, E.T., Baylis, G.C., & Leonard, C.M. (1985). Role of low and high spatial frequencies in the face-selective responses of neurons in the cortex in the superior temporal sulcus in the monkey. *Vision Research, 25*, 1021–1035.

Rolls, E.T., Judge, S.J., & Sanghera, M.K. (1977). Activity of neurones in the inferotemporal cortex of the alert monkey. *Brain Research, 130*, 229–238.

Ross, W.D., & Mingolla, E. (1994). Grouping effects in visual search. *Investigative Opthalmology and Visual Science, 35*(4), 2081.

Rossi, A., & Paradiso, M.A. (1995). Feature-specific effects of selective visual attention. *Vision Research, 35*, 621–634.

Royden, C.S., Wolfe, J.M., Konstantinova, E., & Hildreth, E.C. (1996). Search for a moving object by a moving observer. *Investigative Opthalmology and Visual Science, 37*(ARVO suppl.).

Rubin, J.M., & Kanwisher, N. (1985). Topological perception: Holes in an experiment. *Perception and Psychophysics, 37*, 179–180.

Saarinen, J. (1993). Shifts in visual attention at fixation and away from fixation. *Vision Research, 33*(8), 1113–1117.

Sagi, D. (1988). The combination of spatial frequency and orientation is effortlessly perceived. *Perception and Psychophysics, 43*, 601–603.

Sagi, D. (1990). Detection of an orientation singularity in Gabor textures: Effect of signal density and spatial-frequency. *Vision Research, 30*(9), 1377–1388.

Sagi, D., & Julesz, B. (1985). Fast noninertial shifts of attention. *Spatial Vision, 1*, 141–149.

Sagi, D., & Tanne, D. (1994). Perceptual learning: Learning to see. *Current Opinion in Neurobiology, 4*, 195–199.

Sanders, A.F. (1970). Some aspects of the selective process in the functional visual field. *Ergonomics, 13*(1), 101–117.

Sanders, A.F., & Brück, R. (1991). The effect of presentation time on the size of the visual lobe. *Bulletin of the Psychonomic Society, 29*(3), 206–208.

Schneider, W., & Eberts, R. (1980). Automatic processing and the unitization of two features. *Report of the Human Attention Research Lab., University of Illinois, #8008*, 1–26.

Schneider, W., & Shiffrin, R.M. (1977). Controlled and automatic human information processing: I. Detection, search, and attention. *Psychological Review, 84*, 1–66.

Scialfa, C.T., Kline, D.W., & Lyman, B.J. (1987). Age differences in target identification as a function of retinal location and noise level: Examination of the useful field of view. *Psychology and Aging, 2*(1), 14–19.

Sekuler, R., & Ball, K. (1986). Visual localization: Age and practice. *Journal of the Optical Society of America A, 3*(6), 864–868.

Shibuya, H., & Bundesen, C. (1993). Efficiency of visual selection in duplex and conjunction conditions in partial report. *Perception and Psychophysics, 45*(6), 716–732.

Shiffrin, M.R., & Schneider, W. (1977). Controlled and automatic human information processing: II. Perceptual learning, automatic attending, and a general theory. *Psychological Review, 84*, 127–190.

Shiffrin, R.M., & Gardner, G.T. (1972). Visual processing capacity and attentional control. *Journal of Experimental Psychology, 93*(1), 72–82.

Shih, S.-I., & Sperling, G. (1996). Is there feature-based attentional selection in visual search? *Journal of Experimental Psychology: Human Perception and Performance, 22*(3), 758–779.

Shulman, G.L. (1990). Relating attention to visual mechanisms. *Perception and Psychophysics, 47*(2), 199–203.

Sireteanu, R., & Rettenbach, R. (1995). Perceptual learning in visual search: Fast enduring but non-specific. *Vision Research, 35*(14), 2037–2043.

Smallman, H.S., & Boynton, R.M. (1990). Segregation of basic color in an information display. *Journal of the Optical Society of America A, 7*(10), 1985–1994.

Smith, S.L. (1962). Color coding and visual search. *Journal of Experimental Psychology, 64*, 434–440.

Snowden, R.J. (1996). Texture segregation and visual search: A comparison of the effects of random variations along irrelevant dimensions. *Investigative Ophthalmology and Visual Science, 37*(ARVO Suppl).

Soraci, S.A. Jr, Franks, J.J., Carlin, M.T., Hoehn, T.P., Hardy, J.K. (1992). A "popout" effect with words and nonwords. *Bulletin of the Psychonomic Society, 30*(4), 290–292.

Stefurak, D.L., & Boynton, R.M. (1986). Independence of memory for categorically different colors and shapes. *Perception and Psychophysics, 39*, 164–174.

Steinman, S.B. (1987). Serial and parallel search in pattern vision. *Perception, 16*, 389–398.

Sternberg, S. (1969). High-speed scanning in human memory. *Science, 153*, 652–654.

Stivalet, P., Marendaz, C., Barraclough, L., & Mourareau, C. (1995). Effect of gravito-inertial cues on the coding of orientation in pre-attentive vision. *Journal of Vestibular Research: Equilibrium and Orientation, 5*(2), 125–135.

Stromeyer, C.F., & Riggs, L.A. (1974). Curvature detectors in human vision? *Science, 184*, 1199–1201.

Stuart, G.W. (1993). Preattentive processing of object size: Implications for theories of size perception. *Perception, 22*(10), 1175–1193.

Sun, J., & Perona, P. (1996a). Early computation of shape and reflectance in the visual system. *Nature, 379*(11 Jan), 165–168.

Sun, J., & Perona, P. (1996b). Preattentive perception of elementary three-dimensional shapes. *Vision Research, 36*(16), 2515–2529.

Suzuki, S., & Cavanagh, P. (1995). Facial organization blocks access to low-level features: An object inferiority effect. *Journal of Experimental Psychology: Human Perception and Performance, 21*(4), 901–913.

Swensson, R.G. (1980). A two-stage detection model applied to skilled visual search by radiologists. *Perception and Psychophysics, 27*(1), 11–16.

Swensson, R.G., & Judy, P.F. (1981). Detection of noisy visual targets: Models for the effects of spatial uncertainty and signal-to-noise ratio. *Perception and Psychophysics, 29*(6), 521–534.

Taylor, S., & Badcock, D. (1988). Processing feature density in preattentive perception. *Perception and Psychophysics, 44*, 551–562.

Theeuwes, J. (1991). Cross-dimensional perceptual selectivity. *Perception and Psychophysics, 50*(2), 184–193.

Theeuwes, J. (1992). Perceptual selectivity for color and form. *Perception and Psychophysics, 51*(6), 599–606.

Theeuwes, J. (1993). Visual selective attention: A theoretical analysis. *Acta Psychologica, 83*, 93–154.

Theeuwes, J. (1994). Stimulus-driven capture and attentional set: Selective search for color and visual abrupt onsets. *Journal of Experimental Psychology: Human Perception and Performance, 20*(4), 799–806.

Theeuwes, J. (1995). Abrupt luminance change pops out; abrupt color change does not. *Perception and Psychophysics, 57*(5), 637–644.

Theeuwes, J., & Kooi, J.L. (1994). Parallel search for a conjunction of shape and contrast polarity. *Vision Research, 34*(22), 3013–3016.

Thomas, J.P., & Gille, J. (1979). Bandwidths of orientation channels in human vision. *Journal of the Optical Society of America A, 69*, 652–660.

Thompson, P. (1980). Margaret Thatcher: A new illusion. *Perception, 9*, 482–484.

Tiana, C., Lennie, P., & D'Zmura, M. (1989). Parallel search for color/shape and color/motion conjunctions. *Investigative Ophthalmology and Visual Science (Suppl.), 30*, 252.

Tipper, S.P., Driver, J., & Weaver, B. (1991). Object centered inhibition of return of visual attention. *Quarterly Journal of Experimental Psychology, 43*A, 289–298.

Titchener, E.B. (1919). *A text-book of psychology.* New York: Macmillan.

Todd, S., & Kramer, A.F. (1994). Attentional misguidance in visual search. *Perception and Psychophysics, 56*(2), 198–210.

Townsend, J.T. (1971). A note on the identification of parallel and serial processes. *Perception and Psychophysics, 10*, 161–163.

Townsend, J.T. (1976). Serial and within-stage independent parallel model equivalence on the minimum completion time. *Journal of Mathematical Psychology 14*, 219–239.

Townsend, J.T. (1990). Serial and parallel processing: Sometimes they look like Tweedledum and Tweedledee but they can (and should) be distinguished. *Psychological Science, 1*, 46–54.

Treisman, A. (1982). Perceptual grouping and attention in visual search for features and for objects. *Journal of Experimental Psychology: Human Perception and Performance, 8*, 194–214.

Treisman, A. (1986). Properties, parts, and objects. In K.R. Boff, L. Kaufmann, & J.P. Thomas (Eds.), *Handbook of human perception and performance,* (1st edn., Vol. 2, pp.37.1–35.70). New York: Wiley.

Treisman, A. (1988). Features and objects: The 14th Bartlett memorial lecture. *Quarterly Journal of Experimental Psychology, 40*A, 201–237.

Treisman, A. (1991). Search, similarity, and integration of features between and within dimensions. *Journal of Experimental Psychology: Human Perception and Performance*, 17(3), 652–676.

Treisman, A. (1992). Spreading suppression or feature integration? A reply to Duncan and Humphreys (1992). *Journal of Experimental Psychology: Human Perception and Performance*, 18(2), 589–593.

Treisman, A. (1993). The perception of features and objects. In A. Baddeley & L. Weiskrantz (Eds.), *Attention: Selection, awareness, and control* (pp.5–35). Oxford: Clarendon Press.

Treisman, A., & Gelade, G. (1980). A feature-integration theory of attention. *Cognitive Psychology, 12*, 97–136.

Treisman, A., & Gormican, S. (1988). Feature analysis in early vision: Evidence from search asymmetries. *Psychological Review, 95*, 15–48.

Treisman, A., & Sato, S. (1990). Conjunction search revisited. *Journal of Experimental Psychology: Human Perception and Performance, 16*(3), 459–478.

Treisman, A., & Souther, J. (1985). Search asymmetry: A diagnostic for preattentive processing of separable features. *Journal of Experimental Psychology: General, 114*, 285–310.

Treisman, A., & Souther, J. (1986). Illusory words: The roles of attention and of top-down constraints in conjoining letters to form words. *Journal of Experimental Psychology: Human Perception and Performance, 12*, 3–17.

Treisman, A., Vieira, A., & Hayes, A. (1992). Automaticity and preattentive processing. *American Journal of Psychology, 105*, 341–362.

Treisman, A.M., & Schmidt, H. (1982). Illusory conjunctions in the perception of objects. *Cognitive Psychology, 14*, 107–141.

Tsal, Y., & Lavie, N. (1988). Attending to color and shape: The special role of location in selective visual processing. *Perception and Psychophysics, 44*, 15–21.

Tsal, Y., Meiran, N., & Lamy, D. (1995). Towards a resolution theory of visual attention. *Visual Cognition, 2*(2/3), 313–330.

Tsal, Y., Meiran, N., & Lavie, N. (1994). The role of attention in illusory conjunctions. *Perception and Psychophysics, 55*(3), 350–358.

Tsal, Y., Shalev, L., Zakay, D., & Lubow, R.E. (1994). Attention reduces perceived brightness contrast. *Quarterly Journal of Experimental Psychology, 47*A(4), 865–893.

Tsotsos, J.K. (1990). Analyzing vision at the complexity level. *Brain and Behavioral Sciences, 13*(3), 423–469.

Tyler, C.W. (1983). Sensory processing of binocular disparity. In C.W. Schor & K.J. Ciuffreda (Eds.), *Vergence eye movements* (pp.199–295). Boston: Butterworth.

Van Orden, K.F. (1993). Redundant use of luminance and flashing with shape and color as highlighting codes in symbolic displays. *Human Factors, 35*(2), 195–204.

Vecera, S.P., & Farah, M.J. (1994). Does visual attention select objects or locations? *Journal of Experimental Psychology: General, 123*(2), 146–160.

Verghese, P., & Nakayama, K. (1994). Stimulus discriminability in visual search. *Vision Research, 34*(18), 2453–2467.

Verghese, P., & Pelli, D.G. (1992). The information capacity of visual attention. *Vision Research, 32*(5), 983–995.

Verghese, P., & Pelli, D.G. (1994). The scale bandwidth of visual search. *Vision Research, 34*(7), 955–962.

Vieira, A., & Treisman, A. (1988). *Automatic search: Changing perceptions or procedures?* Paper presented at the Psychonomic Society Annual Meeting, Chicago.

Virzi, R.A., & Egeth, H.E. (1984). Is meaning implicated in illusory contours. *Journal of Experimental Psychology: Human Perception and Performance, 10*, 573–580.

von der Heydt, R., & Dursteler, M.R. (1993). Visual search: Monkeys detect conjunctions as fast as features. *Investigative Ophthalmology and Visual Science, 34*(4), 1288.

Von Grünau, M., & Dubé, S. (1994). Visual search asymmetry for viewing direction. *Perception and Psychophysics, 56*(2), 211–220.

Wang, Q., & Cavanagh, P. (1993). Acquired familiarity effects in visual search with Chinese characters. *Investigative Ophthalmology and Visual Science, 34*(4), 1236.

Wang, Q., Cavanagh, P., & Green, M. (1994). Familiarity and pop-out in visual search. *Perception and Psychophysics, 56*(5), 495–500.

Ward, R., Duncan, J., & Shapiro, K. (1996). The slow time-course of visual attention. *Cognitive Psychology, 30*(1), 79–109.

Ward, R., & McClelland, J.L. (1989). Conjunctive search for one and two identical targets. *Journal of Experimental Psychology: Human Perception and Performance, 15*(4), 664–672.

Westheimer, G. (1979). The spatial sense of the eye. *Investigative Ophthalmology and Visual Science, 18*, 893–912.

Westland, S., & Foster, D.H. (1996). A line-target-detection model using horizontal–vertical filters. In A. Gale, & K. Carr (Eds.), *Visual search III*. Basingstoke, UK: Taylor & Francis.

Williams, D., & Julesz, B. (1989). The significance of closure for texture segregation. *Investigative Ophthalmology and Visual Science, (Suppl.). 39.*

Wilson, H.R. (1986). Responses of spatial mechanisms can explain hyperacuity. *Vision Research, 26*, 453–469.

Wolfe, J.M. (1986). Stereopsis and binocular rivalry. *Psychological Review, 93*, 269–282.

Wolfe, J.M. (1992a). "Effortless" texture segmentation and "parallel" visual search are *not* the same thing. *Vision Research, 32*(4), 757–763.

Wolfe, J.M. (1992b). The parallel guidance of visual attention. *Current Directions in Psychological Science, 1*(4), 125–128.

Wolfe, J.M. (1993a). Guided Search 2.0: The upgrade. *Proceedings of the Human Factors and Ergonomics Society, 37*, 1295–1299.

Wolfe, J.M. (1993b). Talking to yourself about *What* is *Where*: What is the vocabulary of preattentive vision? Commentary on Jackendorf and Landau, BBS Article. *Behavioral and Brain Sciences, 16*(2), 254–255.

Wolfe, J.M. (1994a). Guided Search 2.0: A revised model of visual search. *Psychonomic Bulletin and Review, 1*(2), 202–238.

Wolfe, J.M. (1994b). Visual search in continuous, naturalistic stimuli. *Investigative Opthalmology and Visual Science, 35*(4), 1328.

Wolfe, J.M. (1996a). Extending Guided Search: Why Guided Search needs a preattentive "item map". In A. Kramer, G.H. Cole, & G.D. Logan (Eds.), *Converging operations in the study of visual selective attention* (pp.247–270). Washington, DC: American Psychological Association.

Wolfe, J.M. (1996b). Post-attentive vision. *Investigative Opthalmology and Visual Science, 37* (ARVO suppl.).

Wolfe, J.M., & Bennett, S.C. (1996). Preattentive object files: Shapeless bundles of basic features. *Vision Research, 37*(1), 25–44.

Wolfe, J.M., & Cave, K.R. (1989). Deploying visual attention: The guided search model. In T. Troscianko & A. Blake (Eds.), *AI and the eye* (pp.79–103). Chichester, UK: Wiley.

Wolfe, J.M., Cave, K.R., & Franzel, S.L. (1989). Guided Search: An alternative to the Feature Integration model for visual search. *Journal of Experimental Psychology: Human Perception and Performance, 15*, 419–433.

Wolfe, J.M., Chun, M.M., & Friedman-Hill, S.R. (1995). Making use of texton gradients: Visual search and perceptual grouping exploit the same parallel processes in different ways. In T. Papathomas, C. Chubb, A. Gorea, & E. Kowler (Eds.), *Early vision and beyond* (pp.189–198). Cambridge, MA: MIT Press.

Wolfe, J.M., & Franzel, S.L. (1988). Binocularity and visual search. *Perception and Psychophysics, 44*, 81–93.

Wolfe, J.M., & Friedman-Hill, S.R. (1992a). On the role of symmetry in visual search. *Psychological Science, 3*(3), 194–198.

Wolfe, J.M., & Friedman-Hill, S.R. (1992b). Part–whole relationships in visual search. *Investigative Ophthalmology and Visual Science, 33*, 1355.

Wolfe, J.M., & Friedman-Hill, S.R. (1992c). Visual search for orientation: The role of angular relations between targets and distractors. *Spatial Vision, 6*(3), 199–208.

Wolfe, J.M., Friedman-Hill, S.R., & Bilsky, A.A. (1994). Parallel processing of part/whole information in visual search tasks. *Perception and Psychophysics, 55*(5), 537–550.

Wolfe, J.M., Friedman-Hill, S.R., Stewart, M.I., & O'Connell, K.M. (1992). The role of categorization in visual search for orientation. *Journal of Experimental Psychology: Human Perception and Performance, 18*(1), 34–49.

Wolfe, J.M., & Pokorny, C.W. (1990). Inhibitory tagging in visual search: A failure to replicate. *Perception and Psychophysics, 48*, 357–362.

Wolfe, J.M., Yee, A., & Friedman-Hill, S.R. (1992). Curvature is a basic feature for visual search. *Perception, 21*, 465–480.

Wolfe, J.M., Yu, K.P., Stewart, M.I., Shorter, A.D., Friedman-Hill, S.R., & Cave, K.R. (1990). Limitations on the parallel guidance of visual search: Color × color and orientation × orientation conjunctions. *Journal of Experimental Psychology: Human Perception and Performance, 16*(4), 879–892.

Yantis, S. (1993). Stimulus-driven attentional capture. *Current Directions in Psychological Science, 2*(5), 156–161.

Yantis, S., & Egeth, H.E. (1994). Visual salience and stimulus-driven attentional capture. *Investigative Ophthalmology and Visual Science, 35*(4), 1619.

Yantis, S., & Gibson, B.S. (1994). Object continuity in apparent motion and attention. *Canadian Journal of Experimental Psychology, 48*, 182–204.

Yantis, S., & Hillstrom, A.P. (1994). Stimulus-driven attentional capture: Evidence from equiluminant visual objects. *Journal of Experimental Psychology: Human Perception and Performance, 20*(1), 95–107.

Yantis, S., & Johnson, D.N. (1990). Mechanisms of attentional priority. *Journal of Experimental Psychology: Human Perception and Performance, 16*(4), 812–825.

Yantis, S., & Jones, E. (1991). Mechanisms of attentional priority: Temporally modulated priority tags. *Perception and Psychophysics, 50*(2), 166–178.

Yantis, S., & Jonides, J. (1996). Attentional capture by abrupt visual onsets: New perceptual objects or visual masking? *Journal of Experimental Psychology: Human Perception and Performance, 22*(6), 1505–1513.

Zacks, J.L., & Zacks, R.T. (1993). Visual search times assessed without reaction times: Changes with aging. *Journal of Experimental Psychology: Human Perception and Performance, 19*(4), 798–813.

Zelinsky, G.J. (1993). *Eye movements during parallel/serial search tasks.* Unpublished PhD, Brown University, Providence, RI.

Zenger, B., & Fahle, M. (1995). *"Missed targets" versus "false alarms": A model for error rates in visual search,* Paper presented at the European Conference on Visual Perception, Teubingen, Germany.

Zhou, W., Chen, L., & Zhang, X. (1992). Topological perception: Holes in illusory conjunction and visual search. *Investigative Ophthalmology and Visual Science, 33*(4), 958 (abs #1326).

Zhou, W., Zhang, X., & Chen, L. (1993). Shape transformation in illusory conjunctions. *Investigative Ophthalmology and Visual Science, 34*(4), 1082.

Zohary, E., & Hochstein, S. (1989). How serial is serial processing in vision? *Perception, 18*, 191–200

CHAPTER TWO

Auditory Attention: The Psychoacoustical Approach

Bertram Scharf
CNRS, Marseille, France and Northeastern University, Boston, USA

I. INTRODUCTION

Recent decades have seen a proliferation of studies of visual attention that have largely displaced the emphasis on auditory attention that prevailed in the 1950s and 1960s with the resurgence of the experimental study of attention (e.g. Broadbent, 1958; Cherry, 1953). Yet it would seem that selective auditory attention presents the greater challenge. Visual attention is closely linked to the position of the head and eyes; normally, visual attention follows the fovea where stimuli are most fully processed. In contrast, the human cochlea (the inner ear) has no equivalent to the fovea and so attention does not seek to focus sound on a particular, favored region of the basilar membrane. Thus, auditory attention is mostly independent of the position of the head and ears, even if some increase in loudness or in signal-to-noise ratio can be achieved by turning the head or cupping the ear. This neutrality with respect to the spatial attributes of sound makes the auditory system an excellent early-warning system, one that is ready to receive and process stimuli from all directions regardless of the organism's current orientation. At the same time, this openness to all the vagaries of the environment makes it especially important that the organism be able to select for devoted processing one among two or more simultaneous sources of sound. Whereas the eyes achieve this selection primarily by aiming the fovea at the object of interest, the ears lack this possibility and must use other means to extricate the wheat from the chaff (cf. Spence & Driver, 1994).

Nonetheless, the auditory and visual systems are alike in that shifts in attention may be either voluntary or involuntary. One can voluntarily choose to attend to one or another section of the visual field, turning the eyes toward that chosen section and focusing the lens appropriately. However, a sudden change in the peripheral field usually attracts attention, and the eyes tend to turn toward that direction. Similarly, one can choose to attend to one or another part of the auditory field, defined both in terms of spatial direction and spectral content. (Spectral content refers to the distribution of amplitude over sound frequency.) Again, a sudden change in an ongoing sound or a new sound usually attracts attention to a previously unattended part of the field.

A frequent example of auditory selectivity is the *cocktail-party effect*, the ability to listen to one speaker among many (Cherry, 1953). The ability is encoded in language in the distinction between listening and hearing (a distinction that appears to be universal even if cocktail parties are not). One *listens* to the person whom one wants to understand; *hearing* does not suffice. Listening is active and voluntary whereas hearing is passive and involuntary. The same distinction is found between looking and seeing, touching and feeling, sniffing and smelling. However, whereas looking and touching and sniffing imply a specific motor activity that reorientates the sensory receptors—the eyes turn, the hands move, the nose sniffs—listening implies an internal state, more akin to alertness. Although one normally turns toward a human speaker when listening, it is to see, to look at the speaker. Thus, one seldom turns to look at a loudspeaker when listening to recorded or broadcast sound. (However, not looking at a loudspeaker emitting unwanted talk may help the processing of wanted talk [Reisberg, Scheiber, & Potemken, 1981].) In general, listening appears not to require the motor activity so usual in the other senses when focusing attention. (Nonetheless, we shall see that in fact a subtle, wholly invisible motor-like activity may also take place in listening.)

If listening is an internal state with no apparent peripheral changes, than is auditory attention, after all, a wholly cognitive act? Is the selection then made in a central nervous system bombarded by a myriad of incoming stimulus-bound excitations, stimuli for which the initial neural processing is uninfluenced by the goals of the organism? In more usual terms, is the selection among competing sounds made late, at a cognitive level far from the ear, rather than early, at the sensory level? This chapter will present evidence that at least some type of auditory selection is made at the receptor, under central control. Such precocious selectivity is possible because each cochlea is innervated by some 1400 *efferent* nerve fibers of the olivocochlear bundle (OCB), which runs from the olivary complex in the brainstem to the cochlea. The OCB is the last stage in the transmission of neural information *from* the auditory centers in the temporal lobe *to* the cochlea (Desmedt,

1975). Thus, the sensory receptors (the hair cells) on the basilar membrane in the cochlea may be prepared in advance to favor one sound over another. The nervous system needs such advance preparation because natural sounds reaching the cochlea are usually so greatly intermixed that if the brain had to do all the sorting, its task would be formidable.

The notion that the efferent fibers of the OCB serve a function in attention dates to the 1950s when the OCB was first described by Rasmussen (1946). An early hypothesis was not that the OCB would help the organism to choose among competing sounds but that it would gate auditory input. An organism seeking to focus on sights or smells would partly shut down auditory input by inhibiting the response of the hair cells. Hernandez-Peon, Scherrer, and Jouvet (1956) published data supporting such a hypothesis. They found that auditory-nerve responses to sounds were reduced when a cat saw a mouse or smelled a fish. Such a reduction meant that the hair cells of the cochlea must have been less active, since it is they that react to sound and then excite the auditory nerve. The authors suggested that the hair cells were being inhibited by the OCB. However, it turned out that various experimental artifacts such as head movements (Marsh, Worden, & Hicks, 1962) could have reduced the amplitude of the stimulus reaching the hair cells, which would then respond less strongly. The stimulus amplitude would have decreased when the cat moved because the sound at the ear became weaker or because the middle-ear muscles contracted. But diverting attention may also cause the middle-ear muscles to contract and attenuate the sound reaching the cochlea (Baust & Berlucchi, 1964; Baust, Berlucchi, & Moruzzi, 1964). Accordingly, attention may have been part of the cause of the reduction of the neural response observed by Hernandez-Peon et al. (1956), but via the middle-ear muscles rather than the efferent nerve.

Taking a different approach, Igarashi et al. (1974) did provide evidence for a role of the OCB in the interaction between seeing and hearing. They showed that cats with a severed OCB were more easily distracted by noise during a visual task than were sham controls. Before the surgery, detection of a light flash was reduced from 80% correct to 50% correct when the animals were exposed to a continuous white noise near 90 dB. After the surgery, detection was reduced to 50% by a noise at only 83 dB. Other cats who underwent the same surgery except that the OCB was spared (a *sham* operation) required a stronger noise (93 dB instead of 90 dB) to reduce performance to 50%. (The small increase in the noise may have resulted from habituation or learning.) Thus, when efferent input is intact, an organism is less susceptible to distraction and interference from noise. It would seem that the outright dismissal of the findings of Hernandez-Peon et al. (1956) as due entirely to uncontrolled experimental artifacts was premature; attention may indeed gate auditory input via efferent input to the cochlea, but more about this later.

Turning down auditory input while attention is riveted on another sense would not necessarily serve an organism's best interests. After all, it is just during preoccupation with visual or olfactory stimuli, that hearing—the other long-distance receiving system—is most needed to signal new events outside the focus of visual or olfactory attention. If anything, one might expect greater rather than less sensitivity to sound. But such sensitivity would be mainly to new sounds and not to the repetitive or continuous sounds used in the experiments of Hernandez-Peon et al. (1956) and of Igarashi et al. (1974). The OCB may act as a nonlinear gating device, reducing the response to loud, monotonous sounds but leaving unaffected the response to weak or new sounds unless auditory detection is the main task at hand. Evidence presented later suggests a subtle role for the OCB at near-threshold levels, one in which the selection of which sounds to process is under central, even cognitive control. This evidence is psychoacoustical in nature; that is, it is based on rigorous auditory tests that require simple responses to well-defined sounds. We return to these issues in section III. First, a brief review and update of earlier work on auditory attention.

II. BRIEF HISTORY AND UPDATE

II.1. William James on Auditory Attention

In his general treatise on psychology, William James (1890) included a chapter on attention that continues to inspire current discourse. Earlier authors are seldom cited. One was John Locke, who in the 17th century explicitly recognized the role of attention in perception. He wrote that while the "mind is intently employed in the contemplation of some objects ... it takes no notice of impressions of sounding bodies made upon the organ of hearing" (Locke, 1929, pp.73–74). In other words, while engrossed in looking, one does not hear sounds arriving at the ears. Locke clearly rejected any notion that the receptor organ, the ear, was affected, but rather "want of sensation ... is not through any defect in the organ, *or that the man's ears are less affected than at other times when he does hear*; but that which" usually produces the sensation "though conveyed in by the usual organ, not being taken notice of in the understanding, ... there follows no sensation." (my italic) In other words, a sound may well produce an effect of some sort in the organism, but unless attended (taken notice of), the sound goes unheard. This approach to attention—a late-selection approach—was based almost entirely on introspection as was William James's own analysis.

James provided much food for thought about attention. Although he gave no experimental evidence of his own, he did refer to measurements of reaction time by Wundt and to keen observations by Helmholtz and G.E. Müller as well as by Wundt and other 19th-century investigators. James hypothesized that attention is based mainly on a conscious effort, probably accomplished by muscular changes in the appropriate sense organ. (This would be an extreme example of early selection.) He quoted both Fechner and Mach (James, 1890, p.436). Fechner argued that, in general, attention sets "in motion ... the muscles which belong to" the different sense organs. Mach suggested that seeking to hear one sound among many is accomplished by "the variable tension of the muscles of the ear." For James, attention allows the organism to select among "several simultaneously possible objects or trains of thought" (1890 pp.403–404). Graphic illustration was provided by Helmholtz's instructions on how to hear out an overtone in a piano chord by first listening to the overtone as an isolated sound, or Wundt's approach which was based on memory of the targeted sound James, (1890, p.440). No attempt was made to support these observations by objective measurements. James wrote that "in listening for ... overtones in a musical sound, the one we attend to sounds probably a little more loud as well as more emphatic than it did before" (1890 p.425). A century later, experimental results (see section III) have become available to support and greatly extend these mainly introspective observations.

II.2. Broadbent's Filter Theory and its Sequel

The first half of the 20th century is thought not to have added much to the understanding of auditory attention. The modern studies of auditory attention are usually traced to the 1950s and the work of Broadbent (1958) and Cherry (1953; Cherry & Taylor, 1954). Broadbent's goals were at first largely of a practical nature. He wanted to determine the best way to arrange sound sources so as to enhance communication in a noisy environment. The results led to his formulation of a filter theory, according to which attention is expressed by filtering out some stimuli and admitting others. The filtering is accomplished primarily on the basis of physical characteristics such as spatial locus, spectral content, temporal characteristics. This was an early-selection theory that placed the filter very early in the auditory system without, however, any physiological specifications, such as those put forth by James (see preceding section). Treisman (1960) pointed out that the filtering was far from perfect and that some information from rejected stimuli could reach consciousness. Aside from this modification, which Broadbent (Broadbent & Gregory, 1963) readily accepted, no other basic change has been made to the filter model within the attention literature although signal-detection theory has provided fruitful insights and notable alterations (e.g. Green & Swets, 1966; Tanner & Norman, 1954). Meanwhile, the major focus of research on attention has shifted to the visual system where the filter model appears under the guise of the spotlight or zoom model, which is readily—although not necessarily—interpreted as an early-selection model.

Much of the research reviewed by Broadbent in 1958 had to do with the perception of speech. The subject's task was either to *shadow* (i.e. repeat) a spoken message as it was heard or to answer subsequent questions about it. The usual experiment presented two or more messages simultaneously or nearly so. Subjects had to respond either to a single message, ignoring the others, or to both (or more) messages. Although none of the paradigms qualifies as a psychoacoustical measurement, the results of many experiments served as the basis for theories about auditory attention and for psychoacoustical experiments to test those theories. Of particular relevance to current ideas about auditory attention are those experiments that required the listener to respond to one of two or more competing messages and which varied such stimulus parameters as sound source and spectral content. For example, it was found that subjects (1) could attend to one ear and ignore the other in earphone listening (e.g. Cherry, 1953), (2) responded better to speech from a loudspeaker when it was not in the same place as other emitting speakers (e.g. Broadbent, 1954; Poulton, 1956), (3) understood speech better with the high sound frequencies taken out when interfering speech was presented that contained only high frequencies (Egan, Carterette, & Thwing, 1954).

One of Broadbent's (1954) experiments illustrates the approach of that era. The goal was to determine how much better subjects could understand one of two competing speech signals when they were spatially separated. Understanding was assessed by having the subjects answer brief spoken questions. The answer was either right or wrong. Results for six groups, each with 12 subjects, showed that two different voices could be kept apart better when the sound sources were physically separated. The subjects could attend to and respond to one voice while ignoring the other provided the voices came from different earphones or different loudspeakers. Although most of the data were based on large separations—loudspeakers 90° apart or left earphone vs right earphone—some data suggested that even putting one loudspeaker on top of another helped listeners, as compared to having both voices come from a single loudspeaker. The question arose as to how much the listener learns about the ignored signal. Cherry (1953) used the shadowing technique (see preceding paragraph). He showed that listeners could readily shadow speech in one earphone while ignoring speech in the other and also that they were unaware of much about the input to the ignored ear. For example, they did not realize that the ignored speech was in a different language (and not in English) nor even that it was played backwards. But they could report whether the speaker in the ignored ear was male or female and they noticed when a pure tone replaced speech. These findings have been confirmed in more recent, better controlled tests (e.g. Wood & Cowan, 1995). Later, Moray (1959) showed that the listener hears his or her own name on the ignored channel about a third of the time that it is presented. This observation has often been cited as supporting the notion that the auditory signal on the ignored channel is processed to a semantic level (i.e. it is encoded in the auditory system as speech) but then discarded at some cognitive level. One alternative explanation is that people are highly sensitive to the ratios among the formants in their own name; hence, a sound containing those components will pass more readily through a peripheral filter whose parameters had been set early in the individual's auditory development.

Treisman and Geffen (1967) also used a shadowing task, but rather than ask for reports, after the fact, about the signal in the ignored ear, they had their subjects make ongoing responses to either ear while shadowing one ear. Accordingly, the subjects had two simultaneous tasks. The primary task was to shadow the right ear and ignore the left ear; the voice of a woman reading from one text went to the right ear and from a different text to the left ear. The secondary task was to tap every time a target word was heard in *either* ear. Subjects scored 86% correct on targets in the shadowed ear and only 8% on targets in the other ear. The authors interpreted the finding, for a variety of reasons, as indicating perceptual or peripheral filtering, i.e. early selection. (See Broadbent, 1971, Chapter 5 for more details and references concerning the filter theory of auditory attention.)

II.3. Evoked Responses and Attention

Over the past two decades, much of the research on auditory attention—mostly on humans—has been carried out by measuring the electrical signals evoked in the nervous system by sound stimulation. These *evoked response potentials* (ERP) are measured at various stages of the auditory nervous system. Results have revealed clear distinctions between the responses evoked by attended sounds and those evoked by unattended sounds, whether attention is directed according to ear, to sound frequency, or to another physical characteristic of the signals. In general, attended signals evoke stronger responses and more quickly than do ignored signals. However, the differences in the responses usually do not show up until some 100 ms after sound onset. A delay of 100 ms suggests that processing is not affected by attention until well within the nervous system, far beyond the cochlea and auditory nerve. Studies using evoked potentials are described in more detail in the chapter by Luck in this volume. (Also see Näätänen, 1992, for a thorough review.)

Although most ERP studies have not revealed an effect of attention on early stages of auditory processing, at least two have; one for the cat, the other for humans. Oatman (1976) measured the responses evoked by clicks in cats before, during, and after a visual discrimination task. During the task the amplitude of evoked responses was significantly reduced in the auditory

nerve. Because middle-ear muscles had been cut and because control measurements showed no change in the acoustic input to the cochlea, it seemed
likely that the reduction was caused by efferent input to the cochlea, thereby
supporting the conclusions of Hernandez-Peon et al. (1956).

Lukas (1981) recorded a significant reduction in the amplitude and
increase in the latency of neural responses evoked by target tone bursts or
pips when human listeners were required to keep track of visual stimuli
instead of keeping track of the tone bursts. The visual task was counting
occasional Qs in a series of Os; the auditory task was to respond every time
the subject heard a target tone pip, which was presented 5% of the time,
with a longer duration than the non-target pips. The auditory and visual
stimuli were the same during both tasks; the tasks differed only in that one
required the subjects to listen (pay attention to the sounds) and the other
required them to look (pay attention to the letters). Figure 2.1 shows that
the neural response to the non-target pips (white bars) was no greater when
subjects were listening than when looking, but the response to target pips
(black bars) was significantly greater when listening. The enhanced
responses occurred less than 3 ms after sound onset and so must have ori-
ginated in the cochlea. The effect cannot be readily ascribed to general
activation because stimulation was identical in the two tasks. Nor can the

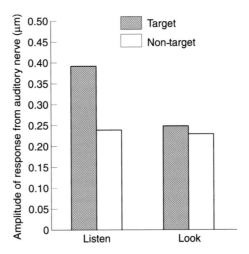

FIG. 2.1.   Amplitude of the response of the auditory nerve to tone pips of longer (targets, black
bars) or shorter (non-targets, white bars) duration. In the "listen" condition, the subjects
counted target pips; in the "look" condition, they counted letters presented visually. Pips and
letters were presented in both conditions. In the look condition, the pips evoked the same
amplitude nerve response whether they were long or short, but in the listen condition the longer
pips evoked a greater amplitude response because they were the targets that were being counted
and attended. This difference is attributed to the effect of attention on cochlear responses.

effect be ascribed to differential action of the middle-ear muscles because the amplitude of the neural response to the non-target pips was the same in both tasks; it is highly unlikely that during the visual task the middle-ear muscles acted to reduce only the input of target pips which were randomly inter-mixed with non-target pips.

Still another way to determine the neural level at which attention influ-ences auditory processing is to measure evoked *otoacoustic emissions*, which are weak sounds produced within the cochlea in response to external sounds. Sometimes referred to as echoes, they are actually new sounds generated by active processes in the cochlea, most likely the result of rapid changes in the size of the outer hair cells. During a visual task, these evoked emissions may be reduced.

Puel, Bonfils, and Pujol (1988) found, in humans, that the otoacoustic emissions evoked by clicks were smaller during a visual task than during relaxation. The visual task, inspired by Lukas (1981), was to count the Qs interspersed in a series of Os. Attention to the visual task could have depressed the emissions in one of two ways: (1) indirectly, by contraction of the middle-ear muscles which would reduce the amplitude of the acoustic stimulus reaching the cochlea or (2) directly, by efferent input via the OCB which could modify the activity of the outer hair cells. Support for the second alternative comes from Giard et al. (1994) who demonstrated that evoked emissions in the frequency band corresponding to attended tones are stronger than those in frequency bands corresponding to unattended tones. The middle-ear muscles could not have caused such a difference among frequency-bands, leaving efferent input to the hair cells as the plausible origin of the depression of the emissions.

II.4. Signal Detection Theory and Auditory Attention

In 1958, Broadbent couched his analysis of attention in terms of informa-tion theory. With the application of signal-detection theory (SDT) to psy-chophysics in the 1960s, Broadbent and Gregory (1963) showed how SDT could distinguish between the effect of attention on sensory sensitivity and on decision criteria. Their subjects had to detect the presence or absence of a tone in bursts of noise presented to one ear. In one condition they had only the detection task, but in another condition, they also had to report six-digit numbers presented to the other ear. The data showed that the subjects used the same response criteria, á, whether or not they were dividing their attention between the two ears. However, the sensitivity index, d', was smaller in the two-task condition than in the simple detection task; subjects missed more tones that had actually been presented and reported more tones that had not been presented. The authors "concluded that diversion of attention away from a stimulus produces an effect resembling a reduction in the intensity of the stimulus." (1963, p.222) In other words, having to respond to digits in one ear made the subjects less sensitive to sounds in the other ear; less attention meant a smaller d'.

Moray and his colleagues (e.g. Moray et al., 1976; Moray & O'Brien, 1967) also used SDT to analyze similar experiments, but the results were less clear cut. Related studies of signal uncertainty generally confined themselves to SDT without explicit concern for attention (e.g. Sorkin, 1965), but contemporary investigators are beginning to assign an important role to attention in studies of stimulus uncertainty and "informational masking" (e.g. Neff, 1995). Few other kinds of experimental studies have made an explicit connection between auditory attention and SDT (for a theoretical discussion see Sperling, 1984 and Sperling & Dosher, 1986). Yet, certain aspects of classical SDT are analogous to concepts in the attention literature. The reasoning goes as follows. All psychophysical tasks require that the subject make a decision, such as whether or not a signal was presented, or whether one sound is louder than another. The decision is based on information within the nervous system, information that is always variable or *noisy*. The noise originates both in the stimulus and in sensory transduction and transmission. It may be trivial, as when a sound to be detected is presented at a high level in the quiet, or it may be extremely significant, as when a tone is presented against a noise background (as in many of the experiments described later). Given noise, the decision process cannot avoid error. However, once the goals of the psychophysical task have been defined (for example, to detect a signal as often as possible or, alternatively, to avoid stating a signal was presented when it wasn't), the optimal decision-making strategy can be defined mathematically. Among other things, an optimal strategy usually means giving different weights to different sensory inputs. In hearing, a broadband noise may be divided into separate frequency bands when the task is to detect a tone against the noise. Accordingly, most weight is given to the channel where the signal is most likely to occur (provided that such information is available). Some theorists (e.g. Buus et al., 1986) have suggested that observers may seek optimal performance by giving zero weight to some channels, which means disregarding or ignoring some channels. Thus, the mathematical abstraction of the optimal decision-making strategy corresponds to the more mechanistic concept of an attentional gate or filter. Whether people actually carry out the optimal weighting or filtering, as has been suggested, is another question.

III. PSYCHOACOUSTICS OF ATTENTION: STIMULUS ATTRIBUTES

Visual studies of the role of attention in the response to simple stimuli have placed great emphasis on spatial locus. Research has shown that knowing where to look for a stimulus in the visual field speeds responses and may improve detection and discrimination (see Chapter 6). Auditory studies have placed similar emphasis on sound frequency. This research has shown that knowing what frequency to listen for improves detection and discrimination, but does not seem to reduce reaction time. In contrast, when information is available about the spatial locus (generally, direction or *azimuth*) of a sound, then reaction time is shorter, although detection and discrimination may not be any better. Finally, a few experiments have examined the possibility that signal processing benefits from knowing the intensity region—for example, whether soft or loud—in which to listen.

Most psychoacoustical studies involving attention have used simple stimuli, such as pure tones and bands of noise. More complex sounds including speech are coming under rigorous investigation, and these studies are considered in section IV. This present section deals separately with three stimulus attributes: frequency, spatial locus, and intensity.

III.1. Frequency

A number of investigations have measured detection or discrimination when attention is directed to a particular frequency region or regions. After a discussion of detection experiments, the more limited results on discrimination are reviewed.

(a) Detection.   In the audiology clinic, a common observation is that a patient has a higher threshold when he or she does not know at what frequency the signal is to be presented than when he or she does know. In the laboratory, Tanner and Norman (1954) seem to have been the first to examine this phenomenon experimentally. They measured the listener's ability to detect a 1000-Hz tone by a 4IFC method; that is, the listener had to indicate which of four brief observation intervals contained the signal. A 1000-Hz tone was presented in one of the four intervals at a level such that the listeners could score about 65% correct, well above the 25% attainable by guessing. After several hundred such trials, the experimenters changed the frequency of the signal to 1300 Hz. Performance went down to 25% correct until the subjects were told that a different frequency was being presented and could hear examples of it. Performance promptly rose to 65% for the 1300-Hz tone (see Fig. 2.2).

The interpretation of this result was that after having heard the 1000-Hz tone many times, listeners were focused on that frequency so that they were less sensitive to signals at other frequencies. But just how narrowly focused were they and just how bad are they in detecting other frequencies?

Greenberg and Larkin (1968) developed their *probe-signal method* to answer the first question. In one experiment, they focused the listeners' attention on a tone at 1100 Hz, by presenting it at a fairly high level on the first two trials of each block; thereafter, the level was set lower so that

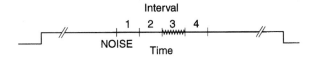

Four-interval forced choice

A. "Listen for 1000-Hz tone burst."

   65% correct

REST PERIOD

B. Tone burst changed to 1300-Hz. Subject NOT informed.

   25% correct

C. Subject NOW informed. "Listen for 1300-Hz burst."

   65% correct

FIG. 2.2.   Subjects indicated in which of four observation intervals a tone burst had been presented. In Part A, the tone burst had a frequency of 1000 Hz and subjects scored 65% correct. In Part B, the subjects continued to try to detect a 1000-Hz tone but now the signal was 1300 Hz, and they scored at chance. In Part C, having been informed of the change in signal frequency and having heard samples of the new tone, they once again scored 65% correct.

listeners could detect the signal on only approximately 80% of the trials. The procedure was two-interval, forced choice (2IFC); the signal was presented in one of two brief observation intervals on every trial, and the listener indicated in which interval he or she heard the sound. After 75 to 100 trials with only the target frequency presented so that the listeners were set on detecting a signal at 1100 Hz, test blocks began. In test blocks, on 23% of the trials, the 1100-Hz tone was replaced by a tone at a different *probe* frequency, which remained the same throughout a single block. Tones at most probe frequencies were not detected. By varying the probe frequency from block to block, Greenberg and Larkin (1968) could map out the range of frequencies surrounding the 1100-Hz target over which signals could be detected. It turned out to be a narrow range, roughly from 1000 to 1200 Hz. For most listeners, frequencies below 1000 and above 1200 Hz were detected close to 50%—chance performance. It was as if the listeners were listening through a bandpass filter centered on 1100 Hz. A bandpass filter lets through signals over a prescribed frequency range better than lower and higher ones.

Varying their probe-signal procedure somewhat, Greenberg and Larkin (1968) obtained very similar results for a target at 1000 Hz, as did Yama and Robinson (1982) for a 500-Hz target. Two points are worth noting. First, measurements were carried out against a continuous background of masking noise which made it easy for the experimenter to set each of the signal frequencies at a level at which it would be detected about 80% of the time when listened for. Second, although lower and higher frequencies were not detected at low levels, they would have been detected had they been presented at higher levels.

In one of their experiments, Greenberg and Larkin (1968) focused their listeners on a target frequency by presenting a cue at that frequency on every trial just prior to the two observation intervals. Scharf et al. (1987) used that procedure exclusively. They obtained the results shown in Fig. 2.3 for three groups of undergraduate students, each group exposed to two different probe frequencies. Figure 2.3 gives the percentage correct as a function of the signal frequency. The filled symbols are from the condition in which the cue was always at 1000 Hz so that listeners were listening for that frequency. When the signal was presented at 1000 Hz they averaged around 90% correct (unfilled symbol at 1000 Hz). When, in the same block of trials, the signal was presented at a different unexpected frequency (black symbols), the percentage correct declined markedly, so that even at a frequency separation as small as 75 Hz (probe signals at 925 and at 1075 Hz), percentage correct was down to around 63%; at 600 and 1500 Hz, performance was at 55%, close to chance. In a control condition, the cue and the signal were always at a probe frequency, e.g. 600 Hz, so that performance at that frequency could be assessed when it was the expected, attended signal. Those results are shown by the unfilled symbols, all of which are around 90%. Thus the very same signal, e.g. 600 Hz, that was hardly detected when it was the unexpected probe was detected very well, on 90% of the trials, when it became the target.

The dotted line in Fig. 2.3 represents the normal, internal auditory filter as measured by procedures very different from the probe-signal method (cf. Patterson, 1974). Among other things, the normal filter shows the spectral extent over which a masking noise interferes with the detection of a tone at the center of the filter. The results of the probe-signal method follow remarkably closely the pattern of the normal filter. This similarity would

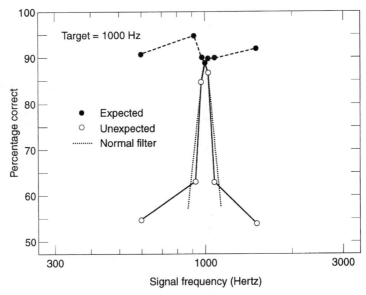

FIG. 2.3.   Percentage correct detection as a function of signal frequency. Subjects listened for a 1000-Hz signal, which was presented on each trial in one of two observation intervals against a continuous noise. On 25% of the trials the signal was at a different frequency; the percentage correct on those trials is indicated by the filled symbols. Performance declined markedly as the actual signal presented became more different from the expected signal at 1000 Hz. The unfilled symbols give the percentage correct at each frequency when that frequency was the expected and attended frequency. The dotted line indicates the shape of the internal auditory filter measured in other kinds of masking experiments.

suggest that attentional filtering is determined at the cochlear level, where signal processing is often likened to a set of bandpass filters. One interpretation of the results in Fig. 2.3 is that the listeners attend through a single one of those bands, which acts as a kind of *attentional filter*. In the example shown, that band would be centered on 1000 Hz. Signals within that band, whose shape is indicated by the normal filter, would be enhanced, or signals outside of it would be suppressed, or enhancement and suppression may complement each other. This is the single-band model of auditory attention (cf. Swets, 1984). As we shall see later, listeners can attend to more than a single band at a time so that the single-band model appears to be a limiting condition of the more general *multi-band model*. Among alternative models are those that ascribe the results more to the response or decision side.

According to one such model, listeners actually hear the probe signals but ignore them because they misidentify them as part of the noise if too different from the expected target signal. Were this the case, it would mean that the probe-signal procedure reveals little about attention. This criticism was based, in part, on the fact that in earlier probe-signal experiments, the listeners were led to believe that only targets would be presented, and no mention was made of probes. Scharf et al. (1987) provided strong evidence against this *heard-but-not-heeded* hypothesis. First of all they told one group of listeners that probes would be presented. If listeners misidentify signals because they expect only the target frequency, then telling listeners about the presence of probes should improve the detection of probes. However, providing such information did not improve the detection of distant probes, which stayed down near chance. Knowledge about probes does not matter much to trained listeners either. Dai, Scharf, and Buus (1991) continued to obtain approximately the same results from a listener, who had completed many hundreds of trials, after telling her about the presence of probes.

Figure 2.4 shows this subject's data at five different target frequencies. At each target many hundreds of trials were run without her knowing about the

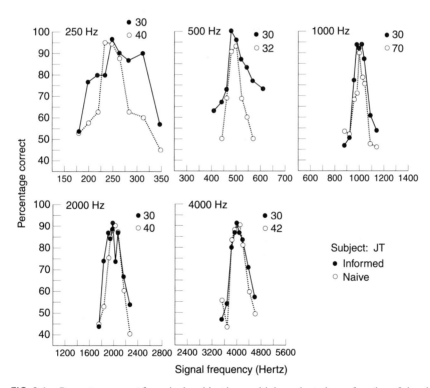

FIG. 2.4.   Percentage correct for a single subject in a multiple-probe task as a function of signal frequency; each panel is for a different target frequency. After the subject was informed that probe signals were being presented, percentage correct on most probes, especially around 250 Hz, improved but not enough to affect radically overall attentional selectivity. (Adapted from Dai, 1989.)

presence of probes (unfilled circles). After being informed about them, she continued to miss most of them (filled symbols) except for some of the probes near 250 Hz. Moreover, in that study the results for one of the experimenters who served as an observer were like those of the other observers. Generally, when experimenters serve as listeners in probe-signal experiments, they do not detect distant probes although they know all about them.

Another prediction of the heard-but-not-heeded hypothesis would be that repeated exposures to easily detected signals at a given frequency would make probes at that frequency subsequently more detectable. However, immediately after having heard a 600-Hz signal as the cue on over 100 trials and having detected it correctly on most of them, listeners were tested in a new series with the same 600-Hz tone now presented as the probe and a 400-Hz tone as the target. Despite their just having heard the 600-Hz tone on so many trials, listeners scored at chance now that it was presented as the probe (Scharf et al., 1987). One would also predict that omitting the cue from every trial would make it less likely that the listener would ignore probe frequencies. But once a listener had become set to listen in a particular frequency region, the absence of the cue did not improve the detection of distant probes (Greenberg & Larkin, 1968; Scharf et al., 1987).

The heard-but-not-heeded hypothesis should also mean that listeners who were not heeding probe signals that occurred on only a minority of trials should be more likely to respond to them if they occurred more often. Such is not the case. The probe can be presented on as many trials as the target, i.e. on 50% of the trials instead of 20% or 25%, without affecting performance (Scharf, 1995). Figure 2.5 gives the means for four listeners who were tested with a target at 1700 Hz, in one session with the probe presented on 25% of the trials and in the other on 50% of the trials. Whether presented as often as the target or only half as often, the probes were detected at chance.

Another test of the heard-but-not-heeded hypothesis is to vary the quality of the signal without changing its frequency locus. The filter model implies that the quality of the signal matters little and that the frequency locus is the primary, perhaps the sole, determinant of how detection will vary with signal level. Frequency locus would matter for the heard-but-not-heeded hypothesis in so far as it means that the probe sounds more or less like the target, but other stimulus attributes like bandwidth and temporal pattern would also matter. To test these differing predictions, Ebata and Scharf (1992) presented a 1000-Hz tone as cue and target and a narrow band of noise centered on 1000 Hz as the probe. In a separate experiment, the converse held; that is, the noise served as cue and target and the tone served as probe. Under both arrangements, 14 listeners in one experiment and 15 in the other detected the probes just as well as the targets despite the large

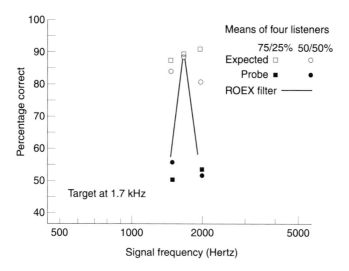

FIG. 2.5.   Percentage correct for four listeners as a function of signal frequency. Unfilled symbols are for expected signals, and filled symbols for unexpected, probe signals. Squares are for sessions in which the targets were presented on 75% of the trials, and probes on 25%; circles are from sessions in which probes were presented on 50% of the trials. In both sessions, probes were detected at near chance levels. Adapted from Scharf, 1995. Reprinted with the kind permission of World Scientific Publishing Co Pte Ltd.

perceptual difference between a tone and a band of noise. Average percentage correct varied between 82 and 89%, with no advantage for targets; in fact, it was for a 1000-Hz tonal probe that the highest score of 89% was achieved.

Sound quality can also be manipulated by using different temporal patterns. In one experiment, the target was a 1000-Hz tone burst presented three times; the single bursts lasted 30 ms and were separated by 130 ms. The probe was presented eight times; the single bursts lasted 12 ms and were separated by 42 ms. In one block, the probe burst had the same frequency, 1000 Hz, as the target pattern, and in another block it had a different frequency, 1700 Hz. (As usual all signals were set to a level at which performance would be close to 90% when they were the targets.) Despite the difference in temporal pattern, the 1000-Hz probe bursts were detected just as well as the target, whereas the 1700-Hz probe bursts were not detected (56% correct). If observers responded only to signals that were like the cue and target, unlike temporal patterns should also have gone unheeded; nor should they have heeded bands of noise when the target was a tone.

Yet another way to vary the nature of a sound is to change its direction in space. Scharf et al. (1986) reported that 1000-Hz probe signals expected from a loudspeaker 45° to the right were detected as well as 1000-Hz targets which came from a loudspeaker 45° to the left (see next section on spatial locus).

A different approach is to make the probe similar to the target in some manner despite their having different frequencies. This was done in one experiment by presenting the target and probe with the same temporal pattern but at different frequencies. Despite having the same pattern as the target, the probes were poorly detected (60% correct). Scharf et al. (1987) also reported that when the probe had the same *periodicity* pitch as the target or was an octave higher, it was detected at chance; in both cases, the probe shared a common attribute—periodicity pitch or octave similarity— with the target and yet performance was not at all helped. So far it seems that the only stimulus attribute to influence detection scores for constant-level probes is tonal frequency.

Schlauch and Hafter (1991) provide some of the clearest evidence against the heard-but-not-heeded hypothesis. In one experiment their cues, presented on every trial, were made up of four simultaneous tones, each separated from its neighbors by a frequency ratio of at least 1:4. (The component frequencies were chosen randomly on each trial from a set of values from 600 to 3570 Hz.) The individual tonal components seldom stood out perceptually from the overall complex. Nonetheless, listeners detected probes at or near the component frequencies but not distant probes, including those falling between the component frequencies. The observers appeared to listen through four bands simultaneously. It is difficult to believe that they ignored those in-between probes because they were unlike any one of the cue components, which were not heard separately to begin with. These results seem especially difficult to square with the heard-but-not-heeded hypothesis.

Results from patients who lack efferent input to the cochlea provide yet another striking piece of evidence against this hypothesis that probes are processed by the auditory system as well as targets but are somehow missed at the decision level. In the final section of this chapter we return to this line of research, which has important implications for the whole basis of attention.

The demonstration by Schlauch and Hafter (1991) that listeners can detect as many as four different probe frequencies was an extension of previous results of MacMillan and Schwartz (1975), confirmed by Dai (1989). Those results showed that listeners who were exposed to two different frequencies during training and told to listen for them would then detect them both but would miss frequencies that were lower, higher, and *in between*. Figure 2.6 gives one set of results for targets at 700 Hz and at 1600 Hz. Circles are the results obtained when only 700 Hz was the target, squares when only 1600 Hz was the target, and filled triangles when both were targets. The targets are detected somewhat less well when there are two

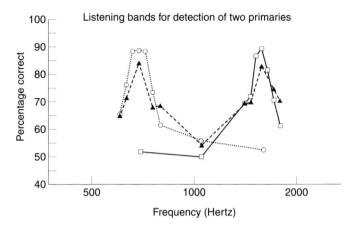

FIG. 2.6. Effect of listening for two distant frequencies on detection. Percentage correct from three listeners is plotted as a function of signal frequency. Circles are for conditions in which the listeners expected signals at 700 Hz, squares for conditions in which they expected 1600 Hz, and triangles for conditions in which they expected signals at both 700 and 1600 Hz. Results from the dual-frequency condition are like the combination of the two conditions with only one expected target frequency, except that performance is somewhat poorer at the target frequencies when listening for both simultaneously. (Adapted from Dai, 1989.)

of them (around 85% correct instead of near 90%), but both are detected in the same block of trials. Moreover, signals lying between them at close to 1000 Hz are not detected. It seems that subjects listen through two filters when the task so requires.

Another way to lead a subject to listen at two frequencies is to gradually increase the level of the probe block by block. Figure 2.7 shows the results for a single subject who was tested on the probe-signal procedure with a target at 1000 Hz and a probe at 600 Hz, presented on half the mixed trials. Results from the first day (1/31) are indicated by the unfilled circles, the second day (2/22) by the filled triangles, and the third day (2/24) by the unfilled square. On the first day, the probe was first presented at 46 dB where it was detected at chance (near 50%). After 50 mixed trials, the level of the probe was increased to 47 dB. Not until it was at 49 dB could it be detected well—above 95%. The rise in performance when the probe level was increased 1 dB from 48 to 49 dB is very large, a gain of 40%, from near chance to near perfect. It is as if the probe, having reached a critical level, began to be heard on some trials and that the listener then switched to a two-tone listening mode as was seen in Fig. 2.6. When the subject came back three weeks later, he was given the probe again at 46 dB and again scored near chance at that level. But already at 47 dB he scored near 90%. Especially revealing is that when he came back two days later, he detected the 46-dB

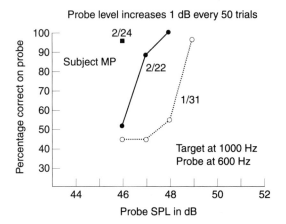

FIG. 2.7.   Change in performance as a function of the level of an unexpected probe at 600 Hz. On January 31, the percentage correct remained around 50% as the probe level was increased from 46 to 48 dB, but it jumped to over 90% for a probe at 49 dB. Three weeks later, percentage correct was near 90% at a level of 47 dB, and two days after that it was above 90% at 46 dB. The subject continued to detect the target at 1000 Hz at between 80 and 90% even after switching to a two-frequency listening strategy.

probe right away at 95% correct. We appear to have succeeded in training the subject to listen for these two probes. During these sessions, similar results were obtained by increasing a probe at 1400 Hz. We do not know how long he would persist in this strategy nor whether it would generalize to other probe frequencies. The ability to focus on several frequency regions at once should not be surprising, because natural sounds contain many frequencies which together determine their nature and identifiability. As we shall see later, this ability may be especially important in speech recognition.

   The fact that subjects can learn to listen for a probe means that they could perhaps adopt such a strategy during a single-probe session and give a distorted picture of the attentional filter. To reduce the likelihood of that happening and also to avoid inter-session variability, Dai (1989; Dai et al., 1991) presented not one other frequency as the probe in a single block, but eight and sometimes as many as 24 other frequencies together with the target. This multiple-probe procedure makes it difficult for the subject to begin to listen to frequencies other than the target; there are just too many of them and each one occurs too infrequently. The procedure allows a rapid mapping out of the attentional filter. Examples of data obtained on individual subjects are shown in Fig. 2.8. Each set of data was collected in a single session lasting about 1.5 hours. The four subjects varied in age from the early 20s to near 40 years. One was a woman. All had had at least some experience in psychoacoustical measurements and two of them were familiar

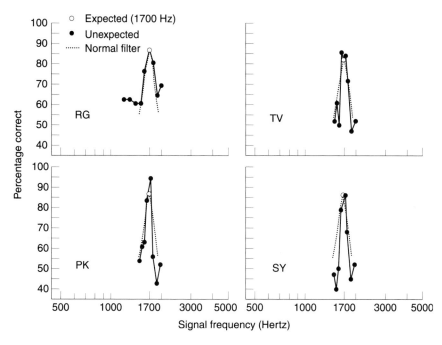

FIG. 2.8. Examples of performance on the multiple-probe task for four individuals. Percentage correct is plotted as a function of signal frequency for the target (unfilled symbol) and for the probe (filled symbols). The ROEX filter (dotted line) derived from other types of masking studies is followed closely by the individual results.

with the purpose of the experiment. The data fall close to the normative internal filter centered on 1700 Hz.

All these experiments were carried out against a background of noise, but selective listening is not confined to signals presented in noise. Ebata, Sone, and Nimura (1968) measured thresholds in the quiet, using a procedure similar to that in a probe-signal experiment, and found that the detection was much poorer when signals were at unexpected frequencies than when at expected frequencies. Their method allowed an estimation of the *effective attenuation* of the unexpected signals which was as much as 6 to 8 dB. In other words, to detect a signal as well when it was unexpected as when expected required that its level be increased 6 to 8 dB. We call this the effective attenuation because performance was like that to be expected had the signals been externally attenuated. Dai et al. (1991) also provided estimates of the effective attenuation by measuring the psychometric functions for targets and probes. In a variation of their multiple-probe procedure, a given block of trials had probes at any one of 24 frequencies and six levels.

Their best estimate of the effective attenuation of distant probes was approximately 7 dB.

In the foregoing experiments, targets and probes always had the same duration. When the durations are different, signals are detected less well, even when at the same frequency as the target. Wright and Dai (1994) found that subjects detected a 295-ms tone poorly when they were expecting a tone at the same frequency but with a duration of only 5 ms. Conversely, subjects detected a 5-ms tone poorly when expecting a tone lasting 295 ms.

Coming back to the question of effective attenuation, we note that the estimate of 7 dB is close to the value of 8 dB reported by Squires, Millyard, and Lindsay (1973) as the attenuation determined from evoked potentials. They measured the cortical potentials evoked by a tone in noise when listeners were making behavioral responses to the signals and when they were reading a book. To evoke a negative potential with the same amplitude, the tone had to be 8 dB greater in the reading condition than in the listening condition.

Although most of the experiments using the probe-signal method have employed a 2IFC procedure, it is also possible to use a yes–no procedure which yields a sensitivity measure d' (cf. Scharf, 1988a). In the yes–no procedure, a signal is presented on only some (e.g. 50%) of the trials, each of which contains a single observation interval. The listener responds "yes" if he or she hears a signal and "no" if not. A yes reponse when a signal was presented is called a hit, and when no signal was presented it is called a false alarm. Results for 12 listeners gave a d' of 2.3 for a target at 1000 Hz (corresponding to a hit rate of near 86%), of 2.0 for a near probe at 1025 Hz, and of 0.6 (31% hit rate) for a distant probe at 1500 Hz. Because d' is based on both hits and false alarms and because false alarms cannot be attributed to the target and probe separately (in the condition in which the target is presented on some trials and the probe on others), some uncertainty accrues to the precise value of d'. Nonetheless, the results are like those obtained with the 2IFC procedure, as can be seen in Fig. 2.9.

In most of the aforementioned experiments, attention was directed to the appropriate frequency region or regions by presenting the target as a cue on every trial or as a clear example prior to a block of trials. In every case the cue was a sound at the same frequency as the target signal. However, it is possible to direct attention by presenting a cue at a frequency different from that of the target, but that stands in a known frequency relation to the target; it is even possible to present visual cues to designate target frequencies. Thus, Swets and Sewall (1961) reported that subjects detected signals that could be at either one of two distant frequencies better when cued as to which frequency would occur either by a sound at the target frequency or by a light. However, in both cases the improvement was small, an average of 5% for the sound cues and 8% for the light cues. (The

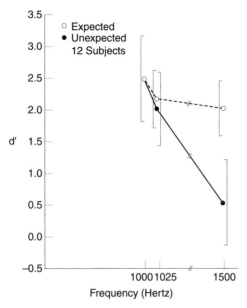

FIG. 2.9. Performance, as measured by the sensitivity index d', in a yes–no task as a function of signal frequency. When listening for a 1000-Hz tone, twelve subjects had a d' of 2.5—indicating very good performance—at that frequency but only 0.5—near chance performance—at 1500 Hz. When 1500 Hz was the expected frequency, d' was up to 2.0. At 1025 Hz, very close to the target, d' was the same whether that frequency was expected or not. Results are similar to those obtained by a 2IFC procedure.

improvement is so small because the listeners were probably already listening for both frequencies in a two-band listening mode.) Hafter, Schlauch, and Tang (1993) obtained much more impressive results with a probe-signal procedure in which the cues were musical 5ths of the targets (where targets were 1.5 times the frequencies of the cues). Results were similar to those obtained with cues at the same frequencies as the targets, the main difference being that the attentional bandwidth was wider with the relative cues, i.e. the effective attenuation increased more slowly with increasing frequency distance of the probe from the target. Yet another way to focus the listener is to present a sequence of ascending or descending frequencies, so that a certain frequency is expected at a given moment in the sequence. Howard et al. (1984) showed that listeners were more sensitive to a signal at the appropriate frequency—as defined by the sequence—than at other frequencies.

A different line of research on selective attention in the frequency domain has put one frequency in one ear and a different frequency in the other ear. Investigators compared divided attention—responses had to be made to signals in both ears—with selective attention—responses had to be made to only one ear. In their review of this area, Puleo and Pastore (1978) pointed out the problems engendered by interaural fusion between simultaneous inputs that were too close in frequency. Nonetheless, separate earphones have been used to vary "spatial locus" as described here in section III.2.

So far we have referred only to how attention affects sensitivity to a sound, the ability to detect it, and have said nothing about how attention may affect speed of responding to a sound. That is because none of the published experiments on the relation between attention and frequency has reported any effects on reaction time. Yet, in the vision literature, the relation between selective attention and spatial locus has been established mainly on the basis of measurements of reaction time (see the chapter by Yantis in this volume). In a typical visual experiment, a cue is given at the beginning of a trial to indicate whether the stimulus is more likely to be to the right or to the left of fixation. Responding is faster when the signal is presented at the more likely location than at the less likely location.

In hearing, sound frequency is translated into place on the basilar membrane of the cochlea and so resembles the direct spatial distribution of visual stimuli on the retina. Consequently, one could reason that responding would be more rapid to sounds at an expected frequency than to sounds at an unexpected frequency. In my laboratory at Northeastern, we tested that possibility by performing an auditory reaction-time experiment with sound frequency taking the place of visual space. Subjects were cued to listen to a weak 1000-Hz tone burst in noise and to respond as rapidly as possible to it or to any other sound. The cue, always a 1000-Hz tone burst, was followed after a variable interval by a burst at 1000 Hz on 75% of the trials and by a burst at one of six other frequencies, between 850 and 1150 Hz, on the other 25% of the trials. Responding to a sound at the cued frequency was no faster than responding to one of the other frequencies. Reaction times were about 300 to 350 ms at all frequencies. After the fact, we realized that it was really not too likely that reaction times would be faster at an expected frequency. Although the tonotopic organization of frequency on the basilar membrane resembles the spatial organization on the retina (albeit limited largely in hearing to a single dimension), the processing of sound is entirely different from that of light. The locus of a light stimulus is directly translated into a corresponding place on the retina. The locus of a sound on the basilar membrane is only approximate and, most important for reaction time, the locus is not set immediately; initially a sound may stimulate a large part of the basilar membrane. The subject responds to the onset of the tone burst, before any frequency analysis can be made. At onset all sounds resemble each other and are "represented" over a large part of the basilar membrane. Accordingly, to measure the possible effects of frequency expectation on reaction time, it would be necessary to prevent the subject from responding to sound onset without any frequency analysis. That could be accomplished by requiring the subject to respond as quickly as possible to a sound at one frequency but not to respond to a sound at a different frequency in catch trials. Using such a paradigm, LaBerge (1970, 1971) did report that reaction time was longer when listeners were confronted with a block of trials in which the frequency in the catch trials was at or near that of a cue tone than when the frequency in the catch trials was far away. However, the role of attention in such a task is not entirely clear.

(b) Discrimination. Many fewer experiments have measured the effect of attention on discrimination than on detection. Watson and his colleagues (e.g. Watson, 1987) have carried out an extensive series of investigations of the effect of attention on the discrimination of complex sounds, and these are considered in section IV. With respect to simple sounds, we review briefly the few experiments on intensity, duration, and frequency discrimination.

Subjects discriminate intensity better when the signal—a pure tone—is presented at the same frequency on every trial than when presented at a different frequency (Mori & Ward, 1991, 1992). It is not simply the mixing of frequencies that impairs discrimination because cuing the frequency on every trial with either an acoustic cue (the tone itself at a lower level) or a visual cue makes discrimination nearly as good as for a constant frequency (Mori & Ward, 1991, 1992, personal communication). Thus, discrimination, like detection, is better when attention can be focused in a particular frequency region; that is not possible if the signal frequency is uncertain.

Focused attention also helps frequency discrimination. Leek, Brown, and Dorman (1991) showed that discrimination was significantly better when one brief tone burst in a sequence of nine, all at different frequencies, was made to stand out. It stood out if it was far enough in frequency from the other tones in the sequence or if it was louder. The greater isolation of the target tone did not facilitate discrimination simply by reducing interference from the neighboring tones; facilitation appeared to result from the subject's being able to focus attention on the target.

Sequences of tone bursts, 50 ms each, were also used by Brochard et al. (1995) to determine how the frequency separation between two or more such sequences affected discrimination of a temporal irregularity. All the tone bursts in a given sequence had the same frequency and the same inter-onset interval (the time from the onset of one burst until the onset of the next): 300, 400, 500, or 700 ms. Initially, a sequence, which lasted nearly four seconds, was presented twice, once with a temporal irregularity and once without. The irregularity was a lengthening or shortening of a single inter-onset interval. Subjects were to say whether the irregularity was in the first or second presentation. Subsequently, the same test was performed but with the initial, target sequence accompanied by one to three other sequences. Each sequence contained tone bursts with different sound frequencies and had a different tempo. Subjects were presented the target sequence at the beginning of each trial and told to attend to that sequence and ignore the others. They could make the discrimination very well, although the percentage change in the inter-onset interval required for discrimination was two to three times greater when more than one sequence was presented at a time. They could not discriminate changes in the other, non-target sequences (as shown in earlier work). Of particular interest in the present context, for the target sequence to stand out, it had to be separated from the other sequences by one to two critical bands, i.e. the frequency of its component tone bursts had to be that different. Once again, subjects appear to listen through an attentional band similar in width to the critical band.

The outcome of the one report (Mondor & Bregman, 1994) of the effects of attention on duration discrimination is equivocal. The authors used a probe-signal procedure and measured performance in a duration-identification task. Although reaction times were faster when the signal was presented at the cued frequency than when presented at a probe frequency, the accuracy of the judgments was no better (once adequate controls were employed).

Given the limited amount of work on attention and auditory discrimination, it is difficult to draw general conclusions. Nonetheless, discrimination, like detection, appears to be better in an attended than in an unattended frequency region.

III.2. Spatial Locus

Everyday observation suggests that we can attend to a sound from one direction and ignore sounds from other directions. However, the competing sounds differ not only in locus but also in spectral and temporal characteristics so that the selection could be based on a stimulus property other than perceived direction. As we saw already, many laboratory experiments have shown that listeners can attend to signals at a particular frequency to improve detection or discrimination. Accordingly, whenever we listen to a sound coming from a certain direction, we may in fact be segregating it from other sounds on the basis of frequency differences (and perhaps of other physical differences).

This skepticism is justified by the failure to demonstrate improved detection or discrimination for sounds that could be selectively attended to only on the basis of their direction (Lowe, 1968; Posner, 1978; Scharf, 1988a), but dividing attention between two directions may reduce detection somewhat (Possamaï, Scharf, Bonnel, & Ward, in preparation). In contrast, spatial selectivity does influence reaction time; responding is faster to sounds from an expected or cued direction than to sounds from an unexpected direction (e.g. Mondor & Zatorre, 1995; Rhodes, 1987; Scharf, 1988a, 1988b; Scharf et al., 1986; Spence & Driver, 1994, 1996).

Before the reaction-time measurements, two experiments on spatial attention and detection are discussed. One by Lowe (1968) used a stimulus-uncertainty paradigm, that by Scharf (1988a) a probe-signal technique.

Lowe (1968) measured the detection in a yes–no procedure under three conditions: (1) the brief tonal signal always came from a loudspeaker to the left, (2) it always came from the right, and (3) it came equally often from left and right. Groups of subjects were tested in the center of a large room, in the presence of a white masking noise from loudspeakers in front and back. Overall sensitivity was no greater when the sound's direction was certain (conditions 1 and 2) than when it was uncertain (condition 3). One interpretation of these results is that knowing in which direction to attend does not increase sensitivity to signals coming from that direction.

Scharf (1988a) used the probe-signal procedure to test the effects of attention more directly. The hypothesis was that listeners would better detect a sound coming from an expected, attended direction than one coming from an unexpected direction. The experiments were carried out in a large anechoic room with one loudspeaker 45° to the subject's left and the other 45° to the right; both speakers were approximately level with the subject's head at a distance of about two meters. The signal was a 1000-Hz, 350-ms tone set to 4 dB above its 71% masked threshold. A 2IFC procedure was used to measure percentage correct detection. The masking noise either came on at the beginning of each trial for 2.3 seconds and stayed on until after the second observation interval, or it came on and off three times during each trial. The noise was 1000 Hz wide, at 60 dB SPL. Every trial began with a cue, which was the same tone as the signal set 4 dB higher so it would be readily heard. In condition 1, the cue and signal came from the left speaker on all trials. In condition 2, the cue always came from the left, while the signal came from the left speaker on 75% of the trials, and from the right speaker on 25%. Finally, in condition 3, the cue and signal came from the right speaker on all trials (the noise still from the left speaker). In conditions 1 and 3, the cue was always valid, meaning that it was at the same location as the signal on all trials. In condition 2, the cue was valid on 75% of the trials and invalid (predicted the incorrect signal direction) on 25% of the trials. Table 2.1 gives the individual and mean results for six subjects.

Detection is no better in the attended direction, which is assumed to be determined by the cue, than in the unattended direction. The percentage correct for the signal from the right side was only 3% greater when the right was the attended target side (condition 3) than when it was the unattended

TABLE 1
Percentage Correct in Probe-signal Procedure for Direction

Subject	Noise	Cond. 1 100% left	Signal Presented in: Cond. 2		Cond. 3 100% right
			75% left	25% right	
1	Continuous	73	83	72	73
2	Continuous	92	92	84	85
3	Continuous	80	87	80	90
4	Continuous	90	95	92	98
	Intermittent	83	81	96	93
5	Intermittent	74	61	86	94
6	Intermittent	83	76	92	98
Mean of 6 Subjects*		81	81	85	88

* Results of subject 4 averaged and included as one score.

probe side (condition 2). In later experiments, the signal duration was shortened to 50 ms so that subjects would be less likely to switch listening from one side to the other during an observation interval. Again, performance was no better for signals from the valid side.

Despite these negative results, the possibility remains that under other experimental conditions, listening in a given direction helps detection. For example, when we presented the masking noise on most trials from one side and the signal from the other side, subjects responded more accurately on trials when the signal came from the usual, expected side. In other terms, on trials where the signal and noise switched sides so that the noise came from the side from which the signal usually came and the signal came from what was usually the noise side, subjects detected the signal less accurately (Possamaï et al., in preparation). However, the better detection of signals from an expected direction was statistically significant only under some stimulus conditions, and the advantage was small. From an ecological point of view, one could argue that the organism should be prepared to detect sounds from all directions at all times, because hearing is our primary early warning system, providing information from parts of the environment outside our visual field.

In contrast to these mostly negative results for the effect of attention on the detection of weak sounds, several experiments have shown that directed spatial attention speeds the response to clearly audible sounds. Rhodes (1987) had her subjects verbally indicate as quickly and accurately as possible which of eight loudspeakers emitted a 100-ms noise burst. The eight loudspeakers were arrayed in a circle around the subject at a distance of 77 cm. Subjects were told to keep attention on the speaker that had just been activated given that 40% of the sounds would be at that locus. The other 60% of the sounds would come from one of the other seven speakers. Responses were fastest to the speaker most recently activated (i.e. were fastest when the sound came again from the same speaker as just previously) and were slower when the sound came from a different speaker. Moreover, the farther the currently activated speaker was from the previously activated speaker, the longer the reaction time. Rhodes interpreted this result as showing a kind of analog map of auditory space such that moving attention from one location to another would take longer as the distance between the two locations increases.

Spence and Driver (1994) pointed out that Rhodes' subjects might have responded more rapidly when the previously activated speaker was activated again because they had to respond by saying the number of the speaker and so would be primed to repeat that same number. Furthermore, the numbers increased with the spacing of the speaker and responding may have been more rapid with neighboring numbers. Such a criticism would not apply to the experiments reported by Possamaï et al. (in preparation; cited in Scharf, 1988a, 1988b). Those experiments, carried out by Scharf, Canévet, Possamaï, and Bonnel (1986), compared reaction times to a tone burst from an expected direction with those to a burst from an unexpected direction. This study was inspired by visual reaction-time experiments which have shown that responses are more rapid to the cued, attended side of fixation than to the non-attended side (see Chapter 6). By analogy, we had our subjects attend in the direction of a loudspeaker 45° to the left. They were told that most signals would come from the left, but that some could come from a loudspeaker 45° to the right. Each trial began with a warning tone burst and light signal to the left. The signals were 1000-Hz, 40-ms tone bursts easily heard at about 60 dB SPL, presented in the quiet in a large anechoic room. On 80% of the trials the warning tone was followed by a signal; the other 20% were catch trials with no signal. When presented, the signal came from the left on 75% of the trials and from the right on 25%. The subject was to respond by pressing a button on a hand-held computer terminal as quickly as possible to a signal, whether from the left or right, and was not to respond if there were no signal. In a second condition the roles of left and right were reversed so that the signal came most often from the right. Finally, in a third condition, signals came equally often from the left and right with the warning cue from a loudspeaker in the middle, directly in front of the listener. Although subjects tended to respond more rapidly to the expected, more frequent side, than to the unexpected side, the differences were small and not significant. However, in a different version of the experiment, in which trials were set so that the warning cue varied from trial to trial, responses were significantly faster even if by a small amount (40 ms or 13%) in the expected direction. (The advantage of varied over blocked conditions has been repeatedly noted in visual experiments on the spatial allocation of attention.) At least two other studies have reported little or no effect of spatial cues on the speed of detecting a sound (Buchtel & Butter, 1988; Spence & Driver, 1994).

The effects of attention were much larger when listeners had not only to respond as quickly as possible but also to discriminate between two sounds. The setup was like that in the third condition described in the preceding paragraph, with two loudspeakers to the left and right and a third directly in front of the listener (see inset of Fig. 2.10). In one series of experiments, the task was to respond as quickly as possible to a 40-ms tone burst at 1000 Hz and not to respond to one at 800 Hz. The 1000-Hz tone burst was presented at the beginning of each trial as a warning sound and was accompanied by a 300-ms flash from a small lamp. The warning sound ended 920 ms before the signal, and the light went off 700 ms before. On 80% of the trials the signal was at 1000 Hz, and on the other 20%, it was at 800 Hz. In one condition, on all trials the warning sound came from the left speaker and the light from a lamp just left of center. Listeners were instructed to attend to the left because signals would come from the left speaker on 75% of the trials, and from the right on only 25%. In a second condition, sides were reversed so that the warning cues and majority of the signals came from the right. In a third,

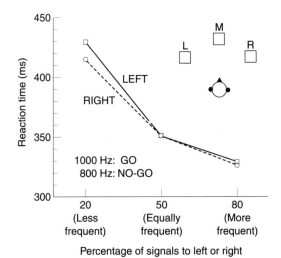

FIG. 2.10.   Time required to respond to a sound as a function of the frequency with which it came from the left or from the right. The task was to respond as quickly as possible to a 1000-Hz tone burst and not to respond to an 800-Hz burst. Reaction time was longest when it came from the least frequently presented direction (20%) and shortest from the most frequently presented direction (80%). It was in between when presented equally often from left and right. From Scharf, 1988a. Reprinted with the kind permission of Karger, Basel.

neutral condition, the cues came from a loudspeaker and lamp directly in front of the listener at 0°, and the signals came from the left on 50% of the trials and from the right on the other 50%. Figure 2.10 shows the results for nine subjects under three conditions, which were run in various orders. Mean reaction time is plotted as a function of the percentage of trials on which the signal came from one side. Results are shown separately for signals coming from the left and from the right. Responses were nearly 100 ms faster to signals from the more frequent side where the cue was valid. When the signals came equally often from left and right (neutral cues), responses were somewhat slower than when the signals came from the more frequent side in the other conditions but were considerably faster than to the less frequent side (invalid cues). Similar results were obtained when subjects had to make a spatial discrimination, responding to a sound from a speaker 60° to one side but not to the same sound from a speaker at 45°; in other words, the subjects had to make a distinction between two speakers on the left and between two speakers on the right on the basis of their locus. The cue effect was no greater when a spatial discrimination was required than when a pitch discrimination was required which disagrees with Rhodes' (1987) prediction that spatial cuing would be beneficial only for spatial discrimination.

These results suggest that attention to a particular direction facilitates discrimination of signals from that direction, and lack of attention impedes discrimination. However, faster responding may reflect better response preparation for one class of signals, for example, those coming most often from a particular direction. Such an interpretation seems unlikely because responses were identical for both directions and because direction was irrelevant to the decision as to whether to respond or not. Moreover, the fact that such preparation speeded up detection little, if at all—although the same response bias ought to have been present—may mean that the faster responding in a discrimination task reflects, at least in part, sensory facilitation. Once again, we point out that these findings suggest that the auditory system, in its role as an early-warning device, is ready to respond to sounds wherever they come from and requires little, if any, prior directional orienting. The processing of sounds, however, is enhanced by such information. Spence and Driver (1994) would add that the enhancement we found results from goal-driven or endogenous orienting (that is, from internal preparation for the signal) in contrast to stimulus-driven or exogenous orienting, by which the stimulus (here the cue) evokes an automatic preparation. Recall that throughout a block of trials, one direction was much more likely than the other so that subjects could listen toward a particular direction throughout a block. Exogenous orienting would be unlikely because the interval between our cue onset and signal onset was so long (700 to 900 ms) and in some experiments only a visual cue which was mainly symbolic, was available. The experiments of Spence and

Driver (1994) permit a distinction between endogenous and exogenous orienting.

Spence and Driver (1994) investigated the effects of cuing on auditory detection, and also on frequency and spatial discrimination. Their primary performance measure was reaction time. They found that the response to a sound was no faster when it came from a cued direction than when it came from an uncued direction, indicating no effect of a spatial cue on the speed of detection. This result is similar to that of Possamaï et al. (in preparation); both studies reported some evidence for a small but usually insignificant cuing effect.

In another experiment, Spence and Driver required the subjects to make a spatial discrimination, that is, to indicate something about the locus of the signal. Because they varied the onset time between cue onset and signal onset (stimulus onset asynchrony or SOA), they could draw inferences about whether the cuing gave rise to endogenous or exogenous orienting. In one experiment, on half the trials they presented valid cues, which came from the same direction as the following signal, and on the other half they presented invalid cues. Reaction time was reduced by valid cues presented 100 ms before the signal. This facilitation occurred even though on half the trials, the cues were invalid and could not be used by the subject to orient attention. On the assumption that the subject cannot shift spatial attention within 100 ms, the faster responses would seem to have resulted from exogenous orienting. However, this automatic facilitation was shortlived; cues that came on 400 or 1000 ms before the signal did not speed the response. This analysis was buttressed by another experiment in which the cue was valid on 75% of the trials. Responses were faster at all SOAs, including valid trials with SOA set to 100 ms, than in the previous experiment. This experiment shows the importance of endogenous orienting and suggests that the automatic drawing of attention toward the cued side can be modulated by the long-term consequences of the cue.

Spence and Driver (1994) also showed that frequency discrimination was faster toward the cued side, when the cue indicated the more likely side and the listener had enough time (at least 400 ms) to shift attention toward that side. However, the advantage was only about 50 ms whereas in Fig. 2.10 (from Scharf, 1988a) the advantage for valid over invalid trials is 90 ms. The difference may be related to the positioning of the loudspeakers relative to the subject (although the two experiments also differed in other respects). Spence and Driver had a speaker on either side of the subject directly opposite the ear at a distance of 40 to 45 cm, whereas Scharf placed the speakers at two meters from the subject, 45° off center. Thus, in the experiments by Spence and Driver, sounds were presented almost as they are in earphone listening which, as the next paragraph shows, gives rise to smaller directional effects. All in all, the results of Spence and Driver (1994) suggest that exogenous spatial orienting speeds spatial discrimination but not frequency discrimination; they also show, together with the results of Scharf (1988a; see also Possamaï et al., in preparation), that endogenous orienting speeds both spatial and frequency discrimination.

Listening to sounds through earphones, subjects respond more rapidly when the sound comes from the expected earphone (as indicated by a preceding cue) than when it comes from the unexpected phone (Mazzucchi & Cattelani, 1983; Murray, Allard, & Bryden, 1988; Quinlan & Bailey, 1995). However, the advantage is small, of the order of 4% for simple reaction times. The advantage increases when the subject must do more than react to sound onset and must indicate, for example, which ear was stimulated. Thus, responding with the left hand to the left ear and with the right hand to the right ear, subjects had reaction times that were over 20% shorter to a sound in the expected phone (Quinlan & Bailey, 1995). Although this outcome resembles the advantage for loudspeaker listening seen in Fig. 2.10, part of the faster responding was surely due to response preparation; that is, when expecting a signal to the left, the left hand was more ready to respond than the right. Nonetheless, despite the subjective difference between the spatial attributes of sounds presented from earphones and from loudspeakers, which probably makes the former less salient, in both cases attention directed to a given locus leads to faster responding.

III.3. Intensity

Section III.1 provided many results showing that subjects can focus attention on a narrow band of frequencies. An analogous band in the intensity domain has been hypothesized by Luce and Green (1978). They assumed that subjects can attend to a range of levels encompassing 10 to 20 dB, for example, sounds between 50 and 70 dB or between 30 and 50 dB, depending on the task. This attention-band hypothesis clarified results from experiments in which listeners identified sounds (Luce & Green, 1978), judged loudness directly (Green & Luce, 1974), or discriminated intensity (Nosofsky, 1983). For example, Nosofsy (1983) had subjects judge whether the second of two successive sounds was louder or softer than the first. Clusters of 10 such trials with soft sounds (levels around 45 dB) alternated with clusters of 10 trials with loud sounds (levels around 75 dB). Averaged over hundreds of trials from each kind of cluster, discrimination by four subjects improved as the number of trials within a cluster increased from the first to the eighth or so. The interpretation was that subjects had to shift attention to loud sounds after having listened during the preceding 10 trials to soft sounds (and vice versa). Shifting the attention band required several trials to be fully effective; with attention poorly focused during the first trials of a new sequence, discrimination suffered.

Although results from various kinds of experiments generally supported an attention-band hypothesis, other explanations of the results—such as changes in response strategies or memory effects—could not be excluded. Moreover, Kornbrot (1980) provided theoretical and empirical evidence that signal-detectability models predict some effects in identification experiments better than the attention-band model. Despite its appeal, the generality of the attention-band model for intensity remains to be clarified.

IV. SELECTIVE ATTENTION FOR SPEECH AND OTHER COMPLEX PATTERNS

A few investigations have shown how expectancies derived from explicit training or from musical and linguistic knowledge can guide listening in a psychoacoustical task.

IV.1. Non-speech Patterns

Watson and his colleagues (e.g. Leek & Watson, 1984; Watson, 1987) have performed a series of experiments in which subjects had to detect or discriminate one tone burst in a sequence of rapidly presented bursts. Thus, Leek and Watson (1984) presented three sequences of nine or ten 45-ms bursts at different frequencies, always in the same order, one burst after the other. The first sequence and either the second or third sequence contained nine bursts and the odd sequence had a tenth burst which could occur in any position. In effect, the subject's task was to detect the presence of that extra burst. Because most of the 10 frequencies differed by more than a critical band and because each one served in turn as the missing target, initially it could be detected only at very high levels. Only after 800 to 1000 trials per component did the subjects learn to detect the extra target at much lower levels. Even then, two of the four subjects could barely detect one of the signals. Lengthening the duration of that burst from 45 to 165 ms led to immediate improvement which was sustained when the duration was set back to 45 ms.

One interpretation of these results is that the initial training had little to do with attention. The subjects learned to discriminate a number of complex patterns but were given no opportunity to focus attention owing to the great signal uncertainly and to the lack of any cues. However, once some learning had taken place, the listener could "attend to specific spectral-temporal regions until" he or she became "competent at hearing the component occurring at that position" (Leek & Watson, 1984, p.1043). Moreover, the learning could be accelerated by making the target more salient, as was done by lengthening a single component. The authors suggest that the learning of speech could involve analogous processes.

Taking advantage of musical experience, Dowling, Lung, and Herrbold (1987) showed that subjects could judge better the pitch of a note in a five-note melody when the target note was at the expected frequency (in terms of the music scale) than when at a different frequency. The authors argued that subjects were listening at an expected frequency and so could process it better, just as we saw in section III.1 that subjects in a pure psychoacoustical task detect and discriminate tones at expected frequencies better than those at unexpected frequencies.

IV.2. Speech

Few investigations have addressed the question of whether a listener's attention to specific acoustical properties influences the perception and recognition of speech. Two such psychoacoustical studies did measure the effect of attending, in one case, to a particular frequency region and, in the other, to a brief temporal segment. A third study examined the effect of distraction on the relative importance of stimulus properties.

Scharf, Dai, and Miller (1988; see also Scharf, 1989) had listeners discriminate a synthesized /da/ from a /ga/ in a single-interval, two-alternative procedure. The syllables differed acoustically only in the frequency region around 2500 Hz. After training on the task in the quiet, in the first condition the subjects heard the syllables in the presence of a masking noise, which reduced performance to near chance. In the next condition, a weak 1000-Hz tone burst was added to the /da/, but not to the /ga/. Despite the tonal cue, discrimination did not improve. In a new condition, instead of a 1000-Hz tone burst a 2500-Hz burst was added, again only to the /da/; performance now improved significantly to 75% correct. It appeared that the subjects had focused on 2500 Hz and could therefore make use of the cue at that frequency but not of the cue at 1000 Hz. In a final condition, the subjects were informed about the 1000-Hz cue and given examples; they then began to use the cue at 1000 Hz, and their scores went up from 58% to 90% correct.

A straightforward interpretation of these results is that initially subjects came to focus attention on the critical 2500-Hz region, which was necessary to discriminate between /da/ and /ga/. The learning was probably automatic. Even when added noise made the discrimination very difficult, they continued to focus on 2500 Hz and could not take advantage of the cue which was arbitrarily located at 1000 Hz. However, they could redirect attention to the 1000-Hz region once they knew that the best information was located there.

Pitt and Samuel (1990) determined the ability of subjects to focus on a brief segment of a spoken word, such as "bandit", which was composed of two syllables. The task was to report as quickly as possible whether or not the word contained a target phoneme (smallest unit of speech that carries meaning), which was indicated by a letter on a computer screen. The target phoneme was a consonant, such as /b/ or /n/. A different word was presented on every trial, but every word was so constructed that the target could have occurred at the beginning or end of either one of the component syllables. Accordingly, the target could have been at any one of four temporal locations in the word. The target was presented on most trials at one of the four locations—the expected location—and only occasionally at one of the three others. Four groups of subjects were tested, each group with a different location as the most likely to contain the target and therefore as the expected location. Reaction times were significantly shorter and errors fewer when the phoneme was heard at the expected location than when heard at one of the three unexpected locations.

These two experiments show that, in listening to speech, people can direct attention toward the frequency or temporal region where the relevant information is located or most likely to be located. However, Gordon, Eberhardt, and Rueckl (1993) have shown that the role of attention in speech is complex. When listeners were required to perform a visual task while discriminating between /pa/ and /ba/, they gave more weight to a frequency component of the speech stimuli than normally and less weight to a temporal component. Normally, under attentive listening, the temporal component is the strong cue for these syllables. Thus, attention determines not only what acoustical properties are processed most fully but also how they influence the coding of the speech.

V. NEUROLOGICAL BASES OF AUDITORY SELECTIVE ATTENTION

Rather than speculate about the possible neurological mechanisms that underlie auditory attention in general, we restrict the discussion to the neurological underpinning of the effects of selective attention in the frequency domain (see section III.1). These attentional effects are likely to reflect events in the cochlea, as they are so closely coupled to the critical band and auditory filter, which are thought to be determined in the inner ear. The neural basis for attentional control of cochlear events would be via the olivocochlear bundle (OCB), the final stage in the neural circuitry that sends messages from the central nervous system to the hair cells of the cochlea. To test the hypothesis that the failure to detect signals at unexpected frequencies requires OCB input, Scharf, Magnan, and Chays (1997) tested patients whose OCB to one ear had been severed during a vestibular neurotomy. (The vestibular nerve, which contains the OCB, is cut to relieve severe vertigo caused by Ménière's disease.) The probe-signal procedure was used to measure the attentional band in the operated ear of over 20 patients. Results were compared to those either from the same ear prior to the vestibular neurotomy or to the other healthy ear.

Although most Ménière's patients have hearing loss in addition to vertigo, some patients had normal auditory thresholds in both ears, before as well as after the operation. Results for one such patient are shown in Fig. 2.11 which has the same format as Fig. 2.3. Percentage correct in the 2IFC detection task is plotted as a function of the frequency of the signal. Data collected the day before the operation are wholly normal; the patient detected unexpected probes less well as their frequency became more different from that of the target at 1000 Hz, and the filled symbols fall along the typical auditory filter contour. Data collected after the operation, over a period of many months, are grossly distorted; the patient detected probes at frequencies far from the target, the very same probes that he had missed earlier. Similar if less dramatic results have been obtained from a number of other patients, either by before–after comparisons or by comparing the operated ear to the healthy ear (Scharf, Magnan, and Chays, 1997).

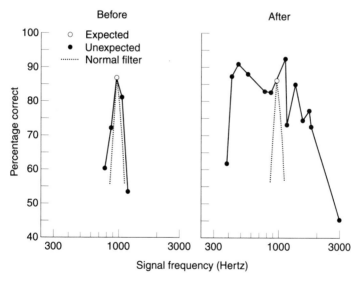

FIG. 2.11.   Percentage correct in a signal-probe experiment as a function of signal frequency for patient SB. The target frequency was 1000 Hz. The left panel shows data collected the day before the OCB was severed; the right panel shows data collected one week after the operation and during the next 10 months. Before the operation, SB missed signals at unexpected frequencies (black circles) in just the same way as depicted by the normal auditory filter (dotted line), with the percentage correct declining rapidly to near chance (50%). After the operation, he detected those same unexpected probes and many farther away, with percentage correct hovering between 70 and 90%. (Adapted from Scharf et al., 1994.)

In almost all the patients the comparison was made with signals and noise presented at the same levels in the operated and unoperated ears. This was possible because only patients with normal or near-normal thresholds were tested and because the detection of targets was unaffected by the operation (Scharf et al., 1993); only the detection of probes improved. One way to understand this outcome is to assume that in normal ears, the basilar membrane in the cochlea is tuned to respond best to signals at expected frequencies and that signals at unexpected frequencies are attenuated the equivalent of 3 or 4 dB (see Fig. 2.7) in a signal-probe procedure with a single probe frequency. This tuning would be accomplished via the OCB. In operated ears without OCB input, the unexpected probes would not be effectively attenuated and so would be detected, leading the patient to adopt a two-signal listening strategy. Normal subjects can readily adopt such a strategy as shown in Fig. 2.6 and in experiments by MacMillan and Schwartz (1975). The effective attenuation at probe frequencies may be achieved by the OCB's innervation of the outer hair cells, which are ana-logous to a miniature motor system; they contract and dilate when stimu-lated. Accordingly, auditory selectivity may also involve a kind of motor control remotely akin to that in vision where the oculomotor system directs the fovea toward the attended stimulus.

VI. SUMMARY AND CONCLUSIONS

Hearing serves two major purposes. First, it provides information about the environment that is often not available to any other sense, and because that information can come from any direction regardless of the organism's spatial orientation, hearing is the primary early-warning system. Second, it is the basis for communication, which in humans is especially important as speech reception. Somewhat orthogonal to these two functions are the questions of how attention operates across the senses and how it operates within hearing. There is the question of how paying attention to, for example, what one is seeing affects what one is hearing. Then there is the question of how attending to one sound or even one property of a sound affects the processing of both the attended and unattended sounds. This way of posing the problems of auditory attention can perhaps help us to make better sense of the many data reviewed in this chapter.

As an early-warning system, hearing must be ready for sounds, even very faint ones, coming from a distant or stealthy source. Consequently, even while engaged in some particular task, whether involving hearing or mainly another sense, the organism must remain sensitive to new sounds. No prior pre-paration is possible because unforeseen sounds from unknown directions are of primary concern. Thus, it is wholly reasonable that experiments show that attending to a particular direction in space does not improve the detection of faint sounds from that direction relative to sounds from unattended directions. And the difficulty in demonstrating a suppression of auditory input that comes along during a non-auditory task is also reasonable, although repetitive sounds may be somewhat reduced, as some studies suggest. On the other hand, the evidence is ample that subjects respond more rapidly to sounds from expected directions than from unexpected directions. In summary, sensitivity does not depend on maintaining attention in a particular direction; attention can be spatially oriented as needed, and responding is most rapid to sounds from the newly attended direction.

Hearing does more than point out where a sound comes from. It helps to tell one sound source from another: the lion (to be avoided) from the lamb (to be pursued). And, as noted, discrimination is better for sounds from an expected direction. But most of the time sounds do not come singly but are embedded in what is often a cacophony. Thus, orienting attention among competing sounds is a major task. Spatial locus is a great help in that selection. However, selectivity is possible for sounds coming from the same direction (or earphone), mainly on the basis of sound frequency, but also on the basis of temporal characteristics and, perhaps, loudness. Focusing attention on a particular frequency region or regions improves detection and discrimination, and along with attention to designated temporal segments enhances the understanding of speech. Focusing on a particular sound frequency most likely is accomplished via efferent input to the cochlea, to the hair cells that transduce sound into neural energy. If true, then part of auditory selective attention is fashioned right at the receptor, and those 19th-century theorists who argued that attention could affect the very muscles of the ear were right, although the "muscles" turn out to be the outer hair cells deep within the inner ear.

ACKNOWLEDGMENTS

The preparation of this chapter was supported in part by a grant (DC00084) from NIH. I thank Richard Ivry for helpful comments on an earlier version.

REFERENCES

Baust, W., & Berlucchi, G. (1964). Reflex response to clicks of cat's tensor tympani during sleep and wakefulness and the influence thereon of the auditory cortex. *Archives Italiennes de Biologie, 102,* 686–712.

Baust, W., Berlucchi, G., & Moruzzi, G., (1964). Changes in the auditory input in wakefulness and during the synchronized and desynchronized stage of sleep. *Archives Italiennes de Biologie, 102,* 657–674.

Broadbent, D.E. (1950). The twenty dials test under quiet conditions. *Applied Psychology Unit Report No. 130* (cited in Broadbent, 1958).

Broadbent, D.E. (1954). The role of auditory localization in attention and memory span. *Journal of Experimental Psychology, 47,* 191–196.

Broadbent, D.E. (1958). *Perception and communication*. London: Pergamon Press.

Broadbent, D.E. (1971). *Decision and stress*. London: Academic Press.

Broadbent, D.E. & Gregory, M. (1963). Division of attention and the decision theory of signal detection. *Proceedings of the Royal Society, 158*, 222–231.

Brochard, R., Drake, C., Botte, M.-C., & McAdams, S. (1995). Focusing attention on one auditory stream does not depend on the number of simultaneous streams. In C.-A. Possamai (Ed.), *Fechner Day 95: Proceedings of the Eleventh Annual Meeting of the International Society for Psychophysics*, (pp.155–160). Marseille: ISP.

Buchtel, H.A. & Butter, C.M. (1988). Spatial attentional shifts: Implications for the role of polysensory mechanisms. *Neuropsychologia, 26*, 499–509.

Buus, S., Schorer, E., Florentine, M., & Zwicker, E. (1986). Decision rules in detection of simple and complex tones. *Journal of the Acoustical Society of America, 80*, 1646–1657.

Cherry, E.C. (1953). Some experiments on the recognition of speech, with one and with two ears. *Journal of the Acoustical Society of America, 25*, 975–979.

Cherry, E.C., & Taylor, W.K. (1954). Some further experiments upon the recognition of speech, with one and with two ears. *Journal of the Acoustical Society of America, 26*, 554–559.

Dai, H. (1989). *Detection of unexpected sounds*. Doctoral dissertation, Northeastern University, Boston.

Dai, H., Scharf, B., & Buus, S. (1991). Effective attenuation of signals in noise under focused attention. *Journal of the Acoustical Society of America, 89*, 2837–2842.

Desmedt, J.E. (1975). Physiological studies of the efferent recurrent auditory system. In W.D. Keidel, & W.D. Neff (Eds.), *Handbook of sensory physiology, Vol. V/2 Auditory system* (pp 219–246). Berlin: Springer-Verlag.

Dowling, W.S., Lung, K.M., & Herrbold, S. (1987). Aiming attention in pitch and time in the perception of interleaved melodies. *Perception and Psychophysics, 41*, 642–656.

Ebata, M., & Scharf, B. (1992). The effect of selective attention on auditory detection. *Journal of the Acoustical Society of Japan (E) 13*, 59–61.

Ebata, M., Sone, T., & Nimura, T. (1968). Improvement of hearing ability by directional information. *Journal of the Acoustical Society of America, 43*, 289–297.

Egan, J.P., Carterette, E.C., & Thwing, E.J. (1954). Some factors affecting multi-channel listening. *Journal of the Acoustical Society of America, 26*, 774–782.

Giard, M.H., Collet, L., Bouchet, P., & Pernier, J. (1994). Auditory selective attention in the human cochlea. *Brain Research, 633*, 353–356.

Gordon, P.C., Eberhardt, J.L., & Rueckl, J.G. (1993). Attentional modulation of the phonetic significance of acoustic cues. *Cognitive Psychology, 25*, 1–42.

Green, D.M., & Luce, R.D. (1974). Variability of magnitude estimates: A timing theory analysis. *Perception and Psychophysics, 15*, 291–300.

Green, D.M., & Swets, J.A. (1966). *Signal detection theory and psychophysics*. Huntington, NY: Krieger.

Greenberg, G., & Larkin, W. (1968). Frequency-response characteristic of auditory observers detecting signals of a single frequency in noise: The probe-signal method. *Journal of the Acoustical Society of America, 44*, 1513–1523.

Hafter, E.R., Schlauch, R.S., & Tang, J. (1993). Attending to auditory filters that were not stimulated directly. *Journal of the Acoustical Society of America, 94*, 743–747.

Hernandez-Peon, R., Scherrer, H., & Jouvet, M. (1956). Modification of selective activity in cochlear nucleus during "attention" in unanesthetized cats. *Science, 123*, 331–332.

Howard, J.H., O'Toole, A.J., Parasuraman, R., & Bennett, K.B. (1984). Pattern-directed attention in uncertain frequency detection. *Perception and Psychophysics, 35*, 256–264.

Igarashi, M. Alford, D.R., Gordon, W.P., & Nakai, V. (1974). Behavioral auditory function after transection of crossed olivo-cochlear bundle in the cat: II. Conditioned visual performance with intense white noise. *Acta Otolaryngol. (Stockh.), 77*, 311–317.

James, W. (1890). *The principles of psychology*. New York: Holt.

Kornbrot, D.E. (1980). Attention bands: Some implications for categorical judgment. *British Journal of Mathematical and Statistical Psychology, 33*, 1–16.

LaBerge, D. (1970). On the processing of simple visual and auditory stimuli at distinct levels. *Perception and Psychophysics, 9*, 331–334.

LaBerge, D. (1971). Effect of type of catch trial upon generalization gradients of reaction time. *Journal of Experimental Psychology, 87*, 225–228.

Leek, M.R., Brown, M.E., & Dorman, M.F. (1991). Informational masking and auditory attention. *Perception and Psychophysics, 50*, 205–214.

Leek, M.R., & Watson, C.S. (1984). Learning to detect auditory pattern components. *Journal of the Acoustical Society of America, 76*, 1037–1044.

Locke, J. (1929). *An essay concerning human understanding*. London: Oxford University Press.

Lowe, G. (1968). Auditory detection and recognition in a two alternative, directional uncertainty situation. *Perception and Psychophysics, 4*, 180–182.

Luce, R.D., & Green, D.M. (1978). Two tests of a neural attention hypothesis for auditory psychophysics. *Perception and Psychophysics, 23*, 363–371.

Lukas, J.H. (1981). The role of efferent inhibition in human auditory attention: An examination of the auditory brainstem potentials. *International Journal of Neuroscience, 12*, 137–145.

MacMillan, N.A., & Schwartz, M. (1975). A probe-signal investigation of uncertain-frequency detection. *Journal of the Acoustical Society of America, 58*, 1051–1058.

Marsh, J.T., Worden, F.G., & Hicks, L. (1962). Some effects of room acoustics on evoked auditory potentials. *Science, 137*, 280–282.

Mazzucchi, A., & Cattelani, R. (1983). Hemispheric prevalence in acoustical attention. *Brain and Cognition, 2*, 1–11.

Mondor, T.A., & Bregman, A.S. (1994). Allocating attention to frequency regions. *Perception and Psychophysics, 56*, 268–276.

Mondor, T.A. & Zatorre, R.J. (1995). Shifting and focusing auditory spatial attention. *Journal of Experimental Psychology: Human Perception and Performance, 21*, 387–409.

Moray, N. (1959). Attention in dichotic listening: Affective cues and the influence of instructions. *Quarterly Journal of Experimental Psychology, 11*, 56–60.

Moray, N., Fitter, M., Ostry, D., Favreau, D., & Nagy, V. (1976). Attention to pure tones. *Quarterly Journal of Experimental Psychology, 28*, 271–283.

Moray, N., & O'Brien, T. (1967). Signal-detection theory applied to selective listening. *Journal of the Acoustical Society of America, 42*, 765–772.

Mori, S., & Ward, L.M. (1991). Listening versus hearing: Attentional effects on intensity discrimination. *Technical Reports on Hearing: Acoustical Society of Japan*, No. H-91–36.

Mori, S., & Ward, L.M. (1992). Listening versus hearing II: Attentional effects on intensity discrimination by musicians. *Technical Reports on Hearing: Acoustical Society of Japan*, No. H-92–48.

Murray, J., Allard, F., & Bryden, M.P. (1988). Expectancy effects: Cost–benefit analysis of monaurally and dichotically presented speech. *Brain and Language, 35*, 105–118.

Näätänen, R. (1992). *Attention and brain function*. Hillsdale, NJ: Lawrence Erlbaum Associates Inc.

Neff, D.L. (1995). Signal properties that reduce masking by simultaneous random-frequency maskers. *Journal of the Acoustical Society of America, 98*, 1909–1920.

Nosofsky, R.M. (1983). Shifts of attention in the identification and discrimination of intensity. *Perception and Psychophysics, 33*, 103–112.

Oatman, L.C. (1976). Effects of visual attention on the intensity of auditory evoked potentials. *Experimental Neurology, 51*, 41–53.

Patterson, R.D. (1974). Auditory filter shape. *Journal of the Acoustical Society of America, 55*, 802–809.

Pitt, M.A., & Samuel, A.G. (1990). Attentional allocation during speech perception: How fine is the focus? *Journal of Memory and Language, 29*, 611–632.

Posner, M.I. (1978). *Chronometric explorations of mind*. Hillsdale, NJ: Lawrence Erlbaum Associate Inc.

Possamaï, C.-A., Scharf, B., Bonnel, A.-M. & Ward, L.M. (in preparation). *Effects of spatial auditory attention on detection and discrimination*.

Poulton, E.C. (1956). Listening to overlapping calls. *Journal of Experimental Psychology, 52*, 334–339.

Puel, J.L., Bonfils, P., & Pujol, R. (1988). Selective attention modifies the active micro-mechanical properties of the cochlea. *Brain Research, 447*, 380–383.

Puleo, J.S., & Pastore, R.E. (1978). Critical-band effects in two-channel auditory signal detection. *Journal of Experimental Psychology: Human Perception and Performance, 4*, 153–163.

Quinlan, P.T., & Bailey, P.J. (1995). An examination of attentional control in the auditory modality: Further evidence for auditory orienting. *Perception and Psychophysics, 57*, 614–628.

Rasmussen, G. (1946). The olivary peduncle and other fibrous projections of the superior olivary complex. *Journal of Comparative Neurology, 84*, 141–219.

Reisberg, D., Scheiber, R., & Potemken, L. (1981). Eye position and the control of auditory attention. *Journal of Experimental Psychology: Human Perception and Performance, 7*, 318–323.

Rhodes, G. (1987). Auditory attention and the representation of spatial information. *Perception and Psychophysics, 42*, 1–14.

Scharf, B. (1988a). The role of listening in the measurement of hearing. In S.D.G. Stephens (Ed.), *Advances in audiology* (pp. 13–26). Basel: Karger.

Scharf, B. (1988b). The effect of listening on hearing: Focused attention in audition. In M. Karjalainen, T. Lahti, & J. Linjama (Eds.), *Proceedings of the Nordic Acoustical Meeting 88* (pp.1–8) Tampere, Finland: The Acoustical Society of Finland.

Scharf, B. (1989). Spectral specifity in auditory detection: The effect of listening on hearing. *Journal of the Acoustical Society of Japan. (E), 10*, 309–317.

Scharf, B. (1995). Adaptation and attention in psychoacoustics. In G.A. Manley, G.M. Klump, C. Köppl, H. Fastl, & H. Oeckinghaus (Eds.), *Proceedings of the 10th International Symposium on Hearing: Advances in Hearing Research* (pp. 365–386) Singapore: World Scientific Publishing Co.

Scharf, B., Canévet, G., Possamaï, C., & Bonnel, A. (1986). Some effects of attention in hearing. *18th International Congress on Audiology*, (p.202) Prague.

Scharf, B., Dai, H., & Miller, J.L. (1988). The role of attention in speech perception. *Journal of the Acoustical Society of America, 84*, S158 (A).

Scharf, B., Magnan, J., & Chays, A. (1997). On the role of the olivocochlear bundle in hearing: Sixteen case studies. *Hearing Research, 103*, 101–122.

Scharf, B., Magnan, J., Collet, L., Ulmer, E., & Chays, A. (1994). On the role of the olivo-cochlear bundle in hearing: A case study. *Hearing Research, 75*, 11–26.

Scharf, B., Nadol, J., Magnan, J., Chays, A., & Marchioni, A. (1993). Does efferent input improve the detection of tones in monaural noise? In R. Verrillo (Ed.), *Sensory research: Multimodal perspectives* (pp.299–306). Hillsdale, NJ: Lawrence Erlbaum Associates Inc.

Scharf, B., Quigley, S., Aoki, C., Peachey, N., & Reeves, A. (1987). Focused auditory attention and frequency selectivity. *Perception and Psychophysics, 42*, 215–223.

Schlauch, R.S., & Hafter, E.R. (1991). Listening bandwidths and frequency uncertainty in pure-tone signal detection. *Journal of the Acoustical Society of America, 90*, 1332–1339.

Sorkin, R.D. (1965). Uncertain signal detection with simultaneous contralateral cues. *Journal of the Acoustical Society of America, 38*, 207–212.

Spence, C.J., & Driver, J. (1994). Covert spatial orienting in auditory: Exogenous and endogenous mechanisms. *Journal of Experimental Psychology: Human Perception and Performance, 20*, 555–574.

Spence, C.J., & Driver, J. (1996). Audiovisual links in endogenous covert spatial attention. *Journal of Experimental Psychology: Human Perception and Performance, 22*, 1005–1030.

Sperling, G. (1984). A unified theory of attention and signal detection. In R. Parasuraman & D.R. Davies (Eds.), *Varieties of attention* (pp.103–181). New York: Academic Press.

Sperling, G., & Dosher, B. (1986). Strategy and optimization in human information processing. In K. Boff, L. Kaufman, & J. Thomas (Eds.), *Handbook of perception and human performance, Vol. I*, pp.2–1 to 2–65. New York: Wiley.

Squires, K.C., Hillyard, S.A., & Lindsay, P.H. (1973). Vertex potentials evoked during auditory signal detection: Relation to decision criteria. *Perception and Psychophysics, 14*, 265–272.

Swets, J. (1984). Mathematical models of attention. In R. Parasuraman & D.R. Davies (Eds.), *Varieties of attention* (pp.183–242). New York: Academic Press.

Swets, J.A., & Sewall, S.T. (1961). Stimulus versus response uncertainty in recognition. *Journal of the Acoustical Society of America, 33*, 1586–1592.

Tanner, W., & Norman, R. (1954). The human use of information: II. Signal detection for the case of an unknown signal parameter. *Transactions of the Institute of Radio Engineering, Professional Group on Information Theory, 4*, 222–227.

Treisman, A. (1960). Contextual effects in selective listening. *Quarterly Journal of Experimental Psychology, 12*, 242–248.

Treisman, A., & Geffen, G. (1967). Selective attention: Perception or response? *Quarterly Journal of Experimental Psychology, 19*, 1–17.

Watson, C.S. (1987). Uncertainty, informational masking, and the capacity of immediate auditory memory. In W.A. Yost, & C.S. Watson (Eds.), *Auditory processing of complex sounds* pp.267–277. Hillsdale, NJ: Lawrence Erlbaum Associates Inc.

Wood, N.L., & Cowan, N. (1995). The cocktail-party phenomenon revisited: Attention and memory in the classic selective listening procedure of Cherry (1953). *Journal of Experimental Psychology: General, 124*, 243–262.

Wright, B.A., & Dai, H. (1994). Detection of unexpected tones with short and long durations. *Journal of the Acoustical Society of America, 95*, 931–938.

Yama, M., & Robinson, D. (1982). Comparison of frequency selectivity for the monaural and binaural hearing systems: Evidence from a probe-frequency procedure. *Journal of the Acoustical Society of America, 71*, 694–700.

CHAPTER THREE

Visual Attention and Eye Movements

James E. Hoffman
University of Delaware, USA

Visual information regarding the spatial layout and identity of objects in our environment requires several kinds of orienting mechanisms. Our eyes have parallel visual axes, providing overlap of the views in each eye, a prerequisite for binocular vision (Julesz, 1971). This arrangement results in an inability to see the approximately 180 degrees of space that lie behind our head. Thus body and head movements are required to access the entire 360 degrees available to us. Similarly, the retina of the eye is nonhomogeneous, containing a foveal area at the center which provides a small area of high-acuity form analysis (one can see a string of about eight letters in this area). Eye movements are required to bring this foveal area to bear on peripheral objects to clearly discern their shapes. These overt orienting mechanisms are, in turn, supplemented by a covert or "hidden" attention system that provides enhanced visual processing of selected areas through internal neural adjustments that can be made much faster than overt orienting (Hoffman, 1975; Posner, 1980).

This chapter reviews evidence supporting the claim that the covert attention system plays an important role in guiding overt orienting based on eye movements. In particular, it appears that eye movements directed to a location in space are preceded by a shift of visual attention to the same location and, furthermore, this coupling of eye movements and attention is mandatory. This relationship holds regardless of whether the eye movement is triggered by an external event such as a sudden movement or onset (exogenous control, see Yantis, 1996) or is "internally" directed by the subject (endogenous control) on the basis of instructions or expectations.

The claim that eye movements are guided by attention does not entail the proposition that these two systems are completely interdependent. It has been known at least since Helmholtz's time that one can attend to peripheral objects without making an eye movement. Helmholtz (1909) noted that he could direct his attention "at will" to different characters printed on a card that was illuminated by a brief electrical spark. The duration of the spark was too short to allow an eye movement to occur so the impression that he could "look" at a given letter must have been due to an internal attentional system being directed at a stored memory representation of the array. These impressions have been confirmed by modern work that has shown that there is indeed a visual copy of briefly presented stimuli that persists for a short time after termination of a stimulus (Sperling, 1960). In addition, a growing body of work (Eriksen & Hoffman, 1972, 1973; Hoffman & Nelson, 1981; Hoffman, Nelson, & Houck 1983; Posner, 1980; Yantis, this volume) shows that observers can direct an internal visual attention mechanism to different areas of visual space even while the eye remains fixed. Thus the relationship between attention and eye movements is one of partial interdependence. Attention is free to move independent of the eyes, but eye movements require visual attention to precede them to their goal.

ATTENTION AND SACCADIC EYE MOVEMENTS

The most heavily researched area involving attentional control of eye movements is in the area of saccades, which are rapid, ballistic changes in eye position that occur at rate of about 3–4 per second (Becker, 1991). This means that we make approximately 230,000 saccades during each waking day! The eye is essentially blind during these movements and information is acquired during the relatively long fixations (approximately 250 msec) that intervene between saccades. Saccades are important during reading and scanning of scenes which require the high-acuity form vision provided by the fovea. As Yarbus (1967) pointed out, the location and sequence of saccades is not random. Subjects scanning the same picture show highly replicable "scan paths" from one day to the next. This sequence, however, can be changed by asking subjects to report on different aspects of the picture such as people's ages, in which case, fixations tend to be restricted to faces.

What is that guides the eye from one fixation to the next? A possibility is that sometime during the course of a fixation, visual attention is allocated to the periphery to determine the location of the next fixation. This location information, in turn, is transmitted to the neural machinery responsible for actually moving the eyes. This proposal, although plausible, is not universally accepted (see for example Klein, 1980; and Klein, Kingstone &

Pontefract, 1992; Klein & Pontefract, 1994) and raises several questions regarding the precise role of visual attention in the planning and execution of saccades. First, it may appear to beg the question of how eye movements are made, by postulating an intelligent controller (visual attention) whose operation itself must then be explained, leading to an "infinite regress" of explanatory mechanisms. Luckily, we will see that this is not entirely the case because a fair amount is known about the mechanisms that guide attention and we can make use of this knowledge in understanding saccades.

Second, this proposal needs to be fleshed out with a number of details. For example, when during fixation does attention begin to "search" the periphery for candidate saccade locations and what happens to processing of fixated material during this period? What determines whether and when the eye will actually begin its movement to the new destination? And finally, how can the role of attention in this process be verified? After all, saccades can now be measured with great accuracy using modern eye-trackers but how can "covert" shifts of attention be detected? We will explore these issues in some detail by examining the control of saccades during reading.

Attention and Reading

Adult readers tend to fixate most of the "content" words (nouns, verbs, adjectives, etc.) in a text although short "function" words (articles, conjunctions, etc.) may be skipped (Just & Carpenter, 1980; Rayner & Pollatsek, 1989). For example, Crowder (1982) points out that readers make about 75 fixations in reading a 100-word text, which indicates that they are reading about 1.33 words per fixation. The duration of each fixation lasts about .25 seconds but varies widely for different words as a function of several factors such as the word's length and frequency in the language, how well it fits into the context of the sentence, and its syntactic and thematic roles (Just & Carpenter, 1980). Just and Carpenter (1980) suggested that readers fixate each word until processing at perceptual, linguistic, and conceptual levels has been completed. According to this model, fixation durations provide a direct estimate of the total time to process each word in the text and therefore provide a useful metric of the cognitive processes involved in reading.

Preview Effects.   The fact that function words located in the periphery of the currently fixated word are skipped, however, indicates that at some point during fixation, readers are obtaining information, not just from the fixated word, but also from the about-to-be-fixated word located in the periphery (also known as the "parafovea"). Subjects are apparently "previewing" words before they are fixated. When these words are short and familiar (such as *of* or *the*), this preview is sufficient to identify the word and allow it to be skipped. However, even when subjects do not skip the word, a preview may be beneficial in reducing the subsequent fixation on the pre-viewed word.

This predication is supported by an experiment reported by Rayner (1975). Consider a reader fixating the first word in the phrase *ship's chart*. During fixation of *ship's*, subjects may preview the upcoming word *chart*. This preview might provide a saving in processing during the subsequent fixation of *chart*. Now consider a situation in which subjects view the first word in the phrase *ship's chyft*. When a saccade is initiated toward the nonword *chyft*, the computer changes it to *chart*. (subjects rarely notice such changes when they occur during the time the eye is in motion). In this case, there shouldn't be any benefits associated with parafoveal preview and, indeed, fixation durations on *chart* were longer relative to the case when *chart* was previewed.

Parafoveal preview effects have also been obtained in an experiment using pictures. Henderson, Pollatsek, and Rayner (1989) presented subjects with a series of displays containing four pictures, each one portraying a common object. Subjects were instructed to fixate each picture in the display in anticipation of a memory test. In the *one object* condition, pictures were presented for inspection one at a time, thus preventing any preview effects. In the *one + next* condition, while the subject fixated one drawing, the next drawing to be fixated was present. This preview shortened the subsequent fixation on the previewed picture. In the *all objects* condition, all four objects were presented simultaneously and remained on the screen during the entire trial. This condition provided no additional preview benefits suggesting that previews are restricted to that object about to be fixated.

Why do preview effects occur? One answer is suggested by examining factors that influence the landing position of saccades. Readers do not simply make a fixed-size saccade after fixating each word but instead adjust the size depending on several aspects of the material to the right of fixation (Rayner & McConkie, 1976). Readers appear to have a *preferred viewing location* in words, which lies between the beginning and middle of the word (O'Regan, 1992; Rayner & Pollatesk, 1989). This position will, of course, depend on the length of the word, and several studies have shown that readers increase the length of their saccades with increases in the length of the peripheral word. In addition, they rarely fixate spaces between words so that if extra spaces are inserted next to the currently fixated word, saccades will be lengthened to skip over these uninformative areas (Abrams & Zuber, 1971).

These considerations suggest that programming of the landing point for a saccade depends on locating the first nonblank character to the right of fixation (indicating the beginning of the word) and then the next blank character (indicating the end of the word). This information can then be used to estimate the length of the word and the corresponding optimal viewing position. The location information can then be passed to the mechanism responsible for programming and executing the saccade. This view suggests that preview benefits may occur simply as a byproduct of the need to pay attention to the periphery to control saccades.

A different answer as to why preview effects occur is offered by Epelboim, Booth, and Steinman (1994, 1996). They reasoned that if spaces between words are critical for guiding the eye during reading, removing spaces should disrupt eye movements and severely impair reading. They presented sentences in which the spaces between words were removed, like this one:

Readingsentenceswithoutspacesmayseemdifficultatfirstbutyoumay finditsurprisinglyeasy.

They found that although this manipulation did slow reading speed by about 30% on average, some subjects showed no slowing at all. In addition, many characteristics of the saccades were similar with spaced and unspaced text. For example, the same subjects that showed a preferred viewing location (PVL) with normal or unspaced text, did so with unspaced text as well. Their data raise the question: If space information is not used to guide the eye to its landing position, then what is? Epelboim et al. suggest that it is recognition of the peripheral word that guides the eye. That is, while fixated on one word, subjects are also processing the peripheral word for the purpose of word recognition. Even when spaces are not present, letter strings can be recognized as words (note that spoken language does not have spaces either!) and this information in turn, may draw attention and the eye to the proper location in the word. This recognition stage is more difficult with filled spaces because errors in segregating the letters into word strings will sometimes occur and therefore reading is a bit slower, but still possible.

Are there any critical observations that point to a resolution of this debate? Rayner and Pollatsek (1996) point out that word-skipping data seem compatible with their view. Short, familiar words are often skipped during reading which is consistent with the idea that peripheral words are recognized only sometimes as opposed to being the usual state of affairs as predicted by the Epelboim et al. model. Nonetheless, the very fact that at least some readers can read normally with space information removed shows that eye guidance in reading *can* be based on more than just perceptual information about word length. It may be that both kinds of information are used to guide saccades during normal reading with perceptual information or word identity information being more or less useful depending on the circumstances. In any case, we should not lose sight of one principle that transcends the particular models being debated: words to the right of the one being fixated are often identified and this fact suggests that visual attention precedes the eye to its destination.

Note that we have assumed that the preview effects observed in these experiments are due to an attentional mechanism directed to the right of the fixated word. This asymmetry to the right is presumably due to the left-to-right pattern of saccades that maps onto the direction in which our language is written. Pollatsek, Bolozky, Well, and Rayner (1981) investigated this claim using bilingual readers fluent in English and Hebrew. These readers showed the usual "asymmetric to the right" span when reading English and an opposite pattern for Hebrew, which is read from right to left. This flexibility strongly implicates visual attention as the mechanism mediating the preview effects.

Models of Saccade Control in Reading.   At this point, one might agree that attention is important in controlling the eye during reading but the details of *how* this might work remain to be specified, and here we need a model that makes testable predictions. A good starting point is the *sequential attention model* of reading that was originally proposed by Morrison (1984) and expanded on by Rayner and Pollatsek (1989) and later by Henderson (1992). According to the this model, fixation begins with attention allocated to the fixated word. Processing of this word continues until it has been identified and integrated into the context of the text (Just & Carpenter, 1980). Attention is then disengaged (Posner, 1980) from the fixated word and reallocated to the periphery, in order to locate the position for the upcoming saccade. This location can presumably be determined using low-level visual features such as spaces to determine the length of the next word. The engagement of attention in the periphery provides direction and amplitude parameters necessary for constructing a motor program, which when executed will move the eye to the attended location. In addition, allocation of visual attention to the periphery, will result in preview benefits for the next fixation. Finally, if the peripheral word is identified before the saccade is executed, the current saccade can be canceled and a new one programmed resulting in a longer saccade that skips the already identified word.

This model highlights several questions about the time course of attention allocation in saccade programming. First, it suggests that the allocation of attention to the periphery occurs late in fixation. This can be tested by manipulating when information necessary for programming the saccade becomes available in the periphery. If peripheral information is only accessed at the end of fixation, there should be a period of time, starting at fixation onset, in which readers are not affected by whether or not peripheral information is available. Morris, Rayner, and Pollatsek (1990) tested this prediction by having subjects read text in which words and inter-word

spaces beyond the fixated word were initially filled in with Xs. Consider the
following schematic displays:

```
(0ms)    Magic XXXXXXXXXXXXXXXXXXXXXX   Spaces Released
(50 ms)  Magic XXXX XXXXXXXXXXXXXXXX

(0 ms)   Magic XXXXXXXXXXXXXXXXXXXXXX   Letters and spaces
(50 ms)  Magic Wand XXXXXXXXXXXXXXXX    released
```

In the *spaces released condition*, subjects initially fixated on the word
"magic". Fifty msec later, the length of the adjacent word was revealed by
"releasing the space information" (accomplished by removing the appropriate Xs). The length but not the identity of the adjacent word was now
available and, as pointed out earlier, this length information may be one
factor used in programming the upcoming saccade. If this information is
used late in the fixation, for example, later than 150 msec after fixation
onset, then a 50 msec delay should not be any different than a 150 msec
delay as long as the information in both cases arrives before programming is
initiated. However, Morris et al. found that word length information was
particularly effective when it was available during the first 50–100 msec of
the fixation, although it continued to have some effect even late in fixation.
This suggests that either saccade programming or the information useful for
saccade programming is accessed early in fixation. According to Morris et
al. (1990), information arriving near the end of the fixation is apparently
used to modify an already existing program rather than building one from
scratch.

In the *letters and spaces released condition*, both the length and identity of
the adjacent word are provided during fixation. Not surprisingly, Morris et
al. found a preview effect in this condition. That is, having the word "wand"
present while fixating "magic" shortened the subsequent fixation on
"wand". This preview was effective only when identity information was
available during the first 50 msec of the fixation on "magic". Like the
saccade length data discussed earlier, the fixation duration data suggest that
it is primarily early in the fixation when the location of the upcoming saccade is determined, perhaps because some time is required for attention to
be fully "engaged" on the fixated word.

In any case, we are still left with the question of the state of attention
during the fixation. There are several possibilities. The location information
acquired early in fixation may be stored in some way to be used later for
saccade programming; saccade programming may be completed immediately, with the "execution" or "go" command coming later; or attention
may be maintained on the location of the upcoming saccade until saccade
programming and execution of the saccade commence at the end of fixation.
This latter possibility seems a bit puzzling because we are assuming that

attention needs to be simultaneously allocated to the fixated word as well as to the location of the upcoming saccade, requiring attention to be in two places at once. We return to this possibility later.

Complementing the aforementioned study, which sought to determine the temporal course of information processing of peripheral information during a fixation, is a study by Blanchard, McConkie, Zola, and Wolverton (1984) which examined processing of the foveal word. Their subjects read short texts while their eye position was monitored. During selected fixations, the word being fixated was briefly masked and then replaced by the same or a different word. This change was made at various times after fixation in an attempt to track the time course of identification of the fixated word. The two possible words differed by a single letter and both fit the context. For example, subjects might read "The underground caverns were meant to house hidden (*bombs, tombs*) but then the construction stopped because of lack of funds." The masking stimulus prevented subjects from detecting the letter change on the basis of apparent movement or other physical cues. Following the sentence, subjects had to choose which of four possible words had been present in the sentence. Two of the choices corresponded to the two critical words.

What would the *sequential attention model* predict for this experiment? Once the initial word has been on long enough to be "identified", attention should switch to the periphery to program the next saccade and the subject should report only the first word. This identification time has been estimated to be about 100 msec (Rayner et al., 1981) so we might expect that once the word change is delayed beyond 100 msec after fixation, the subject will simply fail to "see" the second word and will always choose the first word. Blanchard et al. (1984) reported that when the arrival of the second word was delayed by as much as 120 msec, subjects generally did report the first word but also frequently reported only the second word or both words. Remarkably, 12% of the times when the second word was reported, it had been presented only during the last 30 msec or less of fixation. These results are complex and open to several interpretations but they do suggest that subjects continue to process information in the fovea throughout the duration of fixation, even quite late when attention might be expected to be allocated to the periphery.

So far the results do not fit easily within the sequential attention model. Information regarding the peripheral word appears to be acquired throughout the fixation but primarily at the beginning, not at the end, as the model assumes. In addition, information regarding the fixated word appears to be acquired throughout the fixation interval, even at the very end when attention should now be firmly fixed on the location of the soon to be executed saccade. Such results are at least suggestive that both the fixated and peripheral words are processed in parallel and that a full commitment of attention to the new fixation location is not made until the very moment prior to the actual eye movement. Before entertaining specific versions of such a model, one additional finding needs to be considered.

Henderson (1992) derived the following prediction from the serial attention model. Suppose that the difficulty of processing the fixated stimulus is increased (referred to as an increase in *foveal load*), for example, by using a low-frequency word. This should prolong the processing of the fixated word but what will be the effect on information acquired from the periphery? Recall that one way to evaluate this is by looking at *preview benefit*, the amount of savings one gets during a fixation by having previewed that word in the preceding fixation. According to the serial attention model, the amount of preview benefit one gets from a peripheral word should be independent of the difficulty of the fixated word. Increased load should prolong the fixation but once processing of the fixated stimulus is completed, attention will be shifted to the periphery for a constant average time prior to the initiation of the saccade, producing a constant preview benefit. In other words, the sequential nature of processing of fovea and periphery prevents the difficulty of one process from influencing the duration of the subsequent process. In contrast, if processing of peripheral and foveal words are proceeding in parallel, and both processes are competing for a limited "supply of attention", it easy to see how increases in difficulty of processing of the foveal word may call on resources that could be used to process the peripheral word.

Henderson and Ferreira (1990) tested these predictions by having subjects read sentences like the following:

(1) Mary bought a chest despite the high price.
(2) Mary bought a trunk despite the high price.

When subjects were fixated on the word *chest* or *trunk*, the word *despite* could either be present in the periphery (*same preview* condition) or it could be replaced by a random letter string (*different preview* condition). The difference in fixation durations on *despite* between these two conditions provides a measure of preview benefit. Notice that *trunk* is a lower-frequency word than *chest* and should therefore be more difficult to identify. As it turns out, *trunk* also led to a smaller preview benefit than did *chest*, contrary to the predictions of the sequential attention model.

The finding that increased difficulty with the foveal word decreases "knowledge" about the peripheral word suggests an explanation in terms of competition for attention. For example, subjects may determine early in fixation the location of the next saccade. A partial allocation of attention to this location may then be established with primary attention remaining on the foveal word. Partial allocation of attention to the periphery provides a convenient way to maintain information about the saccade goal (similar to what Pylyshyn, 1989, 1994, calls a "FINST" mechanism for spatial indexing). It also accounts for why information about the peripheral and foveal words are both available throughout fixation. On those occasions when peripheral attention is adequate to identify the peripheral word (a likely occurrence for short, high-frequency words), attention may be reallocated to the following word, resulting in word skipping. Finally, the amount of attention available for processing of peripheral information would depend on the difficulty of the foveal word and hence the amount of attention it required.

Henderson (1992) pointed out that postulating divided attention introduces its own set of difficulties. At the time he wrote his chapter, there was little in the way of convincing evidence that subjects can divide their attention between two separated spatial locations and this continues to be an area of controversy in attention research. Pylyshyn (1989, 1994) showed that subjects can track multiple objects simultaneously without including areas between the tracked objects. Yantis (1992) provided evidence that this occurs only when subjects see the dots as the vertices of a single object moving on the screen. Kramer and Hahn (1995) however, provided direct evidence for divided visual attention in a paradigm requiring subjects to simultaneously compare two shapes in different locations. Subjects were able to do this while excluding irrelevant shapes located between the two comparison shapes. So the possibility of divided spatial attention cannot be excluded.

Second, in the sequential allocation model, the eye movement was triggered by a clearly defined criterion, namely identification of the foveal word. The parallel model would need some sort of control structure spelled out so that eye movements could be triggered at appropriate times. Third, the parallel model would predict that increasing difficulty of peripheral processing should affect processing of the foveal word and this apparently does not occur (Henderson, 1992). This latter difficulty can be handled by simply assuming that it is the "primary" locus of attention that determines how attention is allocated among competing inputs.

Summary.   What can we conclude about the role of attention in guiding the eye during reading? One clear finding that has emerged from this line of work is that during fixation, readers attend to and acquire information about the word lying to the right of the currently fixated word. This information includes length, shape, and sometimes identity. These characteristics affect the subsequent saccade but exactly how and when attention plays a role is still a matter of speculation. Evidence favors the idea that attention is divided between the fixated and peripheral words throughout fixation but much more research will be required to determine if this is the case. We now turn to the question of whether the coupling between attention and saccades that we have observed in reading is one of convenience or necessity.

Can Attention and Saccades be Directed to Different Locations?

Evidence Favoring the Dissociation of Attention and Saccades. The research reviewed earlier suggests that attention normally precedes the eye to its destination. However, the possibility remains that this relation is one of convenience and that under suitable conditions, subjects could be induced to send their eyes and their spatial attention to different locations. This possibility has been investigated by several different researchers using some variant of a dual-task paradigm. Subjects are given two tasks: they are to move their eyes to one location as quickly as possible and, in addition, try to detect or identify a visual target presented in close temporal proximity to the saccade. The target can occur in the same location as the saccade goal or at varying distances. Accuracy on the target detection task serves as an indirect measure of attention allocation because accuracy and speed of target detection and identification is generally superior at the locus of attention and drops with increasing distance (Eriksen & Hoffman, 1972, 1973; Hoffman & Nelson, 1981; Yantis, this volume). If saccades and attention can be dissociated in space, then subjects should be able to attend to one location (verified by superior target performance at that location) while making a saccade to another.

Klein (1980) reported one of the first attempts to experimentally dissociate movements of the eyes and attention. We will extensively review one of his experiments, both because his results are often cited as showing that this dissociation is possible and because it will make it clear that subjects' strategies in the dual-task paradigm play a powerful role in the pattern of results. Klein proposed a particular version of the relation between attention and eye movements known as the *oculomotor readiness theory* which holds that movements of attention are mediated by activity in brain areas that are responsible for moving the eyes. For example, attention to a particular location is accomplished by constructing a program suitable for moving the eyes to that location. This saccade program, in turn, produces the enhancement effects at the attended location. This theory makes two predictions which are the basis of his experiments. First, subjects who are preparing to make a saccade to a location should also be better at detecting signals at that location relative to other locations in the visual field. Second, attention to a location should lead to preparation of a corresponding saccade program resulting in fast saccades to that location.

The attentional enhancement predicted to accompany saccades was examined in Klein's first experiment. Subjects faced a computer screen and were told that on each trial, they would have to perform one of two tasks. In the saccade task, they were to move their eyes in a particular direction (for example, right) if an asterisk was presented on the screen. In the detection task, they were to release a response key if a dot brightened. The display consisted of three evenly spaced dots, one in the center and the other two falling 8° on either side of the center. After trial initiation, one of three events could occur: (1) the left or right dot brightened for 100 msec, (2) an asterisk replaced either the left or right dot, or (3) no change occurred, which constituted a catch trial. Note that this is not strictly a dual-task paradigm because subjects make only one response per trial. However, the important point is that they must prepare for both tasks because they do not know which one they will be performing until the display appears.

Consider the predictions of the oculomotor readiness theory. Suppose that the subject is instructed to favor the saccade task over the manual task, and is told to move to the right as soon as the asterisk is detected (remember that the asterisk can occur on either the left or right and, in both cases, signals a saccade to the right). They should be attending to the right before the trial begins because there is an oculomotor readiness to move to the right and this produces allocation of attention in this direction. Therefore, detection of the brightening of the dot (reflected in manual RTs) should be faster when it is occurs on the right side.

Contrary to the oculomotor readiness theory, manual detection latencies were the same regardless of their relationship to the direction of the saccade. Subjects were no faster at detecting a signal on the right side of the display when they were preparing a saccade in that direction than when they were instructed to saccade to the left. Single-task control conditions verified that when subjects were *instructed* to attend to the left or right in the absence of a saccade task, they showed the usual attention effects found previously in this paradigm (Posner, 1980), verifying that the detection task was sensitive to the direction of attention.

Although this result seems to offer a clear and simple test of the theory, there are several reasons to be cautious in accepting the conclusions. First, there were large delays in the speed of both responses in dual-task conditions compared to the single-task controls (approximately 90 msec for the saccade task and 125 msec for the manual task)[1]. If subjects were primarily

---

[1] A second difficulty is associated with the large delays of the manual response in dual-task conditions. Pashler (1989, 1994) has shown that the response to the second of two tasks presented in close temporal proximity is often delayed, relative to a single-task condition. The increase in second task RT appears to be due to a mechanism that is capable of selecting a single response at a time. Earlier processes in the second task can proceed in parallel with processing of the first task, but once the response selection stage is reached, processing must wait until response selection for the first task is completed. Notice that at some point, perceptual processes in the second task may be finished but a response cannot be selected until the response selection in the first task is finished. This "dead time" in the second task means that factors that slow perceptual processes down will not show up in second task RT because they spill over into the dead time. Therefore, manipulations, such as attention, which affect RT in single-task conditions, may not appear in dual-task conditions.

preparing the saccade task, it should have been delayed only a small amount or not at all (see Kowler, Anderson, Dosher, & Blaser, 1995, and Hoffman & Subramaniam, 1995 reviewed later in this section for evidence supporting this assertion). But notice that in the dual-task blocks, unlike the controls, one of two kinds of peripheral visual events could occur unpredictably: a brightening of the dot or an onset of the asterisk. Subjects may well have had to attend to the peripheral event in order to determine which signal had occurred. In single-task conditions, simple detection of any visual event in the periphery was enough to initiate a response. Therefore, it is possible that subjects were not prepared to make a saccade in a particular direction in dual-task trials but chose a strategy of first determining which task was required (manual or saccadic) before programming the appropriate response. Without this saccade preparation, the predictions of the oculo-motor readiness theory cannot be tested.

Second, the use of a peripheral visual event (the onset of the asterisk) to signal the subject to make a saccade would be expected to automatically attract attention to that location (Yantis, 1996). Therefore, even if subjects were preparing a saccade to the left location, and were attending to that location as part of the saccade preparation process, the onset of an asterisk on the right would essentially abolish this attentional set by reorienting attention to the right. The same difficulty holds for the second experiment which also failed to find any link between attention and saccades. Other investigators (e.g. Crawford & Mueller, 1992; Remington, 1980) have also used peripheral visual signals to indicate the direction of saccades. Even in cases where target detection does appear to be enhanced at the saccade goal, one can not conclude that attention normally precedes saccades. Such an enhancement effect of a peripheral visual signal would be expected even if subjects were not making a saccade and therefore is not relevant to the question of whether attention and saccades can be dissociated.

Evidence for a Role of Attention in Saccades.   The preceding analysis suggests several methodological requirements for research addressing this issue. First, it is probably best to signal the initiation of a saccade with a nonvisual signal. Visual signals will tend to draw attention automatically (see Yantis, this volume) and may disrupt the attentional allocation established by instructions. Second, subjects may adopt various strategies for combining the two tasks and this possibility needs to be assessed.

Shepard, Findlay, and Hockey (1986) used an improved methodology to study this issue. They used a central arrow cue pointing to a box on the left or right of fixation to indicate the target of the saccade, avoiding the capture effects associated with peripheral cues. Attention was manipulated by varying the probability of a target occurring in the left or right box. Thus, subjects could be instructed to move their eyes to the left while target probabilities favored attending to the right. In these conflict situations, subjects detected targets more quickly when they occurred in the saccade target location, not the position favored by the probability manipulation. When saccades were not required, the probability manipulation had the expected effect of speeding responses to signals on the probable side. Shepard et al. concluded that making a saccade requires that attention be allocated to the saccade target location. Although this experiment is an improvement over previous methods, it too has a flaw that suggests caution. The target was left on the screen until subjects responded, so that targets located in the direction of the saccade were foveated. Because average saccade latencies were shorter than manual RTs, at least part of the advantage for targets appearing in the direction of a saccade could have been due to faster processing of foveal signals compared to peripheral signals.

Hoffman and Subramaniam (1995) used the central cuing procedure of Shepard et al. together with short target durations to eliminate the target foveation problem. Their method is shown in Fig. 3.1. On dual-task trials, subjects were instructed to make a saccade to one of the four fixation boxes as soon as they heard a tone. The direction of the saccade was constant for the entire session. The saccade task was emphasized and subjects were

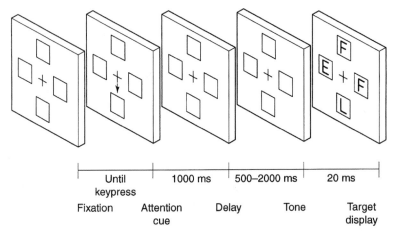

Until keypress	1000 ms	500–2000 ms	20 ms
Fixation	Attention cue	Delay	Tone	Target display

FIG. 3.1.   Procedure used by Hoffman and Subramaniam (1995) in Experiment 2. Subjects were to make an eye movement to a specified peripheral box on each trial. After trial initiation, they were presented with a central arrow cue (duration = 1000 msec) indicating the likely position of a target (*L* or *T*). After a variable warning interval (500–2000 msec) a tone was presented as a signal to initiate the saccade. 20 msec later a letter array was presented containing the target and three distractors. After completing the eye movement, subjects have to indicate which target had been presented. (From "Saccadic eye movements and visual selective attention" by J.E. Hoffman & B. Subramaniam, 1995, *Perception and Psychophysics, 57*, 787–795.) Reprinted with the kind permission of the Psychonomic Society, Inc.

encouraged to achieve saccade latencies comparable to those obtained in a control condition in which this task was performed alone. Subjects were able to do this, indicating that they were optimally prepared to make a saccade in the instructed direction at the beginning of each trial. Prior to each trial, they were also shown a central arrow pointing to one of the four boxes which indicated the likely position of a target letter. One of two targets (*L* or *T*) could occur and nontarget positions were filled with distractors (an *E* or an *F*). Subjects made their choice as to which target had been presented after the saccade. Target presentation was brief (14 msec) so that the letter display was gone by the time subjects made their eye movement.

The data are shown in Table 3.1, separated according to whether the target occurred in the location indicated by the cue (cue–target match) or the location corresponding to the saccade goal (saccade–target match). Also shown are data for a control condition in which subjects performed the detection task by itself. In the detection-only block, target detection was best in the cue–target match condition, indicating that subjects used the arrow to attend to the cued position with a resulting enhancement in target discrimination. In the dual-task condition, subjects sometimes faced a conflict. The arrow cue directed them to allocate their attention to one location while their saccades were directed to another. If visuospatial attention is required to execute a saccade, targets should be discriminated best when they occur at the location of the saccade goal and the arrow cue should be ineffective in directing attention. The data in Table 3.1 show this pattern. Targets were discriminated 13% better when they occurred in a location to which subjects were preparing to move their eyes. In contrast, the attention arrow was ineffective even though it continued to provide valid information about the likely location of the target (Schneider & Duebel, 1995 report similar results).

TABLE 3.1

Results from Experiment 2 of Hoffman and Subramaniam (1995)

	Detection-only Block	Dual-task Block	
		Saccade–Target Match	Saccade–Target Mismatch
Cue–Target Match	79.3	86.6	73.4
Cue–Target Mismatch	66.93	86.4	70.4

Percent correct target discrimination in the detection-only and dual-task blocks. On saccade–target match trials, the target was located at the goal position for the saccade. On cue–target match trials, the target was located at the position indicated by the central arrow cue. (From "Saccadic eye movements and visual selective attention" by J.E. Hoffman & B. Subramaniam, 1995, *Perception and Psychophysics, 57,* 787–795.)

Subjects did not simply ignore the arrow cue indicating the likely target location. Saccade latencies were slightly shorter when the directions of attention and saccade agreed than when they disagreed, suggesting that subjects were allocating some attention to the arrow cue. This experiment probably represents one point on a trade-off function relating saccade latency and target discrimination performance. Emphasis on the saccade task resulted in attentional allocation that was dominated by the location of the saccade goal, and saccades were only slightly delayed when there was a conflict between the two tasks. Increasing attention to the target discrimination task should be accompanied by increases in performance on that task at a cost of slower eye movements.

Kowler et al. (1995) have recently evaluated the nature of this trade-off function in terms of the *attention operating characteristic* or AOC (Sperling & Dosher, 1986; Sperling & Melchner, 1978). In their experiment, subjects were presented with a circular array of eight letters and a simultaneous central arrow cue pointing to one of the eight locations. The arrow cue indicated the goal of the saccade that was to be initiated at display onset. Throughout the block of trials subjects were to report the identity of the letter occurring at a fixed position in the display. The saccade arrow sometimes agreed with this location, but on *conflict* trials it indicated a different position. In the *random* saccade condition, the cue indicating the direction of the saccade changed from trial to trial. In the *fixed* saccade condition, the arrow pointed to the same location for all trials in a block. In the latter condition, subjects knew both the locations of the letter target and saccade goal prior to target onset. If it is possible to attend to one location and make an eye movement to another, this condition should provide the optimal conditions for its occurrence.

In different blocks of trials, subjects were given instructions emphasizing either the saccade or letter task. For example, in one condition, subjects were instructed to emphasize the letter task, prolonging the saccade latency only as much as needed to achieve perfect identification performance. In another condition, saccade latencies were to be kept as short as possible. In a third condition, both tasks were to be performed together with equal emphasis. Performance of each task was also evaluated in single-task control conditions. Evaluating performance in each condition as task emphasis is changed should reveal the nature of the trade-off that exists when subjects make a saccade to one location while trying to attend to another.

The results are shown in Fig. 3.2, which graphically shows the trade-off in performance between the two tasks. The dotted rectangles provide a reference for evaluating dual-task interference. Points located on the axes represent single-task performance levels. For example, points on the y axis represent performance in the letter identification task when subjects are not required to make saccades. Similarly, the open rectangle on the x axis

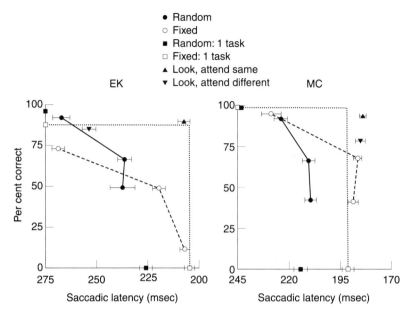

FIG. 3.2.   Results from Experiment 4 of Kowler et al. (1995). (From "The role of attention in the programming of saccades" by E. Kowler, E. Anderson, B. Dosher, & E. Blaser, 1995, *Vision Research, 35*, 1897–1916.) Reprinted with kind permission of Elsevier Science Ltd, The Boulevard, Langford Lane, Kidlington OX5 1GB, UK.

represents the average saccade latency when letter identification was not required. The intersection of these points (upper right corner of graph) represents the "independence point"; the expected dual-task performance if both tasks can be performed together as well as each task is performed alone. If the two tasks are incompatible, we should see dual-task interference, in which performance on one or both tasks is reduced compared to their single-task levels. This would be reflected in dual-task data that lie "inside" the rectangle defined by the single-task performance levels. Each condition in the experiment (*fixed* or *random*) produces a set of points that constitute an *AOC function*.

Several notable features of the AOCs can be seen in Fig. 3.2. For both subjects, the AOCs in both the random and fixed conditions lie inside the rectangle defining "interference-free" dual-task performance. For example, consider the *random* condition for subject EK (solid circles). The upper left point represents performance when the perceptual task (letter identification) was emphasized, and indeed accuracy is close to that achieved when this was the sole task. The saccade latency here is about 265 msec. In contrast, when the saccade task is emphasized, letter performance drops by 43% and saccade latency is improved by about 30 msec. This trade-off holds for both conditions (*random* and *fixed*) for both subjects. The nature of this trade-off is illuminated by two additional observations. In separate blocks, subjects were given a "final opportunity" to try to perform both tasks together as well as they were performed separately. Subjects were encouraged to try to combine both tasks to achieve performance comparable to single-task conditions. The upward-pointing triangle represents performance in this block when the letter and saccade goal were in the same location ("look, attend same"). The downward-pointing triangle shows corresponding performance when these locations were different ("look, attend different"). The "same" condition leads to joint performance close to the independence point. When different locations were to be attended, performance of one or the other task suffered. This shows that dual-task interference is not due to some general inability to do both tasks together, because subjects were quite good at combining tasks when attention and saccades were to be directed to the same location. The difficulty appears to be due to competition for a specific limited resource, a spatial attention mechanism that can be allocated to one location at a time.

One additional aspect of the AOCs shown in Fig. 3.2 is striking. Notice that as the emphasis is shifted from favoring the saccade task to equal emphasis on both tasks, there is a substantial improvement in letter identification with little or no cost in terms of saccade latency (the AOCs in this region appear as vertical lines). In other words, there are diminishing returns of allocating attention to the saccade task. Some attention is beneficial but more does not help. In contrast, the letter task seems quite sensitive to attention, with large changes in performance accompanying each change in task emphasis. Kowler et al. account for these features in terms of a temporal model of the effects of attention on saccades. Suppose that there is a critical period, late in the fixation in which attention plays an important role in saccade generation. For example, attention may have to be switched to the saccade goal just before a "go" signal is issued to initiate saccade execution. Attending to the saccade goal before this critical period does not produce any benefits in terms of saccade latency, and reduces the discriminability of information at other locations. When subjects are trying to do both tasks together (equal emphasis condition), a good strategy would be to keep attention on the relevant letter location until the critical period for saccade initiation arrives, at which time attention would be switched to the saccade goal. Increasing emphasis on the saccade task might cause subjects to start attending to the saccade goal prior to the critical period, with a resulting loss in letter identification accuracy and little improvement in saccade latency.

Summary.   Let us pause at this point and try to draw some conclusions about the relationship between visual attention and saccadic eye movements. The section on attention and reading pointed to two important conclusions. First, saccades appear to be guided by information in the periphery of the fixated word. Either the word's physical characteristics, its identity, or both help the reader program the saccade to fall on an optimal viewing position in the word. Second, the data were suggestive that readers divide their attention between the fixation and the saccade goal and consequently, continue to process information about the fixated and peripheral words throughout fixation.

Research with the dual-task paradigm shows that the link between attention and saccades is mandatory. Attention must be allocated to the saccade goal at some point prior to saccade execution. The time course of attentional allocation is not known but Kowler et al. (1995) offer an interesting speculation. They suggest that attention must be shifted to the saccade goal during a critical time period that may occur late in fixation. In addition, they speculate that this attention shift will initiate a saccade only if it is accompanied by a "go signal"; otherwise the eye is inhibited from moving. If this go signal can be set to trigger automatically with shifts of attention, one might account for the smooth and effortless coupling of attention and saccades that seems to characterize many ordinary activities such as reading.

This model is similar to the divided attention model in that both models propose that a shift of attention to the saccade goal is one of the critical events that triggers the execution of a saccade. Each model also faces a difficulty. In the Kowler et al. model, how does attention "know" where to shift? In other words, what mechanism finds the critical location for the upcoming saccade and preserves that information until saccade execution? This question is even more puzzling in the case of reading, where there is no attention cue to indicate the landing point of the eye; instead this must be gleaned from various aspects of the peripheral word, such as its identity and length. Is this information delivered by "preattentive mechanisms" or is attention allocated to the periphery for this purpose? The parallel model proposes that attention is divided between the fixation point and the periphery throughout the fixation interval. Saccade initiation would correspond to a rapid shift of attention from fixation to the peripheral location being indexed by a partial allocation of attention. The problem here is that only certain shifts of attention should produce saccades and it is clear that subjects can shift attention to different locations in the visual field without an accompanying saccade (Yantis, this volume).

Clearly, the parallel model requires an additional mechanism that acts as a switch, allowing a shift of attention to produce a saccade in one case but not another, similar to the "go signal" proposed by Kowler et al. A possible candidate for this mechanism is to be found in the idea of "attentional disengagement" (Posner, 1995). Posner (1995) suggests that before attention can be switched to a new location it must be actively disengaged from its current location. It may be that subjects maintain fixation by engaging attention on the fixated object. The swift "all or none" allocation of attention that triggers saccades may be possible only when attention has been disengaged from its current focus. Interestingly, the phenomenon of *express saccades* offers direct support for this conjecture.

Express Saccades

Express saccades have a mean latency in the range of 100 msec compared to about 225 msec for "normal saccades" (Fischer & Weber, 1993). Express saccades are found in the so-called *gap paradigm* (Saslow, 1967) in which the fixation stimulus is turned off at various times prior to the appearance of a peripheral target which serves as the goal for the saccade. According to Fischer and Weber, the termination of the fixation point allows subjects to disengage attention before the appearance of the target. Once attention is disengaged, the appearance of the peripheral target produces a shift of attention and an express saccade. It is the elimination of the "disengage operation" from the normal saccadic RT which results in the short latency characteristic of express saccades. Fischer and Weber (1993) review a large number of findings supporting the attentional disengagement theory. Their view has, however, generated a vigorous critique. Some investigators have failed to observe express saccades in the gap paradigm (Kingstone & Klein, 1993a). Others have suggested that removing the fixation point provides a warning signal that speeds RTs according to well-known principles governing all speeded reactions (Reuter-Lorenz, Hughes, & Fendrich, 1991). Still others have accepted that the gap paradigm does result in faster RTs over and above warning effects but have pointed out that there is little or no evidence of a role for attention in producing these effects (Kingstone & Klein, 1993b)

The research presented earlier showing a relationship between attention and saccades is consistent with the occurrence of the gap effect and the interpretation in terms of attentional disengagement. The notion that disengagement must precede a change in the direction of attention is an important component of Posner's (1980) theory of orienting. He suggests that a peripheral signal triggers a disengagement of attention from a fixation stimulus, movement of attention to the new stimulus, and a subsequent engagement at the new location. Duncan, Ward, and Shapiro (1994) have recently shown that the time to disengage attention (what they call "dwell time") can be surprisingly long, in some of their experiments as long as 500 msec. (see Hoffman, 1978, 1979 for similar arguments).[2]

The preceding arguments suggest that time to disengage attention from fixation is at least a reasonable explanation for the reduction in saccadic latency that is associated with removal of fixation prior to onset of the

---

[2] Dwell time has been studied by sequentially presenting subjects with two shapes to be recognized. It can be estimated by progressively increasing the delay of the second figure until it no longer suffers interference from the first. Dwell time probably includes the time required to identify the first figure as well as to disengage attention.

target. What is needed is some direct evidence that these same conditions also result in rapid shifts of *attention* to the target, otherwise we cannot be sure that attention is involved in the gap effect. Mackeben and Nakayama (1993) provided such a demonstration. Their paradigm is shown in Fig. 3.3. Subjects viewed a central fixation point which in the gap condition went off 200 msec prior to the appearance of a circular cue in the periphery. The cue

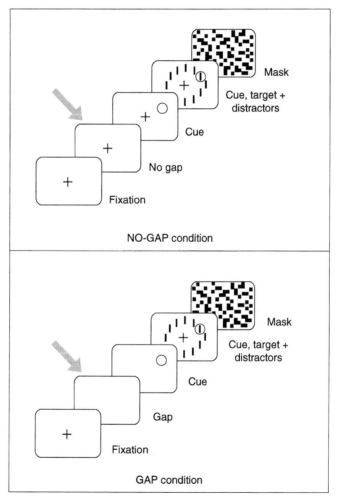

FIG. 3.3. Procedure used by Mackeben and Nakayama, 1993. In the no-gap condition the fixation cross remained on throughout the trial. In the gap condition, the fixation was removed prior to the appearance of the cue (a circle). The cue indicated the position of a target (vernier acuity line) embedded in distractors (vertical lines). (From "Express attentional shifts" by M. Mackeben & K. Nakayama, 1993, *Vision Research, 33*, 87.) Reprinted with kind permission of Elsevier Science Ltd, The Boulevard, Langford Lane, Kidlington OX5 1GB, UK.

was followed at variable intervals by a display containing a target in the cued position together with 17 distractors. The target was a line with a vernier offset while the distractors were vertical lines. The subjects' task was to determine the direction of offset in the target. The target display was followed by a mask and the measure of interest was discrimination accuracy. In the no-gap condition, the fixation stimulus remained on throughout the trial.

Results are shown in Fig. 3.4. It can be seen that providing a gap before the onset of the cue improved performance with short cue–target SOAs, presumably because attention was in a "disengaged state" and could be quickly captured by the cue. Additional experiments varied the gap duration while holding cue–target SOA constant and found that the optimal gap was approximately 200 msec, which agrees with results by Fischer and colleagues for the optimal express saccade gap. In addition, a variety of control conditions ruled out the possibility that the gap effect was due to warning effects. This is a fairly direct demonstration that a gap has the predicted effect on the visual attention system. A more direct approach would be to try to measure attention shifts in the gap paradigm when subjects are actually making saccades, much as in the dual-task experiments reviewed earlier. In the meantime, debate continues on the occurrence and meaning of express saccades (see Kingstone & Klein, 1993a, 1993b; Reuter-Lorenz et al., 1991; Tam & Stelmach, 1993)

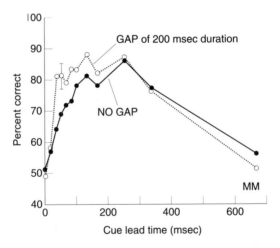

FIG. 3.4.   Results from Experiment 1 of Mackeben and Nakayama (1993). Percent correct discrimination of the target as a function of cue lead time for the gap and no-gap conditions. (From "Express attentional shifts" by M. Mackeben & K. Nakayama, 1993, *Vision Research*, *33*, 87.) Reprinted with kind permission of Elsevier Science Ltd, The Boulevard, Langford Lane, Kidlington OX5 1GB, UK.

The Premotor Theory of Attention

The research reviewed to this point shows clearly that spatial attention is a critical component of the programming and execution of saccadic eye movements. There are many possible mechanisms by which this link could be achieved. For example, there may be a "general" spatial attention mechanism that is capable of indexing locations in visual space. This mechanism can be used to provide coordinates to any system that needs spatial location information including perception, reaching, locomotion, eye movements, etc. This model is consistent with the finding that there are cells in the parietal cortex that increase their firing rate when an animal attends to a location independent of the task being carried out (Wurtz, Goldberg, & Robinson, 1980). In this model, there is no special relationship between visual attention and the eye movement system.

An alternative view is illustrated by the oculomotor readiness hypothesis proposed by Klein (1980) and a related theory, the *premotor theory of attention* proposed by Rizzolatti et al. (e.g. Rizzolatti, Riggio, Dascola, & Umiltà, 1987; Rizzolatti, Riggio, & Sheliga, 1994). According to these theories, there is no response-independent representation of space being activated by an attentional mechanism. Instead there are many different representations of space, each responsible for particular motor actions such as reaching, eye movements, etc. Attending involves activating motor routines in the area appropriate for the response system being employed.

Because of the close association between visual attention and saccades (we usually look at the object of our attention) visual attention should be strongly related to activity in those brain mechanisms involved in eye movements. In particular, these theories hold that shifts of attention are accomplished by preparing an eye movement program to execute a saccade to the attended location via activity in oculomotor areas such as the superior colliculus (SC). The SC is a subcortical brain area that has both visual and motor functions and is particularly important in generating saccades. For example, the SC has indirect outputs to the motor areas that actually move the eyes and stimulation of SC cells can produce saccades. It also has cells that are visual rather than motor. These cells receive inputs from the retina along a pathway separate from the set of neurons that proceed from the retina through the geniculate to the visual cortex. In addition, the SC and several areas of cortex are heavily interconnected, allowing for two-way communication.

This anatomical arrangement suggests the possibility that the visual cells in the SC could perform certain visual functions, such as detecting the sudden onset of a stimulus in the visual field, and directly program a saccade to that location. In cases where saccades are generated by an intention to move the eyes to a location without any abrupt onsets, cortical mechanisms could send the necessary information to the SC so that, once again, an appropriate saccade program could be compiled. Finally, when subjects are attending to a location in the absence of a saccade, information may still be sent to the SC, resulting in a saccade program but, in this case, the program is inhibited from being executed. The preparation of this program, however, enhances the sensitivity of purely visual cells in the SC, perhaps by feedback from the motor neurons to the visual cells. Presumably, it is the enhanced response of these visual cells that produces enhanced detection and identification of attended objects, although this enhancement would also have to be fed back to the visual cortex, because SC cells would not, by themselves, be able to accomplish processes such as object recognition, which are affected by visual attention.

As we have seen, recent experiments (Hoffman & Subramaniam, 1995; Kowler et al., 1995) have shown that the two predictions derived from the premotor hypothesis are supported: saccades to a location entail attending to that location, and attention to an area speeds saccades to that area. It was not necessary, however, to assume that attending *without* saccade generation involved any activity specifically connected with saccades (although this is certainly a possibility). This suggests that one needs to look for other aspects of behavior that might be uniquely related to the oculomotor system and see whether these hold true of covert orienting as well. The *meridian effect* has been proposed as one such signature of oculomotor activity (Rizzolatti et al., 1987).

Rizzolatti et al. (1987) presented subjects with a linear string of four boxes (oriented either vertically or horizontally) so that two boxes were located in each visual field. A central cue pointed to one of the boxes, indicating the likely position of a target flash to be detected. Subjects were to press a key as soon as they detected the appearance of the target regardless of its location. The focus of the analysis was on the costs associated with invalid trials, that is trials in which the target was presented in an uncued box. Rizzolatti et al. found that costs were greater when the invalid position was in the opposite hemifield from the cue, compared to the same-hemifield case, even when distance between attended and unattended locations was held constant across the two conditions. According to the authors, target detection was especially slow when attention had to cross either the vertical or horizontal meridian to locate the target. Note that the meridians separate the visual field into left vs right and top vs bottom. The muscles that move the eyes are also arranged in pairs so that one set moves the eyes left and an opposing set moves them right. An oculomotor program needs to specify both the direction (left vs right, for example) and amplitude of the movement (how far left or right).

Consider the case in which subjects are cued to attend to a location in the left visual field. Attending is accomplished by compiling a saccade program specifying the direction and amplitude parameters required to actually move the eyes to the attended location. On invalid trials, in which the target does not occur at the cued position, this saccade program must be modified so that its parameters reflect the new location. In the case of invalidly cued targets occurring in the right visual field, the direction parameter must be changed, whereas in the case of same-hemifield targets, it is the amplitude that must be modified. There is evidence that saccades are programmed in a hierarchical fashion, with direction being specified first, followed by an amplitude parameter (Becker & Jurgens, 1979). Once programmed, changes in direction require a new program to be constructed from scratch, whereas a change in amplitude requires only a change in a parameter. In the Rizzolatti et al. (1987) study, invalid locations in the same visual field would involve changes in amplitude (which might be accomplished quickly) whereas crossing a meridian involves a change in direction and hence a change in the entire program (which might take longer than a change in a parameter value). This scheme provides a clever explanation of the meridian effect based on changes in saccade programming.

One additional finding regarding the meridian effect is relevant. It is only observed with endogenous cues; costs associated with exogenous cues do not show a meridian effect (Reuter-Lorenz & Fendrich, 1992). According to Rizzolatti et al. (1995), this is compatible with their theory. Exogenous cues may exert their effects by directly stimulating cells in the SC and causing a saccade program to be set up in a "wholistic" manner; that is, the exogenous cue can program a saccade to its location without separately specifying direction and amplitude. Therefore, the costs associated with modifying such a program (i.e. constructing a new one directed to the location of the invalidly cued target) should be independent of same vs different hemifields. Although this explanation might seem *post hoc* and convenient, there is some evidence that exogenously cued saccades are programmed in a "wholistic" fashion compared to the hierarchical specification of direction and amplitude associated with endogenously cued saccades (Abrams & Jonides, 1988).

Reuter-Lorenz and Fendrich (1992) provided an alternative explanation of the meridian effect and its dependence on exogenous cues. They pointed out that exogenous cues tend to produce fairly narrow attentional fields compared to endogenous cues (Shepard & Mueller, 1989). This makes some sense in that exogenous cues specify the attended area "directly" whereas endogenous cues (such as an arrow pointing to another location), require the observer to estimate where attention should be allocated (Logan, 1995). This estimation process would be expected to be approximate and error-prone. Therefore central cues would tend to activate large areas and, if the size of these areas was limited by anatomical divisions such as horizontal and vertical meridians (Hughes & Zimba, 1985; but see Egly & Homa, 1991 for qualifications on this result), the meridian effect would be obtained for central or endogenous cues. Notice that in this explanation, the costs associated with invalid cues are not due to realignments of attention, but rather the amount of enhancement that unattended signals receive. Exogenous cues, which produce a tight focus of attention on the cued area, will not produce enhancement of large areas and therefore will not lead to meridian effects.

Summary.   Findings reviewed earlier showing that saccades are preceded by shifts of attention are compatible with predictions of the premotor theory. Such predictions are not unique to this theory; they are also compatible with the assumption of a central attentional control mechanism that sends spatial coordinates to the saccade generation system. One does not need to add the further assumption that shifts of attention in the absence of saccades necessarily involved the saccade system. A similar situation holds for phenomena such as the meridian effect which can be accounted for by both theories.

More direct tests of the premotor theory would examine whether damage to the SC results in impaired covert orienting as well as impaired eye movements. Rafal et al. (1988) investigated this possibility by examining patients with progressive supranuclear palsy, a degenerative disorder that attacks the superior colliculus (SC), among other structures. These patients displayed a deficit in making voluntary saccades, particularly in the vertical direction. Rafal et al. found a similar deficit in shifting attention in the vertical direction in response to exogenous cues, suggesting a common role for the SC in exogenous orienting and saccades. Rafal, Smith, Krantz, Cohen, and Brennan (1990) studied a group of hemianopic patients who were functionally blind in one hemifield due to destruction of part of their striate cortex. The retinotectal pathway leading to the SC is intact in these patients and we might expect that orienting to exogenous cues might also be intact. Rafal et al. demonstrated that this was the case by presenting a saccade target in their good field together with a visual signal in the blind field. Although these subjects were unaware of the signal in their blind field, it slowed their saccade to the signal in their good field, probably because it competed with the target for exogenously triggered attention. These two experiments together make a strong case for the proposition that the geniculostriate pathway may play a key role in mediating awareness of visual stimuli while the older retinotectal pathway, which includes the SC, plays a role in orienting to exogenous signals. Desimone, Wessinger, Thomas, and Schneider (1989) directly tested this proposition by showing that focal lesions in the SC of monkeys produced deficits in covert orienting to stimuli occurring in the receptive fields of the lesioned cells (see also Gattass & Desimone, 1992).

This suggests that, as the premotor readiness hypothesis predicts (Rizzolotti et al., 1987), brain structures directly concerned with saccade generation may also be important in some aspects of covert orienting in the absence of eye movements. However, this appears to be true only for exogenous cuing. There is no evidence that endogenously directed attention depends on the SC. The claim that the SC is involved in orienting to exogenous cues but not endogenous cues is supported by the phenomenon of inhibition of return which we review in the next section.

Inhibition of Return

Exogenous cues produce an initial enhancement of information at the cued location, followed a few hundred msec later by a period of inhibition in which detection of visual signals is impaired. Posner and Cohen (1984) called this phenomenon *inhibition of return* (IOR). They suggested that attention is initially drawn to the location of the exogenous cue and then withdrawn after the contents of the location have been determined. It is this withdrawal of attention that generates IOR and it represents a bias against *attending* to the same location more than once within some time period. Such a mechanism would be useful in visual search, for example, where having searched a location, one should avoid immediately searching it again.

The inhibition that follows withdrawal of attention from a location increases the latency of both manual and saccade responses. A close link between IOR and saccade programming is suggested by the finding that IOR occurs following exogenous cues regardless of the task; endogenous cues produce IOR only when the subject prepares or executes a saccade to the attended location (Rafal, Calabresi, Brennan, & Sciolto, 1989). This difference in susceptibility to IOR has been taken as evidence that exogenous and endogenous attention may be mediated by different mechanisms (Klein et al. 1992). The findings are consistent with the claim that exogenous cues automatically initiate saccade programming in the superior colliculus. Endogenous orienting does not invariably produce saccade programming but can when this is the appropriate response.

What is the basis for IOR? Abrams and Dobkin (1994) considered two different loci for the IOR effect. The slowing of signal detection at previously attended locations could be the result of inhibition of early perceptual processing at the previously attended position, or it could be due to effects on the response system. They separated these different contributions with the following method. The subject's attention was attracted to a peripheral location by a brief flash and then it was drawn back to fixation by another transient. Withdrawal of attention from the peripheral location should have produced an IOR for that location. This was tested by requiring subjects to make a saccade, either to the previously cued position or to a new one. The direction of the saccade was indicated either by an arrow at fixation (endogenous cue) or a peripheral flash (exogenous cue). The endogenous cue does not involve presenting a signal at the peripheral location, so any inhibition found here would be attributed to the response system rather than perceptual processes. In contrast, the exogenous cue involved both perceiving the peripheral signal as well as responding. They found a small IOR for the endogenous cue, consistent with a role for purely response level processes, and a larger effect for the exogenous cue, indicating an additional contribution to IOR by factors important for signal detection.

There is also evidence that part of the IOR is defined in "object-based" coordinates rather than retinotopic or environment-based coordinates. Tipper, Driver, and Weaver (1991) had subjects view two boxes on either side of a fixation box. Attention was drawn to one box by an exogenous cue (a brightening of the box) and drawn back to fixation by another transient. The two peripheral boxes were then rotated about the fixation point by 180°. A signal appeared randomly in one of the two boxes and subjects had to press a key as soon as they detected it. They were slower in detecting signals in the *box* that had been cued even though the uncued box was at the same *retinal* location as the previous cue. Apparently, some aspect of IOR is "attached" to the object and moves with it to new locations (see also Tipper, Weaver, Jerreat, & Burak, 1994)

Abrams and Dobkin (1994) showed that when a previously cued object moves to a new location, subjects are slower to respond to exogenous signals that are part of the object. In contrast, if they are cued to move their eyes to the box by a central arrow, there is no IOR. They concluded that the IOR associated with the saccade system was defined in retinal or environmental coordinates and that IOR associated with stimulus detection was defined in object-based coordinates. They took this as supporting evidence for Klein's (1980) position that selection mechanisms for saccades are not dependent on perceptual attention. However, the perceptual IOR in these experiments could be due to object perception processes that are *location-invariant* and do not reflect the operation of visual attention. That is, there is no evidence that the slower detection of the signal in object-based coordinates is particularly due to difficulties in *attending to the location* of the object. A better test would be to see if other signals that are nearby the object but not part of it are also impaired, as would be expected if there is a difficulty in *spatial attention*. There is nothing in the object-based IOR effect that shows it involves any location-specific processes at all.

Summary.   The inhibition of return phenomenon is compatible with the claim that a single spatial attention mechanism is important for both perceptual processes and the programming/execution of saccades. There appears to be a perceptual component of IOR that is object-centered and does not specifically affect the saccade system. A second component of IOR occurs when attention is cued exogenously, and reveals itself in longer latency saccades to the previously attended location. The close relationship between exogenous cuing and the saccade system suggests that exogenous cues may directly activate local saccade programs in the superior colliculus. Saccade programming can also be activated by endogenous processes but only when the subject intends to make a saccade. This program, whether executed or not, slows down subsequent saccades to the same location. In addition, detection of signals associated with the cued object are inhibited and this inhibition moves with the object to new locations.

ATTENTION AND PURSUIT EYE MOVEMENTS

Saccades are not the only variety of eye movement and although they have been the subject of most of the studies on attention and eye movements, there has been important work on pursuit and vergence eye movements as well. Pursuit or smooth eye movements serve to keep a moving target stable on the retina, reducing image blur and maintaining the position of the object in the fovea. Because the world will usually contain a variety of moving and stationary stimuli at any given moment, observers need a mechanism for choosing which stimulus will be pursued and which ignored. Similar to the case with saccades, visual attention provides such a mechanism. Kowler, Van Der Steen, Taminga, and Collewijn (1984) presented observers with two identical random dot patterns, one moving and the other stationary. In different conditions, observers were instructed to attend to the moving or stationary pattern. Results showed that the behavior of the eye (moving or stationary) was determined almost completely by the attended pattern, demonstrating that the smooth oculomotor subsystem receives an input from a voluntary attention system.

Later work by Kowler and colleagues (Khurana & Kowler, 1987; Kowler & Zingale, 1985) was aimed at determining whether the attentional mechanism affecting pursuit eye movements was the same one involved in enhancing perception of attended areas. Khurana and Kowler (1987) presented subjects with four horizontal strings of letters moving across the screen from left to right at two different velocities. Subjects were instructed to pursue two rows having a particular velocity. At a point midway in their trajectory, the letters in all four rows were briefly replaced by a target array containing two digits, one in an attended row (the row being pursued) and one in an unattended row. Subjects were to report the identity and locations of both digits. Search performance was strongly influenced by pursuit, with target detection accuracy about 35% better for the target rows than the unattended "background" rows. Of course, this result might be due to the relatively stable retinal image in the case of pursued letters as opposed to the retinal smear that might accrue to background letters. The authors reject this possibility by considering those cases where tracking was less than perfect, resulting in retinal velocity for attended letters as well. Even when retinal velocity was comparable for target and background rows, attended targets maintained a substantial edge over background rows.

In subsequent experiments, subjects were instructed to try to pay attention to one row, e.g. the slow one, while tracking the fast one. Subjects were unable to fully comply with this instruction, as performance on the attended row was not as good as it was when the row was also the target for pursuit eye movements. Subjects could improve their target detection on the "attended" but untracked rows only by sacrificing pursuit performance on the other row. These results suggest that there is a single visual attention mechanism shared by pursuit eye movements and perceptual tasks.

ATTENTION AND VERGENCE EYE MOVEMENTS

Vergence eye movements occur when both eyes converge to fixate a near target or diverge to fixate a far target. The fixated stimulus will fall on corresponding retinal points (the fovea of each eye) while objects located closer and further from fixation will have disparate retinal images. This disparity, in turn, is processed by the binocular cells of the visual cortex and leads to a perception of depth. As many objects located at various depths are available to serve as targets for a vergence eye movement, the observer must be able to choose the target voluntarily. It seems likely that visual attention is the required mechanism, especially as attention can be deployed to different locations in stereo space (Hoffman & Mueller, 1994).

Erkelens and Collewijn (1991) verified that observers have voluntary control over which stimulus will control vergence. In their experiment, observers fixated a long vertical bar which was flanked on either side by shorter vertical bars, one having crossed disparity (appearing in front of the fixation) and the other, uncrossed disparity (appearing behind fixation). Image stabilization was employed so that eye movements did not change the position of images in either eye. Subjects were instructed to change fixation to either the left or right bar and their vergence changed according to the binocular disparity of the attended bar. Notice here that vergence changes are being initiated by the depth of the attended stimulus and are not due to changes in positions of the retinal images, as they have been stabilized. Thus, the vergence eye movement system, like the saccadic and pursuit systems, appears to be under control of a voluntary attentional system which determines the targets for these various eye movements. It remains to be shown that vergence eye movements are accompanied by an enhancement in perceptual processing of the vergence target.

CONCLUSIONS

The results reviewed here support the claim that visuospatial attention plays an important role in the programming and execution of eye movements including saccades, smooth pursuit, and vergence movements. Eye movements are not random but, instead, are guided by information extracted from the periphery prior to movement. Spatial attention appears to be the mechanism providing this guidance. The evidence favors the parsimonious view that there is a single covert orienting mechanism responsible for both perceptual enhancement and programming of eye movements. This evidence comes in several different guises including: the asymmetric perceptual span in reading, the perceptual enhancement of information at the goal of a saccade, express saccades, and inhibition of return. The details of exactly how attention is used to guide the eye, however, are a still a matter of speculation. Here is a short list of issues still outstanding: What peripheral information is used to guide the eye: spaces, word identity, or both? When is this information accessed by attention? When is attention shifted to the saccade goal? How is the location of the saccade goal maintained until saccade generation?

Attentional guidance of eye movements may also help explain how perception and action are coordinated during overt orienting, For example, Currie et al. (1995) recently reported that changes in some of the details of a complex scene that occur during a saccade often go unnoticed. The exception is when such changes involve regions of the scene that are the target of a saccade. They suggest that scene details in the region of the saccade goal are attended and stored in short-term visual memory and are then available for comparison to the perceptual information available at fixation following the saccade. This comparison mechanism offers a novel explanation for the stability of perception during eye movements (McConkie & Currie, 1996). As long as the eye generally lands in the attended area and the world does not move during saccades, the contents of short-term visual memory and current fixation will match. Thus, attention plays a role in guiding the eye to informative areas of a scene, as well as in integrating the separate "snapshots" provided by a moving eye.

ACKNOWLEDGEMENTS

Preparation of this chapter was supported by a grant from the McDonnell-Pew Program in Cognitive Neuroscience. I am grateful to Lou French for helpful comments on an earlier draft of this chapter.

REFERENCES

Abrams, R.A., & Dobkin, R.S. (1994). Inhibition of return: Effects of attentional cueing on eye movement latencies. *Journal of Experimental Psychology: Human Perception and Performance, 20*, 467–477.

Abrams, R.A., & Jonides, J. (1988). Programming saccadic eye movements. *Journal of Experimental Psychology: Human Perception and Performance, 14*, 428–443.

Abrams, S.G., & Zuber, B.L. (1971). Some temporal characteristics of information processing during reading. *Reading Research Quarterly, 8*, 40–51.

Becker, W. (1991). Saccades. In R.H.S. Carpenter (Ed.), *Eye movements* (pp.95–137), Boca Raton, FL: Macmillan.

Becker, W., & Jurgens, R. (1979). An analysis of the saccadic system by means of double step stimuli. *Vision Research, 19*, 967–983.

Blanchard, H.E., McConkie, G.W., Zola, D., & Wolverton, G.S. (1984). Time course of visual information utilization during fixations in reading. *Journal of Experimental Psychology: Human Perception and Performance, 10*, 75–89.

Crawford, T.D., & Mueller, H.J. (1992). Spatial and temporal effects of spatial attention on human saccadic eye movements. *Vision Research, 32*, 293–304.

Crowder, R.G. (1982). *The psychology of reading.* New York: Oxford University Press.

Currie, C., McConkie, G.W., Carlson-Radvansky, L.A., & Irwin, D.E. (1995). *Maintaining visual stability across saccades: Role of the saccade target object.* Technical Report UIUC-BI-HPP-95-01. The Beckman Institute, University of Illinois, Champaign, IL.

Desimone, R., Wessinger, M., Thomas, L., & Schneider, W. (1989). Effects of deactivation of lateral pulvinar or superior colliculus on the ability to selectively attend to a visual stimulus. *Society of Neuroscience Abstracts, 15*, 162.

Duncan, J., Ward, R., & Shapiro, K. (1994). Direct measurement of attentional dwell time in human vision. *Nature, 369*, 313–315.

Egly, R., & Homa, D. (1991). Reallocation of visual attention. *Journal of Experimental Psychology: Human Perception and Performance, 17*, 142–159.

Epelboim, J., Booth, J.R., & Steinman, R.M. (1994). Reading unspaced text: Implications for theories of eye movements. *Vision Research, 34*, 1735–1766.

Epelboim, J., Booth, J.R., & Steinman, R.M. (1996). Much ado about nothing: The place of space in text. *Vision Research, 36*, 465–470.

Eriksen, C.W., & Hoffman, J.E. (1972). Temporal and spatial characteristics of select encoding from visual displays. *Perception and Psychophysics, 12*, 201–204.

Eriksen, C.W., & Hoffman, J.E. (1973). The extent of processing of noise elements during selecting encoding from visual displays. *Perception and Psychophysics, 14*, 156–160.

Erkelens, C.J., & Collewijn, H. (1991). Control of vergence: Gating among disparity inputs by voluntary target selection. *Experimental Brain Research, 87*, 671–678.

Fischer, B., & Weber, H. (1993). Express saccades and visual attention. *Behavioral and Brain Sciences, 16*, 553–567.

Gattass, R., & Desimone, R. (1992). Stimulation of the superior colliculus (SC) shifts the focus of attention in the macaque. *Society for Neuroscience Abstracts, 18*, 703.

Helmholtz, H. (1909/1962). *Treatise on physiological optics (3rd edn.).* [J.P.C. Southall (Ed.).] New York: Dover.

Henderson, J.M. (1992). Visual attention and eye movement control. In K. Rayner (Ed.), *Eye movements and visual cognition* (pp.260–283). New York: Springer-Verlag.

Henderson, J.M., & Ferreira, F. (1990). Effects of foveal processing difficulty on the perceptual span in reading: Implications for attention and eye movement control. *Journal of Experimental Psychology: Learning, Memory, and Cognition, 16*, 417–429.

Henderson, J.M., Pollatsek, A., & Rayner, K. (1989). Covert visual attention and extrafoveal information use during object identification. *Perception & Psychophysics, 45*, 196–208.

Hoffman, J.E. (1975). Hierarchical stages in the processing of visual information. *Perception and Psychophysics, 18*, 348–354.

Hoffman, J.E. (1978). Search through a sequentially presented visual display. *Perception and Psychophysics, 23*, 1–11.

Hoffman, J.E. (1979). A two-stage model of visual search. *Perception and Psychophysics, 25*, 319–327.

Hoffman, J.E., & Mueller, S. (1994, November). *An in-depth look at attention.* Paper presented at the 35th annual meeting of the Psychonomic Society, St. Louis, MO.

Hoffman, J.E., & Nelson, B. (1981). Spatial selectivity in visual search. *Perception and Psychophysics, 30*, 283–290.

Hoffman, J.E., Nelson, B., & Houck, M.R. (1983). The role of attentional resources in automatic detection. *Cognitive Psychology, 51*, 379–410.

Hoffman, J.E., & Subramaniam, B. (1995). Saccadic eye movements and visual selective attention. *Perception and Psychophysics, 57*, 787–795.

Hughes, H., & Zimba, L.D. (1985). Spatial maps of directed attention. *Journal of Experimental Psychology: Human Perception and Performance, 11*, 409–430.

Julesz, B. (1971). *Foundations of cyclopean perception.* University of Chicago Press.

Just, M.A., & Carpenter, P.A. (1980). A theory of reading: From eye fixations to comprehension, *Psychological Review, 87*, 329–354.

Khurana, B., & Kowler, E. (1987). Shared attentional control of smooth eye movement and perception. *Vision Research, 27*, 1603–1618.

Kingstone, A., & Klein, R.M. (1993a). What are human express saccades? *Perception and Psychophysics, 54*, 260–273.

Kingstone, A., & Klein, R.M. (1993b). Visual offsets facilitate saccadic latency: Does predisengagement of visuospatial attention mediate the gap effect? *Perception and Psychophysics, 19*, 1251–1265.

Klein, R. (1980). Does oculomotor readiness mediate cognitive control of visual attention? In R.S. Nickerson (Ed.), *Attention and performance VIII* (pp.259–276). Hillsdale, NJ: Lawrence Erlbaum Associates Inc.

Klein, R.M., Kingstone, A., & Pontefract, A. (1992). Orienting of visual attention. In Rayner, K. (Ed.), *Eye movements and visual cognition* (pp.46–65). New York: Springer-Verlag.

Klein, R.M., & Pontefract, A. (1994). Does oculomotor readiness mediate cognitive control of visual attention? Revisited! In C. Umiltà & M. Moscovitch (Eds.), *Attention and performance XV* (pp.333–350), Cambridge, MA: MIT Press.

Kowler, E., Anderson, E., Dosher, B., & Blaser, E. (1995). The role of attention in the programming of saccades. *Vision Research, 35*, 1897–1916.

Kowler, E., Van Der Stein, J., Tamminga, E.P., & Collewijn, H. (1984). Voluntary selection of the target for smooth eye movement in the presence of superimposed, full field stationary and moving stimuli. *Vision Research, 24*, 1789–1798.

Kowler, E., & Zingale, C. (1985). Smooth eye movements as indicators of selective attention. In M.I. Posner & O.S.M. Marin (Eds.), *Attention and performance XI* (pp.285–300). Hillsdale, NJ: Lawrence Erlbaum Associates Inc

Kramer, A., & Hahn, S. (1995). Splitting the beam: Distribution of attention over non-contiguous regions of the visual field. *Psychological Science, 6*, 381–386.

Logan, G.D. (1995). Linguistic and conceptual control of visual attention. *Cognitive Psychology, 28*, 1–72.

Mackeben, M., & Nakayama, K. (1993). Express attentional shifts. *Vision Research, 33*, 85–90.

McConkie, G.W., & Currie, C.C. (1996). Visual stability across saccades while viewing complex pictures. *Journal of Experimental Psychology: Human Perception and Performance, 22,* 563–581.

Morris, R.K., Rayner, K., & Pollatsek, A. (1990). Eye movement guidance in reading: The role of parafoveal letter and space information. *Journal of Experimental Psychology: Human Perception and Performance, 16,* 268–281.

Morrison, R.E. (1984). Manipulation of onset in reading: Evidence for parallel programming of saccades. *Journal of Experimental Psychology: Human Perception and Performance, 10,* 667–682.

O'Regan, J.K. (1992). Optimal viewing position in words and the strategy–tactics theory of eye movements in reading. In K. Rayner (Ed.), *Eye movements and visual cognition* (pp.333–354). New York: Springer-Verlag.

Pashler, H. (1989). Dissociations and dependencies between speed and accuracy: Evidence for a two-component theory of divided attention in simple tasks. *Cognitive Psychology, 21,* 469–514.

Pashler, H. (1994). Dual-task interference in simple tasks: Data and theory. *Psychological Bulletin, 116,* 220–244.

Pollatsek, A., Bolozky, S., Well, A.D., & Rayner, K. (1981). Asymmetries in the perceptual span for Israeli readers. *Brain and Language, 14,* 174–180.

Posner, M.I. (1980). Orienting of attention. *Quarterly Journal of Experimental Psychology, 32,* 3–25.

Posner, M.I. (1995). Attention in cognitive neuroscience: An overview. In M.S. Gazzaniga (Ed.), *The cognitive neurosciences* (pp.615–624). Cambridge, MA: MIT Press.

Posner, M.I., & Cohen, Y. (1984). Components of visual orienting. In H. Bouma & D.G. Bouwhuis (Eds.), *Attention and performance X* (pp.531–556). Hove, UK: Lawrence Erlbaum Associates Ltd.

Pylyshyn, Z.W. (1989). The role of location indexes in spatial perception: A sketch of the FINST spatial-index model. *Cognition, 32,* 65–97.

Pylyshyn, Z.W. (1994). Some primitive mechanisms of spatial attention. *Cognition, 50,* 363–384.

Rafal, R., Calabresi, P., Brennan, C., & Sciolto, T. (1989). Saccade preparation inhibits reorienting to recently attended locations. *Journal of Experimental Psychology: Human Perception and Performance, 15,* 673–685.

Rafal, R., Smith, J., Krantz, J., Cohen, A., & Brennan, C. (1990). Extrageniculate vision in hemianopic human saccade inhibition by signals in the blind field. *Science, 250* (4977), 118–121.

Rafal, R.F., Posner, M.I., Friedman, J.H., Inhoff, A.W., & Bernstein, E. (1988). Orienting of visual attention in progressive supranuclear palsy. *Brain, 111,* 267–280.

Rayner, K. (1975). Parafoveal identification during a fixation in reading. *Acta Psychologica, 39,* 271–282.

Rayner, K., Inhoff, A.W., Morrison, R.E., Slowirczek, M.I., & Bertera, J.H. (1981). Masking of foveal and parafoveal vision during eye fixations in reading. *Journal of Experimental Psychology: Human Perception and Performance, 7,* 167–179.

Rayner, K., & McConkie, G. (1976). What guides a reader's eye movements? *Vision Research, 16,* 829–837.

Rayner, K., & Pollatsek, A. (1989). *The psychology of reading.* Englewood Cliffs, NJ: Prentice Hall.

Rayner, K., & Pollatsek, A. (1996). Reading unspaced text is not easy: Comments on the implications of Epelboim et al.'s (1994) study for models of eye movement control in reading. *Vision Research, 36,* 461–465.

Remington, R.W. (1980). Attention and saccadic eye movements. *Journal of Experimental Psychology: Human Perception and Performance, 6,* 726–744.

Reuter-Lorenz, P.A., & Fendrich, R. (1992). Oculomotor readiness and covert orienting: Differences between central and peripheral precues. *Perception and Psychophysics, 52*, 336–344.

Reuter-Lorenz, P.A., Hughes, H.C. & Fendrich, R. (1991). The reduction of saccadic latency by prior offset of the fixation point: An analysis of the gap effect. *Perception and Psychophysics, 49*, 167–175.

Rizzolatti, G., Riggio, L., Dascola, I., & Umiltà, C. (1987). Reorienting attention across the vertical and horizontal meridians: Evidence in favor of a premotor theory of attention. *Neuropsychologia, 25*, 31–40.

Rizzolatti, G., Riggio, L., & Sheliga, B.M. (1994). Space and selective attention. In C. Umiltà & M. Moscovitch (Eds.), *Attention and performance XV* (pp.231–265), Cambridge, MA: MIT Press.

Saslow, M.G. (1967). Effects of components of displacement-step stimuli upon latency of saccadic eye movement. *Journal of the Optical Socieety of America, 57*, 1024–1029.

Schneider, W.X., & Deubel, H. (1995). Visual attention and saccadic eye movements: Evidence for obligatory and selective spatial coupling. In J.M. Findlay, R. Kentridge, & R. Walker (Eds.), *Eye movement research: Mechanisms, processes, and applications* (pp.317–324). New York: Elsevier.

Shepard, M., Findlay, J.M., & Hockey, R.J. (1986). The relationship between eye movements and spatial attention. *The Quarterly Journal of Experimental Psychology, 38A*, 475–491.

Shepard, M., & Mueller, H.J. (1989). Movement versus focusing of visual attention. *Perception and Psychophysics, 46*, 146–154.

Sperling, G. (1960). The information available in brief visual presentations. *Psychologica Monographs, 74*, (11, Whole No. 498)

Sperling, G., & Dosher, B.A. (1986). Strategy and optimization in human information processing. In K.R. Boff, L. Kaufman, & J.P. Thomas (Eds.), *Handbook of perception and human performance* (*Vol. I, Sensory processes and perception*, Ch. 2). New York: Wiley.

Sperling, G., & Melchner, M.J. (1978). Visual search, visual attention, and the attention operating characteristic. In J. Requin (Ed.), *Attention and performance VII* (pp.675–686). Hillsdale, NJ: Lawrence Erlbaum Associates Inc.

Tam, W.J., & Stelmach, L.W. (1993). Viewing behavior: Ocular and attentional disengagement. *Perception and Psychophysics, 54*, 211–222.

Tipper, S., Driver, J., & Weaver, B. (1991). Object-centered inhibition of return of visual attention. *Quarterly Joural of Experimental Psychology, 43*A, 289–298.

Tipper, S., Weaver, B., Jerreat, L., & Burak, A. (1994). Object-based and environment-based inhibition of return of visual attention. *Journal of Experimental Psychology: Human Perception and Performance, 20*, 478–499.

Wurtz, R.H., Goldberg, M.E., & Robinson, D.L. (1980). Behavioural modulation of visual responses in the monkey: Stimulus selection for attention and movement. *Progress in Psychobiology and Physiological Psychology, 9*, 43–83.

Yantis, S. (1992). Multielement visual tracking: Attention and perceptual organization. *Cognitive Psychology, 24*, 295–340.

Yimtis, S. (1996). Attentional capture in vision. In M. Coles, G. Logan, & A. Kramer (Eds.), *Converging operations in the study of visual selective attention*. Washington, DC: American Psychological Association.

Yarbus, A.L. (1967). *Eye movements and vision*. New York: Plenum Press.

CHAPTER FOUR

Attentional Limitations in Dual-task Performance

Harold Pashler
University of California, USA

James C. Johnston
NASA Ames Research Center, Moffett Field, USA

INTRODUCTION

People's ability (or inability) to do different activities or tasks at the same time is a topic of much interest not only to psychologists, but also to the proverbial "person in the street". It is natural to wonder about what we as human beings can and cannot do. An understanding of our limitations should also have practical value, because the intelligent design of human/machine systems depends as much on knowing the capabilities of people as it does on knowing the capabilities of machines. Human performance limits have played an important role in catastrophes that have occurred in aviation and other fields; a better understanding of those limits might help in designing systems and procedures that can minimize the frequency of such disasters.

Simultaneous performance of different tasks is intellectually intriguing as well. The limitations on simultaneous cognition may provide important clues to the architecture of the human mind. The notion that dual-task performance limitations have implications about the "unity of the mind" occurred to people long before the present era of information-processing psychology. In the late nineteenth century, for example, the educated public was fascinated with a phenomenon called "automatic writing", in which people were claimed to be able to write prose while carrying out other tasks (see Koutstaal, 1992).

This chapter provides an overview of research on attentional limitations in dual-task performance. The organization of the chapter follows a plan that is typical in present-day psychology: we begin with mental processes at the "front end" (i.e. analysis of incoming sensory stimuli), and then proceed to more "central" processes (e.g. decision-making, memory storage, memory retrieval, and action planning).

What is meant by "attentional limitations"? A formal definition of the term "attention" is not presently available, nor is it likely that a compelling definition can be arrived at from *a priori* considerations alone. However, it seems sensible to start with at least some rough characterization of what sort of phenomena we describe as attentional. In this spirit, we offer two criteria that a performance limitation must satisfy to be called attentional. First, the limitation must not be a direct consequence of the structure of the human body or its sensory or motoric apparatus. By this criterion, our inability to drink a cup of coffee and type at the same time is not attentional (at least not exclusively attentional), nor is our inability to read a word in the newspaper 10 degrees off fixation (as this is a consequence of the low density of photoreceptors in the periphery of the retina). Second, an inability to perform two tasks at the same time to a given criterion of performance is attentional only if a person could voluntarily perform either task alone to that criterion under essentially the same conditions. By this criterion, our inability to comprehend two spoken messages at the same time probably does qualify as attentional, while our inability to read two superimposed visual words (one masking the other) probably would not.

Roughly speaking, then, attentional limits are caused by limitations on those parts of mental machinery or processes that are normally subject to voluntary control or direction. We can use this definition without assuming (as ordinary language seems to assume) that that these limitations reflect a single underlying entity or process called Attention. From a scientific point of view, that assumption is probably best regarded as mere folklore; attentional limitations may turn out to reflect a great variety of mechanisms or processes.

Overview of Theories of Dual-task Interference

Before turning to empirical findings, we begin by considering a few theoretical ideas and concepts that have been widely applied in trying to understand attentional limitations. The first concept is that of a strict processing *bottleneck*. This refers to the idea that certain critical mental operations are carried out sequentially, and must be carried out sequentially. When this limitation applies, a bottleneck arises whenever, in a dual-task situation, two tasks require a critical mental operation at the same point in time. This kind of account is generally referred to as a bottleneck or single-channel model. The most obvious explanation for the existence of bottlenecks, if they do in fact exist, would be that the mind/brain contains only a single device or mechanism capable of carrying out the operation(s) in question. Other interpretations are possible, however. For instance, two operations that are carried out in different neural machinery might inhibit each other, thereby making it possible for only one or the other to operate at any given time. Naturally, there could be not just one, but two or more distinct bottlenecks associated with different types of mental operations, and bottlenecks might depend not only on the type of mental operation to be performed but also on the types of material to be processed and the extent to which the operation had been practiced.

Many theorists have argued for a less discrete analysis of dual-task performance limitations. They have suggested that there may be one or more pools of processing "resources" (sometimes equated with "effort" or "mental fuel") that can be divided up among different tasks or stimuli in a graded fashion. That is, when more processing resources are devoted to one task or stimulus this leaves a little less for others. On this account, processing for different tasks proceeds in parallel but the rate or efficiency of the processing depends on the capacity available to the task (among other factors). This conception will be referred to as *capacity sharing*. The single-channel bottleneck and capacity-sharing models provide very different pictures of our mental machinery; in the single-channel conception, certain aspects of mental processing are invariably sequential, while in the capacity view, processing on different tasks is simultaneous but occurs more slowly due to the reduction in available resources.

A third interpretation of attentional limitations attributes interference to *crosstalk* or other impairment in performance that hinges directly on the specific content of the information being processed. It has long been suggested that when two tasks are more similar, performing them together causes more interference than would be the case with very different tasks (e.g. Paulhan, cited by James, 1890). Some theorists have suggested that even when there is adequate machinery to carry out different tasks at once, keeping processing streams separate may be an important cause of dual-task interference. This predicts that the interference depends on the similarity or confusability of the mental representations involved in each task (e.g. Navon & Miller, 1987). This kind of theory is not entirely incompatible with the idea of a bottleneck. One could suppose, for example, that certain mental operations operate sequentially precisely because if they were allowed to run concurrently, crosstalk would occur (see Kinsbourne, 1981, for suggestions along these lines).

The three broad approaches sketched here do not exhaust the space of possible theories of dual-task performance. Further alternatives can be considered, and various hybrids can be constructed out of the models just mentioned. However, the concepts of capacity, bottleneck, and crosstalk provide an adequate framework for appreciating the research described in the remainder of this chapter and we will defer consideration of more complicated models until the empirical motivation for complications has emerged.

EMPIRICAL EVIDENCE ON LIMITATIONS

We turn now to the empirical evidence on human dual-task performance limitations, beginning with sensory and perceptual analysis and moving from there to more central processes. This review is necessarily incomplete but fairly representative of a large and growing literature.

Perceptual Processing Limitations

As mentioned in the Introduction, the earliest information-processing theories of attention tended to assume very severe limitations in perceptual processing. Broadbent's Filter Theory, for example, contended that people are unable to identify more than a single spoken word at one time. In the late 1960s and early 1970s, several theorists proposed a radical departure from this approach, arguing that sensory and perceptual processes are subject to no attentional limitations whatever. This new view was termed the "late-selection theory of attention" (referring to the idea that selection occurs only after all stimuli are identified unselectively). At first glance, this notion might strike the reader as absurd: surely an organism's capacity to do anything must be limited. It should be kept in mind, however, that attentional limits are only one factor potentially limiting performance. Claiming that attentional limitations on perception do not exist does not, therefore, imply that perceptual systems do a "perfect" job of analyzing a stimulus or that people can recognize an unlimited number of objects at the same time; it merely implies that these systems analyze any one stimulus just as effectively whether other stimuli are being processed at the same time or not.

Whether plausible or not, the late-selection account rested from its inception on a rather thin evidence base from its inception. The main support for the theory consisted of demonstrations that, even when people try to ignore certain stimuli (e.g. letters to the left or right of fixation, words spoken to an unattended ear), these stimuli are nonetheless analyzed semantically, at least to some extent (e.g. Eriksen & Hoffman, 1973). Naturally, the fact that to-be-ignored stimuli are sometimes analyzed does not imply that there are no attentional capacity limitations, especially when the evidence of unwanted processing involves only a few simple stimuli like letters.

More direct empirical assessments of capacity limitations in perceptual processing involve "divided attention" tasks in which people try to identify a number of objects simultaneously. The most obvious task to use for this purpose is one that requires observers to report all the stimuli they can (e.g. to read off a display of briefly exposed letters). This "whole report task" was first studied in detail by Sperling (1960). Sperling's findings disclosed that limitations in storing or retaining stimuli in short-term memory often prevent stimuli from being reported even when conditions would allow them all to be identified successfully (see also Estes & Taylor, 1964). To assess perceptual capacities apart from memory limitations, one needs a task that allows subjects to demonstrate what they have identified without having to hold much information in memory.

For this reason, most contemporary research on visual processing capacity limitations has relied on detection or search tasks (Estes & Taylor, 1965). In these experiments, people report the presence or absence of a prespecified target somewhere in a search display or, in some cases, choose which of several alternative targets was present. As Wolfe describes in Chapter 1, when the number of distractors in search displays is increased, response times generally increase too. This increase is much greater when the target and distractor differ only in some subtle or complex fashion, e.g. when they consist of the same parts but arranged differently (e.g. Logan, 1994) or when targets and distractors vary along some continuous dimension like length or orientation and the difference between them is subtle (e.g. Treisman, 1991). This finding strongly suggests the existence of capacity limits in perceptual analysis. For technical reasons, however, the inference is not absolutely secure. For purely statistical reasons, accuracy falls as the number of items to be searched is increased (basically because each distractor represents an additional opportunity for a "false alarm"). Increases in response times could potentially occur because people compensate for this by taking longer with larger display set sizes, not because capacity limitations arise (Duncan, 1980a; Palmer, 1994).

Detection studies that focus on the accuracy rather than speed of visual search performance have also been carried out, usually using objects briefly exposed and followed by pattern masks; pattern masks serve to curtail visual persistence and ensure that visual analysis takes place immediately rather than at the subject's convenience. One particularly incisive experiment from the point of view of assessing capacity limitations was carried out by Shiffrin and Gardner (1972). They required observers to search a display of four alphanumeric characters for a target character (each item followed by a mask). In the Simultaneous Condition, all four characters were flashed at the same time. In the Successive Condition, they were flashed one or two at a time, with pauses in between flashes. If capacity limitations were at work, the successive condition should provide an important advantage: each item can benefit from more capacity than it could in the simultaneous condition, where capacity must be divided up among all four items. What Shiffrin and Gardner observed, however, was essentially no difference in accuracy between the two conditions. This striking finding has been replicated by a number of other investigators (e.g. Duncan, 1980b), and argues strongly that at least four characters can be processed in parallel without attentional limitations.

Although the result is consistent with the strong claims of late-selection theories, further experimentation using the same technique showed that capacity limitations arise whenever processing load is increased beyond a certain point. When the target/background discrimination is more difficult or larger display set sizes are used, for example, accuracy in the simultaneous condition is often substantially worse than in the successive condition (Duncan, 1987; Kleiss & Lane, 1986). This finding fits well with the results of speeded search tasks (see Wolfe's Chapter 1) and refutes the late-selection theory discussed earlier.

What causes processing limitations in perceptual analysis? Unfortunately, at present we have few clues to help in answering this interesting question. Recent studies of the time course of interference, and of the correlation between performance on simultaneous discrimination tasks, suggests that capacity overload may typically produce graded capacity sharing rather than sequential processing (Duncan, Ward, & Shapiro, 1994; Miller & Bonnel, 1994). There is no evidence that performance limitations result from crosstalk in processing multiple items, because the interference seems to be comparable whether the tasks involve similar or different sorts of judgments (Duncan, 1993). However, interference is clearly worse when inputs involve a single sensory modality (e.g. audition or vision) compared to inputs presented in different modalities (Treisman & Davies, 1973).

These observations suggest several tentative conclusions. Identifying stimuli probably requires processing resources that are specific to a particular sensory modality. Particular perceptual discriminations require different amounts of processing capacity, depending on the difficulty of a given discrimination. Different objects can be analyzed in parallel and independently, but only so long as total capacity demands are not exceeded. When they are exceeded, perceptual analysis becomes less efficient, perhaps typically resulting in parallel processing at reduced efficiency.

How do these capacity limits affect our perception of the sights and sounds of less austere displays such as those we usually encounter in daily life? Here our knowledge is sadly limited. Studies in which observers look at rapid sequences of pictures (many frames presented per second in the same part of the visual field) reveal that people can comprehend a scene very rapidly (subject, of course, to acuity limits of the periphery). For example, observers can fairly reliably detect an object out of place in scenes viewed at rates of approximately 100–200 msec per picture (Biederman, Teitelbaum, & Mezzanotte, 1983). The fact that processing is rapid does not imply that it is free of capacity limitations, of course; any given object in a scene may be identified more slowly than it would be in isolation. It seems reasonable to suspect that this is so, based on the laboratory studies described earlier, but there are so many differences between perception of scenes and visual search involving letters and symbols that this is only a conjecture.

Central Processing Limitations

What sort of processing limitations arise at central levels of the cognitive system, i.e. in the neural/mental machinery responsible for thinking, decision making, and planning actions? To isolate limitations in central processing, we need experimental methods that do not overload perceptual limitations. One simple precaution is to use tasks whose perceptual requirements are relatively slight. Given the results described earlier, another natural precaution is to use different input modalities in each task (typically vision and audition), making it less likely that any single perceptual mechanism will be overloaded. These precautions are sensible, but not definitive; the locus of any particular dual-task interference cannot be assumed *a priori*.

Before turning to the empirical literature, it is worth pausing momentarily to ask what ordinary experience might teach us, if anything. Most of us have reflected on the fact that we sometimes seem able to perform two daily tasks at the same time, e.g. carrying on a conversation and driving a car. At some crude level of description, this is certainly possible: the car does not end up in a ditch and our friends are (usually) not offended. What does this tell us about the extent of concurrent mental processing? Although the car is certainly moving while the driver is speaking, often it would continue on a perfectly reasonable trajectory for several seconds without any action whatever on the part of the driver. As for the conversation, even under normal circumstances, conversing involves intermittent behavior and partially redundant messages. Therefore, the brute fact that people drive and converse does not necessarily indicate that parallel processing of all aspects of language processing and driving is possible. Our casual observations would be equally consistent with the possibility that our brains do what single-processor computers often do to juggle multiple tasks or users: work on one task at a time, but alternate rapidly between them in order to respond to inputs in a timely fashion.

Computer time-sharing normally requires that the computer must be able to "buffer" (hold in temporary memory) a considerable amount of information. Computers usually have buffers both for inputs that have not yet been fully processed and for outputs that have been planned but not yet carried out, as well as various internal buffers. As it happens, human beings are also equipped with a variety of memory buffers that seem roughly suitable for such a "buffer and switch" processing strategy (Baddeley, 1986).

Ordinary experience, then, provides little insight as to which mental operations can occur at the same instant; laboratory studies are plainly needed to sort this out. Research in the lab has confirmed the casual observation that people can sometimes perform two continuous tasks concurrently with only modest loss in performance, when these tasks involve no obvious conflicts in input or output modality. Examples include playing the piano and shadowing spoken words (Allport, Antonis, & Reynolds, 1972) and, for a skilled typist, typing a manuscript while shadowing (Shaffer, 1975). Even more remarkably, Spelke, Hirst, and Neisser (1976) were able to train subjects to take dictation (speech input, manual output) while reading aloud (visual input, vocal output). In each of these cases, dual-task performance was very good, although error rates were usually somewhat higher than in the single-task conditions.

Although tasks like typing and reading aloud might seem to require more continuous cognitive activity than driving of conversing, smooth combination of these tasks might still reflect a switching strategy. One factor that might facilitate switching is sometimes termed "chunking": after people have practiced a task like typing, they seem able to plan and execute larger and larger response units. For a skilled typist, for example, the primary or highest-level unit at which actions are planned is probably the word rather than the individual letter. Several observations support this idea. For example, the "eye–hand span" (the lag between which letter a typist fixates and which letter they are typing at the same instant) is considerable, and grows longer as a typist acquires expertise (Salthouse & Saults, 1987).

Suppose, then, that seemingly continuous activities like typing actually involve discontinuous planning of relatively large output "chunks". In that case, if people can smoothly perform two such tasks concurrently, this may be because the planning operations are occurring at different moments, not because the two tasks are performed completely independently. Consider the analogy of a person doing the laundry and cooking dinner. Although few people can load the laundry and stir a frying pan at the same instant, for example, nonetheless one can sometimes schedule things so that the dinner and the laundry are both completed at roughly the same time that they would be if carried out by themselves. At a finer time-scale, the same may be true for the central operations involved in tasks like typing and reading aloud.

In the light of these possibilities, to determine whether people can carry out different central mental operations independently, we need to look at the speed with which they can respond to individual stimuli presented close together in time. Buffering and switching may suffice to produce continuous behavioral streams but the lag between individual stimuli and the corresponding responses should nonetheless provide telltale indications of delay. To detect these signs, we need to use experimental designs in which stimuli are presented at discrete moments in time, and to determine the latency of responses that are unambiguously related to particular stimuli.

A rather austere type of experiment fits these requirements. This design involves discrete trials; the subject must, on each trial, perform two tasks, responding to each of two different stimuli presented in rapid succession (S1 and S2). The interval between the onset of the two stimuli (known as the stimulus onset asynchrony, or SOA interval) is varied, typically from short intervals of 50 ms or so up to intervals of half a second or longer. This kind of experiment was apparently first tried by Telford (1931), and since then hundreds of studies have confirmed a very basic result: as the SOA between two stimuli is shortened, responses to the second stimulus are delayed, often by hundred of milliseconds. This finding is observed with almost all tasks involving choice (i.e. response uncertainty), although some exceptions and potential exceptions will be discussed later.

Why should there be such a delay? A natural interpretation is that subjects are unable to carry out certain processing involving the second stimulus until they have finished with the first. When the effect was first observed, some thought it was analogous to the refractory period of neurons—after producing a neural spike, neurons are temporarily inhibited from firing again for a very brief period. Although the delays in the behavioral case are usually much longer than the neural refractory period, and although the two phenomena differ in other important respects, the delay in responding to the second of two stimuli has been christened the Psychological Refractory Period (or PRP) effect, and for better or worse, the term has stuck. We will use the term PRP Paradigm to refer to the method, leaving open the question of whether the analogy to neural refractoriness is illuminating or not.

Let us look more closely at an actual PRP experiment. For convenience we will use a study of our own (Pashler & Johnston, 1989, Experiment 1). The experiment was carried out with a microcomputer. Subjects were required to perform two completely unrelated choice response-time tasks. For Task 1, the stimuli were a 300 Hz tone and a 900 Hz tone. Subjects responded by pressing one of two adjacent keys on a keyboard with fingers of the left hand. For Task 2, the stimuli were the letters "A", "B", or "C"; subjects responded by pressing one of three adjacent keys with fingers of the right hand. Each trial began with subjects fixating a mark at the center of the CRT screen. After 1000 ms this mark was extinguished, and after another 200 ms one of the two possible tones for Task 1 sounded for 33 ms. After a variable SOA (50, 100, or 400 ms) one of three Task 2 stimuli appeared on the CRT screen. Subjects were instructed to respond rapidly and accurately on both tasks, but the instructions particularly emphasized the importance of responding rapidly on Task 1. In a control condition, subjects were asked to perform only Task 1; Task 2 stimuli were presented, but subjects did not respond to them.

Figure 4.1 shows results from the experiment. The solid curve shows mean RT for Task 1 in the dual-task condition. It was about 600 ms

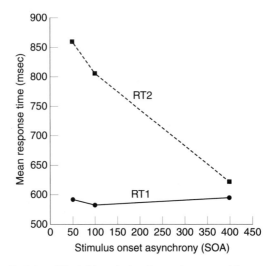

FIG. 4.1.   RT for Task 1 and Task 2 in a dual-task experiment requiring separate responses to a tone (first stimulus) and a letter (second stimulus). Stimulus onset asynchrony refers to the time between onset of tone and letter. RT1 is time for response to tone; RT2 is time for response to letter. (Data from Experiment 1, Pashler & Johnston, 1989.) The slowing of RT2 at shorter SOAs is referred to as the psychological refractory period (PRP) effect.

regardless of the SOA delay in presenting the Task 2 stimulus. The dashed curve shows RT2 in the dual-task condition. Unlike many functions, this one is easiest to think about starting from the right-hand side. At the longest SOA (400 ms), when the two tasks could generally be done sequentially, RT2 was a little over 600 ms. But at the shortest SOA (50 ms), when both stimuli need to be processed at almost the same time, RT2 was several hundred ms higher—about 850 ms. The fact that subjects are delayed several hundred ms in making the response to that letter stimulus (the PRP effect) is what we would expect from the "buffer and switch" strategy discussed earlier. Note that the dual-task interference found here is clearly evident only in RT data; the data show no increase in errors on Task 2 at short SOAs (in fact subjects made more errors at the longest SOA).

Although RT1 in the dual-task condition was little influenced by SOA, it was consistently slower than the response time for the same task performed alone in a control condition. This is a typical finding, and many theorists attribute it to the difficulty in attaining an optimal level of preparation for both tasks (cf. Gottsdanker, 1980; Pashler, 1994). If this is correct, we should expect slowing even if Task 2 were omitted altogether on some trials, and this has been observed as well (Ruthruff & Pashler, submitted).

As mentioned earlier, the basic PRP result—a dramatic slowing in RT for the second task, when stimuli for both tasks are presented in rapid succession—has been replicated many times, with a variety of different tasks (for reviews of early work, see Bertelson, 1966, and Smith, 1967). These results have suggested to many investigators that the mind may, in certain respects at least, contain a "single-channel" information processor, capable of working on only one task at a time. The simplest version of such an account would claim that all aspects of the second task are delayed until all aspects of the first task are finished. The data in Fig. 4.1 show, however, that both tasks are often completed in less time than the sum of the time it would for each task to be performed in isolation. (The average time elapsed from S1 to R2 was 909 ms at the shortest SOA, while the times to perform each task alone were roughly 590 and 500 ms.) At a very crude level, then, there are signs of overlapping processing. This suggests that if there is a bottleneck, it probably involves some but not all of the processes involved in carrying out the two tasks. The earliest proponent of a bottleneck, Welford (1952, 1980), suggested that single-channel processing occurred in the central stages of each task—stages that he termed "stimulus–response translation". This *central bottleneck model* is at least grossly consistent with the data from the experiment we have been looking at.[1]

Recent evidence provides more definitive evidence about the validity of the single-channel hypothesis. Two separate issues can be distinguished: first, whether PRP interference is attributable to a bottleneck at all; and second, if it is, what the functional locus of this bottleneck might be.

Is PRP Interference Caused by a Bottleneck?

Although many early researchers favored a bottleneck explanation for PRP interference, others advocated a capacity-sharing analysis. For example, in his book *Attention and Effort*, Kahneman (1973) proposed that PRP interference typically reflects a slowdown in processing that occurs when general processing capacity is shared between tasks at short SOAs. Assuming (as seems reasonable) that reduced capacity results in slower processing, this readily accounts for the basic PRP effect.

Several further pieces of evidence have sometimes been taken to support a capacity account. Kahneman noted that in many PRP studies, responses were slower not only on Task 2, but also on Task 1. Capacity theory, because it treats Task 1 and Task 2 symmetrically, has a natural account for RT1 slowing when it occurs. As capacity is divided between both tasks, processing for each task should operate at a slower than normal rate, resulting in delays of both responses. Bottleneck theory itself provides no account of RT1 slowing, but it can be amended to do so in a reasonable fashion. For one thing, subjects given no instruction to keep the first task response as fast

---

[1] He also suggested that monitoring the response occupied the single channel as well.

as possible might sometimes switch to working on Task 2 before finishing Task 1. For another, subjects may often "group" the two responses, i.e. withhold the first response until the second response has been selected. Both of these strategies are likely to be under some degree of conscious control, and indeed, when subjects are told to produce R1 as fast as possible (as in the experiment described earlier), there is little sign of R1 slowing.

Although capacity theories have not been shown to make particularly distinctive predictions,[2] the central bottleneck model does make very detailed predictions. Fig. 4.2 shows the model graphically, with time running from left to right and the upper three connected boxes representing Task 1 and the lower three boxes representing Task 2. In the spirit of Sternberg's (1969) stage analysis, it is assumed that processing on each task can be divided into three general stages, with each stage normally commencing as soon as the preceding stage is finished. We will discuss later and in more detail what might be accomplished in each stage, but for now one can think of stage A as "early" stimulus processing, stage B as central processing, and stage C as "late" response-related processing (each of these could be sub-divided into further stages, naturally, but for present purposes this is not necessary). The assumption of a central bottleneck can be stated slightly more formally, as follows: (1) any stage A or stage C can proceed on each task regardless of what is happening on the other tasks, but(2) stage B can operate for only one task at a time. If stage 1B is running, stage 2B cannot run and vice versa. From this, one can derive equations for both RTs:

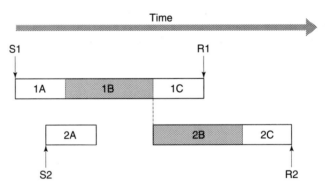

FIG. 4.2. Sequence of processing stages hypothesized in most general versions of the central bottleneck model of PRP effect. Stages 1A, 1B, and 1C comprise Task 1, while 2A, 2B, and 2C comprise Task 2. A fundamental constraint is that processing in the shaded stages cannot operate simultaneously; hence, a bottleneck arises when S1 and S2 are presented close together in time, as they are here; stage 2B cannot begin until stage 1B has been completed.

---

[2] But see McLeod (1977) for an example one highly restricted version of capacity-sharing theory that might make stronger predictions.

(i) $RT1 = 1A + 1B + 1C$

(ii) $RT2 = Max(1A + 1B + SW, SOA + 2A) + 2B + 2C - SOA$

Note that RT1 is simply the sum of the component stage times for Task 1. However for Task 2, the central stage 2B cannot begin until both the resources required by the central stage are released (determined by $1A + 1B + SW$, where SW is any switching time required to move central resources from Task 1 to Task 2; in the figure $SW = 0$) *and* early stimulus processing in Task 2 is finished, providing the information input to stage 2B, (determined by $SOA + SW$). Because of the "and" relation, RT2 on any given trial is determined by whichever of these two terms is greater.

In exploring this model, let us begin with the (surely unrealistic) simplifying assumption that stages times are deterministic. It then follows that a graph of RT2 against SOA should look like Fig. 4.3 [elbow curve]. To the right of the elbow, at longer SOAs, there is never a wait for the central resources to be released from Task 1, so SOA has no effect on RT2. At short SOAs, RT2 is always determined only by how rapidly stage 2B finishes. The time at which S2 is presented no longer affects when R2 occurs, so the combined interval from the beginning of S1 to R2—which is equal to $SOA + A2$—is a constant. This means that for every one millisecond increase in SOA, RT2 decreases by one millisecond. Thus we arrive at the very specific prediction that the graph of RT2 against SOA should have a left segment with a slope of –1, a right segment with a slope of 0, and a bend at the point where the processor and the results of stage 2A become available simultaneously.

If we allow stage durations to vary stochastically, the graph of the mean RT2 against SOA should look more like the dotted curve: the elbow is now

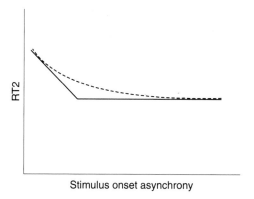

Stimulus onset asynchrony

FIG. 4.3. Shape of function relating RT2 (vertical axis) to SOA (horizontal axis), as predicted by a deterministic version of the bottleneck model (solid line) and a more realistic version that assumes stochastic variation in stages durations (approximated with dotted line).

smoothed out by trial-to-trial variation. There may be some portion of the curve on the left with a slope of –1, but only if there is range of SOAs over which stage 2B always waits on completion of central stages in Task 1. There will be some range of SOAs on the right of the curve over which the slope will be 0 if, over this range, stage 2B never waits on completion of the central stages in Task 1.

One clear prediction of this model is that a graph of RT2 against SOA should be declining but positively accelerated. This is virtually always found. The prediction that a –1 slope occurs at very short SOAs is often at least approximately true (the slope is –1.06 for the Pashler & Johnston data shown in Fig. 4.1) and sometimes very precisely true. In an experiment of McCann and Johnston (1989) to be discussed shortly, where an unusually large amount of data was obtained by testing the same subjects over six days, four different curves of this kind had measured slopes between SOA 50 and SOA 150 of –1.02, –1.00, –1.00, and –.97. Note that if Task 1 is relatively fast and/or stage 2A requires unusually lengthy processing, then –1 slopes may not be obtained. Note also that the prediction does not hold if subject sometimes take time out from Task 1 to do some processing on Task 2, or use a grouping strategy.

A more realistic version of the model assumes that stage times have stochastic variability. This makes predictions about how RT1 and RT2 covary across trials. Generally speaking, anything that causes stage 1B to finish later (anything slowing stages 1A or 1B) will "push on" RT2 as well as RT1. This leads to the prediction that RT1 and RT2 will be positively correlated. High positive correlations are indeed observed at short SOAs (Gottsdanker & Way, 1966; Pashler & Johnston, 1989). More recently, it has often been noted that at long SOAs, RT2 tends to be influenced only by unusually long RT1s, whereas at shorter SOAs, it is influenced by progressively shorter and shorter RT1s (e.g. Pashler, 1989; Pashler & O'Brien, 1993).

The prediction that longer times for stages 1A and 1B will "push" onto RT2 at short SOAs but not at long SOAs also holds if these stages in Task 1 are lengthened by experimental manipulations rather than spontaneous variability. McCann and Johnston (1989) manipulated the difficulty of stimulus processing on Task 1, using a factor that increased RT1 by 29 ms. The effect of this Task 1 difficulty factor on RT2 was 30 ms at SOA 50, 28 ms at SOA 150, 16 ms at SOA 300, and only 2 ms at SOA 800. (These results are an average over two different types of Task 1, one auditory and one visual; virtually the same pattern was observed in each case.) This is just the pattern predicted by central bottleneck theory. Although capacity theory can predict effects of the difficulty of one task on performance in another, a millisecond for millisecond "propagation" of Task 1 effects onto RT2 at short SOAs is a hallmark of a true bottleneck.

Perhaps the most striking predictions from central bottleneck theory arise when difficulty of Task 2 is manipulated, however. Suppose that, by means of some difficulty manipulation, we increase the duration of some processing stage on Task 2 by k ms. What does the model predict? The predictions differ, depending on whether the manipulated stage occurs before or after the "gap" in the timeline for Task 2. This gap in the timeline represents the postponement of stage B of Task 2 until the completion of stage B in Task 1. The top panel of Fig. 4.4 shows what the model predicts if we manipulate the duration of stage 2B. As the change is after the "gap" is over, the consequence is simply that RT2 increases by the same amount k by which stage 2B was lengthened. Hence the prediction is that RT2 will be increased by k regardless of SOA. Thus, the effect of the stage manipulation will be additive with the effect of SOA on RT2.

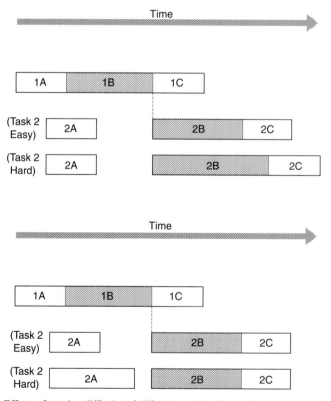

FIG. 4.4. Effects of varying difficulty of different aspects of stage 2 on sequence of processing stages with a short SOA. Top Panel: increasing difficulty of stage 2B simply adds a constant to RT2 (the same constant would be added at a long SOA, where the two tasks are effectively sequential). Bottom Panel: increasing difficulty of stage 2A does not affect second response time at all, if the SOA were very long, however, this would not be the case.

The bottom panel of Fig 4.4 shows what to expect if we increase the duration of stage 2A by k ms. As long as stage 2A still ends before stage 1B, the factor effect onto RT2 will be washed out. In operations research, this is known as "absorption into slack". Following Schweickert (1978) we can call the mental wait state in the diagram "cognitive slack", and the disappearance of factor effects on stage 2B phenomena at short SOAs can then be dubbed "absorption into cognitive slack".

Several predictions follow from this analysis. Overadditive interactions of factor effects and SOA (i.e. larger difficulty effects at shorter SOAs) are not predicted by the mechanism described here. Rather, absorption into slack (underadditivity) is expected for factors affecting early stages of Task 2, while additivity is predicted for factors affecting late stages. In fact, overadditive interactions seem rare in the literature. In the Pashler and Johnston (1989) study, the predictions of underadditivity and additivity were confirmed. In this study, the effect of altering the intensity of Task 2 stimuli, which plainly should affect an early stage of processing, was almost entirely absorbed into slack at short SOAs. An effect of intensity of about 30 ms was reduced to only 5 ms. We also found that the effect of repetition of Task 2 stimulus, which mainly affects the more central stage of S–R mapping (Pashler & Baylis, 1991) was additive with SOA. Underadditive interactions involving manipulations that affect early stimulus processing have also been reported by Johnston, McCann, and Remington (1996) and de Jong (1993).

Additive effects for other manipulations of central decision-making and response-selection operations have been reported by McCann and Johnston (1992), Ruthruff, Miller, and Lachmann (1995), Van Selst and Jolicoeur (1995), McCann and Johnston (1989), and Carrier and Pashler (1996). Dutta and Walker (1995) and McCann and Johnston (1989) found that this additivity persists over at least several sessions of practice, so the bottleneck is not caused by any simple failure to remember the task instructions.

In summary, recent research has provided new and subtle evidence for the existence of a central bottleneck in dual-task performance, at least at low and intermediate levels of practice in "ordinary" choice RT tasks (a distinction that will be clarified later under the heading "Exceptions to the PRP effect"). So far, there does not appear to be any solid body of data that poses substantial problems for bottleneck theory. Obviously, new data might change this situation and force revisions of the model; it seems implausible, however, that any more refined model will have no resemblance to what we have been describing so far.

Locus of PRP Bottleneck

We have seen that there is considerable evidence that a central bottleneck is a principle cause of PRP interference. "Central" is a vague notion, however, and it would certainly be desirable if the bottleneck could be pinpointed with more precision than that. The main consideration that led Welford (1952) to hypothesize a central bottleneck years ago was the fact that PRP interference arises with pairs of tasks that do not use the same input modality (e.g. one task may be visual and the other auditory). Since then, it has been found with various combinations of different output modalities, too (e.g. a manual response and a vocal response). This suggests, but does not prove, that the interference originates in processes that are neither perceptual nor motoric in character.

The methodology described in the preceding section suggests a way to pinpoint the locus of interference with more precision: by manipulating the time taken for a particular mental operation, one can determine whether this operation is subject to the central bottleneck. When applied to the second task in the PRP design, if the variable has effects that combine additively with SOA, then it must affect a stage at or after the point where the bottleneck begins (or to be more precise, there can be no effective bottleneck[3] after that stage). It seems natural to start with choice reaction time tasks, but the method can be perfectly well applied to more complex and interesting cognitive tasks that require stages and operations not present in choice reaction time.

An early attempt to use this logic was carried out by Keele (1973), who compared RT2 for simple and choice RT tasks (as Donders noted over a century ago, RTs are slower for choice than for simple RT). Karlin and Kestenbaum (1968) had found that difference between the two was smaller when the task was placed second in the PRP paradigm than when the tasks were performed in isolation. Keele assumed that the RT difference between choice and simple RT reflected "decision" or "memory retrieval", and inferred that these operations were not delayed by the first task. Hence, he concluded that the PRP effect must originate from a delay in initiating or producing responses (rather than choosing them, as suggested earlier). This reasoning can be questioned. First, there is little reason to assume that simple and choice RT differ only in the presence of any single stage or stages (see Goodrich et al., 1990; Pashler, 1994). Second, the issue may now be moot in any case; Van Selst (1996) made repeated attempts to replicate Karlin and Kestenbaum's finding of underadditivity, but instead found additivity.

A number of other variables in choice RT have been investigated more recently using this design. As described earlier, Pashler and Johnston (1989) found that stimulus repetition effects in a choice RT task were additive. As repetition is likely to affect response selection (Pashler & Baylis, 1991), this

---

[3] By "no effective bottleneck", we mean no bottleneck that is producing slowing within the experiment itself.

suggests that the bottleneck is at or prior to that operation (translation, in Welford's terminology). McCann and Johnston (1992) found additive results using another factor likely to affect the duration of the response selection stage—the "naturalness" of the S–R mapping rule. For instance, in one of their experiments, three sizes of objects were either mapped onto the fingers of one hand in a consistent order (e.g. 1–2–3) or an arbitrary order (e.g. 3–2–1). In another experiment, naturalness of the S–R mapping was manipulated by having subjects respond with a left or right key press to either an arrow (natural mapping) or the letters M and T (arbitrary mapping). Both experiments found that the natural mapping was faster than the unnatural mapping by the same amount at short SOAs (where the PRP delayed RT2) as at long SOAs where the bottleneck did not occur.

So far, then, we can conclude that there is, in choice tasks at least, no bottleneck *after* the S–R mapping stage. This, of course, is fully compatible with the possibility of a bottleneck located at the stage of S–R mapping itself and/or a bottleneck at some prior stages. The fact that varying the difficulty of central processing in the *first* task causes a delay in R2 (Pashler, 1984; Smith, 1969) rejects the idea that the bottleneck is completely prior to response selection. We are left, therefore, with two alternatives: the bottleneck is only in response selection, or it is in response selection plus certain earlier operations—presumably those concerned with stimulus analysis.

Recent evidence suggests that when stimulus analysis is made sufficiently difficult (in certain ways, at least), it too can become subject to the central bottleneck. Johnston and McCann (submitted) used a task requiring an "analog" (i.e. nondiscrete) perceptual judgment as Task 2. In one of their experiments, this task involved pressing one of two keys depending on whether a cross was to the left or right of the center of a circle. Here, the S–R mapping process (i.e. response selection) can be assumed to take as input the left-vs-right classification. Johnston and McCann varied the difficulty of deriving this code by putting the cross either slightly or quite substantially off center. At long SOAs, this variable produced an 88 ms increase in RT2. At short SOAs, this was reduced to 64 ms. Hence, less than one third of the difficulty effect was absorbed into slack. The fact that absorption into slack was far from complete suggests that a considerable amount of input classification was held up by the bottleneck.

In follow-up experiments, Johnston and McCann used a different Task 2: judging whether a rectangle was fat or thin. Four progressively wider stimuli were used—"very thin", "somewhat thin", "somewhat fat", and "very fat". Subjects had to classify the first two as thin and the other two as fat. Responses were substantially faster for the two extreme stimuli compared to the intermediate cases; this difference was the difficulty manipulation of interest. In these experiments, the Task-2 difficulty effect was very close to additive with SOA, implying postponement of the corresponding processing stage(s). Thus, for this task at least, the bottleneck seems to include operations in Task 2 that occur before S–R translation. It has also been found that when perceptual processing on Task 2 includes complex mediating operations such as mental rotation, these operations are (usually or largely) unable to proceed during the bottleneck (Ruthruff et al., 1995).

In another set of studies, McCann and Johnston (1989 and submitted) examined variables that prolong letter identification. While intensity effects are fully absorbed, as described earlier, these effects might be affecting stages of visual analysis prior to actual identification. McCann and Johnston (submitted) squeezed letters to make them either very squat or very narrow, while keeping the stroke widths and contrast constant. In another experiment, the tilt of component strokes (for instance the diagonal segments in the letter "A" were rotated inward so the character looked a bit like a teepee). The task required subjects to identify the letters. At long SOAs, both experiments showed about a 30 ms slowing of RT2 for the distorted forms. At short SOAs, however, there was complete absorption into slack, i.e. RTs for distorted and undistorted were no different. These results show that some stimulus processing beyond primitive visual feature extraction can occur on Task 2 while critical stages of Task 1 are executed.

We are led to conclude, therefore, that the bottleneck ordinarily encompasses response selection in choice RT tasks and, when present, certain other perceptual operations as well, such as analog comparisons and mental rotation. Some caution is in order, however, as only a fairly modest number of results are available using this method. Like a paleontologist with only a few skulls at hand, we should be cautious about jumping to broad conclusions on the basis of a few studies. The locus-of-slack method is based on assumptions that cannot presently be tested wholly independently of the method. Nonetheless, the method so far has produced consistent and sensible patterns of results, namely underadditive interactions—indicating absorption into slack—for factors one would independently have judged to be perceptual (e.g. visual degradation, letter identification), and additive effects for factors independently believed to affect S–R mapping. This pattern follows naturally from the central bottleneck model, and it is hard to see which other accounts would predict it.

PRP AND OTHER ASPECTS OF ATTENTION

What is the relationship of the central bottleneck revealed in the experiments just described and the very general notion of Attention? As noted at the beginning of this chapter, attention is a diffuse concept. Perhaps the most prominent idea associated with the term is perceptual selectivity: our ability to choose one object from among many for "awareness", memory, and the control of action. In trying to relate the central bottleneck to attention it seems natural to start by asking whether the machinery that controls perceptual selection plays some role in our inability to choose different responses at the same time. For example, if shifts in attention were carried out by the same central machinery as response selection and other centrally demanding operations, attentional shifts should represent a bottleneck along with response selection and other mental operations.

Several recent sets of studies offer converging ways of addressing this question. One set of experiments used a hybrid methodology, with a speeded first task and an unspeeded second task (Pashler, 1991). The first task required a rapid choice response to a tone, while the second required the observer to shift attention within the visual field based on the nature of a cue presented by the experimenter. In this second task, the display of letters contained an arrow or bar indicating a single item that the observer should attempt to remember and later, at his or her leisure, report. The entire display was followed by a mask. To perform this second task beyond a minimum level[4] one must shift attention to the cued location and store the appropriate item in short-term memory; because the mask appears so quickly, there is barely enough time to complete this on most trials. As in a PRP experiment, the key manipulation was SOA; at very short SOAs, the attention shift would be called for just as the planning of a response to the tone was under way, whereas at long SOAs, it would not have to begin until the first task had been completed (at least on most trials). The results showed, however, that the accuracy of letter report was unaffected by SOA. This implies, then, that response selection and attention shifting occurred in parallel, and thus that the central bottleneck does not encompass shifting visual attention.

Converging evidence for this conclusion comes from recent work by Johnston, McCann, and Remington (1996). Recall that the PRP results described earlier argue that letter identification is not normally subject to the central bottleneck, i.e. identification of letters in Task 2 can proceed without waiting for central processing in Task 1 to be completed (McCann & Johnston, 1989; Johnston et al., 1996). Johnston et al. carried out several new experiments using essentially the same logic to see if letter identification is held up by spatial attention delays. Their results indicated that it is. These results suggest a model in which letter identification requires spatial attention (and therefore occurs *after* spatial attention in tasks where spatial attention is initially directed away from the letters) but does not require whatever limited machinery underlies the central bottleneck. The fact that letter identification would wait for spatial attention but does not have to wait for this central machinery strongly suggests that the two reflect different underlying systems or mechanisms; Johnston, McCann and

---

[4] The minimum level is actually higher than chance, because people may unselectively store as many items as they can (Sperling, 1960).

Remington (1995) dubbed these "input attention" and "central attention". This conclusion fits nicely with the results of the hybrid speeded/unspeeded task results described in the previous paragraph. Using the terminology of Johnston et al., those results could be described as showing that input attention can be shifted while central attention is occupied with a different task. Both results imply the same fundamental point: that input attention cannot *be* central attention.

Does PRP Slowing Reflect Only a Single Bottleneck?

So far, we have talked as if the PRP effect stems from a single bottleneck (i.e. there is one set of operations constrained so that no operation in that set can overlap with any other in the set). It would obviously be unwise to assume this, however; as with a complex computer system, the brain might have various processors each individually capable of handling only one input at a time. If so, there could be various processor conflicts resulting in various bottlenecks. If the dual-task methodologies described here are applied to a wide variety of tasks involving complex spatial, linguistic, and other cognitive functions, as it seems likely they will be, it is quite possible that a number of bottlenecks will be discovered.

At present, however, a single bottleneck seems sufficient to account for the response delays observed in "standard" PRP designs involving pairs of choice RT tasks. In fact, results from these paradigms are difficult to square with the existence of multiple bottlenecks. The reason is that, as noted earlier, any Task-2 factor that slows a stage prior to the *last* bottleneck will show absorption into slack. Given the robust patterns of additivity observed in many studies, there cannot be "slack" *beyond* the stage manipulated. Nonetheless, there is reason to believe that the processes involved in producing distinct manual responses have the potential to conflict under certain circumstances, introducing a second, independent source of interference. It seems likely, however, that this potential is latent rather than actual in most experiments. To see why, consider some results by Pashler and Christian (unpublished), which involved a PRP task. The duration of the Task-1 response was manipulated: some stimuli required just a single keypress, while others required a series of several keypresses. Naturally, it took more time to finish the series than it took to perform a single keypress. When R2 was a vocal response, however, RT2 was barely affected by this manipulation; on trials where R1 was a sequence, R2 was often emitted while R1 was still under way. Thus, executing the manual responses in Task 1 did not hold up Task 2 (consistent with the idea that the central bottleneck encompasses response selection not response production). On the other hand, when R2 was a (right-hand) *manual* response, R2 was generally held up until the left-hand response sequence was completed. Thus, it seems that producing a stream of manual responses can potentially engender a second bottleneck in addition to the central bottleneck. However, in the typical PRP experiment with two discrete keypress responses, the first keypress is completed so quickly that there is no conflict between R1 and R2, making this limitation moot.[5] Naturally, daily life may include many situations where this conflict is not moot and does affect performance.

Why a Bottleneck?

So far we have talked about the existence of bottlenecks and their locus, but little has been said about *why* the human mind should be limited in this fashion. We can do little more than speculate here, but some of the possibilities are quite interesting. One interpretation of a bottleneck—so obvious that it is sometimes assumed to be equivalent to the concept of a bottleneck—is that the brain contains only a single piece of machinery capable of performing the critical operations that generate the bottleneck (response selection, retrieval, decision making, etc.). This is a parsimonious interpretation, but not the only possible one, and it may not even be the most plausible. For many decades it has been known that the brain relies on massive parallel processing at the level of individual neurons. There is also good reason to believe that different cortical areas are heavily specialized for carrying out different cognitive functions. However, different cortical areas are generally interconnected, so even if different mental operations are carried out in different neural modules, inhibitory interactions between modules might prevent parallel processing. That is, there might be a "lockout" operation whereby activity in one area suppresses processing in other areas.

Why would such a lockout occur? One possibility is that it might be a functional adaptation designed to prevent crosstalk or confusion. As noted in the introduction, some researchers have argued that crosstalk is *the* essential source of dual-task interference. In the PRP design, at least, this does not fit the facts: pairs of tasks show extreme interference (queuing of central processing) even when they use different input and output modalities, and involve completely different "domains" of cognition (e.g. spatial vs verbal vs lexical information processing; see Pashler, 1994). It is possible, however, that mutual inhibition might occur even with completely dissimilar tasks precisely because the possibility of crosstalk cannot always be excluded; that is, processing lockout might occur whether or not crosstalk actually arises simply because it *might* arise.

Another possibility is that attentional limitations in the control of action may exist to prevent the organism from producing incompatible motor

---

[5] One exception may be when the tasks are simple rather than choice RT (see De Jong, 1993).

actions, presumably with harmful results. Allport (1989, p. 649), for example, hypothesized the need to maintain "coherent and univocal control of action". One problem with this perfectly reasonable-sounding idea, at least as an explanation for the central bottleneck, is that in many dual-task experiments, subjects *can* in fact execute distinct motor plans at the same time. Indeed, casual observation confirms that people often talk while picking things up, for example. What seems to be blocked is simultaneous planning, rather than simultaneous execution, of motor responses. It is not clear how this would prevent incoherent or conflicting actions. Further-more, it is not clear that there really is any general process that prevents incoherent or conflicting actions. While motor responses are being produced they are susceptible to both modification and inhibition, although naturally modifications are not instantaneous (Logan & Burkell, 1986). Furthermore, there seems to be no general constraint that prevents people from "willing" and initiating two physically incompatible actions in rapid succession; when this happens, the result is in some ways a compromise of the two (de Jong, 1995). Late modifications of ongoing behavior may, from time to time, cause what we would judge to be action errors, but these need not neces-sarily have disastrous consequences. Baars and Motley (1976) have argued persuasively that Spoonerisms and other speech errors often occur when speech plans are changed after the plans have already been partly carried out.

EXCEPTIONS TO THE PRP EFFECT?

If there were no fundamental constraint preventing central stages of mul-tiple tasks from being carried out simultaneously, one might expect that exceptions to PRP interference would be encountered frequently. But in fact, amidst the hundreds of studies in this area, only a handful of excep-tions have been noted. These examples appear to be cases where two con-ditions are met: (1) modality conflicts in perceiving and responding are avoided, and (2) one or both tasks are unusually "easy" in some intuitive sense. (In fact, these two conditions are probably necessary but not suffi-cient to avoid PRP interference.) These exceptions have generally been interpreted as indicating that certain specific neural pathways are capable of bypassing the central bottleneck.

Greenwald (1972) and Greenwald & Shulman (1973) reported finding virtually no PRP interference when a special relationship between stimuli and responses was present in both tasks. For example, in Greenwald and Shulman (1973), Task 1 required moving a switch right to a right arrow and left to a left arrow, while Task 2 required subjects to say "A" to the spoken signal "A", and "B" to the spoken signal "B". Greenwald and Shulman suggested that these tasks produced little PRP interference because they did not require the normal process of mapping arbitrary stimuli onto responses. They argued that in these experiments, the stimuli generated a mental code that was already in the right format to select the response. It is certainly not implausible that there is some direct relation between the stimulus and response codes for "right" and "left", and it has long been suspected that listening and speaking speech codes for the same word are closely connected. McLeod and Posner (1984) found similar results when one task involved immediate verbal repetition (shadowing) and argued that there may be a small number of "privileged loops" that bypass the main path for stimulus–response mapping.

A few other exceptions have been reported more recently. Pashler, Carrier, and Hoffman (1993) found that PRP essentially disappeared when Task 2 required shifting eye position to the location of a stimulus. Johnston and Delgado (1993) found virtually no PRP when Task 2 was a simple tracking task in which subjects controlled the position of a circle and tried to keep it over a moving stimulus cross. The dynamics required leftward or rightward movements of a joystick in response to leftward and rightward movements of the stimulus cross. Note that both the eye movement task and the tracking task involved extremely "natural" stimulus–response mapping rules.

Johnston and Delgado (1993) found that PRP interference could be avoided when tracking served as Task 2 even though Task 1 required an arbitrary mapping of spoken stimulus words to spoken response words. The authors speculated that what is critical for avoiding a PRP is only that the second task be able to bypass the bottleneck channel; if it can, it should not matter whether Task 1 occupies that channel or not. In a more speculative vein, Johnston and Delgado suggested that there might be two requirements for avoiding PRP interference. The first is that subjects be able to conceive of Task 2 responses as "pre-authorized" prior to any particular movement. In the tracking task, no new "respond now" command is required for each response. Second, in line with previous theorizing, there must be a natural mapping of stimulus and response codes so that lower-level systems can carry out the pre-authorized responses without central mechanisms. In the case of tracking, what is required is that the brain use closely related spatial coordinate systems for the location of stimuli and the location of the action-consequences of responses. If either of these conditions is not met, higher-level systems will be needed either to authorize responding or to accomplish the S–R mapping, and a PRP will be produced.

WHERE IS THE BOTTLENECK ANATOMICALLY?

Although purely behavioral methods have taken us a considerable distance, it would obviously be desirable if our partial functional understanding of dual-task performance limitations could be tied to underlying brain structures and processes. Eventually one might hope to be able to record neural events indicative of bottlenecks and capacity sharing. This goal is as yet unrealized, but an initial step was taken in a recent study that measured event-related potentials during a PRP experiment (Osman & Moore, 1993). These authors found that the lateralized readiness potential over motor cortex associated with R2 was delayed to approximately the same extent as the RT itself. The result suggests that the lateralized readiness potential occurs at the completion of response selection, a view that seems to fit a number of other findings.

Other clues about the neural locus of PRP interference have emerged from recent studies of an unusual class of neurological patients—so-called "split-brain" patients in whom the connections between the cortical hemispheres have been surgically severed. If the central bottleneck described earlier has a cortical locus, split-brain patients should have two separate response-selection devices and exhibit no PRP effect whenever the two tasks are confined to separate hemispheres. However, using lateralized stimuli and responses, Pashler et al. (1994) observed a more or less normal PRP effect in four split-brain patients. They suggested that the structures causing the PRP bottleneck might therefore have a sub-cortical source, as connections at these brain levels remain intact in split-brain patients.

Examining one of the four split-brain patients studied by Pashler et al. (patient JW), Ivry, Franz, Kingstone, and Johnston (in press) confirmed the occurrence of PRP interference even when different input and response modalities were used for the two tasks. However, they have also obtained findings suggesting that the bottleneck may have a different locus for patient JW than it has for normals. In one experiment, Ivry et al. tested for the effects of inconsistent mapping rules in each task, using a method first employed by Duncan (1979). Both tasks required subjects to press an upper or a lower key in response to an upper or lower light. Sometimes, however, the S–R mapping for a task was the natural "compatible" mapping (upper light to upper button, lower light to lower button), whereas sometimes it was an unnatural, "compatible" mapping (upper light to lower button, lower light to upper button). Not surprisingly, subjects took longer to make a response when they used the compatible mapping than when they used the incompatible mapping. In a dual-task experiment with normal subjects, Duncan found that when the compatible mapping must be used on one task and the incompatible mapping on the other, responses in both tasks are slowed. In a PRP design, one would expect that having to switch from one mapping rule to another would slow Task 2 responses, as indeed it does. Interestingly, the inconsistency also slows responses on the *first* task; evidently, the alternation between rules impairs preparation of both tasks.

With patient JW, Ivry et al. used two conditions from Duncan's design. In one condition both Task 1 and Task 2 used compatible mappings (hence a consistent relationship between the mappings). In the other condition, Task 1 used a compatible mapping and Task 2 used an incompatible mapping. Normal subjects showed results like Duncan's. Although the only difference between the two conditions was in the mapping rule used in Task 2, both RT1 and RT2 were substantially lengthened. However, for patient JW, changing the mapping rule on Task 2 to an incompatible mapping substantially lengthened RT2 but had almost no effect on RT1. Thus it appears that for this patient, the hemisphere doing the compatible mapping was not affected by the fact that the other hemisphere was using an inconsistent mapping rule. There was one further difference between normals and patient JW. The variation in mapping rule on Task 2 constitutes a Task 2 difficulty variable so we can apply the locus of slack analysis. As this manipulation presumably affects the duration of the S–R mapping stage we should expect to find no absorption into slack, as in several experiments described earlier. This is essentially what Ivry et al. found for the normal subjects. For patient JW, however, the effect of the change in Task 2 mapping on RT2 was about 200 ms at the longest SOA but only about 40 ms at the shortest SOA. Thus almost all of the effect of the task 2 S–R mapping variable on RT2 was absorbed into slack. This indicates that for this patient—but not for normals—the bottleneck locus is after the S–R mapping stage.

Pashler et al. had inferred that as patient JW and normals both show a PRP bottleneck, this bottleneck is probably in an anatomical structure that is intact in JW; hence that the normal bottleneck is subcortical in origin. However, the new results challenge this conclusion, by suggesting that the bottleneck in patient JW may arise at a different processing stage than it does in normals. Therefore we cannot necessarily assume that the anatomical locus of the bottleneck in patient JW corresponds to the anatomical locus of the bottleneck in normals. There are at least two possible interpretations of these results.

The first is that patient JW's data reveal a bottleneck that exists in normals, but is normally "latent", in very much the same sense that manual response production bottleneck was argued to be latent in the typical PRP experiment with dual manual responses.[6] That is, as patient JW has no bottleneck at the stage of response selection (a conclusion suggested by the virtual elimination of the inconsistency effect in this patient), a bottleneck at a later stage (perhaps some brief stage of initiating responses) emerges—a bottleneck that is normally concealed in normals by queuing of the earlier response selection stage.

---

[6] To be slightly more formal: even if stage J in Task 1 and stage J in Task 2 cannot be performed simultaneously, this may be only a latent conflict if, due to the timing of preceding stages, and due to possible bottlenecks arising in these earlier stages, it will never happen that the input to stage J in Task 2 will be ready before stage J in Task 1 has been completed.

A second possibility is that the separation of patient JW's cortical hemispheres may have removed all central bottlenecks, removing any internal obstacles to parallel performance on both tasks. However, as JW was studied years after his surgery, he may have acquired novel strategies to prevent the two sides of his brain from acting incoherently. For instance, what would happen if one side of his brain decided it wanted to continue moving a spoonful of soup to his mouth to eat, while the other side decided to command the other hand to push away from the table so he could get up and do something else entirely? Conceivably, patient JW has had to learn some strategy for letting his hemispheres take turns at controlling his overt actions, a strategy that carries over to his performance in the PRP paradigm. Ironically, then, the suggestion that central bottlenecks are not structural but merely strategic may have some validity, but only for split-brain patients and not for intact individuals.

Although the attempt to characterize the source of PRP interference in functional terms has been going on for about half a century, attempts to uncover the physiological/anatomical locus of central interference has barely begun. With recent advances in brain imaging technologies, we may be able to look forward to new insights on this question.

ATTENTIONAL LIMITS IN MEMORY

Many theorists have assumed that attentional capacity limitations can be equated in one fashion or another with short-term memory (STM). Although some writers have questioned the empirical validity of the concept of short-term memory, there is a formidable body of evidence for the idea that information can be stored in a transient form that is distinct from permanent memory (see Pashler & Carrier, 1996, for a review). This evidence argues for a multiplicity of short-term memory systems rather than a single system, however. There is also evidence that short-term storage usually reflects brain systems specialized for carrying out specific cognitive functions aside from short-term memory (e.g. language comprehension, motor control, visual perception). For this reason, we use the term "STM" here to refer to various different systems in which information can be held transiently—systems that may well have other functions besides memory.

It has long been supposed that there is a close and important connection between "attention" and short-term retention. For one thing, people have selective control over what information they hold onto for immediate report. Some illustrations of this are found in the classic partial-report experiments involving audition (Darwin, Turvey & Crowder, 1972) and vision (Sperling, 1960). Here, subjects were able to transfer items into short-term memory on the basis of some cued attribute like the position or color of a letter.

What sorts of attentional limitations is STM subject to? One way to address this question is to see whether information can be transferred into STM while a person carries out a centrally demanding operation in an unrelated task—e.g. planning an action of some kind. Is the transfer of information into STM subject to the same central bottleneck responsible for the PRP effect described in the preceding section?[7] A number of investigators have presented lists of words while people performed a concurrent task, and later tested memory for the word using the "free recall" task (repeating the items back in any order). Murdock (1965), for example, had subjects listen to a spoken list while rapidly sorting cards, and then attempt free recall. The so-called "recency effect" (memory for the last-presented items) was quite intact, suggesting that the sorting task did not prevent words from being stored in STM. Anderson and Craik (1974) made similar observations using a list of spoken words presented while subjects performed a concurrent visual/manual choice reaction-time task.

Other evidence also argues that storage in visual short-term memory is relatively free of central capacity demands. One experiment that explored this issue required subjects to make a rapid choice response to a tone; at some point during or after the choice task, a pattern of black and white squares was flashed briefly, followed immediately by a mask. Subjects were able to maintain good performance regardless of the temporal overlap of the two tasks, suggesting that information about the patterns was stored in visual STM while the response to the tone was being planned (Pashler, 1993b).

What about simply holding onto information already in STM? Passively retaining a memory load slows responses in concurrent speeded tasks to some extent (Logan, 1978). However, it does not severely impair performance in difficult reasoning and comprehension tasks (Baddeley & Hitch, 1977). It is an odd fact that researchers have very frequently assumed that STM storage drains "general processing resources". The results just described would seem to test this assumption and reject it. On the other hand, beginning to rehearse information that has just been stored in STM (which intuitively feels more like carrying out an action rather than merely maintaining a state) does seem to produce substantial interference that lasts for a short time (Naveh-Benjamin & Jonides, 1984).

What about long-term memory (LTM)? As with short-term memory, when someone deliberately ignores a stimulus there is often little trace of that stimulus evident in later tests of long-term memory (Moray, 1959; Rock & Guttman, 1981). However, unlike with STM, concurrent tasks that

---

[7] The alert reader will notice that evidence already described suggests that there could not be any complete interference of this sort, in the experiments combining speeded responses with attention shifts.

impose central processing demands clearly reduce the flow of information into LTM. Evidence arguing for this conclusion comes from experiments described earlier in which people listened to words while carrying out con-current sorting tasks. Although recency (reflecting predominantly STM) was unaffected, recall of items from earlier parts of the list (reflecting pre-dominantly LTM) was much reduced (Anderson & Craik, 1974; Murdock, 1965). Further evidence comes from recent studies in which people carried out speeded choice tasks while items to be remembered were presented (Carrier & Pashler, unpublished data). When the concurrent tasks involved speeded responses to tones, and there was a short interval between the response to a tone and the occurrence of the next tone, subsequent memory for material read during the tone task suffered substantially. This was true whether the material consisted of word lists or sequences of faces, and whether memory was measured with recall or recognition. This result reinforces the earlier observation that profound dual-task interference may occur without the materials involved in the two tasks being discernibly similar. This suggests competition for a relatively general mechanism or some process of mutual inhibition.

The fact that the flow of information into long-term memory is impaired by concurrent central demands would suggest that memory storage is sub-ject to the very same central bottleneck as the PRP. However, measures of accuracy of memory storage, unlike reaction time, do not tell us whether the concurrent task completely prevents the memory storage, or merely slows it. Empirically, dual-task manipulations generally reduce memory performance without bringing it down to chance levels. Before leaving this topic, it should be mentioned that some reports in the literature have concluded that sec-ondary tasks do not reduce memory storage. Usually, these studies have involved concurrent tasks that require only intermittent central processing. For example, Tun, Wingfield, and Stine 1991) found that a concurrent choice reaction-time task did not reduce later recall of spoken prose pas-sages. However, the concurrent task involved responding to letters that were presented only once every three to seven seconds, a task that would be expected to occupy central processing machinery for only a tiny fraction of the total time.

So far, we have talked about storing information in memory; we turn now to *retrieving* information that has already been stored in long-term memory. Experiments requiring people to carry out memory retrieval together with a concurrent task have led to conflicting conclusions. On the one hand, Park, Smith, Dudley, and Lafronza (1989) found that an audi-tory/manual concurrent task impaired concurrent (verbal) free recall. On the other, Baddeley et al. (1984) combined a sorting task with memory retrieval, and found that the difficulty of the sorting had little effect on the success of retrieval, although it did increase response latencies. Baddeley et al.

concluded that interference affected the production of responses but not the actual memory retrieval process.

More fine-grained analyses are necessary to discriminate between interference in production and interference in retrieval. As described earlier, the PRP method is particularly well suited for this. Carrier and Pashler (1996) combined a manual response to a tone (Task 1) with retrieval of a paired associate in response to a visually presented cue word (Task 2) in a PRP design. There was a PRP effect (slower responses in the paired-associate task at shorter SOAs). The duration of the memory retrieval was manipulated in various ways. These manipulations slowed second-task RTs, and the slowing was roughly additive with SOA (Carrier & Pashler, 1996). Following the logic described earlier, this implies that memory retrieval, but not response production or any other stage in the second task after memory retrieval, was delayed when the first task was being performed. This in turn suggests that the central bottleneck described earlier encompasses memory retrieval. One is led to suspect, then, that the inability to select two responses at the same time (response selection bottleneck) is just a special case of a general constraint on retrieving associations in memory, not a limitation particularly tied to motor programming or action.

CONCLUDING COMMENTS

One general theme of this chapter is that examining dual-task performance in detail reveals that our cognitive machinery is subject to more severe limitations than we might have suspected from casual observation. Although perceptual machinery seems capable of identifying more than a single object at a time, it is subject to capacity limits that become evident when the stimulus load is increased beyond a fairly modest level. In the realm of memory retrieval and action planning, a different and more central form of limitation seems to arise. The evidence presently available suggests that overlap in the central operations of different tasks simply does not occur except for a few special cases of extremely compatible stimulus–response mappings. Sufficient practice may get around this limitation, but this has not yet been demonstrated; several thousand trials of practice in rather simple choice reaction-time tasks seem insufficient.

It should be noted that the idea of obligatory serial central processing is quite consistent with a great deal of parallel processing, for several reasons. First, central processing in one task can clearly overlap with both perceptual analysis and production of motor responses in another task (as Fig. 4.2 makes plain). Second, planning of a response to a given stimulus seems to overlap with continuing perceptual analysis of that stimulus (Levy & Pashler, 1995). Thus, at the very moment we are planning an action based on preliminary perceptual conclusions about some objects, these conclusions may be refined and even overturned. This implies that the boxes in stage diagrams of the sort shown in Fig. 4.2 should be seen as depicting a stream of processing that results in a given response, not the totality of the processing of a given stimulus that the nervous system may carry out. Third, at least in the case of dissimilar motor responses (e.g. vocal and manual responses), two independent streams of outputs can often be produced. This is demonstrated in the continuous-task experiments described at the beginning of the chapter, and confirmed in the PRP experiments that combined sequences of responses in one task and punctate responses in a second task (Pashler & Christian, unpublished). Fourth, even though the use of different inputs to select different responses to each input requires sequential processing, when several inputs select a *single* response this lookup can be carried out in a single mental operation. This is demonstrated in the so-called coactivation effect observed by Miller (1982), and is also seen in people's ready ability to solve crossword puzzles using completely unrelated cues to "home in on" a target in memory.[8]

Therefore, the central bottleneck argued for in this chapter does not conflict with casual observations that people often read a newspaper while riding an exercise bicycle, for example, or move a cup of coffee away from their lips while speaking. Nor does it conflict with the idea that different brain areas—some specialized more for stimulus-related processing, some more for response-related processing—usually work continuously and concurrently. What these results do suggest, however, is that in certain important respects our mind may nonetheless work a bit like a digital computer with switching and buffering capabilities, and that fine-grained measurements of performance in dual-task situations can reveal many non-obvious facts about the timing of underlying mental/neural events.

REFERENCES

Allport, A. (1989). Visual attention. In M.I. Posner (Ed.), *Foundations of cognitive science* (pp. 631–682). Cambridge, MA: MIT Press.

Allport, D.A., Antonis, B., & Reynolds, P. (1972). On the division of attention: A disproof of the single-channel hypothesis. *Quarterly Journal of Experimental Psychology, 24*, 225–235.

Anderson, C.M.B., & Craik, F.I.M. (1974). The effect of a concurrent task on recall from primary memory. *Journal of Verbal Learning and Verbal Behavior, 13*, 107–113.

Baars, B.J., & Motley, M.T. (1976). Spoonerisms as sequencer conflicts: Evidence from artificially elicited errors. *American Journal of Psychology, 89*, 467–484.

Baddeley, A., Lewis, V., Eldridge, M., & Thomson, N. (1984). Attention and retrieval from long-term memory. *Journal of Experimental Psychology: General, 113*, 518–540.

Baddeley, A.D. (1986). *Working memory*. Oxford: Oxford University Press.

Baddeley, A.D., & Hitch, G. (1977). Recency reexamined. In S. Dornic (Ed.), *Attention & performance VI* (pp. 647–667). Hillsdale, NJ: Lawrence Erlbaum Associates Inc.

---

[8] For a discussion of the implications of this for cognitive architecture, see Pashler (1993a).

Bertelson, P. (1966). Central intermittency twenty years later. *Quarterly Journal of Experimental Psychology, 18*, 153–163.

Biederman, I., Teitelbaum, R.C., & Mezzanotte, R.J. (1983). Scene perception: A failure to find a benefit from prior expectancy or familiarity. *Journal of Experimental Psychology: Learning, Memory, and Cognition, 9*, 411–429.

Carrier, M., & Pashler, H. (1996). The attention demands of memory retrieval. *Journal of Experimental Psychology: Learning, Memory, and Cognition, 21*, 1339–1348.

Darwin, C.J., Turvey, M.T., & Crowder, R.G. (1972). An auditory analogue of the Sperling partial report procedure: Evidence for brief auditory storage. *Cognitive Psychology, 3*, 255–267.

de Jong, R. (1993). Multiple bottlenecks in overlapping task performance. *Journal of Experimental Psychology: Human Perception and Performance, 19*, 965–980.

de Jong, R. (1995). Perception–action coupling and S–R compatibility. *Acta Psychologica, 90*, 287–299.

Duncan, J. (1979). Divided attention: The whole is more than the sum of its parts. *Journal of Experimental Psychology: Human Perception and Performance, 5*, 216–228.

Duncan, J. (1980a). The demonstration of capacity limitation. *Cognitive Psychology, 12*, 75–96.

Duncan, J. (1980b). The locus of interference in the perception of simultaneous stimuli. *Psychological Review, 87*, 272–300.

Duncan, J. (1987). Attention and reading: Wholes and parts in shape recognition—A tutorial review. In M. Coltheart (Ed.), *Attention and performance XII: The psychology of reading* (pp. 36–61). Hove, UK: Lawrence Erlbaum Associates Ltd.

Duncan, J. (1993). Similarity between concurrent visual discriminations: Dimensions and objects. *Perception and Psychophysics, 54*, 425–430.

Duncan, J., Ward, R., & Shapiro, K. (1994). Direct measurement of attentional dwell time in human vision. *Nature, 369*, 313–315.

Dutta, A., & Walker, B.N. (1995, November). *Persistence of the PRP effect: Evaluating the response-selection bottleneck.* Paper presented at the 36th annual meeting of the Psychonomic Society, Los Angeles, California.

Eriksen, C.W., & Hoffman, J.E. (1973). The extent of processing of noise elements during selective encoding from visual displays. *Perception and Psychophysics, 14*, 155–160.

Estes, W.K., & Taylor, H.A. (1964). A detection method and probabilistic models for assessing information processing from brief visual displays. *Proceedings of the National Academy of Sciences, 52*, 446–454.

Estes, W.K., & Taylor, H.A. (1965). Visual detection in relation to display size and redundancy of critical elements. *Perception and Psychophysics, 1*, 9–15.

Goodrich, S., Henderson, L., Allchin, N., & Jeevaratnam, A. (1990). On the peculiarity of simple reaction time. *Quarterly Journal of Experimental Psychology: Human Experimental Psychology, 42A*, 763–775.

Gottsdanker, R. (1980). The ubiquitous role of preparation. In G.E. Stelmach & J. Requin (Eds.), *Tutorials in motor behavior* (pp. 355–371). Amsterdam: North-Holland Press.

Gottsdanker, R., & Way, T.C. (1966). Varied and constant intersignal intervals in psychological refractoriness. *Journal of Experimental Psychology, 72*, 792–804.

Greenwald, A.G. (1972). On doing two things at once: Time-sharing as a function of ideomotor compatibility. *Journal of Experimental Psychology, 100*, 52–57.

Greenwald, A., & Shulman, H. (1973). On doing two things at once: II. Elimination of the psychological refractory period. *Journal of Experimental Psychology, 101*, 70–76.

Ivry, R.B., Franz, E., Kingston, A., & Johnston, J.C. (in press). The PRP effect in a split-brain patient: Response uncoupling despite normal interference. *Journal of Experimental Psychology: Human Perception and Performance.*

James, W. (1890/1950). *The principles psychology. Vol 1.* New York: Dover.

Johnston, J.C. & Delgado, D. (1993, November). *Bypassing the single-channel bottleneck in dual-task performance.* Paper presented at the 34th annual meeting of the Psychonomic Society.

Johnston, J.C. & McCann, R.S. (1997). *On the focus of dual-task interference: Is there a bottleneck at the stimulus classification stage?* Manuscript submitted for publication.

Johnston, J.C., McCann, R.S. & Remington, R.W. (1995). Chronometric evidence for two types of attention. *Psychological Science, 6,* 365–369.

Johnston, J.C., McCann, R., & Remington, R. (1996). Selective attention operates at two processing loci. In A. Kramer & G. Logan (Eds.), *Essays in honor of Charles Eriksen* (pp.439–458). American Psychological Association.

Kahneman, D. (1973). *Attention and effort.* New York: Prentice Hall.

Karlin, L., & Kestenbaum, R. (1968). Effects of number of alternatives on the psychological refractory period. *Quarterly Journal of Experimental Psychology, 20,* 167–178.

Keele, S.W. (1973). *Attention and human performance.* Pacific Palisades, CA: Goodyear.

Kinsbourne, M. (1981). Single channel theory. In D. Holding (Ed.), *Human Skills* (pp. 65–89). Chichester, UK: Wiley.

Kleiss, J.A., & Lane, D.M. (1986). Locus and persistence of capacity limitations in visual information processing. *Journal of Experimental Psychology: Human Perception and Performance, 12,* 200–210.

Koutstaal, W. (1992). Skirting the abyss: A history of experimental explorations of automatic writing in psychology. *Journal of the History of the Behavioral Sciences, 28,* 5–27.

Levy, J., & Pashler, H. (1995). Does perceptual analysis continue during selection and production of a speeded response? *Acta Psychologica, 90,* 245–260.

Logan, G.D. (1978). Attention in character classification tasks: Evidence for the automaticity of component stages. *Journal of Experimental Psychology: General, 107,* 32–63.

Logan, G.D. (1994). Spatial attention and the apprehension of spatial relations. *Journal of Experimental Psychology: Human Perception and Performance, 20,* 1015–1036.

Logan, G.D., & Burkell, J. (1986). Dependence and independence in responding to double stimulation: A comparison of stop, change and dual-task paradigms. *Journal of Experimental Psychology: Human Perception and Performance, 12,* 549–563.

McCann, R.S., & Johnston, J.C. (1989, November). *The locus of processing bottlenecks in the overlapping tasks paradigm.* Paper presented at the 1989 meeting of the Psychonomic Society, Atlanta, Georgia.

McCann, R.S., & Johnston, J.C. (1992). Locus of the single-channel bottleneck in dual-task interference. *Journal of Experimental Psychology: Human Perception and Performance, 18,* 471–484.

McLeod, P. (1977). Parallel processing and the psychological refractory period. *Acta Psychologica, 41,* 381–391.

McLeod, P., & Posner, M.I. (1984). Privileged loops from percept to act. In H. Bouma & D.G. Bouwhuis, (Eds.), *Attention and performance X.* Hove, UK: Lawrence Erlbaum Associates Ltd.

Miller, J. (1982). Divided attention: Evidence for coactivation with redundant signals. *Cognitive Psychology, 14,* 247–279.

Miller, J., & Bonnel, A.M. (1994). Switching or sharing in dual task line length discrimination? *Perception and Psychophysics, 56,* 431–446.

Moray, N. (1959). Attention in dichotic listening: Affective cues and the influence instructions. *Quarterly Journal of Experimental Psychology, 11,* 56–60.

Murdock, B.B. (1965). Effects of a subsidiary task on short-term memory. *British Journal of Psychology, 56,* 413–419.

Naveh-Benjamin, M., & Jonides, J. (1984). Maintenance rehearsal: A two-component analysis. *Journal of Experimental Psychology: Learning, Memory, and Cognition, 10,* 369–385.

Navon, D., & Miller, J. (1987). Role of outcome conflict in dual-task interference. *Journal of Experimental Psychology: Human Perception and Performance, 13*, 435–448.

Osman, A., & Moore, C. (1993). The locus of dual-task interference: Psychological refractory effects on movement-related brain potentials. *Journal of Experimental Psychology: Human Perception and Performance, 19*, 1292–1312.

Palmer, J. (1994). Set-size effects in visual search: The effect of attention is independent of the stimulus for simple tasks. *Vision Research, 34*, 1703–1721.

Park, D.C., Smith, A.D., Dudley, W.N., & Lafronza, V.N. (1989). Effects of age and a divided attention task presented during encoding and retrieval on memory. *Journal of Experimental Psychology: Learning, Memory, and Cognition, 15*, 1185–1191.

Pashler, H. (1984). Processing stages in overlapping tasks: Evidence for a central bottleneck. *Journal of Experimental Psychology: Human Perception and Performance, 10*, 358–377.

Pashler, H. (1989). Dissociations and dependencies between speed and accuracy: Evidence for a two-component theory of divided attention in simple tasks. *Cognitive Psychology, 21*, 469–514.

Pashler, H. (1991). Shifting visual attention and selecting motor responses: Distinct attentional mechanisms. *Journal of Experimental Psychology: Human Perception and Performance, 17*, 23–1040.

Pashler, H. (1993a). Doing two tasks at the same time. *American Scientist, 81*, 46–55.

Pashler, H. (1993b). Dual-task interference and elementary mental mechanisms. In D. Meyer & S. Kornblum (Eds.), *Attention and performance XIV* (pp. 245–264). Cambridge, MA: MIT Press.

Pashler, H. (1994). Overlapping mental operations in serial performance with preview *Quarterly Journal of Experimental Psychology, 47*, 161–191.

Pashler, H., & Baylis, G.C. (1991). Procedural learning: II. Intertrial repetition effects in speeded-choice tasks. *Journal of Experimental Psychology: Learning, Memory, and Cognition, 17*, 33–48.

Pashler, H., & Carrier, M. (1996). Structures, processes and flow of control. In E.L. Bjork, & R.A. Bjork (Eds.), *Handbook of perception and cognition: Memory* (2nd edn. pp. 3–29). San Diego, CA: Academic Press.

Pashler, H., Carrier, M., & Hoffman, J. (1993). Saccadic eye movements and dual-task interference. *Quarterly Journal of Experimental Psychology, 46A*, 51–82.

Pashler, H., & Christian, C. (1997). *Dual-task interference and motor response production.* Unpublished manuscript.

Pashler, H., & Johnston, J.C. (1989). Interference between temporally overlapping tasks: Chronometric evidence for central postponement with or without response grouping. *Quarterly Journal of Experimental Psychology, 41A*, 19–45.

Pashler, H., Luck, S.J., Hillyard, S.A., Mangun, G.R. & Gazzaniga, M. (1994). Sequential operation of disconnected cerebral hemispheres in split-brain patients. *Neuroreport, 5*, 2381–2384

Pashler, H., & O'Brien, S. (1993). Dual-task interference and the cerebral hemispheres. *Journal of Experimental Psychology: Human Perception and Performance, 19*, 315–330.

Rock, I., & Guttman, D. (1981). The effect of inattention on form perception. *Journal of Experimental Psychology: Human Perception and Performance, 7*, 275–285.

Ruthruff, E., Miller, J., & Lachmann, T. (1995). Does mental rotation require central mechanisms? *Journal of Experimental Psychology: Human Perception and Performance, 21*, 552–570.

Ruthruff, E., & Pashler H. (submitted) Dual-task central bottleneck: Structural or strategic?

Salthouse, T.A., & Saults, J.S. (1987). Multiple spans in transcription typing. *Journal of Applied Psychology, 72*, 187–196.

Schweickert, R. (1978). A critical path generalization of the additive factor method: Analysis of a Stroop task. *Journal of Mathematical Psychology, 18*, 105–139.

Shaffer, L.H. (1975). Multiple attention in continuous verbal tasks. In P.M.A. Rabbitt & S. Dornic (Eds.), *Attention and performance V*. New York: Academic Press.

Shiffrin, R.M., & Gardner, G.T. (1972). Visual processing capacity and attentional control. *Journal of Experimental Psychology, 93*, 78–82.

Smith, M.C. (1967). Theories of the psychological refractory period. *Psychological Bulletin, 67*, 202–213.

Smith, M.C. (1969). The effect of varying information on the psychological refractory period. In W.G. Koster (Ed.), *Acta Psychologica, 30*, 220–231

Spelke, E., Hirst, W., & Neisser, U. (1976). Skills of divided attention. *Cognition, 4*, 215–230.

Sperling, G. (1960). The information available in brief visual presentations. *Psychological Monographs: General and Applied* (Whole No. 498, 1–29).

Sternberg, S. (1969). The discovery of processing stages: Extensions of Donders' method. In W.G. Koster (Ed.), *Attention and performance II* (pp.276–315). Amsterdam: North Holland.

Telford, C.W. (1931). The refractory phase of voluntary and associative responses. *Journal of Experimental Psychology, 14*, 1–36.

Treisman, A. (1991). Search, similarity, and integration of features between and within dimensions. *Journal of Experimental Psychology: Human Perception and Performance, 17*, 652–676.

Treisman, A., & Davies, A. (1973). Dividing attention to ear and eye. In S. Kornblum (Ed.), *Attention and performance IV*. (pp.101–117) New York: Academic Press.

Tun, P.A., Wingfield, A., & Stine, E.A.L. (1991). Speech-processing capacity in young and older adults: A dual-task study. *Psychology and Aging, 6*, 3–9.

Van Selst, M., & Jolicoeur, P. (1995). Can mental rotation occur before the dual-task bottleneck? *Journal of Experimental Psychology: Human Perception and Performance, 20*, 905–921.

Van Selst, M. (in press). Decision and response in dual-task interference. *Cognitive Psychology*

Welford, A.T. (1952). The "psychological refractory period" and the timing of high speed performance: A review and a theory. *British Journal of Psychology, 43*, 2–19.

Welford, A.T. (1967). Single channel operation in the brain. *Acta Psychologica, 27*, 5–22.

Welford, A.T. (1980). The single-channel hypothesis. In A.T. Welford (Ed.), *Reaction time* (pp.215–252). New York: Academic Press.

CHAPTER FIVE

Attention and Inhibition

Bruce Milliken
McMaster University, Ontario, Canada

Steven P. Tipper
University of Wales, Bangor, UK

Although our senses are inundated with information from the world around us, only a small portion of that information is relevant to our goal-driven thought and behavior. As a result, intelligent behavior requires that we process information selectively. From a phenomenological perspective, it appears that this selectivity is achieved by an enhancement of processing of relevant information; the targets of our attention—sometimes external objects, other times internal thoughts—seem to dominate our mental activity.

At the same time, introspection about attention may well reflect a description of the end product of attentive analysis, rather than a mechanistic explanation of how that end product came to be. This distinction between attention as an effect and attention as a cause was made long ago by William James, and has since played a prominent role in a number of theoretical treatments of attention (see Desimone & Duncan, 1995; Johnston & Dark, 1986; Johnston & Hawley, 1994). For example, LaBerge (1995) carefully distinguishes between the *expression* of attention, and the *mechanism(s)* by which that expression is achieved. Although attention is widely presumed to be expressed as an enhancement of processing of relevant information, the mechanisms that give rise to this relative enhancement continue to be debated among attention researchers.

In the present chapter, we focus on an issue of wide and enduring interest in the field of psychology; that attentive processing of relevant information may be achieved by mechanisms that impede the processing of irrelevant information. Although this issue cannot be addressed in its entirety in a single chapter, we attempt to meet two objectives in the discussion that follows. The first objective is to demonstrate the historical resilience of the view that inhibitory processes play a role in selective attention. To this end, we highlight three landmark contributions to the attention literature that make a strong collective argument for the utility of mechanisms that impede the processing of irrelevant information. At the same time, the second objective of this chapter is to point out that linking specific behavioral effects with inhibitory attentional mechanisms is an inherently complex task. To address this objective, we discuss results from a range of human behavioral studies in which deficits in the processing of irrelevant information have been measured.

THREE LANDMARKS

As already mentioned, the research contributions discussed in this section were chosen as representative of the steady and continued interest in the issue of inhibitory attentional processes. However, the choice of contributions was also meant to reflect a distinct trend in the approach used to study inhibitory mechanisms in attention. In particular, whereas early work on this issue relied strictly on human experimental data, results from computational and neurophysiological studies now supplement data garnered from human behavioral studies. As will be apparent in the second section of the chapter, it has become increasingly evident that an understanding of the role of inhibitory mechanisms in attention will require such converging approaches.

Filter Theory: Broadbent (1958)

One of the first modern theories of attention was Donald Broadbent's (1958) filter theory. Broadbent viewed the central nervous system as akin to a single communication channel with limited capacity. As such, his filter theory was designed to explain how some of the information processed by our senses is discarded before reaching the limited capacity channel. To effect this discarding of irrelevant information, Broadbent proposed that certain physical properties of stimuli (e.g. spatial location, pitch) are analyzed in parallel, with the products of this analysis then being stored in a short-term memory buffer called the S system. A selective filter then ensures that only the behaviorally relevant contents of the S system are subject to further attentive analysis by the P system. Stimuli not selected for attentive analysis are presumed to decay passively within the S system in a matter of seconds.

Note that Broadbent (1958) did not use the term "inhibition" to refer to the selective filter. Indeed, he argued (p.306) that "to use hypothetical constructs made up from physiological terms is to lay oneself open to the danger of having one's psychological theory disproved by some irrelevant physiological research". To be clear, our interest here is in mechanisms that function to directly impede the processing of irrelevant information. Broadbent's filter clearly satisfies this criterion, as may an attentional mechanism that is meant to map onto a known mechanism of neural inhibition. Their putatively common function motivates the treatment of both in this chapter.

An important prediction of Broadbent's filter model is that processing of unattended material should not proceed to the level at which semantic information is accessed. However, shortly after publication of Broadbent's model, several investigators reported evidence that semantic access is, at least sometimes, achieved for unattended stimuli (e.g. Moray, 1959; Treisman, 1960). For example, Moray (1959) reported that subjects occasionally recognize their own name when it is inserted in an unattended message during a shadowing task. Results such as this one prompted some to modify the notion of a selective filter (e.g. Treisman, 1960) and others to abandon it completely (Deutsch & Deutsch, 1963; Neisser, 1967).

Lateral Inhibition: Walley and Weiden (1973)

To abandon the notion of a filter completely requires an alternative hypothesis to explain how central processes are protected from information overload. For example, Neisser (1967) forwarded a view of attention that differentiates between two stages of processing. As in Broadbent's (1958) filter model, the first stage analyzes multiple inputs in parallel, the products of which are stored in sensory memory. However, the second stage is an active encoding process that constructs a conscious representation of selected information from sensory memory. Neisser called this encoding process "analysis by synthesis", and its most important feature is that it can effectively encode only a limited amount of information at any one time. By this view, irrelevant information is often prevented access to central processes because the process that provides that access is occupied with the encoding of other information. Neisser's (1967) view, then, represents one way in which irrelevant information can be prevented from overloading central mechanisms without it being actively filtered.

However, Walley and Weiden (1973, p.286) suggested that such a theory evades a fundamental question: what prevents irrelevant sources of information from competing for access to this encoding process?

> Unless one postulates a mechanism which prevents the encoding of one input during the encoding of another, it appears that the rejected input should produce an information overload and more interference than appears to be the case.

Their response to this problem was a model that integrated work from both behavioral and neurophysiological studies of attention. An important property of their model distinguished it from others that had been proposed up to that time. In particular, Walley and Weiden suggested that the latter stages of encoding could conceivably occur in parallel across a range of inputs. Note that the assumption of serial processing in these latter stages was widely presumed necessary to explain how information overload is avoided. To deal with this potential problem, Walley and Weiden (1973) suggested that there must be a mechanism to ensure that encoding of one input actively interferes with the encoding of other similar inputs.

The mechanism that they proposed to fulfil this role was lateral inhibition. Lateral inhibition is a mechanism by which activity in a neural unit at one level of a system reduces the activity of neighboring units at the same level of the system. The inhibitory effect often varies with distance, such that stronger inhibitory effects are associated with more closely neighboring units. In early vision, lateral inhibition is useful because it enhances the neural response in regions of contrast, thereby providing information concerning, for example, where one object ends and another begins. More generally, lateral inhibition serves to accentuate differences in the activity of neighboring neurons.

Walley and Weiden (1973) assumed that similarities among external stimuli are represented in the cortex by the physical proximity of their neural representations. If this is the case, then lateral inhibitory connections among neural units at the highest levels of an hierarchical pattern-recognition system would help to ensure that a single highly activated representation of a target input would dominate over those associated with similar, but distracting, sources of input. These inhibitory interactions were presumed to produce *cognitive masking*, an analogue to sensory masking that was widely believed to be caused by inhibitory interactions at lower levels in the processing hierarchy. Importantly, the degree of cortical lateral inhibition was argued to be related to arousal, which in turn could be modulated either voluntarily or reflexively. Walley and Weiden described a series of neural network simulations to back these claims. Together, their theoretical and computational work demonstrated that lateral inhibitory mechanisms could comprise the filter necessary to protect an organism from information overload.

Single Cell Recordings: Moran and Desimone (1985)

Visual processing that leads to object recognition is known to proceed along a pathway from striate cortex (V1) through prestriate areas (e.g. V4), and on to the inferior temporal cortex (IT; Felleman & Van Essen, 1991; Ungerleider & Mishkin, 1982). The receptive fields of neurons increase in size along this pathway, which means that cells respond to stimulation from an increasingly wide portion of the visual field as one progresses from V1 to V4 to IT. This being the case, the need to filter irrelevant sources of input becomes crucial at later stages in this pathway.

Evidence of this filtering in V4 and IT was reported by Moran and Desimone (1985). Their evidence derives from single cell recordings in the visual cortex of rhesus monkeys. Their procedure involved isolating a single cell, mapping out its receptive field, and noting which types of stimuli (among bars of varying colors, orientations, and sizes) were effective, and which ineffective, in producing a strong response from the cell. In an experimental trial, one effective and one ineffective stimulus were both displayed within the receptive field of the cell, but at different spatial locations. The monkeys had received prior training by which they learned to attend to one of the locations or the other.

When the monkey attended to the location of the effective stimulus, the cell fired at a high rate. However, when the monkey attended to the location of the ineffective stimulus the firing rate of the cell was attenuated. Note that this attenuation occurred despite the fact that the effective stimulus remained within the receptive field of the cell. Further, cells that demonstrated this attenuated firing rate were observed both in IT and V4, where filtering of irrelevant input is presumed to be most important, but not in V1 (but see Motter, 1993).

In a separate condition of the same study the effective stimulus was displayed within the receptive field, while the ineffective stimulus was displayed just outside the receptive field of the target cell. In this condition the cell fired at a high rate both when the effective stimulus was attended, and when the ineffective stimulus was attended. In other words, the response of the target cell to the effective stimulus within its receptive field was modulated only when attention was devoted to an ineffective stimulus that was also within the receptive field of the target cell. Importantly, the modulation was such that the firing rate of the target cell was attenuated when an ineffective stimulus within its receptive field was attended. This finding suggests that *attention was not enhancing the response to attended stimuli, but rather that it was gating the neural response to unattended stimuli.*

Summary

This section has outlined three landmarks within the attention literature. Collectively, they share the view that a critical role of the attention system is to protect central mechanisms from interference caused by irrelevant input. As such, impeded processing of unattended information, as well as enhanced processing of attended information, is deemed important. We now turn to a wider discussion of experimental methods that have been used to measure the consequences of attending to one event on processing of another event. Such methods are perhaps best differentiated from one another by reference to the function of attentive processing in each. For example, attention may be employed to generate an expectation, attention may be used to concentrate on the ongoing processing demands of a primary task, or attention may be used to direct behavior selectively toward one of a number of competing events.[1]

ATTENTION AS EXPECTATION

When attention is used to generate an expectation for a stimulus of a particular category, responses to stimuli from an unexpected category are often less efficient. Posner and Snyder (1975) demonstrated this phenomenon using a same–different letter matching task. Each experimental trial began with a prime stimulus that was either a letter or a plus sign. The following stimulus contained two target letters, and the subject's task was to discriminate whether these target letters were the same or different. On either 20% or 80% of the trials the prime was *valid*; that is, the prime letter corresponded to one or both of the target letters. In the 80% valid condition, subjects would do well to *expect* the prime letter to reappear as one of the targets. By contrast, in the 20% valid condition, there would be little to motivate the subject to generate such an expectation.

Facilitation effects in the Posner and Snyder (1975) study were defined as the difference in response time between valid and neutral (plus sign as prime) trials, and inhibition effects as the difference in response time between invalid and neutral trials. Importantly, although facilitation effects were observed in both the 20% and 80% valid conditions, they were larger in the 80% condition. Posner and Snyder (1975) suggested that the relatively small facilitation effects in the 20% valid condition could be attributed to the automatic activation of the pathway associated with the prime. However, the larger facilitation effects in the 80% valid condition were attributed to a combination of automatic pathway activation and a controlled expectation of repetition.

On the other hand, inhibition effects were observed only in the 80% valid condition, and then only at prime–target stimulus onset asynchronies (SOAs) of approximately 200 ms or greater. As a result, Posner and Snyder (1975) suggested that automatic activation from the prime acts as a one-way set (or expectation), facilitating processing of expected stimuli, but not inhibiting processing of unexpected stimuli. In contrast, conscious attention to the prime results in a two-way set, both facilitating the processing of expected stimuli, and inhibiting the processing of unexpected stimuli.

---

[1] The reader is referred to LaBerge (1995) for a detailed analysis of what he refers to as the "manifestations" of attention. The functions of attentive analysis described here are intended to correspond loosely to these manifestations.

Neely (1977) addressed a similar issue using a semantic priming procedure. This procedure also involved presentation of a category name as a prime stimulus, and a category exemplar as a target stimulus. The task was to decide whether the target item was a word or a non-word. Importantly, subjects were instructed to expect target items to be from a different category than the prime. For example, when presented with the prime word "building" they were told to expect the target item to be a body part, such as "heart". Similarly, when presented with the prime word "body" they were told to expect the target item to be a building part, such as "door". Indeed, two-thirds of the time the target item was a member of the category subjects had been instructed to expect. The results from these two conditions in the Neely (1977) study are depicted in Fig. 5.1. Facilitation and inhibition effects were computed using prime displays with a row of Xs as a control condition. Note that at prime–target SOAs of less than approximately 400 ms, facilitation effects were observed for target items from the same category as the prime. However, at longer prime–target SOAs facilitation effects were observed for expected target items (e.g. "door" following "body"), and inhibition effects were observed for target items from the same category as the prime (e.g. "heart" following "body"). Although similar to the results reported by Posner and Snyder (1975), these data suggest that inhibitory effects of expectation can in fact be driven by a controlled expectancy in favor of an invalid target item.

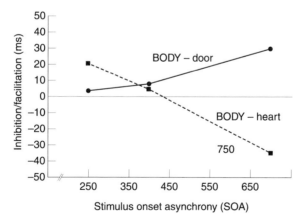

FIG. 5.1.   Lexical decision times reported by Neely (1977). Note that at short stimulus onset asynchronies (SOAs) responses were faster to targets in the same category as the prime than in the neutral condition. However, at longer SOAs responses were faster to targets in the attended (or expected) category. Copyright © 1977 by the American Psychological Association. Adapted with permission from Neely, J.H. (1977). Semantic priming and retrieval from lexical memory: Roles of inhibitionless spreading activation and limited-capacity attention. *Journal of Experimental Psychology: General, 106*, 226–254.

At this point, it is worth considering the sense in which the term "inhibitory" is applied to the effects described. To the extent that conscious expectation derives from attentional processes, these effects do depict an impoverished ability to process unattended information. However, there is no guarantee that this decrement in performance is determined directly by processes that impede processing of unattended stimuli. One may be tempted to ignore this problem, and use the term "inhibitory" as a description of any effect characterized by slowed responses to unattended stimuli. However, the disadvantage of this approach should be obvious. In particular, if our theoretical focus is attentional mechanisms that act directly on unattended input, then our empirical focus should be experimental phenomena that tap such processes, rather than experimental phenomena characterized by a particular pattern of data.

For example, it may be that inefficient responses to unexpected stimuli (Neely, 1977; Posner & Snyder, 1975) are not produced directly by a mechanism that impedes the encoding of an unexpected event. Instead, the enhanced processing associated with an expectation may necessarily put representations of unexpected stimuli at a competitive disadvantage. For example, assume that expectation for a target provides a head start for that target in a competitive process, and that response time is determined by the time required for the target response to achieve some criterion amount of advantage in this competitive process. With these assumptions in place, it should be clear that the time required to respond to an event should be greater when a competing stimulus has been given a head start, than when no competing stimulus has been given a head start. Thus, a cost in the processing of an unexpected event could conceivably be explained by direct reference only to the head start, or expectation, for a highly probable event.

Note that this alternative explanation does not rule out the possibility that inhibitory mechanisms modulate the processing of unexpected events. Rather, alternative explanations serve as a reminder that the relation between a measured empirical effect and its theoretical explanation is inferred rather than observed. As a result, the case favoring one particular hypothesis often rests on converging evidence from a variety of empirical approaches. To that end, evidence garnered recently from studies of event-related potentials in attentional cuing tasks have begun to provide support for the notion that unexpected events may indeed be subject to active inhibitory processing (Eimer, 1994; Luck et al., 1994).

ATTENTION TO A PRIMARY TASK

Trying to do too many tasks at once often ensures that those tasks are performed less efficiently than if they were done one at a time. Attention researchers often study this issue by measuring performance on a secondary task that overlaps temporally with a primary task by varying degrees. Much research has shown that, to the extent that primary and secondary tasks overlap temporally, response to the secondary task suffers (Pashler, 1984; Posner & Boies, 1971; Welford, 1952). Such a result clearly fits within the class of phenomena defined by deficits in processing of unattended events. Once again, however, it is worth considering whether such effects can be satisfactorily explained without reference to an attentional mechanism that directly impedes processing of unattended input. Indeed, neither of the two most common explanations of dual-task deficits makes direct reference to inhibitory processes.

For example, attention has been conceptualized by some to be a limited pool of resources that is drawn on by the cognitive processes required to perform tasks (Kahneman, 1973), with demanding tasks drawing more resources. Performance on a secondary task will then be limited by the demands of a primary task, as the resources remaining in the limited pool may not be sufficient to deal optimally with the secondary task. Thus, poor performance on a secondary task may reflect a depletion of resources, rather than the active inhibition of processing of unattended stimuli.

An alternative to the limited central resource interpretation of dual-task deficits assumes that an attentional bottleneck is created by a stage of processing that is inherently serial in nature. If that serial stage is occupied by the processing demands of a primary task, then the corresponding processing stage in the secondary task may be postponed (see McCann & Johnston, 1992; Pashler & Johnston, 1989; Welford, 1952). This postponement, in turn, may underlie poor performance on a secondary task when there is sufficient temporal overlap of primary and secondary tasks. Such a postponement would be consistent with Neisser's (1967) analysis by synthesis view of attention described earlier. Recall that Neisser (1967) forwarded this view as an alternative to filtering notions of attention (Broadbent, 1958; Treisman, 1960). From this discussion it should be apparent that the source of dual-task processing deficits is relevant to the central concern of this chapter. This close relation is yet more transparent in the following discussion of one particular dual-task procedure.

Dual-target Detection in Rapid Serial Visual Presentation

The method of rapid serial visual presentation (RSVP) involves the presentation of stimuli, such as letters or words, one at a time in rapid succession. The stimuli are presented at a rate of approximately 10 items per second in a single location on a computer monitor. At this rate of presentation, one often has the impression that the stimuli are briefly recognized as they appear, but then are subject to rapid forgetting. At the same time, it is relatively easy to select and remember one item from the stream based on its predefined color, letter case, or category (Potter, 1976, 1993). Of relevance here are problems associated with selecting and remembering more than a single target in the stream.

Broadbent and Broadbent (1987) asked subjects to identify two target words embedded within an RSVP stream of distracting words. The targets were indicated by a row of hyphens above and below both words. The critical independent variable was the temporal interval between the onset of the two targets. Broadbent and Broadbent (1987) found that subjects had great difficulty reporting both targets correctly when the temporal interval between the two was less than about 400 ms (see also Reeves & Sperling, 1986; Weichselgartner & Sperling, 1987). They attributed this effect to an effortful, attention-demanding identification process that follows detection of a target item. Cast in the light of this experimental paradigm, the central issue addressed in this chapter concerns how attention to a first target impedes the identification of a second target (see also Duncan, 1980).

An important boundary condition of this effect was subsequently reported by Raymond, Shapiro, and Arnell (1992). Their procedure (Raymond et al., 1992; Experiment 2) is depicted in Fig. 5.2. Subjects were presented with an RSVP stream of letters. One of the letters was white and the rest were black on the gray background of a computer monitor. A single

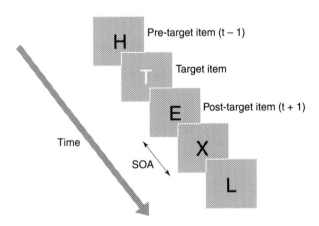

FIG. 5.2. The procedure used by Raymond, Shapiro, and Arnell (1992; Experiment 2). Subjects were shown an RSVP stream that contained 7–15 pre-target items and 8 post-target items. The stimulus onset asynchrony (SOA) was 90 ms. The subject's task was to identify the white target letter (the "T") and to detect whether the probe "X" appeared in the stream. Copyright © 1992 by the American Psychological Association. Adapted with permission from Raymond, J.E., Shapiro, K.L., & Arnell, K.M. (1992). Temporary suppression of visual processing in an RSVP task: An attentional blink? *Journal of Experimental Psychology: Human Perception and Performance*, 18, 849–860.

white letter in the stream was designated the *target*, and a black X was designated the *probe*. On experimental trials, subjects were asked to identify the white letter and to indicate whether the probe (the black X) appeared in the stream following the target. In fact, the probe appeared on half of the trials. On control trials, subjects were not required to identify the target item, and instead were asked to indicate only whether the probe appeared. The data from this experiment are displayed in Fig. 5.3.

Two aspects of these data are noteworthy. First, probe detection performance was very poor in the experimental condition when the probe appeared 2, 3, 4, or 5 temporal positions away from the target. In this respect the data are consistent with previously reported research (Broadbent & Broadbent, 1987; Weichselgartner & Sperling, 1987). Second, this deficit in detection did not occur for identical stimuli presented in the control condition. Because the deficit in probe detection occurs only when subjects must respond to more than a single target, the effect appears to have an attentional rather than purely sensory basis. This distinction prompted Raymond et al. (1992) to refer to the effect as an *attentional blink*.

The boundary condition of note was observed in a subsequent experiment (Raymond et al., 1992; Experiment 3). Raymond et al. used a similar method to that just described, with the exception that the first temporal interval following the target (position t + 1; see Fig. 5.2) was left blank.

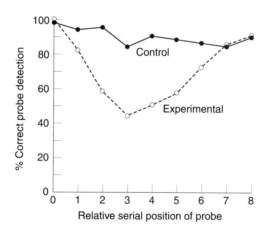

FIG. 5.3.   The data reported by Raymond, Shapiro, and Arnell (1992; Experiment 2) Note that subjects experienced considerable difficulty in reporting the appearance of the X when it occurred at post-target positions 2 through 5. Copyright © 1992 by the American Psychological Association. Adapted with permission from Raymond, J.E., Shapiro, K.L., & Arnell, K.M. (1992). Temporary suppression of visual processing in an RSVP task: An attentional blink? *Journal of Experimental Psychology: Human Perception and Performance, 18,* 849–860.

Interestingly, with this slight modification in procedure, the attentional blink was substantially smaller. Removal of the second post-target item, and removal of both the second and third post-target items, on the other hand, resulted in a probe detection deficit comparable to that observed with no blank temporal intervals.

Raymond et al. (1992) explained the attentional blink in terms similar to those of Broadbent and Broadbent (1987). In particular, they suggested that detection of a target letter within the RSVP stream occurs pre-attentively. Subsequent identification of the target is thought to require a more demanding encoding process by which the target item gains entry to a visual short-term memory buffer (VSTM). However, because of the rapid rate of presentation of items in the stream, attention to the target item also allows entry of the first post-target item to VSTM. Raymond et al. argued that when more than one item is held in VSTM there exists the possibility of a conjunction error (Treisman & Gelade, 1980). The notion of conjunction errors follows from the logic that features of items in VSTM may float freely in the absence of an attentive act that conjoins them. Thus, in the brief period that follows entry of both items to VSTM, the identity of the first post-target item may be incorrectly conjoined with the color of the target item. Of course, this would lead to an inaccurate response to the target. As a result, and to combat further conjunction errors, Raymond et al. suggested that entry of subsequent post-target items to VSTM may be suppressed until the target item has been conjoined with its color.

By the Raymond et al. (1992) account, then, the attentional blink does not occur when the first post-target item is replaced with a blank interval because the attentional blink is an inhibitory response to the potential for confusion created by the first post-target item. More generally, attention to a target item is purported to be facilitated by a process that impedes the visual processing of distractors.

However, Chun and Potter (1995) recently demonstrated that an attentional blink can be observed when subjects are required to identify two target letters in a RSVP stream of distracting digits or symbols, and in which all the targets and distractors are the same color. Note that with this procedure the deficit in post-target processing cannot be attributed to the potential for error in combining color and shape attributes. Chun and Potter (1995) also observed the attentional blink to be sensitive to the global and local similarity of targets to distractors. They defined local similarity as that relating targets to the items that followed them, and global similarity as that relating targets to other distractors that made up the RSVP stream. Thus, the attentional blink was observed to be larger when searching for two letters among digits than when searching for two letters among non-alphanumeric symbols (e.g. =, %, ?), and larger when the item following a letter target was a digit than when it was a symbol.

Chun and Potter (1995) forwarded a two-stage model for the attentional blink that differs from that of Raymond et al. (1992) in the following important way. Whereas Raymond et al. suggested that subjects respond to potential confusion by suppressing the visual processing of following distractors, Chun and Potter suggest that the attentional blink is determined by a limited-capacity second stage of processing that consolidates representations of items detected by a first stage of processing. Thus, if a second target item appears during consolidation of a first target item, then the second target becomes vulnerable to interference by subsequent items in the stream. As mentioned earlier, such a model presumes that the poor efficiency of processing of unattended stimuli occurs not because processing of those stimuli is targeted by an inhibitory process, but rather because an encoding process is capacity-limited.

A third alternative account of the attentional blink has been forwarded by Shapiro and Raymond (1994; see also Raymond, Shapiro, & Arnell, 1995; Shapiro, Raymond, & Arnell, 1994). This account presumes that the attentional blink results from competition for retrieval among representations in VSTM. To understand this account of the attentional blink one must first consider two simple criteria by which items gain entry to VSTM. One way in which an item can gain entry to VSTM is by virtue of a match with an attentional template (Duncan & Humphreys, 1989), with better matches receiving a greater weighting in VSTM. The second constraint on entry to VSTM is provided by temporal limits on our ability to segregate relevant from irrelevant items in the RSVP stream. With these constraints in mind, both the target and probe items in an RSVP sequence are presumed to gain entry to VSTM on the basis of their match with a template that depicts the target of the visuo-temporal search process. Further, the first post-target and first post-probe items are likely candidates for entry to VSTM on the basis of their temporal proximity to the target and probe.

Shapiro and Raymond (1994) argue that if the probability of retrieval of an item from VSTM is determined by its relative weighting, by its similarity to other items in VSTM, and by the number of other items in VSTM, then many of the properties of the attentional blink can be accounted for. For example, the attenuation of the attentional blink with the elimination of the first post-target item may occur because fewer items compete for retrieval from VSTM. The time course of the attentional blink can be explained by either the exit of a strong competitor (e.g. the target) from VSTM to a more durable memory store, or by the decaying of weightings of a weaker competitor (e.g. the $t + 1$ item) across time.

Given the relatively neat mapping of the two previous accounts (Chun & Potter, 1995; Raymond et al., 1992) onto separate views of the source of processing deficits for unattended stimuli, it is worth considering where the Shapiro and Raymond (1994) account fits within the context of other material presented in this chapter. To this end, note that retrieval of the target item is presumed to depend on a competitive process within VSTM. Although the mechanisms by which this competition is resolved are not made explicit, lateral inhibitory connections among like representations within VSTM would be useful in such a role, and would make this account generally compatible with Walley and Weiden's (1973) view.

To summarize, subjects experience considerable difficulty in detecting more than a single target within an RSVP stream when the targets appear within approximately 400 ms of one another. A variety of theoretical accounts of this processing deficit have been proposed. Of interest in this chapter is how each of these accounts protects central mechanisms from interference caused by irrelevant input. One of the accounts (Raymond et al., 1992) posits an explicit inhibitory process, a second (Chun & Potter, 1995) posits a bottleneck created by a capacity-limited stage of processing (see also Jolicoeur & Dell'Aqua, 1997), and a third (Shapiro & Raymond, 1994) posits a competitive retrieval process, to account for the processing deficit associated with post-target items. These three accounts of the attentional blink map well onto more general issues raised in considering the role of processes that impede the encoding of irrelevant stimuli. As such, there is reason to be optimistic that further research using this paradigm will help to distinguish among these models.

ATTENTION AS SELECTION: ITEM-SPECIFIC EFFECTS

As should be clear, the attribution of empirical effects to processes that directly impede the encoding of unattended information is often qualified by alternative theories. Many such alternatives attribute processing costs to indirect by-products of attending target information, rather than to direct consequences of ignoring distracting information. In particular, we have described how slow responses to unexpected stimuli may be caused by interference from expected stimuli, and how poor performance on a secondary task may reflect the unavailability of a critical processing stage caused by demands of a primary task. This form of alternative account is ruled out by the two phenomena discussed next, as the costs in performance are specific to stimuli that were presented previously. For this reason, these two behavioral phenomena have garnered wide interest. Nevertheless, as with the other behavioral phenomena discussed earlier, the relation between empirical effects and putative inhibitory attentional mechanisms remains complex.

Negative Priming

One of the most often used tools for investigating selective attention is the Stroop task (Stroop, 1935). In the original version of this task subjects were asked to name the ink color of each member of a list of words presented on cards. In one such list the words themselves corresponded to colors. Subjects were asked to name the ink color in which each of the words was presented. For example, the correct response to the word BLUE written in green ink would be "green". When the color word conflicted with the ink color in which it was drawn, as in the example just given, naming times were significantly slower than for control lists that contained an equal number of solid colored squares. This result suggests that the identity of the color word interferes with naming of the incompatible ink color.

An extension of this method reported by Dalrymple-Alford and Budayr (1966) is of particular relevance here. They used an experimental list in which the ink color of each item corresponded to the ignored color word of the immediately previous item. For example, the word BLUE written in red ink was followed by the word YELLOW written in blue ink. For ease of description we shall call this an *ignored repetition* list, as what is repeated for consecutive items is the color of the previously ignored word. In another type of list there was no relation between either the ink color or word of consecutive items in the list. In these *control* lists the word GREEN written in red ink might have been followed by the word YELLOW written in blue ink. Dalrymple-Alford and Budayr (1966) noted that subjects identified the ink color of words in ignored repetition lists more slowly than those in control lists (see also Neill, 1977).

This phenomenon was shown to have wide generality by Tipper and colleagues (Allport, Tipper, & Chmiel, 1985; Tipper, 1985; Tipper & Cranston, 1985). In these experiments subjects were asked to respond to one of two overlapping stimuli, such as letters or line drawings, in each of two consecutive displays. The details of this method are depicted in Fig. 5.4. One of the overlapping items was designated the target and the other the distractor. Thus, subjects were required to identify the red item, first in the *prime* display, and then again in the *probe* display. In the control condition the prime and probe items were unrelated to one another, in the attended repetition condition the prime and probe targets were identical, and in the ignored repetition condition the prime distractor and probe target were identical.

Two aspects of the data typically observed in such an experiment are of particular note. First, response times in the attended repetition condition are often significantly shorter than those in the control condition; second, response times in the ignored repetition condition are significantly longer than those in the control condition. Note that the latter result parallels that reported by Dalrymple-Alford and Budayr (1966; Neill, 1977), and contradicts the notion that response to a probe item is invariably facilitated by previous presentation of the same or a related item. As such, Tipper (1985) labeled this phenomenon negative priming.

The qualitatively different effects in the attended and ignored repetition conditions suggest that selection of a target item may be achieved both by

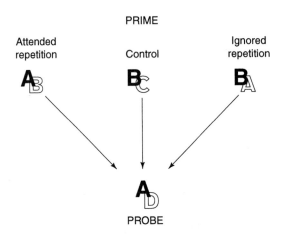

FIG. 5.4.   A prototypical procedure used to measure negative priming. Target letters are drawn in solid characters, and distractor items are drawn in outline characters. In the actual experiments the stimuli are often displayed in different colors. Subjects are required to identify the target in both the prime and probe displays. Negative priming is defined by slower responses to the probe target in the ignored repetition than in the control condition.

enhanced activation of representations of target items and by active inhibition of representations of ignored items. The logic underlying this conclusion is straightforward. If the internal representation of a prime distractor is inhibited, and if the effect of this inhibition lingers across the interval between prime and probe, then response times on ignored repetition trials may provide an index of this inhibition (Neill, 1977; Tipper, 1985). The contrast between this account of selection and that forwarded by Broadbent (1958) is worth consideration. Whereas Broadbent (1958) proposed that representations of ignored items decay passively from sensory memory, the negative priming effect suggests that representations of ignored items may be actively suppressed below a tonic level of activity.

In the years since it was first reported, interest in negative priming has increased remarkably. One of the reasons for this interest is that diminished negative priming has been observed in a number of clinical and developmental populations. For example, negative priming has been shown to be less robust in children (Tipper, Bourque, Anderson, & Brehaut, 1989), the elderly (Hasher, Stoltzfus, Zacks, & Rypma, 1991; McDowd & Oseas-Kreger, 1991; Tipper, 1991; but see Sullivan & Faust, 1993), obsessionals (Enright & Beech, 1990), subjects who report high cognitive failure (Tipper & Baylis, 1987), schizophrenics (Beech, Powell, McWilliams, & Claridge, 1989), depressed patients (Benoit et al., 1992), and Alzheimer's patients (Sullivan, Faust, & Balota, 1995). It has been argued that these individual differences indicate that cognitive processing in these populations is characterized by a deficiency in inhibition of irrelevant information.

A second reason for the wide interest in negative priming is that it has been demonstrated in a wide variety of experimental contexts. Negative priming has now been reported in tasks requiring spatial localization (Tipper, Brehaut, & Driver, 1990), reaching (Tipper, Lortie, & Baylis, 1992), same–different matching (DeSchepper & Treisman, 1996; Neill, Lissner, & Beck, 1990), counting (Driver & Tipper, 1989), semantic categorization (Tipper & Driver, 1988), and lexical decision (Fuentes & Tudela, 1992; Yee, 1991). Clearly, if the negative priming effects observed across this array of tasks are determined in the same manner, then negative priming may provide a measure of the efficiency of a process that is critical to general cognitive function.

Having outlined an argument in support of the link between negative priming and inhibitory attentional mechanisms, it is important to note that there are alternative explanations of this phenomenon as well. Such alternatives have found favor in evidence that contradicts the simplest of distractor inhibition models, such as that introduced earlier. In the remainder of this section we discuss three such empirical issues, and highlight the implications of these issues for the distractor inhibition interpretation of negative priming.

The Role of Probe Interference.   Lowe (1979) demonstrated that negative priming in the Stroop task often depends on properties of the probe task. In one particular study, negative priming was observed when the probe display contained a conflicting Stroop color–word stimulus, but positive priming was observed when the probe display contained four solid colored disks (but see Neill & Westberry, 1987). This result is puzzling in that a simple inhibition account of negative priming, like that described at the beginning of this section, presumes that negative priming is determined during the prime task, and merely measured by the probe task. By this view, it is not immediately clear why negative priming should depend on anything other than properties of the prime task.

Tipper and Cranston (1985) observed a similar result in a letter identification version of the negative priming paradigm. As a result, they concluded that the simplest of distractor inhibition accounts was untenable. Instead, they suggested that inhibitory mechanisms may not actually suppress the activation state of a distracting item's representation, but may block the translation of an otherwise active perceptual code into an accessible response code. Further, they suggested that when the probe task requires the subject to make a selective response to one of two sources of information, the "selection state" adopted by subjects in the prime task is carried over to the probe task. The response block is presumed to be a critical element of this selection state, and thus plays a role in determining the response of the subject in the probe task. However, when the probe task does not require a selective response to one of two items, the selection state may be abandoned. The active perceptual code of the ignored distractor may then produce positive priming effects.

In fact, the response blocking account has been reasonably successful in accounting for what is now a complex literature. At the same time, it does not provide a full account of when negative priming does, and when negative priming does not depend on probe interference (Fuentes & Tudela, 1992; Moore, 1994; Neill, Terry, & Valdes, 1994; Neill & Westberry, 1987; Yee, 1991). Although other alternative accounts of this dependence have since been suggested (see Houghton & Tipper, 1994; Moore, 1994; Neill, Valdes, Terry, & Gorfein, 1992) it seems safe to say that this property of negative priming remains an enigma.

The Time Course of Negative Priming. If negative priming were determined by an inhibitory mechanism with properties similar to those at the neural level, then it should dissipate relatively quickly following response to the prime. Although preliminary data concerning this issue did not provide a consistent picture (see Neill & Westberry, 1987; Tipper et al., 1991b), data reported recently by DeSchepper and Treisman (1996; Treisman & DeSchepper, 1996) demonstrate clearly that negative priming can have a long duration. They reported negative priming effects that persisted for a lag of *thirty days* between the time a novel item was ignored and the time it reappeared as the probe target item.

An effect of this nature merits close examination. The procedure used by DeSchepper and Treisman (1996) is depicted in Fig. 5.5. Subjects were asked to discriminate whether one of two overlapping shapes was the same as or different from a standard shape that was displayed to the side of the comparison pair. Consistent with many previous examinations of negative priming, one of the overlapping pair of shapes was displayed red, and the other green. It is noteworthy that the stimuli used by DeSchepper and Treisman (1996) were meaningless shapes that can be presumed not to have been experienced by the subjects prior to the experiment. That negative priming can be found for novel, meaningless shapes suggests that it can involve retrieval of representations that are created at the time such shapes are first encountered and ignored, rather than the suppression of abstract, long-term memorial representations (see also Neill et al., 1992).

Contrasts with Attended Repetition Effects. A third important property of negative priming is its qualitatively different nature from more conventional repetition priming effects. This contrast has been demonstrated explicitly by comparing negative priming on ignored repetition trials to

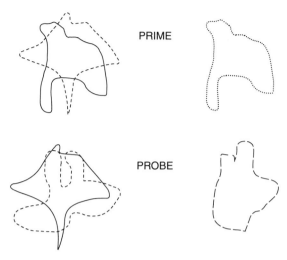

FIG. 5.5.   The procedure used by DeSchepper and Treisman (1996). Subjects were asked to compare the green shape (solid line) on the left to the standard shape (dotted line) on the right, and respond either *same* or *different*. Note that the target shape in the probe trial is identical to the distractor shape (dashed line) in the prime trial. The trial depicted here is one that would be used in the ignored repetition condition.

positive priming on attended repetition trials (Lowe, 1979; Tipper, 1985). Note how central this result is to the issue being addressed in this chapter. If attention functions both by enhancing the processing of relevant information, and by impeding the processing of irrelevant information, then qualitatively different attended and ignored repetition effects would appear to directly tap the complementary nature of these processes.

Once again, however, the current empirical story on this property of negative priming is complex. In particular, it is not always the case that attended repetition effects are qualitatively different from ignored repetition effects. For example, in tasks that require the subject to report the spatial location of a target item researchers have reported negative priming effects in both attended and ignored repetition conditions (e.g. Shapiro & Loughlin, 1993). A similar result has been observed in a task requiring word identification (Sullivan, Faust, & Balota, 1995). Note that if both attended and ignored repetition conditions can lead to negative priming, then these effects cannot be presumed to tap complementary attentional processes that enhance processing of targets and impede processing of distractors under all circumstances. There appear to be two general solutions to this problem. One solution assumes that, when negative repetition effects occur in both ignored and attended repetition conditions, they must be determined by different attentional processes; one that impedes processing of ignored stimuli, and another that impedes processing of previously attended stimuli (see the next section on Inhibition of Return). A second possible solution assumes that slowed responses to both attended and ignored repetition conditions are determined by the same attentional process, and that therefore, both are less directly related to prime task processing than has been widely presumed.

Summary.   Negative priming has been demonstrated in many different experimental contexts (see Fox, 1995: May, Kane, & Hasher, 1995; Neill, Valdes, & Terry, 1994 for several more detailed reviews). This generality suggests that the mechanism that causes negative priming may play an important and ubiquitous role in selective attention. At the same time, several empirical issues that have surfaced within the negative priming literature make it clear that the attribution of negative priming to an inhibitory attentional mechanism is not straightforward. Nevertheless, the stark qualitative contrast between attended and ignored repetition effects, when it is observed, maps directly onto the notion of complementary excitatory and inhibitory selection mechanisms. Future work on this issue would do well to focus on this contrast.

Inhibition of Return

The most common method of studying selective attention requires subjects to respond to a target event presented with one or more distractors. However, attention also plays an important selective role in modulating the effect of past experience on current behavior. In particular, although behavior is commonly most efficient when directed toward familiar events, unpredictable situations often require an ability to orient attention toward novel or surprising events (see Johnston & Hawley, 1994). This property of our attentional system appears to play a critical role in determining an empirical effect known as inhibition of return. This phenomenon was discovered and named by Posner and Cohen (1984) within the context of a research program aimed at the study of orienting behavior (see Posner, 1978, 1980; Posner, Snyder, & Davidson, 1980). A brief introduction to an attentional orienting procedure is provided here as context for the subsequent discussion of inhibition of return.

In a typical attentional orienting study, a trial contains two critical events: an attentional cue and a target. Subjects are required to respond as quickly as possible by pressing a single response button upon the onset of the target event. The target may be a small, luminous rectangle displayed against the dark background of a computer monitor, and it appears either to the left or right of the point on the screen that subjects fixate at the beginning of each trial.

Attentional cues are commonly classified as one of two types. An *endogenous* attentional cue provides information about the likely occurrence of a subsequent target. For example, prior to the appearance of the target an arrow may appear at fixation pointing either to the left or to the right. A valid arrow cue is one that points to the location of the subsequent target, whereas an invalid arrow cue is one that points in the other direction. If the proportion of valid cues is high relative to invalid cues, then less time is required to detect a validly cued than invalidly cued target.

Endogenous attentional cues have sometimes been described as push cues; that is, they are presumed to elicit a voluntary push of attention to the cued location. In contrast, *exogenous* attentional cues are described as capturing, or pulling, attention to the cued location automatically. An exogenous cuing procedure is depicted in Fig. 5.6. The cue itself is an abrupt luminance increment of one of the two peripheral locations marked on the computer screen. Subsequent to the cue, a small solid square appears in one of the three locations. Properties of attentional orienting are then inferred on the basis of response time differences to targets appearing in cued (valid), uncued (invalid), and central (neutral) locations.

Posner and Cohen (1984) reported a study that used exogenous cuing, and in which the target appeared with high probability (0.6) in the central location, and with low probability (0.1) in both the cued and uncued peripheral locations. On the remaining trials (0.2) no target was displayed. These catch trials were included to ensure that subjects were actually waiting until the appearance of the target to initiate a response. Onset of the target

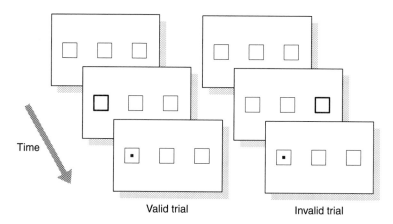

Valid trial   Invalid trial

FIG. 5.6.   The three boxes in each display depict potential locations of the target event. The abrupt luminance increment that served as the exogenous cue is depicted by the enlarged outline of one of the peripheral boxes in each of the middle two displays. The subject's task is to press a single response button upon the onset of the target, depicted by the small square inside the left box in the bottom of the display.

occurred at varying SOAs relative to the cue. The results from this experiment are shown in Fig. 5.7.

Note that when the onset of the cue was followed shortly thereafter (100 ms) by the onset of the target, detection times were faster at the cued than at the uncued location. However, when the interval between cue onset and target onset was 300 ms or greater, detection times were reliably slower at the cued than the uncued location. This latter phenomenon is known as inhibition of return. Inhibition of return has since been observed in report of the onset of auditory targets (e.g. Reuter-Lorenz, Jha, & Rosenquist, 1996), eye movements to a cued location (e.g. Abrams & Dobkin, 1994), in detection of repeated color targets (Law, Pratt, & Abrams, 1995), when discriminating targets from non-targets, (e.g. Pratt, 1995), and when making temporal order judgments (Gibson & Egeth, 1994). Clearly, like negative priming, inhibition of return is a pervasive experimental phenomenon.

The time course of the exogenous cuing effect displayed in Fig. 5.7 was explained by Posner and Cohen (1984) in the following manner. The peripheral cue is presumed to attract attention to its location automatically, leading to relatively fast detection of targets that appear at that location shortly after the cue. This facilitation effect is not observed at longer cue–target SOAs because the longer interval gives attention sufficient time to return to the central location. Indeed, precisely the opposite effect occurs at longer SOAs. The relatively slow detection of cued targets at long SOAs is

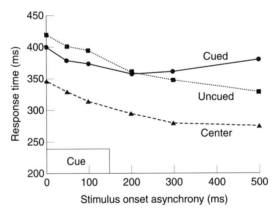

FIG. 5.7.   The data reported by Posner and Cohen (1984). Note that response times to targets at cued locations are faster than at uncued locations for short cue-target stimulus onset asynchronies (SOAs), but slower than at uncued locations for longer SOAs. We thank the International Association for The Study of Attention and Performance for permission to adapt Figure 32.2 from Posner, M.I., & Cohen, Y. (1984). Components of visual orienting. In H. Bouma & D.G. Bouwhuis (Eds.), *Attention and performance X: Control of language processes*. Hove, UK: Lawrence Erlbaum Associates Ltd.

presumed to reflect a bias against returning attention to regions of space that have been previously attended. Although its precise determinants are a matter of considerable debate, the utility of such a bias is quite clear. Generally speaking, a bias that favors novelty may play a critical role in preventing perseverative types of error in behavior.

A more specific form of this hypothesis posits that the novelty bias evolved as an adaptive search routine (Klein, 1988). For example, when searching for food, one would be rewarded for covering a maximum amount of territory in as little time as possible. Inhibiting return to already attended locations would ensure that valuable time is spent searching new locations rather than those that have already been searched. Yet, despite the intuitive appeal of this hypothesis, researchers have been unsuccessful in demonstrating a direct relation between inhibition of return and visual search (Klein & Taylor, 1994; Wolfe & Pokorny, 1990).

The Attentional Basis of Inhibition of Return.   The attribution of inhibition of return to an attentional mechanism presumes that it is not caused at a peripheral sensory level; for example, by forward masking. In fact, experiments by Posner and Cohen (1984), and others conducted since, have ruled out a simple sensory masking account of inhibition of return. For example, whereas forward masking usually dissipates within 100 ms of the presentation of a first stimulus, inhibition of return can be observed with intervals between the cue and target that are much longer than one second (Maylor, 1985; Posner & Cohen, 1984; Rafal, Calabresi, Brennan, & Sciolto, 1989). Also, inhibition of return is not defined by the area of the retina that is stimulated by the peripheral cue (Posner & Cohen, 1984). Indeed, Tipper, Driver, and Weaver (1991a) demonstrated that inhibition of return can be tied to abstract *object-based* co-ordinates, rather than to spatial co-ordinates. In their study, one of two peripheral boxes was cued and then both boxes moved in a 90° arc that was centered on the middle of the display. Thus, at the onset of the target the boxes were above and below the middle of the display rather than left and right. Despite this movement, detection times were slower for targets that appeared in the box that had been cued.

Inhibition of Return and Oculomotor Programming.   Despite the data just described, the role of sensory factors was not summarily dismissed by researchers of inhibition of return. One reason for this hesitancy was that inhibition of return was known to occur for exogenous (abrupt peripheral onset) but not for endogenous attentional cues (arrow pointing left or right; Posner, Rafal, Choate, & Vaughan, 1985). This result forces one of two conclusions about the relation between inhibition of return and attentional orienting. One possibility is that endogenous and exogenous orienting are fundamentally different from one another (see Briand & Klein, 1987; Jonides, 1981; Maylor, 1985), that inhibition of return is caused specifically by exogenous orienting, and that this explains why inhibition of return occurs with one but not the other orienting procedure. A second possibility is that endogenous and exogenous orienting are fundamentally similar to one another, but that inhibition of return is indirectly rather than directly related to orienting in general. In fact, the latter of these possibilities led to studies on the role of eye movements and oculomotor programming in inhibition of return.

As mentioned earlier, when subjects maintain fixation centrally, inhibition of return occurs following an exogenous attentional cue, but not following an endogenous attentional cue. However, Posner et al. (1985) noted that this distinction disappears when subjects are asked to move their eyes in the direction indicated by an attentional cue, rather than keeping their eyes fixed centrally. Thus, inhibition of return occurs if either a central arrow or an abrupt onset cues a peripheral target location, as long as subjects move their eyes to that location, and then back to fixation before appearance of the target (Posner et al., 1985).

Rafal et al. (1989) subsequently reasoned that inhibition of return may not be a direct result of exogenous orienting, but rather that it may occur because a peripheral exogenous cue automatically activates the oculomotor system. In support of this theory, Rafal et al. (1989) observed inhibition of return not only when eye movements were made in response to a central, endogenous cue, but also when an eye movement was simply planned on the basis of a central cue, not made, and then "cancelled" by the subject. Thus, Rafal et al. argued that inhibition of return may not occur directly because of the orienting response to an exogenous cue, but instead may occur because an exogenous cue leads to the automatic programming of an eye movement to its location.

Summary.   Inhibition of return is a robust phenomenon that appears to reflect a form of bias favoring novelty (for recent reviews see Klein & Taylor, 1994; Rafal & Henik, 1994). This novelty bias can be seen as a form of impedance to processing of stimuli that correspond to previously attended events. In this sense, it may play an important role in preventing perseverative types of error. At the same time, there remains considerable debate as to the most appropriate theoretical account of inhibition of return. An oculomotor–based explanation of inhibition of return does well in accounting for data from the majority of inhibition of return studies that employ spatial uncertainty. At the same time, recent evidence suggests that inhibition of return may occur in tasks that do not employ spatial uncertainty (Law et al., 1995), and further that not all forms of spatial inhibition of return are best accounted for by the oculomotor hypothesis (e.g. Abrams

& Dobkin, 1994). As such, in the case of inhibition of return as well, the relation between empirical effect and inhibitory process is a complex one.

CONCLUSION

A fundamental issue in the study of attention concerns the fate of unattended information. In particular, a theory of attention must explain how intelligent, goal-relevant behavior proceeds in the face of inundation from goal-irrelevant information. In the first section of this chapter, three contributions to the attention literature were described. These contributions were chosen for discussion because each deals directly with the problem just described. From this discussion it should be clear that the conceptual simplification of attention into complementary sets of mechanisms—some enhancing processing of relevant information, others impeding processing of irrelevant information—is a resilient and useful one.

An important enterprise for experimental psychologists is that of developing relatively simple experimental paradigms by which such inhibitory processes can be examined in humans. In the second section of this chapter we described several such empirical paradigms, all of which demonstrate that attending, in its various forms, to sources of relevant information can produce a decrement in the ability to respond to sources of irrelevant information. In this sense, all of these experimental paradigms are candidates to help us understand the role that inhibitory mechanisms play in selective attention.

At the same time, in all of the human experimental research described in this chapter the relationship between empirical effects and inhibitory mechanisms is subject to debate. In some cases, an apparent impedance of processing of distractor information may actually reflect an indirect effect of the enhanced processing of target information. In others, a seemingly transparent link between an empirical effect and an inhibitory attentional mechanism has been occluded by findings that leave one skeptical about any simple relation between theory and data.

One perfectly valid justification for the difficulties encountered in attributing empirical effects to inhibitory mechanisms is that it is an ambitious enterprise. In particular, juxtaposition of the terms "attention" and "inhibition" invites speculation about the relation between higher–order mental constructs and their physiological determinants. The breadth of this issue is such that convergence from a variety of experimental methods may be the only satisfactory approach. In fact, one of the factors that has lengthened the life of this theoretical issue is the broad interest that exists in inhibitory attentional mechanisms across a range of methodological disciplines within psychology. This interest is reflected in recent studies that have employed event-related potentials (e.g. Eimer, 1994, Luck et al., 1994,

Mangun, 1995), single cell recordings in primates (e.g. Chelazzi, Miller, Duncan, & Desimone, 1993; Desimone, Miller, & Chelazzi, 1994; Moran & Desimone, 1985; Motter, 1993, 1994a, 1994b), and neuro-imaging (e.g. Haxby et al., 1994) to address some of the issues raised here.

The ambitiousness of the theoretical issue, however, should not paralyze the behavioral researcher. Critical evaluation of models based on behavioral data remains a worthwhile exercise. With this in mind, we make the following observation. To some extent, interpretive problems associated with the phenomena described here may be symptomatic of a more general issue that experimental psychologists have confronted for years. In particular, whether implicitly or otherwise, we often make the assumption that cognitive machinery sits still while we measure it. As such, behaviors studied in the laboratory, such as the speed of response to a probe event, are often assumed to be determined before the point in time at which we introduce our measuring instrument. In reality, the brain is a dynamic organism. Thus, although some experimental effects may be largely determined in the prospective manner described here, others may be determined by processes that occur only upon onset of the probe event itself.

If this logic seems somewhat opaque, imagine the following situation. You are sitting at the kitchen table eating dinner when your roommate challenges you with the following question: Is the light inside the refrigerator on or off? Being an empiricist, you walk over to the refrigerator, open the door, evaluate the status of the light, close the door, and then tell your roommate that the light is indeed on! The flaw in logic appears obvious in this case, because of our *a priori* familiarity with how refrigerator lights function. However, we do not have the same *a priori* knowledge of how attention functions. As a result, we may neglect the wide array of retrospective processes that may be elicited by a probe event, and that therefore make up part of the effect that we measure. As it applies to the present research area, we should remain aware that a probe event may not innocuously measure the effect of a previous inhibitory process. More generally, we ought to be aware that the act of measurement may contaminate the measurement itself.[2]

At the same time, there is no reason to exclude inhibitory mechanisms from the set used to explain how behavior may be determined at the time it is measured. Indeed, a probe event may initiate a series of events in which inhibitory processes play a defining role. Such an approach suggests that attentional processes may be inextricably related with memory retrieval processes (see Anderson & Bjork, 1994). The role of inhibitory processes at

---

[2] The first author thanks Ben Bauer for the reminder of this useful analogy, although ultimately, thanks are likely due to the author of a textbook read long ago by both of us, which we have not been able to track down.

the interface of attention and memory systems is now being addressed with success in neurophysiological studies (Desimone, Miller, & Chelazzi, 1994; Chelazzi et al., 1993). Human experimental studies that directly address the interaction of attention and memory systems may well prove equally worthwhile.

ACKNOWLEDGEMENTS

The writing of this chapter was supported by a Natural Science and Engineering Research Council of Canada (NSERC) post-doctoral fellowship awarded to the first author, and NSERC operating grants awarded to both authors. We thank Karen Arnell and an anonymous reviewer for comments on an earlier version of this chapter.

REFERENCES

Abrams, R.A., & Dobkin, R.S. (1994). Inhibition of return: Effects of attentional cuing on eye movement latencies. *Journal of Experimental Psychology: Human Perception and Performance, 20*, 467–477.

Allport, D.A., Tipper, S.P., & Chmiel, N. (1985). Perceptual integration and post-categorical filtering. In M.I. Posner & O.S.M. Marin (Eds.), *Attention and performance XI* (pp.107–132). Hillsdale, NJ: Lawrence Erlbaum Associates Inc.

Anderson, M.C. & Bjork, R.A. (1994). Mechanisms of inhibition in long-term memory: A new taxonomy. In D. Dagenbach & T. Carr (Eds.), *Inhibitory processes in attention, memory, and language.* Orlando, CA: Academic Press.

Beech, A.R., Powell, T.J., McWilliams, J., & Claridge, G.S. (1989). Evidence of reduced "cognitive inhibition" in schizophrenia. *British Journal of Clinical Psychology, 28*, 110–116.

Benoit, G., Fortran, L., Lemelin, S., LaPlante, L., Thomas, J., & Everett, J. (1992). L'attention selective dans la depression majeure: Ralentissement clinique et inhibition cognitive. *Canadian Journal of Psychology, 46*, 41–52.

Briand, K., & Klein, R.M. (1987). Is Posner's "beam" the same as Treisman's "glue"? On the relationship between visual orienting and feature integration theory. *Journal of Experimental Psychology: Human Perception and Performance, 13*, 228–241.

Broadbent, D.E. (1958). *Perception and communication.* London: Pergamon Press.

Broadbent, D.E., & Broadbent, M.H.P. (1987). From detection to identification: Response to multiple targets in rapid serial visual presentation. *Perception and Psychophysics, 42*, 105–113.

Chelazzi, L., Miller, E.K., Duncan, J., & Desimone, R. (1993). A neural basis for visual search in inferior temporal cortex. *Nature, 363*, 345–347.

Chun, M.M., & Potter, M.C. (1995). A two-stage model for multiple target detection in rapid serial visual presentation. *Journal of Experimental Psychology, 21*, 109–127.

Dalrymple-Alford, E.C., & Budayr, B. (1966). Examination of some aspects of the Stroop color–word test. *Perceptual and Motor Skills, 23*, 1211–1214.

DeSchepper, B., & Treisman, A. (1996). Visual memory for novel shapes: Implicit coding without attention. *Journal of Experimental Psychology: Learning, Memory, and Cognition, 22*, 27–47.

Desimone, R., & Duncan, J. (1995). Neural mechanisms of selective visual attention. *Annual Review of Neuroscience, 18*, 193–222.

Desimone, R., Miller, E.K., & Chelazzi, L. (1994). The interaction of neural systems for attention and memory. In C. Koch & J.L. Davis (Eds.), *Large-scale neuronal theories of the brain* (pp.75–91.). Cambridge, MA: MIT Press.

Deutsch, J.A., & Deutsch, D. (1963). Attention: Some theoretical considerations. *Psychological Review, 70,* 80–90.

Driver, J., & Tipper, S.P. (1989). On the nonselectivity of "selective" seeing: Contrasts between interference and priming in selective attention. *Journal of Experimental Psychology: Human Perception and Performance, 15,* 304–314.

Duncan, J. (1980). The locus of interference in the perception of simultaneous stimuli. *Psychological Review, 87,* 272–300.

Duncan, J., & Humphreys, G. (1989). Visual search and stimulus similarity. *Psychological Review, 96,* 433–458.

Eimer, M. (1994). "Sensory gating" as a mechanism for visuospatial orienting: Electrophysiological evidence from trial by trial cuing experiments. *Perception and Psychophysics, 55,* 667–675.

Enright, S.J., & Beech, A.R. (1990). Obsessional states: Anxiety disorders or schizotypes? An information processing and personality assessment. *Psychological Medicine, 20,* 621–627.

Felleman, D.J., & Van Essen, D.C. (1991). Distributed hierarchical processing in the primate visual cortex. *Cerebral Cortex, 1,* 1–47.

Fox, E. (1995). Negative priming from ignored distractors in visual selection: A review. *Psychonomic Bulletin and Review, 2,* 145–173.

Fuentes, L.J., & Tudela, P. (1992). Semantic processing of foveally and parafoveally presented words in a lexical decision task. *Quarterly Journal of Experimental Psychology, 45*A, 299–322.

Gibson, B., & Egeth, H. (1994). Inhibition of return to object-based and environment-based locations. *Perception and Psychophysics, 55,* 323–339.

Hasher, L., Stoltzfus, E.R., Zacks, R.T., & Rypma, B. (1991). Age and inhibition. *Journal of Experimental Psychology: Learning, Memory and Cognition, 17,* 163–169.

Haxby, J.V., Horwitz, B., Ungerleider, L.G., Maisog, J.M., Pietrini, P., & Grady, C.L. (1994). The functional organization of human extrastriate cortex: A PET–rCBF study of selective attention to faces and locations. *Journal of Neuroscience, 14,* 6336–6353.

Houghton, G., & Tipper, S.P. (1994). A model of inhibitory mechanisms in selective attention. In D. Dagenbach & T. Carr (Eds.), *Inhibitory processes in attention, memory, and language.* Orlando, CA: Academic Press.

Johnston, W.A., & Dark, V. (1986). Selective attention. *Annual Review of Psychology, 37,* 43–75.

Johnston, W.A., & Hawley. K.J. (1994). Perceptual inhibition of expected inputs: The key that opens closed minds. *Psychonomic Bulletin & Review, 1,* 56–72.

Jolicoeur, P., & Dell' Acqua, R. (1997). *From the attentional blink to the psychological refractory period: Empirical and theoretical unification of two paradigms.* Manuscript submitted for publication.

Jonides, J. (1981). Voluntary vs automatic control over the mind's eye's movement. In J.B. Long & A.D. Baddeley (Eds.), *Attention and performance IX* (pp.187–203). Hillsdale, NJ: Lawrence Erlbaum Associates Inc.

Kahneman, D. (1973). *Attention and effort.* New York: Prentice Hall.

Klein, R.M. (1988). Inhibitory tagging system facilitates visual search. *Nature, 334,* 430–431.

Klein, R.M., & Taylor, T. (1994). Categories of cognitive inhibition with reference to attention. In D. Dagenbach & T. Carr (Eds.), *Inhibitory processes in attention, memory, and language.* Orlando, CA: Academic Press.

LaBerge, D. (1995). *Attentional processing. The brain's art of mindfulness.* Cambridge, MA: Harvard University Press.

Law, M.B., Pratt, J., & Abrams, R.A. (1995). Color-based inhibition of return. *Perception and Psychophysics, 57,* 402–408.

Lowe, D.G. (1979). Strategies, context and the mechanisms of response inhibition. *Memory and Cognition, 7,* 382–389.

Luck, S.J., Hillyard, S.A., Mouloua, M., Woldorff, M.G., Clark, V.P., & Hawkins. H.L. (1994). Effects of spatial cuing on luminance detectability: Psychophysical and electrophysiological evidence for early selection. *Journal of Experimental Psychology: Human Perception and Performance, 20,* 887–904.

Mangun, G.R. (1995). Neural mechanisms of visual selective attention. *Psychophysiology, 32,* 4–18.

May, C.P., Kane, M.J., & Hasher, L. (1995). Determinants of negative priming. *Psychological Bulletin, 118,* 35–54.

Maylor, E.A. (1985). Facilitatory and inhibitory components of orienting in visual space. In M.I. Posner & O.S.M. Marin (Eds.), *Attention and performance XI* (pp.189–204). Hillsdale, NJ: Lawrence Erlbaum Associates Inc.

McCann, R.S., & Johnston, J.C. (1992). Locus of the single-channel bottleneck in dual-task interference. *Journal of Experimental Psychology: Human Perception and Performance, 18,* 471–484.

McDowd, J.M., & Oseas-Kreger, D.M. (1991). Aging, inhibitory processes, and negative priming. *Journal of Gerontology: Psychological Sciences, 46,* 340–345.

Moore, C.M. (1994). Negative priming depends on probe–trial conflict: Where has all the inhibition gone? *Perception and Psychophysics, 56,* 133–147.

Moran, J., & Desimone, R. (1985). Selective attention gates visual processing in the extrastriate cortex. *Science, 229,* 782–784.

Moray, N. (1959). Attention in dichotic listening: Affective cues and the influence of instructions. *Quarterly Journal of Experimental Psychology, 11,* 56–60.

Motter, B.C. (1993). Focal attention produces spatially selective processing in visual cortical areas V1, V2, and V4 in the presence of competing stimuli. *Journal of Neurophysiology, 70,* 909–919.

Motter, B.C. (1994a). Neural correlates of attentive selection for color or luminance in extrastriate area V4. *Journal of Neuroscience, 14,* 2178–2189.

Motter, B.C. (1994b). Neural correlates of feature selective memory and pop-out in extrastriate area V4. *Journal of Neuroscience, 14,* 2190–2199.

Neely, J.H. (1977). Semantic priming and retrieval from lexical memory: Roles of inhibitionless spreading activation and limited-capacity attention. *Journal of Experimental Psychology: General, 106,* 226–254.

Neill, W.T. (1977). Inhibition and facilitation processes in selective attention. *Journal of Experimental Psychology: Human Perception and Performance, 3,* 444–450.

Neill, W.T., Lissner, L.S., & Beck, J.L. (1990). Negative priming in same–different matching: Further evidence for a central locus of inhibition. *Perception and Psychophysics, 48,* 398–400.

Neill. W.T., Terry, K.M., & Valdes, L.A. (1994). Negative priming without probe selection. *Psychonomic Bulletin and Review, 1,* 119–121.

Neill, W.T., Valdes, L.A., & Terry, K.M. (1994). Selective attention and the inhibitory control of cognition. In F.N. Dempster & C.J. Brainerd (Eds.), *New perspectives on interference and inhibition in cognition.* New York: Academic Press.

Neill, W.T., Valdes, L.A., Terry, K.M., & Gorfein, D.S. (1992). The persistence of negative priming: II. Evidence for episodic trace retrieval. *Journal of Experimental Psychology: Learning, Memory, and Cognition, 18,* 993–1000.

Neill, W.T., & Westberry, R.L. (1987). Selective attention and the suppression of cognitive noise. *Journal of Experimental Psychology: Learning, Memory, and Cognition, 13,* 327–334.

Neisser, U. (1967). *Cognitive psychology.* New York: Appleton.

Pashler, H. (1984). Processing stages in overlapping tasks: Evidence for a central bottleneck. *Journal of Experimental Psychology: Human Perception and Performance, 10,* 358–377.

Pashler, H., & Johnston, J.C. (1989). Chronometric evidence for central postponement in temporally overlapping tasks. *Quarterly Journal of Experimental Psychology, 41A*, 19–45.

Posner, M.I. (1978). *Chronometric explorations of mind.* Hillsdale, NJ: Lawrence Erlbaum Associates Inc.

Posner, M.I. (1980). Orienting of attention. The VIIth Sir Frederick Bartlett lecture. *Quarterly Journal of Experimental Psychology, 32A*, 3–25.

Posner, M.I., & Boies, S.J. (1971). Components of attention. *Psychological Review, 79*, 391–408.

Posner, M.I., & Cohen, Y. (1981). Components of visual orienting. In H. Bouma & D.G. Bouwhuis (Eds.), *Attention and performance X: Control of language processes.* Hove, UK: Lawrence Erlbaum Associates Ltd.

Posner, M.I., Rafal, R.D., Choate, L.S. & Vaughan, J. (1985). Inhibition of return neural basis and function. *Journal of Cognitive Neuropsychology, 2*, 211–228.

Posner, M.I., & Snyder, C.R.R. (1975). Attention and cognitive control. In R.L. Solso (Ed.), *Information processing and cognition: The Loyola Symposium.* Hillsdale, NJ: Lawrence Erlbaum Associates Inc.

Posner, M.I., Snyder, C.R.R., & Davidson, B.J. (1980). Attention and the detection of signals. *Journal of Experimental Psychology: General, 109*, 160–174.

Potter, M.C. (1976) Short-term conceptual memory for pictures. *Journal of Experimental Psychology: Human Learning and Memory, 2*, 509–522.

Potter, M.C. (1993). Very short-term conceptual memory. *Memory and Cognition, 21*, 156–161.

Pratt, J. (1995). Inhibition of return in a discrimination task. *Psychonomic Bulletin and Review*, 117–120.

Rafal, R.D., & Henik, A. (1994). The neurology of inhibition. In D. Dagenbach & T. Carr (Eds.) *Inhibitory processes in attention, memory, and language.* Orlando, CA: Academic Press.

Rafal, R.D., Calabresi, P., Brennan, C., & Sciolto, T. (1989). Saccade preparation inhibits reorienting to recently attended locations. *Journal of Experimental Psychology: Human Perception and Performance, 15*, 673–685.

Raymond, J.E., Shapiro, K.L., & Arnell, K.M. (1992). Temporary suppression of visual processing in an RSVP task: An attentional blink? *Journal of Experimental Psychology: Human Perception and Performance, 18*, 849–860.

Raymond, J.E., Shapiro, K.L., & Arnell, K.M. (1995). Similarity determines the attentional blink. *Journal of Experimental Psychology: Human Perception and Performance, 21*, 653–662.

Reeves, A., & Sperling, G. (1986). Attention gating in short-term visual memory. *Psychological Review, 93*, 180–206.

Reuter-Lorenz, P.A., Jha, A.P., & Rosenquist, J.N. (1996). What is inhibited in inhibition of return? *Journal of Experimental Psychology: Human Perception and Performance, 22*, 367–378.

Shapiro, K.L., & Raymond J.E. (1994). Temporal allocation of visual attention: Inhibition or interference? In D. Dagenbach & T. Carr (Eds.), *Inhibitory processes in attention, memory, and language.* Orlando, CA: Academic Press.

Shapiro, K.L., Raymond, J.E., & Arnell, K.M. (1994). Attention to visual pattern information produces the attentional blink in rapid serial visual presentation. *Journal of Experimental Psychology: Human Perception and Performance, 20*, 357–371.

Shapiro K.L., & Loughlin, C. (1993). The locus of inhibition in the priming of static object: Object token versus location: *Journal of Experimental Psychology: Human Perception and Performance, 19*, 352–363.

Stroop, J.R. (1935). Studies of interference in serial verbal reactions. *Journal of Experimental Psychology, 18*, 643–662.

Sullivan, M.P., & Faust, M.E. (1993). Evidence for identity inhibition during selective attention in old adults. *Psychology and Aging*, *8*, 589–598.

Sullivan, M.P., Faust, M.E., & Balota, D. (1995). Identity negative priming in old adults and individuals with dementia of the Alzheimer's type. *Neuropsychology*, *9*, 537–555.

Tipper, S.P. (1985). The negative priming effect: Inhibitory effects of ignored primes. *Quarterly Journal of Experimental Psychology*, *37A*, 571–590.

Tipper, S.P. (1991) Less attentional selectivity as a result of declining inhibition in older adults. *Bulletin of the Psychonomic Society*, *29*, 45–47.

Tipper, S.P., & Baylis, G.C. (1987). Individual differences in selective attention: The relation of priming and interference to cognitive failure. *Personality and Individual Differences*, *8*, 667–675.

Tipper, S.P., Bourque, T., Anderson, S., & Brehaut, J.C. (1989). Mechanisms of attention: A developmental study. *Journal of Experimental Child Psychology*, *48*, 353–378.

Tipper, S.P., Brehaut, J.C., & Driver, J. (1990) Selection of moving and static objects for the control of spatially-directed action. *Journal of Experimental Psychology: Human Perception and Performance*, *16*, 492–504.

Tipper, S.P., & Cranston, M. (1985). Selective attention and priming: Inhibitory and facilitatory effects of ignored primes. *Quarterly Journal of Experimental Psychology*, *37A*, 591–611.

Tipper, S.P., & Driver, J. (1988). Negative priming between pictures and words: Evidence for semantic analysis of ignored stimuli. *Memory and Cognition*, *16*, 64–70.

Tipper, S.P., Driver, J., & Weaver, B. (1991). Object-centered inhibition of return of visual attention. *Quarterly Journal of Experimental Psychology*, *37A*, 591–611.

Tipper, S.P., Lortie, C., & Baylis, G.C. (1992). Selective reaching: Evidence for action-centered attention. *Journal of Experimental Psychology: Human Perception and Performance*, *18*, 891–905.

Tipper, S.P., Weaver, B., Cameron, S., Brehaut, J.C., & Bastedo J. (1991). Inhibitory mechanisms of attention in identification and localization tasks: Timecourse and disruption. *Journal of Experimental Psychology: Learning, Memory, and Cognition*, *17*, 681–692.

Treisman, A., & DeSchepper, B. (1996). Object, tokens, attention, and visual memory. To appear in T. Inni & J.L. McClelland (Eds.), *Attention and performance XVI* (pp.15–46). Cambridge, MA: MIT Press.

Treisman, A., & Gelade, G. (1980). A feature integration theory of attention. *Cognitive Psychology*, *12*, 97–136.

Treisman, A.M. (1960). Contextual cues in selective listening. *Quarterly Journal of Experimental Psychology*, *12*, 242–248.

Ungerleider, L.G. & Mishkin, M. (1982). Two cortical visual systems. In J. Ingle, M.A. Goodale, R.J.W. Mansfield (Eds.), *Analysis of visual behavior* (pp.549–586). Cambridge, MA: MIT Press.

Walley, R.E., & Weiden, T.D. (1973). Lateral inhibition and cognitive masking: A neuropsychological theory of attention. *Psychological Review*, *80*, 284–302.

Weichselgartner, E., & Sperling, G. (1987). Dynamics of automatic and controlled visual attention. *Science*, *238*, 778–780.

Welford, A.T. (1952). The "psychological refractory period" and the timing of high-speed performance: A review and a theory. *British Journal of Psychology*, *43*, 2–19.

Wolfe, J.M., & Pokorny, C.W. (1990). Inhibitory tagging in visual search: A failure to replicate. *Perception and Psychophysics*, *48*, 357–362.

Yee, P.L. (1991). Semantic inhibition of ignored words during a figure classification task. *The Quarterly Journal of Experimental Psychology*, *43A*, 127–153.

CHAPTER SIX

Control of Visual Attention

Steven Yantis
Johns Hopkins University, Baltimore, USA

Vision allows organisms to know the contents and layout of their local environment. Its major function is object recognition. Experimental evidence accumulated over the last 30 years suggests that in many (but not all) cases, the visual system accomplishes object recognition by visually selecting a relevant or salient part of the visual image (e.g. the cluster of features constituting an object or located in a region of space) and operating only on that cluster, then selecting another part of the image, and so forth. This strategy reduces the complexity of object recognition by limiting it to only one or a small number of elements at a time. The mechanism that accomplishes selection is called visual attention, and this chapter is concerned with how visual attention is deployed within an image as a function of image properties and observer goals.

A major distinction that has guided research in this area, and one that will provide an organizing principle for this chapter, is whether attention is goal-driven, controlled in a "top-down" fashion, or stimulus-driven, controlled in a "bottom-up" fashion. This distinction has been recognized at least since William James first introduced it a century ago in his seminal book, *The principles of psychology* (1890). James characterized this distinction in terms of "active" and "passive" modes of attention, respectively.

Attention is said to be goal-driven (in James' words, "active") when it is controlled by the observer's deliberate strategies and intentions. For example, if one is looking for a particular type of cereal at the supermarket, and that cereal is known to have a yellow box, then yellow boxes in general are likely to be selected by attention and recognized. In contrast, attention is said to be stimulus-driven (or "passive") when it is controlled by some salient attribute of the image that is not necessarily relevant to the observer's perceptual goals. For example, if cereal boxes in one part of the aisle all tended to be blue, then a single red box among them might seem to "pop out" of the background and draw attention automatically.

Although the distinction between goal-driven and stimulus-driven control of attention is important, it is equally important to recognize that any given act of attention typically involves some combination of the two attentional modes. One of the themes of this chapter is how the two types of attentional control are coordinated to yield coherent visual performance.

Psychologists have devised a number of techniques for assessing how goal-driven and stimulus-driven selection occur. Perhaps the most revealing and widely used of these is *visual search* (see Wolfe, this volume). Visual search tasks require observers to view a display containing multiple elements and to find a prespecified *target* element among several *distractor* elements. Experimenters typically measure response time (RT) during visual search to assess the efficiency with which a target is detected or identified. In such tasks, it is useful to distinguish between the *defining attribute* of the target and its *reported attribute* (Duncan, 1985). The defining attribute is what the observer must search for during the task; it may be simple, such as the color or orientation of a bar, or complex, such as the conjunction of two or more features (e.g. large red vertical bar). The reported attribute is often simply the target's presence or absence, but in many instances it may be the name of the target or some attribute other than the defining one. When an observer is required to report the orientation of the red bar, the defining attribute is color and the reported attribute is orientation.

When experimental psychologists study attention, they must take certain precautions in order to ensure that the observed empirical effects are attentional and not due to some other, nonattentional, factors. For example, in everyday life it is standard to look at what we wish to attend to. The relationship between attention and eye movements is complex (see Hoffman, this volume); therefore in most of the experiments reviewed in this chapter subjects are required to maintain fixation and to attend to stimulus events "out of the corner of their eyes." When the maintenance of fixation is crucial to the interpretation of the experiment, eye movements are monitored. The stimuli are typically positioned so that variation in visual acuity with retinal eccentricity is minimized (for example, they might be arranged in a circle centered at the fixation point, so all the stimuli are equidistant from the center of gaze).

In the following sections, I will review evidence concerning goal-driven and stimulus-driven selection, respectively. In each case, evidence from visual search and other paradigms will reveal aspects of these two modes of attentional control. We will find that they are by no means independent of one another, and in a concluding section I will discuss how stimulus-driven and goal-driven selection complement one another in vision.

GOAL-DRIVEN VISUAL SELECTION

The modern study of visual attention began in the late 1960s (although several earlier studies will be noted) with investigations of how much control observers have in attending to relevant objects and ignoring irrelevant ones, and this was explored with a cuing paradigm in which relevant objects or locations were indicated visually. Later, interest developed in the distribution of attention in 2- and 3-dimensional space, and how attention is shifted from one location to another. In this section, each of these issues is addressed in turn.

Attention to Spatial Locations

The first well-known claim that observers can direct attention to locations in space other than their current point of fixation was made by Helmholtz (1866/1925). He performed an experiment in which a picture was placed in a light-tight box containing a pair of holes through which the picture could be viewed, and a pair of pinholes on the opposite wall that served as fixation points. The picture was illuminated briefly by a spark. This experiment was carried out in a series of studies of depth perception, but Helmholtz (1866/1925, p.455) made the following observation in passing:

> It is a curious fact, by the way, that the observer may be gazing steadily at the two pinholes and holding them in exact coincidence, and yet at the same time he can concentrate his attention on any part of the dark field he likes, so that when the spark comes, he will get an impression about objects in that particular region only. In this experiment the attention is entirely independent of the position and accommodation of the eyes, or indeed, of any known variations in or on the organ of vision. Thus it is possible, simply by a conscious and voluntary effort, to focus the attention on some definite spot in an absolutely dark and featureless field. In the development of a theory of the attention, this is one of the most striking experiments that can be made.

This observation was not pursued with rigorous experimentation until nearly a century later, and the earliest attempts to do so yielded negative results. For example, Mertens (1956) had observers view dim flashes of light under two conditions: "general attention" in which the flash could appear in any of four peripheral locations, and "special attention" in which the flash would appear in a single known location on each trial. Observers were required to press a button when they were able to see the light flash. The author found that the ratio of intensities for the general and special attention conditions required to achieve 25%, 50%, and 75% correct detections was 1.02, 1.11, and 1.18, respectively; that is, in all three cases the intensity required for a given level of performance in the general attention condition was greater than that in the special attention condition, implying an advantage for the latter. Nevertheless, Mertens (1956, p.1070) concluded that there was "practically no influence of the attention upon the probability of observation". He argued that the ratios for the two higher proportions, which seem to show clear attentional effects, should be ignored because of possible response bias effects. As van der Heijden (1992) and others have pointed out, however, Mertens's conclusion and the reasoning on which it is based are not entirely convincing.

A second failure to observe attentional effects was reported more than a decade later by Grindley and Townsend (1968). In their experiments, subjects were to report the orientation (up, down, left, or right) of a briefly flashed T appearing in one of four locations. They compared a condition in which the location of the T was known in advance to one in which it was not, and found essentially no advantage in accuracy when location was known in advance (at least when there was only a single item in the display; with multiple distracting characters present, foreknowledge did improve performance). Grindley and Townsend (1968) concluded that attention to location does not improve discriminability within single-item displays.

So the first two attempts to measure an attentional advantage after Helmholtz's original observation met with apparent failure. However, in many subsequent experiments, an attentional advantage was observed. Advantages were found both in how accurately subjects could detect or identify a briefly-presented object (e.g. Bashinski & Bacharach, 1980; Egly & Homa, 1984; Shaw & Shaw, 1977; Van der Heijden & Eerland, 1973), and in how rapidly subjects could detect or identify an above-threshold stimulus (e.g. Jonides, 1981; Posner, 1980; Posner, Snyder, & Davidson, 1980; Shaw, 1978).

Among the earliest studies to exploit Helmholtz's observation about one's ability to direct attention "by a conscious and voluntary effort" was a study concerned not with attention at all, but with perceptual memory. Sperling (1960) was interested in measuring the duration and capacity of visual memory, and so he invented the *partial report technique*. In a typical partial report experiment, an array of letters (say, three rows of four letters each) was illuminated very briefly, and this was followed by a tone (either immediately or after a delay). The tone could be high, medium, or low in pitch. Subjects were to report the contents of the top row if the high tone sounded, and so forth for the other two tones. The purpose of the procedure was to avoid requiring subjects to recall the contents of the entire array, which took time during which visual memory of the array might be decaying. In partial report, subjects had to report only part of the array, but their "readout" of the contents of the array had to come from visual memory, because the tone did not sound until the array had physically disappeared. A modification of this procedure was carried out by Averbach and Coriell (1961); in their experiments, a single letter was cued after the offset of the array with a circle surrounding the location that had been occupied by the cued letter. For our purposes, the interesting part of these experiments is that subjects could easily direct their attention to the relevant location in the remembered array and read out its contents.[1]

Criteria other than spatial location can also be used to direct attention in the partial report task, including differences in color or brightness (von Wright, 1968). For example, if an array containing half red items and half green items (randomly interspersed) is flashed very briefly, and a partial report cue is then presented (say, a high tone means report the red items and a low tone the green items), then subjects can successfully direct attention to the cued subset. However, more complex criteria, such as whether an item is a letter or a digit, cannot be used. This suggests that only "sensory" factors are useful in directing attention, but that more meaning-based factors, which require prior identification, cannot.

The earliest direct studies of the control of visual attention in the modern era were reported by C. W. Eriksen and his students in the early 1970s. They were concerned with an issue that remains unresolved today: to what extent are visual objects identified *before* attentional selection rather than after? This question is an extension of a debate that began in the early 1960s concerning the locus of selection in audition, the so-called early- vs late-selection debate. On one side, it was argued that only very simple stimulus attributes (e.g. pitch of a voice) can be detected preattentively and used to direct attention (Broadbent, 1958); on the other side, it was argued that stimuli are completely identified preattentively, and that attentional limitations arise only when a response must be selected (e.g. Deutsch & Deutsch, 1963). So the question as formulated by Eriksen and colleagues in the domain of vision was this: if an observer focuses attention on an object with the goal of identifying that object, to what extent will nearby but to-be-ignored objects interfere with the identification process?

In their experiments (e.g. Eriksen & Hoffman, 1973), subjects viewed a display containing multiple letters arranged in a circle so that all the letters were the same distance from the fixation point. At various moments before the letters appeared, a bar marker was presented. The bar marker indicated one of the display locations that would contain a letter. The subjects were

---

[1] The reader may be interested to know that Sperling (1960) and others (see Coltheart, 1980, for a comprehensive review) found that visual sensory memory has a very high capacity (that is, almost all of what is seen is remembered), but the contents of that memory decay rapidly, in less than one second.

required to identify the letter that was indicated by the bar marker (the *target*) and to ignore all the other letters in the display (*distractors*). Subjects were to push one switch if the target was (say) *A* or *U*, and another switch if the target was *H* or *M*. The distractors could appear at different distances from the target, and they could have various identities. Typically, most of the distractors were response-neutral (i.e. letters to which no response was ever required).

The critical comparison in this experiment was the time required to press the button when a nearby distractor's response assignment was compatible with that of the target (e.g. target *A*, nontarget *U* displays) vs when it was incompatible (e.g. target *A*, nontarget *H* displays). The effect of target compatibility could be measured as a function of the distance between the target and the critical distractor and of the duration between the onset of the bar marker and the onset of the display.

Eriksen and Hoffman (1973) made several observations. First, they found that the identity of the distractor did matter: responses were slower when adjacent distractors were incompatible with the target than when they were compatible. Second, the interference produced by incompatible distractors decreased as the distance between the distractor and the target decreased, and it also decreased as the time between the onset of the bar marker and the onset of the display decreased. These findings suggested that subjects require some time to localize the bar marker so as to focus attention on the indicated location, and that the attended region was limited in spatial extent. Yantis and Johnston (1990), using a variant of this paradigm, concluded that attention can be very efficiently focused, given optimal conditions, suggesting that early selection is at least possible under certain conditions.

In the late 1970s and early 1980s, Posner and colleagues (e.g. Posner, 1978, 1980; Posner et al., 1980) developed a technique for exploring top-down control over attention that extended the paradigm used by Eriksen. In Posner et al. (1980), for example, subjects were required to detect the onset of a light appearing in one of four horizontally arrayed positions, and to press a button to indicate their detection (simple detection and not identification was required). At the start of each trial, a digit appeared at fixation indicating which of the four locations (1, 2, 3, or 4) was likely to contain the light. Subjects were told that the light would appear in the cued location on 79% of the trials (these are referred to as *valid-cue* trials), and in each of the other locations on 7% of the trials (*invalid-cue* trials). On some trials, a plus sign appeared instead of a digit; this indicated that the light was equally likely to appear in all four positions (*neutral-cue* trials). Posner et al. (1980) found that responses were fastest when the light appeared in the expected location, slowest when it appeared in an unexpected location, and intermediate when all locations were equally likely. The magnitude of the RT benefit (i.e. the difference between the valid-cue RT and the neutral-cue RT) was approximately the same as the RT cost (i.e. the difference between the neutral-cue RT and the invalid-cue RT).[2]

In closing this section, let us return to the initial failures to observe attentional effects, the experiments of Mertens (1956) and Grindley and Townsend (1968). The many subsequent studies in which effects of directed attention *were* observed leave us with a puzzle: why did Mertens, and Grindley and Townsend fail to find evidence for directed attention? One possible answer lies in a critical methodological difference between these two studies and almost every other study discussed in this section. In both of these studies, the stimuli to be identified or detected were presented in an otherwise blank visual field. If the function of attention is to select relevant information from the visual field, then one might not expect to observe attentional effects in these special circumstances. A review of the literature by Shiu and Pashler (1994), together with their own targeted experiments, corroborate this idea. Attention effects are usually observed only when other, potentially competing, visual stimuli are present in the display.

Spatial Distribution of Attention

The experiments of Eriksen, Posner, and their colleagues established that attention could be directed to a spatial location, and that this location has a limited spatial extent. Several subsequent studies have explored the distribution of attention in space under different conditions. Among the earliest of these experiments was one reported by Engel (1971). Subjects viewed a blank display with a fixation point in it. A visual noise field of randomly oriented densely distributed line segments was flashed; somewhere in the noise was a randomly oriented L-shaped figure (or, in other experiments, a U-shape or a small square). Subjects were required to report the location and orientation of the L. Engel found that performance was good for targets near the point of fixation and declined with eccentricity. This is not too surprising, given the known variation in visual acuity with retinal eccentricity. He defined a "conspicuity area" within which performance was

---

[2] Shaw (1984) has pointed out a difficulty in the simple detection procedure used by Posner and others. In this task, subjects merely have to press a button when a dot or other simple change in the display is detected. Catch trials are included in which no stimulus appears to ensure that subjects respond to the stimulus and do not anticipate its appearance (subjects are instructed not to respond on catch trials). It is possible for subjects in a simple detection task to adjust their decision criterion so that they are willing to respond on the basis of less sensory information in the cued location (because they know that location is more likely to contain a target event), and this could account, at least in part, for their increased speed. This criterion shift problem is ameliorated (but not eliminated) when the task requires subjects to perform a discrimination (e.g. is the target a T or an L?), because errors in perception can then be observed directly. It is worth keeping this issue in mind while reading later in the chapter about other studies that use simple detection.

perfect with no foreknowledge of location and outside of which performance was imperfect; the conspicuity area was a horizontally oriented ellipse centered at fixation (see Fig. 6.1). He then provided subjects with perfect preknowledge about where the target stimulus would be presented; in this case, the observer only had to report the orientation of the stimulus. The region within which the target could be seen under these conditions, termed the "visibility area," was more than twice as large as the conspicuity area. Finally, Engel examined the effect of providing an "attention point" at some position in the visual field; subjects were informed that the target was most likely to occur at this point, but it could appear elsewhere. Observers were required to maintain fixation on the center of the display. Subjects' performance improved when the stimulus appeared near the attention point, and it declined only slightly when the target appeared in other locations within the previously defined visibility region. The conspicuity region simply bulged outward in the direction of the attention point.

Hoffman & Nelson (1981) provided additional evidence concerning the distribution of attention during visual search. Subjects were required to carry out two tasks simultaneously. The first task was to determine which of two target letters appeared in a sequence of briefly flashed four-letter displays. During one of the frames a small U-shaped character appeared in one of four orientations adjacent to one of the letters in one of the frames. The second task was to report the orientation of the U. In different conditions the relative importance of the letter task and the orientation task was varied, providing data to construct a *performance operating characteristic* (POC) which characterizes the performance trade-off between any two tasks (Navon & Gopher, 1979; Sperling & Melchner, 1978).

Hoffman and Nelson (1981) found that when the U was not adjacent to the target letter, there was a substantial performance trade-off between the

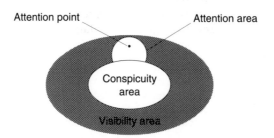

FIG. 6.1.   The visibility, conspicuity, and attention areas as conceived by Engel (1971). In the conspicuity area, targets can be seen without foreknowledge of location. In the visibility area, targets can be seen with perfect locational foreknowledge, and the attention area represents a "bulge" in the conspicuity area when there is imperfect foreknowledge of location. Adapted from Vision Research, Vol 11, F.L. Engel, *Visual conspicuity, directed attention, and retinal locus*, pp.563–576. Copyright © 1971, with kind permission from Elsevier Science Ltd, The Boulevard, Langford Lane, Kidlington OX5 1GB, UK.

tasks. That is, an emphasis on the letter task substantially reduced performance in the U task and vice versa. However, when the U was adjacent to the target position, the trade-off was more restricted; that is, subjects performed well on the U task even if the letter task was emphasized. Hoffman and Nelson concluded that in standard visual search tasks, attention is directed to the spatial region containing the target stimulus. To the extent that other relevant stimulus information is nearby, performance on tasks requiring that other information benefits.

LaBerge (1983; LaBerge & Brown, 1986) attempted to assess the shape of the attended region. He required subjects to perform two tasks on each trial, one right after the other. The first task required them to determine whether a string of five letters briefly flashed at fixation was a male name or not (the word task) or, in a separate experiment, whether the middle letter in the letter string was a consonant or a vowel (the letter task). The letter string was followed on some trials by a probe dot appearing at one of the five locations previously occupied by the letter string. Subjects were required to press a button as quickly as possible when they detected the probe dot. The first (word or letter) task was intended to produce a specific distribution of attention, and the second (probe) task was then used to map out that distribution. LaBerge predicted that the word task would require subjects to distribute attention roughly evenly across the entire letter string, while the letter task would require subjects to focus attention on the central position in the letter string. He assumed that the distribution of attention produced by the letter or word task would be reflected in RT to detect the probe stimulus. It was: RT to the probe on word trials did not differ as a function of probe position; RT on letter trials, however, was fastest for probes occurring at the middle location and slowest for the extreme positions, producing a V-shaped function.

A related study was reported at about the same time by Downing and Pinker (1985). Subjects were required to detect a spot of light that appeared in one of 10 outline boxes arranged horizontally on a computer screen. Subjects were required to press a button as quickly as possible after one of the boxes was filled in (again, simple RT; see footnote 2). The digits 1–10 were displayed immediately above each box corresponding to the position of that box in the horizontal array. At the start of each trial, a numeral appeared at fixation indicating the likely location of the target that was about to appear (cued trials) or indicating that all positions were equally likely to contain the target (neutral trials). On 18% of the cued trials, no target appeared; these catch trials were included to ensure that subjects were responding to the stimulus and not anticipating its appearance. Of the remaining cued trials, the target appeared in the cued location 70% of the time and in one of the uncued locations 30% of the time. Subjects were encouraged to focus attention on the cued location so as to minimize RT to detect the target.

Downing and Pinker measured the distribution of attention for a given cue condition by examining RT costs and benefits relative to the neutral baseline RT (see discussion of Posner et al., 1980, in the last section) so that differences in RT due to acuity would be factored out. The results revealed a distribution of attention that was similar to the one reported by LaBerge (1983): there was a V-shaped function surrounding the attended location such that targets appearing closer to the cued location were detected more rapidly than targets appearing farther from the cued location. Interestingly, Downing and Pinker (1985) found that the distribution was modulated in this way only within a hemifield; RT costs and benefits in the hemifield contralateral to the cued location did not vary with distance from the cued location. Furthermore, the attentional gradient was sharpest near to fixation and became shallower when a peripheral location was attended.

Shaw (1978; Shaw & Shaw, 1977) explored a parallel model of attention allocation to spatial locations. Shaw analyzed a visual search task in which there were n objects in the display; the probability that the target would appear in location j was p_j, $j = 1, 2, \ldots n$. According to her capacity allocation model (CAM), there exists a fixed total capacity for visual processing (denoted ϕ) that must be distributed over spatial locations, and the time required to identify a stimulus is a monotonically decreasing function of the capacity allocated to it (i.e. more capacity, faster identification). Shaw derived an optimal allocation function given a probability distribution (the set of p_js) and the total capacity ϕ. She then tested the assumptions of the CAM in an experiment with two different probability distributions and found almost identical estimates for the value of ϕ. She concluded that the CAM characterizes performance in visual search tasks of the sort she analyzed.

One can interpret Shaw's (1978) capacity allocation model as a mechanism that samples from the visual field according to the probability distribution of likely target locations. More samples per unit time are taken at likely locations, and fewer at unlikely locations. Only a limited number of samples may be taken per unit time. This analysis comes directly from the theory of optimal search developed during World War II in which limited search resources (e.g. aircraft) had to be allocated to searching for military assets (Koopman, 1957).

Attending to 3-D Space

The experiments reviewed so far suggest that observers can attend to locations in space according to task demands, and that the distribution of attention is at least somewhat graded. All the studies reviewed so far have dealt with stimuli that lie in the picture plane, which is not, of course, characteristic of real-world scenes. This led naturally to the question of whether attention could also be directed selectively in 3-D space. The question has significant implications for determining the representational basis of visual selection: if selection is early, before a 3-D representation is constructed, then one might expect not to observe selectivity in 3-space. Several studies have explored the allocation of attention in 3-D space, with seemingly inconsistent results. Recently, however, a consensus has emerged about this elusive issue.

Among the earliest studies of attention in 3-D space was Experiment 1 of Downing and Pinker (1985), whose Experiment 2 in 2-D space was reviewed earlier. Downing and Pinker had subjects view a real 3-D scene (this was not a computer-generated simulation, which is a real break from common practice these days) containing four lights mounted on stalks and placed on a table. Viewing was monocular,[3] and the table was covered with textured cloth to enhance the monocular depth cues available in the scene. In any given block of trials, the lights were placed in four of eight defined locations on the table, four near locations and four far locations in two curved rows. The near and far locations were selected so that corresponding lights in the near and far rows fell on corresponding retinal locations (e.g. the leftmost light position in the near and far rows fell along the same line of sight). A typical arrangement for a block of trials would have lights in the near, far, near, and far rows, respectively, going from left to right. In the center of the display table was an LED that could display a digit. On each trial, subjects fixated the central LED, which then displayed a digit from 0 to 4, where 0 meant all positions were equally likely to contain a light (the neutral cue), and 1–4 meant that the corresponding light (numbered from left to right) was highly likely to be illuminated. Subjects were instructed to attend to the cued position (without moving their eyes) and to press a key when any of the lights was illuminated. The light appeared in the cued location on 79% of the trials, and in one of the uncued locations on 21% of the trials. The cue duration was randomly selected from the range 400–800 ms. No light appeared on 26% of the trials; these catch trials were meant to ensure that subjects did not anticipate the stimulus.

The experimental design permitted Downing and Pinker to assess detection RT for trials in which the light appeared in an uncued location as a function of the retinal distance between the lights and as a function of the distance in depth between the lights. In other words, if light 1 is cued, and a light appeared in location 2, does it matter whether the light in location 2 was at the same depth as light 1? To answer this question, Downing and Pinker computed the costs associated with detecting a light in an unattended

---

[3] The near and far lights were outside of Panum's Area (the region within which binocular images can be fused) and this would have caused double images if the lights were viewed binocularly.

location. They did this by subtracting the RT to detect a light in an unattended location from the RT to detect a light in that same location when they were not selectively attending anywhere (i.e. when they had received the neutral "0" cue). These costs were then plotted as a function of where the stimulus appeared relative to the cued location separately for same-depth and different-depth trials. If attention could be directed only to a retinal location and not to a specific depth, then these two functions should be superimposed.

That was not the case. First, as expected, costs increased with increases in 2-D separation. For example, when location 1 was cued, costs were greater if the stimulus appeared in location 4 than if it appeared in location 2. More importantly, costs for different-depth trials were greater than for same-depth trials. For example, if location 1-near was cued, costs for location 4-far were greater than costs for location 4-near. This result suggests that attention did rely on a representation containing depth information.

A more recent study by Gawryszewski, Tiggio, Rizzolati, and Umiltà (1987) was reported in which attention to locations in 3-D space was measured, and reliable costs and benefits to locations at different depths were also observed. It is important to note that the study of Gawryszewski et al. (1987), like that of Downing and Pinker (1985) employed real-world 3-D displays.

Several other studies, all using computer-generated stereoscopic displays, have been reported in which attention did not appear to be directed to locations in 3-D space. For example, Iavecchia and Folk (1996) found no effect of whether a target stimulus in an uncued location was in the same depth plane as the cued location.

Ghirardelli and Folk (1996) have also recently reported no attentional effect of the depth plane in which a stimulus appears. In their study, observers viewed a stereoscopic display in which one of two possible characters (e.g. A or H) was presented, and they had to decide as quickly as possible which character was presented. On each trial, two possible stimulus locations were defined by a pair of location markers; one of the location markers was brightened for 100 ms, and after an additional 50 ms, a target character appeared in one of the two marked locations. The target appeared in the cued (brightened) location on 80% of the trials and in the uncued location on 20% of the trials.

The location markers appeared either at the same depth (i.e. with zero disparity) but in different x–y positions (i.e. left and right of the fixation point), or at the same x–y position (i.e. at fixation) but in different depth positions (with crossed disparity, in front of the fixation point, or uncrossed disparity, behind the fixation point). The former condition is similar to standard spatial cuing procedures (e.g. Posner et al., 1980). The key question asked by Ghirardelli and Folk (1996) was whether observers could selectively attend to one of two positions that differed only in depth.

The answer was clear. When the two locations differed in x–y coordinates, there were significant benefits when the target appeared in the cued location and significant costs when it appeared in an uncued location (both relative to a neutral condition). This is consistent with many previous studies showing the same thing. However, when the two locations differed only in depth and not in x–y location, there were no costs or benefits at all. It was as if subjects could attend to both locations simultaneously. Ghirardelli and Folk (1996) concluded that observers cannot selectively attend to different locations in 3-D space if they do not also differ in 2-D retinal projection.

This leaves us with an apparent inconsistency: some studies (e.g. Downing & Pinker, 1985; Gawryszewski et al., 1987) have provided evidence that it is possible to attend to locations in 3-D space, while others (e.g. Ghirardelli & Folk, 1996; Iavecchia & Folk, 1995) suggest that attention cannot be directed selectively to locations in 3-D space. One difference between these two sets of studies is that the former involved real-world scenes (objects placed at different physical depths relative to the observer), while the latter involved computer-generated simulations of depth. However, a recent report by Hoffman and Mueller (1994) suggests that this is not the key difference. Instead, Hoffman and Mueller (1994) argue that what is crucial is whether there exist well-defined perceptual objects to which attention can be directed in advance. In their study, the to-be-attended locations were defined by placeholder objects, one of which transformed into the target object. In this case, observers were evidently able to attend selectively to a cued object that differed from the uncued object only in depth. Hoffman and Mueller (1994) concluded that object-based selection may operate on a representation that contains depth information.

In summary, the studies reviewed in this section suggest that, although attention cannot be directed to empty locations in 3-D space, attention to objects at different 3-D locations may be possible.

Shifts of Attention

The work reviewed so far has been concerned with determining how attention is distributed in space at a given moment in time. This leaves open the question of how attention is shifted from one location to another. Before reviewing some of the relevant studies, it will be useful to sketch the space of possibilities. One dimension along which models of attention shifts differ is whether the movement of attention is continuous or discrete. A continuous model holds that attention should be conceived as something like a spotlight: it "illuminates" a restricted convex region of the image, it permits information from the image to pass only from that region, and it moves continuously from one location to the next as a spotlight sweeps across the surfaces that it illuminates as it moves. This is contrasted with a "gradient" or "zoom-lens" model according to which the size but not the location of the attended region may change continuously; according to these models, changes in location occur discontinuously (for example, the "amount" of attention at one location might gradually decline as the "amount" at another location increases). One can imagine various hybrid possibilities as well.

Among the first to examine this question were Shulman, Remington, and McLean (1979). The experiment was designed to test a prediction of the class of spotlight models: When attention moves from one location to another, it "illuminates" intervening locations. Therefore, we might expect that responses to objects that lie on the presumed path of an attention movement should be facilitated by attention at some point during the course of the attention movement. Certain aspects of the data obtained by Shulman et al. were consistent with the analog spotlight hypothesis, and the authors concluded that the spotlight hypothesis was supported. However, Yantis (1988) and Eriksen and Murphy (1987) have pointed out that other aspects of their data are difficult to reconcile with the spotlight hypothesis. These inconsistencies have not yet been clarified empirically, and so evidence concerning the "attention to intervening locations" hypothesis remains uncertain.

Most of the remaining evidence about the mechanisms for shifts of attention concerns the timecourse of attentional shifts. One prediction of a continuous spotlight hypothesis is that if the spotlight of attention moves at a constant rate, then it should take longer to shift attention a long distance than to shift it a short distance.[4] This was the focus of an experiment reported by Remington and Pierce (1984). Subjects were required to detect the onset of a light appearing at one of two locations to the right or left of fixation; the eccentricity was either 2° or 10° on any given trial. At various moments in time before the light flashed, an arrowhead appeared at the fixation point indicating the side on which the light was likely to appear. On some trials, instead of an arrowhead, a neutral cross, providing no spatial information, appeared instead. The purpose of the neutral cross cue was to provide subjects with a warning about when the target flash would appear without also providing them with spatial information about where to direct attention. In this way, Remington and Pierce could separately estimate the timecourse of the spatially specific attentional effect uncontaminated by changes in readiness or arousal that are also known to accompany a cuing

---

[4] Of course, movements of attention could move at a variable velocity (e.g. attention could move faster the farther it has to go) and still be continuous. However, the constant velocity assumption is a reasonable starting point.

signal (e.g. Bertelson, 1967; Posner & Boies, 1971). Subtracting the non-spatial warning effect from the spatially specific attentional effect, Remington and Pierce (1984) found that response times improved to a minimum, asymptotic, level as the cuing interval increased, and that the asymptotic level occurred at the same cuing interval for different distances. They concluded that the time required for a shift of attention does not depend on the distance over which attention must be shifted.[5] This result undermines a simple attentional spotlight hypothesis that assumes a constant-velocity trajectory.

Several additional experiments have corroborated the findings of Remington and Pierce (1984). Kwak, Dagenbach, and Egeth (1991) presented displays consisting of two letters and required subjects to judge whether they were the same or different. The two letters appeared on the circumference of an imaginary circle with radius 4.5°; the distance between the letters varied from one trial to the next. In their Experiment 2, the letters were rotated Ts and Ls; evidence from Experiment 3 of Kwak et al. (1991) and elsewhere (e.g. Egeth & Dagenbach, 1991) strongly indicates that these letters are processed strictly sequentially, which makes them useful for assessing movements of attention. If attention moves with a fixed velocity, then responses should be slower when the letters are far apart than when they are close together. The data revealed no such variation with distance, however. Kwak et al. (1991) concluded in favor of time-invariant shifts of visual attention. Kröse and Julesz (1989) drew similar conclusions based on data from a paradigm in which response accuracy, rather than response time, was the dependent variable.

These experiments are based on the notion that attention must be directed to a location in space with a fixed "attentional aperture." Eriksen and St. James (1986) proposed an alternative "zoom-lens" model of attentional focus. According to the zoom-lens model, attention is directed to a region of space the size and location of which changes with task demands. If a subject is required to focus attention on a single location indicated by a bar marker, the locus of attention begins in a diffuse state, so that the entire display is attended (in preparation for the appearance of the bar marker), and then it "zooms in" on the indicated location over time. If multiple contiguous locations are relevant, attention can be distributed over the larger region containing those locations, but at some loss in speed. Eriksen and St. James (1986)—using a procedure similar to that of Eriksen and Hoffman (1973), described earlier—probed the interference produced by incompatible distractors at various moments in time after the onset of the

---

[5] An earlier study by Tsal (1983) had similar logic but came to a different conclusion. However, Tsal's experiments failed to include the critical neutral-cue control condition. See Yantis (1988) for a discussion.

bar marker, and found that the spatial extent over which interference occurred decreased over time as predicted by the zoom-lens model.

A consistent but incomplete picture emerges, then, concerning shifts of visual attention. They clearly do not take more time as the distance to be traversed increases. This result casts some doubt on a simple spotlight metaphor. However, little enough is known about the principles governing shifts of visual attention, so that not much more can be said with confidence. This difficult issue requires more theoretical and empirical analysis.

STIMULUS-DRIVEN CONTROL OF ATTENTION

The evidence reviewed in the previous section shows that people are able to deploy attention to relevant objects or regions of space when they wish to do so. We now turn to the evidence concerning how stimulus events that are not explicitly represented in the observer's state of attentional readiness may capture or otherwise modulate attention. At issue is the extent to which stimulus events can control the distribution of attention independently of the goals and intentions of the observer.

As I stated earlier, William James wrote about attention in his classic *Principles of psychology* a century ago, and he noted that certain kinds of events are likely to automatically draw attention. Referring to this variety of attention as passive and immediate, he said that certain stimuli have a "directly exciting quality;" examples include "strange things, moving things, wild animals, bright things, pretty things, metallic things, words, blows, blood, etc., etc., etc." (James, 1890, pp.416–417). In this section, we will examine recent empirical evidence that clarifies what sorts of stimulus events do capture attention in a stimulus-driven fashion.

Attentional Capture by Spatial Cues

As we saw earlier, attention can be directed voluntarily to spatial locations by informative visual cues (e.g. Eriksen & Hoffman, 1973; Posner et al., 1980). It was initially assumed that a salient display change in the visual periphery would capture attention automatically; Jonides (1981) set out to test this assumption empirically. Jonides used a visual search task in which subjects viewed an array of eight letters arranged in a circle so that each letter in the array was equidistant from the fixation point. Every array contained either an *L* or an *R*, and subjects were to determine which of these targets was present by pressing the corresponding left or right button. Shortly before the letter array appeared, an arrowhead cue appeared indicating one of the display locations. On some trials the cue was valid and indicated the location in which the target letter eventually appeared, and on others it was invalid. The arrowhead cue appeared either at fixation (a central cue) or near the letter location that it indicated (a peripheral cue).

The question of interest was whether these two different cue types had different effects on the deployment of attention. Jonides speculated that the peripheral cue would capture attention "automatically", whereas the central cue would require voluntary effort to direct attention to the indicated location. Three criteria for automaticity were used to assess the automaticity of the central and peripheral cue. An automatic process does not require significant mental capacity, it is resistant to suppression, and it does not require deliberate intent on the part of the observer to have its effect (Shiffrin & Schneider, 1977).

Jonides examined these criteria in three experiments; I will describe his Experiment 2 in which resistance to suppression was measured. The cue validity in this experiment was 12.5%; because there were eight letters in each array, the cue provided no predictive information about the likely location of the target (i.e. $1/8 = .125$). One group of subjects was instructed to attend deliberately to the cued location on each trial (the "attend" group), and a second group was explicitly told that the cue was uninformative and should therefore be ignored (the "ignore" group).

According to the automaticity hypothesis, the central cue should affect the distribution of attention only when subjects deliberately adopt a strategy to use the cue, but the peripheral cue should affect the distribution of attention whether subjects choose to use it or not. That is exactly what happened. In the "attend" group, there was a substantial effect of cue validity for both central and peripheral cues—although the magnitude of the difference between invalid cue RT and valid cue RT was larger for peripheral cues (95 ms) than for central cues (61 ms). This shows that subjects can choose to use either type of cue if they wish. In the "ignore" group, however, the effect of cue validity was very different for central and peripheral cues. There was no difference in response time for valid and invalid central cues (2 ms *slower* for valid central cues), but a substantial validity effect for peripheral cues (98 ms). These results showed that while central cues are effective only when subjects adopt a strategy to use the cues, peripheral cues capture attention even when subjects deliberately attempt to ignore the cues. Experiments 1 and 3 of Jonides (1981) provide converging evidence for the automaticity of peripheral cues.

A decade later, Remington, Johnston, and Yantis (1992) set out to define the limits of the conclusions drawn by Jonides (1981). They asked how effectively such peripheral display changes capture attention when there is a substantial incentive actively to ignore the cue. In the critical conditions of their experiments, the cue *never* appeared in the target location, and this negative contingency was emphasized in the instructions. Subjects were to identify a target character appearing in one of four locations arranged in a diamond configuration above, below, and to the left and right of fixation. On each trial a "cue" appeared around one of the four possible target locations (here I use quotation marks around the word cue to remind the reader that the peripheral stimulus did not always provide information about the upcoming target location and in those cases would not be considered a cue in standard usage). The cue consisted of a highly salient array of four small crosses surrounding the potential target location. In *SAME* blocks, the cue always indicated the target location, and subjects were encouraged to use the cue to direct attention to the indicated location; in *DIF* blocks, the "cue" never indicated the target location (in fact, the cue told subjects that the target was certain to appear in one of the three *other* locations), and subjects were exhorted to ignore the cue and attend elsewhere if possible. In addition, there were blocks of trials in which all locations were cued (*ALL* blocks) and blocks in which none were cued (*NONE* blocks); in both of these conditions there was no information about where the target might appear.

This manipulation tests a stronger version of the automaticity hypothesis than that tested by Jonides (1981): here, subjects were actively attempting to suppress the cued location; in Jonides (1981), the target could sometimes appear in the cued location, so although subjects may not have been actively using the cues, they were probably not actively attempting to suppress them, either. Remington et al. (1992) found that even when the cues were explicitly to be ignored, subjects were unable to do so. Response time in DIF blocks were always slower than in the SAME, NONE, and ALL blocks; this is what one would expect if attention was drawn to the cue even in the DIF blocks when the cue was explicitly to be ignored.

Several studies have pursued the difference between attentional capture by cues adjacent to the object to be attended versus deliberate attentional deployment based on cues that indicate a location other than themselves; one distinguishing characteristic of these two types of cuing is the timecourse with which attention is deployed. It has generally been found that peripheral cues tend to draw attention rapidly, but release it rather quickly; in contrast, deliberate attentional deployment based on central or indirect cues takes longer to occur but can persist for several hundred ms. For example, Müller and Rabbitt (1989) asked subjects to identify and localize a briefly flashed target letter. Preceding the appearance of the target at various points in time, one of two cuing events occurred: an arrowhead appeared at fixation pointing toward the target's location, or a box surrounding the target location brightened briefly. Like Jonides (1981), Müller and Rabbitt (1989) found that (compared to the central arrowhead) the peripheral cue was resistant to suppression even when it was known to be irrelevant. Furthermore, they found that the timecourse of attentional deployment for the two cues was also different: RT to peripherally cued targets reached a minimum at relatively short cuing intervals (i.e. the interval from the onset of the cue to the onset of the target), and then increased again; in contrast,

RT to centrally cued targets improved more slowly with cuing interval, reaching an asymptote later and remaining at the faster level for some time.

An interesting violation of this pattern was reported by Warner, Juola, and Koshino (1990). Subjects practiced a cued letter identification task for many sessions. Early in practice, the standard pattern was observed: identification of targets in uncued location was slower than targets in cued locations, even if the uncued location was the likely location of the target. However, after about 4500 trials, subjects were able to direct attention to a location opposite the cue very efficiently. Somehow practice was able to overcome the natural tendency for attention to be captured by a peripheral cue.

The distinction between attention to a peripheral cue and a central indicator has been reported by other labs using somewhat different paradigms. Nakayama and Mackeben (1989) required subjects to search for a complex target in an array of as many as 64 elements. The array was presented briefly and then masked. At various moments in time before array onset, a square appeared at the location that would eventually contain the target. Nakayama and Mackeben recorded detection accuracy as a function of the cuing interval and found that accuracy started at a level just above chance for very short cuing intervals, then increased to a peak at cuing intervals of approximately 150 ms, and then fell to an asymptotic but well above chance level. A similar pattern of results was reported by Cheal and Lyon (1991).

The results of all three of these studies (Cheal & Lyon, 1991; Müller & Rabbitt, 1989; Nakayama & Mackeben, 1989) led the authors to conclude that there exist two separate attentional mechanisms. One mechanism responds to peripheral events, draws attention automatically and rapidly, and then dissipates rapidly. The second mechanism is voluntary, requires effort, and has a slower timecourse. Overall performance in the experiments is thought to reflect the superposition of both mechanisms.

Not all investigators subscribe to this view. However, there is good evidence that attentional deployment based on central (symbolic, indirect) cues is different in potency and timecourse than attentional capture by peripheral (direct) cues. At the end of the chapter, I will return to this issue in a discussion of the interaction between top-down and bottom-up control of attention.

Attentional Capture and Visual Salience

Certain visual stimuli are subjectively salient. The clearest examples are objects that differ substantially from their surround in some simple visual feature. For example, a red element will stand out from a background of uniformly green elements. It is not enough that the element differs from the background elements, however: a unique red element will not be subjectively salient if the background consists of multicolored elements, even if none of them is red. So salience requires two conditions: a stimulus that differs from its immediate surround in some dimension, and a surround that is reasonably homogeneous in that dimension (Duncan & Humphreys, 1989). Stimuli that satisfy these criteria are termed *feature singletons.*

Singletons are easy to find in visual search. For example, Egeth, Jonides, and Wall (1972) found that visual search for a *4* in a background of *C*s or vice-versa was very efficient: RT to find the target did not increase as the number of nontargets in the array was increased. Indeed, this is one of the central facts to be explained by theories of visual search (Treisman & Gelade, 1980; Wolfe, 1984; see Wolfe, this volume, for further details).

The efficiency of visual search for a feature singleton led to the assumption that such stimuli capture attention. One manifestation of this assumption is the terminology that is sometimes applied to feature search: feature singletons are said to "pop out" of the display. One must keep in mind, however, that in most feature search tasks, the subject is actively seeking the feature in question; one cannot conclude that a feature for which the observer is deliberately searching captures attention because of the likely involvement of top-down strategies and mechanisms. In this section, several studies are reviewed that cast light on the circumstances under which feature singletons do capture attention. The studies will be divided into two types: those suggesting that feature singletons typically do not capture attention when they are known to be irrelevant to the search task, and those suggesting that when one type of feature singleton (say, a color singleton) is relevant to the search task, then another, irrelevant, singleton (say an orientation singleton) may capture attention despite intentions to the contrary.

Feature Singletons Do Not Always Capture Attention.   Only a handful of studies has been carried out to test directly whether feature singletons capture attention when they are completely irrelevant to the task at hand. However, the results have been clear and consistent. Jonides and Yantis (1988) had subjects search through an array of letters for a prespecified target letter; the total number of letters in each display was varied from trial to trial. Each trial contained one letter that differed from all the rest in some way. For example, in one condition, one of the letters was red and the rest were green (and for half the subjects the reverse was true). In another condition, one letter was bright and the rest were dim. In all cases, the position of the unique element was uncorrelated with the position of the target. For example, during trials in which there were seven letters, the target was the bright element on one-seventh of the trials and it was one of the dim elements on the remaining six-sevenths of the trials. The experimental design thereby included no inducement to deliberately attend to the unique element.

The critical observation was whether RT depended on whether the target happened to be the unique element or not. If feature singletons capture attention, then they should do so even when they are uninformative about the location of the upcoming target. (The logic is the same as that used by Jonides, 1981, when he found that peripheral cues capture attention even when they are known to be uninformative about the target's location.) Jonides and Yantis (1988) found that feature singletons, unlike peripheral cues, do not capture attention when they are irrelevant. RT to unique (e.g. bright) targets did not differ from RT to the nonunique (e.g. dim) targets. Hillstrom and Yantis (1994) performed a similar experiment in which the unique feature was motion. Subjects searched for a target letter among nontargets; one letter in each display exhibited motion (they used five different forms of motion, including oscillation, moving internal texture, and small moving elements revolving around the critical letter). Hillstrom and Yantis (1994) first ensured that the features they used were indeed salient by running a version of the visual search experiment in which the moving element was *always* the target, and subjects were encouraged to guide attention to the moving element to speed search. In this case, all five types of motion yielded very efficient search with RTs that did not increase with the number of letters in the array. They then ran a version of the experiment in which the location of the moving element was uncorrelated with the target; in this case, the time required to find the target was no greater when it happened to be the moving element than when it was one of the stationary elements.

Yantis and Egeth (1994) recently reported a similar result using simpler stimuli (oriented colored bars). They extended the findings of Jonides and Yantis (1988) and Hillstrom and Yantis (1994) by showing that response times to singleton targets are highly sensitive to the informativeness of the singleton. The correlation between the location of the singleton element and the target varied for several different groups of subjects. In addition to a group with no correlation and a group with a perfect correction (the results for which were the same as in the studies summarized earlier), they included groups with three intermediate degrees of correlation. The visual search function for singleton targets reflected decreasing influence of the number of nontargets as the correlation between the locations of the singleton and target letters increased (and hence, as the informativeness of the singleton increased). This suggests that subjects were able to use the contingencies contained within an experimental design to guide attention deliberately and in some sense optimally, even with salient feature singletons as the carrier of that information.

Folk and Annette (1994) speculated that the reason Jonides and Yantis (1988) did not observe attentional capture by color or brightness singletons was that the feature density in their displays was too low, leading to reduced feature contrast (the same objection could also be leveled at the studies of Hillstrom & Yantis, 1994, and Yantis & Egeth, 1994.) To test this idea, Folk and Annette performed an experiment similar to those of Jonides and Yantis (1988) but they increased the feature density by including between the letters in the search array randomly positioned dots whose color matched the nonunique color in the display. In this way, the uniquely colored element was much closer to elements with a contrasting color, yielding a sharper color contrast than in the earlier studies. Folk and Annette found, however, that this did not change the results: irrelevant color singletons still did not capture attention. Together, the results described in this section provide strong evidence that feature singletons do not capture attention in a purely bottom-up fashion.

Attentional Control in Singleton Search.   A somewhat different story about the attentional effects of feature singletons emerges when observers are actively searching for a singleton. One of the first studies to address this issue directly was reported by Pashler (1988). Subjects were required to search for a circle target in an array of tilted lines (or vice-versa). On any given trial, they did not know whether the target would be a circle in a background of tilted lines or a tilted line in a background of circles. The subjects' primary task, then, was to find and report the location of the form singleton. Two of the elements in each display were colored red, and the rest were green; subjects were informed that the color singletons were irrelevant to their task and should be ignored (the form singletons were never red). Pashler found that localization accuracy for the form singleton decreased in the presence of the two irrelevant color singletons. Evidently Pashler's subjects could not ignore the color singletons when searching for form singletons.

A corroborating result was reported by Theeuwes (1992). Observers were required to report the orientation of a line segment (vertical or horizontal) that was located within one of several colored shapes (red and green diamonds and circles) arranged on the circumference of an imaginary circle centered at fixation (Fig. 6.2, top). The target element was always contained within a form that differed from all the other forms in shape or color. Within a given block of trials, for example, the target would always appear within a circle; all the other forms in each trial were diamonds. This induced subjects to direct attention to the shape singleton on each trial and then make a horizontal/vertical judgment about the line contained therein. On some trials, all the forms had the same color (e.g. green; represented by the solid lines in Fig. 6.2); on other trials, one form had a unique color (e.g. red; represented by the dashed lines in Fig. 6.2). The color singleton, when present, was always in a location that differed from the location of the shape

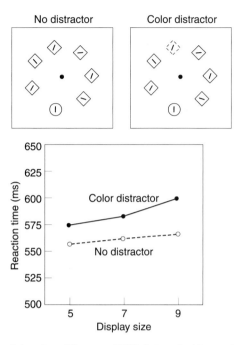

FIG. 6.2. Stimuli and data from Theeuwes (1992) (adapted with permission). Top: A vertical or horizontal bar appeared within a green circle (the other bars were all oblique). On the left, all the diamonds are green (solid lines); on the right, one of the diamonds is red (dashed lines). Subjects were to report the orientation of the bar in the circle. Bottom: The presence of the irrelevant color singleton slowed responses to the bar. Reprinted with the kind permission of the Psychonomic Society, Inc.

singleton. Color variation was known to be irrelevant to the task and subjects were strongly encouraged to ignore the color singleton if it occurred. Theeuwes (1992) found that orientation responses were always substantially slower in the presence of the color singleton than in its absence (Fig. 6.2, bottom), strongly suggesting that subjects could not ignore the color singleton in this task. (It is worth noting that this finding was not symmetrical: responses to color-defined targets were not slowed by the presence of a shape singleton, a finding Theeuwes attributed to differing degrees of salience in the shape and color domains.) Several other studies have yielded similar results and conclusions (e.g. Theeuwes, 1991a; Folk, Remington, & Johnston, 1992, Experiment 4).

On the face of it, the results described here, suggesting that singletons do capture attention and cannot be ignored, are at odds with those described in the last section suggesting that singletons can be ignored easily. How can this apparent discrepancy be explained? The critical difference between the experiments described in the last section and those in this section is this: in all the former studies, singletons were completely irrelevant to the task (the targets were difficult-to-discriminate stimuli that required scrutiny to find), while in the latter studies, the targets were defined as feature singletons. Bacon and Egeth (1994) have argued persuasively that subjects in experiments like those of Theeuwes (1992) and Pashler (1988) adopt a strategy they call *singleton-detection mode*. This strategy relies on a feature-contrast detector to guide attention (see Nothdurft, 1993, for relevant evidence). The feature-contrast detector provides information about the locations in the display with high feature contrast (i.e. locations in which neighboring elements differ in some dimension like color) but it does not provide information about what dimension is producing the contrast. In singleton-detection mode, subjects direct attention to the most salient feature contrast in the display; this strategy is presumed to be very efficient when the target is a singleton. However, when there are one or more other, irrelevant, singletons in the display, attention may sometimes be directed to the wrong location.[6]

To test this idea, Bacon and Egeth (1994) performed several experiments modeled after those of Theeuwes (1992). They first replicated the findings reported by Theeuwes (1992). They then changed the design slightly so that singleton-detection mode would no longer be an effective strategy. In one experiment, for example, they did this by including three instances of the target feature in the display; now the target was not a singleton (i.e. its feature contrast with the rest of the display was low), so singleton-detection mode was inefficient. In this case, the presence of a potentially distracting singleton in another dimension had no discernable effect. Bacon and Egeth concluded that when subjects adopt a different strategy, irrelevant singletons no longer capture attention.

Folk et al. (1992) proposed a framework for conceptualizing the interaction between a subject's strategies and the extent to which stimulus features capture attention. According to their proposal, subjects adopt an *attentional control setting* that determines what stimulus features will control the deployment of attention in any given task. Bacon and Egeth's (1994) singleton detection mode might be considered an instance of an attentional control setting. The idea is that when an observer adopts a deliberate state of attentional readiness for some feature or feature set, then stimuli that are consistent with that feature will tend to receive attention, and stimuli that are not consistent with it will not.

Folk et al. (1992) carried out several experiments to test their idea. The experiments required subjects to identify a target that was defined as

---

[6] Of course, this raises the question of why subjects continue to use singleton detection mode when irrelevant singletons may appear. It is possible that search is less effortful in this case even though attention may sometimes be misdirected.

possessing a particular feature (e.g. the target might be the only red element in an array of white elements, or the target might be the only element in the display with an abrupt onset). Shortly before the target appeared, a distracting "cue" was presented at a different location.[7] The cue either matched the target feature (if the target was uniquely red, so was the cue) or it did not (if the target was uniquely red, the cue might be a unique abrupt onset). Folk et al. found that the cue disrupted performance (i.e. slowed responses) only when it matched the target's defining feature (and hence, by assumption, the subject's attentional control setting). When the cue did not match the attentional control setting, it did not disrupt performance.

Folk et al. (1992) also found that the disruptive effects of a cue extended to feature values other than ones that were identical to the target's defining feature. For example, if the target was defined as uniquely red, than a uniquely green cue also captured attention. This finding corroborates and extends the finding of Theeuwes (1992) described earlier, and led Folk et al. to speculate that there might be categories of features (e.g. all color singletons) that could serve as a joint attentional control setting, and any singleton within that category would control the deployment of attention. This is a refinement of Bacon and Egeth's (1994) singleton-detection mode according to which any singleton will capture attention with a potency that is proportional to the salience of that feature.

The attentional control setting idea of Folk et al. (1992) can account for an impressive range of results. Some of the specific claims made by Folk et al. (1992) have been contested, however. For example, Folk et al. argued (see Folk, Remington, & Wright, 1994, for additional evidence) that there is a basic distinction between static discontinuities (e.g. shape and color singletons) and dynamic discontinuities (e.g. motion and onset singletons). Theeuwes (1994) reported experiments using a visual search task without spatial cues in which search for a target defined by a static discontinuity was disrupted by the presence of a dynamic discontinuity and vice versa. This finding casts doubt on the static/dynamic distinction proposed by Folk et al. (1992).

Another contested claim made by Folk et al. is that all instances of attentional capture are mediated by an attentional control setting. Yantis (1993b) objected that attentional capture by abrupt visual onset occurs even without a corresponding state of attentional readiness (see the next section for details). Folk et al. (1993) responded by speculating that, in the absence of a simple attentional set, there may exist a "default" attentional control

---

[7] As before, I enclose the word "cue" in quotation marks because the term is not used by Folk et al. in the usual way. The "cue" serves only a distracting function (and subjects were clearly informed of this).

setting for abrupt onset, and the default setting may control the deployment of attention in certain tasks.

These objections notwithstanding, Folk et al. (1992) have contributed to an understanding of attentional control by offering a framework for characterizing the interaction between deliberate attentional strategies and nondeliberate attentional capture. I will return to this important issue at the end of the chapter.

Attentional Capture by Abrupt Visual Onsets

In a 1976 article, Breitmeyer and Ganz discussed the role of transient and sustained visual channels in visual pattern masking and information processing. Late in the article, they speculated that one role for the transient channels (i.e. visual channels specialized for the detection of abrupt luminance change over time) might be to direct attention to regions or events in the image that exhibit change; they argued that such events are likely to be significant for behaving organisms because they may require rapid identification and response. Shortly thereafter, Todd and Van Gelder (1979) tested a version of this hypothesis by measuring eye movement latencies to visual stimuli that either did or did not contain abrupt visual onsets. They found that latencies to stimuli with abrupt onsets were faster than to those without abrupt onset, and argued that the speculation of Breitmeyer and Ganz (1976) was consistent with this finding.

Abrupt Visual Onsets Capture Attention.   Yantis and Jonides (1984) extended this idea to explore a specifically attentional version of the hypothesis. They used a visual search task to ask whether an abrupt onset stimulus captures attention automatically. The logic was similar to that used by Jonides (1981): to what extent will an abrupt onset stimulus enjoy an advantage in visual search even when there is no incentive for subjects to deliberately attend to it?

The stimuli used by Yantis and Jonides (1984) are illustrated in Fig. 6.3 (top). Each trial began with the presentation of the target letter for that trial (not shown), followed by a set of figure-eight placeholders similar to the seven-segment characters in a digital clock. The placeholders were present for one second, and were replaced by an array of letters. The letters were formed from a subset of the seven segments. All but one of the letters appeared in locations that previously were occupied by figure-eight placeholders; two line-segments were removed to reveal letters in those locations. These letters were termed *no-onset* stimuli. One letter appeared in a previously blank location; this letter was called an *onset* stimulus.

Subjects were required to press one button if the target letter was present in the array, and another button if it was absent. Display sizes of two and

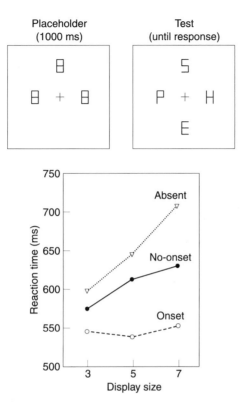

FIG. 6.3.   Stimuli and data from Yantis and Jonides (1984; Jonides & Yantis, 1988). Top: An array of figure-eight placeholders appears for 1000 ms, and is followed by an array of letters. One letter appears in a previously blank location (the onset letter), while the remaining letters appeared in locations previously occupied by figure-eight placeholders. These no-onset letters are revealed by the removal of camouflaging line-segments. Bottom: Response times for trials in which the target is the onset letter, one of the no-onset letters, or is absent. Data are from Jonides and Yantis (1988): (Adapted with permission). Reprinted with the kind permission of the Psychonomic Society, Inc.

four letters were used in the experiment. As Wolfe (this volume) states, when the target–distractor discrimination is difficult, then response time typically increases with display size, reflecting an attentionally demanding search. The letters in the experiments of Yantis and Jonides (1984) were designed to be difficult to discriminate, providing a context within which attentional capture might be observed.

A critical feature of the experimental design was that the onset letter was no more likely to be the target than was any other letter in the display. In particular, the target happened to coincide with the onset letter only randomly (i.e. on $1/d$ of the trials, where d is display size). This design minimized subjects' incentive to attend deliberately to the onset location.[8] Thus it was possible to assess the extent to which the onset letter captured attention in a purely stimulus-driven fashion.

Mean RT to correctly detect the target letter for the various conditions of the experiment is shown in the bottom of Fig. 6.3. Four relevant observations can be made. First, when the target was an abrupt-onset stimulus, RT did not increase with display size. Second, when the target was one of the no-onset letters, RT increased significantly with display size. Third, when the target was absent, RT increased even more steeply with display size. Finally, the slope of the target-absent function is approximately twice that of the target-present function for no-onset targets. The last three observations are consistent with a serial self-terminating search strategy for the no-onset letters according to which the letters are scanned one at a time and a response is made when the target is found or after the display is scanned exhaustively and no target is found. The flat display-size function for onset targets strongly suggests that the onset stimulus was identified first during the search, and a response was made after that single identification if the target was the onset letter. This is the prediction of attentional capture by abrupt onset.

New Perceptual Objects Capture Attention.   The speculation by Breitmeyer and Ganz (1976) that motivated the experiments of Yantis and Jonides (1984) was that any stimulus that strongly activated the transient visual channels would capture attention. According to this account, the presentation of a luminance increment is critical in drawing attention; this is called the *luminance-increment account*. Yantis and Hillstrom (1994) considered an alternative account for attentional capture by abrupt onsets, motivated by recent object-based theories of visual selection. According to object-based theories, the representational basis for visual selection is not a specific region of space, but a perceptual object (Duncan, 1984; Kahneman, Treisman, & Gibbs, 1992; Kanwisher & Driver, 1992; see also Wolfe, this volume). According to the *new-object account*, the appearance of a new perceptual object requires the creation of an object representation, and this in turn triggers a shift of attention to the new object.

The luminance-increment account and the new-object accounts are both consistent with the results of Yantis and Jonides (1984) because the abrupt onset stimuli were new objects that exhibited luminance increments. In order to distinguish between the two hypotheses, Yantis and Hillstrom (1994)

---

[8] Indeed, as shown earlier, when a highly salient stimulus (e.g. a red element among green ones) is known by subjects to be uninformative about target location, it is routinely ignored by subjects (e.g. Jonides & Yantis, 1988; Yantis & Egeth, 1994). This provides converging evidence that this experimental design effectively eliminates any top-down intention to direct attention to the unique (in this case, onset) location.

performed experiments that were very similar in design to those of Yantis and Jonides (1984) except that they used objects that were defined by equiluminant discontinuities in motion, depth, or texture. For example, the motion-defined letters were constructed as follows: the screen was filled with randomly placed dots, and windows were defined in the shape of the desired letters (e.g. figure-eights). The dots within the windows moved at a constant speed to the left, and the background dots remained stationary. The contours of the letters were thus defined by a motion discontinuity, but there was no difference in the mean luminance of the letters and the background. A trial started with figure-eight placeholders for one second followed by an array of letters, one appearing in a background location and the others revealed by removing subsets of the line segments making up the figure-eights. Thus when a new object appeared, there was no localized change in the luminance at that location.

The luminance-increment account predicts that such a stimulus will not capture attention, whereas the new-object account predicts that it will. The experiments revealed that new objects do capture attention even without a luminance increment. Yantis and Hillstrom (1994) concluded that a luminance increment is not necessary to capture visual attention.

Overall, the experiments we have carried out lead us to conclude that the appearance of a new perceptual object is an important perceptual event that has significant consequences for the deployment of attention. It is important to emphasize that new objects do not have absolute control over attention (e.g. Koshino, Warner, & Juola, 1992; Theeuwes, 1991b, 1995; Yantis & Jonides, 1990). Nevertheless, the visual system appears to be predisposed to attend to objects that require the creation of a new perceptual object representation.

INTERACTION OF GOAL-DRIVEN AND STIMULUS-DRIVEN ATTENTION

The experiments reviewed in this chapter reveal some of the properties that characterize both goal-driven and stimulus-driven attentional control. Attention can be directed to locations in space "by a conscious and voluntary effort," as Helmholtz suggested. It can also be captured by abrupt onset and other stimulus events. Perhaps more importantly, the experiments show that attentional control results from an interaction between the observer's intentions and the properties of the image.

A complete understanding of control requires a specification of the nature of that interaction. We have touched on several varieties of interaction in this chapter. One is exemplified by the experiments of Pashler (1988), Theeuwes (1992), Folk et al. (1992), and Bacon and Egeth (1994). When an observer is searching for a featural singleton, then even to-be-ignored singletons will capture attention. This suggests that subjects adopt a perceptual set to attend to any feature discontinuity (Nothdurft, 1993). However, when an observer searches for a more complex object (e.g. a rotated T in a background of rotated Ls), then irrelevant featural singletons will not capture attention. When the target of search cannot be localized on the basis of contrast in a single feature, then subjects do not enter singleton detection mode.

When an observer directs attention to a spatial location in advance of a display, then visual events that would otherwise capture attention will generally fail to do so. Evidence for this fact was provided by Yantis and Jonides (1990), Koshino et al. (1992), and Theeuwes (1991b, 1995). In these studies, observers were cued to attend to a location that was likely to contain a target stimulus; the appearance of an abrupt onset stimulus in another (to-be-ignored) location did not capture attention. However, that same stimulus did capture attention (and thereby affected performance) when attention could not be focused elsewhere in advance.

Stimulus-driven attentional control is both faster and more potent than goal-driven attentional control (e.g. Jonides, 1981; Nakayama & Mackeben, 1989). A likely reason for this difference is the necessary translation or decision process that is required in goal-driven control: if attention is to be voluntarily directed to a location, then the cue or instruction indicating the to-be-attended location must be perceived and decoded to determine which location it indicates. Sometimes the decoding process is straightforward (e.g. an arrowhead indicating a location) but sometimes it is more symbolic (e.g. a tone or a numeral indicating a location). When the stimulus itself captures attention, however, no such translation is required; attention is directly and immediately deployed.

The interactions between goal-driven and stimulus-driven aspects of attentional control are well characterized by the notion of attentional control settings as proposed by Folk et al. (1992; Folk et al., 1994). It is safe to assume that any alert observer viewing a natural scene has a complex constellation of goals and expectations about what they are about to see. When searching for a specific object, the attentional set is likely to include properties of the desired object. But even when walking down the street with no particular search goal in mind, the observer will seek to avoid obstacles and to walk toward his or her destination. He or she may have a mild interest in, say, architecture. In addition, there appear to be some "default" or "hard-wired" control settings, such as the predisposition to attend to new perceptual objects. All of these internal aspects of the observer will contribute to a multidimensional attentional control setting that will in part determine what aspects of the scene are selected for identification and possible memory storage. For example, image features whose motion trajectories are likely to intersect with the observer's own will receive attention, as will (perhaps) the gargoyles on the building across the street and the dog that appears from behind a mailbox. The deployment of attention in an image is determined by an interaction between the properties of the image and the observer's set of attentional goals.

ACKNOWLEDGEMENT

Preparation of this chapter was supported by a grant from the National Institute of Mental Health (R01-MH43924).

REFERENCES

Averbach, E., & Coriell, A.S. (1961). Short-term memory in vision. *Bell Systems Technical Journal, 40*, 309–328.

Bacon, W.F., & Egeth, H.E. (1994). Overriding stimulus-driven attentional capture. *Perception and Psychophysics, 55*, 485–496.

Bashinski, H.S., & Bacharach, V.R. (1980). Enhancement of perceptual selectivity attention to spatial locations. *Perception and Psychophysics, 28*, 241–248.

Bertelson, P. (1967). The time course of preparation. *Quarterly Journal of Experimental Psychology, 19*, 272–279.

Breitmeyer, B.G., & Ganz, L. (1976) Implications of sustained and transient channels for theories of visual pattern masking, saccadic suppression, and information processing. *Psychological Review, 83*, 1–36.

Broadbent, D.E. (1958) *Perception and communication.* Oxford: Pergamon Press.

Cheal, M.L., & Lyon, R.D. (1991). Central and peripheral precuing of forced-choice discrimination. *Quarterly Journal of Experimental Psychology, 43*A, 859–880.

Coltheart, M. (1980). Iconic memory and visible persistence. *Perception and Psychophysics, 27*, 183–228.

Deutsch, J.A., & Deutsch, D. (1963). Attention: Some theoretical considerations. *Psychological Review, 70*, 80–90.

Downing, C.J., & Pinker, S. (1985) The spatial structure of visual attention. In M. Posner & O. Martin (Eds.), *Attention and performance XI* (pp.171–187). Hillsdale, NJ: Lawrence Erlbaum Associates Inc.

Duncan, J. (1984). Selective attention and the organization of visual information. *Journal of Experimental Psychology: General, 113*, 501–517.

Duncan, J. (1985). Visual search and visual attention. In M.I. Posner & O.S. Marin (Eds.), *Attention and performance XI* (pp.85–106). Hillsdale, NJ: Lawrence Erlbaum Associates Inc.

Duncan, J., & Humphreys, G.W. (1989). Visual search and stimulus similarity. *Psychological Review, 96*, 433–458.

Egeth, H.E., & Dagenbach, D. (1991). Parallel versus serial processing in visual search: Further evidence from subadditive effects of visual quality. *Journal of Experimental Psychology: Human Perception and Performance, 17*, 550–559.

Egeth, H., Jonides, J., & Wall, S. (1972). Parallel processing of multielement displays. *Cognitive Psychology, 3*, 674–698.

Egly, R., & Homa, D. (1984). Sensitization of the visual field. *Journal of Experimental Psychology: Human Perception and Performance, 10*, 778–793.

Engel, F.L. (1971). Visual conspicuity, directed attention and retinal locus. *Vision Research, 11*, 563–576.

Eriksen, C.W., & Hoffman, J.E. (1973). The extent of processing noise elements during selective encoding from visual displays. *Perception and Psychophysics, 14,* 155–160.

Eriksen, C.W., & Murphy, T.D. (1987). Movement of attentional focus across the visual field: A critical look at the evidence. *Perception and Psychophysics, 42,* 299–305.

Eriksen, C.W., & St. James, J.D. (1986). Visual attention within and around the field of focal attention: A zoom lens model. *Perception and Psychophysics, 40,* 225–240.

Folk, C.L., & Annett, S. (1994). Do locally defined feature discontinuities capture attention? *Perception and Psychophysics, 56,* 277–287.

Folk, C.L., Remington, R.W., & Johnston, J.C. (1992). Involuntary covert orienting is contingent on attentional control settings. *Journal of Experimental Psychology: Human Perception and Performance, 18,* 1030–1044.

Folk, C.L., Remington, R.W., & Johnston, J.C. (1993). Contingent attentional capture: A reply to Yantis (1993). *Journal of Experimental Psychology: Human Perception and Performance, 19,* 682–685.

Folk, C.L., Remington, R.W., & Wright, J.H. (1994). The structure of attentional control: Contingent attentional capture by apparent motion, abrupt onset, and color. *Journal of Experimental Psychology: Human Perception and Performance, 20,* 317–329.

Gawryszewski, L.D.G., Riggio, L., Rizzolatti, G., & Umiltà, C. (1987). Movements of attention in the three spatial dimensions and the meaning of "neutral" cues. *Neuropsychologia, 25,* 19–29.

Ghirardelli, T.G., & Folk, C.L. (1996). Spatial cuing in a stereoscopic display: Evidence for a "depth-blind" attentional spotlight. *Psychonomic Bulletin and Review, 3,* 81–86.

Grindley, G.C., & Townsend, V. (1968). Voluntary attention in peripheral vision and its effects on acuity and differential thresholds. *Quarterly Journal of Experimental Psychology, 20,* 11–19.

Helmholtz, H. von (1925). *Treatise on physiological optics* (3rd edn., Vol. III, J.P.C. Southhall, Ed. & Trans.). Washington, DC: The Optical Society of America. [Original work published 1866.]

Hillstrom, A.P., & Yantis, S. (1994). Visual motion and attentional capture. *Perception and Psychophysics, 55,* 399–411.

Hoffman, J.E., & Mueller, S. (1994, November). *An in depth look at visual attention.* Paper presented at the 35th Annual Meeting of the Psychonomic Society, St. Louis.

Hoffman, J.E., & Nelson, B. (1981). Spatial selectivity in visual search. *Perception and Psychophysics, 30,* 283–290.

Iavecchia, H.P., & Folk, C.L. (1995). Shifting visual attention in sterographic displays: A minecourse analysis. *Human Factors, 36,* 606–618.

James, W. (1890). *The principles of psychology* (Vol. 1). New York: Henry Holt & Co.

Jonides, J. (1981). Voluntary versus automatic control over the mind's eye's movement. In J.B. Long & A.D. Baddeley (Eds.), *Attention and performance IX* (pp.187–203). Hillsdale, NJ: Lawrence Erlbaum Associates Inc.

Jonides, J., & Yantis, S. (1988). Uniqueness of abrupt visual onset in capturing attention. *Perception and Psychophysics, 43,* 346–354.

Kahneman, D., Treisman, A., & Gibbs, B.J. (1992). The reviewing of object files: Object-specific integration of information. *Cognitive Psychology, 24,* 175–219.

Kanwisher, N., & Driver, J. (1992). Objects, attributes, and visual attention: Which, what and where. *Current Directions in Psychological Science, 1,* 26–31.

Koopman, B.O. (1957). The theory of search: III. The optimum distribution of searching effort. *Operations Research, 5,* 613–626.

Koshino, H., Warner, C.B., & Juola, J.F. (1992). Relative effectiveness of central, peripheral, and abrupt-onset cues in visual search. *Quarterly Journal of Experimental Psychology, 45*A, 609–631.

Kröse, B.J.A., & Julesz, B. (1989). The control and speed of shifts of attention. *Vision Research, 29,* 1607–1619.

Kwak, H.-W., Dagenbach, D., & Egeth, H. (1991). Further evidence for a time-independent shift of the focus of attention. *Perception and Psychophysics, 49,* 473–480.

LaBerge, D. (1983). The spatial extent of attention to letters and words. *Journal of Experimental Psychology: Human Perception and Performance, 9,* 371–379.

LaBerge, D., & Brown, V. (1986). Variations in size of the visual field in which targets are presented: An attentional range effect. *Perception and Psychophysics, 40,* 188–200.

Mertens, J.J. (1956) Influence of knowledge of target location upon the probability of observation of peripherally observable test flashes. *Journal of the Optical Society of America, 46,* 1069–1070.

Müller, H.J., & Rabbitt, P.M.A. (1989). Reflexive and voluntary orienting of visual attention: Time course of activation and resistance to interruption. *Journal of Experimental Psychology: Human Perception and Performance, 15,* 315–330.

Nakayama, K., & Mackeben, M. (1989). Sustained and transient components of focal visual attention. *Vision Research, 29,* 1631–1647.

Navon, D., & Gopher, D. (1979). On the economy of the human-processing system. *Psychological Review, 86,* 214–255.

Nothdurft, H.C. (1993). Saliency effects across dimensions in visual search. *Vision Research, 33,* 839–844.

Pashler, H. (1988). Cross-dimensional interaction and texture segregation. *Perception and Psychophysics, 43,* 307–318.

Posner, M.I. (1978). *Chronometric explorations of mind.* Hillsdale, NJ: Lawrence Erlbaum Associates Inc.

Posner, M.I. (1980). Orienting of attention. *Quarterly Journal of Experimental Psychology, 32,* 3–25.

Posner, M.I., & Boies, S.J. (1971). Components of attention. *Psychological Review, 78,* 391–408.

Posner, M.I., Snyder, C.R.R., & Davidson, B.J. (1980). Attention and the detection of signals. *Journal of Experimental Psychology: General, 109,* 160–174.

Remington, R.W., Johnston, J.C., & Yantis, S. (1992). Involuntary attentional capture by abrupt onsets. *Perception and Psychophysics, 51,* 279–290.

Remington, R.W., & Pierce, L. (1984). Moving attention: Evidence for time-invariant shifts of visual selection attention. *Perception and Psychophysics, 35,* 393–399.

Shaw, M., & Shaw, P. (1977). Optimal allocation of cognitive resources to spatial locations. *Journal of Experimental Psychology: Human Perception and Performance, 3,* 201–211.

Shaw, M.L. (1978). A capacity allocation model for reaction time. *Journal of Experimental Psychology: Human Perception and Performance, 4,* 586–598.

Shaw, M.L. (1984). Division of attention among spatial locations: A fundamental difference between detection of letters and detections of luminance increments. In H. Bouma & D.G. Bonwhuis (Eds.), *Attention and performance X* (pp.109–120). Hove, UK: Lawrence Erlbaum Associates Ltd.

Shiffrin, R.M., & Schneider, W. (1977). Controlled and automatic human information processing: II. Perceptual learning, automatic attending, and a general theory. *Psychological Review, 84,* 127–190.

Shiu, L.-P., & Pashler, H. (1994). Negligible Effects of spatial precuing on identification of single digits. *Journal of Experimental Psychology: Human Perception and Performance, 20,* 1037-1054.

Shulman, G.L., Remington, R.W., & McLean, J.P. (1979). Moving attention through visual space. *Journal of Experimental Psychology: Human Perception and Performance, 5,* 522–526.

Sperling, G. (1960). The information available in brief visual presentations. *Psychological Monographs, 74,* 1–29.

Sperling, G., & Melchner, M.J. (1978). The attention operating characteristic: Examples from visual search. *Science, 202*, 315–318.

Todd, J.T., & Van Gelder, P. (1979). Implications of a transient-sustained dichotomy for the measurement of human performance. *Journal of Experimental Psychology: Human Perception and Performance, 5*, 625–636.

Theeuwes, J. (1991a). Cross-dimensional perceptual selectivity. *Perception and Psychophysics, 50*, 184–193.

Theeuwes, J. (1991b). Exogenous and endogenous control of attention: The effect of visual onsets and offsets. *Perception and Psychophysics, 49*, 83–90.

Theeuwes, J. (1992). Perceptual selectivity for color and form. *Perception and Psychophysics, 51*, 599–606.

Theeuwes, J. (1994). Stimulus-driven capture and attentional set: Selective search for color and visual abrupt onsets. *Journal of Experimental Psychology: Human Perception and Performance, 20*, 799–806.

Theeuwes, J. (1995). Temporal and spatial characteristics of preattentive and attentive processing. *Visual Cognition, 2*, 221–233.

Treisman, A., & Gelade, G. (1980). A feature-integration theory of attention. *Cognitive Psychology, 12*, 97–136.

Tsal, Y. (1983). Movements of attention across the visual field. *Journal of Experimental Psychology: Human Perception and Performance, 9*, 523–530.

Van der Heijden, A.H.C. (1992). *Selective attention in vision.* New York: Routledge, Chapman, & Hall.

Van der Heijden, A.H.C., & Eerland, E. (1973). The effects of cuing in a visual signal detection task. *Quarterly Journal of Experimental Psychology, 25*, 496–503.

von Wright, J.M. (1968). Selection in immediate visual memory. *Quarterly Journal of Experimental Psychology, 20*, 62–68.

Warner, C.B., Juola, J.F., & Koshino, H. (1990). Voluntary allocation versus automatic capture of visual attention. *Perception and Psychophysics, 48*, 243–251.

Wolfe, J.M. (1994). Guided search 2.0: A revised model of visual search. *Psychonomic Bulletin & Review, 1*, 202–238.

Yantis, S. (1988). On analog movements of visual attention. *Perception and Psychophysics, 43*, 203–206.

Yantis, S. (1993a). Stimulus-driven attentional capture. *Current Directions in Psychological Science, 2*, 156–161.

Yantis, S. (1993b). Stimulus-driven attentional capture and attentional control settings. *Journal of Experimental Psychology: Human Perception and Performance, 19*, 676–681.

Yantis, S., & Egeth, H.E. (1994). Visual salience and stimulus-driven attentional capture. *Investigative Ophthalmology and Visual Science, 35*, 1619.

Yantis, S., & Hillstrom, A.P. (1994). Stimulus-driven attentional capture: Evidence from equiluminant visual objects. *Journal of Experimental Psychology: Human Perception and Performance, 20*, 95–107.

Yantis, S., & Johnston, J.C. (1990). On the locus of visual selection: Evidence from focused attention tasks. *Journal of Experimental Psychology: Human Perception and Performance, 16*, 135–149.

Yantis, S., & Jonides, J. (1984). Abrupt visual onsets and selective attention: Evidence from visual search. *Journal of Experimental Psychology: Human Perception and Performance, 10*, 601–621.

Yantis, S., & Jonides, J. (1990). Abrupt visual onsets and selective attention: Voluntary versus automatic allocation. *Journal of Experimental Psychology: Human Perception and Performance, 16*, 121–134.

CHAPTER SEVEN

Neurophysiology of Selective Attention

Steven J. Luck
University of Iowa, USA

INTRODUCTION

Why Neurophysiology?

At any given moment, the human brain is confronted with a multitude of inputs: sounds from many sources; tactile sensations from the entire surface of the body; visual inputs from a huge array of retinal receptors; a variety of smells and tastes; and internally generated thoughts, emotions, memories, and images. Most of these inputs are irrelevant at any given moment, however, and it is therefore more efficient to focus our limited cognitive processing resources on a subset of the available information and ignore the rest; this is the primary role of selective attention in information processing. Although this selection process is usually conceptualized as a cognitive phenomenon that falls exclusively within the domain of psychology, neuroscientists have also become interested in the topic of selective attention in recent years. Before I begin describing their discoveries, however, I would like to consider why neuroscientists have become interested in attention and why psychologists are becoming interested in neurophysiological studies of attention.

To understand the recent interest of neuroscientists in attention, it is useful first to review some important developments in the areas of sensory anatomy and physiology. During the past 20 years, scientists have discovered over 30 separate areas of primate visual cortex that contribute to different aspects of visual perception, including depth perception, motion discrimination, spatial frequency analysis, color processing, and face recognition. As shown in Fig. 7.1a, visual information enters the nervous system in the retina, travels through a relay station called the lateral geniculate nucleus (LGN), and enters the cerebral cortex at the back of the head in an area named V1 (also known as "striate cortex" because of a prominent striation [stripe] that demarcates this area). From this starting point, information branches off and travels forward into the many specialized visual areas that are located in the posterior half of the brain (called "extrastriate" visual areas). As the information travels forward from striate cortex into extrastriate cortex, the features coded by single neurons change from simple bars and edges to more complex attributes of object identity (see Fig. 7.1b).

At the same time that neurophysiologists were discovering this posterior-to-anterior flow of visual information, neuroanatomists were mapping the connections between visual areas, and they discovered something unexpected: wherever a forward connection existed from a lower-level area to a higher-level area, there was also an extensive backward connection from the higher-level area back to the lower-level area (see Rockland, Saleem, & Tanaka, 1994; Rockland & Van Hoesen, 1994; Van Essen, 1985). If visual processing consists of the transformation of simple representations in posterior visual areas into complex representations in anterior visual areas, then what could explain the ubiquitous anterior-to-posterior connections that were so obvious in the anatomy? One likely answer is that these backward "feedback" connections allow top-down cognitive processes like attention to exert control over visual processing. Indeed, computational models of the visual system have frequently relied on top-down processing to solve certain computational problems that arise in simple feedforward systems (e.g. McClelland & Rumelhart, 1981; Mozer, 1991). Unfortunately, however, most studies of visual physiology are conducted with anesthetized animals in whom many of these top-down processes are shut down, potentially eliminating half of the inputs into each visual area. Several neurophysiologists have therefore developed methods to measure neural activity in awake monkeys so that the important effects of attention and other top-down factors can be assessed, as will be discussed later.

There are two other aspects of visual anatomy and physiology that have also led neuroscientists to become interested in attention. First, many studies have shown that the different features of a stimulus, such as its color and its shape, may be coded by different neurons, and these neurons may be located in very different areas of visual cortex. This form of stimulus coding is very efficient, allowing the brain to form representations of many different types of stimuli without devoting a different set of neurons to each combination of features that might be encountered. However, this coding scheme requires a mechanism for linking together the different features that

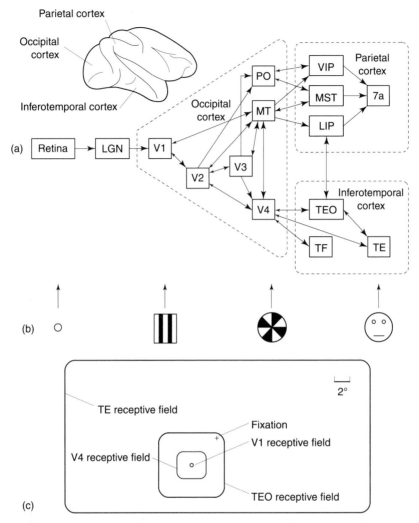

FIG. 7.1. (a) Diagram of several of the major visual areas and their interconnections in the macaque monkey (adapted from Desimone & Ungerleider, 1989). Large arrowheads represent feedforward connections and small arrowheads represent feedback connections. Information enters the retina, passes through the lateral geniculate nucleus (LGN) of the thalamus, and enters cortex in area V1. From area V1, the information diverges into an upper pathway that travels into the parietal lobes and a lower pathway that travels into the ventral portion of the temporal lobes. This diagram shows only a subset of the known areas and connections; for a more complete listing, see Felleman and Van Essen (1991). (b) Examples of the stimuli to which neurons in the various visual areas are sensitive. Neurons in the retina will produce large responses to simple spots of light and neurons in area V1 typically respond well to bars and gratings, whereas neurons in areas V4 and TE are selective for progressively more complex stimuli. (c) Typical receptive field sizes in several visual areas in the object recognition pathway (based on data from Boussaoud, Desimone, & Ungerleider, 1991; Desimone & Schein, 1987). Each outlined region represents the area in which an appropriate stimulus will elicit responses from a typical neuron in a given part of the visual system. In area V1, for example, a neuron may respond to a stimulus only if it falls within a .5° × .5° .5 ara, whereas a neuron in area TEO may respond to a stimulus anywhere within a 10° × 10° area.

define a single object, and many researchers have proposed that attentional processes are responsible for solving this "binding problem" (Crick & Koch, 1990; Desimone, Wessinger, Thomas, & Schneider, 1990; Mozer, 1991; Niebur, Koch, & Rosin, 1993; Treisman & Gelade, 1980). A related characteristic of the visual system is the progressive increase in receptive field sizes that is observed as information flows forward through the visual system (see Fig. 7.1c). The receptive field of a neuron is the area of space to which the neuron is sensitive: an individual neuron in the initial cortical visual area (V1), for example, will respond only to stimuli presented within a very restricted area, whereas an individual neuron in the final area of visual cortex (TE) will respond to stimuli presented almost anywhere within the central region of visual space. The large receptive fields that are present in anterior visual areas also help the brain to code stimuli efficiently, because separate neurons are not needed to indicate the presence of a given stimulus at each possible location. Unfortunately, large receptive fields can lead to ambiguous responses because most natural scenes are likely to contain multiple objects within a single large receptive field. For example, if a neuron that codes blue stimuli is presented with a blue object and a red object simultaneously within its receptive field, its response will indicate that a blue object is present but it cannot indicate which of the two objects is blue. This is really just another form of the binding problem, and may also be solved by means of attentional mechanisms.

In addition to answering questions concerning the role of attention in neural processing, neurophysiological studies of attention have also provided a useful source of information about how attention operates at the psychological level. In particular, neurophysiological techniques provide an alternative means of measuring the effects of attention on perceptual processing. Many questions in the study of attention address the nature of the processing that is allocated to attended versus unattended stimuli, but behavioral responses such as button presses or verbal reports have two major limitations when questions of this nature are addressed. First, in order to compare the processing of attended and unattended stimuli with behavioral measures, it is often necessary to require responses for both attended and unattended stimuli; requiring a response for an unattended stimulus may make it impossible for subjects to ignore these stimuli fully. Second, behavioral responses occur only after a long series of perceptual, decision, and motor processes, and attention-related changes in overt responses may be difficult to attribute to a particular process within that series. For example, if subjects are unable to report the identity of an unattended stimulus, how can we tell whether they failed to perceive this stimulus or whether they perceived it but simply failed to store it in memory for later report? Neurophysiological techniques can be used to provide measurements of the individual processes between a stimulus and a response, and can therefore provide a relatively direct means of assessing the effects of attention on specific perceptual processes.

Neurophysiological Techniques for Studying Attention

Most neurophysiological studies of attention have employed one of three methodologies: (1) direct electrical recordings of individual neurons in monkeys; (2) indirect electrical recordings of large groups of neurons in humans; or (3) noninvasive measurements of regional cerebral blood flow in humans. The first of these, the single-unit recording technique, is conceptually the simplest but is probably the most difficult in practice. With this technique, it is possible to record the output of a neuron, which is a momentary voltage impulse or "spike" that begins in the cell body and travels down the length of the axon to the terminals, where neurotransmitter chemicals are released to pass the signal on to other neurons. The voltage spikes can be recorded by inserting a tiny electrode into the brain until the tip of the electrode is near enough to a neuron's body to pick up its spikes; this is called an "extracellular" recording, because the electrode remains outside the neuron. Fortunately, there are no pain receptors within the brain, so the electrode can be inserted without any anesthesia.

When an appropriate visual stimulus is presented, a neuron in visual cortex will respond with a burst of spikes, and the so-called "firing rate" during this burst (the number of spikes per second) is used as a measure of extent to which the stimulus is registered by the neuron. For example, some neurons prefer blue stimuli and will fire vigorously when a blue stimulus is presented, but may give no response to a red stimulus. Because the responses of a given neuron may vary from trial to trial, the average response over a large number of trials is typically computed in the form of a poststimulus histogram, as shown in Fig. 7.2a. This histogram shows how the average firing rate varies over time during the interval following stimulus onset, and provides a convenient means of displaying the time course of sensory processing within a single neuron.

It is not usually possible to insert electrodes into the human brain,[1] but there are alternative techniques that can be used to record the electro-

---

[1] Intracranial recordings are sometimes obtained from epilepsy patients who are undergoing evaluation for surgical removal of the epileptic focus. In this procedure, strips of electrodes may be placed on the cortical surface or depth electrodes may be inserted directly into the cortex. The electrodes may be left in place for several days, during which they are used to find the epileptic focus so that it can be removed, and to identify critical areas of cortex (e.g. language areas) so that they can be avoided. In some cases, the patients also agree to participate in experiments designed to assess the electrophysiology of cognition (e.g. Allison et al., 1993; McCarthy, Wood, Williamson, & Spencer, 1989; Nobre, Allison, & McCarthy, 1994), but these experiments are necessarily limited by the condition and availability of the patients.

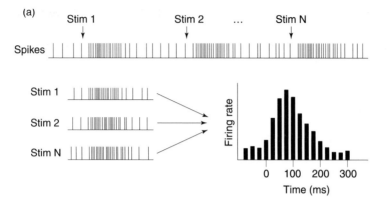

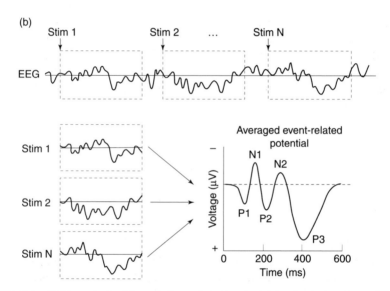

FIG. 7.2. (a) Data obtained in recordings of single-unit activity. In single-unit recordings, a train of spikes is recorded from a single neuron while stimuli are presented (the spikes are represented as vertical lines in this diagram). If the stimuli are effective in stimulating the neuron, the neuron's firing rate increases for a brief period following stimulus onset. The neuron's average response can be visualized by computing a poststimulus histogram, which plots the average number of spikes in each successive time bin following stimulus onset. (b) Data from the ERP technique. In these recordings, the electroencephalogram (EEG) is recorded from the surface of the scalp while stimuli are presented. Each stimulus evokes a sequence of voltage fluctuations (i.e. an ERP), but these fluctuations are normally obscured by the much larger EEG. To visualize the small ERP response, a signal-averaging technique is used: the EEG segments following individual stimuli are extracted from the incoming data, lined up with respect to stimulus onset, and then averaged together. Any voltage fluctuations that are consistently elicited by the stimulus will remain in this average, whereas any random voltage fluctuations will be eliminated if enough trials are averaged together. The resulting waveform consists of a set of positive and negative peaks that follow the onset of the stimulus (represented as time zero on the X-axis). Note that, by convention, negative is plotted upward and positive is plotted downward.

physiological activity non invasively from humans. In particular, if an electrode is placed on the scalp, the well-known electroencephalogram (EEG) can be recorded as a sequence of voltage fluctuations. The EEG consists of the sum of many different sources of electrical activity within the brain, and much of it is unrelated to the processing of specific stimuli. However, some of the activity within the EEG does reflect the brain's response to individual sensory, cognitive, or motor events, and these specific responses are known as event-related potentials or ERPs. Unlike single-unit spikes that reflect the output of a neuron, ERPs arise from the electrical potentials that are produced when a neuron receives input in the form of neurotransmitters. When a large number of neurons receive inputs at the same time, the resulting electrical potentials sum together and spread through the conductive media of the brain, the skull, and the scalp, where they contribute to the overall EEG. These potentials are very small, both in absolute terms and in relation to the overall EEG, but it is possible to measure them with high precision by means of a process called signal averaging, which is shown in Fig 7.2b. In this procedure, many individual stimuli are presented, and the segment of EEG following each stimulus is extracted and lined up with respect to the moment of stimulus onset. The EEG segments are then simply averaged together into a single waveform. Any activity that is consistently time-locked to stimulus onset across trials will remain in this average, whereas any activity that is unrelated to the stimulus will be random from trial to trial and will therefore average out (given a sufficient number of trials). This procedure is analogous to the creation of poststimulus histograms in single-unit recordings, as shown in Fig. 7.2a.

The result of the averaging process is an average ERP waveform, which is typically displayed as a plot of voltage over time (note that, by convention, negative is plotted upward and positive is plotted downward in plots of ERP waveforms). The ERP waveform consists of a number of positive and negative voltage deflections or "components", each of which is named for its polarity (P for positive or N for negative) and its position within the waveform (for example, "P1" for the first positive component or "P105" to indicate the exact time of the peak). Each component reflects activity from a different set of brain areas, and a large number of different components can be observed under different conditions (see Donchin et al. 1986; Hillyard & Kutas, 1983; Hillyard & Picton, 1987). Because the time course of a component indicates the period during which the corresponding brain area is active, the early components reflect sensory processing and the later components reflect higher cognitive processes and motor-related activity. In addition, the distribution of voltage over the surface of the head for a component is related to the anatomical location of its generator source (i.e the area of cortex in which the component was initially generated); the measured scalp distribution of a component can therefore be used to compute a rough estimate of its intracerebral source. Thus, ERPs can be used as a continuous measure of processing between a stimulus and a response, providing information about the time course and neuroanatomical substrates of cognitive processing.

In the past few years, new techniques have been developed for measuring neural activity in humans that provide much greater neuroanatomical precision than the ERP technique, although with a concomitant loss in information about the time course of activation. These techniques are based on a phenomenon first described by Roy and Sherrington in the 1890s: when neurons in a brain region are stimulated and start firing at an increased rate, there is an increase in blood flow to that region. By measuring localized changes in cerebral blood flow, therefore, it is possible to infer the presence of changes in neural firing. Until recently, the best technique for measuring changes in local blood flow was positron emission tomography (PET). In a PET scan, a small amount of a radioactively labeled marker (usually water) is injected into the bloodstream and travels to the brain, where it flows into different regions in proportion to the local blood flow. Specialized detectors are then used to measure the radiation emitted from each area, which allows the creation of 2- or 3-dimensional images of blood flow. By subtracting a scan obtained during a resting state from a scan obtained during a task, the brain regions that are activated during that task can be visualized, as shown in Fig. 7.3. Recently, a new blood flow measurement technique has been developed that has better spatial resolution than PET and does not require

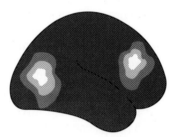

FIG. 7.3. Example of the type of data acquired in a positron emission tomography (PET) experiment. In these experiments, blood flow is measured during a baseline condition and an active condition. For example, subjects may passively view a stream of visual stimuli in the baseline condition and actively look for targets in the same stimulus stream in the active condition. The blood flow image obtained during the passive condition is then subtracted from the blood flow image obtained during the active condition, and the resulting image shows the increase in blood flow in specific brain areas during the active condition. In this figure, brain areas that did not exhibit significant increases in blood flow are shown in dark gray and areas that exhibited significant increases are shown in lighter shades of gray, with progressively lighter values indicating larger increases in blood flow during the active condition.

the injection of radioactive isotopes. This technique is based on the magnetic resonance imaging (MRI) method that has been used for many years to create static images of brain structure; because the new technique is used to study function as well as structure, it has been named functional magnetic resonance imaging (fMRI). The physics of this technique are quite complex, but in essence it uses differences in the magnetic properties of oxygenated and deoxygenated hemoglobin molecules to detect changes in blood flow that can be localized to areas as small as one cubic millimeter.

Although PET and fMRI scans allow very precise localization of changes in neural activity, they provide little information about the time course of activation because changes in blood flow are relatively slow (in the range of 5–10 seconds compared to a few milliseconds for changes in neural firing rates). They also require extremely complex scanners and, in the case of PET, a cyclotron to create radioactive isotopes, and are therefore very expensive. In contrast, the ERP technique provides temporal resolution in the millisecond range and is relatively inexpensive, but lacks the anatomical precision of PET and fMRI. Single-unit recordings allow both high temporal resolution and precise anatomical localization, but these recordings are typically limited to nonhuman animals, who require months of training to learn tasks that humans find trivial and whose visual systems may operate somewhat differently from the human visual system. In addition, recording from awake, behaving monkeys is technically very challenging and requires expensive animal care and surgical facilities. It is also impractical to record from more than a single electrode in most cases, making it difficult to study a large number of brain areas. Thus, each of the major methods used for studying the neurophysiology of attention has both benefits and limitations, and different techniques are therefore appropriate for answering different questions.

We now turn to the application of these techniques to questions about selective attention.

THE LOCUS OF SELECTION

Initial Behavioral Evidence

Most cognitive psychologists agree that selective attention is used to filter out irrelevant information, allowing cognitive processing resources and behavioral outputs to be concentrated on a small number of relevant sources of information. Although there is widespread agreement about this general view of attention, there has been a great deal of debate about which cognitive processes are limited and the stage at which attention selects the relevant inputs. Some early theorists, such as Broadbent (1958) and Treisman (1969), proposed that attention operates at an early stage of processing, allowing only selected inputs to be perceived and recognized.

Others, however, argued that all incoming sensory events receive equal perceptual processing, and proposed that attention operates at a late stage of processing to regulate the flow of information into decision processes, memory, and behavioral output systems (Deutsch & Deutsch, 1963; Norman, 1968). In the subsequent decades, many other scientists have addressed this issue of the "locus of selection," and some debate continues today.

Many of the early experiments on selective attention were related to the "cocktail-party effect," the common phenomenon of being unable to understand anything in a room full of people speaking unless attention is focused on one speaker at a time. A particularly provocative investigation of this phenomenon was reported by Moray (1959), who played passages of prose into one ear and required subjects to "shadow" (verbally repeat) these passages. While subjects shadowed the information in one ear, irrelevant verbal information was also presented in the other ear. When tested on their ability to recall or recognize the irrelevant information 30 seconds later, subjects showed no evidence of having heard anything in the ignored ear. The experiment was replicated with several different types of irrelevant material, including numbers and simple words, but subjects were unable to recall material from the ignored ear even if it was repeated many times. Moray found one exception, however: if a subject's own name was presented in the ignored ear, this stimulus was very likely to be detected, just as one is likely to detect one's own name being mentioned in an unattended conversation at a cocktail party. Thus, Moray provided evidence that information from an irrelevant source may be recalled under some conditions but not others, depending on its intrinsic value to the subject.

Results such as these have been used as evidence for "late-selection" models of attention, which propose that stimuli are identified in both the attended and ignored ears, followed by the selection of important stimuli for decision, memory, and action. Normally, only the to-be-shadowed information is considered important, and this is the information that is typically remembered. However, the subject's own name may also be intrinsically interesting, and will be remembered even if it is presented in the ignored ear. According to this view, the failure of subjects to recall words or numbers from the ignored ear is the result of selective storage of attended information in memory and not a result of selective perception. However, these findings are also compatible with "early-selection" models, in which attention is presumed to suppress the perceptual processing of ignored stimuli. According to these models, the poor memory performance for words in the ignored ear occurs because of degraded perceptual processing for stimuli in that ear. The recognition of the subject's own name in the face of this perceptual suppression can be explained by experiments showing that one's own name can be recognized more easily than other words when presented at low intensities relative to the background noise (Howarth & Ellis, 1961).

In other words, perceptual processing is suppressed for all unattended information, but subjects can still identify easily perceived stimuli such as their names.

In the decades following these early experiments, a large number of psychological experiments have been conducted to test the early- and late-selection models of attention, and virtually everyone now agrees that attentional selection may occur at late processing stages, at least under some conditions. However, many researchers believe that attention also operates at an early stage in certain circumstances (e.g. under conditions of high perceptual load; see Lavie, 1995), but this has been difficult to establish unequivocally: for almost every behavioral finding that has been used as evidence for early selection, an alternative late-selection explanation has been proposed (see, for example, Duncan, 1980; Duncan & Humphreys, 1992; Luck et al., 1996). In part, this is due to the fact that behavioral responses reflect the product of both early and late stages of processing, making it difficult to demonstrate that a change in behavioral output is due to a change in processing at a particular stage.

As discussed previously, neurophysiological measures can be particularly useful for determining the stage at which an experimental manipulation affects processing, and these measures are therefore very appropriate for distinguishing between early and late selection. If attention operates at an early stage to attenuate the processing of irrelevant information, then the initial physiological responses in sensory cortical areas should be smaller for ignored stimuli than for attended stimuli. Conversely, if relevant information is selected only after perceptual processing is complete, then the initial sensory-evoked responses should be the same for attended and ignored stimuli.

Auditory ERP Experiments

During the 1960s and early 1970s, several experiments were conducted to determine whether selective attention affects the early sensory ERP components, but these experiments had various methodological shortcomings that made their results difficult to interpret. In 1973, however, Steve Hillyard and his colleagues developed an experimental design that allowed an unambiguous assessment of the effects of selective attention on auditory ERPs (Hillyard, Hink, Schwent, & Picton, 1973). In this experiment, which is diagrammed in Fig. 7.4, subjects were instructed to attend to the left ear in some trial blocks and the right ear in others. A rapid sequence of tone pips was presented, with half of the stimuli presented in each ear; to make the discrimination between the two ears even easier, the tones were presented at a different pitch in each ear. Subjects were instructed to monitor the attended ear and press a button whenever a slightly higher-pitched target

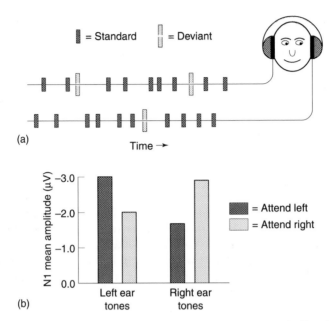

FIG. 7.4. Experimental paradigm (a) and results (b) from the study of Hillyard et al. (1973). Subjects listened to streams of tone pips in the left ear and right ear. Most of the tones were a standard frequency (800 Hz in the left ear and 1500 Hz in the right ear), but occasional deviant tones were presented at a slightly higher frequency (840 Hz left; 1560 Hz right). Subjects were instructed to attend to the left ear for some trial blocks and to the right ear for others, and counted the number of deviant tones in the attended ear. The average N1 amplitude was measured for the standard tones and used as an index of sensory processing. Left ear tones elicited a larger N1 wave when attention was directed to the left ear than when attention was directed to the right ear; conversely, right ear tones elicited a larger N1 wave when attention was directed to the right ear than when attention was directed to the left ear.

tone was detected in that ear, which occurred infrequently and unpredictably. Higher-pitched tones were also presented occasionally in the ignored ear, but subjects were instructed not to respond to these "unattended deviants."

In some prior ERP experiments, subjects were required to respond to all attended stimuli and withhold responses to all unattended stimuli. As a result, any differences in the ERPs evoked by attended and unattended stimuli could have been due to motor-related activity that was present for the attended ERPs but absent for unattended ERPs. Hillyard et al. (1973) avoided this problem by presenting nontarget stimuli in both the attended and unattended ears and focusing their analyses on these nontargets. Because the target and nontarget stimuli presented in the attended ear were difficult to discriminate from each other, but easy to discriminate from stimuli in the ignored ear, subjects focused attention on all of the stimuli within the to-be-attended ear and ignored all stimuli within the other ear. As a result, it was presumed that the same initial selection processes would be applied to both targets and nontargets in the attended ear. The main experimental question was therefore whether the early sensory ERP components evoked by a nontarget stimulus presented in the attended ear would be larger than those evoked by a nontarget stimulus presented in the unattended ear.

The sensory ERP components are highly sensitive to the physical characteristics of the evoking stimulus. As a result, one cannot legitimately compare the ERP evoked by an attended tone in the left ear with an unattended tone in the right ear: any differences between these ERPs could be due to differences between the two ears that have nothing to do with attention. The design employed by Hillyard et al. (1973) circumvents this problem by allowing the ERP elicited by the same physical stimulus to be compared under different psychological conditions. For example, the ERP evoked by a left nontarget during attend-left blocks can be compared with the ERP evoked by the same left nontarget during attend-right blocks. Because the same stimulus is used in both cases, any differences in the ERPs between the attend-left and attend-right conditions must be due to differences in attentional processing.

In many attention experiments, the investigators compare an "active" condition in which the subject responds to the stimuli with a "passive" condition in which the subject completely ignores the stimuli and engages in a distracting activity such as reading a book. Frequently, however, the task in the active condition is much more demanding than the distraction task in the passive condition, leading to greater overall arousal during the active condition. If we compare the ERPs in the two conditions, any differences might be due to these global arousal differences rather than selective changes in stimulus processing. Although this might be interesting, arousal-related changes in ERPs tell us little about *selective* attention. To ensure that differences in global arousal would not interfere with their study, Hillyard et al. (1973) compared ERPs evoked during equally difficult attend-left and attend-right conditions rather than active and passive conditions.

Now that we have discussed the logic behind the study of Hillyard et al. (1973), let us consider the results. As shown in Fig.7.4b, the N1 component was found to be larger for attended stimuli than for unattended stimuli. Specifically, the N1 elicited by left-ear tones was larger when the left ear was attended than when the right ear was attended, and the N1 elicited by right-ear tones was larger when the right ear was attended than when the left ear was attended. These effects began approximately 60–70 ms after stimulus onset and peaked at approximately 100 ms poststimulus, clearly within the time period of sensory processing. In addition, this early modulation of sensory activity was observed for both target and nontarget stimuli, indicating that stimuli from the attended ear were selected for enhanced processing before they were fully identified. On the basis of these findings, Hillyard and colleagues concluded that attention was operating at an early stage of processing to enhance the sensory processing of stimuli presented in the attended ear. Thus, this study provided strong evidence for the early-selection hypothesis.

More detailed information about the time course and neural origins of auditory selective attention has been provided in a series of recent studies by Woldorff and colleagues (Woldorff, Hansen, & Hillyard, 1987; Woldorff & Hillyard, 1991; Woldorff et al., 1993), who used a slightly modified version of the paradigm developed by Hillyard et al. (1973). These experiments were designed to optimize the focusing of attention and to provide extremely precise ERP recordings, thus allowing the investigators to determine the earliest time point at which attention can influence sensory processing. To optimize the focusing of attention, Woldorff used very fast trains of stimuli, analogous to the high information rates found in human speech, thus overloading the auditory system so that subjects were forced to "tune out" information from the unattended ear. In addition, the difficulty of the target/nontarget discrimination (a loudness discrimination) was carefully adjusted to provide uniformly high levels of difficulty for all subjects. Finally, a combination of fast stimulation rates and long recording sessions allowed the collection of many thousands of trials, providing a very high signal-to-noise ratio in the ERP recordings.

The very first ERP components evoked by an auditory stimulus can be seen within 10 ms of stimulus onset and are called the "brainstem evoked responses" because they are generated in the auditory relay stations of the brainstem. As shown in Fig.7.5a, Woldorff and colleagues found that these initial sensory responses were completely unaffected by attention, which indicates that the selection of information from the attended ear occurs sometime after the earliest stages of sensory transmission. When the same ERPs are plotted on a longer time base, the later ERP components can be observed. As in the study of Hillyard et al. (1973), the N1 component was larger for stimuli presented in the attended ear than for stimuli presented in the unattended ear (see Fig.7.5c). This was not the earliest effect, however. In the range of the so-called "midlatency" components (20–50 ms post-stimulus), the attended-stimulus ERPs contained a more positive voltage deflection than the unattended-stimulus ERPs (see Fig.7.5b). The mid-latency components appear to reflect the initial activation of auditory cortex, and so this effect in the 20–50 ms time range suggests that selective attention modulates either the very first cortical responses or the transmission of auditory information from the thalamus to the cortex (see Woldorff et al., 1993, for a detailed analysis of the generator sources of the midlatency and N1 attention effects).

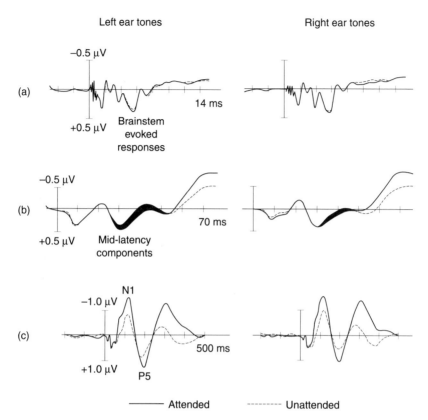

FIG. 7.5.   ERP waveforms elicited by left ear and right ear tones in the experiments of Woldorff and colleagues (Woldorff et al., 1987; Woldorff & Hillyard, 1991). The three rows of this figure show data from the same trials, but recorded on different time scales and with different filters to show different ERP components: (a) the brainstem evoked responses on a scale of 2 ms per time division; (b) the midlatency components on a scale of 10 ms per time division; and (c) the long latency components on a scale of 100 ms per time division. The brainstem responses were virtually identical when attention was directed toward or away from the ear to which the tone was presented. For the midlatency components, however, the amplitude was more positive from approximately 20–50 ms (shaded region) when attention was directed toward the ear of the stimulus. The N1 and P2 components were also enhanced by attention, as in the study of Hillyard et al. (1973). Adapted with permission from Woldorff et al. (1987) and Woldorff and Hillyard (1991). Reprinted with kind permission from Elsevier Science Ireland Ltd, Bay 15K, Shannon Industrial Estate, Co. Clare, Ireland.

To summarize, the studies of Hillyard, Woldorff, and others have shown that attending to information in one ear and ignoring information in the other causes a difference in the sensory ERP responses evoked by the attended and ignored stimuli (Giard, Perrin, Pernier, & Peronnet, 1988; Hillyard, et al., 1973; Woldorff, et al., 1987; Woldorff & Hillyard, 1991;

Woldorff et al., 1993; Woods & Clayworth, 1987). Specifically, attention modulates sensory-evoked activity beginning around 20 ms after stimulus onset, probably in primary auditory cortex, and also modulates the amplitude of later components such as the N1 wave. These results provide clear support for early-selection theories of attention, which propose that attention is used to select relevant sources of input at an early stage in order to enhance perceptual processing.

Visual ERP, PET, and Single-unit Experiments

The locus-of-selection issue has also been addressed in the visual modality with the ERP technique, and many of these experiments have used a visual version of the paradigm developed by Hillyard et al. (1973) for studying auditory attention. In the visual attention paradigm, which is shown in Fig.7.6a, subjects fixate a central point and direct attention either to the left visual field (LVF) or the right visual field (RVF). Streams of bars are flashed in the LVF and RVF, and most of these bars are a standard size. Smaller deviant bars are presented occasionally, and subjects are required to press a button when they detect a deviant bar in the attended visual field. As in the auditory attention paradigm, the ERPs elicited by the standard stimuli are examined instead of the ERPs elicited by the targets in order to avoid contamination by any motor-related ERP components. In order to make sure than any changes in the ERP components are due to internal attentional mechanisms rather than external shifts in eye position toward the attended location, subjects are required to fixate a central point during these experiments, and trials contaminated by eye movements are excluded from the ERP averages.

Many experiments of this type have been conducted by the Hillyard group and by other investigators (e.g. Eason, Harter, & White, 1969; Mangun & Hillyard, 1988, 1990; Mangun, Hillyard, & Luck, 1993; Neville & Lawson, 1987; Rugg, Milner, Lines, & Phalp, 1987; Van Voorhis & Hillyard, 1977), and the typical results are presented in Fig.7.6b. Attended stimuli elicit larger sensory-evoked ERP waves than unattended stimuli beginning with the first major visual ERP component, the P1 wave, which typically onsets between 60 and 90 ms poststimulus and peaks between 100 and 130 ms poststimulus.[2] Visual information typically reaches primary

---

[2] It is important to note that similar naming conventions are used for both auditory and visual ERP components, and both types of waveforms therefore have components with the same names. These names are purely descriptive, and ERP components from different modalities with the same name are not necessarily the same component in any physiological or psychological sense. For example, the first major negative component is named "N1" in both auditory and visual ERP waveforms, but the auditory and visual N1 components arise from different areas of the brain and reflect different neurophysiological processes.

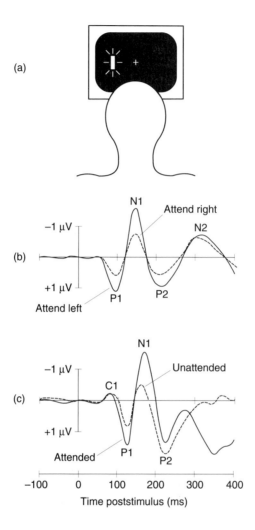

FIG. 7.6. Stimuli and results from a typical visual ERP attention paradigm. (a) Streams of bars are presented at locations in the left and right visual fields; most of these bars are a standard size, but smaller deviant bars are occasionally presented. Subjects fixate a central point and direct attention to the left location on some trial blocks and to the right location on others. Subjects are instructed to press a button whenever a deviant bar is detected on the attended side. (b) Idealized responses to a standard bar in the left visual field. The P1, N1, and P2 components elicited by this left stimulus are larger when attention is directed to the left than when attention is directed to the right (a complementary pattern is observed for stimuli in the right visual field). (c) Results from the study of Gomez Gonzales et al. (1994), in which the C1 component—which appears to be generated in primary visual cortex—could be observed. Although the P1 and N1 components were strongly modulated by attention, there were no significant attention effects for the C1 component, indicating that spatial selective attention operates after the arrival of information into primary visual cortex. Adapted from Luck (1995).

visual cortex (area V1) approximately 40–60 ms after stimulus onset, and the time course of the P1 attention effect therefore indicates that attention begins to influence stimulus analysis during the early stages of cortical processing.

Under certain conditions, it is possible to record an ERP component that precedes the P1 wave and appears to be generated in primary visual cortex (area V1). The effects of attention on this component, which is called the "C1" wave, have been examined in two recent experiments (Gomez Gonzales et al., 1994; Mangun et al., 1993). As shown in Fig.7.6c, the amplitude of this component is the same for attended and unattended stimuli, whereas the later P1 and N1 components are larger for attended stimuli than for unattended stimuli. Thus, although the P1 and N1 effects indicate that visual attention operates at a *relatively* early stage of processing (i.e. within 150 ms of stimulus onset), the effects of attention in the visual modality do not begin until after information from a stimulus has passed through primary visual cortex. This contrasts with the auditory modality, where attention appears to influence processing beginning as early as primary auditory cortex.

Although it is clear that the P1 and N1 components do not arise from primary visual cortex (Clark, Fan, & Hillyard, 1995; Mangun et al., 1993), it has been difficult to determine exactly where they are generated and thereby assess the precise neuroanatomical locus of selection in the visual modality. Unfortunately, it is generally quite difficult to localize the generators of ERP components, especially components arising from visual cortex, which contains more than 30 separate visual processing areas and has a very complex 3-dimensional organization. To provide more precise neuroanatomical localization, Heinze and his colleagues recently conducted an experiment in which they obtained both ERP and PET data using a paradigm similar to that shown in Fig.7.6a (Heinze et al., 1994). When subjects attended to the stimuli, there was an increase in blood flow in an area of visual cortex on the base of the occipital lobe, and this effect was larger in the hemisphere that received direct inputs from the side of the display that was attended (i.e. the contralateral hemisphere). A P1 attention effect was also observed in the ERP recordings, and the estimated generator of this effect was quite close to the locus of the PET attention effect (see Fig. 7.7). Although it is currently impossible to prove that these PET and ERP attention effects reflect the same neurophysiological events, these results provide reasonably convincing evidence that visual attention influences sensory processing in extrastriate visual cortex within 100 ms of stimulus onset, consistent with early-selection models of attention.

Although Heinze et al. (1994) were able to identify a precise neuroanatomical site where attention influences sensory processing, their results reveal relatively little about the specific changes in processing produced at

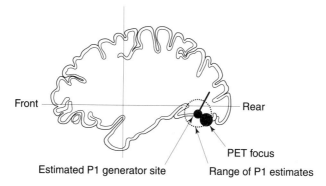

FIG. 7.7. Location of the PET attention effect and estimated location of the P1 attention effect in the study of Heinze et al. (1994). The small dark circle represents the best estimate of the P1 generator location, and the line extending from this circle represents the orientation of the estimated current dipole. The broken circle surrounding this generator shows the range of generator solutions that were compatible with the observed data. The larger dark circle represents the location of the PET attention effect. Although the PET and P1 effects were not identical in location, the PET effect was within the error range of the P1 effect. These results are therefore consistent with the proposal that the P1 attention effect is generated in the extrastriate visual areas located on the ventral surface of the occipital lobe.

that site by attention. For example, it is important to know what sorts of processes are normally conducted in the attention-sensitive brain region and exactly how these processes are changed by attention. Most of our knowledge of the specific sensory processes carried out in the different visual areas has been obtained from macaque monkeys, however, and we are just beginning to be able to determine which areas of the human brain are homologous to specific areas within macaque visual cortex. As a result, it is difficult to combine our detailed knowledge of the visual processes carried out in specific areas of macaque visual cortex with our initial mapping of the areas that are affected by attention in humans. Although future technical improvements may allow these two sets of data to be combined more directly, at present single-unit recordings provide the only technique for measuring the precise effects of attention in well-characterized areas of visual cortex.

Several single-unit studies of visual attention have been conducted in the last decade (Chelazzi, Miller, Duncan, & Desimone, 1993; Moran & Desimone, 1985; Motter, 1993; Wurtz, Richmond, & Newsome, 1984), and one of these studies was adapted directly from the paradigm used in the ERP and PET studies described earlier (Luck, Chelazzi, Hillyard, & Desimone, 1997). In this study, recordings were obtained from V1, V2, and V4 in macaque monkeys; these areas are primarily responsible for the early and intermediate stages of visual object recognition and process features such as color, orientation, and spatial frequency (for more information on these areas, see Desimone & Ungerleider, 1989; Felleman & Van Essen, 1991; Maunsell & Newsome, 1987; Van Essen, 1985). Consistent with the ERP and PET results, no consistent effects of attention were observed in area V1. In areas V2 and V4, however, significant attention effects were observed for many neurons, as shown in Fig. 7.8. In these neurons, the response to a stimulus was larger when it was attended than when attention was directed to another location, just as the P1 component in previous ERP experiments was larger for attended stimuli than for unattended stimuli. In addition, this effect was present immediately at the onset of sensory-evoked activity (c. 60 ms poststimulus in area V4), and appeared to consist of a simple increase in the size of the sensory response, which is also similar to the P1 effects observed in ERP experiments. These results demonstrate that attended-location information is selected for preferential

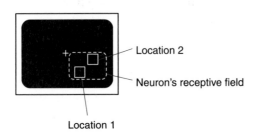

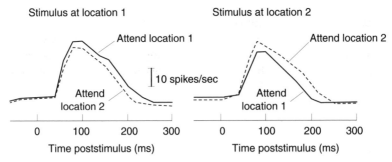

FIG. 7.8. Single-unit attention effects from area V4 (Luck et al., 1997). The monkey fixated the central cross and attended either to location 1 or location 2, which were positioned so that they were both inside the receptive field of the cell being recorded. The poststimulus histograms shown in this figure represent an average of 28 neurons that showed significant effects of attention. Note that the response to a stimulus at location 1 was larger when location 1 was attended than when location 2 was attended, and the response to a stimulus at location 2 was larger when location 2 was attended than when location 1 was attended. These effects were absent when only one of the two locations was inside the receptive field.

processing during the processing of basic stimulus features such as color and orientation.

Although the single-unit data were largely consistent with the ERP and PET studies, there was one important difference. In the single-unit study, attention modulated the size of the sensory response only when both the attended and unattended locations were inside the receptive field of the neuron being recorded; no sensory modulation was observed if one location was inside the receptive field and the other was outside. In addition, these effects were much stronger when the attended and unattended stimuli were presented simultaneously rather than sequentially. This pattern of results was considered surprising by many researchers, but it is not really so surprising when one considers the ambiguous nature of the information coded by individual neurons. Specifically, when two stimuli are simultaneously presented inside a neuron's receptive field, the neuron's output could reflect either the attended stimulus or the unattended stimulus (this is the same "binding problem" that was discussed earlier). As a result, it is computationally useful to suppress information arising from the unattended location so that it is not confused with attended information. When only one location is inside the receptive field, however, the neuron's output clearly reflects information arising from that one location and no suppression is necessary. This pattern of results is quite different from the pattern observed in ERP experiments, however, in which P1 and N1 attention effects have been observed with stimulus locations that were too far apart to fall within a single V2 or V4 receptive field. One possible explanation for this discrepancy is that the ERP attention effects may reflect activity in a part of the human brain that is homologous to macaque inferotemporal cortex, where neurons have very large receptive fields and are strongly influenced by attention (Chelazzi et al., 1993; Moran & Desimone, 1985).

To summarize, the locus-of-selection issue has been addressed in the visual modality using the ERP, PET, and single-unit methodologies, and although it can be difficult to compare results directly across techniques, these studies have yielded converging evidence that attention begins to select visual information at a relatively early time (c. 60 ms poststimulus) and a relatively early neuroanatomical locus (extrastriate visual cortex; see, however, Motter, 1993), consistent with a mechanism that selects information during the intermediate stages of object recognition. Selection appears to occur at a somewhat later time in the visual modality than in the auditory modality, but this difference may simply reflect the greater amount of time required for the initial sensory transduction and integration in the retina. In any case, these neurophysiological studies of attention provide clear support for the early-selection hypothesis in both the auditory and visual modalities.

NEUROPHYSIOLOGICAL STUDIES OF CUING AND SEARCH

Although the experimental paradigm used in the experiments described earlier has been very useful for studying the neural substrates of attention, it is substantially different from the paradigms typically used by cognitive psychologists to study attention. In recent years, however, neurophysiologists have begun to explore the two paradigms used most commonly in psychological studies of attention, namely spatial cuing and visual search (Chelazzi et al., 1993; Eimer, 1994a; Luck, Fan, & Hillyard, 1993b; Luck & Hillyard, 1994, 1995; Luck et al. 1994b; Mangun & Hillyard, 1991). As will be described next, these studies have provided new information about the mechanisms of attention that are used by the visual system when performing these tasks. Before discussing these findings, however, it is necessary to describe the cuing and search paradigms as they have been used by psychologists.

In the spatial cuing paradigm, each trial consists of a cue stimulus followed by a target stimulus, and the subject is required to respond to the target (see Fig. 7.9a). The cue indicates the probable location of the target, allowing subjects to focus attention on this location before the onset of the target (the cue typically precedes the target by several hundred milliseconds). On the majority of trials (called "valid" trials), the target appears at the location indicated by the cue; responses to these targets are typically fast and accurate because the target falls inside the focus of attention. On a small percentage of trials (called "invalid" trials), the target appears at an uncued location; responses to these targets are typically slow and inaccurate

---

FIG. 7.9. Opposite. (a) Examples of cue and target stimuli in the spatial cuing study of Mangun and Hillyard (1991). Each trial began with a cue arrow presented at fixation, and this was followed after an 800-ms delay by a target bar that appeared either at the location indicated by the cue (valid trial) or at the opposite location (invalid trial). In one experiment, subjects pressed one of two buttons to indicate whether the target bar was tall or short (choice RT). In a second experiment, subjects simply pressed a single button as soon as a bar appeared (simple RT). (b) Results from the choice RT experiment. RTs were faster and the P1 and N1 were larger on valid trials than on invalid trials (note that negative voltages are plotted upward). (c) Results from the simple RT experiment. The same RT and P1 effects were observed in this experiment, but there was no significant N1 difference between valid and invalid trials. (d) Stimuli used in the visual search study of Luck et al. (1993). Subjects attended to red on some runs and green on other runs, and pressed one of two buttons to indicate whether the item drawn in the attended color (the target) was an upright T or an inverted T. A small, white, outline square was presented as a probe stimulus 250 ms after the onset of the search array, and this probe was completely task-irrelevant. (e) ERP results from the search experiment. As in the choice RT cuing experiment, both the P1 and N1 components were larger for probes presented within the focus of attention (at the location of the target) than for probes presented outside the focus of attention (at the location of a nontarget). Adapted from Mangun and Hillyard (1991), and Luck (1995).

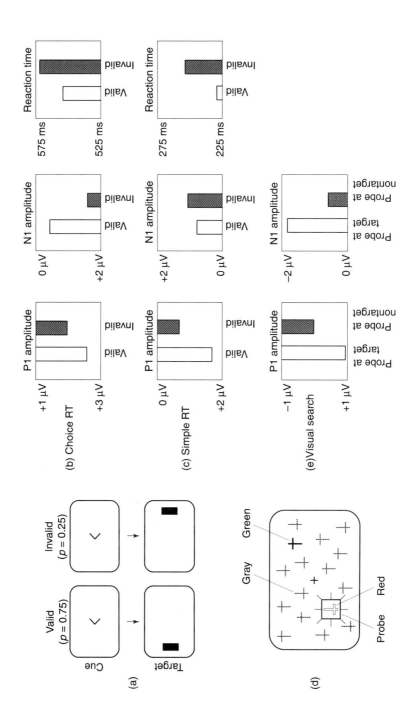

because the target falls outside the focus of attention. Thus, this task provides a direct technique for measuring perceptual processing inside and outside the focus of attention (for more information, see Cheal, Lyon, & Gottlob, 1994; Hawkins et al. 1990; Jonides, 1981; Posner, 1980).

The visual search paradigm provides a somewhat less direct means of comparing the processing of attended and ignored stimuli, but it is much more similar to the tasks that the visual system must perform in natural settings. In this paradigm, subjects are presented with arrays containing multiple stimulus elements, and they must indicate whether or not a target item is present within the array, much like the task of looking for a friend in a crowd. In many cases, the amount of time required to detect the target item increases as the number of elements in the array increases. This is usually taken as evidence that attention moves in a series of shifts from one item to the next until the target is found, at which point a response is made; this is called a "serial search" process. During a serial search, the number of distractor items that are examined before the target is found typically increases as the number of items in the array increases, and this explains the finding that reaction times (RTs) increase as the number of items in the array increases.[3] Under certain conditions, however, subjects can detect the target quickly no matter how many distractors are present, which indicates that an item-by-item search is not necessary; this is called a "parallel search" process. An enormous number of visual search experiments have been conducted in the last 15 years, and a great deal has been discovered about the conditions under which search proceeds in serial or in parallel (summarized by Wolfe, this volume; see also Duncan & Humphreys, 1989; Enns & Rensink, 1991; Treisman & Gelade, 1980; Treisman & Souther, 1985; Wolfe, 1994).

One of the most basic questions addressed by neurophysiological studies of cuing and search is whether the visual system uses the same or different mechanisms of attention in these very different tasks. Although cuing and search are the most commonly used paradigms in the study of visual attention, there have been surprisingly few studies aimed at determining whether they actually tap into the same mechanisms of attention. One reason for this is that it is difficult to determine from behavioral performance data whether the same mechanisms of attention operate in different tasks. For example, even if both tasks lead to some particular change in performance, this change might arise from different mechanisms in the two paradigms. With neurophysiological measures, however, it is possible to measure individual sensory processes in relative isolation, making it possible

---

[3] Although many investigators assume that results of this nature indicate that subjects are performing a serial search of the array, there are other search mechanisms that could produce this same pattern of results (Bundesen, 1990; Mordkoff, Yantis, & Egeth, 1990; Townsend, 1990).

to determine whether attention influences the same specific processes across paradigms. For example, if attention affects the same set of ERP components in both spatial cuing and visual search, then this would provide good evidence that similar attentional mechanisms operate in both paradigms. In addition, neurophysiological measures can also be used to determine whether the same attentional control structures are active across paradigms, which would provide additional evidence for a common set of mechanisms. Let us now consider some recent pieces of evidence indicating that the same sensory processes are modulated by attention and the same attentional control structures are active in both the spatial cuing and visual search paradigms.

Attention Effects in the Spatial Cuing Paradigm

Mangun and Hillyard (1991) recorded ERPs in a set of spatial cuing experiments to determine whether early-selection mechanisms operate in this paradigm. In their first experiment, subjects were cued to the left or right visual field by means of an arrow and were then required to press a button to indicate whether a subsequent target stimulus was a tall bar or a short bar (see Fig. 7.9a). This is called a "choice reaction time" or "choice RT" task because subjects must choose between multiple target alternatives and then make a speeded response. The target bar appeared at the cued location on 75% of trials and at the uncued location on 25% of trials. Consistent with previous studies, shorter reaction times were observed on valid trials than on invalid trials (see Fig. 7.9b). Although many investigators have explained such results by postulating increased sensory efficiency at the cued location (e.g. Bashinski & Bacharach, 1980; Hawkins et al., 1990; Posner, Snyder, & Davidson, 1980), proponents of the late-selection hypothesis have shown that such results can also be explained by changes in postsensory decision or motor processes (Duncan, 1980; Shaw, 1984; Sperling & Dosher, 1986). If these results were caused by an attentional modulation of sensory processes, then larger sensory-evoked ERP components would be expected on valid trials than on invalid trials. This is exactly the pattern that Mangun and Hillyard found. As shown in Fig. 7.9b, both the P1 and N1 components were larger for targets appearing at the cued location than for targets appearing at the uncued location, indicating that the faster responses observed on valid trials were due, at least in part, to facilitated sensory processing.

Mangun and Hillyard (1991) also conducted a second experiment in which all of the target bars were identical and subjects simply pressed a single button upon detecting a bar (a "simple RT" task). As shown in Fig. 7.9c, responses were again faster on valid trials than on invalid trials in this experiment. In addition, the P1 component was again larger on valid trials than on invalid trials, consistent with an early locus of selection. However, the N1 component was not significantly different on valid and invalid trials in this experiment. This difference between the P1 and N1 components has two implications. First, the P1 and N1 attention effects appear to reflect separate mechanisms of attention that can be activated independently rather than being two different manifestations of a single early change in sensory processing. Second, the absence of the N1 attention effect in the simple RT experiment suggests that the attentional process reflected by the N1 component may be involved in discriminative processing at the attended location. We will return to these issues later.

Attention Effects in the Visual Search Paradigm

To determine whether the same mechanisms of attention operate across paradigms, Luck et al. (1993) recorded ERPs during a visual search task. In order to measure the P1 and N1 components at the attended (target) and unattended (distractor) locations during visual search, however, this experiment had to overcome two methodological obstacles. First, stimuli in the spatial cuing task are presented at the attended and unattended locations on separate trials and therefore elicit separate ERP waveforms, whereas the targets and distractors are presented simultaneously during visual search and elicit a single ERP waveform containing contributions from both attended and unattended items. To provide separate waveforms corresponding to the target and distractor locations, task-irrelevant "probe" stimuli were presented at the locations of individual items within the visual search arrays (see Fig. 7.9d). The ERPs elicited by these probe stimuli were used as measures of sensory processing at the probed location, which was the location of the target on some trials and the location of a distractor on other trials. A second problem with the search paradigm is that it is difficult to determine where attention is focused at any given moment during a serial search; to solve this problem, the targets in this experiment were presented in a unique color that could be localized immediately. To ensure that attention would be focused on the target item once it was localized, subjects were required to discriminate the shape of the target item, which was a highly demanding task. Thus, although subjects were not explicitly cued to a particular location, the demands of the task implicitly required subjects to focus attention on the target item. After the search array was displayed for 250 ms—providing subjects with sufficient time to find the target—the probe stimulus was presented either at the target location or at the location of a distractor item on the other side of the array. Trials on which the probe was presented at the location of the target item were analogous to valid trials in a cuing experiment, because the ERP-eliciting stimulus was presented within the focus of attention; trials on which the probe was presented at a distractor location were analogous to invalid trials, because the ERP-eliciting stimulus was presented outside the focus of attention.

As discussed earlier, one cannot legitimately compare the ERPs elicited by two different physical stimuli in an attention experiment, because any differences in the waveforms could be explained by the physical stimulus differences rather than the effects of attention. One cannot, therefore, compare the ERP elicited by a probe presented at the location of a uniquely colored target item with the ERP elicited by a probe presented at the location of one of many identically colored distractor items. To provide a well-controlled comparison, two uniquely colored items were presented within each array (a red item and a green item) and different colors served to define the target on different runs (i.e. the red item was the target for some runs and the green item was the target for others). This design allowed a comparison between the ERP elicited by a probe at the location of the red item when attention was directed to that red item and the ERP elicited by a probe at the location of the same red item when attention was directed to the green item on the opposite side of the array (and vice versa for probes presented at the location of the green item).

Figure 7.9e displays the results from this experiment, and shows that both the P1 and N1 components were larger for probes presented at the location of the target item than for probes presented at the location of the nontarget item on the opposite side of the array. These results are very similar to the results obtained by Mangun and Hillyard (1991) during the choice RT spatial cuing task, and this similarity indicates that attention influences the same sensory processes during both visual search and spatial cuing. This is an important conclusion, because it indicates that we can legitimately integrate the results from cuing and search experiments into a single theory of attention (see also Briand & Klein, 1987; Prinzmetal, Presti, & Posner, 1986; Treisman, 1985).

Suppression and Facilitation in Cuing and Search

Although the studies just described indicate that attention modulates the same sensory processes in both the cuing and search paradigms, it is possible that these similar effects are actually caused by different mechanisms of attention in the two paradigms. One way to provide additional evidence that both paradigms employ the same mechanisms would be to show that the finer details of the attentional modulations are also similar across paradigms. Evidence of this nature was provided recently by studies that examined whether attention operates by facilitating processing at the attended location or by suppressing processing at the unattended location.

The P1 and N1 attention effects discussed earlier have typically been described as reflections of facilitated processing at the attended location, but they could just as easily represent a suppression of processing at the unattended location. Recently, Luck et al. (1994b) provided evidence indicating that although the N1 attention effect does reflect attended-location facilitation, the P1 effect actually reflects unattended-location suppression. This conclusion was reached on the basis of a cuing experiment that included neutral trials as well as valid and invalid trials. On the valid and invalid trials, an arrow cue was used to direct attention to one of four possible target locations, where the target was likely to occur. On neutral trials, four arrows appeared (pointing at all four locations), indicating that the target could occur with equal probability at any of these locations. These trials provided a baseline condition in which attention was presumably unfocused or diffusely focused over the entire set of locations. As shown in Fig. 7.10a, the P1 was suppressed on invalid trials compared to these neutral trials, but no P1 facilitation was observed on valid trials compared to neutral trials. Conversely, the N1 component was enhanced on valid trials compared to neutral trials, but no N1 suppression was observed on invalid trials. Thus, the P1 attention effect appears to reflect a specific suppression of processing at the unattended locations whereas the N1 attention effect appears to reflect a specific facilitation of processing at the attended location.

To test whether this same pattern of suppression and facilitation is also present in the visual search paradigm, Luck and Hillyard (1995) conducted a visual search study that was very similar to the search experiment just described (Luck et al., 1993b), but also included trials that were analogous to neutral trials. In this experiment, the two uniquely colored items in the search arrays were selected at random on each trial from a set of four possible colors (red, green, blue, and purple). When an item of the attended color was present, subjects pressed a button to indicate its shape, as in the previous experiment; when the attended color was absent from the display, no response was required. On target-absent trials, attention was presumably unfocused or diffusely focused, making these trials comparable to the neutral trials of the cuing experiment. These trials were used as a baseline for comparison with trials on which the probe was presented at the location of the target (analogous to valid trials) or trials on which the probe was presented at the location of a distractor item on the opposite side of the array from the target (analogous to invalid trials). As in the cuing experiment, the P1 was suppressed for probes presented on the opposite side of the array from the target compared to the neutral-like target-absent trials, but was not enhanced for probes presented at the target location (see Fig. 7.10b). The N1, in contrast, was enhanced for probes presented at the target location compared to target-absent trials, but was not suppressed for probes presented on the opposite side of the array from the target. These results are extremely similar to the results from the cuing experiment, and this simi-

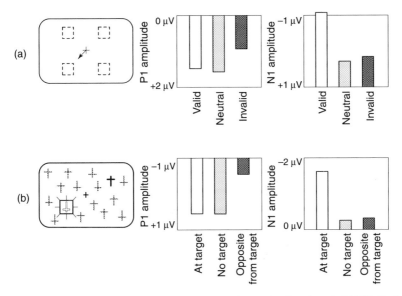

FIG. 7.10.   (a) Stimuli and results from the spatial cuing study of Luck et al. (1994b). Each trial began with a cue presented at fixation, and this was followed after a 200–500-ms delay by a masked luminance target. The cue pointed to a single location on most trials, indicating the most likely location for the subsequent target. On neutral trials, however, the cue pointed to all four locations, indicating that the target could occur equiprobably at any of the locations. The P1 component was suppressed on invalid trials compared to neutral trials, but was not facilitated on valid trials compared to neutral trials. The N1 component, in contrast, was facilitated on valid trials but was not suppressed on invalid trials. (b) Results from the visual search experiment of Luck and Hillyard (1995). This experiment was identical to the search experiment of Luck et al. (1993b), except that the two colored items within the search array were selected at random from a set of four possible colors. Subjects attended to one of the four colors, and pressed a button to indicate the orientation of the item presented in this color when the attended color was present in the array. When the attended color was absent, subjects made no response. The same pattern of P1 suppression and N1 facilitation was observed in this experiment. Adapted from Luck (1995).

larity provides additional evidence that the same mechanisms of attention operate during both cuing and search.

Attentional Control Structures in Cuing and Search

Evidence for a shared set of attentional mechanisms in the cuing and search paradigms has also been provided by studies of the brain structures that are responsible for controlling the focus of attention (see also Driver, this volume). One of the most important of these control structures is the parietal lobe: stroke patients with damage to this area often show impairments in directing attention to the side of space represented by the damaged hemisphere (the "contralesional" side of space). This disorder is called "hemispatial neglect" because the patients may totally neglect all information arising from one side of space. Posner and his colleagues have examined the performance of these neglect patients in spatial cuing experiments (Posner, Cohen, & Rafal, 1982; Posner, Walker, Friedrich, & Rafal, 1984), and have shown that these patients are specifically impaired when they are cued to the intact visual field but the target appears in the impaired field. This result suggests that the parietal lobe is involved in disengaging attention: when the parietal lobe in one hemisphere is damaged, it becomes difficult to disengage from the intact side of space in order to detect targets presented on the impaired side (for a somewhat different interpretation, see Kinsbourne, 1987).

A very similar pattern of results has also been reported in a visual search task (Eglin, Robertson, & Knight, 1989). When neglect patients perform a serial search, their performance is comparable to normal control subjects as long as the target is placed in the intact visual field: as the number of elements in the intact field increases, reaction time increases at a normal rate. Patients also show fairly normal performance for targets placed in the contralesional visual field as long as there are no distractors in the intact field. When distractors are present in the intact field, however, the detection of targets in the impaired field shows two striking abnormalities. First, reaction times are several seconds longer for targets in the impaired field than for targets in the intact field when distractors are present in both fields. Second, responses to targets in the impaired field become increasingly slow as more distractor items are added to the intact field. These results suggest that the patients are unable to disengage attention from the intact field, and search through the intact field several times before finally orienting attention to the impaired field. Because it takes longer to search the intact field when there are more distractors in that field, reaction times for targets in the impaired field are strongly affected by the number of distractors in the intact field. These results show that the hemispatial neglect syndrome produced by damage to the parietal lobes has comparable effects in both the spatial cuing and visual search paradigms.

Another important attentional control structure is the corpus callosum, the long belt of nerve fibers that connects the left and right hemispheres, and recent studies have shown that damage to this structure also has comparable effects in the cuing and search paradigms. These experiments utilized "split-brain" patients who had previously undergone surgical transection of the corpus callosum for the purpose of treating epilepsy. After this operation, the left and right hemispheres become largely independent, and can communicate only indirectly via their connections with subcortical structures. Because of this separation, split-brain patients are commonly used to examine differences in function between the left and right hemispheres. However, they are also very useful for assessing the extent to which subcortical structures are involved in cognitive processes. If a cognitive process is exclusively cortical, then the two hemispheres in a split-brain patient should be able to perform that process independently. If a process involves subcortical structures, however, then the two hemispheres may compete for access to those structures, leading to interference between the hemispheres. This line of reasoning was used to examine the role of subcortical structures in attentional processing.

The left hemisphere receives direct inputs from the right visual field and the right hemisphere receives direct inputs from the left visual field. In most people, information from a given hemifield can eventually reach both hemispheres by traveling through the corpus callosum, but the information remains in a single hemisphere in split-brain patients. As a result, each hemisphere of a split-brain patient should be able to search its own visual field independently of the other hemisphere if attention is controlled by cortical mechanisms. This is exactly what was found when split-brain patients performed a serial search task, as shown in Fig. 7.11a. In this experiment (Luck, Hillyard, Mangun, & Gazzaniga, 1994a), the search items were divided between the left and right visual fields on some trials (bilateral arrays) and were located entirely within a single visual field on others (unilateral arrays). Reaction times increased for both the split-brain patients and normal control subjects as more items were added to a given field, and for normal subjects the rate of increase was the same for both unilateral and bilateral arrays. For split-brain patients, however, the rate of increase was approximately twice as great for unilateral arrays as for bilateral arrays, indicating that they could search twice as fast when the stimuli were divided between the two hemispheres. This result suggests that the two separated hemispheres of the split-brain patients were able to search the bilateral arrays independently, resulting in a more efficient search than was possible when the stimuli were restricted to a single hemisphere. These findings indicate that attention is coordinated across the two hemispheres in normal subjects by means of the corpus callosum.

A similar set of findings was also obtained from split-brain patients in a study of spatial cuing (Mangun et al., 1994). If the separated hemispheres of split-brain patients have their own independent attentional systems, as indicated by the aforementioned search experiment, then it should be possible to cue each hemisphere to its own visual field without any interference from the other hemisphere. This proposal was tested by presenting split-brain patients with a target stimulus that was preceded by either a cue in the left visual field, a cue in the right visual field, or a bilateral cue in both fields (see Fig. 7.11b). In both normal and split-brain subjects, responses on single-cue trials were faster when the cue was valid than when it was invalid.

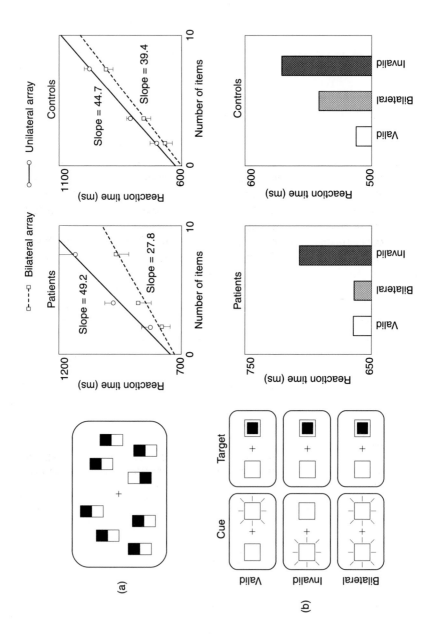

288

On bilateral-cue trials, normal subjects exhibited intermediate reaction times, presumably because the two visual fields were competing for attention. Split-brain patients, in contrast, were just as fast on bilateral-cue trials as they were on valid single-cue trials, indicating that they were able to attend to both visual fields simultaneously. These results provide yet another example of similarities between the neural systems involved in cuing and search.

These split-brain studies provide evidence that the coordination of attentional processing between the left and right hemispheres is controlled by the direct callosal connections between the hemispheres rather than subcortical structures. However, this does not imply that subcortical structures are not important in the control of attention within a given hemisphere. Indeed, there is substantial evidence indicating that two specific subcortical structures—the superior colliculus and the pulvinar—play important roles in attention. The superior colliculus is best known for its role in the programming of saccadic eye movements, and given the important links between eye movements and attention, it is not surprising that this structure also plays a role in attention. Specifically, the superior colliculus appears to be involved in automatically orienting attention when a new stimulus suddenly appears. The pulvinar is a nucleus within the thalamus, but does not serve as a simple sensory gateway like the better-known thalamic nuclei. Instead, it appears to receive both cortical and subcortical inputs and has outputs projecting widely throughout the cortex; these outputs appear to be important for the suppression of ignored information that can be observed in the cortex. These roles of the superior colliculus and the pulvinar in attention have recently been described in great detail by LaBerge (1995).

FIG. 7.11.   Opposite. (a) Stimuli and results from the visual search study of Luck et al. (1994a). The distractor items in the search arrays were blue-over-red rectangles and the target was a red-over-blue rectangle. Each array consisted of two, four, or eight items, and these were either distributed evenly across both visual fields (bilateral arrays) or concentrated in a single hemifield (unilateral arrays). Subjects pressed a left-hand button if the target was present in the left visual field, pressed a right-hand button if the target was present in the right visual field, and made no response if the target was absent. Average reaction times for detecting the target are presented for a group of four split-brain patients and a group of six normal control subjects. (b) Stimuli and results from the spatial cuing study of Mangun et al. (1994). Two boxes and a fixation point were continuously present on the display. On each trial, one or both of the boxes flashed briefly, which cued the subject to the probable location of the subsequent target stimulus. The target was filled square, and subjects pressed one of two buttons to indicate the color of this square. The data shown here reflect responses made with the hand controlled by the hemisphere that directly received the target information, and are averages from three split-brain patients and ten control subjects. Adapted from Luck et al. (1994a) and Mangun et al. (1994).

CONCLUSIONS

This chapter has discussed two key issues within the study of attention that have been addressed in detail by neurophysiologists, namely the locus of selection and the relationship between the visual search and spatial cuing paradigms. Studies of the locus of selection—especially those using variants on the paradigm developed by Hillyard et al. (1973)—have provided strong evidence that attention may operate at an early, sensory stage to select relevant inputs for preferential processing. This selection may occur in the primary sensory cortex as early as 20 ms poststimulus in the auditory modality, and may occur in secondary sensory cortical areas as early as 60 ms poststimulus in the visual modality. In both modalities, intermediate-level perceptual processes are conducted at these times and in these cortical locations, so these attentional modulations clearly reflect early-selection mechanisms. It is important to remember, however, that the existence of early-selection mechanisms does not preclude the existence of late-selection mechanisms: early selection may be limited to conditions of information overload, in which efficient perceptual processing requires a reduction in the amount of sensory information being processed.

Although the most detailed neurophysiological evidence for early selection has been obtained using the paradigm developed by Hillyard et al. (1973), the same early-selection mechanisms observed in that paradigm also appear to operate in paradigms used more commonly by cognitive psychologists, such as visual search and spatial cuing. The conclusion that the same attentional mechanisms operate across these very different paradigms is heartening, because it indicates that theories of attention can validly draw on evidence obtained from both paradigms. However, the findings on which this conclusion is based also add a complication to theories of attention, because they also indicate that both tasks use multiple mechanisms of attention. This conclusion is based primarily on the dissociations that have been observed between the P1 and N1 attention effects. Specifically, the N1 attention effect appears to reflect a facilitation of processing of attended information and is present only when subjects must perform a discrimination, whereas the P1 attention effect appears to reflect a suppression of unattended information and is present in both detection and discrimination tasks. There are additional dissociations between these attention effects as well (reviewed by Luck, 1995), and it now seems clear that these two ERP attention effects reflect independent mechanisms of attention that are used under different conditions and have different effects on sensory processing. Because neurophysiological techniques allow the subcomponents of sensory processing to be recorded in relative isolation, they lead quite naturally to the differentiation of a seemingly unitary process such as attention into a set of separable component mechanisms. The challenge for the future will be to integrate these neurophysiological findings into theories of attention at the cognitive level.

REFERENCES

Allison, T., Begleiter, A., McCarthy, G., Roessler, E., Nobre, A.C., & Spencer, D.D. (1993). Electrophysiological studies of color processing in human visual cortex. *Electroencephalography and Clinical Neurophysiology, 88,* 343–355.

Bashinski, H.S., & Bacharach, V.R. (1980). Enhancement of perceptual sensitivity as the result of selectively attending to spatial locations. *Perception and Psychophysics, 28,* 241–248.

Boussaoud, D., Desimone, R., & Ungerleider, L.G. (1991). Visual topography of area TEO in the macaque. *Journal of Comparative Neurology, 306,* 554–575.

Briand, K.A., & Klein, R.M. (1987). Is Posner's "beam" the same as Treisman's "glue"? On the relation between visual orienting and feature integration theory. *Journal of Experimental Psychology: Human Perception and Performance, 13,* 228–241.

Broadbent, D.E. (1958). *Perception and communication.* New York: Pergamon Press.

Bundesen, C. (1990). A theory of visual attention. *Psychological Review, 97,* 523–547.

Cheal, M.L., Lyon, D.R., & Gottlob, L.R. (1994). A framework for understanding the allocation of attention in location-precued discrimination. *Quarterly Journal of Experimental Psychology, 47*A, 699–739.

Chelazzi, L., Miller, E.K., Duncan, J., & Desimone, R. (1993). A neural basis for visual search in inferior temporal cortex. *Nature, 363,* 345–347.

Clark, V.P., Fan, S., & Hillyard, S.A. (1995). Identification of early visual evoked potential generators by retinotopic and topographic analyses. *Human Brain Mapping, 2,* 170–187.

Crick, F., & Koch, C. (1990). Towards a neurobiological theory of consciousness. *Seminars in Neuroscience, 2,* 263–275.

Desimone, R., & Schein, S.J. (1987). Visual properties of neurons in area V4 of the macaque: Sensitivity to stimulus form. *Journal of Neurophysiology, 57,* 835–868.

Desimone, R., & Ungerleider, L.G. (1989). Neural mechanisms of visual processing in monkeys. In F. Boller & J. Grafman (Eds.), *Handbook of neuropsychology* (pp.267–299). Amsterdam: Elsevier.

Desimone, R., Wessinger, M., Thomas, L., & Schneider, W. (1990). Attentional control of visual perception: Cortical and subcortical mechanisms. *Cold Spring Harbor Symposium on Quantitative Biology, 55,* 963–971.

Deutsch, J.A., & Deutsch, D. (1963). Attention: Some theoretical considerations. *Psychological Review, 70,* 80–90.

Donchin, E., Karis, D., Bashore, T.R., Coles, M.G.H., & Gratton, G. (1986). Cognitive psychophysiology and human information processing. In M.G.H. Coles, E. Donchin, & S.W. Porges (Eds.), *Psychophysiology: Systems, processes and applications* (pp.244–267). New York: Guilford Press.

Duncan, J. (1980). The locus of interference in the perception of simultaneous stimuli. *Psychological Review, 87,* 272–300.

Duncan, J., & Humphreys, G.W. (1989). Visual search and stimulus similarity. *Psychological Review, 96,* 433–458.

Duncan, J., & Humphreys, G. (1992). Beyond the search surface: Visual search and attentional engagement. *Journal of Experimental Psychology: Human Perception and Performance, 18,* 578–588.

Eason, R., Harter, M., & White, C. (1969). Effects of attention and arousal on visually evoked cortical potentials and reaction time in man. *Physiology and Behavior, 4,* 283–289.

Eglin, M., Robertson, L.C., & Knight, R.T. (1989). Visual search performance in the neglect syndrome. *Journal of Cognitive Neuroscience, 1,* 372–385.

Eimer, M. (1994a). An ERP study on visual spatial priming with peripheral onsets. *Psychophysiology*, *31*, 154–163.

Eimer, M. (1994b). "Sensory gating" as a mechanism for visuospatial orienting: Electrophysiological evidence from trial-by-trial cuing experiments. *Perception and Psychophysics*, *55*, 667–675.

Enns, J.T., & Rensink, R.A. (1991). Preattentive recovery of three-dimensional orientation from line drawings. *Psychological Review*, *98*, 335–351.

Felleman, D.J., & Van Essen, D.C. (1991). Distributed hierarchical processing in the primate cerebral cortex. *Cerebral Cortex*, *1*, 1–47.

Giard, M.H., Perrin, F., Pernier, J., & Peronnet, F. (1988). Several attention-related wave forms in auditory areas: A topographic study. *Electroencephalography and Clinical Neurophysiology*, *69*, 371–384.

Gomez Gonzales, C.M., Clark, V.P., Fan, S., Luck, S.J., & Hillyard, S.A. (1994). Sources of attention-sensitive visual event-related potentials. *Brain Topography*, *7*, 41–51.

Hawkins, H.L., Hillyard, S.A., Luck, S.J., Mouloua, M., Downing, C.J., & Woodward, D.P. (1990). Visual attention modulates signal detectability. *Journal of Experimental Psychology: Human Perception and Performance*, *16*, 802–811.

Heinze, H.J., Mangun, G.R., Burchert, W., Hinrichs, H., Scholz, M., Münte, T.F., Gös, A., Scherg, M., Johannes, S., Hundeshagen, H., Gazzaniga, M.X., & Hillyard, S.A. (1994). Combined spatial and temporal imaging of brain activity during visual selective attention in humans. *Nature*, *372*, 543–546.

Hillyard, S.A., Hink, R.F., Schwent, V.L., & Picton, T.W. (1973). Electrical signs of selective attention in the human brain. *Science*, *182*, 177–179.

Hillyard, S.A., & Kutas, M. (1983). Electrophysiology of cognitive processing. *Annual Review of Psychology*, *34*, 33–61.

Hillyard, S.A., & Picton, T.W. (1987). Electrophysiology of cognition. In F. Plum (Ed.), *Handbook of physiology, higher functions of the nervous system section 1: The nervous system: Vol. V. Higher functions of the brain, Part 2* (pp.519–584). Bethesda, Maryland: Waverly Press.

Howarth, C.I., & Ellis, K. (1961). The relative intelligibility threshold for one's own name compared with other names. *Quarterly Journal of Experimental Psychology*, *13*, 236–239.

Jonides, J. (1981). Voluntary versus automatic control over the mind's eye's movement. In J.B. Long & A.D. Baddeley (Eds.), *Attention and performance IX* (pp.187–203). Hillsdale, NJ: Lawrence Erlbaum Associates Inc.

Kinsbourne, M. (1987). Mechanisms of unilateral neglect. In M. Jeannerod (Ed.), *Neurophysiological and neuropsychological aspects of spatial neglect. Advances in psychology, Vol. 45* (pp. 69–86). Amsterdam: Elsevier.

LaBerge, D. (1995). *Attentional processing*. Cambridge, MA: Harvard University Press.

Lavie, N. (1995). Perceptual load as a necessary condition for selective attention. *Journal of Experimental Psychology: Human Perception and Performance*, *21*, 451–468.

Luck, S.J. (1995). Multiple mechanisms of visual-spatial attention: Recent evidence from human electrophysiology. *Behavioural Brain Research*, *71*, 113–123.

Luck, S.J., Chelazzi, L., Hillyard, S.A., & Desimone, R. (1997). Neural mechanisms of spatial selective attention in areas V1, V2, and V4 of macaque visual cortex. *Journal of Neurophysiology*, *77*, 24–42.

Luck, S.J., Fan, S., & Hillyard, S.A. (1931). Attention-related modulation of sensory-evoked brain activity in a visual search task. *Journal of Cognitive Neuroscience*, *5*, 188–195.

Luck, S.J., & Hillyard, S.A. (1994). Spatial filtering during visual search: Evidence from human electrophysiology. *Journal of Experimental Psychology: Human Perception and Performance*, *20*, 1000–1014.

Luck, S.J., & Hillyard, S.A. (1995). The role of attention in feature detection and conjunction discrimination: An electrophysiological analysis. *International Journal of Neuroscience, 80*, 281–297.

Luck, S.J., Hillyard, S.A., Mangun, G.R., & Gazzaniga, M.S. (1994a). Independent attentional scanning in the separated hemispheres of split-brain patients. *Journal of Cognitive Neuroscience, 6*, 84–91.

Luck, S.J., Hillyard, S.A., Mouloua, M., Woldorff, M.G., Clark, V.P., & Hawkins, H.L. (1994b). Effects of spatial cuing on luminance detectability: Psychophysical and electrophysiological evidence for early selection. *Journal of Experimental Psychology: Human Perception and Performance, 20*, 887–904.

Luck, S.J., Hillyard, S.A., Mouloua, M., & Hawkins, H.L. (1996). Mechanisms of visual-spatial attention: Resource allocation or uncertainty reduction? *Journal of Experimental Psychology: Human Perception and Performance, 22*, 725–737.

Mangun, G.R., & Hillyard, S.A. (1988). Spatial gradients of visual attention: Behavioral and electrophysiological evidence. *Electroencephalography and Clinical Neurophysiology, 70*, 417–428.

Mangun, G.R., & Hillyard, S.A. (1990). Allocation of visual attention to spatial location: Event-related brain potentials and detection performance. *Perception and Psychophysics, 47*, 532–550.

Mangun, G.R., & Hillyard, S.A. (1991). Modulations of sensory-evoked brain potentials indicate changes in perceptual processing during visual-spatial priming. *Journal of Experimental Psychology: Human Perception and Performance, 17*, 1057–1074.

Mangun, G.R., Hillyard, S.A., & Luck, S.J. (1993). Electrocortical substrates of visual selective attention. In D. Meyer & S. Kornblum (Eds.), *Attention and performance XIV* (pp.219–243). Cambridge, MA: MIT Press.

Mangun, G.R., Luck, S.J., Plager, R., Loftus, W., Hillyard, S.A., Handy, T., Clark, V.P., & Gazzaniga, M.S. (1994). Monitoring the visual world: Hemispheric asymmetries and subcortical processes in attention. *Journal of Cognitive Neuroscience, 6*, 267–275.

Maunsell, J.H.R., & Newsome, W.T. (1987). Visual processing in monkey extrastriate cortex. *Annual Review of Neuroscience, 10*, 363–401.

McCarthy, G., Wood, C.C., Williamson, P.D., & Spencer, D.D. (1989). Task-dependent field potentials in human hippocampal formation. *Journal of Neuroscience, 9*, 4253–4268.

McClelland, J.L., & Rumelhart, D.E. (1981). An interactive activation model of context effects in letter perception: Part 1. An account of basic findings. *Psychological Review, 88*, 375–407.

Moran, J., & Desimone, R. (1985). Selective attention gates visual processing in the extrastriate cortex. *Science, 229*, 782–784.

Moray, N. (1959). Attention in dichotic listening: Affective cues and the influence of instructions. *Quarterly Journal of Experimental Psychology, 11*, 56–60.

Mordkoff, J.T., Yantis, S., & Egeth, H.E. (1990). Detecting conjunctions of color and form in parallel. *Perception and Psychophysics, 48*, 157–568.

Motter, B.C. (1993). Focal attention produces spatially selective processing in visual cortical areas VI, V2 and V4 in the presence of competing stimuli. *Journal of Neurophysiology, 70*, 909-919.

Mozer, M.C. (1991). *The perception of multiple objects.* Cambridge, MA: MIT Press.

Neville, H.J., & Lawson, D. (1987). Attention to central and peripheral visual space in a movement detection task: I. Normal hearing adults. *Brain Research, 405*, 253–267.

Niebur, E., Koch, C., & Rosin, C. (1993). An oscillation-based model for the neuronal basis of attention. *Vision Research, 18*, 2789–2802.

Nobre, A.C., Allison, T., & McCarthy, G. (1994). Word recognition in the human inferior temporal lobe. *Nature, 372*, 260–263.

Norman, D.A. (1968). Toward a theory of memory and attention. *Psychology Review, 75*, 522–536.

Posner, M.I. (1980). Orienting of attention. *Quarterly Journal of Experimental Psychology, 32*, 3–25.

Posner, M.I., Cohen, Y., & Rafal, R.D. (1982). Neural systems control of spatial orienting. *Philosophical Transactions of the Royal Society of London, B298*, 187–198.

Posner, M.I., Snyder, C.R.R., & Davidson, B.J. (1980). Attention and the detection of signals. *Journal of Experimental Psychology: General, 109*, 160–174.

Posner, M.I., Walker, J.A., Friedrich, F.J., & Rafal, R.D. (1984). Effects of parietal lobe injury on covert orienting of visual attention. *Journal of Neuroscience, 4*, 1863–1874.

Prinzmetal, W., Presti, D.E., & Posner, M.I. (1986). Does attention affect visual feature integration? *Journal of Experimental Psychology: Human Perception and Performance, 12*, 361–369.

Rockland, K.S., Saleem, K.S., & Tanaka, K. (1994). Divergent feedback connections from areas V4 and TEO in the macaque. *Visual Neuroscience, 11*, 579–600.

Rockland, K.S., & Van Hoesen, G.W. (1994). Direct temporal-occipital feedback connections to striate cortex (V1) in the macaque monkey. *Cerebral Cortex, 4*, 300–313.

Rugg, M.D., Milner, A.D., Lines, C.R., & Phalp, R. (1987). Modulation of visual event-related potentials by spatial and non-spatial visual selective attention. *Neuropsychologia, 25*, 85–96.

Shaw, M.L. (1984). Division of attention among spatial locations: A fundamental difference between detection of letters and detection of luminance increments. In H. Bouma & D. Bouwhuis (Eds.), *Attention and performance X* (pp.109–121). Hove, UK: Lawrence Erlbaum Associates Ltd.

Sperling, G., & Dosher, B.A. (1986). Strategy and optimization in human information processing. In K.R. Boff, L. Kaufman, & J.P. Thomas (Eds.), *Handbook of perception and human performance* (pp.2–65). New York: Wiley.

Townsend, J.T. (1990). Serial vs. parallel processing: Sometimes they look like Tweedledum and Tweedledee but they can (and should) be distinguished. *Psychological Science, 1*, 46–54.

Treisman, A. (1969). Strategies and models of selective attention. *Psychological Review, 76*, 282–299.

Treisman, A. (1985). Preattentive processing in vision. *Computer Vision, Graphics, and Image Processing, 31*, 156–177.

Treisman, A., & Gelade, G. (1980). A feature-integration theory of attention. *Cognitive Psychology, 12*, 97–136.

Treisman, A., & Souther, J. (1985). Search asymmetry: A diagnostic for preattentive processing of separable features. *Journal of Experimental Psychology: General, 114*, 285–310.

Van Essen, D.C. (1985). Functional organization of primate visual cortex. In A. Peters & E.G. Jones (Eds.), *Cerebral cortex* (pp.259–329). New York: Plenum Press.

Van Voorhis, S.T., & Hillyard, S.A. (1977). Visual evoked potentials and selective attention to points in space. *Perception and Psychophysics, 22*, 54–62.

Woldorff, M., Hansen, J.C., & Hillyard, S.A. (1987). Evidence for effects of selective attention to the midlatency range of the human auditory event-related potential. In R. Johnson, J.W. Rohrbaugh, & R. Parasuraman (Eds.), *Current trends in event-related potential research* (pp.146–154). Amsterdam: Elsevier.

Woldorff, M., & Hillyard, S.A. (1991). Modulation of early auditory processing during selective listening to rapidly presented tones. *Electroencephalography and Clinical Neurophysiology, 79*, 170–191.

Woldorff, M.G., Gallen, C.C., Hampson, S.A., Hillyard, S.A., Pantev, C., Sobel, D., & Bloom, F.E. (1993). Modulation of early sensory processing in human auditory cortex during auditory selective attention. *Proceedings of the National Academy of Sciences, 90*, 8722–8726.

Wolfe, J.M. (1994). Guided search 2.0: A revised model of visual search. *Psychonomic Bulletin and Review, 1*, 202–238.

Woods, D.L., & Clayworth, C.C. (1987). Scalp topographies dissociate N1 and Nd components during auditory attention. In J.R. Johnson J.W. Rohrbaugh, & R. Parasuraman (Ed.), *Current trends in event-related potential research* (pp.155–160). Amsterdam: Elsevier.

Wurtz, R.H., Richmond, B.J., & Newsome, W.T. (1984). Modulation of cortical visual processing by attention, perception and movement. In G.M. Edelman, W.E. Gall, & W.M. Cowan (Eds.), *Dynamic aspects of neocortical function* (pp.195–217). New York: Wiley.

CHAPTER EIGHT

The Neuropsychology of Spatial Attention

Jon Driver
University College London, UK

The most basic finding in neuropsychology is that brain damage can dramatically impair some mental functions (e.g. disrupting just particular aspects of vision, or of language, or of memory) while leaving others relatively intact. By studying the patterns of spared and impaired functions after brain injury, neuropsychologists seek to learn which mental functions can operate independently in the brain, such that damage to one need not impair others. They may also hope to gain a privileged view of a single process when operating in isolation, in the absence of a second process that normally obscures the details of the first. By correlating the site of a lesion with its effects on performance, neuropsychologists can also try to relate particular mental functions to specific brain regions. Finally, identifying the spared and impaired functions in detail for particular patients may lead to more effective rehabilitation of their disorder.

As with any single method, there are many potential pitfalls for the neuropsychological approach. A damaged brain might reorganise itself to some extent, or patients might resort to idiosyncratic strategies in an attempt to circumvent their disorder. This could undermine attempts to derive models of normal function from studies of dysfunction after brain damage. A second problem is that damage to one area of the brain can have effects in other connected areas. As a result, even when damage to one particular area invariably impairs some process, it can be mistaken to conclude that this area is the sole substrate for that process.

Despite such potential problems, the neuropsychological approach has already proved highly fruitful in the study of vision, language, memory, and motor control, where it has succeeded in isolating numerous component processes that can each be associated with particular neural networks (e.g. McCarthy & Warrington, 1990). Research on these topics has illustrated that the potential pitfalls for neuropsychological methods can largely be avoided by combining neuropsychological analysis with other techniques (e.g. with the behavioral study of normal performance; or with functional neuroimaging of normal brain activity during particular tasks, etc.). The logic of this *convergent* approach is that while every method has its potential pitfalls, these are different for different methods. Hence any conclusion is considerably strengthened when results from several different methods all converge on it.

With this in mind, I shall review recent neuropsychological studies of spatial attention, examining whether the evidence from brain-damaged patients can shed further light on some of the major issues that have occupied the literature on normal attention (and conversely, whether these normal issues can be fruitfully applied to the patients). Although the neuropsychological study of attention has a short history in comparison with that for language or memory, current knowledge does suggest that a convergent approach to attention may prove equally fertile.

The various chapters in this book illustrate that "attention" is a broad term, encompassing many different mental and neural processes, with perhaps the only common factor being that all concern the selective processing of information. Some authors (e.g. Allport, 1993) have seen this broadness as a handicap to research, because when one theorist refers to "attention", they may not have the same referent in mind as another theorist. However, from the perspective of a neuropsychologist interested in attention, the situation may differ little from that when studying language or memory. Nobody disputes that an ability like language is made up of many component processes, each of which can lead to different forms of aphasia or dyslexia when disrupted by brain injury; and likewise for memory and the various forms of amnesia. Similarly, there may be numerous component processes behind our attentional abilities, and correspondingly many possible disorders of attention. For simplicity, the present chapter focuses only on neuropsychological deficits that have been attributed to disorders specifically in the *spatial orienting* of attention.

A normal person can readily turn their eyes, head, or body toward stimuli of interest, in order to process them in further detail. For instance, we may fixate a stimulus so that it now falls on the foveal region of the retina, where receptors have highest visual acuity; or we may feel it with the fingers of our preferred hand, which have highest tactile acuity. Such shifts in receptors are referred to as *overt* orienting. Experimental evidence from normals, described later, shows that we can also direct our attention *covertly* toward particular stimuli, without shifting receptors (as when "looking out of the corner" of our eyes). Stimuli can be judged more efficiently when covertly attended in this way, even though they remain on the same part of the receptor surface.

At least three disorders after brain damage are thought to result from impairments in such overt and covert orienting abilities. Two of these, termed *extinction* and *neglect*, are fairly common following unilateral brain injury, especially to the right hemisphere (Vallar, 1993). The third disorder, *Balint's syndrome*, is associated with bilateral damage, particularly involving the parietal lobe (Balint, 1909; De Renzi, 1982). The hallmark of all three disorders is that the patient responds normally to stimuli in some restricted region, while appearing oblivious to equivalent stimuli in other regions, under circumstances where peripheral sensory or motoric losses (e.g. blindness or paralysis) can be ruled out as explanations for the impairment. In extinction and neglect, stimuli toward one particular side of space often go unacknowledged (in particular, toward the *contralesional* side, i.e. opposite the lesion). In Balint's syndrome, the patient seems spatially dis-orientated, and to be aware of only one object at any one moment, which may be on either side.

It is important to note from the outset that not all extinction patients are identical, and likewise for neglect and for Balint patients. Indeed, the differences between patients can often be as informative as the similarities. Nevertheless, patients usually must exhibit some defining characteristics to be labeled as suffering from one of these disorders. Although there is some dispute over which defining characteristics are most critical, I will briefly discuss those characteristics that are usually considered diagnostic. I will also introduce possible accounts for each generic disorder, in terms of impaired attention.

EXTINCTION

Extinction is a fairly common neurological sign following unilateral brain damage. It is classically associated with right-parietal damage, but can be seen in some form after various unilateral lesions (Driver, Mattingley, Rorden, & Davis, 1997; Vallar et al., 1994). Patients suffering from extinction are able to judge single stimuli presented on either side quite normally, but when presented with two concurrent stimuli they fail to judge the one further toward the contralesional side. This was first observed by Oppenheim (1885), and further investigated by Anton (1899). Extinction has since been regularly observed in vision, audition, and touch (e.g. Bender, 1952). It is often tested for in the clinic using stimuli produced by the clinician's own hands, an informal method called "confrontation".

For instance, vision might be tested by having the patient directly face and fixate the clinician's nose (so that the clinician can readily see where the patient's eyes are pointing). The clinician then stretches his or her own hands out on either side, so that one falls in the patient's left visual field and one in the patient's right visual field. The patient's task is to detect sudden movement (e.g. finger-wiggling) by either of the clinician's outstretched hands, while always looking straight ahead at the clinician's nose. A patient with right-hemisphere damage, and consequent left extinction, can detect an isolated hand movement in their right visual field (which anatomically projects initially to the intact left hemisphere); and likewise can detect an isolated hand movement in their left visual field (which projects initially to the damaged right hemisphere). However, if the clinician moves both hands at the same time, the left extinction patient will characteristically miss the movement in the left visual field, even though this event would have been detected in isolation. Tactile extinction can similarly be demonstrated by having the clinician touch the patient on either or both sides, and auditory extinction by the clinician making finger-snaps on either or both sides, in an unseen manner.

These informal confrontation measures of extinction provide a surprisingly reliable clinical test for unilateral brain damage (e.g. Vallar et al., 1994). However, they are unsatisfactory experimentally, as stimulus presentation is ill-controlled, fluctuating with the clinician's dexterity. Fortunately, the basic method of presenting stimuli on either or both sides, while requiring central fixation, can easily be adapted for use with computer-generated stimuli, so that the timing, salience, and location of events can be precisely controlled. The basic phenomenon of extinction (i.e. missing contralesional stimuli in just the double-stimulation condition) is readily observed with such computerised methods (e.g. Baylis, Driver, & Rafal, 1993; Di Pellegrino & De Renzi, 1995; Ward, Goodrich, & Driver, 1994), and can be measured more sensitively in this way.

For instance, patients who initially show extinction under the clinical procedure of confrontation often appear to recover over the initial months following their brain injury (especially if this was a stroke which, for metabolic reasons, initially produces a widespread disruption of brain activity that gradually resolves into a focus of abnormal tissue). Eventually extinction may no longer be observed when tested with hand movements. However, extinction can usually still be revealed using computer tests (Baylis et al., 1993; Ward et al., 1994); it is simply that the patient has now recovered to the extent that briefer displays are required to elicit extinction than can be produced by hand. Even with longer displays, contralesional stimuli might still be easier to detect when isolated than when paired with an ipsilesional event, but once performance becomes perfect ("reaches ceiling") in the double-stimulation condition, it then becomes impossible to observe any greater ease for the isolated condition. These methodological short-comings of ceiling effects are well known in the normal experimental literature. Unfortunately, they are often overlooked in the neurological literature on attention, a point to which I shall return. Ceiling effects can easily be avoided in computerized extinction tests, by reducing display duration until performance becomes imperfect.

Many authors (e.g. Baylis et al., 1993; Di Pellegrino & De Renzi, 1995), regard extinction as primarily a deficit in covert spatial attention, for several reasons. First, the intact performance for single contralesional events is often held to show that basic sensory processing is intact for the impaired side. The left-extinction patient is evidently not entirely blind, deaf, or insensitive on the left side, as they can report isolated sights, sounds, or touches there. These go undetected only when they must "compete for attention" with concurrent events toward the ipsilesional side.

Second, extinction can be dramatically reduced on double-stimulation trials if the patient is told to ignore any ipsilesional event, reporting only the contralesional events (Di Pellegrino & De Renzi, 1995; Karnath, 1988). This strengthens the idea that contralesional events suffer only when they must compete for attention with *relevant* ipsilesional events. Such competition is usually considered to affect covert rather than overt attention in extinction, as the patient must face and fixate centrally throughout the test, and the use of brief displays rules out any useful role for eye movements.

Finally, the phenomenon of extinction has a suggestive parallel with a robust finding in the normal attention literature, as originally pointed out by Ward et al. (1994). In a variety of tasks, healthy subjects are able to monitor for an occasional target event in two separate streams of information (e.g. rapid series of heard words, or seen characters) even when the streams come from two different locations. Moreover, they may do so as efficiently as when monitoring a single stream (Eriksen & Spencer, 1969; Ostry, Moray, & Marks, 1976; Shiffrin & Gardner, 1972), but with one important exception. Normal performance in monitoring two streams usually breaks down when two *targets* are presented at the same time, one in each stream (Duncan, 1980, 1985; Moray, 1975; see Pashler, 1995, for a concise review). Typically, one or other of two brief targets will be missed when presented concurrently. The usual interpretation is that, while normal subjects can divide their attention across incoming *nontargets* from two streams, and can thus detect a single target in either stream, they nevertheless have great difficulty in attending to two *targets* simultaneously (Duncan, 1980).

This seems analogous to the dilemma of extinction patients. They also exhibit a difficulty only with two concurrent target events, having no problem when a single target appears in just one stream (e.g. on the contralesional side) paired with a nontarget in the other stream/side (i.e.

with an entirely irrelevant item on the ipsilesional side, as in the Karnath, 1988, study; or with just a non-event on the ipsilesional side, as when only a contralesional target is presented in total isolation). Extinction may differ from the normal difficulty with multiple targets only in severity and spatial specificity. Extinction can be so severe that even a temporally extended salient event (such as a hand movement) can go quite undetected, whereas a normal subject would miss only one of two concurrent targets if they were very brief. Furthermore, one can reliably predict *which* of two concurrent targets will be missed by an extinction patient (i.e. the one further to the contralesional side), whereas this may be unpredictable in a normal subject. Nonetheless, it seems plausible to characterize extinction as a spatially specific exaggeration of the normal difficulty in attending to multiple targets, caused by a bias in attention toward the ipsilesional side.

Kinsbourne (1977, 1993) has suggested a simple neural mechanism for controlling the lateral direction of both overt and covert spatial attention, which could produce such a bias toward the ipsilesional side of space following unilateral injury. His account stems from basic anatomical and physiological facts which apply to many species, including humans. First, sensory pathways are typically "crossed", so that information from one side of space projects to the opposite hemisphere. As we have seen, the left visual field projects initially to the right hemisphere, and the right visual field to the left hemisphere. Similarly, touch information from the left and right sides of the body project to the right and left hemispheres respectively. Finally, while auditory sensory pathways are less fully crossed, the left and right ears do have stronger inputs to the right and left hemispheres respectively.

Motor pathways have analogous crossing. Thus, the right hand and left hand are primarily controlled by the left and right hemispheres respectively. Moreover, physiological stimulation studies in animals, together with lesions studies in animals and humans, demonstrate that left turns of the body, head, and eyes primarily involve activity in right-hemisphere structures, whereas right turns primarily involve left-hemisphere activity.

These basic facts led Kinsbourne (1977, 1993) to propose that the two hemispheres induce opposing contralateral orienting tendencies when activated. Stimuli on the left activate the right hemisphere, thus inducing a leftward turn toward them, while stimuli on the right activate the left hemisphere, inducing a right turn. To some extent, humans can also choose which way to turn, regardless of any stimulation. To account for this voluntary control, Kinsbourne must additionally propose that an intention to turn in one direction corresponds to a deliberate activation of regions in the appropriate (contralateral) hemisphere. Which way the person actually orients will then depend on the *relative* activation of regions in the two hemispheres, produced by stimuli and/or by intentions. The person will orient toward the side opposite the more active hemisphere, and will do so further as the relative difference in activity increases.

Kinsbourne (1993) has further argued that similar opponent principles apply in the control of *covert* spatial attention, as well as for overt orienting (although different regions within the hemispheres may well be responsible in the covert case). Thus, the appropriate right-hemisphere lesion could bias covert as well as overt orienting toward the right side of space. Such an account can provide a natural explanation for the basic phenomenon of extinction, primarily because the account stresses the *relative* activity of the two hemispheres, as explained next.

Specifically, a lesion to one side of the brain may be expected to result in less activity than normal in response to the stimuli that project to that hemisphere; that is, stimuli toward the contralesional side of space. As a result, stimuli on this side should produce less (covert and overt) orienting than usual, on Kinsbourne's account. However, the crucial point is that this disadvantage will be largely immaterial when a contralesional event is presented *in isolation*, because it then has no rival stimulus to compete with. Although it may produce less activity than normal, any activity at all should result in some orienting toward it, as there is no stimulus to induce an opposing orienting tendency. By contrast, on a double-stimulation trial, the contralesional event now has to compete with an ipsilesional event. The disadvantage for the contralesional side should thus become more apparent, and hence produce extinction, because in *relative* terms the ipsilesional event will now be strongly favored and the contralesional event correspondingly disadvantaged.

Extinction is not only found between events in different visual fields. If two events are presented *within* the "good" ipsilesional field, the stimulus that is further toward the contralesional direction may be extinguished (Kinsbourne, 1977). Kinsbourne (1993) explains this by proposing that more peripheral items produce a greater relative difference in activation between the hemispheres than more central items; in other words, the further that a stimulus is in one direction, the more it will activate the contralateral hemisphere over the ipsilateral. As a result, hemispheric competition will produce a dynamic *directional* bias, rather than a static impairment for fixed regions of the visual field. This directional bias will favor stimuli that are relatively ipsilesional over those that are relatively contralesional, within each visual field as well as between fields. This model provides a general account for the most basic phenomena of extinction. However, Kinsbourne's model needs considerable elaboration to account for the more detailed findings that we consider later.

UNILATERAL NEGLECT

Like extinction, neglect is relatively common following unilateral brain injury, especially after large lesions to the right parietal lobe (Vallar, 1993). The earliest clinical descriptions of neglect date from the nineteenth century (e.g. Hughlings Jackson, 1876), but detailed case-studies scarcely began until the 1940s (e.g. Paterson & Zangwill, 1944), and the possible relevance of neglect for models of normal attention was not widely appreciated until the 1980s (e.g. Posner, Walker, Friedrich, & Rafal, 1984).

As in extinction, neglect patients fail to acknowledge or respond appropriately for stimuli toward the contralesional side under the appropriate circumstances. However, neglect can be apparent on a wide range of measures in addition to the extinction test (although many of these measures also rely on ipsilesional events competing with contralesional events). Neglect patients are usually severely disabled by their disorder in everyday life; by contrast, a mild extinction patient may show little impairment to the casual observer in daily behavior, perhaps because the temporally extended nature of many real-world tasks allows them to circumvent their difficulty with concurrent discrete target events.

On casual observation, neglect patients may have their eyes, head, and/or body noticeably turned toward the ipsilesional side (although they may be capable of turning contralesionally when asked to do so). They may ignore people who approach or address them from the contralesional side; may fail to eat food toward the contralesional side of their plate; may omit contralesional words or letters when reading text; may fail to groom the contralesional side of their body; and if mobile, may collide with contralesional objects, and get lost when navigating because of a propensity to turn ipsilesionally at each junction (see Bisiach & Vallar, 1988, for review). Furthermore, they may be frustratingly unaware (so-called anosagnosia) of their contralesional deficits.

Common clinical tests for neglect in visual behavior include cancellation tasks (where the patient is given a page with various items distributed across it, asked to mark them all with a pen, and typically fails to mark items toward the contralesional side); bisection tasks (where the patient is given some stimulus, such as a horizontal line, and asked to mark its center, typically placing the mark well to the ipsilesional side); and drawing tasks (where the patient is asked either to draw an object (e.g. a clockface) from memory, or to copy a presented drawing, tending to omit contralesional elements in both cases). Examples of neglect in each of these informal tests are shown in Fig. 8.1.

Neglect, as defined by an impairment for more contralesional stimuli, has also been observed in auditory, tactile, and proprioceptive tasks. Patients may fail to respond to contralesional sounds, or may mislocate them

(a)

(b)

(c)

(d)

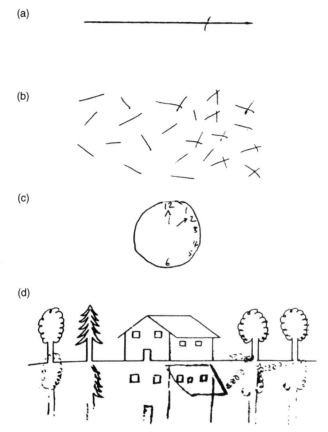

FIG. 8.1. Examples of left neglect after right-hemisphere damage in several informal paper-and-pencil tasks: (a) Line bisection; the patient marks well to the right of true center; (b) Line cancellation; the patient fails to mark lines toward the left of the page; (c) Drawing from memory; details on the left of the object are omitted; (d) Copying; the original drawing is shown above, with the patient's reproduction below (adapted from Gainotti et al., 1972). Note that details on the left of each object are miscopied, rather than just details to the left of the entire scene.

towards the ipsilesional side (so-called allochiria; Bisiach, Cornacchia, Sterzi, & Vallar, 1984); they may fail to explore contralesional space in the tactile modality (Bisiach, Capitani, & Porta, 1985) and they may misjudge the proprioceptively sensed position of their own limbs when these are towards the contralesional side of space (Vallar, Antonucci, Guariglia, & Pizzamiglio, 1993).

Many authors consider extinction to be just a mild form of neglect (see Driver et al., 1997), and clinical textbooks often suggest that extinction persists as the patient gradually recovers from the more florid symptoms of neglect that can be apparent in the early weeks after their initial stroke or trauma (e.g. Heilman, Watson, & Valenstein, 1985). Others argue that extinction and neglect may be fundamentally distinct disorders (e.g. Di Pellegrino & De Renzi, 1995), citing observations that patients can show neglect on the tasks just described and yet no extinction, or vice versa. These two complimentary patterns of selective impairment provide what is known as a "double dissociation". Such a pattern is often taken by neuropsychologists as firm evidence that the dissociated tasks reflect distinct processes (e.g. Shallice, 1988).

However, the reported dissociations between neglect and extinction have not as yet ruled out the possible methodological problem of ceiling effects that was raised earlier. For instance, the patients who showed neglect on paper-and-pencil tests, yet no extinction on confrontation, might well have shown extinction if brief computerized displays had been employed instead. Equally, the paper-and-pencil tests for neglect can sometimes be insensitive, also due to ceiling effects. For instance, the relative difficulty of canceling contralesional items can be overlooked in a patient who eventually cancels all the items, but labors over the more contralesional ones. Their contralesional difficulty would be totally obscured in standard cancellation scores, which consider only how many items were marked on completion of the task, rather than the timing, accuracy, or effortfulness of each mark.

Nonetheless, it should be acknowledged that neglect patients typically exhibit strikingly abnormal performance in fairly naturalistic, temporally extended tasks (see examples in Fig. 8.1), whereas extinction patients may show an impairment only in one very constrained task (i.e detecting two concurrent targets). This difference mirrors the differing degrees of impairment in everyday life for the two broad classes of patient, and suggests that more processes may be disrupted in those patients who show signs of neglect as well as extinction.

Naturalistic tasks like drawing, at which many neglect patients are impaired, are necessarily more complex and unconstrained than the more "artificial" measure of extinction. One consequence is that it can be hard to identify exactly which component processes are impaired in tasks like copying or cancelation, as compared with more restricted tasks like the extinction measure. One obvious way in which most neglect measures differ from the extinction test is that the patient is allowed (indeed, often required) to explore the stimulus in the neglect measures, often by moving their eyes, head, or hand across the scene. The neglect tests might therefore be more sensitive to any deficits in active exploration (be this overt or covert) toward one side of space (Karnath & Fetter, 1995). In general, the standard neglect tests have a more substantial motoric component than the extinction test (see Driver et al., 1997; Mattingley & Driver, 1977).

There is now abundant evidence for double dissociations between the various traditional measures of neglect themselves. That is, a patient can show severe neglect on one measure (e.g. cancellation), but not on another (e.g. line bisection; Halligan & Marshall, 1992). Such dissociations raise the possibility that neglect is a multi-component disorder (Rafal, 1994), as has previously been concluded for aphasia, amnesia, and most of the other neurological syndromes that had been closely analyzed prior to detailed studies of neglect. In other words, the majority of neglect patients may suffer from impairments to a large number of spatially selective processes, with only a minority of patients suffering from damage to restricted subsets of these multiple component processes.

However, it remains controversial whether some of the dissociations already reported for neglect (e.g. between cancellation and bisection tasks) reflect a distinction between two fundamentally separate aspects of spatial cognition. Instead, they may just reflect the different ways in which two crude measures of the same underlying deficit can become insensitive. An analogy with a very different area of psychology, namely the measurement of intelligence, may help to explain the methodological point here. The fact that bisection and cancellation tasks usually both reveal neglect can be considered analogous to IQ testers finding that two types of items on their test-battery (say, visual versus verbal problems) usually both provide a reasonable measure of general intelligence across most people. However, on closer inspection of individual performance, the IQ tester may then find that some people do better on visual problems than verbal, while others do the reverse. Ought they to conclude that there is no such thing as general intelligence (or in our case, neglect), but rather many different abilities? Or should they conclude instead that both types of question (or in our case, both measures of neglect) provide approximate measures of an underlying factor, with each measure being approximate for different reasons, because every measure involves some unique process in addition to the underlying factor of interest?

Such disputes continue over the correct interpretation for the various dissociations that have already been found within neglect patients (see the various opinions in Halligan & Marshall, 1994a). Nevertheless, there is an increasing consensus that various aspects of neglect may be attributable to deficits in corresponding aspects of attention (e.g. Rafal, 1994; Robertson & Marshall, 1993). The rationale for invoking attention is reminiscent of that for the case of extinction; primarily, that peripheral sensory or motoric losses do not provide a complete account of the contralesional deficit, for several reasons.

First, while many neglect patients do have sensory impairments, such as visual field losses ("hemianopia") for the affected side, florid neglect can nevertheless be observed in the complete absence of any such sensory impairment (Halligan, Marshall, & Wade, 1990). Conversely, purely hemi-anopic patients rarely show neglect in everyday life, nor in paper-and-pencil tests, as they can compensate for their blind region simply by moving their eyes. Thus, peripheral sensory loss seems inadequate as an explanation for neglect.

Second, while many neglect patients are hemiplegic (paralysed on the contralesional side of their body), this is by no means true for all of them, and conversely hemiplegia need not lead to neglect. A hemiplegic patient can still move their ipsilesional limbs toward the contralesional side of space, likewise their body, head, and eyes. In principle, the same is true for most neglect patients, but unlike a purely hemiplegic patient they will often fail to make such movements spontaneously, and may exhibit preserved motor behavior toward contralesional items only when explicitly cued to do so. Thus, *peripheral* motor impairments on the contralesional side seem inadequate as a complete explanation for neglect, although raised thresholds for overt responding toward contralesional events seem likely.

Faced with the striking abnormalities in neglect patients' performance, and with the apparent inadequacy of purely sensory or motoric explana-tions, one is compelled to postulate a bias in some spatially selective pro-cess(es) which intervene between initial sensation and ultimate response. Processes of this kind seem very close to most existing definitions of spatial attention (although it must be admitted that such definitions are a little vague). The temptation to invoke an ipsilesional attentional bias becomes even stronger given findings that neglect can be temporarily ameliorated by manipulations that encourage the patient to attend toward the contrale-sional side (e.g. Riddoch & Humphreys, 1983, for line bisection). Much rehabilitative effort has been based on such observations, repeatedly encouraging the left neglect patient to look, scan, or attend leftward (e.g. Diller & Riley, 1993). Unfortunately, current findings suggest that such therapies tend to produce only limited improvements, which remain closely tied to the intervention setting (Robertson & Marshall, 1993). The essential problem in neglect may be that while the patient can, in principle, look or attend toward the contralesional side, they usually fail to do so sponta-neously.

The neglect I have described thus far might be largely due to failures just in *overt* orienting toward the contralesional side, and ipsilesional biases in fixation scanning are indeed well documented in neglect patients (e.g. Karnath & Fetter, 1995; Walker, Findlay, Young, & Lincoln, 1996). However, two classic findings demonstrate that covert factors can also be involved. Bisiach and Luzatti (1978) observed that neglect can sometimes arise even in *imagery* tasks. Their patients had to describe verbally the buildings in a familiar cathedral square (from their home city), when first imagining themselves facing toward the cathedral. The patients, with left neglect after right-hemisphere damage, named buildings on the right from this imagined perspective, but tended to omit buildings on the left. They were later asked to perform the same task, but now imagining themselves on the opposite side of the square, facing away from the cathedral. They tended to omit buildings on the left from this new perspective—that is, those that had previously fallen on the right and had then been recalled!

Such neglect in the imagination has since been confirmed with many other patients and tasks. However, in some cases imaginal neglect has been found without any ostensive neglect in visual behavior (Guariglia, Padovani, Pantano, & Pizzamiglio, 1993), or vice versa (Anderson, 1993), suggesting that imaginal neglect may be a separable problem from the other forms of neglect. Nevertheless, when observed, imaginal neglect clearly cannot be attributed solely to a failure in *overtly* orienting receptors toward contralesional target items, as no target items are physically present on any receptors during the imaginal task.

A final demonstration that covert factors can be involved in neglect provides perhaps the best rationale for considering it (at least partly) to be an attentional deficit. Neglect patients can show specific abnormalities in components of covert spatial attention, as operationally defined by performance measures. Posner (e.g. 1980) introduced one performance method for studying covert shifts of spatial attention in normal subjects, which has since been widely used. In basic form, the subject must detect or discriminate a visual target which can appear in various locations (say, on the left or on the right). The subject's attention is cued to one location or another (e.g. by an uninformative event at that location, or by an instruction that the target is most likely there), but central fixation must be maintained throughout. Even though the subject does not make any eye movement, the robust finding is that a variety of judgments is more efficient for targets at the cued location ("valid" trials) than for targets appearing elsewhere ("invalid" trials). This normal performance benefit on valid trials is usually attributed to a covert shift of spatial attention toward the cued locus.

Posner et al. (1984) administered variants on this cuing task to patients with unilateral parietal damage, suffering from various degrees of neglect and extinction. They found that these patients showed the normal pattern of facilitation following valid cues, for targets in either visual field. That is, the patients were able to shift their covert attention when cued to do so, even in the contralesional direction. However, the patients were abnormally slow to judge contralesional targets if these were preceded by an invalid cue to the ipsilesional side. Posner et al. attributed this result to a specific difficulty in "disengaging" attention from relatively ipsilesional locations once covert attention had been drawn there.

This basic pattern of abnormally poor performance for contralesional targets after invalid ipsilesional cues has since been replicated in further unilateral parietal patients (e.g. Posner, Walker, Friedrich, & Rafal, 1987), and the extent of the abnormality has been shown to correlate with clinical measures of neglect severity (Morrow & Ratcliffe, 1987). However, the specific interpretation in terms of a "disengage" difficulty has been disputed (Cohen, Farah, Romero, & Servan-Schreiber, 1994; Rorden, Mattingley, Karnath, & Driver, 1997). Nevertheless, the result does demonstrate an abnormality in covert attention, as operationally defined, in neglect patients. Note that this abnormality has some striking parallels with extinction. In particular, the deficit for targets at contralesional locations is most pronounced when they must compete with ipsilesional locations (i.e. after an ipsilesional rather than contralesional cue). For this reason, the result can be given a similar explanation as for extinction, in terms of hemispheric competition based on relative activation (Kinsbourne, 1993; Cohen et al., 1994).

BALINT'S SYNDROME

This cluster of deficits was first described by Balint (1909), although similar cases have since been reported (e.g. Baylis, Driver, Baylis, & Rafal, 1994; Driver, Goodrich, Ward, & Rafal, 1996; Holmes & Horrax, 1919; Humphreys & Riddoch, 1993; Luria, 1959). It is associated with symmetrical bilateral lesions, involving the posterior parietal lobe or parieto-occipital junction. It is less common than the unilateral deficits discussed so far, if only because bilateral lesions are rarer. As originally described, Balint's syndrome is extraordinarily disabling, and involves three major deficits.

First, there may be severe difficulties in spatial localization; for example, as suggested by gross misreaching toward visual objects. Second, there may be "fixity of gaze"; that is, a difficulty in executing saccades or in tracking a moving event once a visible item has been fixated. Third, there is a characteristic tendency for visual experience to be dominated by just one object at a time (termed "simultanagnosia"). This can be apparent in the patients' descriptions of what they see (e.g. "When I see your spectacles I cannot see your face"); in their everyday behavior (e.g. failing to light a cigarette because when they see the match they reportedly cannot see the cigarette, and vice versa); and also in their psychophysical performance.

For instance, they may be able to judge whether a stimulus is square or rectangular (when each display comprises just one object) yet be quite unable to compare the length of equivalently extended but unconnected lines (because the display now comprises multiple objects; Holmes & Horrax, 1919). They may also be able to read individual words (presented in isolation as single objects), yet be unable to identify the component letters individually on a visual basis, even for words that are correctly read (because when the letters must be considered individually, each word now comprises several objects; Baylis et al. 1994).

There are now grounds for suspecting that the three major characteristics of Balint's syndrome may be dissociable (De Renzi, 1982); for instance, patients may show just misreaching without the other two problems. It may be that the three deficits often co-occur simply because the brain regions involved in each deficit share some anatomical relation, which may have little to do with their cognitive function. For instance, three functionally separable brain regions or networks might in principle all be sustained metabolically by common blood vessels, in which case a major stroke would be likely to damage all three networks together even though they share no functional relation.

It is for this kind of reason that neuropsychologists often place more faith in *dis*sociations (i.e. observations of which processes can be impaired independently) than in *as*sociations (i.e. which processes tend to be impaired together). Some anatomical factor, such as a common blood vessel, might also produce frequent but nevertheless non-functional associations in neglect, or in any other disorder for that matter. In practice, we often have some useful knowledge of the relevant blood vessels, and of other anatomical interconnections, and so may be able to assess the plausibility of any particular association being of this non-functional kind. Nevertheless, in principle one can always question the interpretation of a neuropsychological association. For instance, while most neglect patients apparently show both a difficulty in ignoring ipsilesional visual distractors (Robertson & Eglin, 1993) and a tendency to err in the ipsilesional direction when reaching for visual objects (Harvey, Milner & Roberts, 1994), there may be no functional relation between these two deficits. The misreaching might be a separate problem, as it may also be in the case of patients suffering from Balint's syndrome.

The grounds for considering components of Balint's syndrome as attentional deficits have been less articulated than for extinction and neglect. To my knowledge, no-one has argued that the misreaching and eye-movement difficulties are specifically attentional, even though both might be considered extreme deficits in overt orienting. However, the simultanagnosic tendency to lock onto individual visual objects has often been regarded as an attentional deficit (e.g. Baylis et al., 1994; Humphreys & Riddoch, 1993), primarily because this aspect of the disorder does not seem reducible to peripheral sensory loss. Particular regions of the visual field may be neglected or reported depending on whether they are linked by a common object to other regions (e.g. Humphreys & Riddoch, 1993; Luria, Pravdina-Vinarskaya, & Yarbuss, 1963). Moreover, the object-based simultanagnosia is not simply due to *overt* orienting factors, as it can be observed in displays too brief to permit eye-movements (Driver et al., 1996). Finally, Balint patients can show specific abnormalities in Posner's cuing measure of covert orienting (Verfaellie, Rapcsak, & Heilman, 1990).

It has been suggested (e.g. Driver et al., 1996; Farah, 1990) that the object-based aspect of Balint's syndrome may just be a form of bilateral rather than unilateral neglect, consistent with the bilateral lesions. Balint patients may suffer from a difficulty in "disengaging" covert attention from one object in order to shift it in *any* other direction, rather than only in the contralesional direction as for the unilateral parietal patients studied by Posner et al. (1987). It should be noted, however, that Kinsbourne's (1977, 1993) account of orienting in terms of hemispheric competition is much less successful in explaining any such "disengage" deficit after bilateral damage than after unilateral damage, as the relative levels of activity in the two hemispheres might remain roughly balanced after symmetric bilateral lesions.

Having introduced the three general deficits of extinction, neglect, and Balint's syndrome, I now turn to consider what light experimental studies of these neurological disorders might shed on some major issues from the *normal* attention literature.

GROUPING EFFECTS ON SPATIAL SELECTIVITY

A recent debate in the normal literature on visual attention (e.g. Baylis & Driver, 1993; Driver & Baylis, 1989; Duncan, 1984; Kanwisher & Driver, 1992) has concerned whether covert attention is directed to unsegmented regions of space, or to segmented perceptual groups that are likely to constitute coherent objects. A common metaphor for covert attention invokes an attentional "spotlight" that "illuminates" relevant areas of space (e.g. Posner, 1980). If taken literally, this metaphor might imply that attention is directed to particular locations with little or no preprocessing of any stimulus structures there.

On the other hand, since the early days of Gestalt psychology it has been well established (Wertheimer, 1923; Pomerantz & Garner, 1973) that human perceptual systems *segment* their input, in order to group together those stimulus elements that are likely to belong to a common object (e.g. grouping together visual elements with common color, motion, or alignment). As our actions must ultimately be selectively directed toward individual objects, some theorists have proposed that it would be efficient for covert attention to operate on segmented objects rather than just on unstructured regions of space (e.g. Driver & Baylis, 1989; Duncan, 1984; Neisser, 1967).

In essence, the recent debate between space-based versus object-based accounts of normal covert attention is just a new variation on a very old question; namely, how much perceptual processing takes place unselectively, *before* attention acts to boost processing for just a subset of the incoming information? The current version of this question focuses on how much grouping of the scene into distinct objects takes place before spatial selection is completed.

In the normal literature, space-based and object-based models of attention have often been presented as mutually exclusive alternatives (e.g. by Driver & Baylis, 1989). However, many hybrid views are possible. For instance, it may be that covert attention does operate within a spatial medium (as argued by Tsal & Lavie, 1993), but that grouping processes modulate the spatial extent of the attended region (Lavie & Driver, 1996). As we shall see, current neuropsychological evidence strongly supports this hybrid view.

To the extent that extinction and neglect are viewed as deficits in attention, their ostensibly spatial nature supports the view that there are space-based components to covert attention, which can be biased toward one side or the other by the appropriate unilateral lesion. However, recent evidence suggests that the extinguished or neglected region can depend strongly on Gestalt grouping factors, as well as on its location. These results imply that grouping still takes place on the extinguished or neglected side, and thus that grouping processes do not depend entirely on the components of spatial attention that are impaired by the brain damage.

Segmentation and Extinction

To my knowledge, at the time of writing, only a few studies have looked for effects of Gestalt grouping on extinction, and these come from my own laboratory. Ward, Goodrich, and Driver (1994) examined two right-hemisphere patients with left extinction, and found that left-sided misses on computerized double-stimulation trials were dramatically reduced if the two concurrent events formed a good perceptual group. For instance, there was less extinction between two horizontally aligned brackets (i.e. a display like "[+]") than between an adjacent bracket plus dot (i.e. "[+ o", or "o +]"). Several normal performance measures have previously shown (e.g. Pomerantz & Garner, 1973) that two aligned brackets tend to be grouped together as a single rectangular object by the visual system. Ward et al. therefore concluded that extinction is reduced when the two concurrent targets can be linked into a single group.

Driver, Goodrich, Ward, and Rafal (1996) similarly showed that visual extinction can be virtually eliminated when the two concurrent targets are literally linked together, using the "bar-bell" versus "two-circle" displays shown in Fig. 8.2. In further studies we have shown that extinction can be similarly modulated by more sophisticated grouping processes than mere

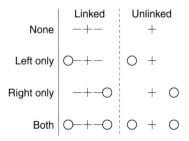

FIG. 8.2. Example stimuli from Driver et al.'s (submitted) study of grouping effects on extinction and on Balint's syndrome. Eight possible displays are illustrated, with the four linked possibilities separated from their four unlinked equivalents by the vertical dotted line. Linked and unlinked displays differed only in whether an uninformative horizontal line was presented together with the circular target events that had to be detected and localized. The patients fixated a central cross, whose position relative to each subsequent display is illustrated. They were then presented with either no circular target event on the two sides, a target on just the left side, on just the right, or on both sides. A right-parietal extinction patient tended to miss left targets only in the unlinked-both displays. Similarly, a bilateral parietal Balint case tended to miss circular targets only in the unlinked-both displays, being equally likely to report just one circle from either side. Both patients' deficit was dramatically reduced in the linked-both displays, presumably because these contain just one object (a bar-bell) rather than two competing objects (the unconnected circles).

visible connectedness or alignment. For instance, two horizontal visual bars produce less extinction when interpreted as the two ends of a single long stick jutting out from either side of a central occluder, rather than as two separate short sticks appearing in front of the same central object (Mattingley, Davis, & Driver, 1997). Equally, two events produce less extinction when together they form a Kanizsa (1979) illusion of a single subjective figure (Mattingley et al., 1997.) Both these effects imply that three-dimensional grouping processes, involved in generating depth interpretations from two-dimensional visual inputs, do not depend on the attentional components that are impaired in extinction patients. This accords with recent proposals that such grouping processes may also operate in a "pre-attentive" manner for normal subjects (Davis & Driver, 1994, in press; Enns & Rensink, 1994).

A further parallel with normal research concerns Duncan's (1984) work. He has found that the performance cost that healthy subjects usually show when they must divide attention across two concurrent targets (Duncan, 1980; Moray, 1975) can be eliminated if the concurrent targets are both attributes of a common object. A similar principle seems to apply for our extinction patients, who show little difficulty with concurrent targets when these are grouped into a single object.

Taken together, these findings suggest the following account. The normal difficulty with multiple concurrent targets is exacerbated in extinction. As in normals, target objects compete for selection. The more ipsilesional of the two objects will usually win this competition in the patients, due to the spatial imbalance produced by their lesion. However, this imbalance has little effect when the two-target events are linked into a common object (e.g. the bar-bell at bottom left of Fig. 8.2), because the two events now become allies rather than competitors for selection. That is, selection of the ipsilesional event now tends to bring the contralesional event with it, because the two events are grouped together.

This general account of extinction is consistent with two broad types of model. First, grouping processes may entirely *precede* spatial attention (as originally proposed by Neisser, 1967), and may thus be totally unaffected by any pathological biases in spatial attention. Second, grouping might *interact* with spatially selective processes, so that both types of operation overlap in time, with each influencing the other (Farah, Wallace, & Vecera, 1993; Humphreys & Riddoch, 1993; Ward et al., 1994). In this way, relatively preserved grouping processes might aid relatively impaired spatial selection in extinction patients. The existing neuropsychological (and normal) evidence has not yet decisively distinguished between these two kinds of model. However, note that on either view the spatial extent of both normal and pathological attention is substantially modulated by grouping processes. Clearly, human covert attention is rather more sophisticated than a simple "spotlight" metaphor implies.

Segmentation and Neglect

As with extinction, the ostensibly spatial nature of neglect might seem consistent with purely space-based models of normal attention. Neglect invariably applies for information toward the contralesional side, and thus might be accounted for by an ipsilesional bias in space-based components of attention. However, as with extinction, recent results suggest that the particular area that is neglected can strongly depend on how the scene is grouped, consistent with models in which grouping processes precede or interact with the spatial selection that is disrupted in neglect.

Suggestive evidence for this comes from the errors in copying made by some neglect patients. In Fig. 8.1d, the left-neglect patient's copy omits details toward the left of each object, but faithfully reproduces the right side of objects that fall well to the left of the scene. One interpretation of such performance would be that the patient's visual system can still segment the scene into distinct objects across both visual fields, with neglect arising only at a later stage of attending to each object in turn to copy its details.

Driver, Baylis, and Rafal (1992) examined this possibility in a single case of left neglect, using a simplified visual-judgment task that was designed to eliminate the possible contributions that eye, head, or hand movements, plus planning processes, might make to abnormal copying performance like that in Fig. 8.1d. As discussed earlier, copying is a naturalistic task that can demonstrate the serious consequences of neglect, and can suggest testable hypotheses, but which remains rather intractable for experimental purposes because of the large number of component processes that may be involved.

In Driver et al.'s simplified task, the left-neglect patient was shown displays like those in Fig. 8.3a and b, comprising a horizontal rectangle divided by a random jagged contour towards its left (Fig. 8.3a) or right (Fig. 8.3b). The smaller of the two resulting areas was bright green, while the larger area was dark red, with the entire rectangle appearing on a black screen. Normal observers unambiguously see the smaller bright-green region in such dis-

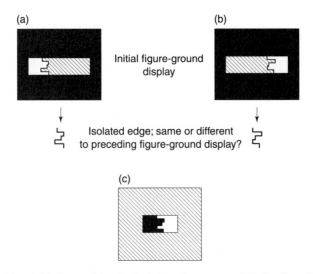

FIG. 8.3.   (a) and (b) give a schematic depiction of two types of display from Driver, Baylis, and Rafal (1992). Each trial began with a figure–ground display against a black screen, comprising a rectangle divided by a random, jagged contour into a large red area (shown with diagonal shading) and a smaller bright green area (shown in white; on the left in a, and on the right in b). Normal observers saw a green figure against a red background in these displays, the jagged edge appearing to belong to just the green shape. The task for a left-neglect patient was to compare the jagged dividing edge in each figure–ground display to an isolated edge which appeared half a second later in the center of the screen (one is shown at the bottom of a, and of b). This isolated edge was equally likely to match (as illustrated) or to differ from the preceding figure–ground display. The left-neglect patient was more accurate at comparing the edges when the initial figure had appeared on the left (as in a) rather than on the right (as in b). This is because the critical jagged edge appears to the right of the green figure in a, but to the left of this figure in b. (c) An ambiguous figure–ground display, which can be seen as a white shape against black, or a black shape against white. Marshall and Halligan (1994) found that their left-neglect patient could reproduce the jagged dividing edge when asked to copy the shape on the left (in this case black), which has the edge on its right, but could not reproduce the very same edge when asked to copy the shape on the right, which has the critical edge on its left.

plays as a figure against a red background, with the dividing jagged contour appearing to belong just to the green shape. The patient's task was to face and fixate the center of each rectangle, while concentrating on the jagged dividing edge for comparison with another jagged edge that appeared immediately afterwards, in total isolation (see bottom of Fig. 8.3a or b) at the center of an otherwise empty black screen. In this way we could measure how well the patient represented edges at particular locations, without requiring him to draw anything, and without allowing him to make any eye-, head-, or hand-movements. All the patient had to do was say whether or not the jagged edge in the initial rectangle matched the subsequent isolated edge.

Our question was how the left-neglect patient's performance would vary as a function of whether the green figure was on the left (Fig. 8.3a) or right (Fig. 8.3b) of the original display. The most straightforward prediction might be for poorer performance when the figure was toward the left (Fig. 8.3a), as here the critical information (i.e. the jagged edge) fell further toward the contralesional (and thus "bad") side of the patient. However, note that in this situation the jagged contour falls toward the ipsilesional (right) side of the small green shape that would be figural for a normal observer. By contrast, when the green figure appeared at the ipsilesional end of the rectangle (and thus to the "good" side of the patient) the jagged edge now fell to the contralesional (left) side of the green figure (see Fig. 8.3b). Thus, if the patient were able to segment figures from ground in both the ipsilesional and contralesional visual fields, with his neglect subsequently applying just to the contralesional side of any figure, he should actually perform worse when judging the contours that originally fell on his "good" ipsilesional side (because these fell on the contralesional side of the figure, see Fig. 8.3b). The results clearly supported this figure-based prediction.

Further evidence consistent with such figure-based neglect has since been reported for another case of left neglect after right-hemisphere damage (Marshall & Halligan, 1994), in a copying task for ambiguous figure–ground displays like the one shown in Fig. 8.3c, which can be seen either as a white shape on a black background, or vice-versa. The patient could accurately copy the jagged edge at the center of each such display when asked to draw the shape on the left side of the display (which has the critical jagged edge on its right), but was quite unable to produce the very same edge when asked to copy the shape on the right side (which has the critical edge on its left).

The results from these two studies suggest that, at least in some cases, neglect can apply to the contralesional side of segmented objects rather than just toward one side of unsegmented space. This implies that segmentation processes precede or interact with those stages of spatial selection at which the neglect arises. It remains to be seen whether this applies for the majority of neglect patients, or for only a specific sub-group. Note that on any account of figure-based neglect in terms of imbalanced hemispheric competition (e.g. Kinsbourne, 1993), one side of a shape must activate a particular hemisphere more than the other side of that shape, even when both sides fall within a single visual field. This remains a physiological possibility, but has yet to be confirmed. Such an explanation would be similar to that proposed for visual extinction within one visual field, except that figure–ground segmentation processes would now also be involved.

The proposal that neglect can apply to one side of segmented shapes immediately raises the question of exactly what divides a shape into its two distinct sides. Driver and Halligan (1991) suggested one possibility, based on research into normal human perception and machine vision. Various authors (e.g. Marr & Nishihara, 1978) have proposed that the visual system describes shapes relative to their principal axis of symmetry and/or elongation, with this axis effectively splitting a shape into two sides. Driver and Halligan tested whether neglect can indeed apply to the contralesional side of a shape's principal axis, using displays like Fig. 8.4a or b, each comprising two nonsense shapes, with one above the other. For many such displays, their left-neglect patient had to judge verbally whether the two shapes were the same or different (this again eliminates the motoric and planning

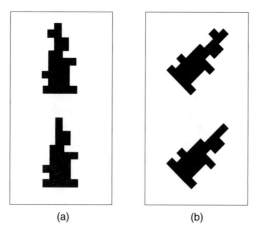

(a)   (b)

FIG. 8.4.   (a) Typical upright display from Driver and Halligan (1991). Their left-neglect patient had to decide whether two black nonsense shapes, one above the other, were the same or different. When different, the discrepancy was only slight. For instance, there is just one additional square element on the left of the top shape in the example shown. The patient tended to miss such differences on the left, while detecting comparable differences on the right. (b) Typical tilted display from the same study. Importantly, the patient continued to miss differences (such as the one illustrated) which fell to the left of the elongated shape's principal axis, even though these differences now fell to the right of the patient.

components of tasks like copying). The shapes were identical on 2/3 of trials, but had a slight difference for the remaining trials, on either the left (as illustrated) or the right.

Unsurprisingly, when the two shapes were upright (Fig. 8.4a) the patient tended to miss differences on the left but not the right, consistent with her left neglect. The critical result was that the *same* differences tended to be neglected (or detected) even when the shapes were both tilted 45° clockwise, so that differences on the top left of the object now fell toward the patient's right (Fig. 8.4b), whereas differences on the bottom right of the shape now fell toward her left. This finding implies that neglect can apply toward the contralesional side of an axis of elongation within a segmented object.

I have since replicated this result in nine further left-neglect patients, and have yet to encounter an exceptional case. Caramazza (personal communication) has similarly corroborated the finding in a case of right-neglect after left-hemisphere damage. Moreover, a similar phenomenon can be observed in left-neglect patients' copying performance, when they omit details along the left of a tilted elongated shape (Halligan & Marshall, 1994b). Finally, Driver, Baylis, Goodrich, and Rafal (1994) have also observed axis-based neglect in a group of right-hemisphere patients, within a purely perceptual task designed to eliminate any possible contribution from eye-movements. Taken together, these findings suggest that axis-based neglect of segmented figures may be a quite general phenomenon, rather than a curio restricted to a few atypical cases. However, further work is needed to determine whether it applies for the majority of cases, or just for a specific subset.

In sum, as with extinction, the ostensibly spatial nature of neglect seems consistent with a bias in spatial components of attention. However, this need not entail that attention is a *purely* space-based phenomenon, as the common spotlight metaphor for normal attention implies. Neglect can be strongly affected by object-segmentation factors, suggesting that such segmentation precedes or interacts with the impaired spatial selection. Thus, the neuropsychological data support neither the purely space-based, nor the purely object-based, models of attention that exist in the normal literature. Instead, they suggest the compromise view that attention acts within a spatial medium, but on a segmented representation.

Segmentation and Balint's Syndrome

The simultanagnosic aspect of Balint's syndrome is almost by definition an impairment with respect to multiple objects, rather than multiple locations. Thus, any attentional account of it seems bound to invoke disrupted attention to objects, or to segmented regions of space, rather than to unsegmented positions in the visual field. A classic Balint patient will readily detect the two circles in the bar-bell of Fig. 8.2 (as they belong to one connected object) but will detect only one circle when the two are unconnected; this was originally shown by Luria (1959), and has since been confirmed and extended by Humphreys and Riddoch (1993) and Driver et al. (1996). Moreover, this pattern of performance can be suprisingly insensitive to the actual spatial separation between the connected or unconnected elements (Humphreys & Riddoch, 1993), confirming the predominance of segmentation factors over spatial factors.

The object-based nature of the attentional deficit in Balint's syndrome has been apparent for some time; the new finding is really that extinction and neglect can be similarly sensitive to segmentation factors. For instance, Driver et al.'s (1996) extinction patient, with right parietal damage, showed an equivalent sensitivity to the bar-bell manipulation shown in Fig. 8.2 as the Balint patient with bilateral parietal damage whom they also tested. The only difference was that the extinction patient would invariably miss the leftmost of two unconnected circles, whereas the Balint patient was as likely to miss an unconnected circle on either side.

As noted earlier, such deficits in Balint patients after bilateral lesions are less readily explained in terms of Kinsbourne's (1993) imbalanced hemispheric competition than the apparently similar deficit in the unilateral extinction patient. I now turn away from the issue of segmentation to consider another area of potential common ground between normal and neuropsychological studies of attention.

MEASURING THE EXTENT OF UNATTENDED AND NEGLECTED PROCESSING

As discussed earlier, there is now abundant evidence in the normal literature (e.g. from the cuing paradigm of Posner, 1980) that covertly attended stimuli can be judged more efficiently than unattended events. This implies that at some stage or stages in the nervous system, attended stimuli are processed more thoroughly. The precise points at which this can happen have long been controversial, as has the fate of unattended stimuli beyond the point where attended stimuli are first favoured. Similar issues arise for the fate of neglected stimuli.

Assessing the extent of processing for unattended stimuli in normals poses a methodological challenge, which has received some quite sophisticated solutions in the normal literature (see the other chapters in this volume). The most basic problem is that if one directly asks a normal person about a stimulus they are requested to ignore, the likelihood is that they will no longer ignore it! Two general solutions have been provided to get around this problem. First, one can try to measure the extent of unattended processing indirectly, without ever asking the person about the information they are meant to ignore, so that it remains irrelevant to them. Second, one can ask the subject a retrospective "surprise" question about events that were not specified as relevant at the time of presentation.

The latter method was employed first in the normal literature, and provides clear results, although the interpretation of these straightforward findings still remains controversial. In the auditory case, if subjects are presented with two spoken messages at once from different locations, and told to concentrate on just one (e.g. to repeat it aloud) they will later recall very little of the irrelevant message when asked surprise questions about it (Cherry, 1953). Typically, they might know that there was another stream of sounds, where it was, and roughly what it sounded like (e.g. male versus female voice), but know nothing about its meaning. Similarly, if normal subjects are presented with multiple visual events, and asked to concentrate on just a subset, when later asked surprise questions about events that were considered irrelevant at the time, they will recall very little (e.g. Neisser & Becklen, 1975; Rock & Guttman, 1981). Typically, they might recall that there were some other events, and perhaps their location or color (Rock et al., 1992) yet be unable to identify them retrospectively. This poor memory can be demonstrated within seconds of initial presentation (Rock et al., 1992; Sperling, 1960).

Such results led to the "early-selection" view that unattended stimuli receive only cursory processing at very peripheral stages of perception (perhaps coding just apparently simple "features" like location, color, or pitch). On this view, unattended stimuli never reach the stages responsible for fully identifying visual objects, or for recognising spoken words. However, the memory findings alone might be reconciled with an alternative "late-selection" view, on which unattended stimuli proceed much further through the system. It can be suggested that unattended stimuli are fully perceived, yet forgotten; or fully processed, yet without reaching full awareness.

Indirect measures of unattended processing were developed to address such possibilities (see Allport, 1993; Kahneman & Treisman, 1984 for overviews). These methods examine the processing of unattended stimuli without requiring any deliberate response to them by the subject. This circumvents the potential problem that the "unattended" stimuli may become attended if specified as relevant. It may also sidestep the potential problem that if unattended stimuli are processed without awareness, deliberate responses to them will not reveal the true extent of this processing. Finally, most indirect measures can be applied at the time of presentation, avoiding the potential problem of forgetting. A wide range of indirect measures has now been employed with normals, ranging from physiological indices of response to irrelevant distractors (e.g. electrical activity measured at the scalp, or autonomic responses measured across the skin) through to behavioral indices of priming or interference from distractors on the speed of deliberate responses to related targets.

The normal literature using these indirect measures of unattended processing is too extensive and complex to be reviewed in full here. However, two major conclusions from it can be stated. First, attention can modulate early sensory responses. For instance, scalp ERPs can be more pronounced for attended stimuli than equivalent irrelevant stimuli within 80 msec of stimulus presentation, and this is thought to reflect differential activity within early areas of visual cortex (Luck, this volume).

Second, despite such early modulation, there is clear evidence that processing of irrelevant stimuli can proceed beyond the stages where this modulation first arises, albeit at attenuated levels. Thus, while a person may have only restricted awareness and memory for events that they ignore, one can nonetheless demonstrate that substantial processing sometimes takes place for them, using interference or priming techniques. These techniques measure the processing of distractors by means of their effect on deliberate responses to targets. As an example of interference, subjects are slower to categorise a target shape when flanked by an irrelevant distractor if the latter shape is associated with an alternative categorization response (Eriksen & Eriksen, 1974). This effect demonstrates that the distractor shape was coded, and it can be found even when the subject is quite unaware of the response-associations of the effective distractors (Miller, 1987). As an example of priming, normal subjects are often slower to respond to a visual object if they have just ignored a related object (Tipper, 1985), even if the distractor and subsequent target were related only in meaning (e.g. after ignoring the word DOG, the subject may be slower to name a picture of a cat; Tipper & Driver, 1988). This implies that the category of the initial distractor was activated to some extent (and perhaps then suppressed, producing the delayed response to subsequent related items). The effect can be found even when subjects are unaware of the identity of the preceding distractor that produces it (Tipper, 1985).

Thus, indirect measures in normals suggest a compromise between extreme early-and late-selection views of unattended processing. Attention apparently can modulate perceptual coding (as early-selection theories emphasize), but nevertheless considerably more perceptual processing can take place for ignored stimuli than would be suggested by normal subjects' ostensive ignorance of them (as emphasized by late-selection theories). These normal findings raise similar possibilities for extinguished and neglected stimuli. To what extent do stimuli on the impaired side continue to be perceptually processed even when a patient is unable to respond to them, or remains quite unaware of them?

Only a few studies to date have used indirect *physiological* indices to examine contralesional processing in neglect. Vallar, Sandroni, Rusconi, and Barbieri (1991) observed visual ERPs in response to contralesional stimuli that two left-neglect patients failed to detect. More recently, Spinelli, Burr, and Morone (1994) reported that while visual ERPs can be found to contralesional stimuli in neglect patients, they typically have a delayed latency relative to the ERPs for comparable ipsilesional stimuli. Such findings are consistent with the view that the deficit in neglect attenuates or delays processing for contralesional stimuli, but does not completely eliminate such processing. Further studies with ERPs and other neuroimaging techniques could be used to address exactly how far neglected stimuli can proceed through the system, by looking for physiological responses that indicate the activation of specific processes, such as visual object recognition, or face perception etc.

Recent behavioral studies suggest that residual processing can include a degree of unconscious object recognition for stimuli toward the contralesional side, in both neglect and extinction patients (see Driver, 1996, for a critical review). These behavioral studies have adapted indirect techniques from the normal attention literature, measuring the processing of contralesional stimuli by means of their impact on deliberate responses to ipsilesional stimuli. Several effects of this kind have now been reported, although it remains to be established how reliable they are across cases, and exactly how different lesions may constrain the degree of residual processing.

Audet, Bub, and Lecours (1991) adapted the interference paradigm of Eriksen and Eriksen (1974), requiring two left-neglect patients to name a target letter presented at fixation. A distractor letter was presented to its left, or above it, and its identity varied. Like normals, both patients were faster to name the fixated target if the distractor above it had the same rather than a different identity to the target (congruence effect). One of the two patients also showed a similar congruence effect when the distractor was on the left, even though he reportedly did not detect the presence of the effective left distractors, as measured by retrospective questioning. This study demonstrates that identification of contralesional stimuli (at least to a level sufficient to determine any congruence between the distractor and target letter) can take place in some but not all neglect patients. It also raises the possibility that this residual processing might be unconscious when found. However, the retrospective test for awareness of the effective contralesional events may have been insensitive, due to forgetting.

Berti and Rizzolatti (1992) also produced initial evidence for unconscious residual processing in the contralesional field. They required seven left-neglect patients to make a speeded animal/vegetable decision for target line-drawings presented in the right visual field, when preceded by a prime line-drawing in the left field. The drawings were presented briefly to preclude any role for overt eye movements during them. The contralesional prime could be identical to the ipsilesional target, from the same category, or from the opposite category. Categorizations of the ipsilesional target were slower in the latter case, even though most patients did not spontaneously report seeing any contralesional event during 24 practice trials that preceded the experiment.

This study also suggests that a degree of object recognition can take place in the contralesional field, possibly without awareness. However, one can again criticize the informal measure of awareness as potentially insensitive. Moreover, while the data clearly show that contralesional objects could be classified to some degree as animal or vegetable, it remains unclear how much visual processing this would require, because the same 14 drawings were repeatedly presented, and thus may have come to be classified on the basis of quite limited information (e.g. just an eye-like feature might be sufficient to merit an animal classification after experience with the limited set of pictures).

A priming study by McGlinchey-Berroth et al. (1993) goes furthest to date in answering these criticisms. They required four patients with left neglect (but no hemianopia), and one patient with left hemianopia (but no neglect) to decide whether a central letter-string was a word or not. This was preceded by two concurrent drawings on either side of fixation, one depicting a common object, while the other was just scrambled lines (see Fig. 8.5a). The drawings were again presented briefly to preclude eye movements during them. The main finding for neglect patients was that judgments of a central word were faster when the preceding meaningful drawing depicted a semantically related object (e.g. a pictured baseball-bat followed by the letter-string BALL). This priming effect was equivalent in size regardless of whether the related picture had been in the ipsilesional or contralesional field. By contrast, no reliable priming was found from the blind field of the hemianopic patient.

The priming from pictures on the affected side in the neglect patients suggests considerable processing for contralesional stimuli, as each picture was shown only once, and could be related to the subsequent target word only in meaning. What about the issue of whether this extensive contralesional processing was truly unconscious? McGlinchey-Berroth et al. addressed this point with a further study. The same neglect patients were again presented with prime displays comprising a drawing of a common object on one side and scrambled lines on the other side, just as before. However, they now had to make an explicit judgment about the meaningful object in this prime display, whereas previously no response had been required to it. The task was to judge which of two subsequent pictures the meaningful prime matched, either the one above fixation or the one below (see Fig. 8.5b). As a group, the patients were above chance at matching when the meaningful prime had been on the right, but at chance when it was on the left, even though left objects had produced equivalent priming to right objects in the preceding experiment.

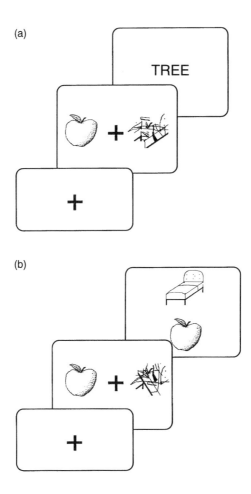

FIG. 8.5. Schematic depiction of a typical sequence of events in one trial from McGlinchey-Berroth et al.'s (1993) priming study (a), and from their matching study (b), with time running from front left to back right in each depicted sequence. In both experiments, the trial began with a fixation point for half a second, followed by a brief presentation of a meaningful drawing in one visual field (illustrated for the left visual field, or LVF) together with scrambled lines in the other field (on the right in the illustrated trials). After an empty 400 msec delay, this was followed by centralized targets which remained visible until a response to them was initiated. In the priming study (a), the drawings were irrelevant to the patients' specific task, which was to judge whether the central letter-string was a word or not. Neglect patients were faster to judge a word after a related drawing (as illustrated by the pictured apple preceding the word TREE), even if the drawing had fallen on the neglected side. In the matching task (b), the initial drawing was now relevant, as the patients had to decide which of the subsequent two targets matched it. They were at chance when the initial meaningful drawing was on the neglected side.

The claim that the contralesional priming reflects unconscious processing thus rests on extrapolation across two separate experiments with slightly different tasks, and on a measure of awareness that concerns identification rather than mere detection of contralesional events. Nevertheless, the McGlinchey et al. (1993) study does show that considerable processing can take place in the contralesional field of neglect patients, as indexed by priming, while the matching task confirms that the extent of this residual processing can be at odds with the patients' very restricted ability to judge the same contralesional stimuli explicitly.

There has been less work on the extent of residual processing in Balint's syndrome than for extinction and neglect. However, some recent results hint that considerable processing may also take place for unreportable stimuli in this class of patients. Rafal and Robertson (1995) provide a preliminary report of congruence effects from undetectable objects on response to detected targets in a Balint case. Coslett and Saffran (1991) had previously reported a Balint case who was better at identifying both stimuli in a con-current pair of words or in a pair of drawings when the two items were related in meaning.

The notion that considerable processing may still take place for patho-logically unattended stimuli in extinction, neglect, and Balint's syndrome is entirely consistent with the evidence discussed earlier for the continued operation of segmentation processes in these disorders. Moreover, the recent work with priming and interference measures provides a further illustration of the potential for fruitful interplay between normal and pathological studies of attention, as these measures have been adapted from the normal literature, and then applied to neuropsychological issues with considerable success.

Although this is encouraging, such methodological adaptations from the normal literature do run the risk of extending past mistakes to the neu-ropsychological domain, as well as previous successes. Interference or priming effects from isolated distractors in the normal literature have in the past often been taken to support extreme late-selection claims that every single one of the numerous stimuli in very complex scenes will *always* be perceived to the same full extent, regardless of the direction of attention (e.g. Tipper & Driver, 1988). Such a claim clearly goes well beyond obser-vations that a single distractor, presented on an otherwise empty back-ground, can be processed to the extent that it exerts a small influence on response to a related target (Lavie & Tsal, 1994). Subsequent work has shown that the extent of processing for distractors by normals actually depends on a variety of complex factors, such as the number of events in the scene, their spatial proximity and grouping, the load imposed by the specified task, and so on (Baylis & Driver, 1992; Lavie, 1995; Yantis & Johnston, 1990).

We should therefore be wary of leaping to any conclusion that perceptual processing is absolutely full and unlimited in the contralesional field of a neglect patient, based just on observations that isolated stimuli in that field can produce priming or interference effects. The extent of residual processing in neglect seems likely to be subject to all the complex factors that influence the extent of unattended processing in normals. We should also recall that neglect and extinction are dynamic directional biases, rather than a static deficit that applies fixedly to an entire visual field (Kinsbourne, 1993). Finally, the extent of residual processing will surely depend on the precise lesion in each particular patient.

Neglect patients typically have relatively diffuse lesions. These tend to focus on right parietal cortex (Vallar, 1993), which is itself a large and heterogeneous region. However, the lesions typically include other areas as well, as the most common aetiology is a stroke involving the middle cerebral artery, which sustains numerous brain regions. Thus, while there is undoubtedly some systematicity to the lesions that produce neglect (Vallar, 1993), no two patients will have identical lesions. It seems very unlikely that the only effect of these diffuse and variable lesions could be to prevent awareness of otherwise fully processed stimuli! Presumably, the extent of residual processing in neglect patients will depend on the exact extent of their residual brain tissue, and thus on the precise details of their lesion.

This potential variability in the extent of residual processing may actually aid rather than hinder future research. We are now able to identify the lesioned areas in individual patients with considerable accuracy, based on techniques such as CT, MRI, PET, or SPECT scanning. We also have independent sources of evidence, other than human-lesion studies, concerning the function of particular brain regions. These come from techniques such as single-cell recording in animals, or functional neuroimaging in healthy people as they carry out various tasks. Such knowledge is particularly advanced for the functions of different components in the visual system (e.g. Zeki, 1993).

We should therefore be able to predict which visual functions will still operate residually for contralesional stimuli in particular neglect or extinction patients, based on the details of their lesion. Moreover, it may ultimately be possible to rehabilitate patients' impaired functions by means of their residual functions. As one example, Mattingley, Bradshaw, and Bradshaw (1994) have recently shown that visual neglect, as measured by line bisection, can be ameliorated in some patients by using visual motion to draw their attention to the contralesional side. Presumably, this is only possible in cases where some residual processing of motion exists.

The existing findings on residual object-recognition in the contralesional field by means of visual shape (Audet et al., 1991; Berti & Rizzolatti, 1992; McGlichey-Berroth et al., 1993) may be broadly consistent with one coarse anatomical distinction between those brain areas that are usually impaired, and those that are spared in most neglect patients. A distinction is often made between "dorsal" (anatomically higher within the skull) and "ventral" (lower) pathways in the primate visual system (Goodale & Milner, 1993; Mishkin, Ungerleider, & Macko, 1983; Ungerleider & Haxby, 1994). The dorsal pathway comprises a sequence of interconnected areas running forward from primary visual cortex in the occipital lobe into the parietal lobe. The ventral pathway also starts in primary visual cortex but runs lower into the temporal lobe. The two pathways were originally distinguished in terms of their anatomical connectivity (although it should be noted that there are some connections between the two). However, most interest has focused on possible differences in their function, as suggested by the effects of lesions in humans and monkeys, and by functional neuroimaging in the former subjects and single-cell recording in the latter subjects.

Such measures have identified the ventral pathway with functions concerning object segregation, and object recognition by shape (Ungerleider & Haxby, 1994). The dorsal pathway has been associated with spatial representation and attention (Mishkin et al. 1983) and/or with the spatial control of action (Goodale & Milner, 1993). Hence, given that the prototypical lesion that induces human neglect primarily involves dorsal areas (Vallar, 1993), one might expect that object segregation and recognition would be largely spared for contralesional stimuli in neglect patients, as the findings I have reviewed suggest. These functions should still take place within intact ventral pathways, with perhaps just spatial awareness and the control of deliberate responses being impaired for stimuli toward the neglected side by the dorsal damage. I return to this idea after considering neuropsychological studies of one final issue that has dominated the normal attention literature.

FEATURE INTEGRATION IN EXTINCTION, NEGLECT, AND BALINT'S SYNDROME

The most influential recent theory of normal visual attention has been Treisman's feature-integration account (e.g. Treisman & Gelade, 1980). In original form, this proposed that simple visual features (e.g. the orientation of edges, their direction of motion, their color etc.) can be coded across the visual field all at once, without any need for focal attention. By contrast, coding the particular combination of features that each object has in a field of many objects was held to require focal attention to the position of each object in turn. This model can be seen as a sophisticated form of early selection. In common with traditional early-selection models, unattended processing is considered restricted to simple physical features. The departure from traditional views is the idea that spatial attention performs one specific function; namely, combining the various features within the attended region into a multidimensional percept.

Evidence initially consistent with this view was provided from a number of different tasks with normal subjects. For instance, in visual search, subjects may detect a target defined by a salient unique feature (e.g. a red item among green, or vertical among horizontal) as rapidly among many nontargets as among a few nontargets (so-called "parallel search", parallel in the sense that the search process can operate over all the items at the same time; see Wolfe, this volume). By contrast, when searching for a target that is unique only in its conjunction of features (e.g. a red vertical item among red horizontal and green vertical nontargets), subjects may be slowed when there are more nontargets, often in a linear fashion (Treisman & Gelade, 1980) implying that every extra item now adds another cycle around some process that takes a particular length of time (so-called "serial search", in which individual items are thought to be inspected one after the other). Such results seem consistent with the hypothesis that while simple features can be coded for all items at once (as in parallel feature search), combining the features of objects may require focal attention to the locus of each object in turn (as in serial conjunction search).

One independent source of initial support for this theory was that normal subjects can apparently miscombine briefly presented features, erroneously conjoining attributes from distinct objects together (so-called "illusory conjunctions"), when prevented from attending serially to the position of each object in turn (Treisman & Schmidt, 1982). Treisman's theory has since attracted considerable research interest, in part because of an apparent similarity between her idea that different visual features are coded independently in preattentive vision, and emerging neuroscience evidence that distinct areas of prestriate visual cortex specialise in coding different visual features (e.g. Cowey, 1985).

In subsequent years, the intense interest in Treisman's theory has led to extensive criticisms and revisions of it, in a substantial literature to which I cannot do full justice here (see Wolfe, this volume, for a review of the visual search evidence). Suffice to say that there have now been several demonstrations that covert attention can affect simple feature coding as well as conjunction coding (e.g. Briand & Klein, 1987; Posner, 1980; Prinzmetal, Presti, & Posner, 1986). There have also been numerous demonstrations that conjunction search can be parallel under some circumstances (see Wolfe, this volume). Moreover, the claim that shape features (such as the different orientations that together make up the occluding edges of an object) require attentional integration in just the same way as features from different dimensions (e.g. orientation plus color) has been particularly questioned (e.g. Davis & Driver, 1994; Enns & Rensink, 1990; Humphreys, Quinlan & Riddoch, 1989).

Despite these many criticisms, covert attention often does produce larger effects on conjunction tasks than on comparable feature tasks (e.g. Prinzmetal et al., 1986). Moreover, while several rival models now exist for the body of normal data generated by tests of feature-integration theory (e.g. Cave & Wolfe, 1990; Duncan & Humphreys, 1989; Humphreys & Müller, 1993; Treisman & Sato, 1990), there are several points in common between these alternatives. First, distinct items in the visual field compete for attention (usually operationalized as some visual short-term memory stage, some inspection process, or control of responding). Second, features on different visual dimensions are initially coded independently. Third, grouping processes modulate the competition for attention (as required to accommodate results such as those discussed earlier in the sections on segmentation). Fourth, attentional competition is usually played out in a spatial medium; typically by means of activity in a "master map" of visual locations, intended to represent the current spatial distribution of attention (see Wolfe, this volume). Thus, there is some consensus in the normal literature, and apparently a substantial germ of truth behind feature-integration theory.

I turn now to consider the neuropsychological literature on this topic, which is scarcer. The most simple-minded prediction that might be derived from feature-integration theory as regards attention deficits is that these deficits should affect only conjunction tasks, not feature tasks. This is clearly not so in most cases; patients with extinction, neglect, and Balint's syndrome can all be impaired in the conscious detection of simple features, as when an extinction patient fails to detect the more contralesional of two wiggling fingers. On the other hand, covert attention is now known to affect coding of features as well as of conjunctions in normals (e.g. Prinzmetal et al., 1986), and thus attentional biases in patients would be expected to influence feature tasks also. The normal findings show only *larger* effects on conjunction than on feature tasks (Prinzmetal et al., 1986). Thus, a more subtle hypothesis can be proposed; attentional deficits might affect both feature and conjunction tasks, but should usually disrupt the latter more substantially.

Cohen and Rafal (1991) tested this possibility in several extinction patients with unilateral parietal injury, with a task of first naming a central digit (to ensure central fixation, and to occupy attention) and then the color and shape of a concurrent peripheral target letter, presented together with a nontarget letter that was always an O but could appear in various colors. The measure of interest was the number of feature errors (e.g. reporting a color that was not presented) and of conjunction errors (e.g. mistakenly ascribing the color of the nontarget O to the target letter) for letters on the ipsilesional versus contralesional side.

The majority of extinction patients simply could not perform this task (Cohen & Rafal, personal communication). They made so many errors for the contralesional target letter (seeing none, and therefore refusing to respond, or just guessing) that the relative proportion of feature and conjunction errors could not be sensibly measured. This poses a methodological problem (the opposite of the ceiling effect discussed earlier) known as a "floor effect". When performance on the feature task (i.e. identifying any color on the contralesional side) is already at chance, no greater difficulty in the conjunction task (i.e. reporting the correct combination of color and shape for just the target letter) can possibly be measured. Such floor effects may obscure greater difficulties with conjunction tasks than feature tasks for many neglect patients.

Cohen and Rafal (1991) also tested one patient who showed only very mild extinction, no longer detectable by confrontation methods but evident in computer tests. Their report concentrated on just this left-hemisphere case. She showed disproportionately many more conjunction errors than feature errors in the contralesional field as compared with the ipsilesional field, after naming the central digit. Cohen and Rafal therefore concluded that her parietal damage had especially impaired feature conjunction for stimuli toward the affected side. This impairment was eliminated when she was presented with the very same displays, but now allowed to ignore the central digit and concentrate just on the peripheral letters. These findings therefore provide another example of extinction (in this case for conjunctions) depending on competition with a *relevant* ipsilesional event (cf. Karnath, 1988).

Riddoch and Humphreys (1987) gave feature and conjunction search tasks to several left-neglect patients, always presenting nontarget stimuli in both visual fields. Reaction times to detect feature targets were scarcely affected by the number of nontargets presented concurrently (as in normals), and there was little difference in the speed of response for contralesional versus ipsilesional feature targets. By contrast, search was slowed by additional nontargets in the conjunction task (as in normals), and contralesional targets were now detected much more slowly than ipsilesional targets. These latency data appear consistent with the strong prediction that only conjunction tasks should be impaired by the attentional deficit. However, the error rates revealed that the patients missed many contralesional targets, but few ipsilesional targets, in both conjunction *and* feature tasks; thus feature performance was not entirely normal toward the affected side.

Eglin, Robertson, and Knight (1989) gave seven neglect patients modified versions of conjunction search and feature search. There was now always one target in each display, with the patient having to locate it by pointing, rather than judging its presence or absence as in the usual task. This modification was intended to circumvent the numerous misses observed by Riddoch and Humphreys (1987), which can complicate the interpretation of reaction-time data. Each display presented stimuli either on just the ipsilesional side of the patient, just the contralesional, or on both sides; although as the patients could move their eyes, and some had hemianopia, every stimulus may ultimately have entered the ipsilesional visual field.

Increasing the number of nontargets delayed the conjunction task more than the feature task, as in normals. This effect was equivalent within ipsilesional displays and contralesional displays (perhaps, as noted, because eye movements took place). Finally, in bilateral displays, responses to contralesional targets were substantially delayed by the addition of nontargets on the ipsilesional side, whereas the addition of contralesional nontargets did not delay responses to ipsilesional targets. This abnormality was much more marked in the conjunction task than in the feature task.

Finally, Arguin, Joanette, and Cavanagh (1993) studied a group of patients with left-hemisphere damage who showed attentional abnormalities in a variant of Posner's (1980) cuing task. They examined feature-and conjunction-search performance for brief displays while ensuring that central fixation was maintained. The patients showed slower search rates in the contralesional field than the ipsilesional field for the conjunction task, but there was no such effect on feature search.

Thus several studies have now shown that spatially specific attention deficits can be more pronounced in conjunction tasks than in feature tasks. However, these studies have not yet established that such an exaggeration of the deficit applies only when feature *conjunction* in particular is required; it might be produced by any manipulation that makes the task more demanding. Indeed, Humphreys and Riddoch (1993) report that search by neglect patients can be impaired disproportionately for contralesional targets by feature-based manipulations that make search harder in normals (e.g. increased target–nontarget similarity, or nontarget heterogeneity; Duncan & Humphreys, 1989). Similarly, Robertson and Eglin (1993) report that contralesional search difficulties in neglect patients are exaggerated when the target is defined only by the absence of a feature (e.g. an O among Qs) rather than by the presence of a unique feature (e.g. a Q among Os). This accords with the greater difficulty of feature-absent searches in normals (Treisman & Gormican, 1988).

There has been little study of visual search or feature integration in Balint's patients. Rafal and Robertson (1995) provide a preliminary report of a Balint patient who detects feature targets more readily than conjunction targets, and can detect a Q among Os, but not an O among Qs. This suggests that which object the Balint patient first locks onto may be determined by some of the same factors that influence attentional capture in normals. As for the possibility of illusory conjunctions, most case reports have stressed that Balint patients correctly integrate the features of the individual objects they experience (e.g. Farah, 1990). However, this conclusion has usually been based on descriptions or judgments concerning the *shape* of particular objects (i.e. their specific conjunction of oriented lines etc.) rather than on assessments of feature conjunction across different dimensions (e.g. linking shapes together with the appropriate colors). Recall that in the normal literature, the hypothesis that attention is required to conjoin the various features of an object within the shape dimension (such as the oriented lines that comprise it) has been particularly criticized (Davis & Driver, 1994; Enns & Rensink, 1990; Humphreys et al., 1989).

Friedman-Hill, Robertson, and Treisman (1995) recently examined the across-dimension conjunction of colours with shapes in a Balint case. The patient made an extraordinarily high rate of illusory conjunctions. When presented with two colored shapes, he was very likely to miscombine the color of one stimulus with the shape of the other in his report, even with quite lengthy exposures. This may be consistent with Treisman's proposal that location plays a special role in attentional feature integration across dimensions. Severe Balint patients are typically unable to locate stimuli accurately, both in their conscious judgments, and in their motor behavior (e.g. grossly misreaching for visual objects). Such loss of location information may preclude knowledge of which color goes with which shape. It will be interesting to examine whether such impairments apply only for conscious knowledge, or also to the residual processing that might be revealed by interference and priming measures.

CONCLUSIONS

I have reviewed recent neuropsychological work relating to three main issues that have dominated the normal literature on visual attention; the relation between segmentation and spatial attention, the extent of unattended processing, and the nature of feature integration. Restrictions on the available space have precluded coverage of a host of further issues thrown up by neuropsychological research, which might usefully broaden the agenda of normal research. These include: possible hemisphere differences in attentional control, which might explain the predominance of left over right neglect; separate attentional systems for different spatial domains; the role of motor programming in producing shifts of attention; and the interactions between multiple sensory modalities in attentional control (see Driver & Mattingley, 1995; Robertson & Marshall, 1993, for reviews of these further issues). Nevertheless, I hope I have covered sufficient material here to indicate the potential fruitfulness of a combined normal and neuropsychological approach to attention.

On the first issue of segmentation, the neuropsychological data strongly suggest that some compromise must be reached between the purely space-based and purely object-based models of attention that have dominated recent normal work. The patient evidence implies that spatial attention is directed within a segmented representation of the visual scene, with at least some of this segmentation taking place preattentively. Recent normal data converge on this conclusion (e.g. Lavie & Driver, 1996).

On the second issue, concerning the extent of processing for unattended/ neglected stimuli, the neuropsychological studies have borrowed usefully from methods in the normal literature, and have provided some compelling examples of thorough implicit processing for stimuli that apparently cannot be reported explicitly. Much further work is required on this topic, however. On the third issue of feature integration, several studies have confirmed that the neurological deficits are more severe in tasks that are more attention demanding, consistent with the initial characterisation of these deficits as attentional in nature.

Can any overarching perspective be presented to accommodate the neuropsychological evidence on all three issues? It may be premature to attempt this. Nonetheless, the current data may be broadly consistent with, on the one hand, the special role often suggested for location in the direction of attention, and in feature integration (both thought to operate in a spatial medium); and on the other hand, the dorsal lesion that is typically involved in the disorders I have reviewed. As discussed earlier, dorsal visual pathways have long been associated with spatial representation, and more recently with the spatial control of action. By contrast, ventral visual pathways have been associated with visual segmentation, with the extraction of visual features such as color, and with recognition of visual objects by means of shape-based access to long-term memory representations.

Against this anatomical background, it may be less surprising to find that implicit segmentation, feature coding, and shape-based recognition (presumed to be ventral functions) can be relatively spared in patients with attentional deficits (due to dorsal lesions). However, this still leaves a striking gap between the extent of such residual processing for contralesional stimuli, and the patients' frequent inability to become aware of these stimuli, or respond overtly to them. This might perhaps be explained if some linkage between ventral properties (e.g. the shape-based identity of an object) and dorsal properties (e.g. the current position, size, and orientation of the ventrally identified object) is required for a person to become fully aware of an object, or to make a deliberate response toward it. Baylis, Driver, and Rafal (1993) have proposed exactly this. Such linkage between dorsal and ventral properties might be seen as an anatomical extension of Treisman's feature-integration idea.

Without the coherent spatial framework that the dorsal pathway normally provides to code the current disposition of objects in the scene, our awareness might be restricted to individual, disembodied objects that cannot be related to each other. This is apparently the dilemma faced by Balint cases. Moreover, if our awareness of the distinction between separate objects is normally based primarily on their differing spatial locations, as argued by the philosopher Leibniz, then we may begin to understand the difficulty that Balint cases have in shifting their attention to new objects, away from the current focus of attention. Essentially, they may have lost the primary spatial means of differentiating new objects from those already attended within a scene. In the case of neglect and extinction patients, such deficits in spatial representation would apply only for items toward the contralesional side, restricting awareness of these objects however full their residual ventral processing might be.

Whatever the truth of such speculations, further study of extinction, neglect, and Balint patients may allow unique insights into the complex interactions between neural subsystems, such as the ventral and dorsal pathways, which take place so profusely and efficiently within the normal system that they are often extremely difficult to unravel.

REFERENCES

Allport, A. (1993). Attention and control: Have we been asking the wrong questions? A critical review of twenty-five years. In D.E. Meyer & S. Kornblum (Eds.), *Attention and performance XIV*. Cambridge, MA: MIT Press.

Anderson, B. (1993). Spared awareness for the left side of internal visual images in patients with left-sided extrapersonal neglect. *Neurology, 43*, 213–216.

Anton, G. (1899). Uber die Selbstwahrnehmung der Herderkrankungen des Gehirns durch den Kranken bei Rindenblindheit und Rindentaubheit. *Archive Psychiatre Nervenkrasse, 32*, 86–111.

Arguin, M., Joanette, Y., & Cavanagh, P. (1993). Visual search for feature and conjunction targets with an attention deficit. *Journal of Cognitive Neuroscience, 5*, 436–452.

Audet, T., Bub, D., & Lecours, A.R. (1991). Visual neglect and left-sided context effects. *Brain and Cognition, 16*, 11–28.

Balint, R. (1909). Seelenhamung des "Schauens", optisches ataxie, raumlische stoung des afmersamkeit. *Monatschrift Psychiatrie und Neurologie, 25*, 51–81.

Baylis, G.C., & Driver, J. (1992). Visual parsing and response competition: The effects of grouping. *Perception and Psychophysics, 51*, 145–162.

Baylis, G.C., & Driver, J. (1993). Visual attention and objects: Evidence for hierarchical coding of location. *Journal of Experimental Psychology: Human Perception and Performance, 19*, 451–470.

Baylis, G.C., Driver, J., Baylis, L., & Rafal, R.D. (1994). Reading of letters and words in a patient with Balint's syndrome. *Neuropsychologia, 32*, 1273–1286.

Baylis, G.C., Driver, J., & Rafal, R.D. (1993). Visual extinction and stimulus repetition. *Journal of Cognitive Neuroscience, 5*, 453–466.

Bender, M.B. (1952). *Disorders in perception*. Springfield, IL: Charles C. Thomas.

Berti, A., & Rizzolatti, G. (1992). Visual processing without awareness: Evidence from unilateral neglect. *Journal of Cognitive Neuroscience, 4*, 345–351.

Bisiach, E., Capitani, E., & Porta, A. (1985). Two basic properties of space representation in the brain. *Journal of Neurology, Neurosurgery, and Psychiatry, 48*, 141–144.

Bisiach, E., Cornacchia, L., Sterzi, R., & Vallar, G. (1984). Disorders of perceived auditory lateralization of the right hemisphere. *Brain, 107*, 37–52.

Bisiach, E., & Luzzatti, C. (1988). Unilateral neglect of representational space. *Cortex, 26*, 307–317.

Bisach, E., & Vallar, G. (1988). Hemineglect in humans. In F. Boller & J. Grafman (Eds.), *Handbook of neuropsychology: Vol. 1.* Amsterdam: Elsevier.

Briand, K., & Klein, R.M. (1987). Is Posner's "beam" the same as Treisman's "glue"?: On the relation between visual orienting and feature integration theory. *Journal of Experimental Psychology: Human Perception and Performance, 13*, 228–241.

Cave, K.R., & Wolfe, J.M. (1990). Modeling the role of parallel processing in visual search. *Cognitive Psychology, 22*, 225–271.

Cherry, E.C. (1953). Some experiments on the recognition of speech with one and with two ears. *Journal of the Acoustical Society of America, 25*, 975–979.

Cohen, A., & Rafal, R.D. (1991). Attention and visual feature integration in a patient with a parietal lobe lesion. *Psychological Science, 2*, 106–110.

Cohen, J.D., Farah, M.J., Romero, R.D., & Servan-Schreiber, D. (1994). Mechanisms of spatial attention: The relation of macrostructure to microstructure in parietal neglect. *Journal of Cognitive Neuroscience, 6*, 377–387.

Coslett, H.B., & Saffran, E. (1991). Simultanagnosia: To see but not two see. *Brain, 113*, 475–486.

Cowey, A. (1985). Aspects of cortical organisation related to selective attention and selective impairments of visual perception: A tutorial review. In M.I. Posner & O.S.M. Marin (Eds.), *Attention and performance XI* (pp.41–62). Hillsdale, NJ: Lawrence Erlbaum Associates Inc.

Davis, G., & Driver, J. (1994). Parallel detection of Kanizsa subjective figures in the human visual system. *Nature, 371*, 791–793.

Davis, G., & Driver, J. (in press). Kanizsa subjective figures can act as occluding surfaces at parallel stages of visual search. *Journal of Experimental Psychology: Human Perception and Performance.*

De Renzi, E. (1982). *Disorders of space exploration and cognition.* New York: Wiley.

Diller, L., & Riley, E. (1993). The behavioural management of neglect. In I.H. Robertson & J.C. Marshall (Eds.), *Unilateral neglect: Clinical and experimental findings.* Hove, UK: Lawrence Erlbaum Associates Ltd.

Di Pellegrino, G., & De Renzi, E. (1995). An experimental investigation on the nature of extinction. *Neuropsychologia, 33*, 153–170.

Driver, J. (1996). What can visual neglect and extinction reveal about the extent of "pre-attentive" processing? In A.F. Kramer, M.G.H. Coles, & G.D. Logan (Eds.), *Convergent methods in the study of visual selective attention.* Washington, DC: American Psychological Association.

Driver, J., & Baylis, G.C. (1989). Movement and visual attention: The spotlight metaphor breaks down. *Journal of Experimental Psychology: Human Perception and Performance, 15*, 448–456.

Driver, J., Baylis, G.C., Goodrich, S.J., & Rafal, R.D. (1994). Axis-based neglect of visual shapes. *Neuropsychologia, 32*, 1353–1365.

Driver, J., Baylis, G.C., & Rafal, R.D. (1992). Preserved figure–ground segregation and symmetry perception in visual neglect. *Nature, 360*, 73–74.

Driver, J., Goodrich, S., Ward, R., & Rafal, R.D. (1996). Object segmentation affects both Balint's syndrome and visual extinction. Manuscript submitted for publication.

Driver, J., & Halligan, P.W. (1991). Can visual neglect operate in object-centred coordinates?: An affirmative single-case study. *Cognitive Neuropsychology, 8*, 475–496.

Driver, J., & Mattingley, J.B. (1995). Normal and pathological selective attention in humans. *Current Opinion in Neurobiology, 5*, 191–197.

Driver, J., Mattingley, J.B., Rorden, C., & Davis, G. (1997). Extinction as a paradigm measure of attentional bias and restricted capacity following brain injury. In P. Thier & H.O.

Karnath (Eds.), *Parietal lobe contributions to orientation in 3D space.* Heidelberg: Springer-Verlag.

Duncan, J. (1980). The locus of interference in the perception of simultaneous stimuli. *Psychological Review, 87,* 272–300.

Duncan, J. (1984). Selective attention and the organization of visual information. *Journal of Experimental Psychology: General, 113,* 501–517.

Duncan, J. (1985). Visual search and visual attention. In M.I. Posner & O.S.M. Marin (Eds), *Attention and performance XI* (pp.85–104). Hillsdale, NJ: Lawrence Erlbaum Associates Inc.

Duncan, J., & Humphreys, G.W. (1989). Visual search and stimulus similarity. *Psychological Review, 96,* 433–458.

Eglin, M., Robertson, L.C., & Knight, R.T. (1989). Visual search performance in the neglect syndrome. *Journal of Cognitive Neuroscience, 1,* 372–385.

Enns, J.T., & Rensink, R.A. (1990). Sensitivity to three-dimensional orientation in visual search. *Psychological Science, 1,* 323–326.

Enns, J.T., & Rensink, R.A. (1992). An object completion process in early vision. *Investigative Ophthalmology and Visual Science, 33,* 1263.

Eriksen, B.A., & Eriksen, C.W. (1974). Effects of noise-letters on identification of a target letter in a nonsearch task. *Perception and Psychophysics, 16,* 143–149.

Eriksen, C.W., & Spencer, T. (1969). Rate of information processing in visual perception: Some results and methodological considerations. *Journal of Experimental Psychology: Monograph, 79,* 1–16.

Farah, M.J. (1990). *Visual agnosia: Disorders of object recognition and what they tell us about normal vision.* Cambridge, MA: MIT Press.

Farah, M.J., Wallace, M.A., & Vecera, S.P. (1993). What and where in visual attention. In I.H. Robertson & J.C. Marshall (Eds.), *Unilateral neglect.* Hove, UK: Lawrence Erlbaum Associates Ltd.

Friedman-Hill, S.R., Robertson, L.C., & Treisman, A. (1995). Parietal contributions to visual feature binding: Evidence from a patient with bilateral lesions. *Science, 269,* 853–855.

Gainotti, G., Messerli, P., & Tissot, R. (1972). Qualitative analysis of unilateral and spatial neglect in relation to laterality of cerebral lesions. *Journal of Neurology, Neurosurgery and Psychiatry, 35,* 545–550.

Goodale, M.A., & Milner, A.D. (1993). Separate visual pathways for perception and action. *Trends in Neuroscience, 15,* 20–25.

Guariglia, C., Padovani, A., Pantano, P., & Pizzamiglio, L. (1993). Unilateral neglect restricted to visual imagery. *Nature, 364,* 235–237.

Halligan, P.W., & Marshall, J.C. (1992). Left visuospatial neglect: A meaningless entity? *Cortex, 8,* 525–535.

Halligan, P.W., & Marshall, J.C., (Eds.) (1994a). Spatial neglect: Position papers on theory and practice. *Neuropsychological Rehabilitation, 4,* 97–240.

Halligan, P.W., & Marshall, J.C. (1994b). Towards a principled explanation of unilateral neglect. *Cognitive Neuropsychology, 11,* 167–206.

Halligan, P.W., Marshall, J.C., & Wade, D.T. (1990). Do visual field deficits exacerbate visuospatial neglect? *Journal of Neurology, Neurosurgery and Psychiatry, 53,* 487–491.

Harvey, M., Milner, A.D., & Roberts, R.C. (1994). Spatial bias in visually-guided reaching and bisection following right cerebral stroke. *Cortex, 30,* 343–350.

Heilman, K.M., Watson, R.T., & Valenstein, E. (1985). Neglect and related disorders. In K.M. Heilman & E. Valenstein (Eds.), *Clinical neuropsychology.* Oxford: Oxford University Press.

Holmes, G. & Horrax, G. (1919). Disturbances of spatial orientation and visual attention with loss of stereoscopic vision. *Archives of Neurology and Psychiatry, 1,* 385–407.

Hughlings Jackson, J. (1876). Case of large cerebral tumour without optic neuritis and with left hemiplegia and imperception. *Royal Opthalmological Hospital Reports, 8,* 434–444.

Humphreys, G.W., & Müller, H.J. (1993). SEarch via Recursive Rejection (SERR): A connectionist model of visual search. *Cognitive Psychology, 25,* 43–110.

Humphreys, G.W., Quinlan, P.T., & Riddoch, M.J. (1989). Grouping processes in visual search: Effects with single-and combined-feature targets. *Journal of Experimental Psychology: General, 118,* 258–279.

Humphreys, G.W., & Riddoch, M.J. (1993). Interaction between space-based and object-based systems revealed through neuropsychology. In D.E. Meyer & S. Kornblum (Ed.), *Attention and Performance XIV.* Hillsdale, NJ: Lawrence Erlbaum Associates Inc.

Kahneman, D., & Treisman, A. (1984). Changing views of attention and automaticity. In R. Parasuraman & D.R. Davies (Eds.), *Varieties of attention.* Orlando, FL: Academic Press.

Kanizsa, G. (1979). *Organization in vision.* New York: Praeger.

Kanwisher, N.G., & Driver, J. (1992). Objects, attributes and visual attention: Which, what and where. *Current Directions in Psychological Science, 1,* 26–31.

Karnath, H. (1988). Deficits of attention in acute and recovered visual hemineglect. *Neuropsychologia, 26,* 27–43.

Karnath, H.O., & Fetter, M. (1995). Ocular space exploration in the dark and its relation to subjective and objective body orientation in neglect patients with parietal lesions. *Neuropsychologia, 33,* 371–377.

Kinsbourne, M. (1977). Hemineglect and hemispheric rivalry. *Advances in Neurology, 18,* 41–49.

Kinsbourne, M. (1993). Orientational bias model of unilateral neglect. In I.H. Robertson & J.C. Marshall (Eds.), *Unilateral neglect: Clinical and experimental findings.* Hove, UK: Lawrence Erlbaum Associates Ltd.

Lavie, N. (1995). Perceptual load as a necessary condition for selective attention. *Journal of Experimental Psychology: Human Perception and Performance, 21,* 451–468.

Lavie, N., & Driver, J. (1996). On the spatial extent of attention in object-based visual selection. *Perception and Psychophysics, 58,* 1238–1251.

Lavie, N., & Tsal, Y. (1994). Perceptual load as a major determinant of the locus of selection in visual attention. *Perception and Psychophysics, 56,* 183–197.

Luria, A.R. (1959). Disorders of "simultaneous perception" in a case of bilateral occipito-parietal brain injury. *Brain, 83,* 437–449.

Luria, A.R., Pravdina-Vinarskaya, E.N., & Yarbuss, A.L. (1963). Disorders of ocular movement in a case of simultanagnosia. *Brain, 86,* 219–228.

Marr, D., & Nishihara, H.K. (1978). Representation and recognition of the spatial organisation of three-dimensional shapes. *Proceedings of the Royal Society of London, B200,* 269–294.

Marshall, J.C., & Halligan, P.W. (1994). The yin and yang of visuo-spatial neglect: A case study. *Neuropsychologia, 32,* 1037.

Mattingley, J.B., Bradshaw, J.L., & Bradshaw, J.A. (1994). Horizontal visual motion modulates focal attention in left unilateral spatial neglect. *Journal of Neurology, Neurosurgery and Psychiatry, 57,* 1228–1235.

Mattingley, J.B., Davis, G., & Driver, J. (1997). Preattentive filling-in of visual surfaces in parietal extinction. *Science, 275,* 671–674.

Mattingley, J.B., & Driver, J. (1997). Distinguishing sensory and motor deficits after parietal damage: An evaluation of response selection biases in unilateral neglect. In P. Thier & H.O. Karnath (Eds.), *Parietal lobe contributions to orientation in 3D space.* Heidelberg: Springer-Verlag.

McCarthy, R.A., & Warrington, E.K. (1990). *Cognitive neuropsychology: A clinical introduction.* San Diego, CA: Academic Press.

McGlinchey-Berroth, R., Milberg, W.P., Verfaellie, M., Alexander, M., & Kilduff, P.T. (1993). Semantic processing in the neglected visual field: Evidence from a lexical decision task. *Cognitive Neuropsychology, 10,* 79–108.

Miller, J. (1987). Priming is not necessary for selective attention failure: Semantic effects of unattended, unprimed letters. *Perception and Psychophysics, 41,* 419–434.

Mishkin, M., Ungerleider, L.G., & Macko, K.A. (1983). Object vision and spatial vision: Two cortical pathways. *Trends in Neuroscience, 6,* 414–417.

Moray, N. (1975). A database for theories of selective listening. In P.M.A. Rabbitt & S. Dornic (Eds.), *Attention and Performance V,* (pp.119–135). New York: Academic Press.

Morrow, L.A., & Ratcliff, G. (1987). Attentional mechanisms in clinical neglect. *Journal of Clinical and Experimental Neuropsychology, 9,* 74–75.

Neisser, U. (1967). *Cognitive psychology.* New York: Appleton.

Neisser, U., & Becklen, R. (1975). Selective looking: Attending to visually specified events. *Cognitive Psychology, 7,* 480–494.

Oppenheim, H. (1885). Ueber eine durch eine klinisch bisher nicht verwerthete Untersuchungsmethode ermittelte Form der Sensibilitatsstoerung bei einseitigen Erkrankugen des Grosshirns. *Neurologisches Centralblatt, 4,* 529–533.

Ostry, D., Moray, N., & Marks, G. (1976). Attention, practice, and semantic targets. *Journal of Experimental Psychology: Human Perception and Performance, 2,* 326–336.

Pashler, H. (1995). Attention and visual perception: Analyzing divided attention. In S.M. Kosslyn & D.N. Osherson (Eds.), *Visual cognition: An invitation to cognitive science,* (2nd ed.). Cambridge, MA: MIT Press.

Paterson, A., & Zangwill, O.L. (1944). Disorders of visual space perception associated with lesions of the right cerebral hemisphere. *Brain, 67,* 331–358.

Pomerantz, J.R., & Garner, W.R. (1973). Stimulus configurations in selective attention tasks. *Perception and Psychophysics, 14,* 565–569.

Posner, M.I. (1980). Orienting of attention. *Quarterly Journal of Experimental Psychology, 32,* 3–25.

Posner, M.I., Walker, J.A., Friedrich, F.J., & Rafal, R.D. (1984). Effects of parietal injury on covert orienting of attention. *Journal of Neuroscience, 4,* 1863–1874.

Posner, M.I., Walker J.A., Friedrich, F.J., & Rafal, R.D. (1987). How do the parietal lobes direct covert attention? *Neuropsychologia, 25,* 135–146.

Prinzmetal, W., Presti, D., & Posner, M.I. (1986). Does attention affect visual feature integration? *Journal of Experimental Psychology: Human Perception and Performance, 12,* 361–370.

Rafal, R.D. (1994). Neglect. *Current Opinion in Neurobiology, 4,* 231–236.

Rafal, R.D., & Robertson, L.C. (1995). The neurology of visual attention. In M. Gazzaniga (Ed.), *The cognitive neurosciences.* Cambridge, MA: MIT Press.

Riddoch, M.J., & Humphreys, G.W. (1983). The effect of cuing on unilateral neglect. *Neuropsychologia, 21,* 589–599.

Riddoch, M.J., & Humphreys, G.W. (1987). Perceptual and action systems in unilateral visual neglect. In M. Jeanneford (Ed.), *Neurophysiological and neuropsychological aspects of spatial neglect.* Amsterdam. Elsevier.

Robertson, I.H., & Marshall, J.C. (1993). *Unilateral neglect: Clinical and experimental findings.* Hove, UK: Lawrence Erlbaum Associates Ltd.

Robertson, L.C., & Eglin, M. (1993). Attentional search in unilateral visual neglect. In I.H. Robertson & J.C. Marshall (Eds.), *Unilateral neglect: Clinical and experimental findings.* Hove, UK: Lawrence Erlbaum Associates Ltd.

Rock, I., & Guttman, D. (1981). The effect of inattention on form perception. *Journal of Experimental Psychology: Human Perception and Performance, 7,* 275–285.

Rock, I., Linnett, C.M., Grant, P., & Mack, A. (1992). Perception without attention: Results of a new method. *Cognitive Psychology, 24,* 502–534.

Rorden, C., Mattingley, J.B., Karnath, H.O., & Driver, J. (1997). Visual extinction and prior entry: Impaired perception of temporal order with intact motion perception after parietal injury. *Neuropsychologia, 35*, 421–433.

Shallice, T. (1988). *From neuropsychology to mental structure.* Cambridge: Cambridge University Press.

Shiffrin, R.M., & Gardner, G.T. (1972). Visual processing capacity and attentional control. *Journal of Experimental Psychology, 93*, 78–82.

Sperling, G. (1960). The information available in brief visual presentations. *Psychological Monographs: General and Applied* (Whole No. 498), 1–29.

Spinelli, D., Burr, D.C., & Morrone, M.C. (1994). Spatial neglect is associated with increased latencies of visual evoked potentials. *Visual Neuroscience, 11*, 909–918.

Tipper, S.P. (1985). The negative priming effect: Inhibitory priming by ignored objects. *Quarterly Journal of Experimental Psychology, 37*A, 571–590.

Tipper, S.P., & Driver, J. (1988). Negative priming between pictures and words in a selective attention task. *Memory and Cognition, 16*, 64–70.

Treisman, A. & Gelade, G. (1980). A feature-integration theory of attention. *Cognitive Psychology, 12*, 97–136.

Treisman, A., & Gormican, S. (1988). Feature analysis in early vision: Evidence from search asymmetries. *Psychological Review, 95*, 15–48.

Treisman, A., & Sato, S. (1990). Conjunction search revisited. *Journal of Experimental Psychology: Human Perception and Performance, 16*, 459–478.

Treisman, A. & Schmidt, H. (1982). Illusory conjunctions in the perception of objects. *Cognitive Psychology, 14*, 107–141.

Tsal, Y., & Lavie, N. (1993). Location dominance in attending to color and shape. *Journal of Experimental Psychology: Human Perception and Performance, 19*, 131–139.

Ungerleider, L.G., & Haxby, J.V. (1994). "What" and "where" in the human brain. *Current Opinion in Neurobiology, 4*, 157–165.

Vallar, G. (1993). The anatomical basis of spatial hemineglect in humans. In I.H. Robertson & J.C. Marshall (Eds.), *Unilateral neglect: Clinical and experimental findings.* Hove, UK: Lawrence Erlbaum Associates Inc.

Vallar, G., Antonucci, C., Guariglia, C., & Pizzamiglio. L. (1993). Deficits in position sense, unilateral neglect, and optokinetic stimulation. *Neuropsychologia, 31*, 1191–1200.

Vallar, G., Rusconi, M.L., Bignamini, L., Geminiani, G., & Perani, D. (1994). Anatomical correlates of visual and tactile extinction in humans: A clinical CT scan study. *Journal of Neurology, Neurosurgery and Psychiatry, 57*, 464–470.

Vallar, G., Sandroni, P., Rusconi, M.L., & Barbieri, S. (1991). Hemianopia, hemianethesia, and spatial neglect. *Neurology, 41*, 1918–1922.

Verfaellie, M., Rapcsak, S.Z., & Heilman, K.M. (1990). Impaired shifting of attention in Balint's syndrome. *Brain and Cognition, 12*, 195–204.

Walker, R., Findlay, J.M., Young, A.W., & Lincoln, N.B. (1996). Saccadic eye-movements in object-based neglect. *Cognitive Neuropsychology, 13*, 569–615.

Ward, R., Goodrich, S., & Driver, J. (1994). Grouping reduces visual extinction: Neuropsychological evidence for weight-linkage in visual selection. *Visual Cognition, 1*, 101–129.

Wertheimer, M. (1923). Untersuchen zu lehre von der Gestalt. *Psychologische Forschung, 1*, 47–58.

Yantis, S., & Johnston, J.C. (1990). On the locus of visual selective attention: Evidence from focused attention tasks. *Journal of Experimental Psychology: Human Perception and Performance, 16*, 135–149.

Zeki, S. (1993). *A vision of the brain.* Oxford: Blackwell.

CHAPTER NINE

Computational modeling of spatial attention

Michael C. Mozer and Mark Sitton
University of Colorado, USA

INTRODUCTION

If we had really huge brains, say the size of watermelons, attention would play a much smaller role in our behavior. Its significance stems primarily from limitations in our processing hardware. We simply do not have sufficient brain capacity to analyze all information that passes through our sense organs, to reason exhaustively about all possible courses of action, and to maintain multiple interpretations of the world. Attentional selection is needed to determine what information will be processed by the available hardware.

Consider the task of recognizing objects in a visual scene. What sort of processing resources would be required to identify all objects in parallel, regardless of their positions, orientations, and size in the scene? If we are familiar with o different objects, and any object can appear in any of p horizontal or vertical positions and r orientations and s scales, the number of different object instantiations is op^2rs. This number would be far larger still if the objects are not rigid. Regardless of the nature of the recognition process, the number of possible object instantiations roughly determines the amount of processing resources required. You can plug in reasonable guesses as to how many object instantiations are possible; 100 million might be a reasonable ballpark figure. If we limit ourselves to one object at a time, however, and the object's position, orientation, and scale are computed first, then the number of object instantiations that have to be considered at once is only *o*, or a number more like 10,000. Ballard (1986) and Tsotsos (1990, 1991) have presented computational complexity analyses of this sort to argue that the combinatorics of vision require some type of attentional selection to reduce the number of possibilities that need to be considered, and that attention can be particularly beneficial when exploiting knowledge of the particular task being faced by the visual system.

In accord with the computational arguments, human vision shows strong limitations on how many objects can be processed and identified in parallel (e.g. Duncan, 1987; Mozer, 1983, 1989; Pashler & Badgio, 1987; Schneider & Shiffrin, 1977; Shiffrin & Gardner, 1972; Treisman & Schmidt, 1982). In general terms, one can conceive of processing of a visual stimulus as occurring along a certain neural *pathway*. If the processing pathways for two stimuli are nonoverlapping, then processing can take place in parallel. But if the pathways cross—i.e. they share common resources or hardware—the stimuli will interact or interfere with one another. One role of attention is to reduce this interference by restricting the amount of information that is processed at once.

In this chapter, we examine the role of spatial attention from a computational perspective. Because the function of attention can be understood only in its relation to visual information processing, we must model not only the attentional system itself, but also the process of object recognition. We begin by presenting a basic model of object recognition, showing that interference prevents the system from reliably processing multiple, complex stimuli, and then we show how a simple mechanism of attentional selection can reduce this interference. Our initial goal will be to present a model that is computationally adequate; that is, a model that has the computational power to perform the sort of visual information processing tasks that people do. Psychologists are most concerned with another issue: whether the model can explain various experimental findings and whether it has any ability to predict the outcome of further experiments. In our view, the demands of computational adequacy and explanatory/predictive power are complementary, and a compelling account should satisfy both, and in so doing, allow one to understand the mechanisms that underlie information processing.

WHAT IS A COMPUTATIONAL MODEL?

Models are often divided into two categories: *descriptive* and *process* models. Descriptive models primarily describe the data obtained from experiments via mathematical equations. In contrast, process models explain the cognitive mechanisms underlying performance in a task. Process models vary in their abstractness, from qualitative verbal descriptions to quantitative computer simulations that embody the cognitive process. Computational models are process models that lean toward the quantitative end of the spectrum.

Computational models come in many varieties. In the area of spatial attention, some models are abstract mathematical characterizations of behavior (e.g. Bundesen, 1990; Sperling & Weichselgartner, 1995), others are algorithmic, describing behavior in a sequence of steps much like a computer program (e.g. Ullman, 1984; Weismeyer & Laird, 1990), and still others, called *connectionist* or *neural network* models, attempt to capture the operation and functional architecture of the brain. Connectionist models are large networks of simple, autonomous, neuron-like processing elements (McClelland, Rumelhart, & Hinton, 1986).

We focus on connectionist models for several reasons. First, connectionist models have proven extremely useful for explaining psychological phenomena in visual perception and attention. Second, while connectionist models do not necessarily describe information processing at a neural level, connectionist models make contact with neurobiological data more readily than do other types of computational models. Third, connectionist models tend to offer a deeper level of explanation than do more abstract frameworks; for example, a mathematical model might treat an attention shift as a primitive operation, whereas in a connectionist model, the attention shift is an emergent consequence of the model's dynamics. Fourth, computer vision research has shown that tasks such as object recognition require massively parallel, distributed processing (e.g. Marr, 1982), of the sort found in connectionist models. Fifth, and perhaps most important, it is our intuition that connectionist models are the *right* level of description for characterizing the essential properties of visual perception and attention. Ultimately, one must trust one's intuition in selecting a set of modeling tools.

Connectionist Models

The basic element of a connectionist model is a neuron-like *processing unit*. Figure 9.1 shows a typical unit. The unit conveys a scalar value, its *activity level*, to other units. The activity level can be thought of as something like the average firing rate of a biological neuron. The activity of unit i is denoted x; The arrow on the right of the figure depicts the flow of activity from the unit. The arrows on the left depict the flow of activity from other units into the unit. The unit's activity is a function of its inputs. In the figure, there are n input lines. To compute its activity, the unit first calculates a weighted sum of its input, called the *net input*,

$$net_i = \sum_{j=1}^{n} w_{ij}x_j,$$

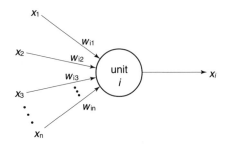

FIG. 9.1.   A connectionist processing unit. The arrows on the left depict inputs to the unit, and the arrow on the right depicts its output.

where w_{ij} is the weighting factor from unit j to unit i. The output of the unit is then a function of the net input:

$$x_i = f(net_i).$$

This *activation function* is typically monotonic and restricts activity between some minimum and maximum value. A common activation function is

$$f(net) = \frac{1}{1 + e^{-net}}.$$

As shown in Fig. 9.2, this activation function maps a net input in the range of $-\infty \rightarrow +\infty$ to activities in the range $0 \rightarrow 1$.

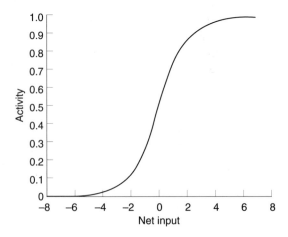

FIG. 9.2.   A typical activation function relating the weighted input to a unit and its output activity.

If a particular weight, say w_{ij}, is zero, unit j will not influence the activity of unit i; if the weight is positive, activity in unit j will tend to produce activity in unit i; and if the weight is negative, activity in unit j will tend to suppress activity in unit i. Positive and negative weights are therefore called *excitatory* and *inhibitory* connections, respectively. Learning in a neural network involves modifying the connection weights which changes the response properties of units. We give an example of connectionist learning in a model we introduce later.

Because it is often important to model the time course of activation, we can add a further constraint to the activation dynamics that the rate at which information can flow from a unit is limited. This is achieved by defining the output of the unit as follows:

$$x_i(t+1) = \tau f(net_i(t)) + (1 - \tau)x_i(t)$$

where t is an index over time, assumed to be quantized into discrete steps, and τ, in the range [0,1], specifies the rate of change. A τ of 0.0 specifies that the rate is infinitely slow, while a τ of 1.0 specifies that the output instantaneously reflects the input state.

Connectionist units can be interconnected to form two basic architectures: *feedforward* and *recurrent*. In a feedforward architecture (Fig. 9.3a), activity flows in one direction, from input units to output units. The architecture shown in the figure is also layered by virtue of the fact that units in one layer communicate only with units in the next layer. In a recurrent architecture (Fig. 9.3b), units are connected in a chain such that activity flows out of a unit, through other units, and can eventually influence activity in the unit itself.

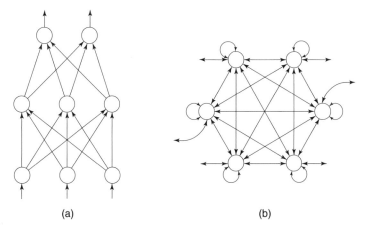

(a)   (b)

FIG. 9.3.   (a) A feedforward architecture in which activity flows from the bottom layer of units to the top layer; (b) A recurrent architecture in which activity flows in cycles.

A BASIC MODEL OF OBJECT RECOGNITION

We begin by introducing a general, relatively noncontroversial connectionist model of visual information processing and object recognition. It may strike experimental cognitive psychologists as unusual to propose a model without reference to specific data. However, the strategy we pursue is to first put forth a mechanism that is sufficient to perform the sort of information processing tasks that we believe are essential to cognition. In the case of visual perception, this includes recognizing objects and making judgments about visual stimuli. Although the model embodies a basic theoretical perspective on visual information processing, we will not attempt to model specific experimental data until the basic framework has been laid out. The point of the model is not to explain object recognition *per se*, but to motivate the need for attention and to study how attention interacts with object recognition. Later, we validate the model as psychologically plausible by showing that it can account for experimental data.

Before describing the model itself, we begin by explaining the input and output of the model. To present a visual stimulus to the model, a pattern of activity is imposed on the model's *retina*. The retina is a collection of *feature maps*. Each feature map is a topographic array of units that detect the presence of a particular visual feature in a particular location of the visual field. The version of the model we will describe has an array of 15 × 15 units in each feature map, and 5 feature maps: oriented line segments at 0°, 45°, 90°, 135°, and line-segment terminators. We refer to these inputs as *primitive features*.[1]

We use a simple font for uppercase letters in which each letter occupies a 3 × 3 region of retina (Mozer, 1991). Figure 9.4 shows the pattern of activity that corresponds to four letters—A, C, D, and X—on the retina. The activity of a feature unit is represented by the shading of the symbol, dark for activity 1.0 or light for activity 0.0.

In the version of the model we have implemented, the model's task is to recognize letters of the alphabet. There is one output unit for each letter. A unit should be active if its corresponding letter is present in any location on the retina.

Figure 9.5 shows a sketch of the model. It is a hierarchical feedforward architecture in which each layer of units feeds to the next layer. The bottom

---

[1] The name "retina" should not be interpreted literally. The primitive feature representation is more like that found in early visual cortical areas than on the human retina. Further, we do not even wish to claim that the coordinate frame of the primitive features is retinotopic. We have simply stated that the features are arranged topographically, but we have not specified whether the feature maps are defined with respect to a coordinate frame that is retinotopic, head-centered, body-centered, or environmental. We avoid this difficult issue because it is not critical to the discussion that follows.

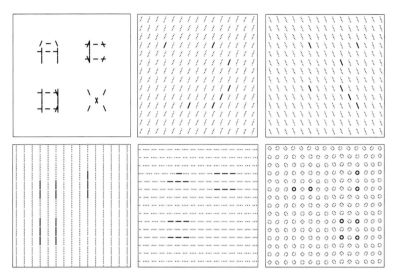

FIG. 9.4. The top left panel shows the set of primitive features that form four letters, A, C, D, and X. The small circles depict terminators. The remaining five panels show the activity in each feature map, with a dark symbol indicating that the corresponding feature unit is active, and a light symbol indicating that the feature unit is inactive.

layer in the figure is the input, the top layer is the output. The basic idea of the architecture is to transform low-level, location-specific visual features into high-level, location-invariant object identities. By "low-level" or "high-level," we mean that the features respond to either simple or complex patterns, respectively; by "location-specific" or "location-invariant," we mean that the feature detector responds to stimuli only in a particular location on the retina or over the entire retina, respectively. The transformation from input to output is accomplished in several stages. At each stage, the number of feature maps increases, the features respond to increasingly more complex patterns, and the region of the retina over which they respond increases. The logic of the architecture is that by increasing the number of feature maps at each layer, information about spatial relations among features in the layer below can be encoded implicitly and hence the explicit representation of spatial relations (i.e the dimensions of the feature maps) can be reduced.

The details of the architecture, not too important for the rest of our presentation, are as follows. Units in a layer receive projections only from a local spatial region of the layer below. Neighboring units in a layer receive projections from neighboring regions of the layer below. Table 9.1 summarizes the architecture. The input layer, layer 1, has an array of 15 × 15 cells of 5 feature types. The output layer, layer 4c, has an array of 1 × 1 cells

Layer

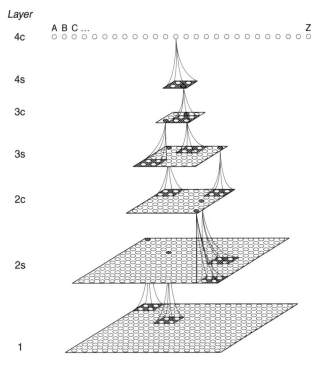

FIG. 9.5. The object recognition model. Each layer is a topographic array of processing units. The bottom layer is the input, the top layer is the output. Activity flows from bottom to top. Each circle represents a *collection* of processing units that detect different features. The connectivity in the network is illustrated by shading a rectangular region in layer *l* and the location in layer *l* + 1 into which this region feeds. Only a small fraction of the connections are depicted.

(i.e there is no explicit representation of location) and 26 feature types (the letters of the alphabet). Between the input and output are three transformation stages, each composed of a "simple" layer and a "complex" layer. The simple layer forms higher-order feature detectors by integrating information over space and feature types in the layer below, while the complex layer integrates only over space, resulting in a representation of the same features with lower spatial resolution. Thus, one will note that the number of feature types in the simple layer is greater than in the layer below, while the number of feature types in the complex layer is the same as in the simple layer. The terms "simple" and "complex" are a reference to cell types in visual cortex.

The ideas embodied in this architecture are traditional. Barlow (1972) and Milner (1974) have described hierarchies of feature detectors for vision. Fukushima and Miyake (1982), Sandon and Uhr (1988; Uhr, 1987), Le Cun et al. (1989), Mozer (1991), and others have built hierarchical connectionist

TABLE 9.1
Architecture of the Recognition Neural Network

Layer	Dimensions	Number of Feature Types	Receptive Field Size	Receptive Field Characteristics
4c	1×1	26	2×2	
4s	2×2	26	2×2	overlapping
3c	3×3	20	2×2	nonoverlapping
3s	6×6	20	2×2	overlapping
2c	7×7	15	2×2	nonoverlapping
2s	14×14	15	2×2	overlapping
1	15×15	5		

architectures for vision tasks. The idea of dividing each stage of the transformation into simple and complex layers comes from Fukushima and Miyake, and Le Cun et al.

Training the Model

We have described the basic pattern of connectivity in the model—which units are connected to which other units. The response of the model also depends on the strength of connections between units, the network weights, which are found by a neural network *training procedure*. We sketch the training procedure but it is not essential to understanding the rest of the chapter.

We first generate a set of *training examples*, each of which consists of an *input pattern* and a *target output*. For instance, given the input pattern shown in Fig. 9.4, the target would be an activity level of one for output units corresponding to A, C, D, and X, and an activity level of zero for all other output units. The training examples included displays containing between one and four letters, 104 examples of each display size. Letters in each example were selected at random and always appeared in one of the four standard positions shown in Fig 9.4.

The goal of the neural network training procedure is to find a set of weights that allow the network to perform correctly on the training examples. That is, when any input pattern in the training set is presented, the network should produce an output pattern closely matching the corresponding target output. This is achieved by a commonly used algorithm called *back propagation* (Rumelhart, Hinton, & Williams, 1986). This algorithm starts with random initial values for the weights and makes small incremental changes to the weights such that with each successive weight change, the network produces outputs that better match the target outputs. In order for units of the same feature type in different locations to respond to the same pattern, their incoming weights must be identical. This is achieved by imposing weight constraints among the units, a common approach for visual object recognition networks (details can be found in Rumelhart et al. 1986).

Performance of the Model

Following training, we can present any single letter in any of the four standard positions and the model will give a strong response to the appropriate letter (output) unit and a weak response to all other letter units. We can quantify the model's performance in terms of *misses* and *false alarms*. A miss occurs when the model fails to activate the output unit corresponding to a letter present in the image above a threshold of .5; a false alarm occurs when the model activates the output unit corresponding to a letter not present in the image above a threshold of .5. By these criteria, the training set of single letters produce a miss rate of 0% and a false alarm rate of 0%. When we test the model on letters presented in novel positions, i.e. not one of the four standard positions, the model shows a fair degree of generalization, achieving a miss rate of 30% and false alarm rate of 5%. This is not surprising, as the local receptive field architecture and the constraints among the neural network weights favor, but do not strongly enforce, translation invariance.[2]

Table 9.2 shows performance on test examples of double, triple, and quadruple letter displays. The test examples were formed by selecting random combinations of distinct letters and selecting a location randomly from among the four standard letter positions. Displays that were used in training were excluded.

Performance drops as the number of stimuli increases. One can understand why this must be the case when one views the model in terms of *processing channels*. Information flowing from one letter position in the input to the output passes through a set of intermediate units. The units

TABLE 9.2
Generalization Performance of the Recognition Neural Network

Number of Letters	Miss Rate	False Alarm Rate
2	10%	0%
3	21%	1%
4	37%	1%

---

[2] *Translation invariance* means that the response of the system is the same regardless of the position of a visual stimulus on the retina.

involved in the processing of one letter position overlap with those involved in the processing of other letter positions, especially at higher layers of the model. The processing channels are thus dependent, and if information is flowing from two channels simultaneously, interference can occur, resulting in the loss of information. Thus, while the model was designed to process visual stimuli in parallel, finite resources result in *capacity limitations.* This motivates the need for some type of attentional processing that can limit the amount of information that the model attempts to handle at once. We now can present an attentional mechanism that performs this function.

A MODEL OF ATTENTIONAL SELECTION

We have described a simple network that can recognize single letters well, and can recognize pairs of letters in parallel for the most part, but as the number of letters increases, the quality of the recognition degrades. On computational grounds, then, some means is required to select a subset of the locations in the visual field where letters appear. By selecting locations sequentially, the attentional system can control the flow of information and prevent the recognition system from being overloaded.

The attentional model we present is most similar to an early-selection model described by Mozer (1991). However, there are many related models in the literature, including Ahmad (1991), Koch and Ullman (1985), LaBerge and Brown (1989), and Sandon (1990). We have attempted to synthesize and incorporate the most promising features of each. The core of the model is a set of units arranged topographically, in one-to-one correspondence with retinal locations. This *attentional map* is depicted in Fig. 9.6, along with the primitive feature maps. (Other details in the figure can be ignored for the time being.) In other models, the attentional map is also referred to as the *priority map* or the *saliency map.* Activity of a unit in the attentional map indicates that units in the corresponding location on the retina are being attended. Attending to a region of the visual field requires activating a compact, contiguous set of units on the attentional map. For the time being, we will not discuss how activity patterns arise in the attentional map. Assume that the activity pattern has been established that indicates attention to a particular region. We will refer to this activity pattern as the *attentional state.*

How might attention control the flow of information in the visual system? The most straightforward notion is to allow the attentional units to *gate the activity flow* from the primitive input features through the object recognition network. If an attentional unit is active, all primitive features at the corresponding location transmit their activities to the recognition network. If an attentional unit is inactive, the activity of primitive features at the corresponding location is not available to the recognition network. This

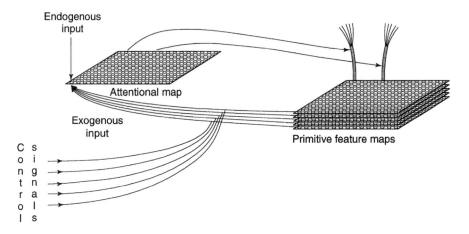

Endogenous
input

Attentional map

Exogenous
input

C s
o i
n g
t n
r a
o l
l s

Primitive feature maps

FIG. 9.6. Each "slab" of circles on the right depicts a primitive feature map, in which the circles represent processing units that respond to a particular feature in a particular location. The slab on the left depicts the attentional map, with a set of units in one-to-one correspondence with the primitive feature maps. Further details of the figure are explained later in the chapter.

is consistent with experimental findings that once a location is selected, all features at that location are processed (Kahneman & Henik, 1981). This gating operation is depicted in Fig. 9.6 for two locations by a convergence of the output from an attention unit onto the bundle of outputs from the primitive features.

A mathematical specification of this gating operation is simple; it basically involves multiplying the activity of the attentional unit by the activity of the primitive feature units. Let a_{xy} denote the activity of a unit at location (x, y) of the attentional map, and suppose this activity level ranges from a minimum of 0.0 to a maximum of 1.0. Let r_{qxy} denote the activity of a primitive feature type q at location (x, y) on the retina. Then the activity from this primitive feature unit that is conveyed to the recognition network, $\hat{r}_{qxy}$, is

$$\hat{r}_{qxy} = a_{xy}(r_{qxy} - \bar{r}) + \bar{r}$$

where $\bar{r}$ is the resting activity level of the primitive feature units. If the attentional unit has activity 0.0, only the resting activity is conveyed. As the attentional unit activity rises to 1.0, the activity conveyed approaches the actual primitive feature activity. This type of multiplicative junction between processing units is common in connectionist models (see e.g. Hinton, McClelland, & Rumelhart 1986).

Information in the unattended field seems not to be completely ignored in at least some situations (e.g. Eriksen & Hoffman, 1973; Gatti & Egeth, 1978;

Shaffer & LaBerge, 1979). This suggests that activity of the primitive feature units in unattended locations should not be completely suppressed, because if it was, unattended information could have no effect on behavior. We will thus suppose that unattended information is attenuated, using a gating function of the form

$$\hat{r}_{qxy} = g(a_{xy})(r_{qxy} - \bar{r}) + \bar{r}$$

where $g(.)$ is a monotonic function, such as

$$g(a) = \lambda + (1 - \lambda)a^{\phi}.$$

For the moment, ignore ϕ. The constant λ determines the degree to which unattended information is passed through the recognition network. With $\lambda = .05$, which we use throughout this chapter, 5% of activity is conveyed even in unattended regions of the visual field. The consequence of a nonzero λ on behavior is not immediately obvious. The fact that 5% of activity is conveyed does not necessarily imply that 5% of unattended objects will be recognized or that their activity will be 5% that of attended objects. This depends in a fundamental way on the operation of the recognition network, and might well interact with familiarity of the unattended stimuli (i.e. the extent to which the recognition network is tuned to processing a particular stimulus) and the nature of task demands (e.g. the information on which responses are based).

The constant ϕ has been included to help suppress the effect of attentional units with weak activity. If $\phi > 1$ and the attentional unit activities are in the range [0,1], small activity values will be squashed more than large activity values. Throughout the chapter, we use $\phi = 4$.

Having described how an attentional state affects processing in the recognition network, we now specify how the model forms attentional states.

Dynamics of the Attentional Network

In a model of location-based selection, the attentional state should indicate a contiguous spatial region on the retina; attentional units within the region should be active and all others inactive. It turns out to be somewhat tricky to design an *elastic-spotlight* model that permits regions of varying size and shape. However, we do not need to deal with this problem right now, because letters are of constant size and are always presented to the model in one of four positions. Consequently, we will describe a simplified implementation that captures the essence of the model but, by its simplicity, is easier to interpret and analyze. In this *rigid-spotlight* model, four attentional states suffice, corresponding to the four quadrants of the retina. To attend to a letter position, say the upper left corner of the retina, all attentional units in that quadrant should have activity 1.0 and all units in the other three quadrants have activity 0.0. Because of the redundancy in this attentional state, we can collapse all attentional units in a quadrant to a single unit.

The rigid-spotlight model requires just four units. What determines how active these units will be? There are two sources of input to the attentional network: exogenous and endogenous. Exogenous input comes from sensory data: in any quadrant where primitive features are present, attention should be directed to that quadrant. This will cause attention to shift to locations where stimuli appear. Endogenous input results from previous learning, priming, or cuing which gives rise to expectations about the location of interesting sensory data. Both exogenous and endogenous input directly activate the appropriate attentional units. In the case of exogenous input, one can think of each primitive feature as having a small-weighted connection to the attentional unit in the corresponding location. In the case of endogenous input, one can think of input from an unspecified source to each attentional unit. This is depicted, for the elastic-spotlight model, in Fig. 9.6.

Because only one attentional unit should be active at a time—corresponding to the selection of a particular location—the units should compete with one another. If each unit has an inhibitory connection to each other unit, the unit that is most active will inhibit all others. This is known in the connectionist literature as a *winner-take-all network* (Feldman & Ballard, 1982; Grossberg, 1976). Additionally, each unit should have an excitatory connection to itself, so that if it is active, it will tend toward the maximum activity level. Figure 9.7 shows a schematic depiction of the attentional model. Algebraicly, the net input to the attentional unit in location (x, y) at time t is:

$$net_{xy}(t) = ext_{xy}(t) + \alpha a_{xy}(t) - \beta \sum_{q,r \neq x,y} a_{qr}(t)$$

and the activity update rule is

$$a_{xy}(t+1) = \tau h(net_{xy}(t)) + (1 - \tau)a_{xy}(t)$$

where $ext_{xy}(t)$ is the external input, endogenous and exogenous, to the attention unit, α is the strength of the excitatory self-connection, β is the strength of the inhibitory connection between pairs of units, and h is a threshold linear function that limits activity to the range $[0,1]$:

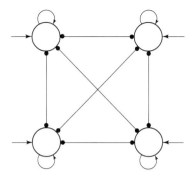

FIG. 9.7.   The rigid-spotlight attentional model. Each attentional unit represents a quadrant of the retina. Each unit is self-excitatory and inhibits each other unit. Each unit receives input from exogenous and endogenous sources. Excitation is represented by connections with arrows, inhibition by connections terminated with small circles.

$$h(net) = \begin{cases} 0 & \text{if } net < 0 \\ net & \text{if } 0 \leq net \leq 1 \\ 1 & \text{if } net > 1 \end{cases}$$

In simulations, we use $\alpha = .4$, $\beta = 3.5$, and $\tau = .2$ for the attentional net. Figure 9.8 shows a graph of the activity over time of four attentional units, given fixed inputs, ext_{xy}. Unit 1 wins the competition and becomes fully active, while the other units are suppressed. Exogenous input to an attentional unit is based on the number of primitive features present in the quadrant represented by the unit. Each feature has a probability ρ of being included in the external input at each time. When detected, the feature contributes a constant σ to the external input. In simulations, we used $\rho = .8$ and $\sigma = .1$.

Curiously, this model does not treat attention as a limited resource of which there is only a finite amount to go around; if we wanted to, we could reduce the value of β so that units would no longer compete so strongly as to shut one another off. The limited resource in this model is found in the object recognition system. Without attentional selection, objects in the visual field will each interfere with the processing of another.

SIMULATIONS OF SPATIAL SELECTION

The Benefit of Attentional Precuing

With the attentional network in place, we can run simulation experiments using the model. Initially, the model is reset to a neutral attentional state in which all attentional units are inactive. A stimulus is presented to the model by introducing a pattern of activity over the primitive features. The primi-

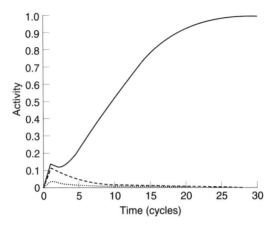

FIG. 9.8.   Activity of four attentional units as a function of time. All units have initial activity 0.0. Unit 1 (solid line) has external input .7, unit 2 (dashed line) has external input .6, and units 3 and 4 (dotted lines) have external input .2.

tive features provide input to the attentional network, leading to activation of attentional units. At first, the inactive attentional network prevents most primitive feature activity from entering the recognition network, but as the competition takes hold in the attentional network, one location becomes preferred and primitive feature units in this location are allowed to pass their activity through the recognition network. Figure 9.9 shows the response of the model when the letter S is presented in the upper left quadrant. The figure depicts both the activity of the attentional unit in the stimulus location and the activity of the letter unit. The time required to activate the letter unit is due to the gradual build-up of activity in the attentional network as well as the slow propagation of activity through the recognition network (as determined by the constant τ).

A simulation trial does not have to begin with a neutral attentional state. If the model has been cued to a location in advance of the trial, endogenous input to the attentional network will sustain activation at that location in the attentional map prior to stimulus onset. When the stimulus is presented, activation from the primitive features will immediately flow through the recognition network. Consequently, one might expect more rapid response to the stimulus.

Posner (1980) has studied a speeded detection task with location precuing. Subjects were asked to detect the onset of a suprathreshold target stimulus at one of several possible locations. Prior to target onset, the subject might be provided with a spatial cue indicating the location in which the target is likely to appear. Subjects were faster to detect the target when a cue was given than when no cue was given. Our description of the model's behavior is consistent

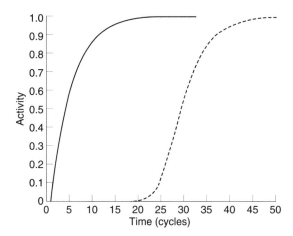

FIG. 9.9. Build-up of activity in an attentional unit (solid line) and the letter S unit (dashed line) in response to the stimulus S.

with this result. Further, Posner manipulated the cue to be either a *valid* or *invalid* predictor of target location. Responses in the valid cue condition were faster than in the *neutral* cue condition, while responses in the invalid cue condition were slower (second column of Table 9.3).[3]

Simulating experimental results even as basic as these nonetheless requires further assumptions about the operation of the model.

1. How do the different cue conditions correspond to states of the model? We assume that in the neutral condition, all attentional units are inactive. A cue—valid or invalid—guides attention endogenously to the cued location prior to presentation of the target.

2. How does the model formulate a response? The detection response must be based on some representation in the model; it could be the primitive input features, on the letter units, or on any level between. We assume that read out is based solely on the outputs of the recognition network.[4] Because the detection response depends only on whether a stimulus is present, not its identity, we assume that the

---

[3] Most of the human data we use for comparison and for setting model parameters has been extracted from figures of the referenced experimental papers, and/or has been averaged over several experiments. Because the details of our simulation experiments do not match the details of the human experiments (e.g. stimuli, presentation conditions), there is little to be gained by trying to determine and model the exact outcome of a specific human experiment.

[4] It may seem strange to read out at a high level when the task does not call for stimulus identification. We find it most parsimonious to make the strong assumption of a single level of read out, and thereby avoid the issue of determining where read out occurs on a task-by-task basis.

TABLE 3
Reaction Time to Detect Target Onset

Cue Condition	Human RT	Model Cycles	Model RT
Valid	230 ms	15.7 cycles	234 ms
Neutral	260 ms	17.5 cycles	256 ms
Invalid	300 ms	20.9 cycles	301 ms

evidence on which a response is based is the total activity of the letter units.

3. When does the model initiate a response? One might assume a response is initiated when the total evidence passes some threshold. If there were no noise in the model, the threshold could be set to zero. However, our recognition model is noisy in that letter units have slight activity even when no stimulus is present. Additionally, most models assume some built-in noise that reflects sources of variability not modeled explicitly. Thus, the threshold should be set as low as possible such that responses can be initiated rapidly and without producing false detections due to noise.

The response generation procedure we adopted is a variant of the procedure used by McClelland and Rumelhart (1981). We describe the general procedure. For each possible response r the model might be asked to make at time t, the *evidence* for the response, denoted $e_r(t)$, is computed. The probability of producing a response r at time t is then:

$$P(r, t) = \frac{\exp(\xi e_r(t))}{\Sigma_s \exp(\xi e_s(t))},$$

where ξ is a constant that translates evidence into response strengths. The numerator is the strength of response r, and the denominator normalizes the probabilities to sum to 1. This rule will always choose a response at each time t it is applied. However, we would like to prevent the model from making a response unless sufficient evidence has accumulated. To do this, we add an additional response category, which we call "no response", that has constant evidence e_{NR}. This constant behaves as a probabilistic threshold; if e_{NR} is large relative to the evidence for the other responses, then the model will likely hold off making a response. e_{NR} is a free parameter of the model, and it essentially controls the speed-accuracy trade-off: the larger e_{NR} is, the more evidence must accumulate before a response is initiated. In all our simulations, $\xi = 10$; in detection tasks, $e_{NR} = .3$ and in discrimination tasks, $e_{NR} = 1.2$, reflecting the fact that more evidence should be required for a discrimination response than a detection response.

Figure 9.10 shows the summed letter unit activity as a function of time for the three cue conditions. Time is measured in *cycles*; each cycle is a single update of the activities of all units in the model. One can clearly see that activity rises most rapidly in the valid cue condition, followed by the neutral cue condition, followed by the invalid cue condition. The third column of Table 9.3 shows the mean number of cycles for the model to initiate a detection response, over a large number of stimulus presentations. The simulation response times are qualitatively in accord with the data. We scaled the model response time in cycles, RT_{model} to real-world response times, $RT_{realworld}$, according to a formula that assumed a fixed number of milliseconds per cycle, γ, and a fixed amount of time, κ, for input pre-processing and motor response:

$$RT_{realworld} = \gamma RT_{model} + \kappa.$$

We chose values for these constants—12.8 for γ and 32.8 for κ—to obtain a reasonable fit to this data. The same constants will be used in all subsequent simulation experiments.[5]

Cohen, Romero, Farah, and Servan-Schreiber (1994) and Jackson, Marrocco, and Posner (1994) have modeled the effect of cues on speeded detection using essentially the same approach—a set of attentional units that

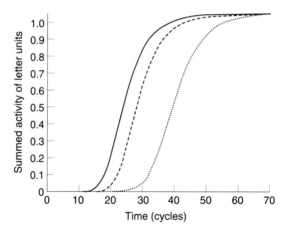

FIG. 9.10. Summed letter unit activity as a function of model *cycles* for the valid (solid line), neutral (dashed line), and invalid (dotted line) cue conditions, averaged over a large number of stimulus presentations. A cycle is a single update of the activities of all units in the model.

---

[5] Surprisingly, some modelers (e.g., Cohen et al., 1994) have allowed themselves the freedom of fitting the results of different experiments with different scaling parameters.

compete to select a location and preactivating units at the cued location. Although the activation dynamics and competition mechanisms vary among the three models, and although Cohen et al. and Jackson et al. do not simulate the perceptual system in any detail, all three models show the same effect. This suggests that the effect is robust under a variety of implementations of the same key notion—that attention is the result of a competition among locations. Jackson et al. have attempted to provide a more neurobiologically plausible mechanism, localizing various components of their model to different brain regions. Both Cohen et al. and Jackson et al. also account for data of neurological patients with attentional disorders by "lesioning" their models in a manner consistent with the form of damage the patients are known to have suffered.

We attempted to extend our model in a somewhat different direction. Shiu and Pashler (1994), summarizing the literature on the effect of advance knowledge of stimulus location in processing single-item displays, concluded that, although a spatial precue results in significant speedups in detection tasks, the effect is more modest in speeded suprathreshold discrimination tasks. We simulated a discrimination task in which the model was given a valid, neutral, or invalid cue, which was followed by one of two visually confusable targets, such as X and Y, and a forced-choice speeded response was required. For the discrimination task, a response cannot be initiated until the model is confident that one stimulus was presented and not the other. This is particularly critical because a stimulus like X will often produce activity for visually confusable letters like Y. Thus, we set the evidence for the X response, e_X, to be the difference in activity between the X and Y units, and symmetrically for the Y response.

After experimenting with parameter values, activation functions, and response functions for over a week, we had to admit defeat: the model always produced a cue-validity effect in the discrimination task that was as large as the effect in the detection task. Figure 9.10 suggests one argument for why this might be. The curves for the three cue conditions appear identical except for a shift in time. Although the figure shows summed activity of all letter units, this is true for the individual unit activity curves too. Any response initiation procedure based on these parallel curves will necessarily produce response times for the cue conditions that differ by the time shift. Thus, the detection cue-validity effect must be the same as the discrimination effect. Although it is theoretically possible that certain parameter settings might result in nonparallel curves, we were unable to discover such settings.

Two lessons might be learned from this exercise. First, the model shows a parameter-independent, qualitative behavior, indicating that it represents a strong, testable theoretical perspective. Large computational models often arouse suspicion because they appear sufficiently malleable that they can be made to account for any piece of data. More often than not, this belief is misguided, as we discuss later. Second, if one has strong confidence in the model, one might question Shiu and Pashler's conclusion from the literature, which is based on studies of Posner (1980) and Posner, Snyder, and Davidson (1980). Although both studies appear to show smaller cue-validity effects for discrimination than detection, this conclusion was not backed up by statistical analyses. Further, the detection and discrimination tasks were performed with different stimulus materials and experimental procedures, making it problematic to compare results directly. (Our simulation results assume that detection and discrimination tasks are carried out under identical stimulus and experimental conditions, except for the response required of subjects.) Resolving whether the model or the characterization of the data is right is beyond the scope of this chapter, but the model—right or wrong—has clearly pointed to an avenue of further investigation.

Time Course of Attention Shifts

In the cue-validity simulation, we assumed that the cue was presented sufficiently far in advance of the target that attention could settle on the cued location prior to the target onset. What happens if the stimulus-onset asynchrony (SOA) between cue and target is varied so that the target is presented before attention becomes fully active at the cued location? Experimental studies have shown that response times decrease monotonically for increasing SOA, up to about 200 ms in both detection and discrimination tasks with peripheral cueing (e.g. Eriksen & Hoffman, 1974; Posner 1980).

Figure 9.11 shows a simulation result for the model on a detection task in which a cue is presented for a varying number of cycles, and is then replaced by a target item to be detected. We assume that the cue initiates activity in the attentional network but not in the recognition network. The same detection procedure is applied as in the cue-validity simulations. Clearly, the model shows the same pattern as human performance.

Effect of Spatial Uncertainty

Speeded response to a visual stimulus is delayed by the presence of irrelevant stimuli, even when sensory interference, discriminability difficulties, and response conflict are ruled out as contributing factors. In a study by Kahneman, Treisman, and Burkell (1983), observers were asked to read as rapidly as possible a word that appeared unpredictably above or below the fixation point. On half the trials, another object was presented on the opposite side of fixation, either a word or a word-sized patch of randomly placed black dots. The mere presence of the second object resulted in a reading time delay of 30–40 msec.

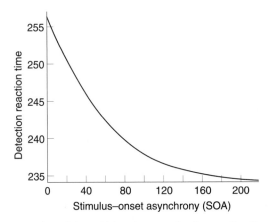

FIG. 9.11.   Response time of the model to detect a stimulus as a function of cue–target SOA. The simulation shows the same pattern as human performance: Response times decrease monotonically for SOAs up to about 200 ms.

We simulated this experiment by presenting a letter in one of the four letter locations and a "black dot patch" in one of the other locations. We assume the black dots activate some unspecified primitive visual features that drive attention to the location of the black dots, as do the other primitive features, but they do not activate the letter features used in the recognition network. We also assume that the letter features provide strong exogenous input to attention, causing attention to eventually select the letter location.[6]

Using the discrimination task, response time of the model was 568 ms in the condition with a letter alone and 605 ms in the condition with a letter and the black dot patch. The explanation for this behavior is straightforward: when the dot patch competes with the letter for attention, the activity of the letter location in the attention network grows more slowly, causing a delay in propagating information through the recognition network.

The Effect of Irrelevant Stimuli

When subjects are asked to make a speeded response to a target letter in a known location, their responses can be influenced by the identities of other letters nearby in the display (e.g. Eriksen & Eriksen, 1974; Eriksen & Hoffman, 1973; Eriksen & Schultz, 1979; Miller, 1991). Consider the task of pressing one response key for the target A or U, and another key for the

---

[6] As we elaborate later, the model requires the ability to modulate the degree to which each primitive feature type can drive attention; in this task, choosing the letter location is desirable, and hence letter features should drive attention more strongly than features of the black dots.

target H or M. Letters can be presented flanking the target which are either *compatible* with the target (i.e. selected from the same response category), *incompatible*, or *neutral* (i.e. not belonging to either response category). Responses are fastest on compatible trials and slowest on incompatible trials (Table 9.4). Flanker effects are significantly reduced when the flankers are presented one degree of visual angle or more from the target, but this may well be due to reduced acuity at greater distances (Egeth 1977).

The flanker effect appears to be a failure of focal attention, in that subjects are unable to prevent the processing of letters adjacent to a target even if the target location is known in advance. This effect can be eliminated under some conditions, however (LaBerge et al., 1991; Yantis & Johnston 1990).

The model has a simple explanation for the flanker effect. When a location is unattended, activity from that location is not completely suppressed; a small amount of activity stemming from that location—represented by the constant λ—is transmitted to and analyzed by the object recognition network. This may result in letter activity that will strengthen the evidence for one response category in the case of compatible flankers or weaken the evidence in the case of incompatible flankers.

We performed a simulation study in which a target letter was presented in a fully attended location, and two flankers appeared in adjacent unattended locations. A large number of trials were run, varying the response sets and the stimulus locations. The response initiation procedure was that of the discrimination task we modeled earlier. The results in the three flanker conditions are shown in Table 9.4. When unattended information is fully suppressed by setting λ to zero, the effect vanishes.

The model has now been shown to account for the results of four quite different phenomena related to selective attention. Although the model produces excellent quantitative fits to the human data, the reader should recognize that there is a bit more going on behind the scenes than we have told you about. For example, in the dot patch experiment, we had the freedom to manipulate the strength of the exogenous input representing the dot patch, enabling us to produce an effect of the right magnitude. Nonetheless, it would be impossible to manipulate the model to alter the

TABLE 9.4
Reaction Time to Target

Distractor Type	Human Data	Model
Compatible	460 ms	459 ms
Neutral	500 ms	493 ms
Incompatible	540 ms	546 ms

qualitative pattern of results; e.g. to cause the effect of attention to diminish as the cue–target SOA increased. At the end of the chapter, we return to the issue of qualitative versus quantitative modeling of data.

ATTENTION AS A SPOTLIGHT?

Spatial attention has been likened to a spotlight (e.g. Eriksen & Hoffman, 1973; Posner 1980). This metaphor implies that attention is allocated to a contiguous, possibly convex, region of the visual field. If the spotlight metaphor is appropriate, then the spotlight should have an adjustable dia-meter (Eriksen & Yeh 1985, LaBerge, 1983). The rigid-spotlight attentional model simulated in the previous section does indeed select a contiguous region, but the region is of fixed size and shape—an entire quadrant of the visual field. We now discuss an implementation of the elastic-spotlight attentional model, which is able to select regions varying in size and shape. In this model, the attentional map has the same dimensions as the retinal map, and a region of the visual field is attended by activating all attentional units in that region.

The elastic-spotlight model is identical to the rigid-spotlight model, except that the dimensions of the attentional map are increased and the computation of the "net input" to the attentional unit at map location (x,y), net_{xy}, is changed to

$$net_{xy}(t) = ext_{xy}(t) + \alpha \sum_{\substack{(i,j)\in \\ NBHD_{xy}}} a_{ij}(t) - \beta(\gamma\bar{a}(t) - a_{xy}(t)),$$

where $ext_{xy}(t)$ is the external input to the attentional unit, as before, $NBHD_{xy}$ is the set of nine locations immediately adjacent to and including (x,y)—the *neighbors*, $\bar{a}$ is the mean activity of units with nonzero activity, α and β are the same constants as before, and γ is an additional constant.

The first term encourages each unit's activity to be consistent with the external input, as before. The second term encourages each unit's activity to be as close as possible to that of its neighbors; if a unit is off and the neighbors are on, the unit will tend to turn on, and vice versa. The third term encourages units having activity below the mean to shut off, and units above the mean to turn on. The constant γ serves as a discounting factor: with γ less than 1, units need not be quite as active as the mean in order to be supported. Instead of using the average activity over *all* units, it is necessary to compute the average over the *active* units. Otherwise, the effect of the third term is to limit the total activity in the network; i.e. the number of units that can turn on at once. This is not suitable because we wish to allow large or small spotlights depending on the external input.

To explain the activation function intuitively, consider the time course of activation. Initially, the activity of all units is reset to zero. Activation then feeds into each unit in proportion to its external input (first term in the activation function). Units with active neighbors will grow the fastest because of neighborhood support (second term). As activity progresses, high-support neighborhoods will have activity above the mean; they will therefore be pushed even higher, while low-support neighborhoods will experience the opposite tendency (third term).

This model has been used to explain data from neurological patients suffering from attentional disorders (Mozer & Behrmann, 1990; Mozer, Halligan, & Marshall, 1997). We have adopted the parameter values from the earlier work: α was set to .11, β to .5, and γ to .11 times the total external input, with lower and upper limits of .75 and 1.0. A feature contributes external input not only to its corresponding attentional unit—as in the rigid-spotlight model, the contribution is σ with probability ρ but also to its

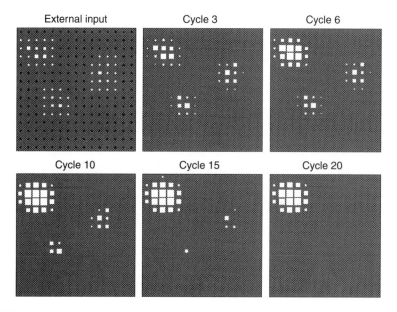

FIG. 9.12. The upper left panel depicts the external input to the attentional model. The panel consists of a 15 × 15 array of squares. The area of a white square corresponds to the amount of external input to the corresponding unit of the attentional model. The small black dots are drawn in locations where the external input is zero, to show the extent of the array. The external input pattern is meant to indicate three objects, the largest one—the one with the strongest external input—is in the upper left portion of the field. The next five panels show the activity as the network settles. By cycle 20, the network has reached equilibrium and has selected the region of the largest object.

neighboring locations with $\sigma_{neigh} = .02\sigma$. The original intent of this blurring was to give the input a more continuous spread of activity.

Figure 9.12 shows an example of the attentional model selecting a single region when the external input specifies three blob-like patterns that represent distinct objects. The region chosen by the model corresponds to the object with the strongest external input. Figure 9.13 shows a similar example when one of the blobs is made larger, and a correspondingly larger region is selected. Comparing the two figures, it is clear that the model can select regions of varying size. Model parameters can also be adjusted to vary the size of its spotlight without changing the input. Figure 9.14 shows the response of the model when the β parameter is raised from 0.5 to 0.7. The external input is the same as in Fig. 9.13, but the region selected is clearly smaller.

Two properties of the network are worth noting. First, the units on the edge of the spotlight tend to have less activity than the units in the center of the spotlight. One is tempted to relate this to the claim that sensitivity falls off gradually at the perimeter of the attended region (Downing & Pinker, 1985; Eriksen & St James, 1986; LaBerge & Brown, 1989). Second, all stimulus locations become active in the initial phase of processing. It is not until competitive mechanisms take reign that a winning location emerges. Thus, the model is unfocused initially, but over the course of time it narrows in on a

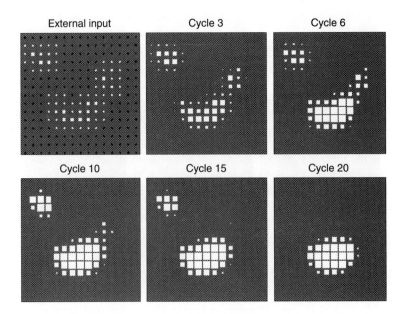

FIG. 9.13.   The response of the attentional model to an external input pattern in which there are three objects, the largest of which is at the bottom and center of the field.

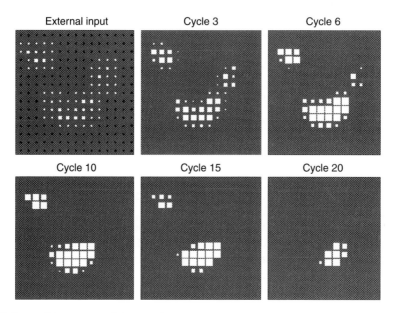

FIG. 9.14. The response of the attentional model when the β parameter is raised from 0.5 to 0.7. The external input is the same as in Fig. 9.13, but the region selected is clearly smaller.

single object. Because the recognition network begins processing immediately—and before the attentional network has settled to equilibrium—it initially tries to handle all information in the field simultaneously. If one were to observe the activity of units in the recognition network, it would appear as if the units responded to unattended stimuli at first, but this activity was eventually suppressed. In single cell studies of monkey visual cortex, this behavior has been observed: 60 msec after stimulus onset a response is triggered in the extrastriate cortex, but not until 90 msec does attention kick in and suppress unattended stimuli (Desimone & Duncan, 1995).

The model was not designed with these data in mind, but it does appear a natural consequence of such a filtering mechanism. One can envision two basic designs: (1) a *cautious* system that does not allow the processing of any information until selection is complete; and (2) an *audacious* system that allows the processing of all information until selection is complete. The audacious system will respond more rapidly, but is more prone to error because items in the visual field may interfere with one another when attention is unfocused. The model, and apparently the primate brain, is audacious. This is a sensible strategy if the cost of slow responses is greater than the cost of occasional errors.

In the simulations described, the initial state of the model was neutral. Essentially, the model was attending nowhere, then a multi-item display appeared which initiated a competition among the stimuli for attention. What if the model is already attending somewhere when the display appears, requiring a shift of attention from one location to another? Figure 9.15 illustrates this situation. Attention fades out from the old location and in to the new. The spotlight metaphor does not seem appropriate for describing the attention shift. If the focus of attention were like a spotlight, one would expect attention to move across the field in an analog fashion, illuminating intervening points along the way. One would also expect that the time required to shift attention would be monotonically related to the distance between foci. The model does not show this behavior either: the time required for attention to shift from a focus at (2,2) to stabilize on a focus at (12,12) is 32 cycles (Fig. 9.15). The time required for a shift half as far—from (2,2) to (7,7)—is also 32 cycles.

Early evidence in the literature did appear to support an analog view of attentional shifts (Shulman, Remington, & McLean, 1979; Tsal, 1983). However, several critiques have appeared of this interpretation of the original data (Eriksen, 1990; Yantis, 1988) and recent experiments suggest that the time to shift attention is independent of the distance traversed and

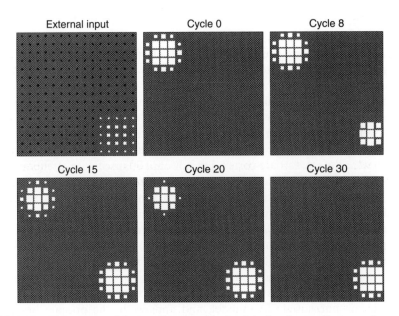

FIG. 9.15.   The response of the attentional model when it is already attending somewhere and the external input changes, triggering an attentional shift. The external input (upper left panel) appears at cycle 0, when the model is in the state depicted in the upper middle panel. The remaining panels show the shift of attention from the upper left corner of the field to the lower right corner.

of the presence of interposed visual obstacles (Sperling & Weichselgartner, 1995). The current consensus is that the spotlight of attention turns off at one location and then on at another (Eriksen, 1990; Kinchla, 1992). Thus, our attentional model, which was not designed to behave this way, appears to capture the key property that attention shifts are discrete and distance-independent.

MODELING VARIOUS SELECTION CRITERIA

We have described several simulations in which the model selects items for report based on location. Other tasks require selection by different properties of the stimulus; for example, reporting the identity of the red letter or the location of the brightest dot. An important aspect of a computational model is that, beyond explaining data, it can also carry out the same sort of operations as can people. Thus, in this section, we endow our model with a mechanism that allows it to perform selection by simple physical attributes such as color or brightness. The mechanism assumes that selection by attributes other than location is nonetheless mediated by location selection, consistent with findings of Snyder (1972), Nissen (1985), and Tsal and Lavie (1988). The mechanism is based on models by Mozer (1991) and Wolfe, Cave, and Franzel (1989).

Earlier, we characterized the input to the model in terms of primitive feature maps. Each map is a spatiotopic array of detectors tuned to a particular feature. Until now, we have only required features of letters—oriented line segments and line terminators—but suppose that the primitive feature maps include other dimensions of the stimulus, such as color and brightness.

To perform selection by arbitrary features, the model needs the ability to specify which of the feature maps provide exogenous input to the attentional network. This is achieved through a set of *control signals*, one per feature map, as shown in Fig. 9.6. The control signals modulate the probability that features in that feature map are detected by the corresponding unit in the attentional map. We referred to this probability earlier as ρ, but we now add the index q to indicate the control signal for feature type q, ρ_q. By default, the ρ_q will have value .8, as we assumed for ρ. The control signals in Fig. 9.6 are shown only for a single location, but the gating is performed at every location across the spatiotopic map.

If the task requires selecting the red item for report, then the system should be configured such that only activity from the "red" feature map drives the attentional network, causing selection of red items. If the display contains only a single red item, it will be selected, activity from all feature types in its spatial location will then be allowed to pass through the recognition network, and the output of the recognition network will be the identity of the red item.

What are the primitive feature dimensions that can drive attention? In addition to edge orientation and termination, color, and brightness, there is evidence to support dimensions such as size, direction and speed of motion, binocular disparity, and three-dimensional surface properties (Driver, McLeod, & Dienes, 1992; Enns, 1990; Hillstrom & Yantis, 1994). Discontinuities or singletons in all of these dimensions appear capable of attracting attention as well (Pashler, 1988; Sandon, 1990; also, see chapter by Yantis, this volume). And multiple spatial scales of resolution must be encoded.[7] By this reckoning, there are at least 15 primitive feature dimensions, and to coarse-code a value on each dimension (e.g. to specify the value "red" on the color spectrum) would require a bare minimum of, say, five feature types, resulting in at least 75 primitive feature types.

Having argued for voluntarily control over which features can drive attention, we must add that this control is certainly limited. Some visual features may attract attention willy nilly (e.g. Jonides & Yantis, 1988; Pashler, 1988; Treisman & Gormican, 1988), indicating that it is difficult or impossible to gate out these features. And, based on evidence we discuss later, there are probably bounds on the visual system's ability to gate in or out various feature types.

In terms of the model, we propose a simple limitation on control over which features can drive attention. Let us allow the control signal, ρ_q, for each feature type q to be continuous in the range [0,1]. The control signal then determines the degree to which a feature type will attract attention. Suppose that each ρ_q has a default setting which has been determined by past experience, based on what features in the environment tend to be most important and need to be responded to quickly. Modulating the value of a ρ_q requires some type of limited resource, let us call it *regulatory juice*. The amount of juice is sufficient to, say, fully open or close one gate, or to make small adjustments in several gates. It may even be that some gates are easier to modulate with a fixed quantity of juice. The point is that the ρ_q cannot be adjusted arbitrarily.

The introduction of control signals into the model allows us to explain selection on the basis of primitive features other than location. The notion of regulatory juice allows us to explain how selection criteria are adjusted in response to task demands. Experimental data are consistent with this notion; e.g. short-term experience performing a task can affect the degree to

---

[7] Our framework makes no strong assumptions about the nature of the primitive visual features. Many features we have listed would not ordinarily be considered "primitive." The framework allows for considerable preattentive parallel visual processing prior to "feature" registration.

which certain feature types drive attention, and this effect can be either excitatory or inhibitory, i.e. increasing or decreasing the ρ_q (Hillstrom, 1995; Maljkovic & Nakayama, 1994). Treating the regulatory juice as a limited resource allows us to account for limitations on attentional selectivity. The general issue of voluntary control over exogenous influences on attention is beyond the scope of this chapter, although we find it difficult to build a computational model without at least specifying the "hooks" for such control from unspecified higher cognitive processes.

THE RELATIONSHIP OF OBJECT-BASED AND LOCATION-BASED ATTENTION

Studies have shown that attention can select stimuli on the basis of object shape or structure (e.g. Behrmann, Zemel, & Mozer, 1996; Duncan, 1984; Egly, Driver, & Rafal, 1994; Kramer & Jacobson, 1991; Vecera & Farah, 1994). For example, Kramer and Jacobson examined the influence of flankers on a target stimulus, similar to the experiments described earlier. When the flankers and the target were considered part of the same object, there was a response-compatibility effect; when the flankers and target were part of different objects, there was no effect, even though the spatial separation between the target and flankers was the same in the two conditions.

The data argue for *object-based* selection: visual features are attended to not on the basis of their spatial location but according to which object they belong to, even if the features are not spatially compact and overlap with features of other objects. Two very different processes could underlie object-based attention. One possibility is that attention is allocated to an object-based representation, perhaps a high-level, abstract representation of object identity. The other possibility is that attention is allocated to a set of spatial locations, possibly noncontiguous, at which features of an object are present. Evidence from Vecera (1994) supports the latter interpretation.

What is the relationship between object-based and location-based attention? Both forms of attention can be observed in the same experiment (Egly et al. 1994), suggesting that the two are not mutually exclusive. Consequently, one must ask which type of attentional selection operates first, or whether there is an interactive process in which both types of selection occur in parallel. Experimental work like that of Kramer and Jacobson (1991) argues that object-based segmentation must precede or interact with location-based selection. Assuming that object-based segmentation is related to perceptual processes that group distinct display elements into coherent regions, additional support for this hypothesis can be found (Driver & Baylis, 1989; Duncan, 1995), and there are several recent theoretical proposals that embody the hypothesis (Grossberg, Mingola, &

Ross, 1994; Humphreys & Müller, 1993; Rensink & Enns, 1995; Trick & Pylyshyn, 1994).

Given that object-based selection involves allocating attention to spatial arrays of features, and that object-based selection operates prior to or simultaneously with location-based selection, the mechanism of attentional gating we have already proposed is adequate to explain object-based selection. We must, however, posit an additional process that segments features of a display according to which object they belong and can guide attention to the locations of a single object's features.

Several computational models have been proposed to segment displays into their component objects. Humphreys and Müller (1993) and Grossberg et al. (1994) have built connectionist models that group display elements on the basis of similarity and spatial proximity. Mozer, Zemel, Behrmann, and Williams (1992) have designed a connectionist model that *learns* which features are likely to be grouped together or apart based on a set of pre-segmented examples. It thus extends the notion from Gestalt psychology of fixed grouping principles to a more dynamic process based on statistics of the environment. (Figure 9.16 shows the model segmenting a simple image.)

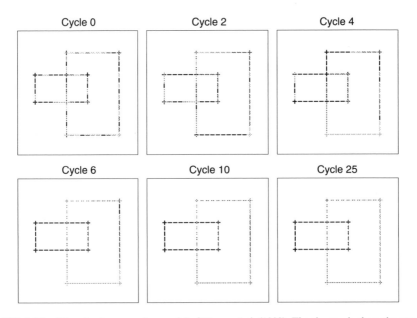

FIG. 9.16.   The adaptive grouping model of Mozer et al. (1992). The six panels show the state of the model at various points in processing a display consisting of two overlapping rectangles. The upper left panel is the initial state of the model; the lower right panel is the final output of the model. Each oriented line segment is a primitive input feature. The coloring of the features indicates the object label assigned to the features. The initially random labeling is transformed into a pattern in which the features of each rectangle have a unique label.

Both types of models use *heuristics* to guide the grouping process, rather than whole-object knowledge. Although the heuristics will not be infallable, the hope is that they will suffice for most segmentation tasks, and even when they fail, recognition processes will be robust to some degree of segmentation error (Enns & Rensink, 1992). This avoids the chicken-and-egg problems of how to segment a display without knowing the component objects, and how to recognize the objects without knowing the segmentation.[8]

Assuming some process has segmented the visual field into feature groups, how do the groups influence attention? Here is one proposal in terms of our model. The attentional model selects a single region—a contiguous set of locations—because each unit in the attentional map inhibits all units outside its neighborhood. However, for object-based attention, the possibility of selecting noncontiguous locations must be allowed. Thus, units representing locations of features of the same group should excite rather than inhibit one another. The result of grouping processes, then, should be to increase temporarily the connection strengths between attentional units that represent grouped locations. The notion of dynamic, short-term weight adjustments in response to grouped features was proposed by von der Malsburg (1981; von der Malsburg & Schneider, 1986).

The eventual attentional state will then be a complex interaction between the dynamic links formed among grouped features and exogenous and endogenous inputs to the attentional network. This brief sketch is hardly a compelling answer to the difficult and important question about how object-based and location-based attention work together. Existing computational models do not directly address how the two forms of attention are integrated, with the exception of preliminary work by Goebel (1993) and Grossberg et al. (1994). This is clearly fertile ground for future exploration and simulation.

---

[8] All segmentation models use some information about objects. The information can be as basic as the fact that two features appearing in a certain spatial relation are more often part of the same object than parts of different objects. The information can be as complex as restrictions on how a feature can appear with respect to all the other features that are part of the object, which we have referred to as *whole-object* knowledge. One can characterize the information along a continuum of what *order* statistics comprise the knowledge. Second-order statistics describe relationships between pairs of features; very high-order statistics are required to describe whole objects. The information used by the Mozer et al. (1992) model is of intermediate order, based on spatially local configurations of features. Vecera (1993) found that upright overlapping block letters are segmented more readily than the same stimuli inverted. This experiment rules out the use of only low-order statistics, such as continuity between pairs of lines, because upright and inverted letters are identical in terms of low-order statistics. Although the use of whole-object knowledge for segmentation could explain the experimental results, the results are also consistent with the use of intermediate-order statistics that are different for upright and inverted letters. For example, English letters are more often open on the right than on the left. Inverted letters violate this configural property.

SIMULATIONS OF VISUAL SEARCH

In the previous three sections, we have discussed diverse aspects of attention: adjustable attentional spotlights, shifts of attention, selection on the basis of object attributes, and the relationship of location-based and object-based attention. All of these aspects must be addressed if we hope to model the vast and complex literature on visual search.

In a visual search task, subjects are commonly asked to detect the presence or absence of a target in a display containing distractor elements. Response time is measured as a function of the number of elements in the display. The shape of this curve indicates something about how subjects perform the search task. Flat curves, in which response time does not increase with the number of elements or increases very gradually (less than about 10 milliseconds per element), is suggestive of a parallel search across the visual field. Curves with steep slopes, in which each additional element increases the response time, are suggestive of a serial search. For example, searching for a vertical bar among horizontal bar distractors produces a flat curve; searching for a plus among vertical and horizontal bar distractors produces a positively sloped curve. Characterizing search using a serial-parallel dichotomy has turned out to be an oversimplification (see chapter by Wolfe, this volume). Response time curves are often nonlinear, and slopes vary across tasks continuously, from flat to steep. It is thus more appropriate to view search on an easy-to-hard continuum.

A variety of promising computational models have been devised to replicate various aspects of the data (Ahmad, 1991; Ahmad & Omohundro, 1991; Gerrissen, 1991; Grossberg et al. 1994; Humphreys & Müller, 1993; Mozer, 1991; Niebur & Koch, 1996; Sandon, 1990). Most of these models are based on feature-integration theory (Treisman & Gelade, 1980; Treisman & Gormican, 1988; Treisman & Sato, 1990) or the guided-search model (Wolfe et al. 1989). We will discuss the processes and mechanisms underlying visual search in terms of the model we have developed for this chapter, but our account overlaps significantly with these theories and earlier computational models. An outline of this account is as follows.

- We assume that the target and distractor sets are known in advance. For each primitive feature type, an analysis must be performed to determine how well the feature discriminates targets from distractors. That is, if all display elements containing (or not containing) the feature are discarded, have we done a good job in eliminating distractors and keeping targets? Consider, for example, searching for a red vertical among blue verticals and blue horizontals. If all red elements are ruled in (or equivalently, all blue elements are ruled out), the target has been reliably separated from the distractors. However, if all verticals are ruled in (or horizontals are ruled out), we are left with a set of elements that includes both targets and distractors.[9]

- The control signals, ρ_q, of highly discriminative feature types should be modulated such that potential target elements will be more likely to capture attention and potential distractor elements will be less likely. In our example of searching for a red vertical among blue verticals and horizontals, ρ_{red} should be increased, causing red elements to drive attention more than blue elements. The modulation of control signals might be subject to a limited amount of regulatory juice. The model also has the flexibility to adjust other parameters that influence its performance, including the diameter of the attentional spotlight, controlled by β, and the response criterion, controlled by e_{NR}.[10]

- When a search display is presented, features in the display will drive the attentional network exogenously, gated by the control signals.

- A competition ensues within the attentional network to select one region. The region may contain one or multiple display elements. The size of the region will depend on the density and arrangement of elements, segmentation and grouping processes, and the adjustable parameter of the attentional network that controls the spotlight diameter.

- As selection takes place, display elements are processed and identified by the recognition network. Even display elements that are commonly thought of as simple features, such as a vertical bar, are processed by the recognition network. The vertical bar is an *object* which might be composed of vertical bar and terminator primitive features.

- The output layer of the recognition network contains a set of units that represent identities of the different display elements that might appear. Target detection would occur using the response initiation procedure of earlier simulations.

- If the target has not been detected by the time that the outputs of the recognition network have stabilized, the selected region is deemed not to contain a target, and attention should be prevented from returning there. This can be accomplished by forcing off the currently active attentional units, possibly by assigning them a strong negative bias that

---

[9] Judging the discriminative power of a feature requires additional assumptions about the nature of the stimulus displays, such as the relative likelihood of various distractors and the relative frequency of target-present trials.

[10] It is a difficult optimization problem to configure the model's parameters so as to minimize errors or response time, especially under the constraint of a finite amount of regulatory juice. Fine-tuning the system parameters is no doubt a matter of learning and experience.

gradually decays back to zero, and resetting the recognition system.[11] [12]

- The attentional state is reset, and this process is repeated until all stimulus locations in the display have been explored, at which point the model reports "target absent." It is possible that the model could quit after only one or a small number of attentional fixations, or, at the other extreme, that it could return to locations to verify the absence of a target.

This is a complicated, ill-specified story, but visual search is a complicated, ill-specified task—ill-specified in the sense that subjects must make a variety of strategic and control decisions that are not part of the task instructions. To simplify our simulation, we will model search in relatively small displays, of up to nine elements. This allows us to avoid limitations on peripheral visual acuity, eye movements, and—as we will show—the need for sequential attentional fixations. We also neglect target-absent data, because modeling performance on these displays requires additional mechanisms which, for example determine when to switch attention, when to quit searching, and how to suppress locations such that they are not repeatedly searched.

Simulation Methodology

For these simulations, we trained a version of the recognition model that recognizes three "objects": a vertical bar, a horizontal bar, and a plus sign. The objects can appear in any of nine locations in the field. Figure 9.17 shows a sample display. Note the distinction between vertical-bar objects and vertical-bar features; the former is composed of the latter. The network was trained on 450 example displays of one to nine elements, similar to those used in the visual search simulations described later. The training set was unbiased in that it contained equal numbers of examples from each condition in the visual search simulations.

During testing, displays are presented to the model with a target and a variable number of distractors. The elements are arranged randomly on the model's retina. The elastic-spotlight attentional network, guided by control signals, selects a subset of the display elements, and the recognition network reports the identities of the selected elements. Although we imagine that

---

[11] A bias is a tonic input to a unit. A negative bias causes the unit to shut off unless there is overwhelming positive input to the unit via excitatory connections from other units.

[12] Although we have not specified the coordinate frame in which the attentional units operate, it seems most natural to interpret it as retinotopic. There is evidence, however, that inhibition of return, the likely mechanism for preventing the human visual system from returning to an already searched location, operates in a coordinate frame that does not depend on eye position (Posner & Cohen, 1984).

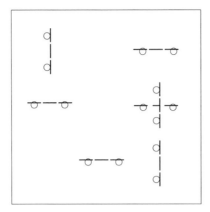

FIG. 9.17. A pattern of activity that corresponds to five bars and a plus in random locations on the model's retina.

detection responses are trigged by the response initiation process described earlier, we took a short cut that is a deterministic approximation to the stochastic process, and simply used a fixed activity threshold, generally around .5, as the all-or-none threshold for initiating a response. If a response has not been initiated within 100 cycles, the model reports "target absent" and is considered to have made an error.[13] The threshold we selected was as low as possible, to produce responses as fast as possible, such that the rate of false detection in target-absent displays was nearly zero.

Simple Feature Search

Searching for an element with a distinctive feature is easy. In a display containing a single vertical target among a variable number of horizontal distractors, response time will be independent of the number of distractors. Our model can explain this finding by assuming that the control signal for the distinctive feature is increased, causing attention to be driven directly to the location of the distinctive feature. Once that location is attended, the object at that location is recognized and a response is made.

We have simulated the search for a vertical among horizontals and a horizontal among verticals. On each simulation trial, the control signal for the primitive feature unique to the target is increased from .8 to 1.0, and the control signal for the primitive feature unique to the distractor is decreased from .8 to 0.

---

[13] The processing involved in deciding the target is absent is undoubtably more complex than this. Indeed, Chun and Wolfe (1996) suggests that absent responses are unlikely to be triggered by a fixed passage of time.

The dashed curve in Fig. 9.18 shows the model's performance on target-present trials as a function of the number of display elements. Response times are not dependent on display size. The model never fails to detect the target.

Theories of visual search generally assume that feature search does not require selective attention, and more strongly, that feature search does not benefit from selective attention. We tested whether this assumption is consistent with our model by forcing attention to be distributed across the visual field. This is achieved by setting $\lambda = 1$, which causes all perceptual data to be fully analyzed by the recognition network, regardless of the attentional state. One might conjecture that if simple feature displays can be processed in parallel and if there is a benefit of allocating attention prior to stimulus onset, as we observed in the cue-validity effect, response times might actually be *faster* with distributed attention. Indeed, there is a statistically reliable benefit for small displays, replicating the cue-validity effect, but there is also a statistically reliable cost for large displays. Cost and benefit are both on the order of 30 ms, and over the various display sizes, they tend to cancel. Thus, the attentional network is not really helping processing for simple feature displays, nor is it hurting, consistent with the traditional view of feature search.

The model offers a nontraditional perspective in two other respects, however. First, simple feature search is viewed as an object recognition task, albeit one that the recognition system has capacity to perform in parallel. Second, while the guided-search model and feature-integration theory consider the role of attentional guidance only in conjunction search,

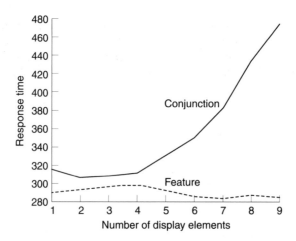

FIG. 9.18.   Time for the model to initiate a detection response as a function of display size for target-present trials in feature (dashed line) and conjunction (solid line) search.

modulation of control signals is critical in our model in feature search. Because the attentional network always acts to select display elements, it is necessary to modulate control signals to select the target features or else the target will be suppressed and may not be detected. It would be a challenge to develop an experimental test that could distinguish this perspective from the traditional view.

Conjunction Search

Subjects are slow to search for an element defined by a conjunction of features, such as a red vertical target among red horizontal and blue and red vertical distractors. An explanation in terms of our model for the difficulty of conjunction search is not obvious. Suppose that control signals were set such that exogenous input from only the red and vertical feature maps was able to reach the attentional network. Locations of red elements would receive a certain amount of input, locations of vertical elements would receive roughly same input, but the locations of red vertical elements would receive twice as much input. The attentional network should reliably select the location of the target, independent of the number of distractors. Regardless of recognition and verification processes, one would expect the response curve to be flat, in contrast to typical human data. Thus, it might seem that our model is too powerful, even though there appear to be at least some conjunction searches that are easy (e.g. color/depth and motion/depth, Nakayama & Silverman, 1986).

One account of the difficulty of conjunction search, suggested by the guided-search model (Wolfe et al., 1989) is to postulate that recognition and attention operate in an intrinsically noisy environment. Although the attentional system should be directed more strongly to the target location than to the distractor locations, the strength of the direction may not be sufficient to overcome noise, and will therefore not be reliable, and serial search will be required. A second account of the difficulty of conjunction search is to postulate limits on the voluntary adjustment of the control signals—the regulatory juice. These two accounts are complementary; weak limits on regulatory juice and a high intrinsic noise level should yield performance similar to that with strong limits on regulatory juice and a low intrinsic noise level. In simulating our model, we discovered that it provides a somewhat different account altogether, which we detail next.

In the canonical conjunction search task, the target is composed of features on two different dimensions. We could simulate this experiment by adding red and blue feature types to the model and then training a net to recognize red and blue verticals and horizontals. We could then use the control signals to bias attention toward the red and vertical feature maps, if the target was a red vertical. Instead, we have chosen to simulate an experiment that is more challenging to the model. Our simulation experiment involves a target plus symbol embedded in a distractor array of verticals and horizontals. Even without modulating the default values of the control signals, the exogenous input to the target location should be twice that of the exogenous input to any of the distractors because the target is composed of twice as many features.[14] It would thus seem that selection should be strongly biased toward the location of the target—a problematic result for the model.

With trepidation, we ran the conjunction search simulation. To our surprise, the model's performance nicely matched the human data, as shown by the solid curve in Fig. 9.18.[15] As the number of display elements increases, response times increase. For small displays, the curve is flat. This is in accord with the finding of Pashler (1987) that nearly flat search slopes can be observed for small displays, and it reflects the fact that the recognition network is able to detect conjunctions in parallel, albeit with limited capacity. Mordkoff, Yantis, & Egeth, 1990, present further experimental evidence of limited-capacity parallel conjunction detection.)

Response times increase with display size for two reasons. First, the competition among elements in the attention network increases. This can be shown by observing how long the attentional network requires to reach a stable state. Second, unattended elements in the display interfere with recognition. This can be shown by comparing performance of the network with $\lambda = 0$, i.e. unattended information fully suppressed, to the standard model, which has $\lambda = .05$. We find that response times are statistically slower with unattended information fully suppressed, 39 ms slower in the case of nine-element displays.

As we did with feature search, we can examine how important selective attention is for conjunction search. Here, we find a very different pattern. Figure 9.19 shows that the model's error rate skyrockets when attention is divided across display elements. No setting of the response threshold can achieve a low error rate over both target present and absent trials. The model cannot reliably detect the plus target without selective attention, consistent with the traditional theories of visual search.

However, our account of conjunction search is in part nontraditional, because it depends on subtle properties of the model—the influence of unattended elements on the detection of attended elements and the dynamics of the attentional model. Simulation studies were critical to dis-

---

[14] The guidance to the target is the same as it would be in the colored bar experiment if the control signals were set up to allow only target features to guide attention, i.e. assuming no limit on the regulatory juice.

[15] By experimentation, we found that the model performed best when the control signals for all feature types were lowered from .8 to .5 and when β was lowered from .10 to .04, creating a narrower focus of attention.

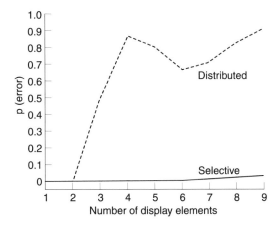

FIG. 9.19. Error rate of the model on target-present trials for conjunction search as a function of display size. The solid line represents the condition in which the attentional network performs selective attention. The dotted line represents the condition in which attention is distributed across the field, i.e. all perceptual data enters the recognition network.

covering that the model behaved correctly and why it did. Although the current simulation did not require postulating noise in the attentional system or limitations on regulatory juice, these factors may contribute to conjunction search performance, and may be necessary in simulations of other experimental findings.

Discussion of Visual Search

In its present form, the model can explain other data relating to visual search, including the findings of faster search in low-density displays (Cohn & Ivry, 1991) and the difficulty of detecting the absence of features (Treisman & Souther, 1985). With minor extensions to the model, a wide variety of other data can be addressed, including response-time curves for target-absent displays, effects of target-distractor contrast (Treisman & Gormican, 1988), search asymmetries (Ivry & Cohen, 1992; Treisman & Gormican, 1988), effects of distractor homogeneity (Duncan & Humphreys 1989), and rapid conjunction search (Wolfe et al., 1989). However, our immediate goal is not to present a comprehensive model of visual search, but rather to begin considering the underlying mechanisms. By addressing data from experimental paradigms as disparate as spatial cuing and visual search, we hope to have convinced the reader of the model's breadth and flexibility. This is the remarkable property of computational models—they can help one to integrate phenomena under a unified framework. The other lesson from these simulations of visual search is that, although the model shows some behavior that one would intuitively expect, other aspects of its behavior were found only via simulation. The model raises some intriguing possibilities, and addressing these possibilities requires further human experimental studies.

THE ROLE OF SELECTIVE ATTENTION

When one adopts a computational perspective, a natural question to ask is what computational role selective attention plays in visual information processing. Four distinct functional roles of attention fall naturally from the computational perspective presented in this chapter.

- *Controlling order of readout.* The attentional system allows the recognition system to selectively access information in the visual field by location. A task requiring sequential responses to items in various locations could not be carried out with the recognition system alone.
- *Reducing crosstalk.* As we illustrated earlier, when the recognition network analyzes multiple items in parallel, interactions within the network cause the processing of one item to interfere with another. Deploying attention to one or a small number of items at once will reduce or eliminate crosstalk.
- *Recovering location information.* The output of the recognition system we developed encodes identities but not locations. Computationally, it makes sense to separate identity from location, because often the same response should be made to a stimulus regardless of where it appears in the visual field. Neurophysiological evidence also suggests that, at least in the responses of individual cells, a great deal of location information is discarded in higher cortical areas involved in object recognition (Tanaka, 1993). And some psychological data suggests that stimulus identity is encoded apart from location (Kanwisher, 1990; Mozer, 1989). Thus, some means of recovering location information is critical. Because the current locus of attention reflects the spatial source of activations in the object recognition system, the attentional system can convey the discarded location information.
- *Coordinating processing performed by independent modules.* The heart of feature-integration theory is the notion that visual stimuli are analyzed by functionally independent modules specialized along certain attribute dimensions such as color, form, and motion. Because these modules operate autonomously, it is imperative to ensure that they coordinate their processing efforts. Otherwise, the system can encounter a *binding problem* in which attributes of multiple objects are simultaneously activated and it cannot be determined which attributes belong together, possibly resulting in illusory conjunctions (Treisman & Schmidt, 1982). By guiding all modules to analyze the same spatial

region, attention can ensure that the attributes of a single object will be bound together.[16]

CONTRASTING THEORETICAL PERSPECTIVES ON SELECTIVE ATTENTION

The key properties of our model are common to most theories of selective attention. We summarize these properties, which collectively we call the *spatial-selection perspective*, as follows.

- Attention operates as a spatial gating mechanism. This is mandatory to perform selection by location.
- The mechanism includes a representation of visual field location—the attentional map—which is distinct from the representation of visual features used for object recognition.
- Attention acts to modulate the activity of visual features such that the signal strength of features at attended locations are enhanced relative to the strength of features at unattended locations.
- Object recognition is limited in capacity. While there may be some capacity to recognize objects in parallel, interference among objects arises which necessitates attentional selection early in the processing stream. Although selection is performed early, unattended information receives some degree of processing and causes some interference with attended information.
- Selection can be performed on the basis of object attributes, if these attributes can be characterized in terms of combinations of primitive features that discriminate the item of interest from other items in the visual field.
- Perceptual grouping operates prior to attentional selection and can influence the deployment of spatial attention.

An alternative theoretical perspective on selective attention has been suggested recently in which competition is ubiquitous and is not limited to competition among locations (Allport, 1993; Desimone & Duncan, 1995; Duncan, 1996; Phaf, Van der Heijden, & Hudson, 1990). We call this the *ubiquitous-competition perspective*, and highlight its the main properties as follows.

- Attention is viewed as the competition among stimulus representations at many loci in the processing stream, from sensory input to response

---

[16] Note that this statement is not as strong as the claim of feature-integration theory that attention is *necessary* to perform all types of binding. Even if intra-dimensional bindings are performed automatically, or if experience might allow inter-dimensional bindings to be performed automatically, or if the modules are only weakly independent, there is still a role for attention to coordinate processing.

formation. Objects might compete within subsystems that represent color, shape, and location information, as well as a subsystem that represents possible actions.

- Within each subsystem, a winner-take-all process results in a gain in activity or representation for one object and a loss for others.
- The competitive mechanisms are integrated such that multiple subsystems tend to work concurrently on the same object.
- Priming of representations within any subsystem acts to guide selection (see also Farah, 1994; Grossberg et al., 1994; Mozer, 1991).
- Selection by location is no more fundamental than selection on the basis of other stimulus or response dimensions.

It is beyond the scope of this chapter to try to resolve the differences between this perspective and the one we have presented. However, we point out that the two are not altogether incompatible. One can accept the primacy of location-based selection, but also allow for competition among higher-order object representations. For example, in the model we have presented, inhibitory connections could be added between units that represent different letters, forcing a selection of a single letter. This competition among identity representations would be useful for response selection; the process could even be primed to a particular letter by pre-activating the appropriate letter unit, in accord with the ubiquitous-competition perspective.

The difference between the two perspectives is primarily one of emphasis, the spatial-selection perspective addressing capacity limitations in object recognition and the ubiquitous-competition perspective focusing on the diverse sorts of cues that can be used for selection. However, the two perspectives suggest quite different mechanisms of selection on the basis of object identity. The ubiquitous-competition perspective allows for competition to operate fairly late in processing among high-level object representations, and then for cooperation among the subsystems to work its way back to select the same object everywhere in the processing stream. The spatial-selection perspective, as we have elaborated, suggests a variety of "quick and dirty" heuristics to guide spatial attention to objects of interest. It remains to be seen which perspective will be most useful in explaining the broad and complex corpus of psychological data on attentional selection.

ISSUES IN COMPUTATIONAL MODELING

We have presented an elaborate computational framework for analyzing and understanding spatial attention. Our goal has not been to convince you that the framework is necessarily correct, but rather that modeling is a valuable exercise that allows one to reason in concrete terms about the computational mechanisms. We suspect that some readers will still be skeptical as to the value of model building. For this reason, we conclude with a discussion of general issues in computational modeling.

Why Build Computational Models?

It goes against the tradition of experimental psychology to construct large, complex computational models with dozens to hundreds of parameters. Nonetheless, as the field matures, computational models should play an increasingly important role, for the following reasons.

- As one tries to explain larger and larger bodies of data and data from diverse experimental paradigms, the complexity of the model must necessarily increase. Computational models with many components and parameters thus become better justified.
- Computational models provide a framework for integrating knowledge from behavioral studies with results from fields such as neuroanatomy and neurophysiology.
- Computational models force one to be explicit about one's hypotheses and assumptions. To test a computational mechanism, it must be specified with precision and detail.
- Computational models provide the ultimate in controlled experimentation. Any simulation experiment can be replicated exactly. Stimulus materials can be generated that differ just on the dimension of interest, without any confounding factors. One can poke at and examine any part of the model. One can precisely lesion or adjust individual components of the model and observe the consequences.
- Computational models can make empirical predictions. The model can be presented with novel stimuli or a novel experimental paradigm, and its performance can be compared to that of human subjects. The ability of the model to predict nontrivial experimental findings that it was not explicitly designed to explain is an indication that the model correctly captures some aspect of cognition. In the best of circumstances, an experiment can be designed to distinguish predictions of one model or model class from another, thereby providing not just support for one model but evidence against another. Of course, the ability to predict experimental results is not unique to computational models.
- Computational models allow one to observe the consequences of interactions among mechanisms. In many models, the effect of changing one component trickles to others. It is difficult to anticipate these effects without computer simulation.
- Computational models help one to understand the trade-offs involved in the design of the cognitive architecture. It is our conviction that limitations in human cognition are not arbitrary, but are the result of

sensible, if not optimal, design decisions given various constraints on the cognitive architecture.

We do not mean to suggest that the mere fact that a model has been implemented in computer simulation gives it some intrinsic value, nor the fact that a model is described qualitatively instead of using equations implies that the model has little value. Any model is useful only to the extent it helps us understand some aspect of cognition.

What Makes a Model Compelling?

A simple model that can explain a large, diverse corpus of data is very compelling. However, characterizing the complexity of a model is not a trivial task. For linear models, the number of parameters is a measure of model complexity and of how many data points it is guaranteed to account for. For nonlinear models such as connectionist models, no such direct relationship exists. Some parameters give the model a lot of flexibility, others practically none. For example, in our model, any individual connection strength in the recognition network can be changed with little effect on the model's qualitative or quantitative behavior; however, a parameter like λ, which determines the degree to which unattended information will be processed, dramatically affects the qualitative behavior of the model.

Perhaps the complexity of a model should be measured in terms of how many basic principles it embodies, rather than the total number of parameters. For example, our recognition model, while it has several thousand parameters, embodies just a few principles—local receptive fields, convergence of information from different regions of the retina, and so forth. The specific number of feature types in each layer and the specific pattern of connectivity is probably not central to the model's qualitative behavior.[17]

One question to ask when evaluating a model is whether more falls out of the model than has been built into it—that is, whether the model has emergent properties. A clear demonstration of emergent properties is when the model can make novel empirical predictions that are eventually validated. However, this is not the only criterion by which a model can be judged as useful. The Occam's Razor argument is that if a simple model can explain complex patterns of data, then there is likely to be some truth in the

---

[17] To determine which aspects of the model are key and which are incidental, one must conduct simulation studies over a variety of different architectures. Unfortunately, this is computation-intensive work, and is seldom done.

model, regardless of whether the data are old or new.[18] Ultimately, it is up to the reader to determine whether the model is indeed simple relative to the amount of data it explains.

When is a Model Right or Wrong?

Odds are that the model is wrong, at least in some detail. This is not to say that the model has no value; it may be one's current best theory, and the only way one has of contemplating mechanisms of behavior. When the model makes a concrete prediction and this prediction is incorrect, one faces the challenge of modifying the model to incorporate the new effect. More often, the model will not be sufficiently well specified to predict the outcome of an experiment; in this case, the model will need to be elaborated to account for results. Thus, over time, the complexity of the model will grow as the corpus of data it can explain grows. If the model is a good one, the model's rate of growth will be far lower than the growth of the corpus. Each time the model is modified or elaborated, it becomes further constrained. Eventually, someone is likely to devise an experiment that the model is simply not suited to explain. At this point, the model has run its useful life, and a fresh conception of the underlying mechanisms is demanded.

What About Other Models That Also Explain the Data?

One question that modelers are constantly asked is: Why should one believe in a particular model when there are probably dozens of models that are just as effective in explaining the corpus of data? The response of modelers is usually amusement; it is extremely difficult to build one model that can explain the data, let alone a hundred. Those who have never built a model often fail to appreciate this fact. The appropriate response is perhaps to challenge the questioner to propose an alternative model. Then, experiments can be devised for which the models make different predictions, or else the models are functionally equivalent.

Depth versus breadth in modeling

Ultimately, one would like a model both broad and deep, "broad" in that it can address a variety of experimental tasks and response paradigms, and "deep" in that it can explain subtleties and quantitative properties of the

---

[18] In model building, the distinction between old and new data is seldom clear. One often constructs the model with particular data in mind, and then discovers that the model, with no or minor changes, can explain other data as well. In this case, the additional data are in fact predicted by the model, even though the data may have been collected and published before the model was developed.

data. Traditionally, psychological models have aimed for depth over breadth, and the cost has been that a model of one phenomenon, say the word superiority effect (McClelland & Rumelhart, 1981) may have little in common with a model of some other phenomenon, say the Stroop task (Cohen, Dunbar, & McClelland, 1990), even though the two models are ostensibly of the same fundamental process, reading, in this case.

We have aimed for breadth in our presentation by discussing data across a variety of experimental tasks and paradigms. A consequence of this choice is a model with multiple components and parameters which can be configured differently for different tasks it is asked to perform. For a particular task, we presented arguments for why the model should be configured a certain way. This "configuration" includes specifying decision criteria, modulating control signals, and adjusting the diameter of the attentional spotlight, and in a more complete model it might also include the vigilance level (the degree to which units are modulated by the attentional network, the parameter λ), exogenous guidance of attention, and priming to bias selection.

When subjects are given verbal task instructions, they are able to configure their perceptual systems appropriately for the task. In addition to producing the right response to a stimulus—whether the response is a foot-tap when a vowel is presented or a spoken report of the number of display items—response criteria are adjusted to trade off speed and accuracy, and performance is optimized, e.g. searching a display in parallel if subjects are capable of doing so. Understanding and modeling this configuration process is a tremendous challenge ahead for the next generation of computational models of human cognition.

ACKNOWLEDGEMENTS

This research was supported by NSF Presidential Young Investigator award IRI-9058450, grant 90–21 from the James S. McDonnell Foundation, and a grant from Lifestyle Technologies. Our thanks to Harold Pashler and James Juola for their fine editorial feedback, and to many helpful discussions with participants in a seminar on computational models of attention, particularly Don Mathis, Clark Fagot, Sigal Adoot, Richard Beach, Gina Cherry, Braden Craig, Julia Fisher, Audrey Guzik, Tracy Hansen, Carol Kealoha, Deb Miller, Bill Raymond, and Eran Tari.

REFERENCES

Ahmad, S. (1991). *VISIT: An efficient computational model of human visual attention* (ICSI Technical Report 91–049). Berkeley, CA: International Computer Science Institute.

Ahmad, S., & Omohundro, S. (1991). Efficient visual search: A connectionist solution. In *Proceedings of the Thirteenth Annual Conference of the Cognitive Science Society* (pp. 293–298). Hillsdale, NJ: Lawrence Erlbaum Associates Inc.

Allport, D.A. (1993). Attention and control: Have we been asking the wrong questions? A critical review of twenty-five years. In D.E. Meyer & S. Kornblum (Eds.), *Attention and performance XIV* (pp.183–218). Cambridge, MA: MIT Press.

Ballard, D.H. (1986). Cortical connections and parallel processing: Structure and function. *The Behavioral and Brain Sciences, 9,* 67–120.

Barlow, H.H. (1972). Single units and sensation: A neuron doctrine for perceptual psychology? *Perception, 1,* 371–394.

Behrmann, M., Zemel, R.S., & Mozer, M.C. (in press). Object-based attention and occlusion: Evidence from normal subjects and a computational model. *Journal of Experimental Psychology: Human Perception and Performance.*

Bundesen, C. (1990). A theory of visual attention. *Psychological Review, 97,* 523–547.

Chun, M.M., & Wolfe, J.M. (1996). Just say no: How are visual search trials terminated when there is no target present? *Cognitive Psychology, 10,* 39–78.

Cohen, J.D., Romero, R.D., Farah, M.J., & Servan-Schreiber, D. (1994). Mechanisms of spatial attention: The relation of macrostructure to microstructure in parietal neglect. *Journal of Cognitive Neuroscience, 6,* 377–387.

Cohen, A., & Ivry, R.B. (1991). Density effects in conjunction search: Evidence for a coarse location mechanism of feature integration. *Journal of Experimental Psychology: Human Perception and Performance, 17,* 891–901.

Desimone, R., & Duncan, J. (1995). Neural mechanisms of selective visual attention. *Annual Review of Neuroscience, 18,* 193–222.

Downing, C.G., & Pinker, S. (1985). The spatial structure of visual attention. In M.I. Posner & O.S.M. Marin (Eds.), *Attention and performance XI* (pp.171–187). Hillsdale, NJ: Lawrence Erlbaum Associates Inc.

Driver, J., & Baylis, G.C. (1989). Movement and visual attention: The spotlight metaphor breaks down. *Journal of Experimental Psychology: Human Perception and Performance, 15,* 448–456.

Driver, J., McLeod, P., & Dienes, Z. (1992). Are direction and speed coded independently by the visual system? Evidence from visual search. *Spatial Vision, 6,* 133–147.

Duncan, J. (1984). Selective attention and the organization of visual information. *Journal of Experimental Psychology: General, 113,* 501–517.

Duncan, J. (1987). Attention and reading: Wholes and parts in shape recognition—A tutorial review. In M. Coltheart (Ed.), *Attention and performance XII* (pp.39–62). Hove, UK: Lawrence Erlbaum Associates Ltd.

Duncan, J. (1995). Target and nontarget grouping in visual search. *Perception and Psychophysics, 57,* 117–120.

Duncan, J. (1996). Coordinated brain systems in selective perception and action. In T. Iaui & J.L. McClelland (Eds.), *Attention and performance XVI.* Cambridge, MA: MIT Press.

Duncan, J., & Humphreys, G.W. (1989). Visual search and stimulus similarity. *Psychological Review, 96,* 433–458.

Egeth, H. (1977). Attention and preattention. In G.H. Bower (Ed.), *The psychology of learning and motivation* (Vol. 11, pp.277–320). New York: Academic Press.

Egly, R., Driver, J., & Rafal, R.D. (1994). Shifting visual attention between objects and locations: Evidence from normal and parietal lesion subjects. *Journal of Experimental Psychology: General, 123,* 161–177.

Enns, J.T. (1990). Three-dimensional features that pop out in visual search. In D. Brogan (Ed.), *Visual search* (pp.37–46). London: Taylor & Francis.

Enns, J.T., & Rensink, R.A. (1992). A model for the rapid interpretation of line drawings in early vision. In D. Brogan (Ed.), *Visual search II.* London: Taylor & Francis.

Eriksen, B.A., & Eriksen, C.W. (1974). Effects of noise letters upon the identification of a target letter in a nonsearch task. *Perception and Psychophysics, 16,* 143–149.

Eriksen, C.W. (1990). Attentional search of the visual field. In D. Brogan (Ed.), *Visual search*. London: Taylor & Francis.

Eriksen, C.W., & Hoffman, J.E. (1973). The extent of processing of noise elements during selective coding from visual displays. *Perception and Psychophysics, 14*, 155–160.

Eriksen, C.W., & Hoffman, J.E. (1974). Selective attention: Noise suppression or signal enhancement? *Bulletin of the Psychonomic Society, 4*, 587–589.

Eriksen, C.W., & Schultz, D.W. (1979). Information processing in visual search: A continuous flow conception and experimental results. *Perception and Psychophysics, 25*, 249–263.

Eriksen, C.W., & St. James, J.D. (1986). Visual attention within and around the field of focal attention: A zoom lens model. *Perception and Psychophysics, 40*, 225–240.

Eriksen, C.W., & Yeh, Y.-Y. (1985). Allocation of attention in the visual field. *Journal of Experimental Psychology: Human Perception and Performance, 11*, 583–597.

Farah, M.J. (1994). Neuropsychological inference with an interactive brain: A critique of the "locality" assumption. *Behavioral and Brain Sciences, 17*, 43–104.

Feldman, J.A., & Ballard, D.H. (1982). Connectionist models and their properties. *Cognitive Science, 6*, 205–254.

Fukushima, K., & Miyake, S. (1982). Neocognitron: A new algorithm for pattern recognition tolerant of deformations and shifts in position. *Pattern Recognition, 15*, 455–469.

Gatti, S.V., & Egeth, H.E. (1978). Failure of spatial selectivity in vision. *Bulletin of the Psychonomic Society, 11*, 181–184.

Gerrissen, J.F. (1991). On the network-based emulation of human visual search. *Neural Networks, 4*, 543–564.

Goebel, R. (1993). Perceiving complex visual scenes: An oscillator neural network model that integrates selective attention, perceptual organisation, and invariant recognition. In S.J. Hanson, J.D. Cowan, & C.L. Giles (Eds.), *Advances in neural information processing systems 5* (pp.903–910). San Mateo, CA: Morgan Kaufmann.

Grossberg, S. (1976). Adaptive pattern classification and universal recoding: I. Parallel development and coding of neural feature detectors. *Biological Cybernetics, 23*, 121–134.

Grossberg, S., Mingolla, E., & Ross, W.D. (1994). A neural theory of attentive visual search: Interactions of boundary, surface, spatial, and object representations. *Psychological Review, 101*, 470–489.

Hillstrom, A. (1995). Singleton pop-out: Facilitation of uniqueness or inhibition of similarity? [Abstract]. *Program of the 36th Annual Meeting of the Psychonomics Society*.

Hillstrom, A.P., & Yantis, S. (1994). Visual motion and attentional capture. *Perception and Psychophysics, 55*, 399–411.

Hinton, G.E., McClelland, J.L., & Rumelhart, D.E. (1986). Distributed representations. In D.E. Rumelhart & J.L. McClelland (Eds.), *Parallel distributed processing: Explorations in the microstructure of cognition: Vol. I. Foundations* (pp.77–109). Cambridge, MA: MIT Press/Bradford Books.

Humphreys, G.W., & Müller, H.J. (1993). SEarch via Recursive Rejection (SERR): A connectionist model of visual search. *Cognitive Psychology, 25*, 43–110.

Ivry, R.B., & Cohen, A. (1992). Asymmetry in visual search for targets defined by differences in movement speed. *Journal of Experimental Psychology: Human Perception and Performance, 18*, 1045–1057.

Jackson, S.R., Marrocco, R., & Posner, M.I. (1994). Networks of anatomical areas controlling visuospatial attention. *Neural Networks, 7*, 925–944.

Jonides, J., & Yantis, S. (1988). Uniqueness of abrupt visual onset in capturing attention. *Perception and Psychophysics, 43*, 346–354.

Kahneman, D., & Henik, A. (1981). Perceptual organization and attention. In M. Kubovy & J.R. Pomerantz (Eds.), *Perceptual organization* (pp.181–211). Hillsdale, NJ: Lawrence Erlbaum Associates Inc.

Kahneman, D., Treisman, A., & Burkell, J. (1983). The cost of visual filtering. *Journal of Experimental Psychology: Human Perception and Performance*, *9*, 510–522.

Kanwisher, N.G. (1990). Binding and type-token problems in human vision. In *Proceedings of the 12th Annual Conference of the Cognitive Science Society* (pp.606–613). Hillsdale, NJ: Lawrence Erlbaum Associates Inc.

Kinchla, R.A. (1992). Attention. *Annual Review of Psychology*, *43*, 711–742.

Koch, C., & Ullman, S. (1985). Shifts in selective visual attention: Towards the underlying neural circuitry. *Human Neurobiology*, *4*, 219–227.

Kramer, A.F., & Jacobson, A. (1991). Perceptual organization and focused attention: The role of objects and proximity in visual processing. *Perception and Psychophysics*, *50*, 267–284.

LaBerge, D. (1983). Spatial extent of attention to letters and words. *Journal of Experimental Psychology: Human Perception and Performance*, *9*, 371–379.

LaBerge, D., & Brown, V. (1989). Theory of attentional operations in shape identification. *Psychological Review*, *96*, 101–124.

LaBerge, D., Brown, V., Carter, M., Bash, D., & Hartley, A. (1991). Reducing the effects of adjacent distractors by narrowing attention. *Journal of Experimental Psychology: Human Perception and Performance*, *17*, 90–95.

Le Cun, Y., Boser, B., Denker, J.S., Hendersen, D., Howard, R.E., Hubbard, W., & Jackel, L.D. (1989). Backpropagation applied to handwritten zip code recognition. *Neural Computation*, *1*, 541–551.

Maljkovic, V., & Nakayama, K. (1994). Priming of pop-out: I. Role of features. *Memory and Cognition*, *22*, 657–672.

Marr, D. (1982). *Vision*. San Francisco: Freeman.

McClelland, J.L., & Rumelhart, D.E. (1981). An interactive activation model of context effects in letter perception: Part I. An account of basic findings. *Psychological Review*, *88*, 375–407.

McClelland, J.L., Rumelhart, D.E., & Hinton, G.E. (1986). The appeal of parallel distributed processing. In D.E. Rumelhart & J.L. McClelland (Eds.), *Parallel distributed processing: Explorations in the microstructure of cognition: Vol. I. Foundations* (pp.3–44). Cambridge, MA: MIT Press/Bradford Books.

Miller, J. (1991). The flanker compatibility effect as a function of visual angle, attentional focus, visual transients, and perceptual load: A search for boundary conditions. *Perception and Psychophysics*, *49*, 270–288.

Milner, P.M. (1974). A model for visual shape recognition. *Psychological Review*, *81*, 521–535.

Mordkoff, J.T., Yantis, S., & Egeth, H.E. (1990). Detecting conjunctions of color and form in parallel. *Perception and Psychophysics*, *48*, 157–168.

Mozer, M.C. (1983). Letter migration in word perception. *Journal of Experimental Psychology: Human Perception and Performance*, *9*, 531–546.

Mozer, M.C. (1989). Types and tokens in visual letter perception. *Journal of Experimental Psychology: Human Perception and Performance*, *15*, 287–303.

Mozer, M.C. (1991). *The perception of multiple objects: A connectionist approach*. Cambridge, MA: MIT Press/Bradford Books.

Mozer, M.C., & Behrmann, M. (1990). On the interaction of selective attention and lexical knowledge: A connectionist account of neglect dyslexia. *Cognitive Neuroscience*, *2*, 96–123.

Mozer, M.C., Halligan, P.W., & Marshall, J.C. (1997). The end of the line for a brain-damaged model of hemispatial neglect. *Cognitive Neuroscience*. *9*, 171–190.

Mozer, M.C., Zemel, R.S., Behrmann, M., & Williams, C.K.I. (1992). Learning to segment images using dynamic feature binding. *Neural Computation*, *4*, 650–666.

Nakayama, K., & Silverman, G.H. (1986). Serial and parallel processing of visual feature conjunctions. *Nature*, *320*, 264–265.

Niebur, E., & Koch, C. (1996). Control of selective visual attention: Modeling the "where" pathway. In D.S. Touretzky. M.C. Mozer, & M. Hasselmo (Eds.), *Neural information processing systems IX.* Cambridge, MA: MIT Press.

Nissen, M.J. (1985). Accessing features and objects: Is location special? In M. I. Posner & O. S. M. Marin (Eds.), *Attention and performance XI* (pp.205–219). Hillsdale, NJ: Lawrence Erlbaum Associates Inc.

Pashler, H. (1987). Detecting conjunctions of color and form: Reassessing the serial search hypothesis. *Perception and Psychophysics, 41,* 191–201.

Pashler, H. (1988). Cross-dimensional interaction and texture segregation. *Perception and Psychophysics, 43,* 307–318.

Pashler, H., & Badgio, P.C. (1987). Attentional issues in the identification of alphanumeric characters. In M. Coltheart (Ed.), *Attention and performance XII: The psychology of reading* (pp.63–82). Hove, UK: Lawrence Erlbaum Associates Ltd.

Phaf, R.H., Van der Heijden, A.H.C., & Hudson, P.T.W. (1990). SLAM: A connectionist model for attention in visual selection tasks. *Cognitive Psychology, 22,* 273.

Posner, M.I. (1980). Orienting of attention. *Quarterly Journal of Experimental Psychology, 32,* 3–25.

Posner, M.I., & Cohen, Y. (1984). Components of visual orienting. In H. Bouma & D. Bouwhuis (Eds.), *Attention and performance X* (pp.531–556). Hove, UK: Lawrence Erlbaum Associates Ltd.

Posner, M.I., Snyder, C.R.R., & Davidson, B.J. (1980). Attention and the detection of signals. *Journal of Experimental Psychology: General, 109,* 160–174.

Rensink, R.A., & Enns, J.T. (1995). Preemption effects in visual search: Evidence for low-level grouping. *Psychological Review. 102,* 101–130.

Rumelhart, D.E., Hinton, G.E., & Williams, R.J. (1986). Learning internal representations by error propagation. In D.E. Rumelhart & J.L. McClelland (Eds.), *Parallel distributed processing: Explorations in the microstructure of cognition: Vol. I. Foundations* (pp.318–362). Cambridge, MA: MIT Press/Bradford Books.

Sandon, P.A. (1990). Simulating visual attention. *Cognitive Neuroscience, 2,* 213–231.

Sandon, P.A., & Uhr, L.M. (1988). An adaptive model for viewpoint-invariant object recognition. In *Proceedings of the Tenth Annual Conference of the Cognitive Science Society* (pp.209–215). Hillsdale, NJ: Lawrence Erlbaum Associates Inc.

Schneider, W., & Shiffrin, R.M. (1977). Controlled and automatic human information processing: I. Detection, search and attention. *Psychological Review, 84,* 1–66.

Shaffer, W.O., & LaBerge, D. (1979). Automatic semantic processing of unattended words. *Journal of Verbal Learning and Verbal Behavior, 18,* 413–426.

Shiffrin, R.M., & Gardner. G.T. (1972). Visual processing capacity and attentional control. *Journal of Experimental Psychology, 93,* 72–83.

Shiu, L.-P., & Pashler, H. (1994). Negligible effect of spatial precuing on identification of single digits. *Journal of Experimental Psychology: Human Perception and Performance, 20,* 1037–1054.

Shulman, G.L., Remington, R., & McLean, J.P. (1979). Moving attention through visual space. *Journal of Experimental Psychology: Human Perception and Performance, 5,* 522–526.

Snyder, C.R. (1972). Selection, inspection, and naming in visual search. *Journal of Experimental Psychology, 92,* 428–431.

Sperling, G., & Weichselgartner, E. (1995). Episodic theory of the dynamics of spatial attention. *Psychological Review, 102,* 503–532.

Tanaka, K. (1993). Neuronal mechanisms of object recognition. *Science, 262,* 685–688.

Treisman, A., & Gelade, G. (1980). A feature-integration theory of attention. *Cognitive Psychology, 12,* 97–136.

Treisman, A., & Gormican, S. (1988). Feature analysis in early vision: Evidence from search asymmetries. *Psychological Review, 95*, 15–48.

Treisman, A., & Sato, S. (1990). Conjunction search revisited. *Journal of Experimental Psychology: Human Perception and Performance, 16*, 459–478.

Treisman, A., & Schmidt, H. (1982). Illusory conjunctions in the perception of objects. *Cognitive Psychology, 14*, 107–141.

Treisman, A., & Souther, J. (1985). Search asymmetry: A diagnostic for preattentive processing of separable features. *Journal of Experimental Psychology: General, 114*, 285–310.

Trick, L.M., & Pylyshyn, Z.W. (1994). Why are small and large numbers enumerated differently? A limited-capacity preattentive stage in vision. *Psychological Review, 101*, 80–102.

Tsal, Y. (1983). Movements of attention across the visual field. *Journal of Experimental Psychology: Human Perception and Performance, 9*, 523–530.

Tsal, Y., & Lavie, N. (1988). Attending to color and shape: The special role of location in selective visual processing. *Perception and Psychophysics, 44*, 15–21.

Tsotsos, J.K. (1990). Analyzing vision at the complexity level. *Brain and Behavioral Sciences, 13*, 423.

Tsotsos, J.K. (1991). Computational resources do constrain behavior. *Brain and Behavioral Sciences, 13*, 506.

Uhr, L. (1987). *Highly parallel, hierarchical, recognition cone perceptual structure* (Technical Report 688). Madison, WI: Computer Sciences Department, University of Wisconsin.

Ullman, S. (1984). Visual routines. *Cognition, 18*, 97–159.

Vecera, S.P. (1993). *Object knowledge influences visual image segmentation.* Proceedings of the Fifteenth Annual Conference of the Cognitive Science Society (pp.1040–1045). Hillsdale, NJ: Lawrence Erlbaum Associates Inc.

Vecera, S.P., & Farah, M.J. (1994). Does visual attention select objects or locations? *Journal of Experimental Psychology: General, 123*, 146–160.

von der Malsburg, C. (1981). *The correlation theory of brain function* (Internal Report 81–2). Goettingen: Department of Neurobiology, Max Planck Institute for Biophysical Chemistry.

von der Malsburg, C., & Schneider, W. (1986). A neural cocktail-party processor. *Biological Cybernetics, 54*, 29–40.

Weismeyer, M., & Laird, J. (1990). A computer model of 2D visual attention. In *Proceedings of the Twelfth Annual Conference of the Cognitive Science Society* (pp.582–589). Hillsdale, NJ: Lawrence Erlbaum Associates Inc.

Wolfe, J.M., Cave, K.R., & Franzel, S.L. (1989). Guided search: An alternative to the feature-integration model for visual search. *Journal of Experimental Psychology: Human Perception and Performance, 15*, 419–433.

Yantis, S. (1988). On analog movements of visual attention. *Perception and Psychophysics, 43*, 203–206.

Yantis, S., & Johnston, J.C. (1990). On the locus of visual attention: Evidence from focused attention tasks. *Journal of Experimental Psychology: Human Perception and Performance, 16*, 135–149.

Author Index

Subject Index

attentional blink, 199–204
abrupt visual onsets
  and attentional capture, 8, 37, 46–47,
  119, 248–251
asymmetries
  in visual search, 25, 49
attention map
  in connectionist network, 351
attention shifts
  smooth versus discrete, 235–238
attentional capture, 1, 8, 37, 46–48,
238–253
attentional limitations
  defined, 156
  in perception and search, 13–74
  in planning actions, 165–181
auditory attention, 75–113
auditory discrimination tasks, 99–100
automatic writing, 155

Balint's Syndrome, 310–312,326, 332–333
  and segmentation, 319–320
bottlenecks
  and dual-task interference, 5–6,
  156–157, 165–181
  causes of, 176–177
  neural locus of, 178–181
bottom-up processing, 43–44

brain scanning techniques and selective
attention, 264–265

capacity-sharing, 18, 51, 157, 166, 199
central attentional limitations, 161, *see
also* bottlenecks
  psychological refractory period (PRP)
  design
chunking, 162
clarity
  and visual attention, 2
closure
  as possible feature, 34–35
coactivation, 185
cocktail party effect, 76, 266
color in visual search, 23–26, 241–248
computational complexity
  and functions of selective
  attention, 341–342
computational models of attention, 258,
341–388
conjunction search, 7, 17, 20–22, 48–51,
329–330, 332, 379–381, *see also* Feature
Integration Theory
connectionist models
  defined, 343–345
corpus callosum, 286–289
crosstalk, 157, 382